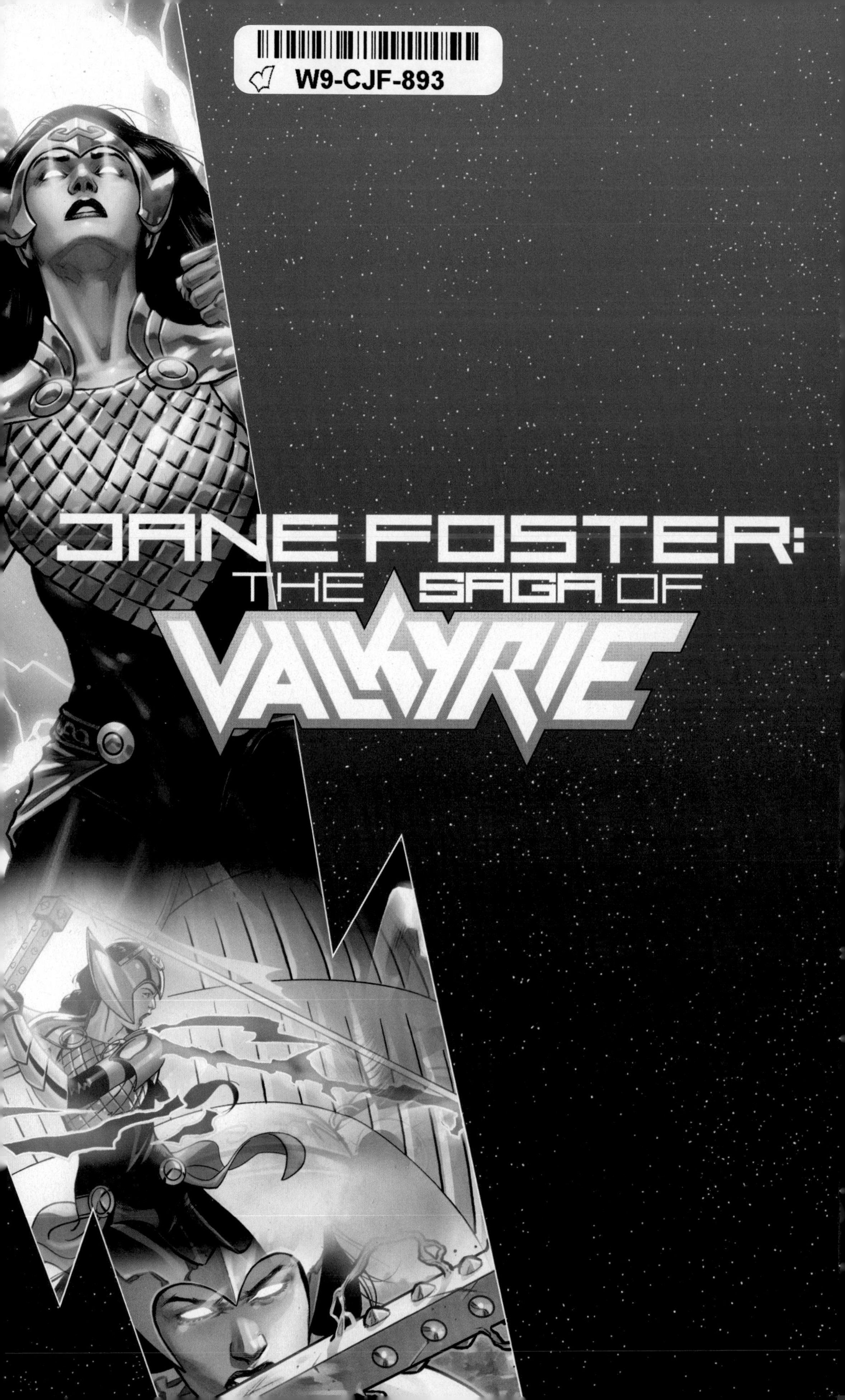

JANE FOSTER: THE SAGA OF VALKYRIE

SPECIAL THANKS TO RUSSELL DAUTERMAN

COLLECTION EDITOR: JENNIFER GRÜNWALD

ASSISTANT EDITOR: DANIEL KIRCHHOFFER

ASSISTANT MANAGING EDITOR: MAIA LOY

ASSOCIATE MANAGER, TALENT RELATIONS: LISA MONTALBANO

VP PRODUCTION & SPECIAL PROJECTS: JEFF YOUNGQUIST

BOOK DESIGNER: STACIE ZUCKER

SENIOR DESIGNER: ADAM DEL RE

SVP PRINT, SALES & MARKETING: DAVID GABRIEL

EDITOR IN CHIEF: C.B. CEBULSKI

JANE FOSTER: THE SAGA OF VALKYRIE. Contains material originally published in magazine form as MIGHTY THOR (2015) #702-706, VALKYRIE: JANE FOSTER (2019) #1-10, MIGHTY THOR: AT THE GATES OF VALHALLA (2018) #1 and WAR OF THE REALMS OMEGA (2019) #1. First printing 2022. ISBN 978-1-302-93482-8. Published by MARVEL WORLDWIDE, INC., a subsidiary of MARVEL ENTERTAINMENT, LLC. OFFICE OF PUBLICATION: 1290 Avenue of the Americas, New York, NY 10104. © 2022 MARVEL No similarity between any of the names, characters, persons, and/or institutions in this book with those of any living or dead person or institution is intended, and any such similarity which may exist is purely coincidental. Printed in Canada. KEVIN FEIGE, Chief Creative Officer; DAN BUCKLEY, President, Marvel Entertainment; JOE QUESADA, EVP & Creative Director; DAVID BOGART, Associate Publisher & SVP of Talent Affairs; TOM BREVOORT, VP, Executive Editor; NICK LOWE, Executive Editor, VP of Content, Digital Publishing; DAVID GABRIEL, VP of Print & Digital Publishing; MARK ANNUNZIATO, VP of Planning & Forecasting; JEFF YOUNGQUIST, VP of Production & Special Projects; ALEX MORALES, Director of Publishing Operations; DAN EDINGTON, Director of Editorial Operations; RICKEY PURDIN, Director of Talent Relations; JENNIFER GRÜNWALD, Director of Production & Special Projects; SUSAN CRESPI, Production Manager; STAN LEE, Chairman Emeritus. For information regarding advertising in Marvel Comics or on Marvel.com, please contact Vit DeBellis, Custom Solutions & Integrated Advertising Manager, at vdebellis@marvel.com. For Marvel subscription inquiries, please call 888-511-5480. Manufactured between 4/15/2022 and 5/17/2022 by SOLISCO PRINTERS, SCOTT, QC, CANADA.

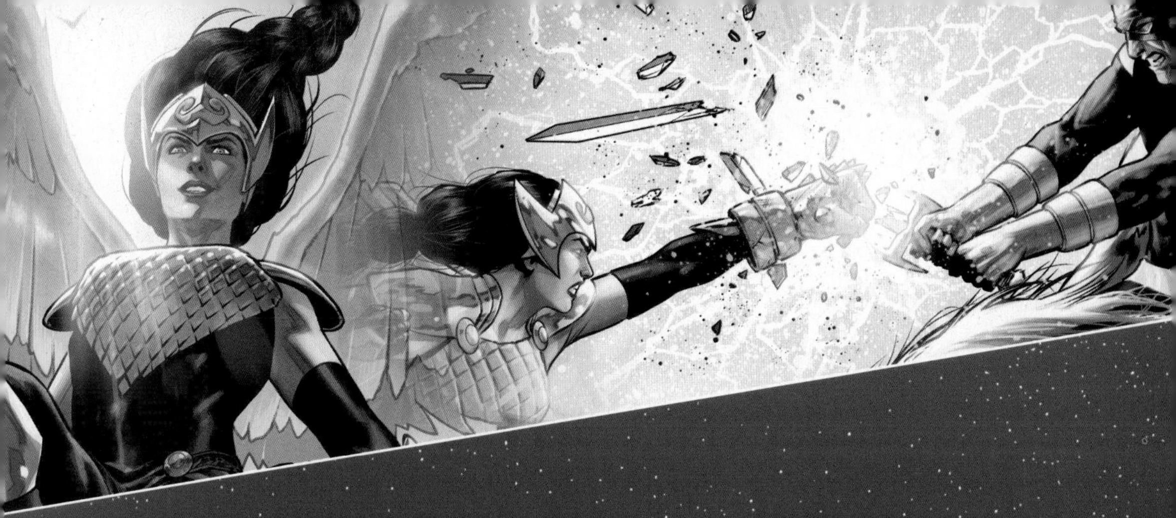

JANE FOSTER: THE SAGA OF VALKYRIE

IGHTY THOR #702-706

RITER: JASON AARON
RTIST: RUSSELL DAUTERMAN
LOR ARTIST: MATTHEW WILSON
VER ART: RUSSELL DAUTERMAN
WITH MATTHEW WILSON (#702-705)

IGHTY THOR: AT THE GATES OF VALHALLA

OMORROW GIRLS"

RITER: JASON AARON
RTIST: JEN BARTEL
LOR ARTIST: MATTHEW WILSON
VER ART: NICK DERINGTON

AR OF THE REALMS OMEGA

OD AND THE DEVIL WALK INTO A CHURCH"

RITER: JASON AARON
RTIST: RON GARNEY
LOR ARTIST: MATT MILLA
VER ART: PHIL NOTO

VALKYRIE: JANE FOSTER #1-5

WRITERS: AL EWING & JASON AARON
ARTISTS: CAFU
WITH RAMÓN K. PÉREZ (#3),
CIAN TORMEY & ROBERTO POGGI (#3)
AND FRAZER IRVING (#3)
COLOR ARTIST: JESUS ABURTOV
COVER ART: MAHMUD ASRAR WITH MATTHEW WILSON (#1-2, #4-5)
& DAVE McCAIG (#3)

VALKYRIE: JANE FOSTER #6-7

WRITERS: AL EWING & JASON AARON
ARTIST: PERE PÉREZ
COLOR ARTIST: JESUS ABURTOV
COVER ART: MAHMUD ASRAR & MATTHEW WILSON

VALKYRIE: JANE FOSTER #8-10

WRITERS: JASON AARON & TORUNN GRØNBEKK
ARTISTS: CAFU (#8) & RAMON ROSANAS (#9-10)
COLOR ARTIST: JESUS ABURTOV
COVER ART: MAHMUD ASRAR & MATTHEW WILSON

TERER: VC's JOE SABINO ASSOCIATE EDITOR: SARAH BRUNSTAD EDITOR: WIL MOSS

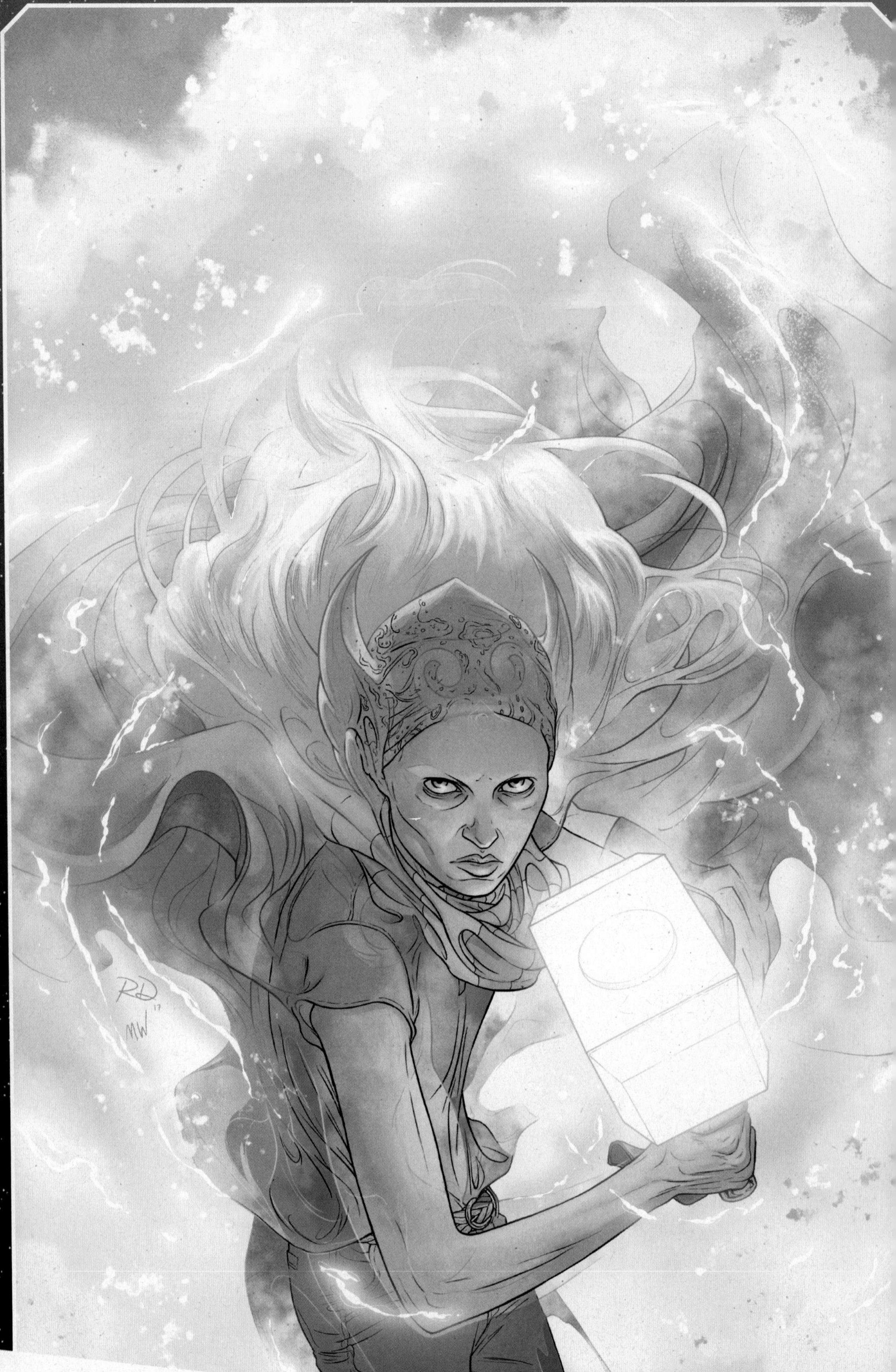

MIGHTY THOR #70[illegible]

When DR. JANE FOSTER lifts the mystic hammer Mjolnir, she is transformed into the Goddess of Thunder, THE MIGHTY THOR! Her enemies are many, as Asgard descends further into chaos and war threatens to spread throughout the Ten Realms. Yet her greatest battle will be against a far more personal foe: the cancer that is killing her mortal form...

MALEKITH and his allies are waging war across the Ten Realms, forcing Jane to neglect her cancer treatments so that Thor can defend the realms. His army killed Karnilla, Queen of the Norns, freeing Malekith from the power of the Fates. And with her dying breath, Karnilla warned Odinson that the death he should fear...is Jane's.

Malekith's plots have unleashed the Mangog — the manifested vengeance of a billion, billion murdered souls. After crushing Volstagg, the new War Thor, and destroying Old Asgard, the Mangog now flies to Asgardia to deliver the ultimate judgment of the gods...

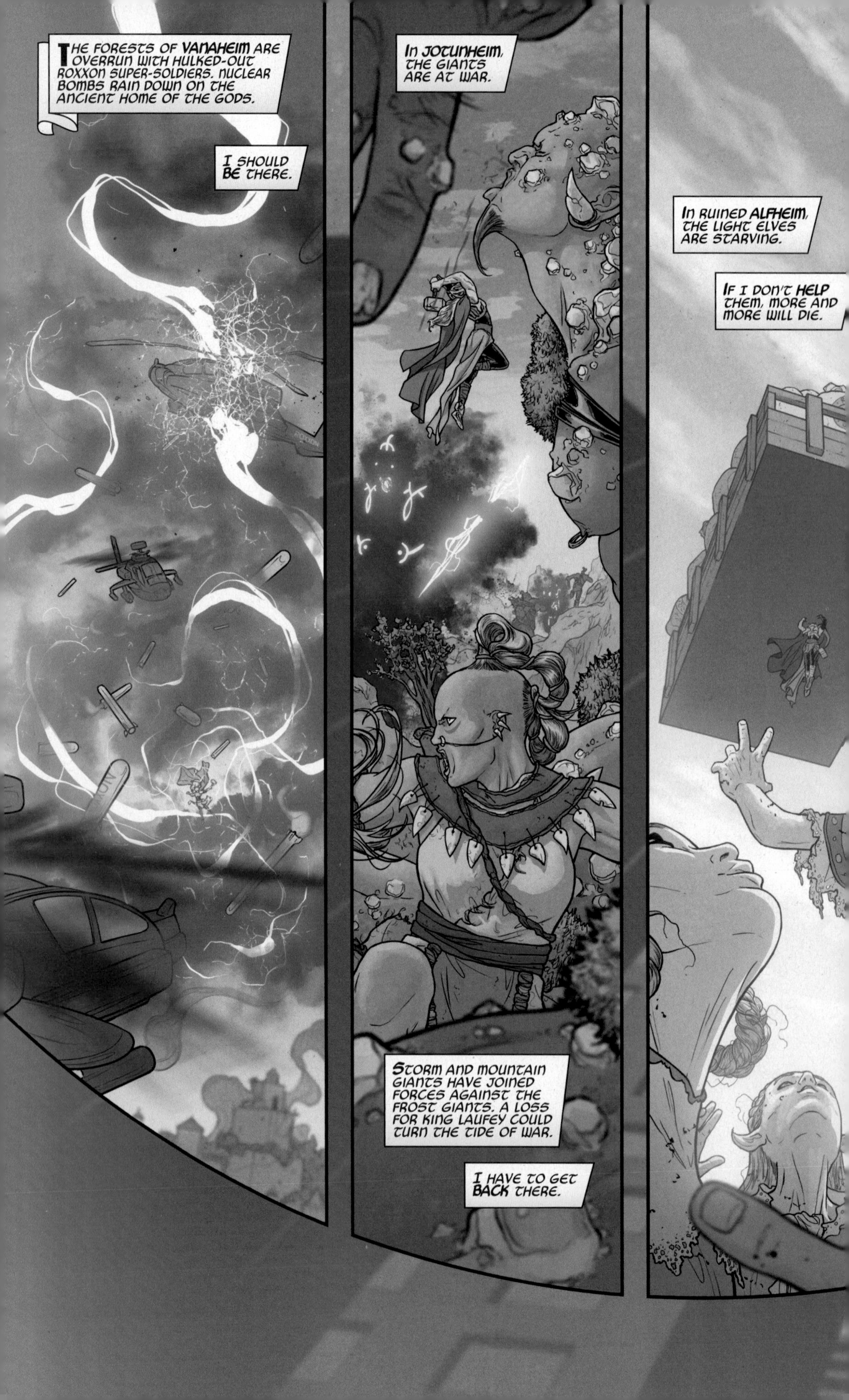
THE FORESTS OF VANAHEIM ARE OVERRUN WITH HULKED-OUT ROXXON SUPER-SOLDIERS. NUCLEAR BOMBS RAIN DOWN ON THE ANCIENT HOME OF THE GODS.
I SHOULD BE THERE.
IN JOTUNHEIM, THE GIANTS ARE AT WAR.
STORM AND MOUNTAIN GIANTS HAVE JOINED FORCES AGAINST THE FROST GIANTS. A LOSS FOR KING LAUFEY COULD TURN THE TIDE OF WAR.
I HAVE TO GET BACK THERE.
IN RUINED ALFHEIM, THE LIGHT ELVES ARE STARVING.
IF I DON'T HELP THEM, MORE AND MORE WILL DIE.

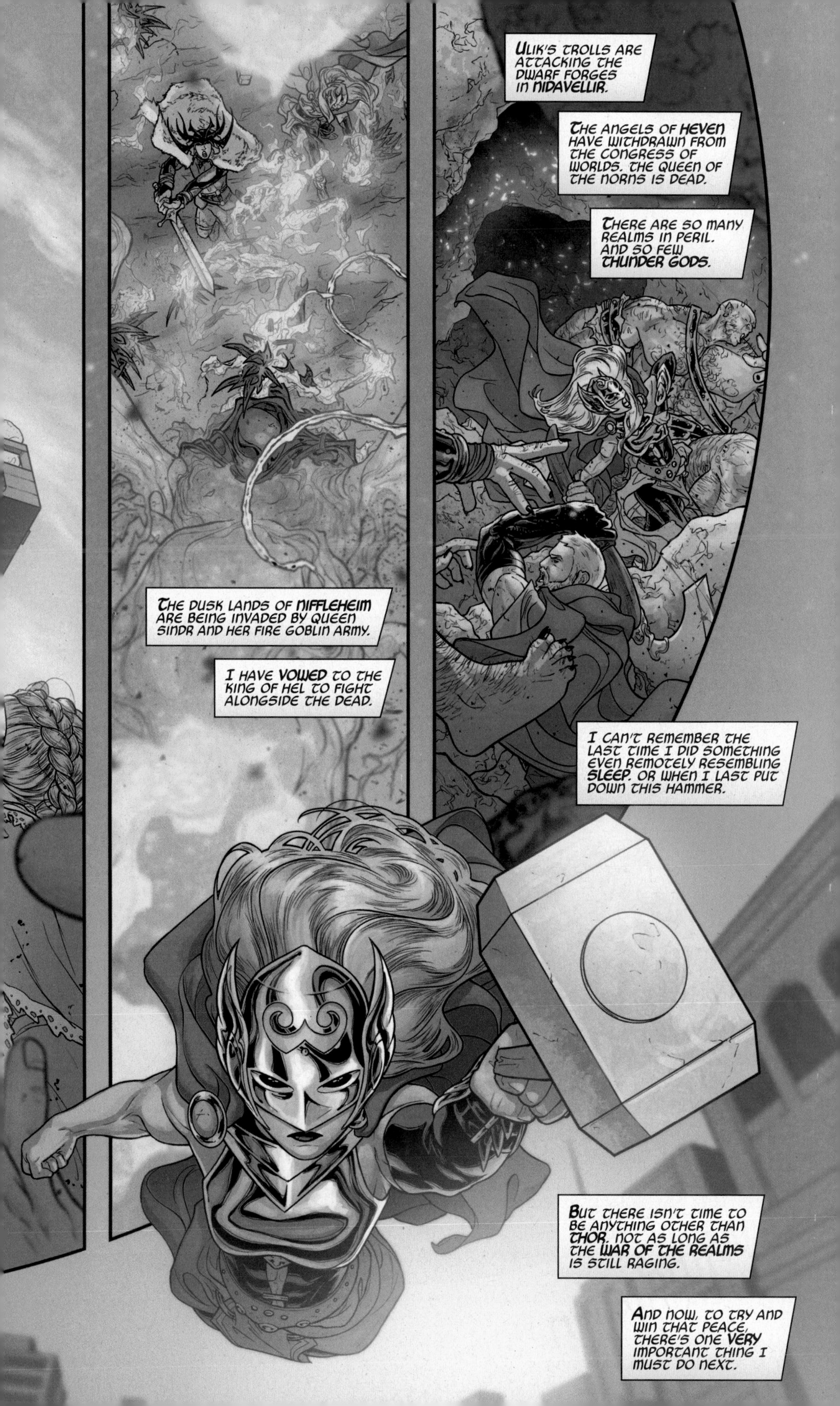

ULIK'S TROLLS ARE ATTACKING THE DWARF FORGES IN NIDAVELLIR.
THE ANGELS OF HEVEN HAVE WITHDRAWN FROM THE CONGRESS OF WORLDS. THE QUEEN OF THE NORNS IS DEAD.
THERE ARE SO MANY REALMS IN PERIL. AND SO FEW THUNDER GODS.
THE DUSK LANDS OF NIFFLEHEIM ARE BEING INVADED BY QUEEN SINDR AND HER FIRE GOBLIN ARMY.
I HAVE VOWED TO THE KING OF HEL TO FIGHT ALONGSIDE THE DEAD.
I CAN'T REMEMBER THE LAST TIME I DID SOMETHING EVEN REMOTELY RESEMBLING SLEEP. OR WHEN I LAST PUT DOWN THIS HAMMER.
BUT THERE ISN'T TIME TO BE ANYTHING OTHER THAN THOR. NOT AS LONG AS THE WAR OF THE REALMS IS STILL RAGING.
AND NOW, TO TRY AND WIN THAT PEACE, THERE'S ONE VERY IMPORTANT THING I MUST DO NEXT.

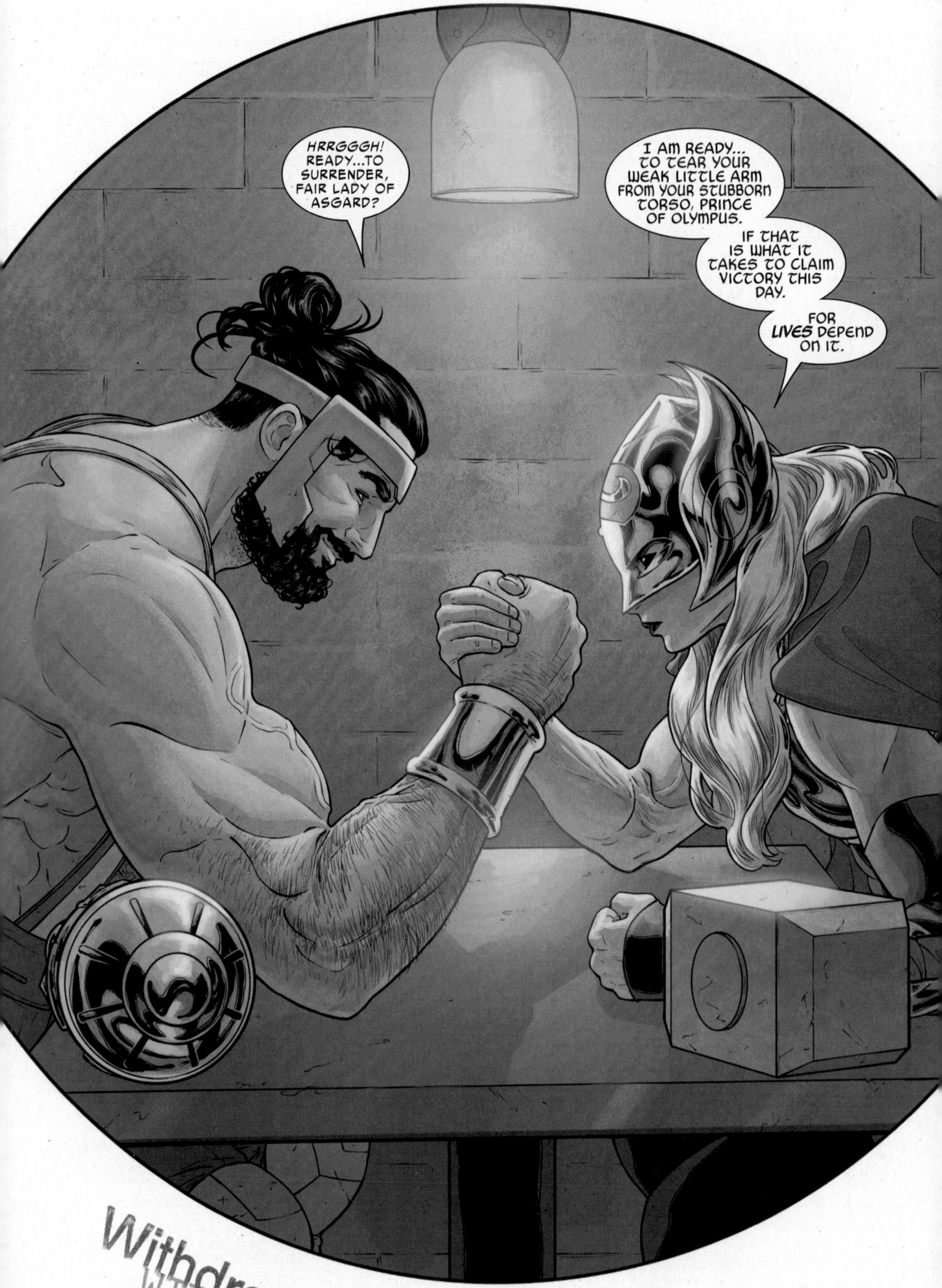
HRRGGGH! READY...TO SURRENDER, FAIR LADY OF ASGARD?
I AM READY... TO TEAR YOUR WEAK LITTLE ARM FROM YOUR STUBBORN TORSO, PRINCE OF OLYMPUS.
IF THAT IS WHAT IT TAKES TO CLAIM VICTORY THIS DAY.
FOR LIVES DEPEND ON IT.

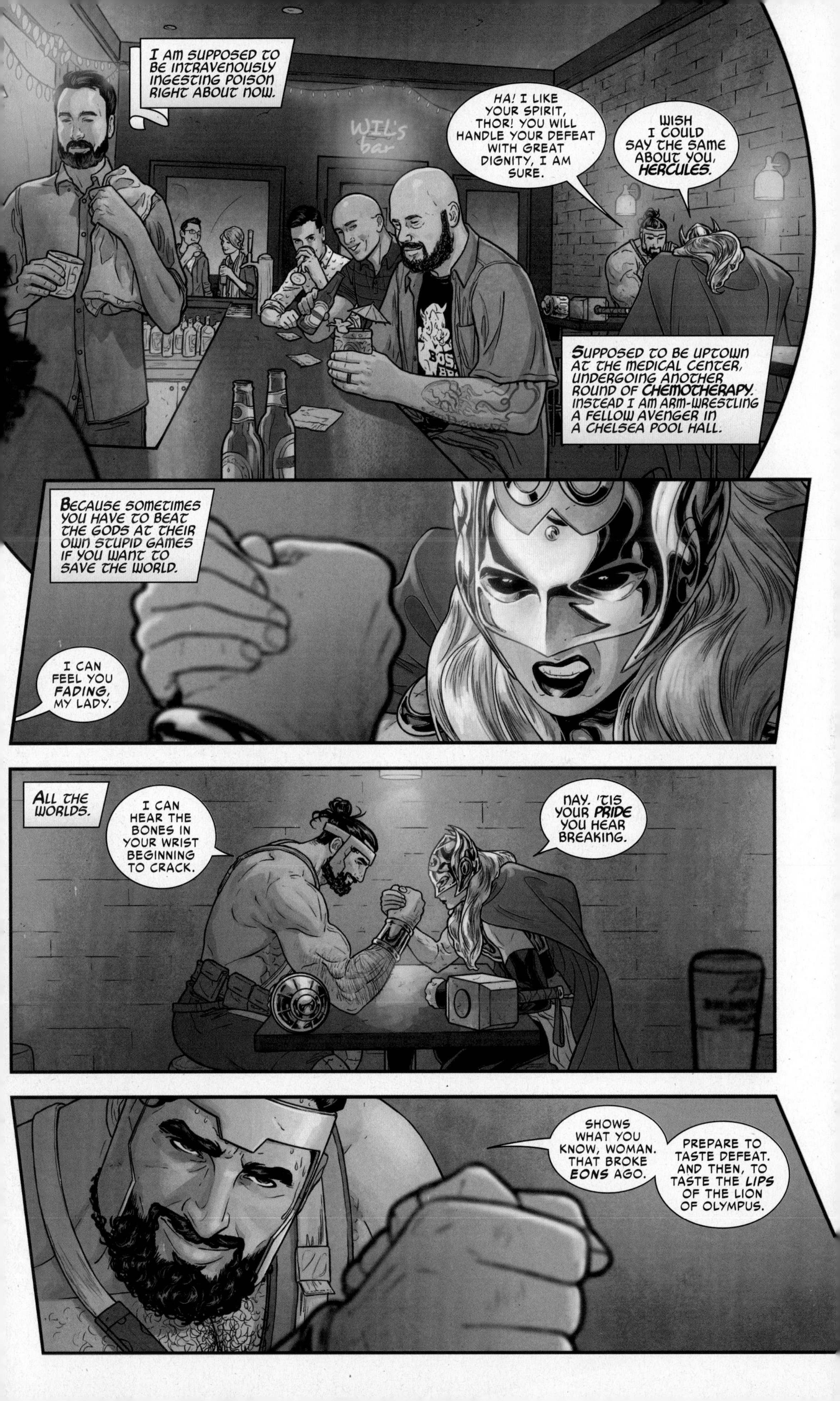
I AM SUPPOSED TO BE INTRAVENOUSLY INGESTING POISON RIGHT ABOUT NOW.
WIL's bar
HA! I LIKE YOUR SPIRIT, THOR! YOU WILL HANDLE YOUR DEFEAT WITH GREAT DIGNITY, I AM SURE.
WISH I COULD SAY THE SAME ABOUT YOU, HERCULES.
SUPPOSED TO BE UPTOWN AT THE MEDICAL CENTER, UNDERGOING ANOTHER ROUND OF CHEMOTHERAPY. INSTEAD I AM ARM-WRESTLING A FELLOW AVENGER IN A CHELSEA POOL HALL.
BECAUSE SOMETIMES YOU HAVE TO BEAT THE GODS AT THEIR OWN STUPID GAMES IF YOU WANT TO SAVE THE WORLD.
I CAN FEEL YOU FADING, MY LADY.
ALL THE WORLDS.
I CAN HEAR THE BONES IN YOUR WRIST BEGINNING TO CRACK.
NAY. 'TIS YOUR PRIDE YOU HEAR BREAKING.
SHOWS WHAT YOU KNOW, WOMAN. THAT BROKE EONS AGO.
PREPARE TO TASTE DEFEAT. AND THEN, TO TASTE THE LIPS OF THE LION OF OLYMPUS.

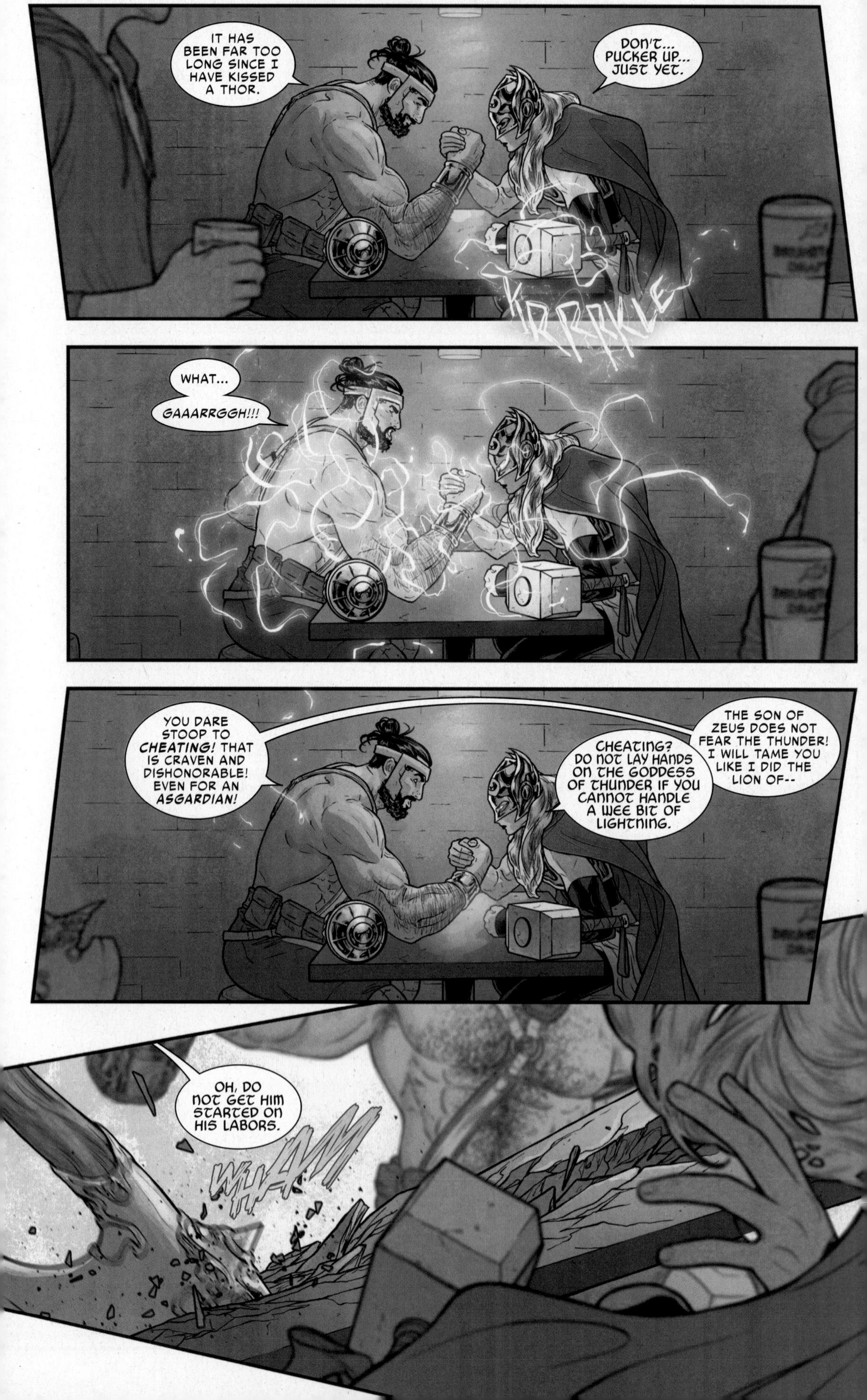

IT HAS BEEN FAR TOO LONG SINCE I HAVE KISSED A THOR.
DON'T... PUCKER UP... JUST YET.
KRRRKLE
WHAT...
GAAARRGGH!!!
YOU DARE STOOP TO CHEATING! THAT IS CRAVEN AND DISHONORABLE! EVEN FOR AN ASGARDIAN!
CHEATING? DO NOT LAY HANDS ON THE GODDESS OF THUNDER IF YOU CANNOT HANDLE A WEE BIT OF LIGHTNING.
THE SON OF ZEUS DOES NOT FEAR THE THUNDER! I WILL TAME YOU LIKE I DID THE LION OF--
OH, DO NOT GET HIM STARTED ON HIS LABORS.
WHAM

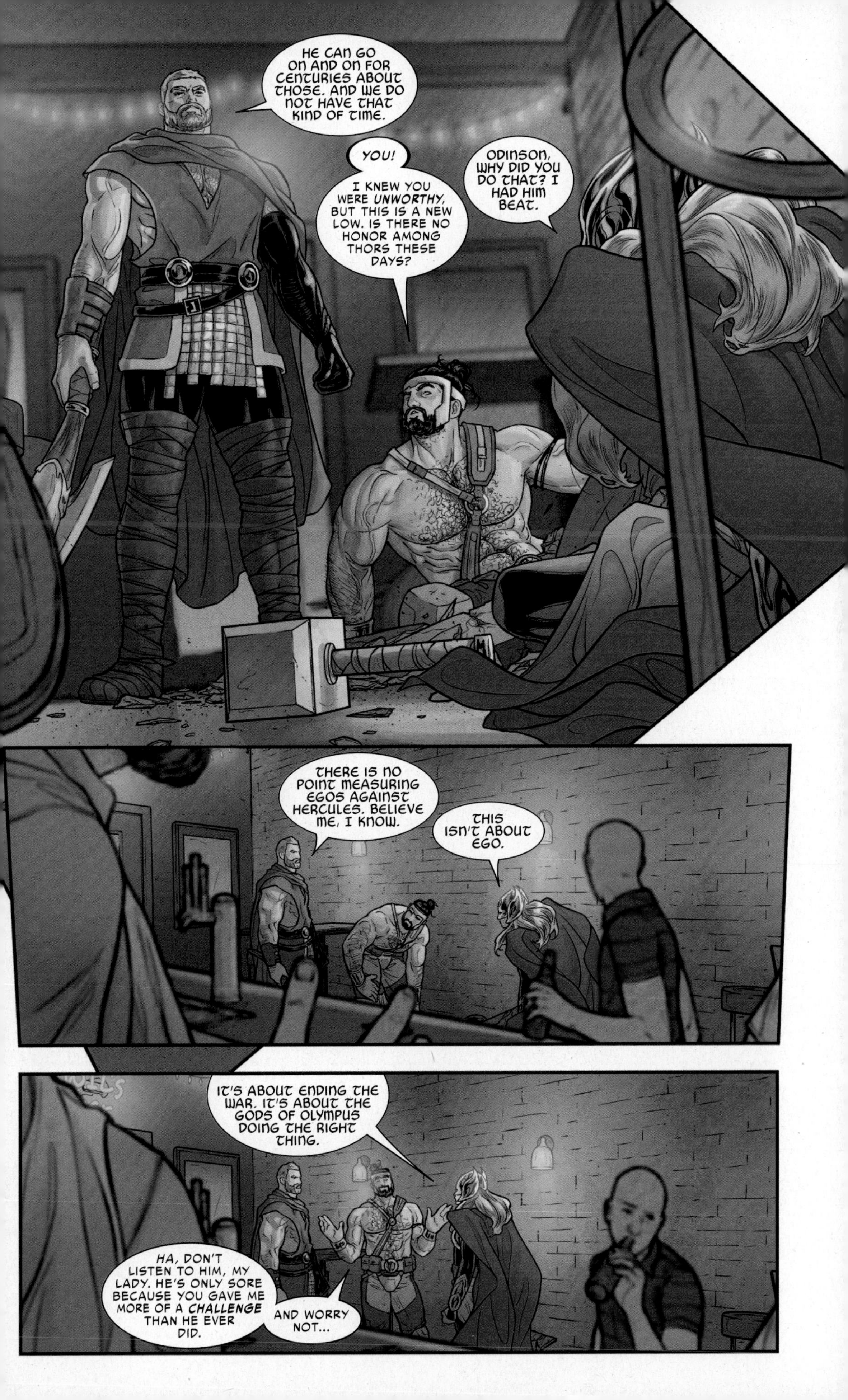
HE CAN GO ON AND ON FOR CENTURIES ABOUT THOSE. AND WE DO NOT HAVE THAT KIND OF TIME.
YOU!
I KNEW YOU WERE *UNWORTHY*, BUT THIS IS A NEW LOW. IS THERE NO HONOR AMONG THORS THESE DAYS?
ODINSON, WHY DID YOU DO THAT? I HAD HIM BEAT.
THERE IS NO POINT MEASURING EGOS AGAINST HERCULES. BELIEVE ME, I KNOW.
THIS ISN'T ABOUT EGO.
IT'S ABOUT ENDING THE WAR. IT'S ABOUT THE GODS OF OLYMPUS DOING THE RIGHT THING.
HA, DON'T LISTEN TO HIM, MY LADY. HE'S ONLY SORE BECAUSE YOU GAVE ME MORE OF A *CHALLENGE* THAN HE EVER DID.
AND WORRY NOT...

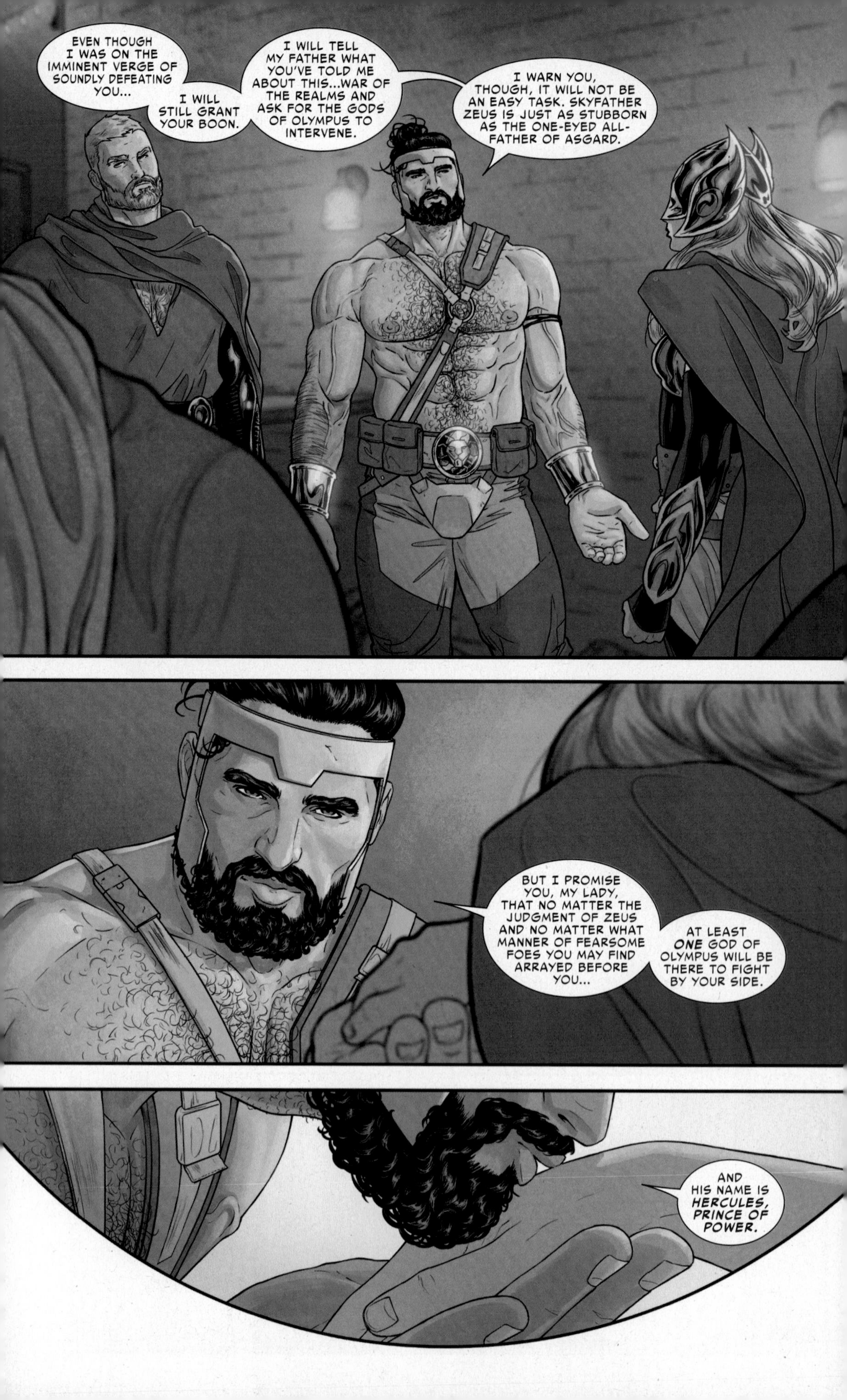
EVEN THOUGH I WAS ON THE IMMINENT VERGE OF SOUNDLY DEFEATING YOU...
I WILL STILL GRANT YOUR BOON.
I WILL TELL MY FATHER WHAT YOU'VE TOLD ME ABOUT THIS...WAR OF THE REALMS AND ASK FOR THE GODS OF OLYMPUS TO INTERVENE.
I WARN YOU, THOUGH, IT WILL NOT BE AN EASY TASK. SKYFATHER ZEUS IS JUST AS STUBBORN AS THE ONE-EYED ALL-FATHER OF ASGARD.
BUT I PROMISE YOU, MY LADY, THAT NO MATTER THE JUDGMENT OF ZEUS AND NO MATTER WHAT MANNER OF FEARSOME FOES YOU MAY FIND ARRAYED BEFORE YOU...
AT LEAST ***ONE*** GOD OF OLYMPUS WILL BE THERE TO FIGHT BY YOUR SIDE.
AND HIS NAME IS ***HERCULES, PRINCE OF POWER.***

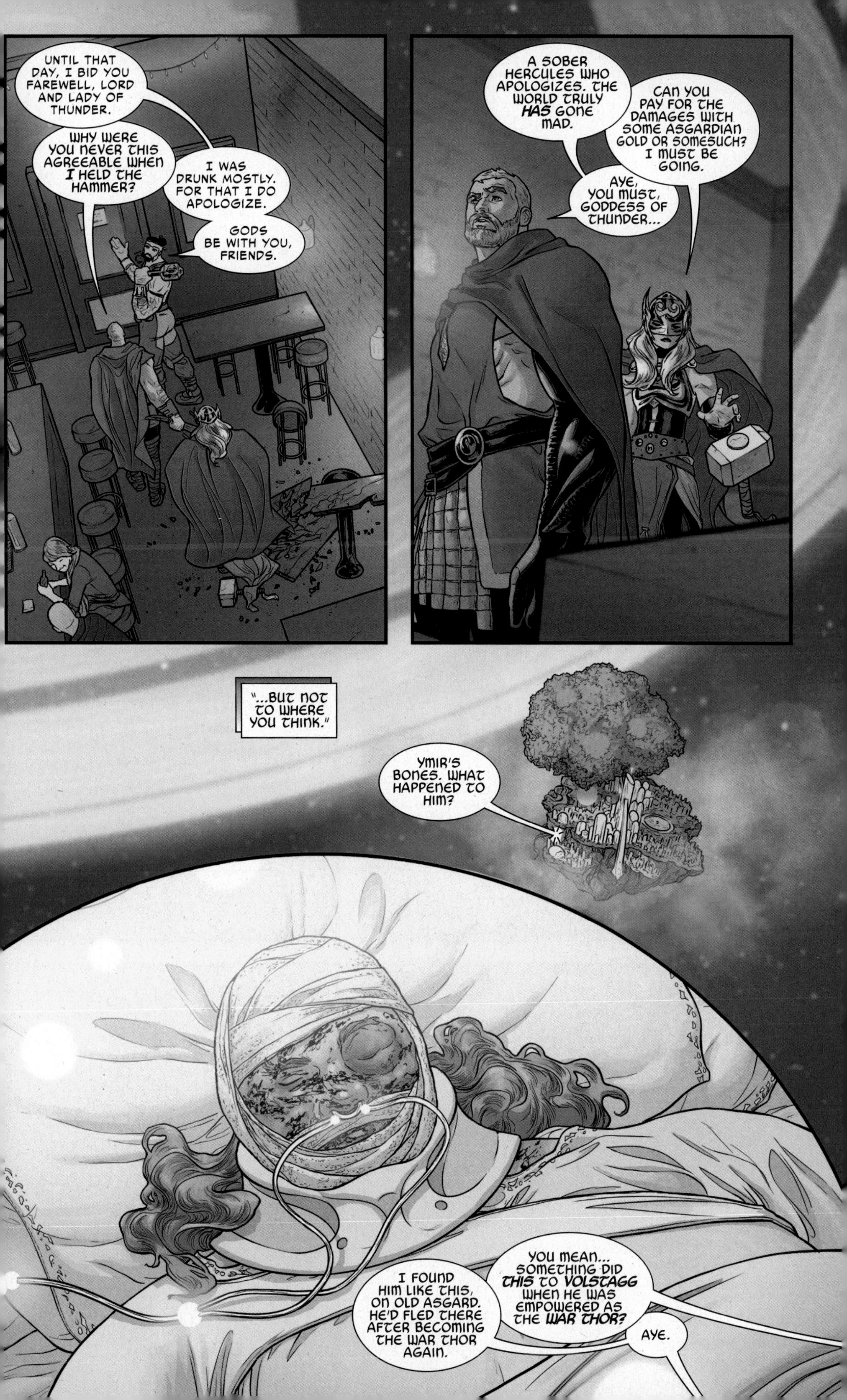

UNTIL THAT DAY, I BID YOU FAREWELL, LORD AND LADY OF THUNDER.
WHY WERE YOU NEVER THIS AGREEABLE WHEN I HELD THE HAMMER?
I WAS DRUNK MOSTLY. FOR THAT I DO APOLOGIZE.
GODS BE WITH YOU, FRIENDS.
A SOBER HERCULES WHO APOLOGIZES. THE WORLD TRULY HAS GONE MAD.
CAN YOU PAY FOR THE DAMAGES WITH SOME ASGARDIAN GOLD OR SOMESUCH? I MUST BE GOING.
AYE, YOU MUST, GODDESS OF THUNDER...
"...BUT NOT TO WHERE YOU THINK."
YMIR'S BONES. WHAT HAPPENED TO HIM?
I FOUND HIM LIKE THIS, ON OLD ASGARD. HE'D FLED THERE AFTER BECOMING THE WAR THOR AGAIN.
YOU MEAN... SOMETHING DID THIS TO VOLSTAGG WHEN HE WAS EMPOWERED AS THE WAR THOR?
AYE.

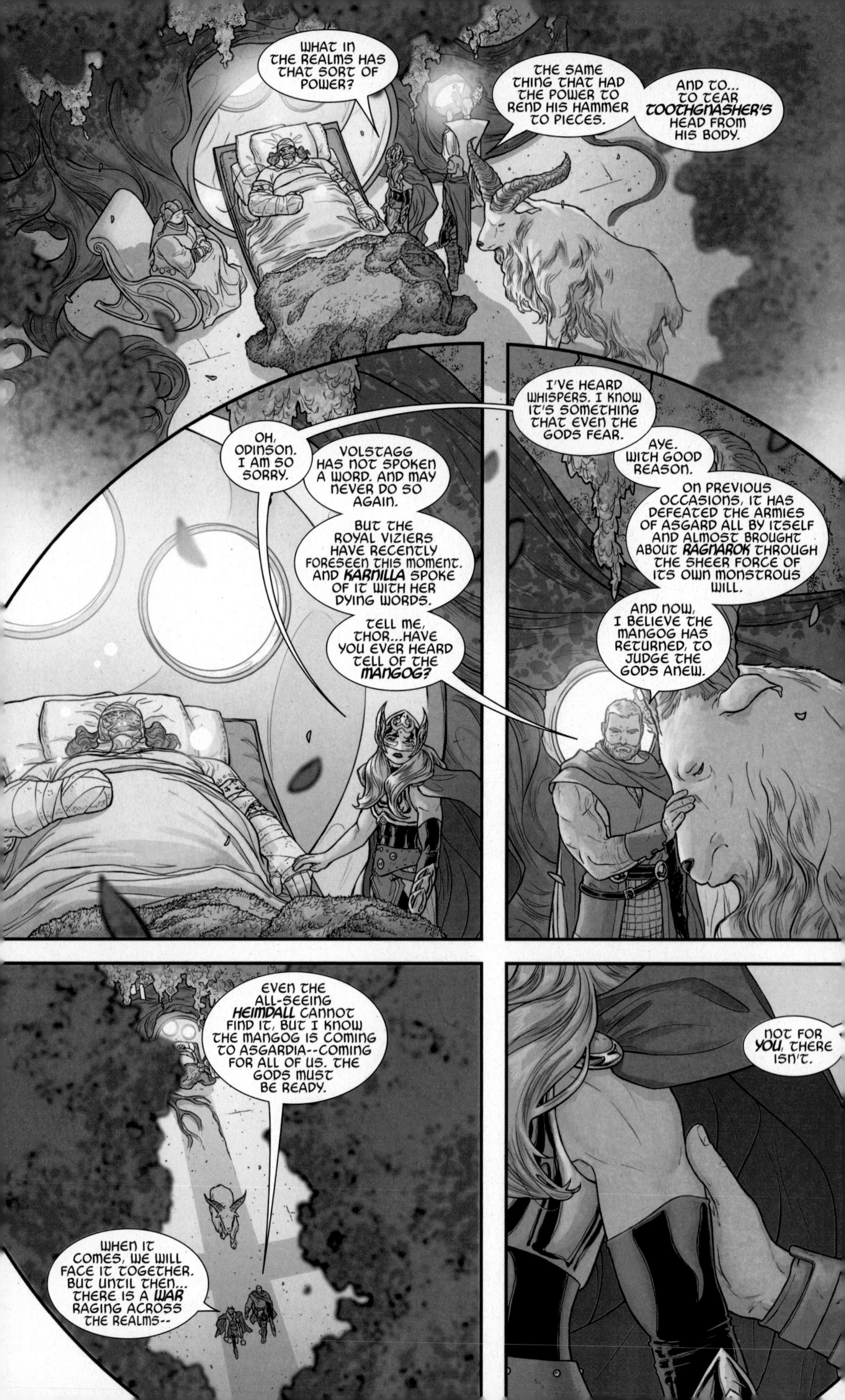
WHAT IN THE REALMS HAS THAT SORT OF POWER?
THE SAME THING THAT HAD THE POWER TO REND HIS HAMMER TO PIECES.
AND TO... TO TEAR TOOTHGNASHER'S HEAD FROM HIS BODY.
OH, ODINSON. I AM SO SORRY.
I'VE HEARD WHISPERS. I KNOW IT'S SOMETHING THAT EVEN THE GODS FEAR.
VOLSTAGG HAS NOT SPOKEN A WORD. AND MAY NEVER DO SO AGAIN.
BUT THE ROYAL VIZIERS HAVE RECENTLY FORESEEN THIS MOMENT. AND KARNILLA SPOKE OF IT WITH HER DYING WORDS.
TELL ME, THOR...HAVE YOU EVER HEARD TELL OF THE MANGOG?
AYE. WITH GOOD REASON.
ON PREVIOUS OCCASIONS, IT HAS DEFEATED THE ARMIES OF ASGARD ALL BY ITSELF AND ALMOST BROUGHT ABOUT RAGNAROK THROUGH THE SHEER FORCE OF ITS OWN MONSTROUS WILL.
AND NOW, I BELIEVE THE MANGOG HAS RETURNED, TO JUDGE THE GODS ANEW.
EVEN THE ALL-SEEING HEIMDALL CANNOT FIND IT, BUT I KNOW THE MANGOG IS COMING TO ASGARDIA--COMING FOR ALL OF US. THE GODS MUST BE READY.
WHEN IT COMES, WE WILL FACE IT TOGETHER. BUT UNTIL THEN... THERE IS A WAR RAGING ACROSS THE REALMS--
NOT FOR YOU, THERE ISN'T.

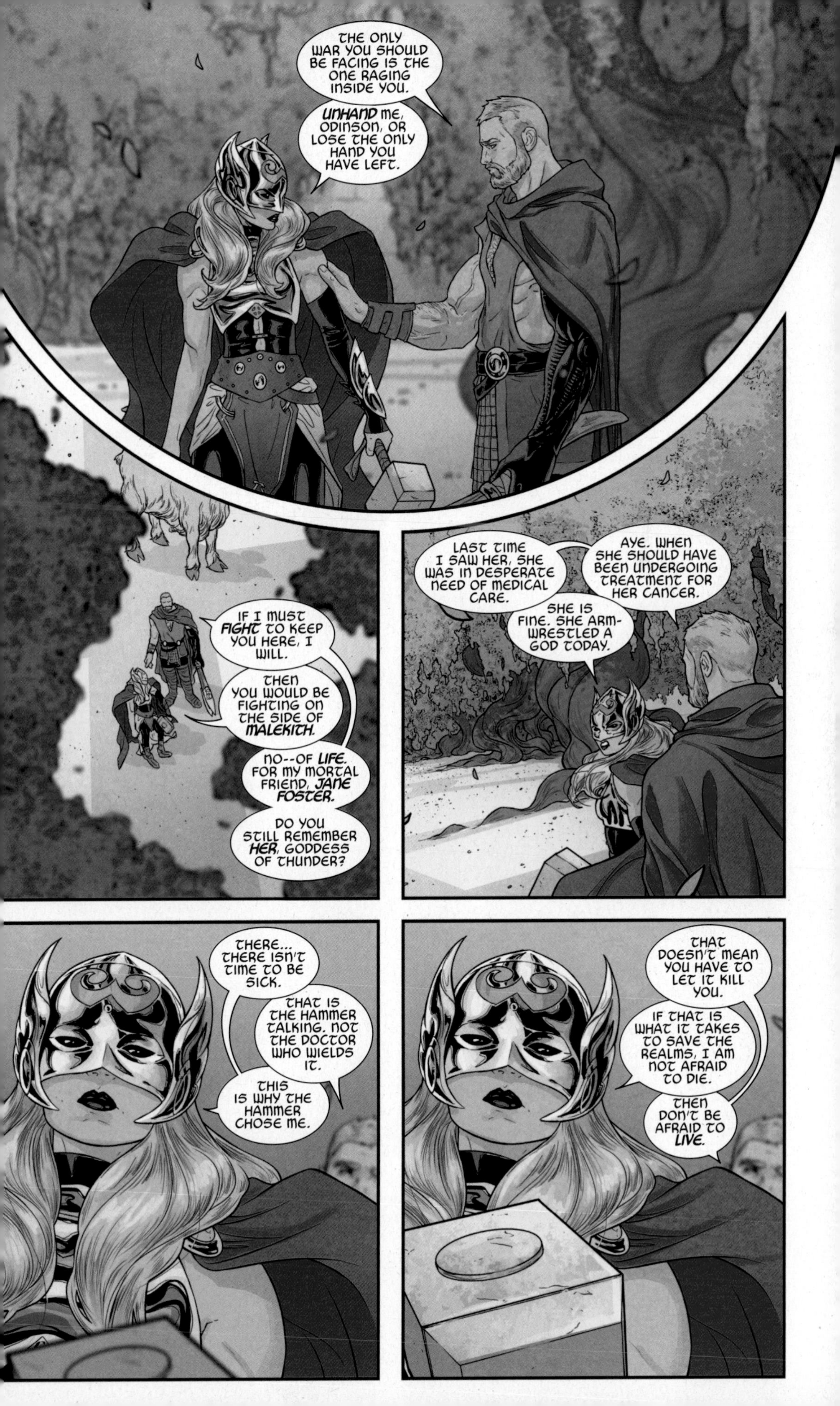
THE ONLY WAR YOU SHOULD BE FACING IS THE ONE RAGING INSIDE YOU.
UNHAND ME, ODINSON, OR LOSE THE ONLY HAND YOU HAVE LEFT.
IF I MUST FIGHT TO KEEP YOU HERE, I WILL.
THEN YOU WOULD BE FIGHTING ON THE SIDE OF MALEKITH.
NO--OF LIFE. FOR MY MORTAL FRIEND, JANE FOSTER.
DO YOU STILL REMEMBER HER, GODDESS OF THUNDER?
LAST TIME I SAW HER, SHE WAS IN DESPERATE NEED OF MEDICAL CARE.
SHE IS FINE. SHE ARM-WRESTLED A GOD TODAY.
AYE. WHEN SHE SHOULD HAVE BEEN UNDERGOING TREATMENT FOR HER CANCER.
THERE... THERE ISN'T TIME TO BE SICK.
THAT IS THE HAMMER TALKING. NOT THE DOCTOR WHO WIELDS IT.
THIS IS WHY THE HAMMER CHOSE ME.
THAT DOESN'T MEAN YOU HAVE TO LET IT KILL YOU.
IF THAT IS WHAT IT TAKES TO SAVE THE REALMS, I AM NOT AFRAID TO DIE.
THEN DON'T BE AFRAID TO LIVE.

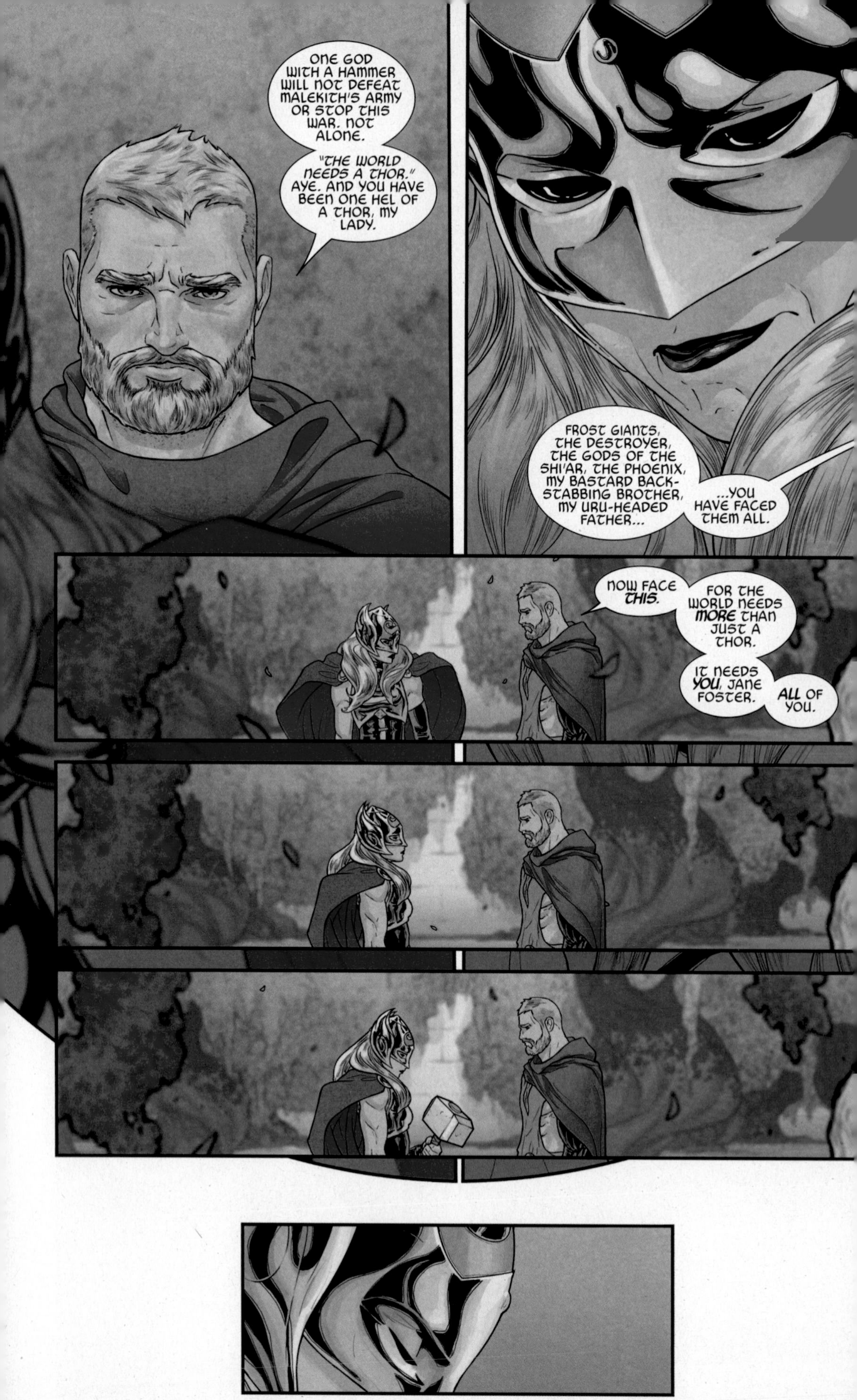
ONE GOD WITH A HAMMER WILL NOT DEFEAT MALEKITH'S ARMY OR STOP THIS WAR. NOT ALONE.
"THE WORLD NEEDS A THOR." AYE. AND YOU HAVE BEEN ONE HEL OF A THOR, MY LADY.
FROST GIANTS, THE DESTROYER, THE GODS OF THE SHI'AR, THE PHOENIX, MY BASTARD BACK-STABBING BROTHER, MY URU-HEADED FATHER...
...YOU HAVE FACED THEM ALL.
NOW FACE THIS.
FOR THE WORLD NEEDS MORE THAN JUST A THOR.
IT NEEDS YOU, JANE FOSTER.
ALL OF YOU.

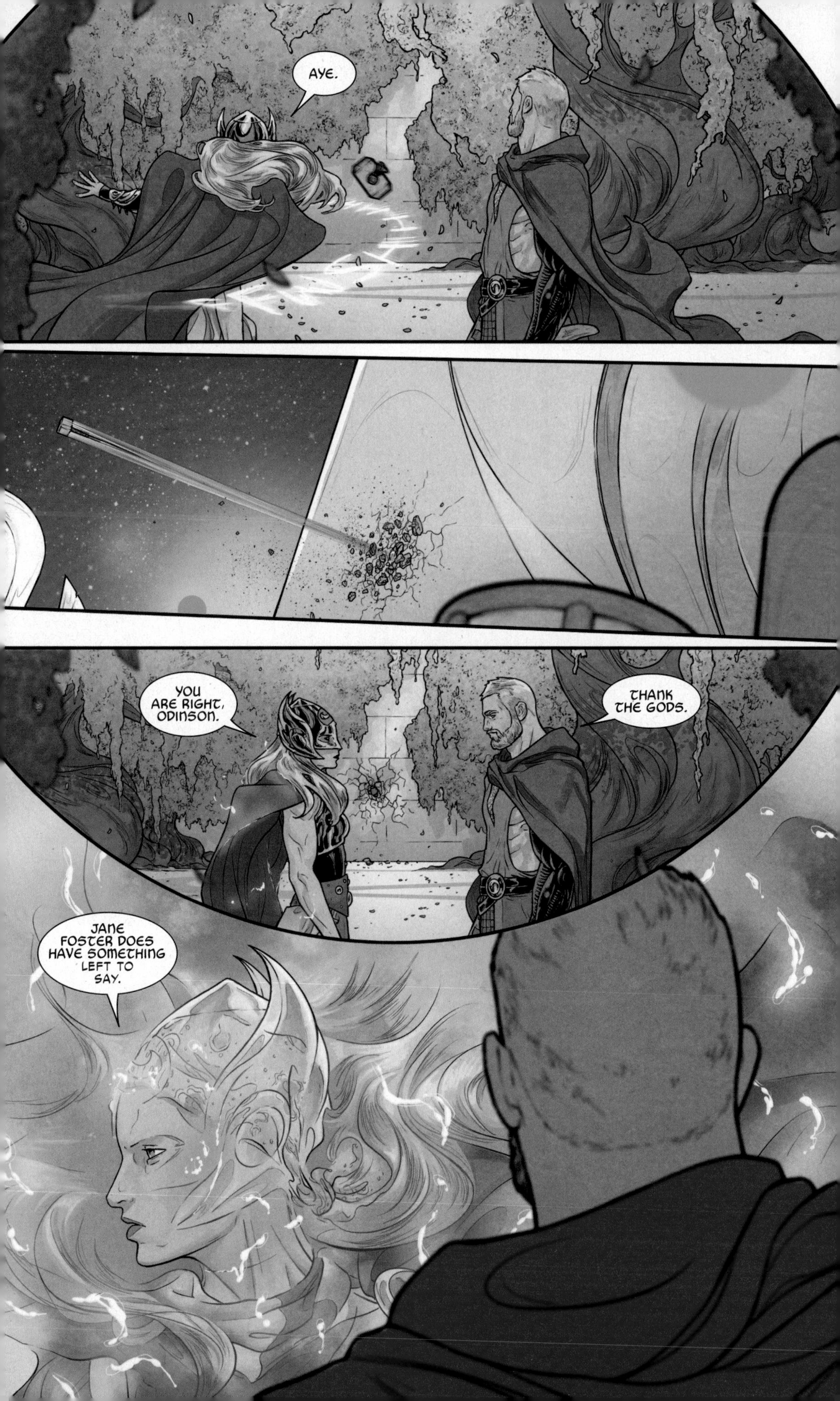
AYE.
YOU ARE RIGHT, ODINSON.
THANK THE GODS.
JANE FOSTER DOES HAVE SOMETHING LEFT TO SAY.

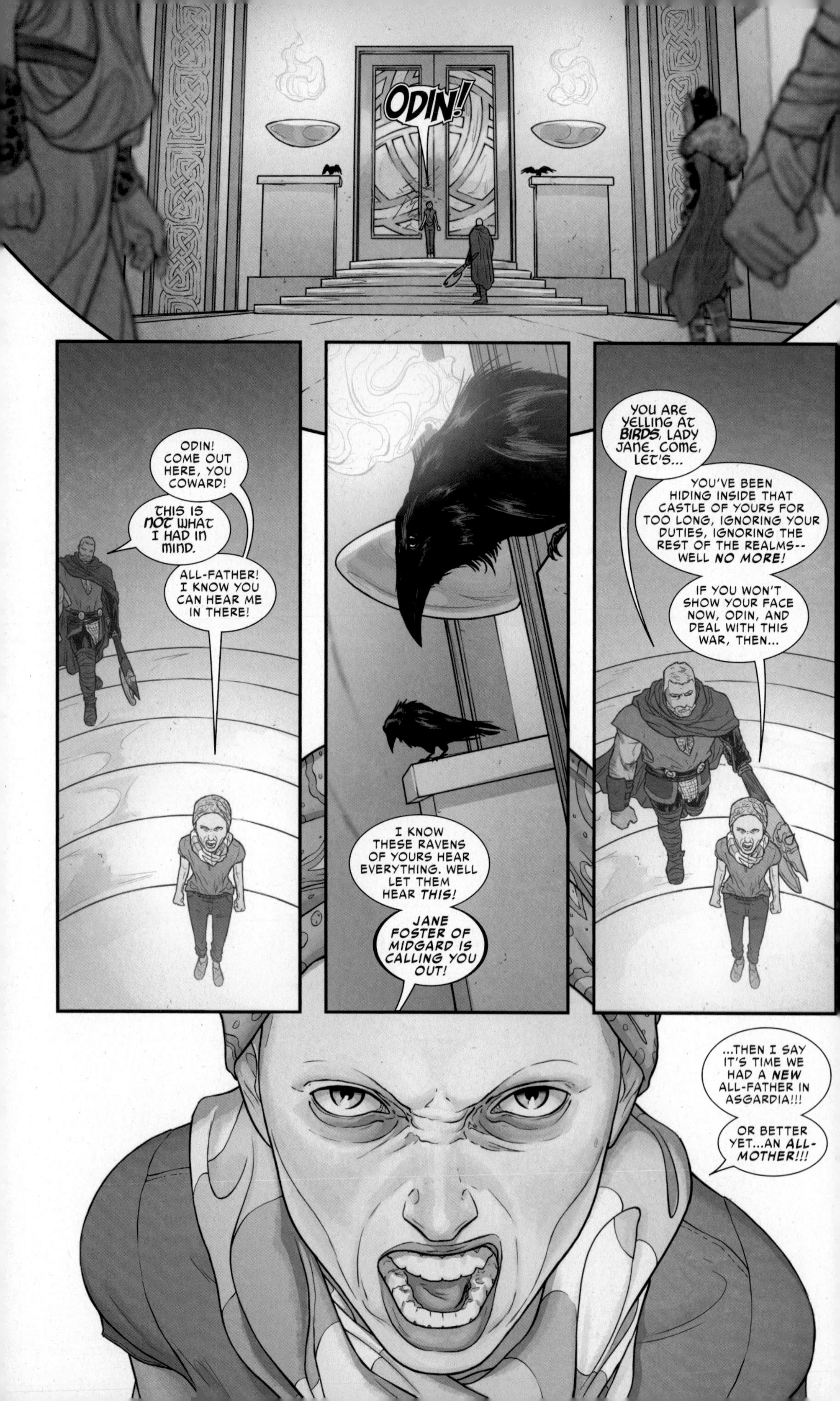

ODIN!
ODIN! COME OUT HERE, YOU COWARD!
THIS IS NOT WHAT I HAD IN MIND.
ALL-FATHER! I KNOW YOU CAN HEAR ME IN THERE!
I KNOW THESE RAVENS OF YOURS HEAR EVERYTHING. WELL LET THEM HEAR THIS!
JANE FOSTER OF MIDGARD IS CALLING YOU OUT!
YOU ARE YELLING AT BIRDS, LADY JANE. COME, LET'S...
YOU'VE BEEN HIDING INSIDE THAT CASTLE OF YOURS FOR TOO LONG, IGNORING YOUR DUTIES, IGNORING THE REST OF THE REALMS-- WELL NO MORE!
IF YOU WON'T SHOW YOUR FACE NOW, ODIN, AND DEAL WITH THIS WAR, THEN...
...THEN I SAY IT'S TIME WE HAD A NEW ALL-FATHER IN ASGARDIA!!!
OR BETTER YET...AN ALL-MOTHER!!!

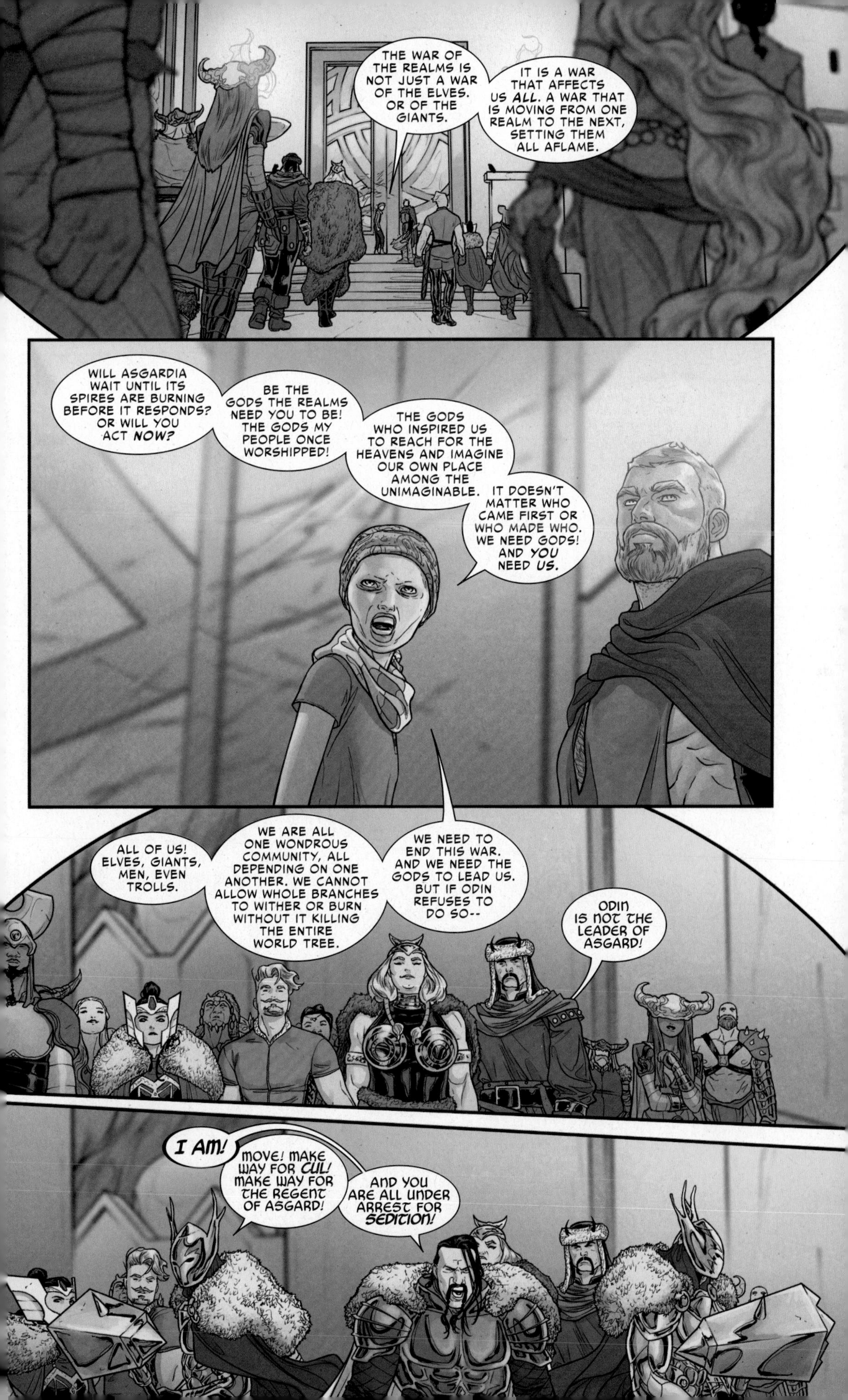
THE WAR OF THE REALMS IS NOT JUST A WAR OF THE ELVES. OR OF THE GIANTS.
IT IS A WAR THAT AFFECTS US ALL. A WAR THAT IS MOVING FROM ONE REALM TO THE NEXT, SETTING THEM ALL AFLAME.
WILL ASGARDIA WAIT UNTIL ITS SPIRES ARE BURNING BEFORE IT RESPONDS? OR WILL YOU ACT NOW?
BE THE GODS THE REALMS NEED YOU TO BE! THE GODS MY PEOPLE ONCE WORSHIPPED!
THE GODS WHO INSPIRED US TO REACH FOR THE HEAVENS AND IMAGINE OUR OWN PLACE AMONG THE UNIMAGINABLE.
IT DOESN'T MATTER WHO CAME FIRST OR WHO MADE WHO. WE NEED GODS! AND YOU NEED US.
ALL OF US! ELVES, GIANTS, MEN, EVEN TROLLS.
WE ARE ALL ONE WONDROUS COMMUNITY, ALL DEPENDING ON ONE ANOTHER. WE CANNOT ALLOW WHOLE BRANCHES TO WITHER OR BURN WITHOUT IT KILLING THE ENTIRE WORLD TREE.
WE NEED TO END THIS WAR. AND WE NEED THE GODS TO LEAD US. BUT IF ODIN REFUSES TO DO SO--
ODIN IS NOT THE LEADER OF ASGARD!
I AM!
MOVE! MAKE WAY FOR CUL! MAKE WAY FOR THE REGENT OF ASGARD!
AND YOU ARE ALL UNDER ARREST FOR SEDITION!

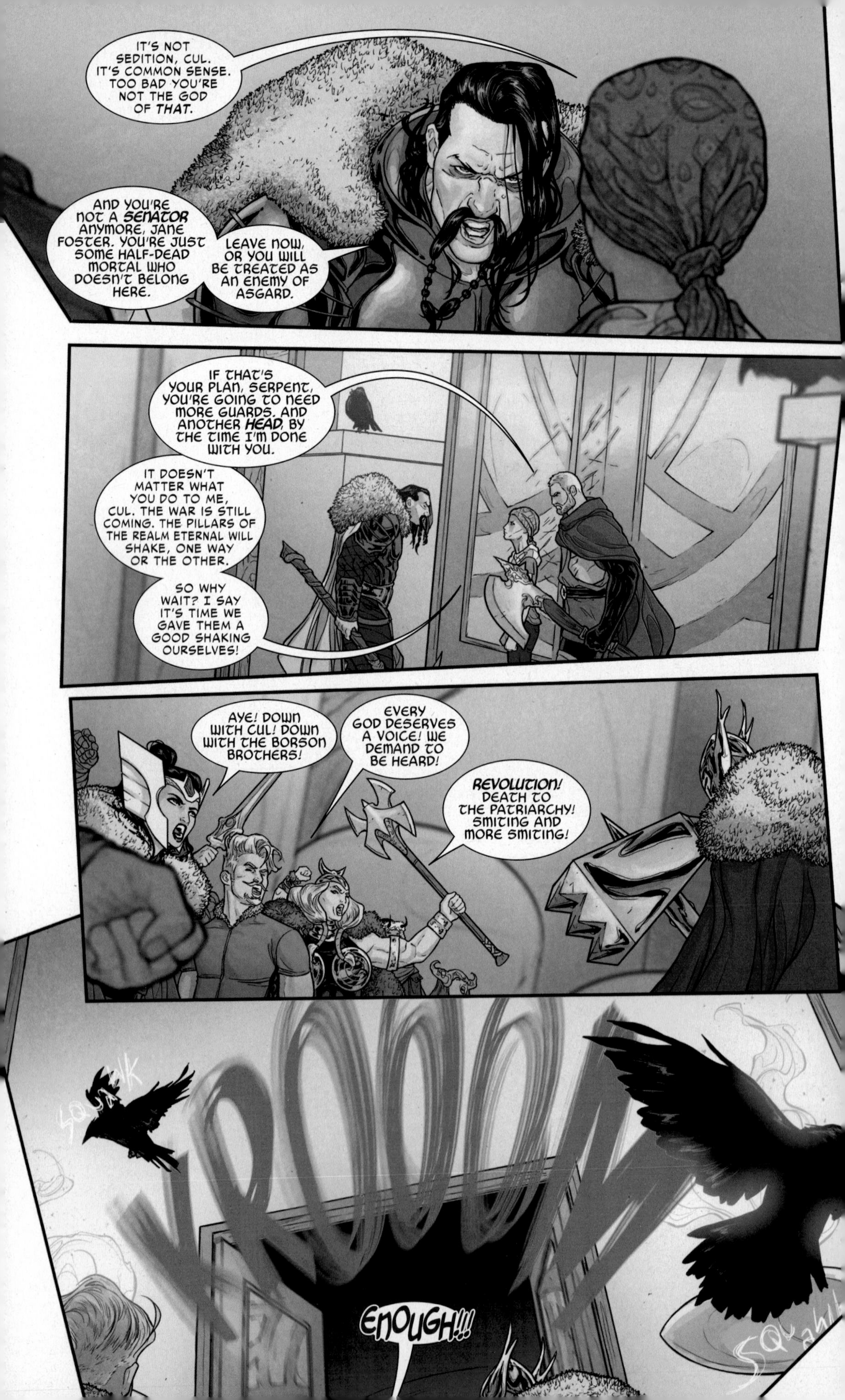
IT'S NOT SEDITION, CUL. IT'S COMMON SENSE. TOO BAD YOU'RE NOT THE GOD OF *THAT*.
AND YOU'RE NOT A ***SENATOR*** ANYMORE, JANE FOSTER. YOU'RE JUST SOME HALF-DEAD MORTAL WHO DOESN'T BELONG HERE.
LEAVE NOW, OR YOU WILL BE TREATED AS AN ENEMY OF ASGARD.
IF THAT'S YOUR PLAN, SERPENT, YOU'RE GOING TO NEED MORE GUARDS. AND ANOTHER ***HEAD***, BY THE TIME I'M DONE WITH YOU.
IT DOESN'T MATTER WHAT YOU DO TO ME, CUL. THE WAR IS STILL COMING. THE PILLARS OF THE REALM ETERNAL WILL SHAKE, ONE WAY OR THE OTHER.
SO WHY WAIT? I SAY IT'S TIME WE GAVE THEM A GOOD SHAKING OURSELVES!
AYE! DOWN WITH CUL! DOWN WITH THE BORSON BROTHERS!
EVERY GOD DESERVES A VOICE! WE DEMAND TO BE HEARD!
REVOLUTION! DEATH TO THE PATRIARCHY! SMITING AND MORE SMITING!
SQUAWK
ENOUGH!!!
SQUAWK

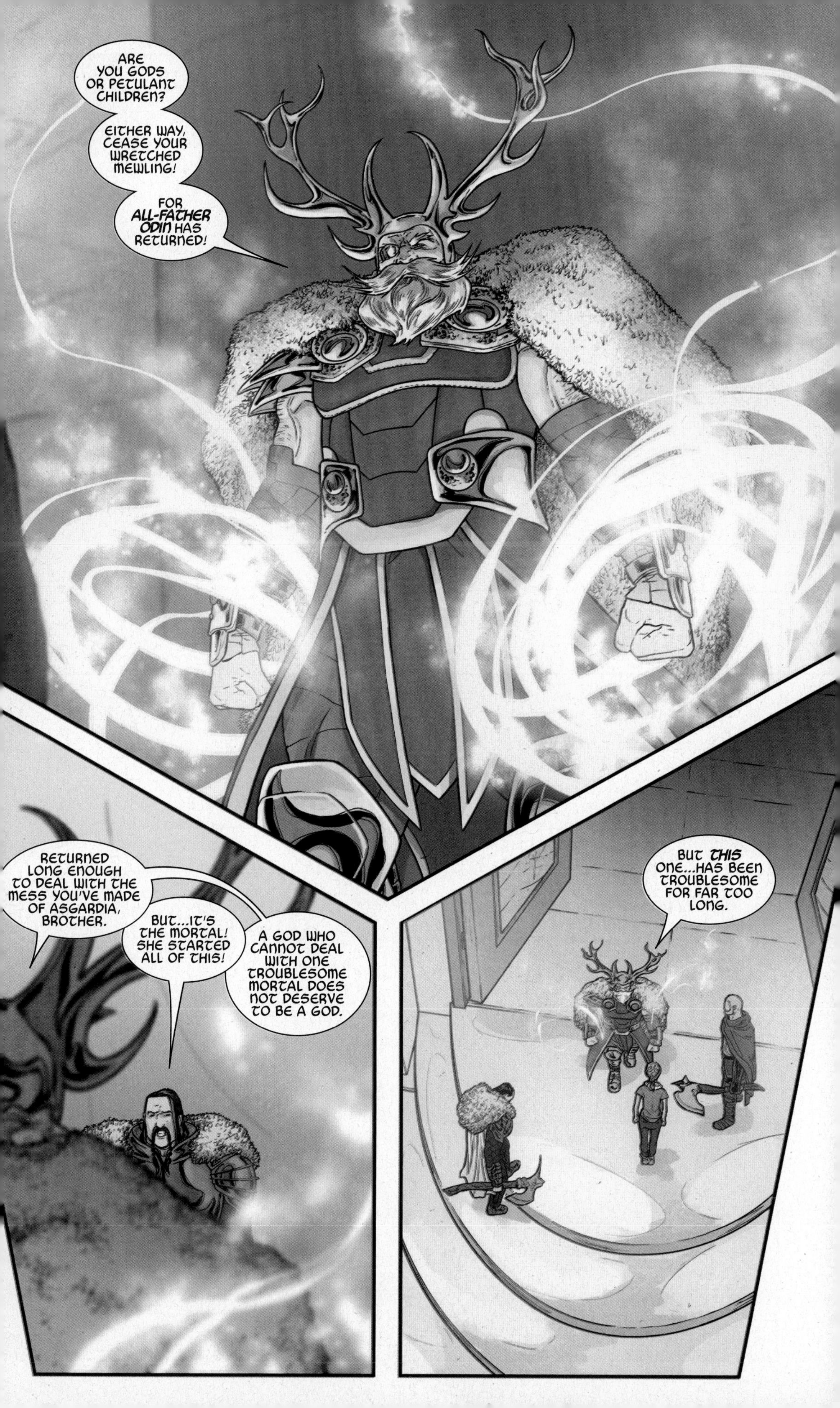
ARE YOU GODS OR PETULANT CHILDREN?
EITHER WAY, CEASE YOUR WRETCHED MEWLING!
FOR ALL-FATHER ODIN HAS RETURNED!
RETURNED LONG ENOUGH TO DEAL WITH THE MESS YOU'VE MADE OF ASGARDIA, BROTHER.
BUT...IT'S THE MORTAL! SHE STARTED ALL OF THIS!
A GOD WHO CANNOT DEAL WITH ONE TROUBLESOME MORTAL DOES NOT DESERVE TO BE A GOD.
BUT THIS ONE...HAS BEEN TROUBLESOME FOR FAR TOO LONG.

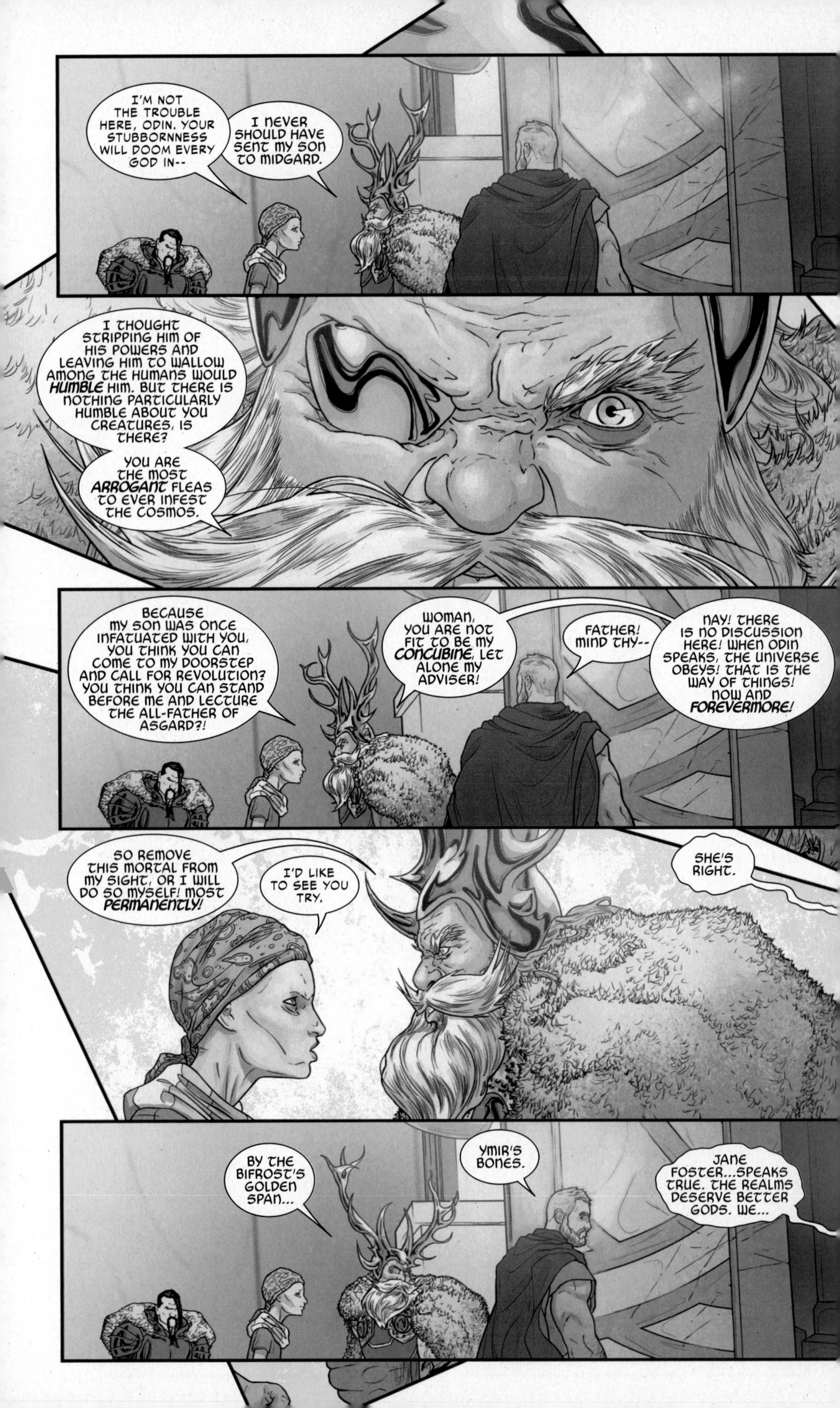
I'M NOT THE TROUBLE HERE, ODIN. YOUR STUBBORNNESS WILL DOOM EVERY GOD IN--
I NEVER SHOULD HAVE SENT MY SON TO MIDGARD.
I THOUGHT STRIPPING HIM OF HIS POWERS AND LEAVING HIM TO WALLOW AMONG THE HUMANS WOULD HUMBLE HIM. BUT THERE IS NOTHING PARTICULARLY HUMBLE ABOUT YOU CREATURES, IS THERE?
YOU ARE THE MOST ARROGANT FLEAS TO EVER INFEST THE COSMOS.
BECAUSE MY SON WAS ONCE INFATUATED WITH YOU, YOU THINK YOU CAN COME TO MY DOORSTEP AND CALL FOR REVOLUTION? YOU THINK YOU CAN STAND BEFORE ME AND LECTURE THE ALL-FATHER OF ASGARD?!
WOMAN, YOU ARE NOT FIT TO BE MY CONCUBINE, LET ALONE MY ADVISER!
FATHER! MIND THY--
NAY! THERE IS NO DISCUSSION HERE! WHEN ODIN SPEAKS, THE UNIVERSE OBEYS! THAT IS THE WAY OF THINGS! NOW AND FOREVERMORE!
SO REMOVE THIS MORTAL FROM MY SIGHT, OR I WILL DO SO MYSELF! MOST PERMANENTLY!
I'D LIKE TO SEE YOU TRY.
SHE'S RIGHT.
BY THE BIFROST'S GOLDEN SPAN...
YMIR'S BONES.
JANE FOSTER...SPEAKS TRUE. THE REALMS DESERVE BETTER GODS. WE...

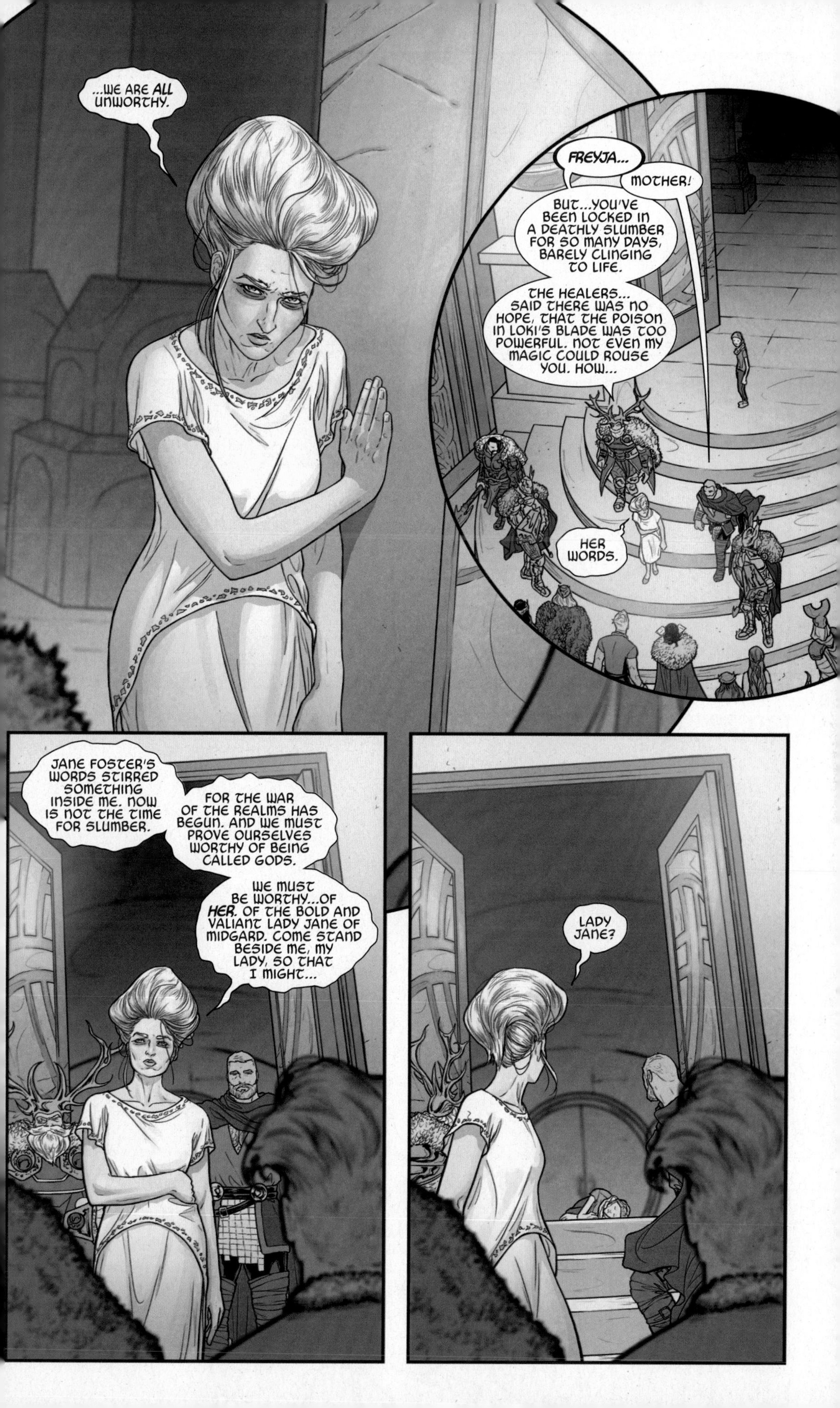
...WE ARE ALL UNWORTHY.
FREYJA...
MOTHER!
BUT...YOU'VE BEEN LOCKED IN A DEATHLY SLUMBER FOR SO MANY DAYS, BARELY CLINGING TO LIFE.
THE HEALERS... SAID THERE WAS NO HOPE, THAT THE POISON IN LOKI'S BLADE WAS TOO POWERFUL. NOT EVEN MY MAGIC COULD ROUSE YOU. HOW...
HER WORDS.
JANE FOSTER'S WORDS STIRRED SOMETHING INSIDE ME. NOW IS NOT THE TIME FOR SLUMBER.
FOR THE WAR OF THE REALMS HAS BEGUN. AND WE MUST PROVE OURSELVES WORTHY OF BEING CALLED GODS.
WE MUST BE WORTHY...OF HER. OF THE BOLD AND VALIANT LADY JANE OF MIDGARD. COME STAND BESIDE ME, MY LADY, SO THAT I MIGHT...
LADY JANE?

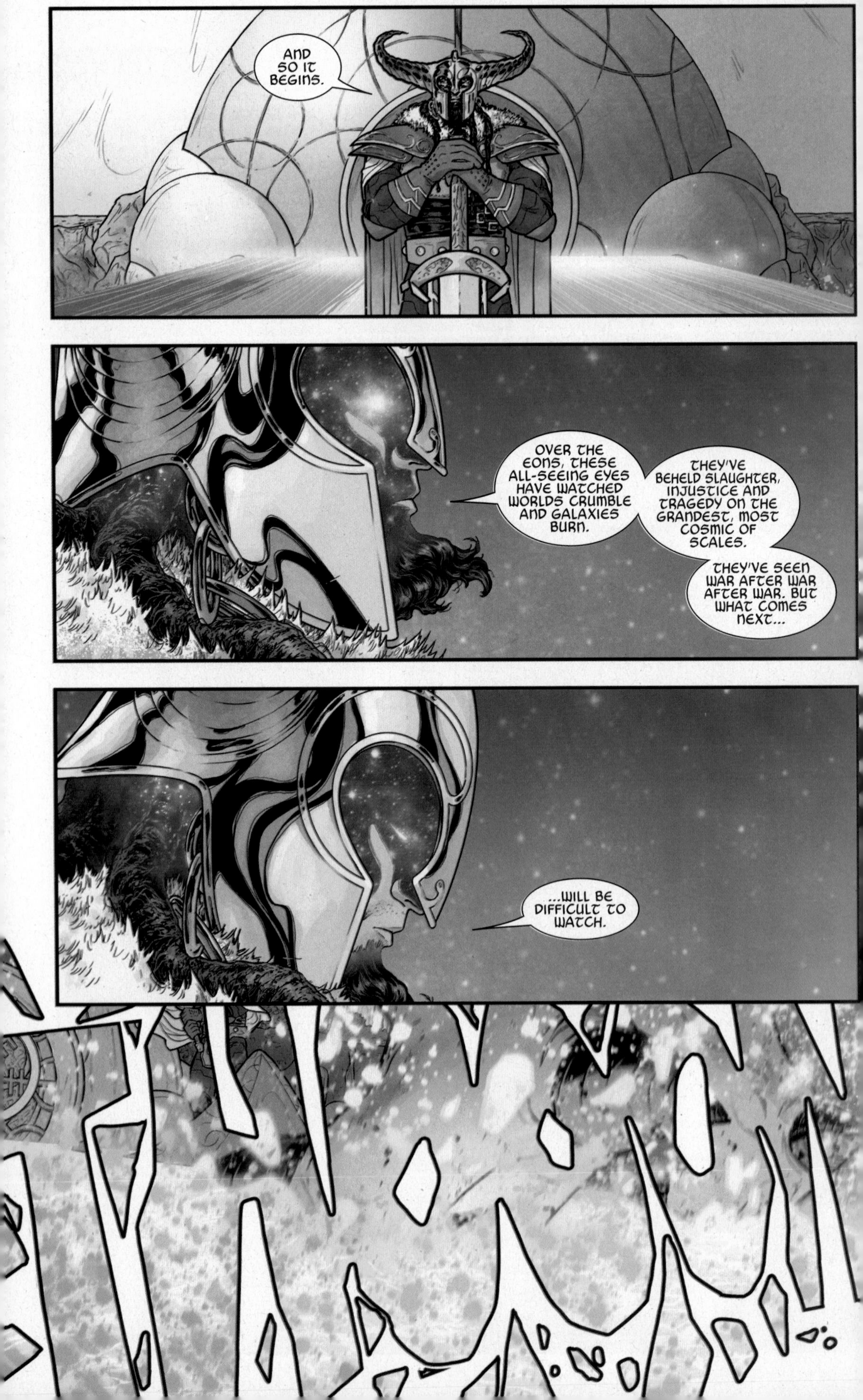
AND SO IT BEGINS.
OVER THE EONS, THESE ALL-SEEING EYES HAVE WATCHED WORLDS CRUMBLE AND GALAXIES BURN.
THEY'VE BEHELD SLAUGHTER, INJUSTICE AND TRAGEDY ON THE GRANDEST, MOST COSMIC OF SCALES.
THEY'VE SEEN WAR AFTER WAR AFTER WAR. BUT WHAT COMES NEXT...
...WILL BE DIFFICULT TO WATCH.

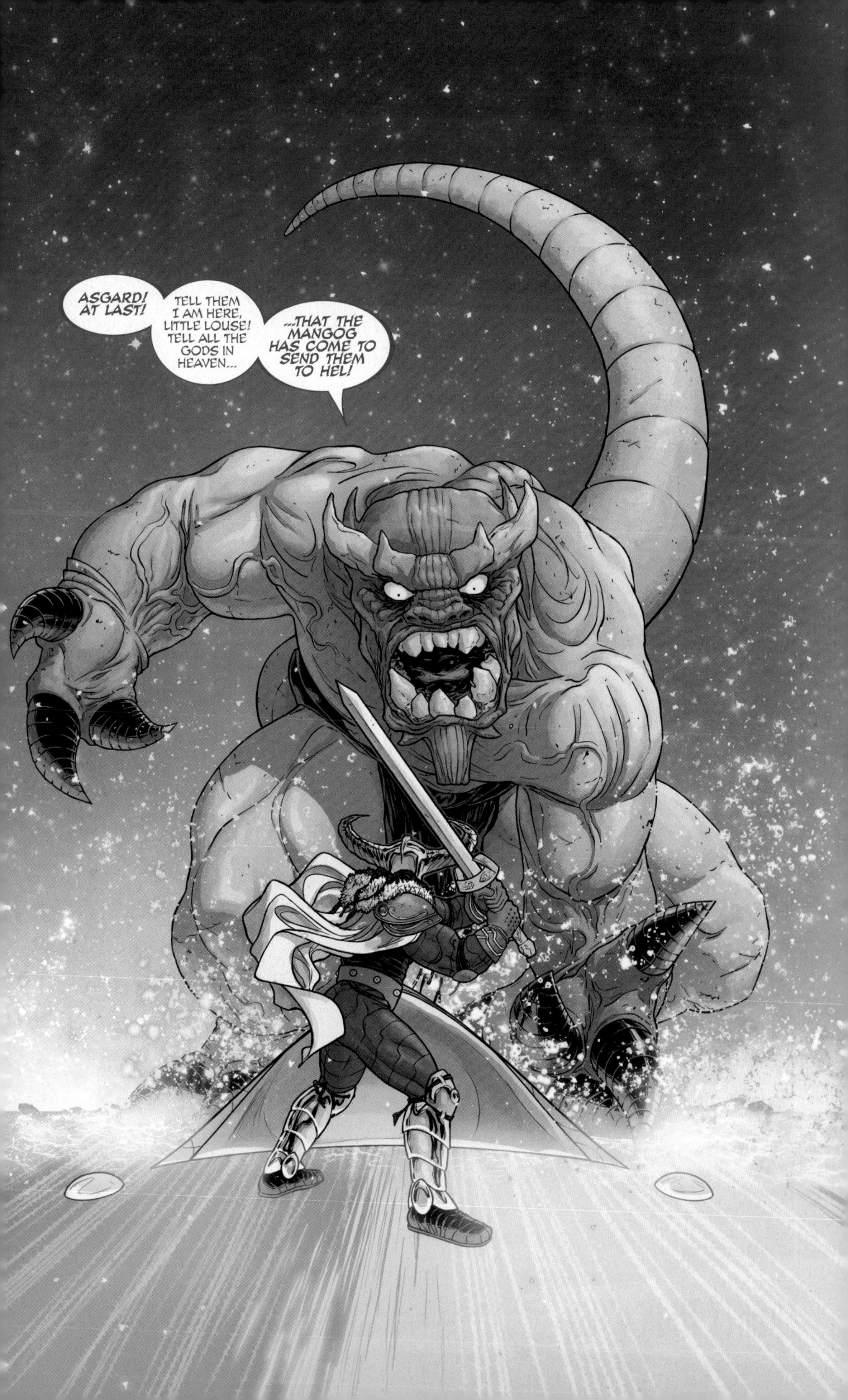
ASGARD! AT LAST!
TELL THEM I AM HERE, LITTLE LOUSE! TELL ALL THE GODS IN HEAVEN...
...THAT THE MANGOG HAS COME TO SEND THEM TO HEL!

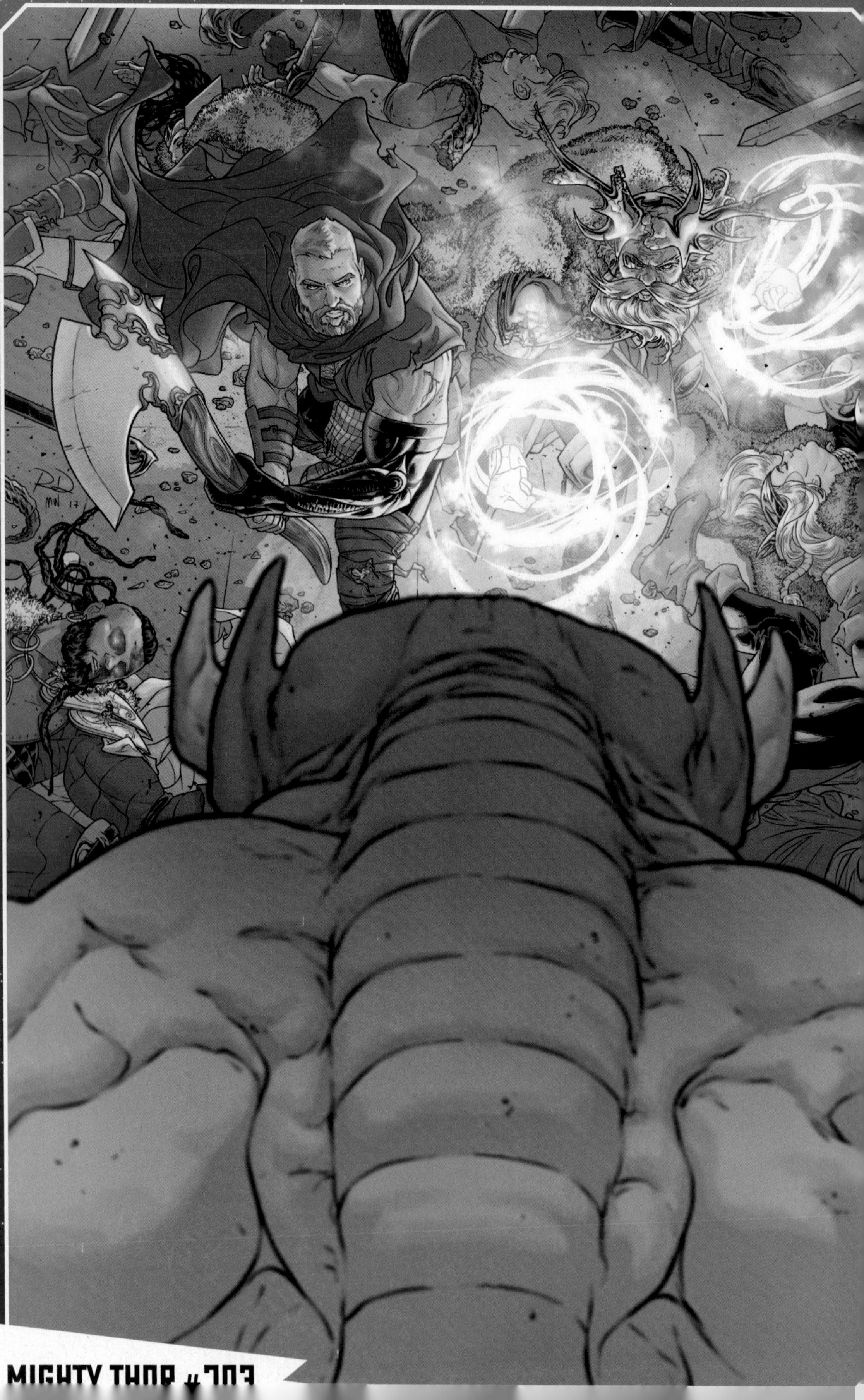

MIGHTY THOR #703

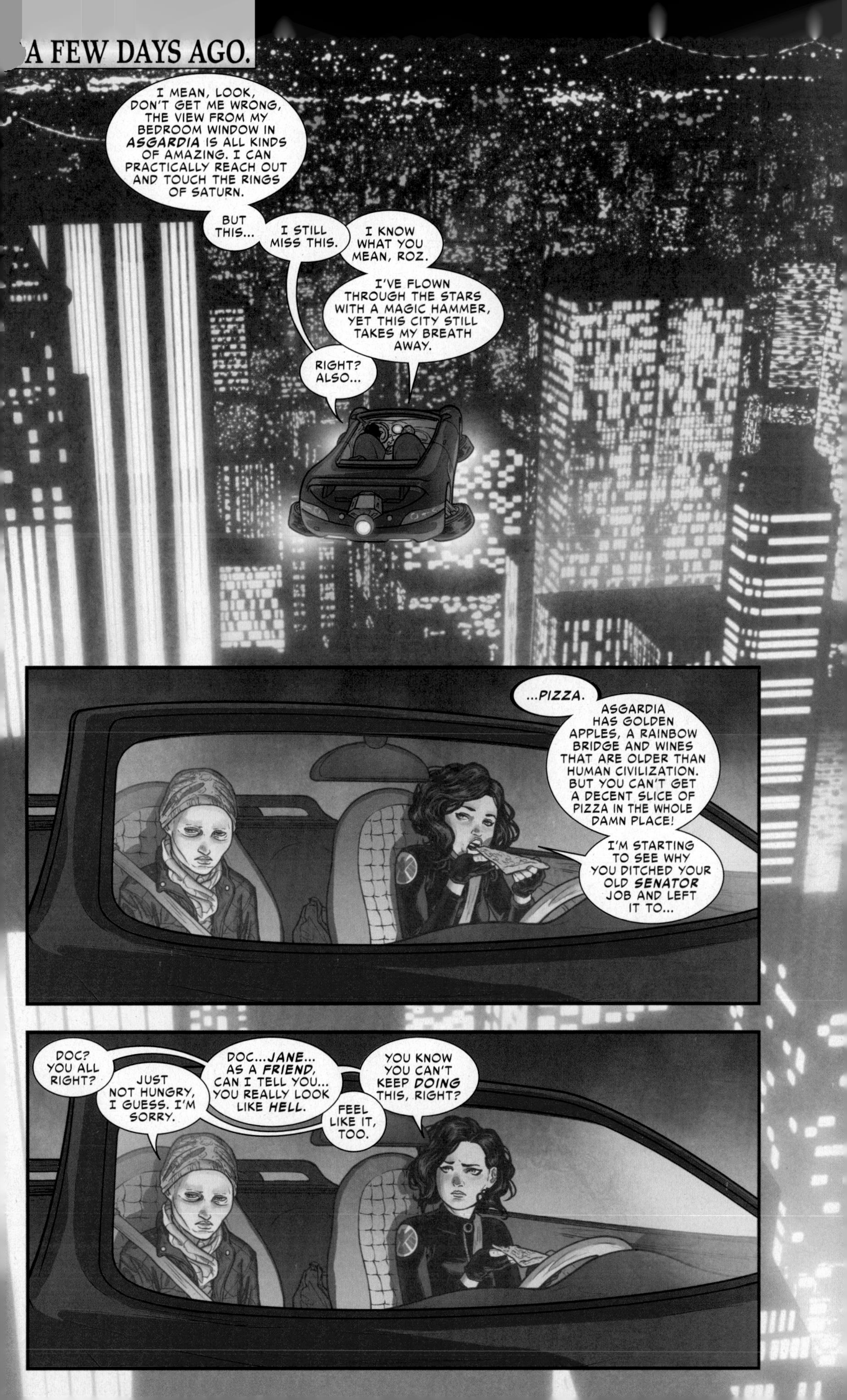
A FEW DAYS AGO.
I MEAN, LOOK, DON'T GET ME WRONG, THE VIEW FROM MY BEDROOM WINDOW IN ASGARDIA IS ALL KINDS OF AMAZING. I CAN PRACTICALLY REACH OUT AND TOUCH THE RINGS OF SATURN.
BUT THIS...
I STILL MISS THIS.
I KNOW WHAT YOU MEAN, ROZ.
I'VE FLOWN THROUGH THE STARS WITH A MAGIC HAMMER, YET THIS CITY STILL TAKES MY BREATH AWAY.
RIGHT? ALSO...
...PIZZA.
ASGARDIA HAS GOLDEN APPLES, A RAINBOW BRIDGE AND WINES THAT ARE OLDER THAN HUMAN CIVILIZATION. BUT YOU CAN'T GET A DECENT SLICE OF PIZZA IN THE WHOLE DAMN PLACE!
I'M STARTING TO SEE WHY YOU DITCHED YOUR OLD SENATOR JOB AND LEFT IT TO...
DOC? YOU ALL RIGHT?
JUST NOT HUNGRY, I GUESS. I'M SORRY.
DOC...JANE... AS A FRIEND, CAN I TELL YOU... YOU REALLY LOOK LIKE HELL.
FEEL LIKE IT, TOO.
YOU KNOW YOU CAN'T KEEP DOING THIS, RIGHT?

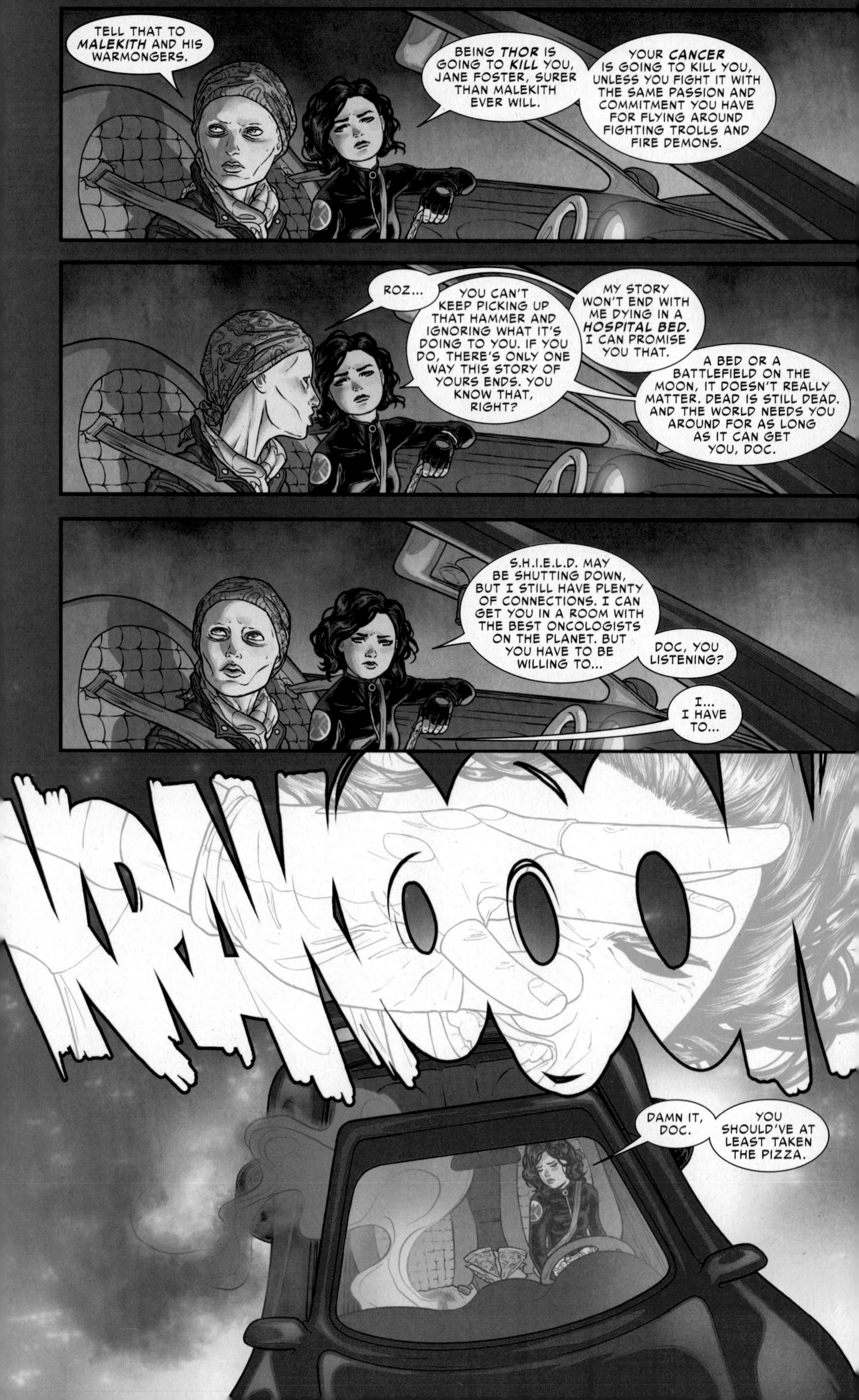
TELL THAT TO MALEKITH AND HIS WARMONGERS.
BEING THOR IS GOING TO KILL YOU, JANE FOSTER, SURER THAN MALEKITH EVER WILL.
YOUR CANCER IS GOING TO KILL YOU, UNLESS YOU FIGHT IT WITH THE SAME PASSION AND COMMITMENT YOU HAVE FOR FLYING AROUND FIGHTING TROLLS AND FIRE DEMONS.
ROZ...
YOU CAN'T KEEP PICKING UP THAT HAMMER AND IGNORING WHAT IT'S DOING TO YOU. IF YOU DO, THERE'S ONLY ONE WAY THIS STORY OF YOURS ENDS. YOU KNOW THAT, RIGHT?
MY STORY WON'T END WITH ME DYING IN A HOSPITAL BED. I CAN PROMISE YOU THAT.
A BED OR A BATTLEFIELD ON THE MOON, IT DOESN'T REALLY MATTER. DEAD IS STILL DEAD. AND THE WORLD NEEDS YOU AROUND FOR AS LONG AS IT CAN GET YOU, DOC.
S.H.I.E.L.D. MAY BE SHUTTING DOWN, BUT I STILL HAVE PLENTY OF CONNECTIONS. I CAN GET YOU IN A ROOM WITH THE BEST ONCOLOGISTS ON THE PLANET. BUT YOU HAVE TO BE WILLING TO...
DOC, YOU LISTENING?
I... I HAVE TO...
KRAKOOOM
DAMN IT, DOC.
YOU SHOULD'VE AT LEAST TAKEN THE PIZZA.

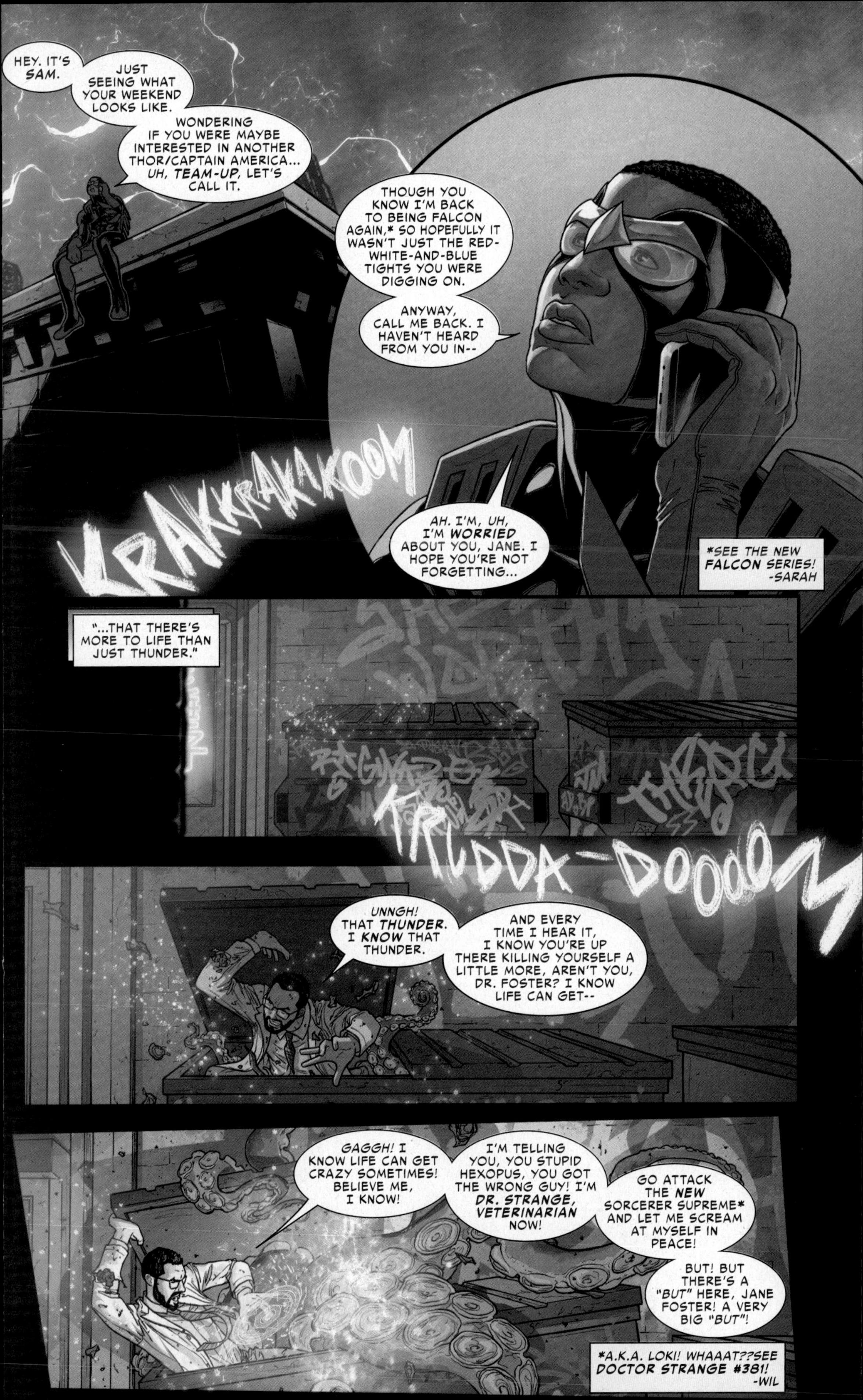
HEY. IT'S SAM.
JUST SEEING WHAT YOUR WEEKEND LOOKS LIKE.
WONDERING IF YOU WERE MAYBE INTERESTED IN ANOTHER THOR/CAPTAIN AMERICA... UH, TEAM-UP, LET'S CALL IT.
THOUGH YOU KNOW I'M BACK TO BEING FALCON AGAIN,* SO HOPEFULLY IT WASN'T JUST THE RED-WHITE-AND-BLUE TIGHTS YOU WERE DIGGING ON.
ANYWAY, CALL ME BACK. I HAVEN'T HEARD FROM YOU IN--
KRAKKRAKAKOOM
AH. I'M, UH, I'M WORRIED ABOUT YOU, JANE. I HOPE YOU'RE NOT FORGETTING...
*SEE THE NEW FALCON SERIES! -SARAH
"...THAT THERE'S MORE TO LIFE THAN JUST THUNDER."
TRUDDA-DOOOOM
UNNGH! THAT THUNDER. I KNOW THAT THUNDER.
AND EVERY TIME I HEAR IT, I KNOW YOU'RE UP THERE KILLING YOURSELF A LITTLE MORE, AREN'T YOU, DR. FOSTER? I KNOW LIFE CAN GET--
GAGGH! I KNOW LIFE CAN GET CRAZY SOMETIMES! BELIEVE ME, I KNOW!
I'M TELLING YOU, YOU STUPID HEXOPUS, YOU GOT THE WRONG GUY! I'M DR. STRANGE, VETERINARIAN NOW!
GO ATTACK THE NEW SORCERER SUPREME* AND LET ME SCREAM AT MYSELF IN PEACE!
BUT! BUT THERE'S A "BUT" HERE, JANE FOSTER! A VERY BIG "BUT"!
*A.K.A. LOKI! WHAAAT??SEE DOCTOR STRANGE #381! -WIL

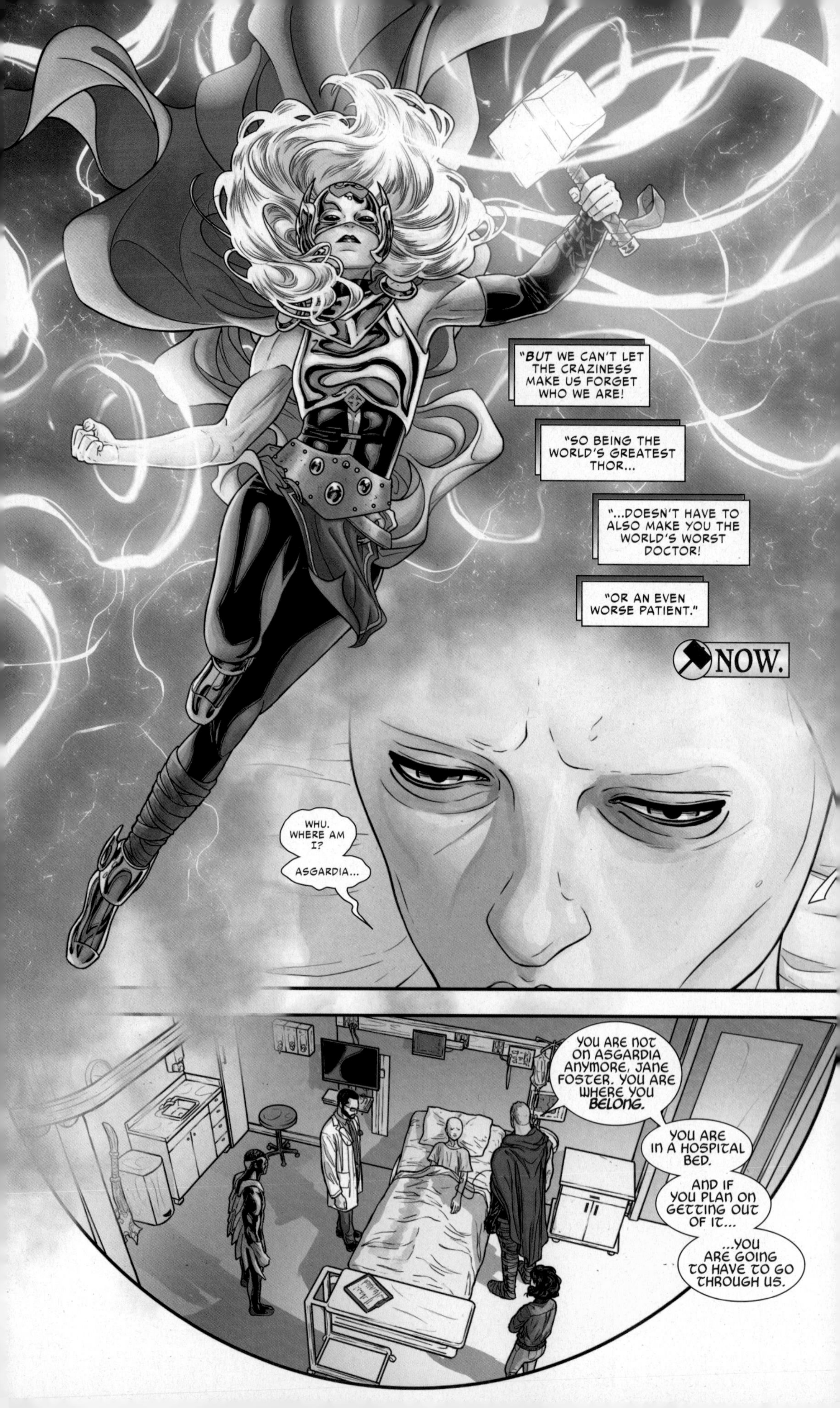

"BUT WE CAN'T LET THE CRAZINESS MAKE US FORGET WHO WE ARE!
"SO BEING THE WORLD'S GREATEST THOR...
"...DOESN'T HAVE TO ALSO MAKE YOU THE WORLD'S WORST DOCTOR!
"OR AN EVEN WORSE PATIENT."
NOW.
WHU. WHERE AM I?
ASGARDIA...
YOU ARE NOT ON ASGARDIA ANYMORE, JANE FOSTER. YOU ARE WHERE YOU BELONG.
YOU ARE IN A HOSPITAL BED.
AND IF YOU PLAN ON GETTING OUT OF IT...
...YOU ARE GOING TO HAVE TO GO THROUGH US.

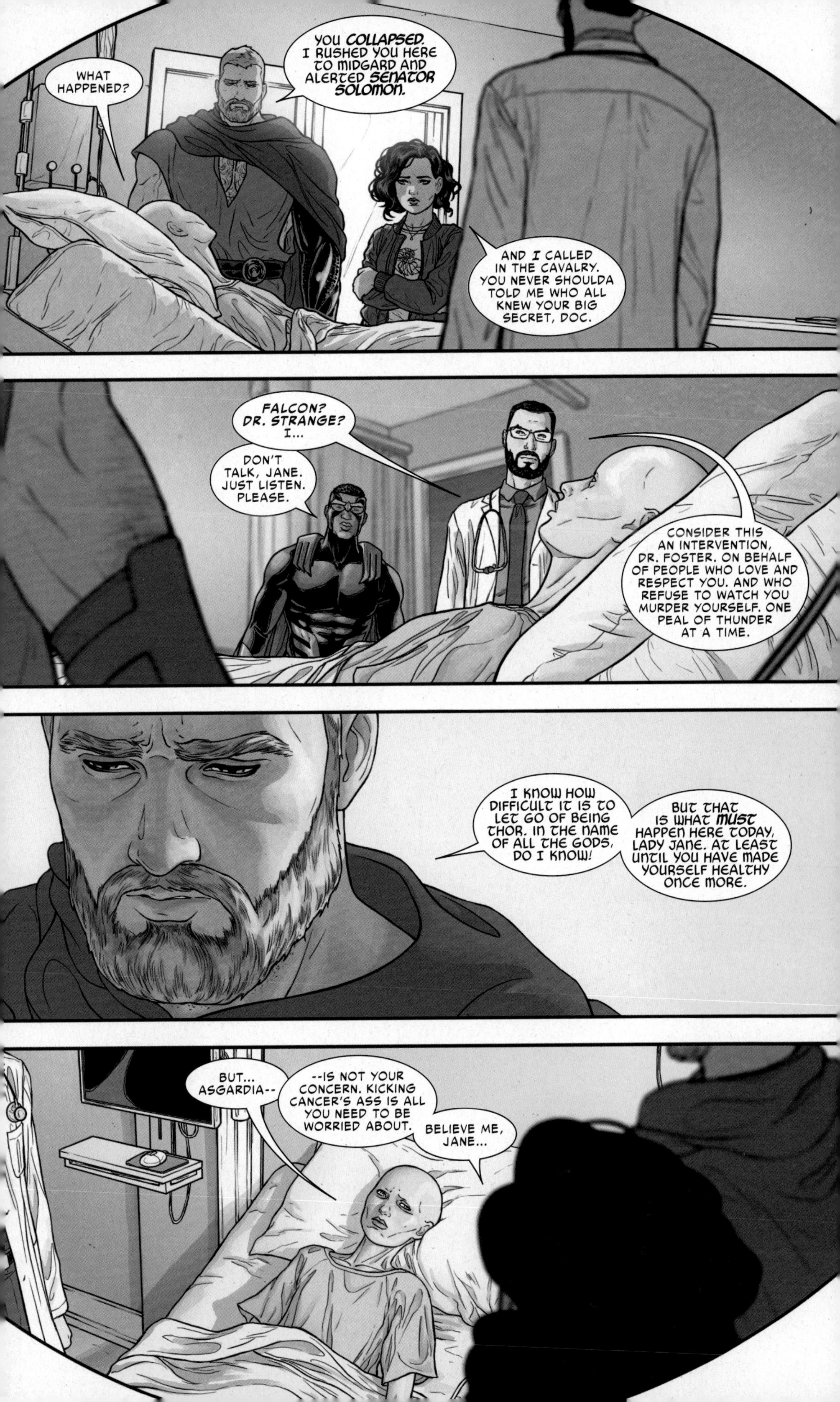
WHAT HAPPENED?
YOU COLLAPSED. I RUSHED YOU HERE TO MIDGARD AND ALERTED SENATOR SOLOMON.
AND I CALLED IN THE CAVALRY. YOU NEVER SHOULDA TOLD ME WHO ALL KNEW YOUR BIG SECRET, DOC.
FALCON? DR. STRANGE? I...
DON'T TALK, JANE. JUST LISTEN. PLEASE.
CONSIDER THIS AN INTERVENTION, DR. FOSTER. ON BEHALF OF PEOPLE WHO LOVE AND RESPECT YOU. AND WHO REFUSE TO WATCH YOU MURDER YOURSELF. ONE PEAL OF THUNDER AT A TIME.
I KNOW HOW DIFFICULT IT IS TO LET GO OF BEING THOR. IN THE NAME OF ALL THE GODS, DO I KNOW!
BUT THAT IS WHAT MUST HAPPEN HERE TODAY, LADY JANE. AT LEAST UNTIL YOU HAVE MADE YOURSELF HEALTHY ONCE MORE.
BUT... ASGARDIA--
--IS NOT YOUR CONCERN. KICKING CANCER'S ASS IS ALL YOU NEED TO BE WORRIED ABOUT.
BELIEVE ME, JANE...

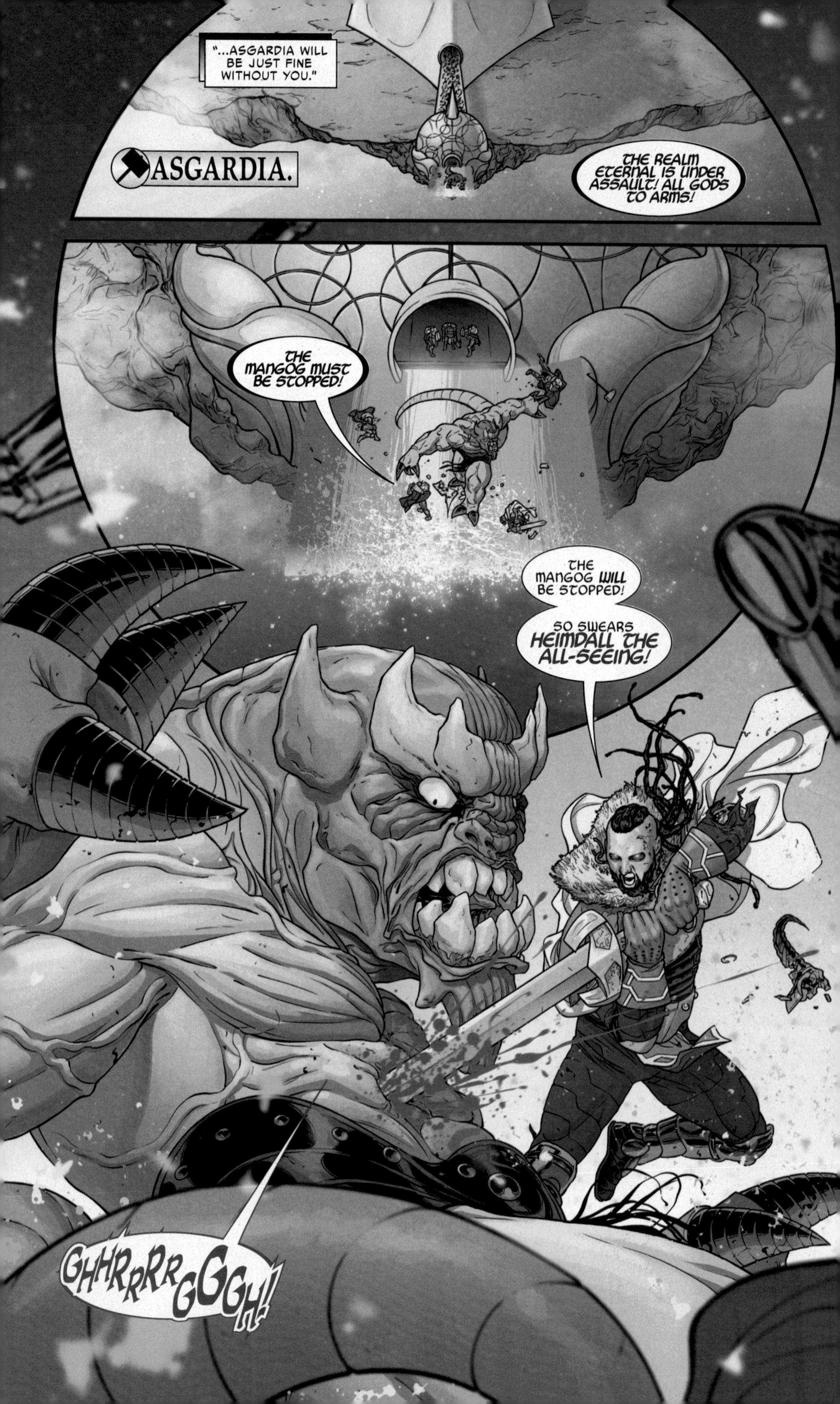
"...ASGARDIA WILL BE JUST FINE WITHOUT YOU."
ASGARDIA.
THE REALM ETERNAL IS UNDER ASSAULT! ALL GODS TO ARMS!
THE MANGOG MUST BE STOPPED!
THE MANGOG WILL BE STOPPED!
SO SWEARS HEIMDALL THE ALL-SEEING!
GHHRRRRGGGH!

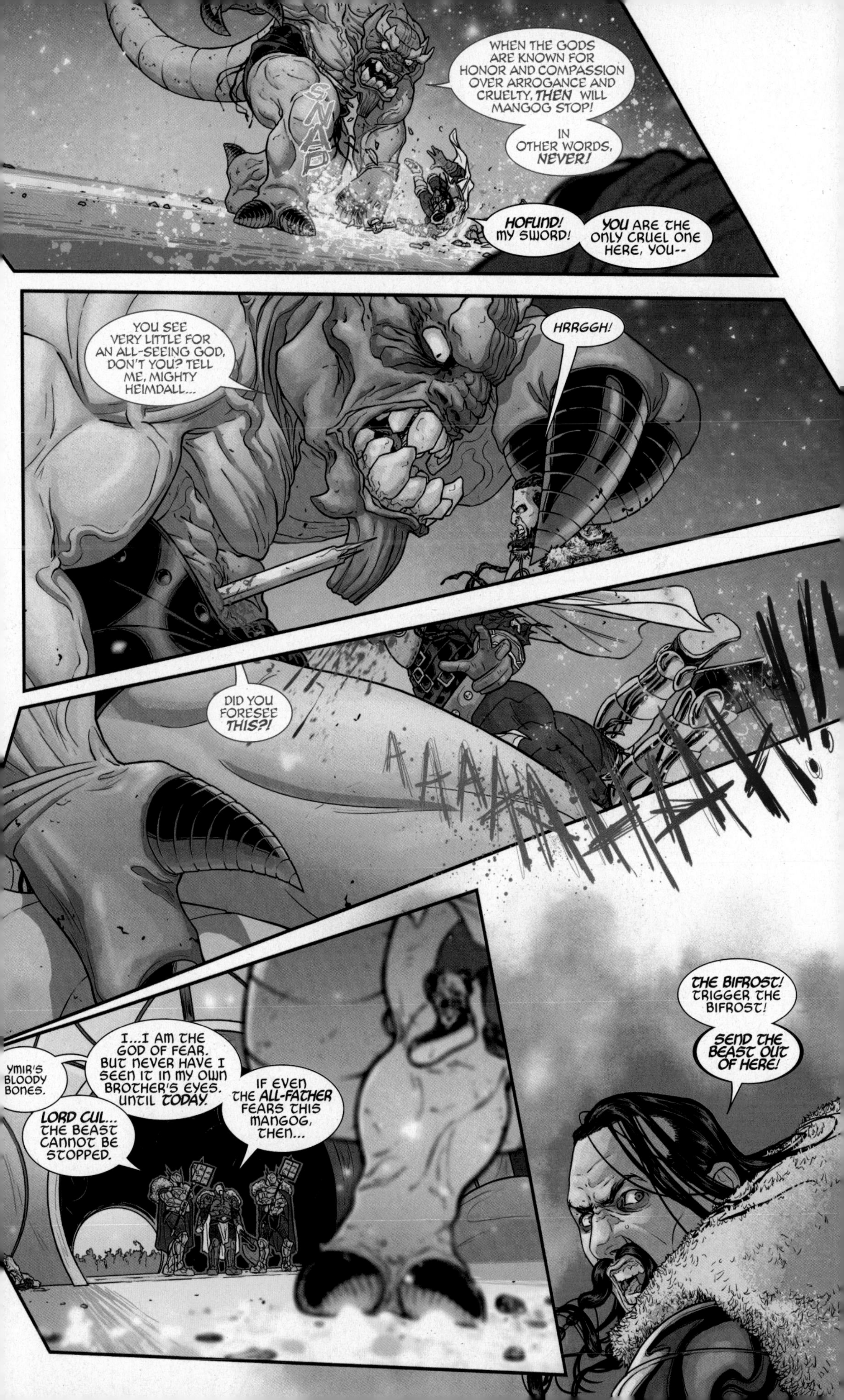
SNAP
WHEN THE GODS ARE KNOWN FOR HONOR AND COMPASSION OVER ARROGANCE AND CRUELTY, *THEN* WILL MANGOG STOP!
IN OTHER WORDS, *NEVER!*
HOFUND! MY SWORD!
YOU ARE THE ONLY CRUEL ONE HERE, YOU--
YOU SEE VERY LITTLE FOR AN ALL-SEEING GOD, DON'T YOU? TELL ME, MIGHTY HEIMDALL...
HRRGGH!
DID YOU FORESEE *THIS?!*
AAAAAHHH!!
YMIR'S BLOODY BONES.
I...I AM THE GOD OF FEAR. BUT NEVER HAVE I SEEN IT IN MY OWN BROTHER'S EYES. UNTIL *TODAY.*
LORD CUL... THE BEAST CANNOT BE STOPPED.
IF EVEN THE *ALL-FATHER* FEARS THIS MANGOG, THEN...
THE BIFROST! TRIGGER THE BIFROST!
SEND THE BEAST OUT OF HERE!

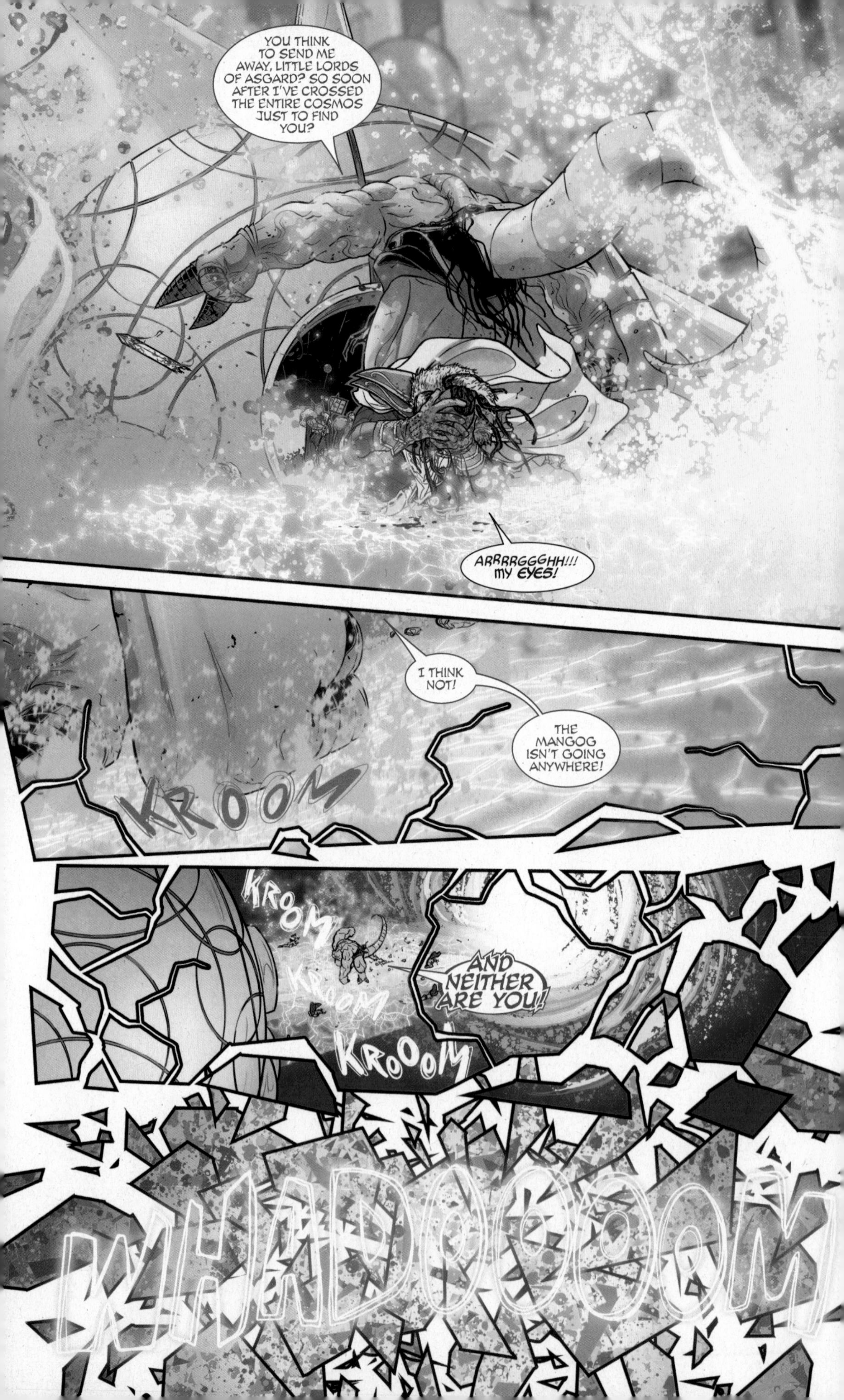
YOU THINK TO SEND ME AWAY, LITTLE LORDS OF ASGARD? SO SOON AFTER I'VE CROSSED THE ENTIRE COSMOS JUST TO FIND YOU?
ARRRRGGGHH!!! MY EYES!
I THINK NOT!
THE MANGOG ISN'T GOING ANYWHERE!
KROOM
KROOM
KROOM
AND NEITHER ARE YOU!
KROOOM
WHADOOOOM

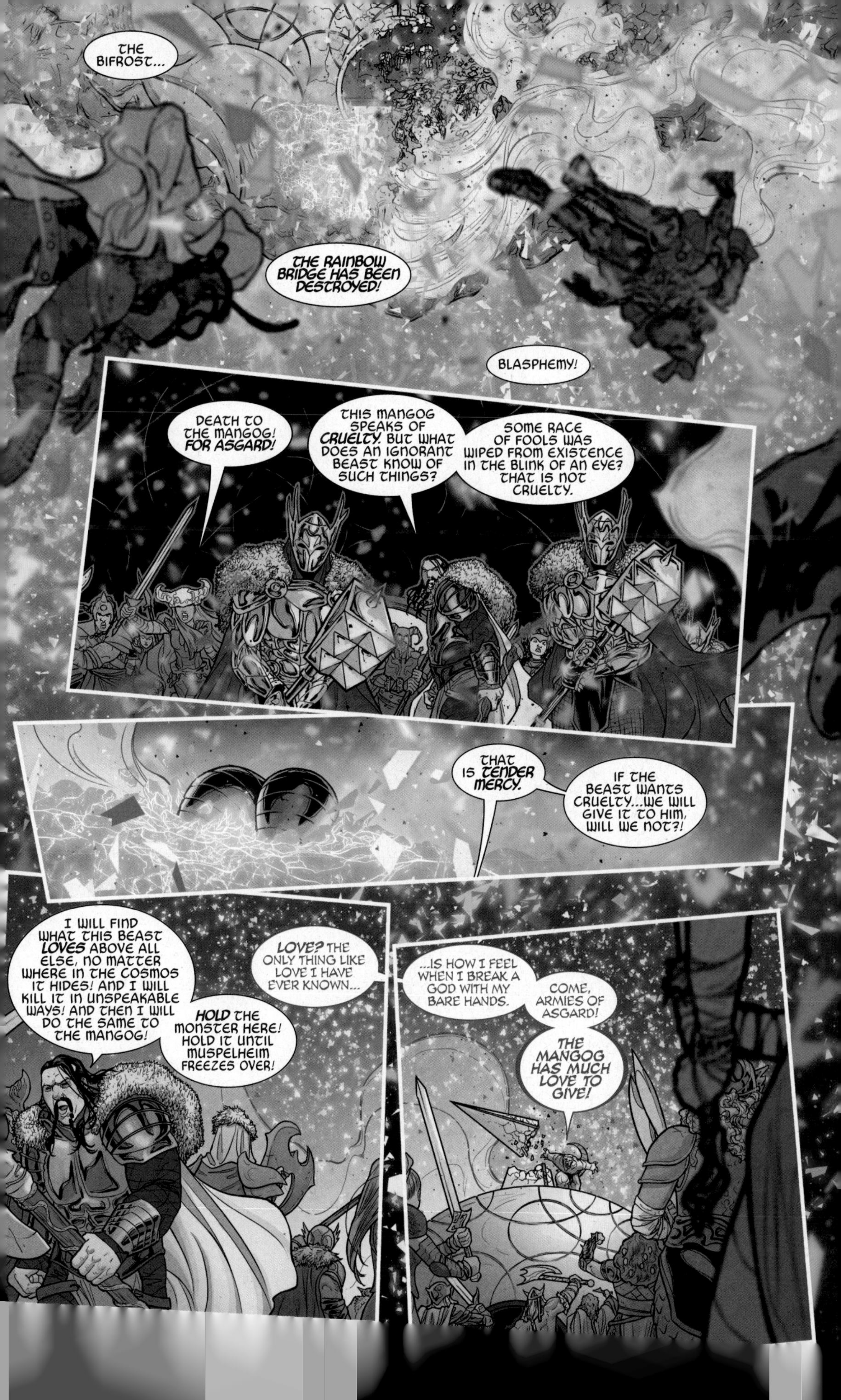

THE BIFROST...
THE RAINBOW BRIDGE HAS BEEN DESTROYED!
BLASPHEMY!
DEATH TO THE MANGOG! FOR ASGARD!
THIS MANGOG SPEAKS OF CRUELTY. BUT WHAT DOES AN IGNORANT BEAST KNOW OF SUCH THINGS?
SOME RACE OF FOOLS WAS WIPED FROM EXISTENCE IN THE BLINK OF AN EYE? THAT IS NOT CRUELTY.
THAT IS TENDER MERCY.
IF THE BEAST WANTS CRUELTY...WE WILL GIVE IT TO HIM, WILL WE NOT?!
I WILL FIND WHAT THIS BEAST LOVES ABOVE ALL ELSE, NO MATTER WHERE IN THE COSMOS IT HIDES! AND I WILL KILL IT IN UNSPEAKABLE WAYS! AND THEN I WILL DO THE SAME TO THE MANGOG!
HOLD THE MONSTER HERE! HOLD IT UNTIL MUSPELHEIM FREEZES OVER!
LOVE? THE ONLY THING LIKE LOVE I HAVE EVER KNOWN...
...IS HOW I FEEL WHEN I BREAK A GOD WITH MY BARE HANDS.
COME, ARMIES OF ASGARD!
THE MANGOG HAS MUCH LOVE TO GIVE!

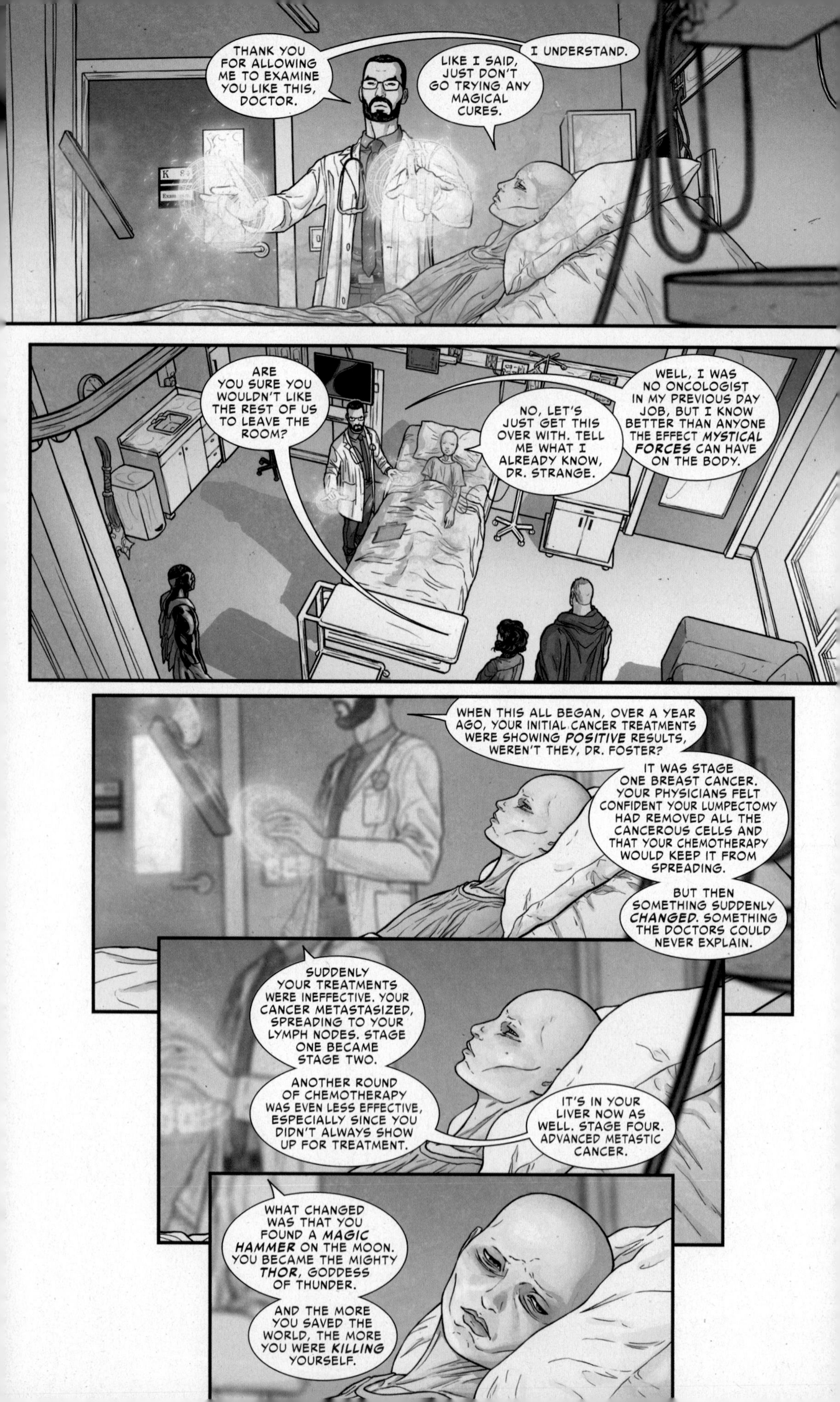
THANK YOU FOR ALLOWING ME TO EXAMINE YOU LIKE THIS, DOCTOR.
I UNDERSTAND.
LIKE I SAID, JUST DON'T GO TRYING ANY MAGICAL CURES.
ARE YOU SURE YOU WOULDN'T LIKE THE REST OF US TO LEAVE THE ROOM?
NO, LET'S JUST GET THIS OVER WITH. TELL ME WHAT I ALREADY KNOW, DR. STRANGE.
WELL, I WAS NO ONCOLOGIST IN MY PREVIOUS DAY JOB, BUT I KNOW BETTER THAN ANYONE THE EFFECT MYSTICAL FORCES CAN HAVE ON THE BODY.
WHEN THIS ALL BEGAN, OVER A YEAR AGO, YOUR INITIAL CANCER TREATMENTS WERE SHOWING POSITIVE RESULTS, WEREN'T THEY, DR. FOSTER?
IT WAS STAGE ONE BREAST CANCER. YOUR PHYSICIANS FELT CONFIDENT YOUR LUMPECTOMY HAD REMOVED ALL THE CANCEROUS CELLS AND THAT YOUR CHEMOTHERAPY WOULD KEEP IT FROM SPREADING.
BUT THEN SOMETHING SUDDENLY CHANGED. SOMETHING THE DOCTORS COULD NEVER EXPLAIN.
SUDDENLY YOUR TREATMENTS WERE INEFFECTIVE. YOUR CANCER METASTASIZED, SPREADING TO YOUR LYMPH NODES. STAGE ONE BECAME STAGE TWO.
ANOTHER ROUND OF CHEMOTHERAPY WAS EVEN LESS EFFECTIVE, ESPECIALLY SINCE YOU DIDN'T ALWAYS SHOW UP FOR TREATMENT.
IT'S IN YOUR LIVER NOW AS WELL. STAGE FOUR. ADVANCED METASTIC CANCER.
WHAT CHANGED WAS THAT YOU FOUND A MAGIC HAMMER ON THE MOON. YOU BECAME THE MIGHTY THOR, GODDESS OF THUNDER.
AND THE MORE YOU SAVED THE WORLD, THE MORE YOU WERE KILLING YOURSELF.

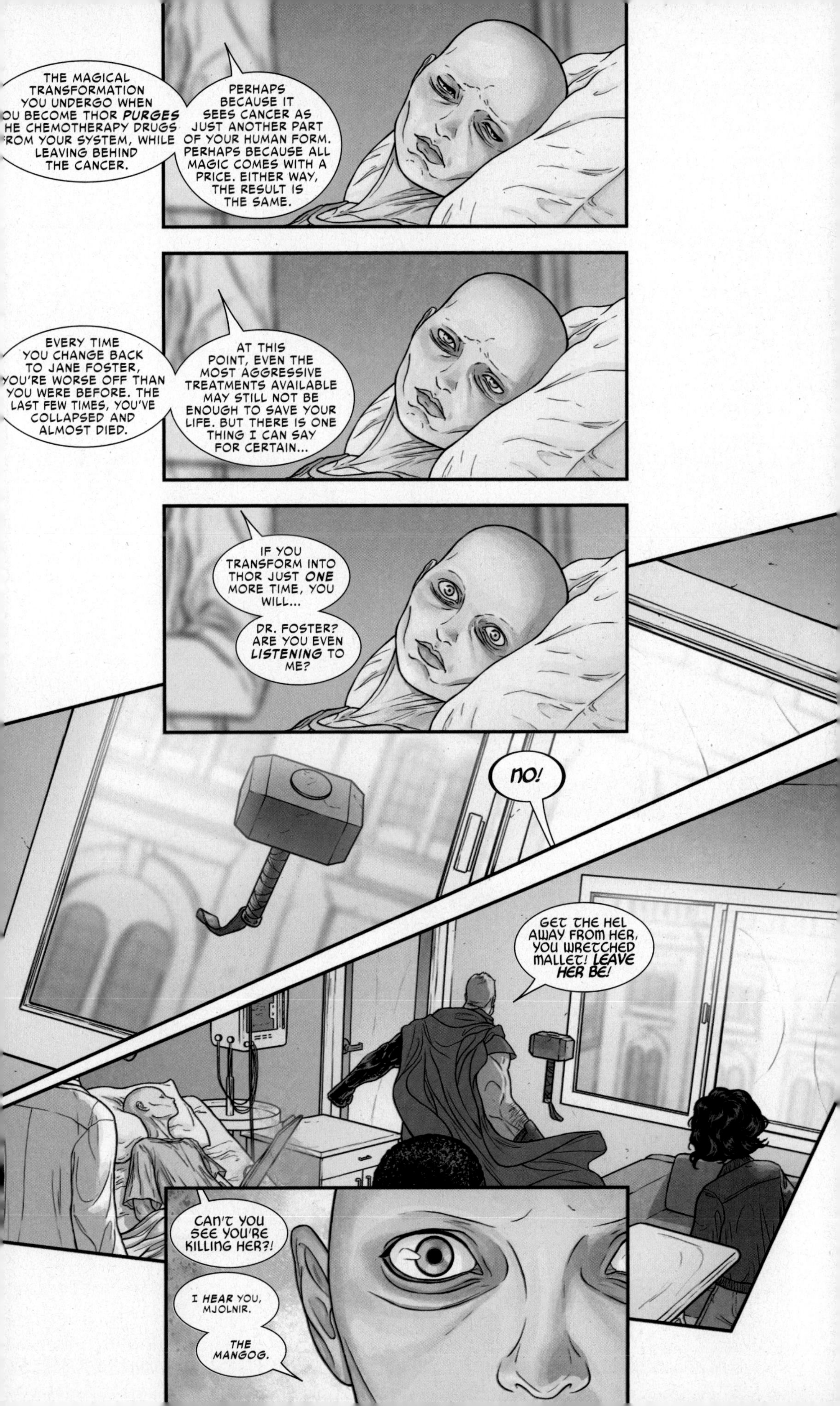
THE MAGICAL TRANSFORMATION YOU UNDERGO WHEN OU BECOME THOR PURGES HE CHEMOTHERAPY DRUGS FROM YOUR SYSTEM, WHILE LEAVING BEHIND THE CANCER.
PERHAPS BECAUSE IT SEES CANCER AS JUST ANOTHER PART OF YOUR HUMAN FORM. PERHAPS BECAUSE ALL MAGIC COMES WITH A PRICE. EITHER WAY, THE RESULT IS THE SAME.
EVERY TIME YOU CHANGE BACK TO JANE FOSTER, YOU'RE WORSE OFF THAN YOU WERE BEFORE. THE LAST FEW TIMES, YOU'VE COLLAPSED AND ALMOST DIED.
AT THIS POINT, EVEN THE MOST AGGRESSIVE TREATMENTS AVAILABLE MAY STILL NOT BE ENOUGH TO SAVE YOUR LIFE. BUT THERE IS ONE THING I CAN SAY FOR CERTAIN...
IF YOU TRANSFORM INTO THOR JUST ONE MORE TIME, YOU WILL...
DR. FOSTER? ARE YOU EVEN LISTENING TO ME?
NO!
GET THE HEL AWAY FROM HER, YOU WRETCHED MALLET! LEAVE HER BE!
CAN'T YOU SEE YOU'RE KILLING HER?!
I HEAR YOU, MJOLNIR.
THE MANGOG.

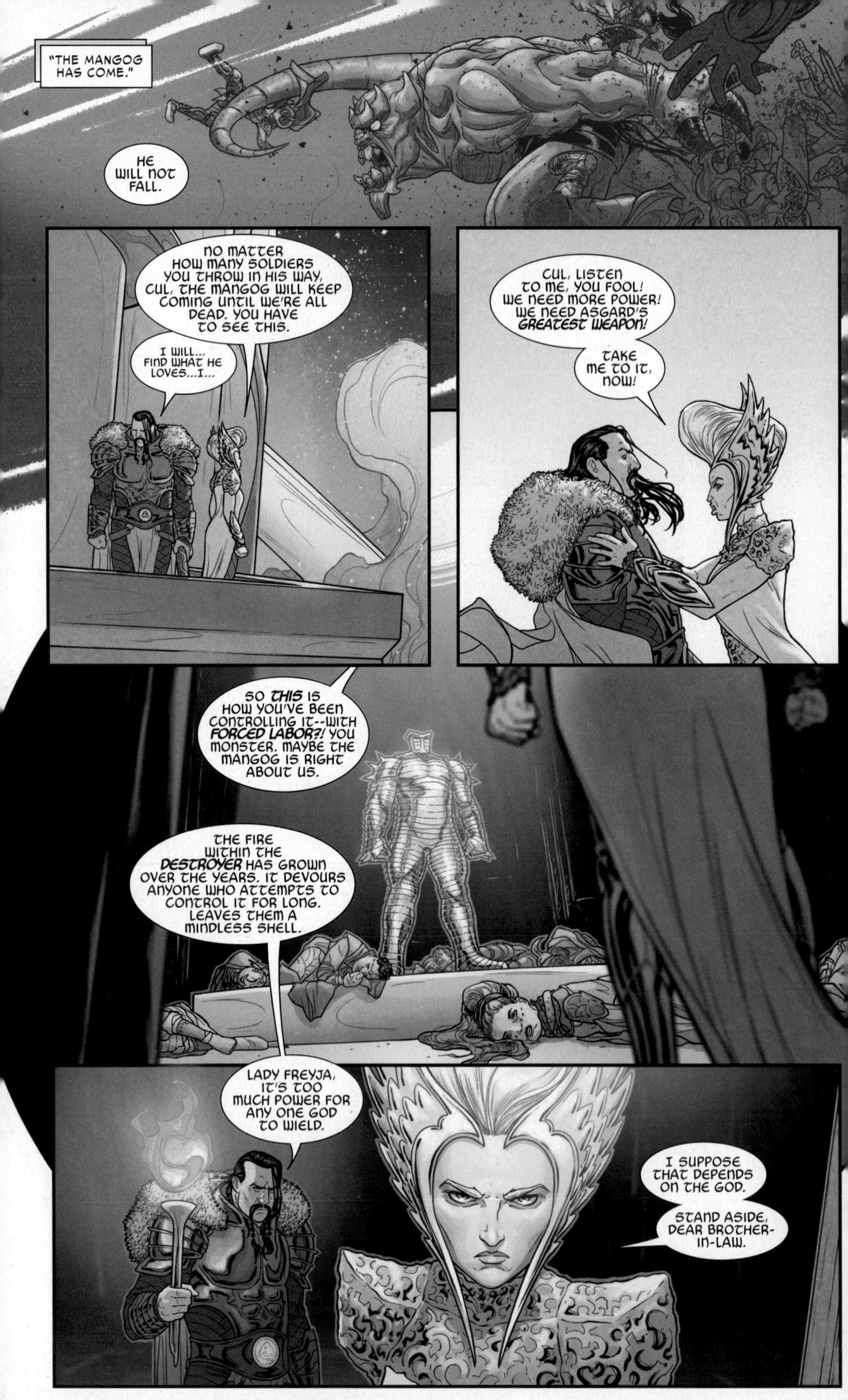
"THE MANGOG HAS COME."
HE WILL NOT FALL.
NO MATTER HOW MANY SOLDIERS YOU THROW IN HIS WAY, CUL, THE MANGOG WILL KEEP COMING UNTIL WE'RE ALL DEAD. YOU HAVE TO SEE THIS.
I WILL... FIND WHAT HE LOVES...I...
CUL, LISTEN TO ME, YOU FOOL! WE NEED MORE POWER! WE NEED ASGARD'S GREATEST WEAPON!
TAKE ME TO IT, NOW!
SO THIS IS HOW YOU'VE BEEN CONTROLLING IT--WITH FORCED LABOR?! YOU MONSTER. MAYBE THE MANGOG IS RIGHT ABOUT US.
THE FIRE WITHIN THE DESTROYER HAS GROWN OVER THE YEARS. IT DEVOURS ANYONE WHO ATTEMPTS TO CONTROL IT FOR LONG. LEAVES THEM A MINDLESS SHELL.
LADY FREYJA, IT'S TOO MUCH POWER FOR ANY ONE GOD TO WIELD.
I SUPPOSE THAT DEPENDS ON THE GOD.
STAND ASIDE, DEAR BROTHER-IN-LAW.

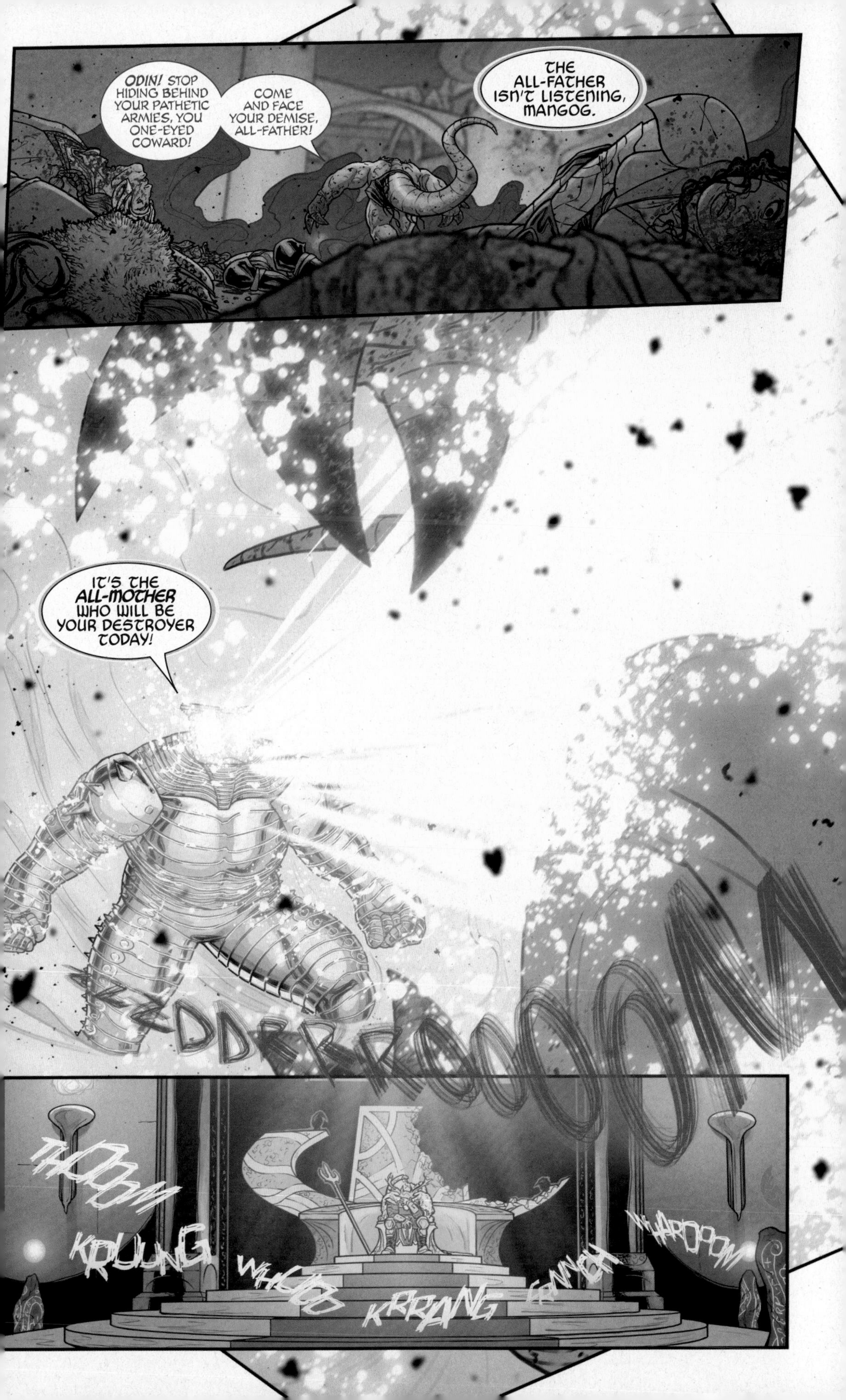

ODIN! STOP HIDING BEHIND YOUR PATHETIC ARMIES, YOU ONE-EYED COWARD!
COME AND FACE YOUR DEMISE, ALL-FATHER!
THE ALL-FATHER ISN'T LISTENING, MANGOG.
IT'S THE ALL-MOTHER WHO WILL BE YOUR DESTROYER TODAY!
ZZDDRRRROOOOOOM
THOOOM
KRUUNG
WHUDD
KRRANG
WHAROOOM

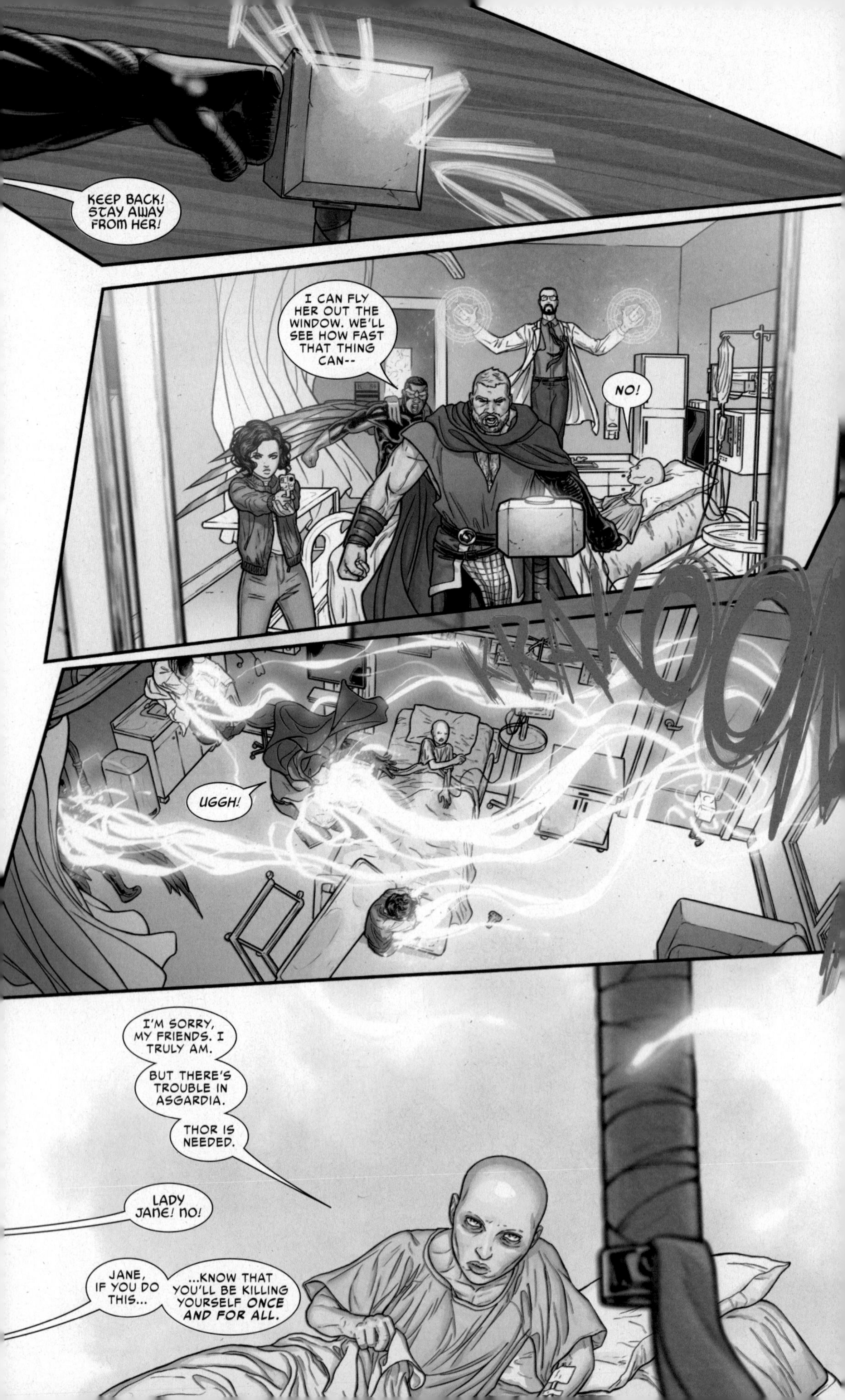
THUNK
KEEP BACK! STAY AWAY FROM HER!
I CAN FLY HER OUT THE WINDOW. WE'LL SEE HOW FAST THAT THING CAN--
NO!
KRAKOOM
UGGH!
I'M SORRY, MY FRIENDS. I TRULY AM.
BUT THERE'S TROUBLE IN ASGARDIA.
THOR IS NEEDED.
LADY JANE! NO!
JANE, IF YOU DO THIS...
...KNOW THAT YOU'LL BE KILLING YOURSELF *ONCE AND FOR ALL.*

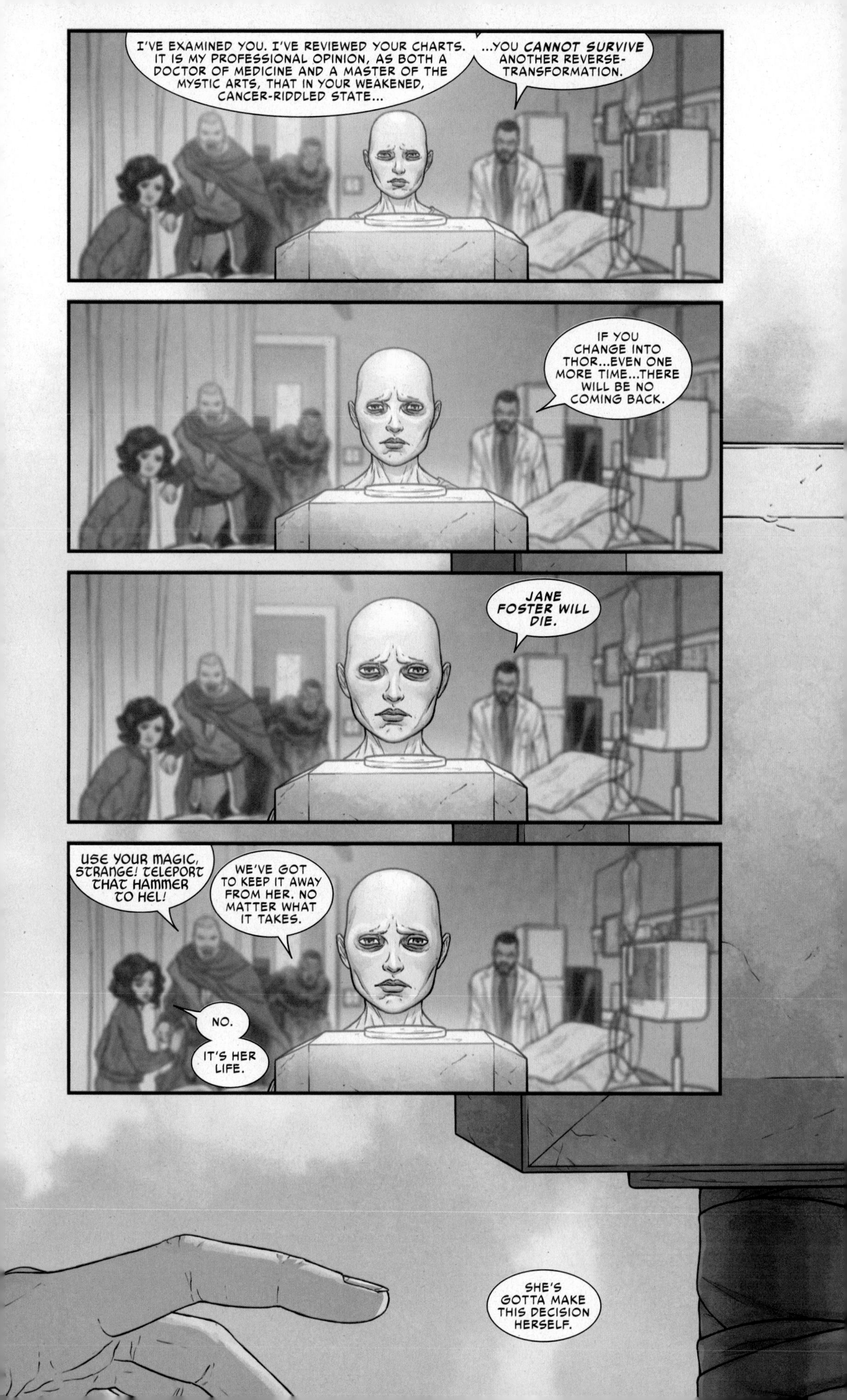
I'VE EXAMINED YOU. I'VE REVIEWED YOUR CHARTS. IT IS MY PROFESSIONAL OPINION, AS BOTH A DOCTOR OF MEDICINE AND A MASTER OF THE MYSTIC ARTS, THAT IN YOUR WEAKENED, CANCER-RIDDLED STATE...
...YOU CANNOT SURVIVE ANOTHER REVERSE-TRANSFORMATION.
IF YOU CHANGE INTO THOR...EVEN ONE MORE TIME...THERE WILL BE NO COMING BACK.
JANE FOSTER WILL DIE.
USE YOUR MAGIC, STRANGE! TELEPORT THAT HAMMER TO HEL!
WE'VE GOT TO KEEP IT AWAY FROM HER. NO MATTER WHAT IT TAKES.
NO.
IT'S HER LIFE.
SHE'S GOTTA MAKE THIS DECISION HERSELF.

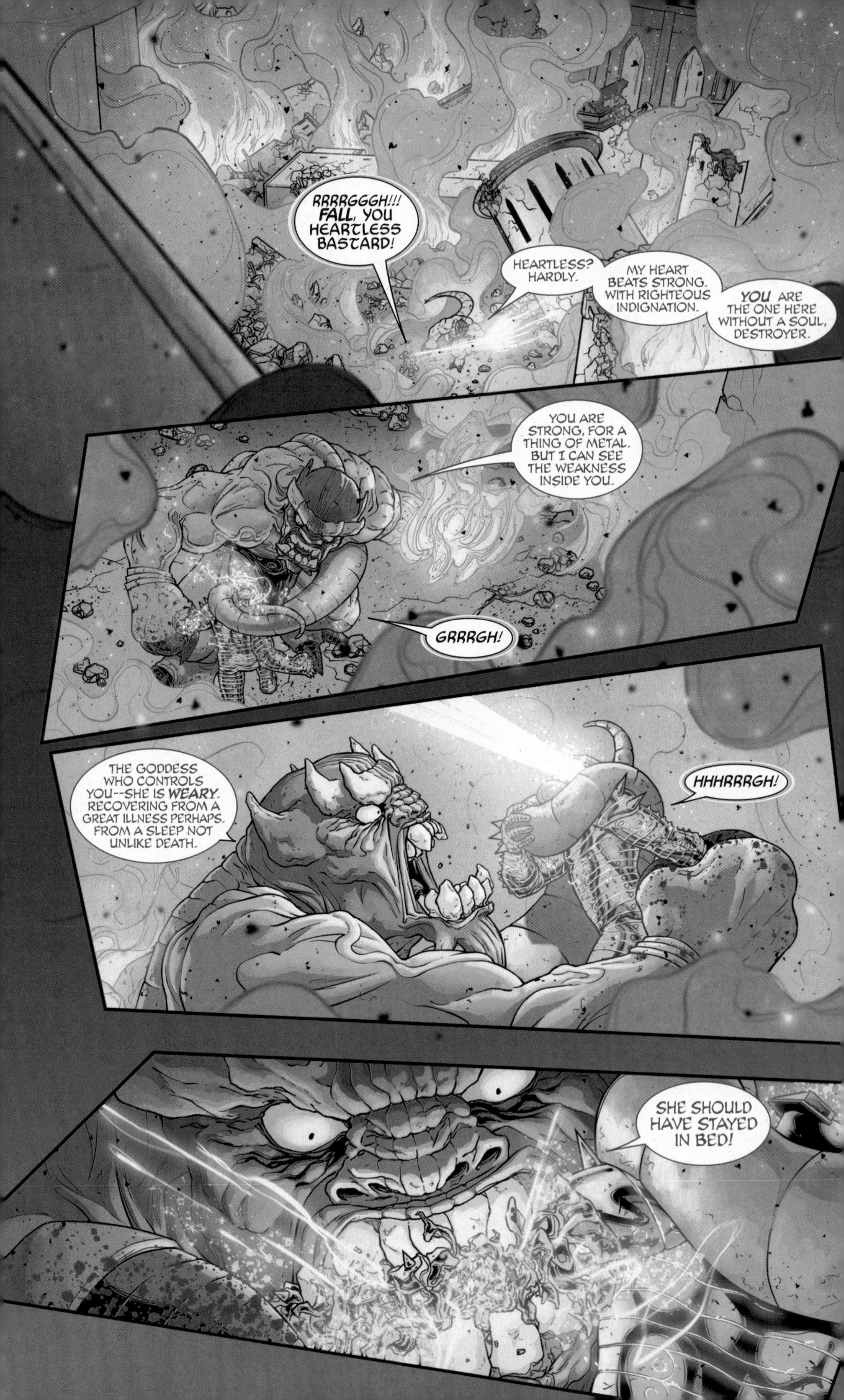
RRRRGGGH!!! FALL, YOU HEARTLESS BASTARD!
HEARTLESS? HARDLY.
MY HEART BEATS STRONG. WITH RIGHTEOUS INDIGNATION.
YOU ARE THE ONE HERE WITHOUT A SOUL, DESTROYER.
YOU ARE STRONG, FOR A THING OF METAL. BUT I CAN SEE THE WEAKNESS INSIDE YOU.
GRRRGH!
THE GODDESS WHO CONTROLS YOU--SHE IS WEARY. RECOVERING FROM A GREAT ILLNESS PERHAPS. FROM A SLEEP NOT UNLIKE DEATH.
HHHRRRGH!
SHE SHOULD HAVE STAYED IN BED!

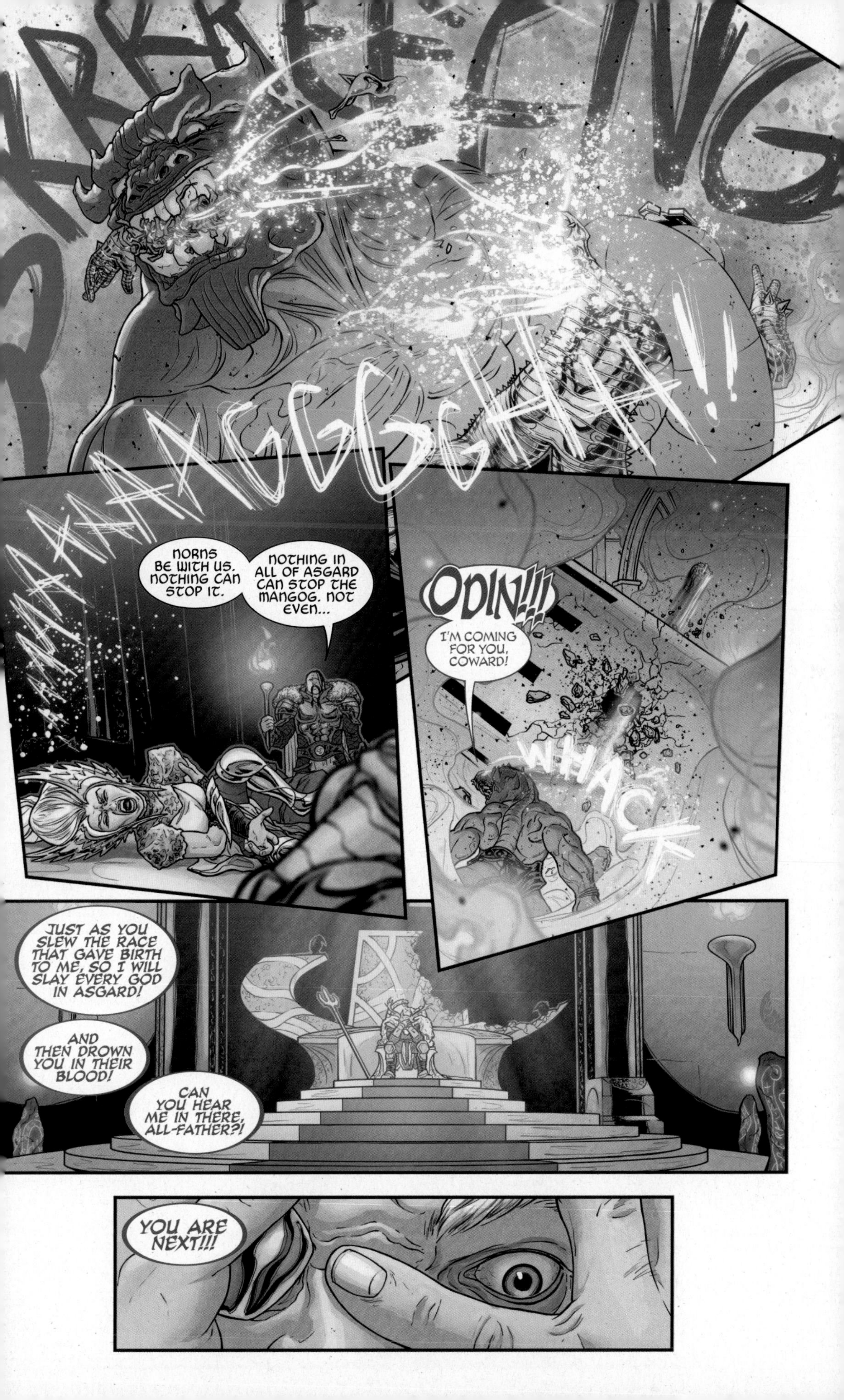

AAAAAGGGHHH!!
NORNS BE WITH US. NOTHING CAN STOP IT.
NOTHING IN ALL OF ASGARD CAN STOP THE MANGOG. NOT EVEN...
ODIN!!!!
I'M COMING FOR YOU, COWARD!
WHACK
JUST AS YOU SLEW THE RACE THAT GAVE BIRTH TO ME, SO I WILL SLAY EVERY GOD IN ASGARD!
AND THEN DROWN YOU IN THEIR BLOOD!
CAN YOU HEAR ME IN THERE, ALL-FATHER?!
YOU ARE NEXT!!!

... JUST PROMISE ME ONE THING...

ANYTHING IN ALL THE HEAVENS.

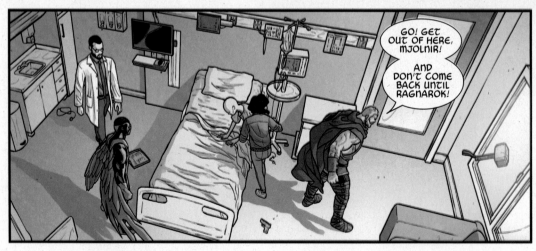

YOU'RE ALL *SOLDIERS* NOW. I'M OFFICIALLY SWEARING YOU IN.

SOLDIERS IN THE *WAR OF THE REALMS.*

MAKE SURE OUR SIDE DOESN'T LOSE.

GO! GET OUT OF HERE, MJOLNIR!

AND DON'T COME BACK UNTIL RAGNAROK!

"THIS MOMENT... WAS INEVITABLE.

"I'VE KNOWN THAT FOR A VERY LONG TIME.

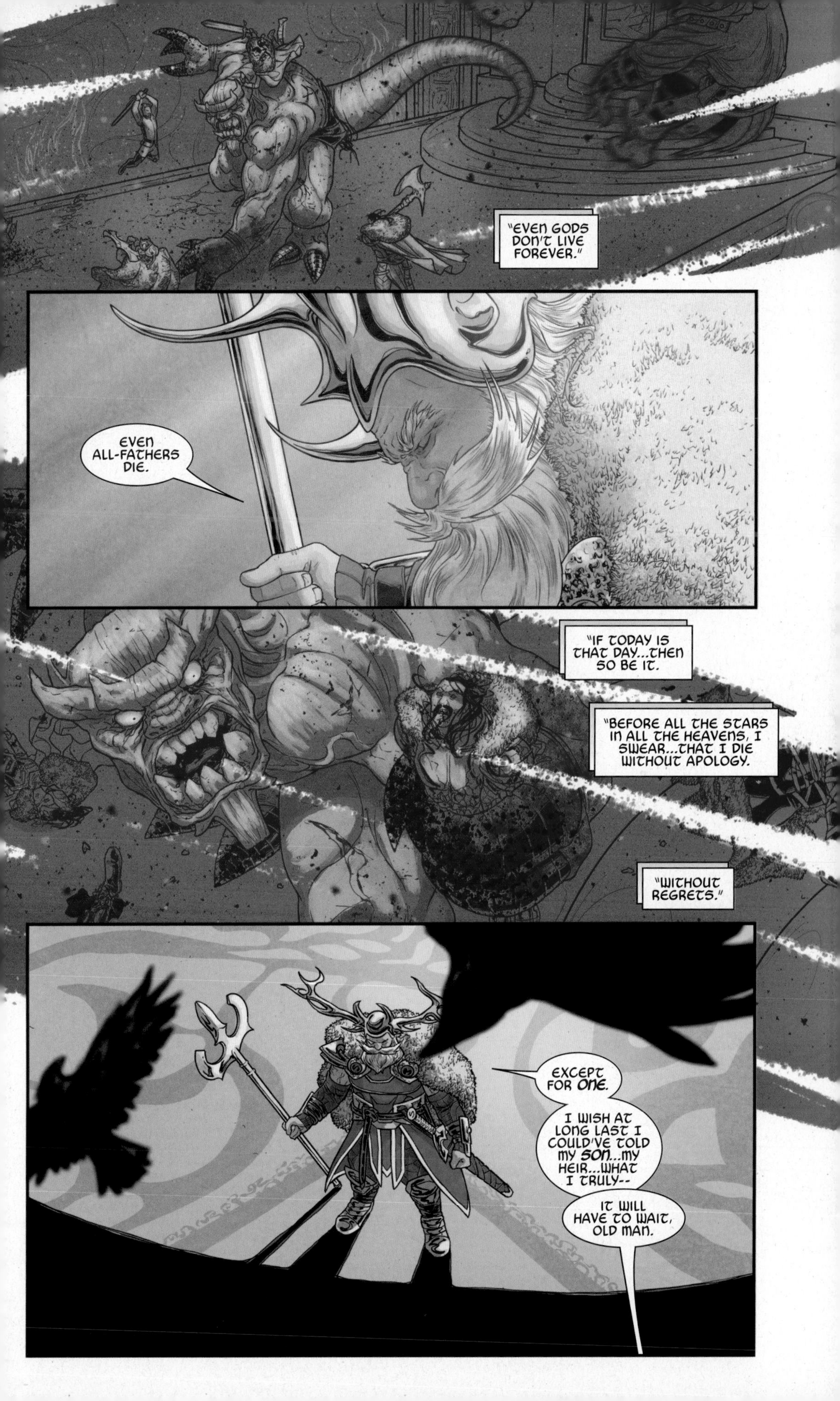

"EVEN GODS DON'T LIVE FOREVER."
EVEN ALL-FATHERS DIE.
"IF TODAY IS THAT DAY...THEN SO BE IT.
"BEFORE ALL THE STARS IN ALL THE HEAVENS, I SWEAR...THAT I DIE WITHOUT APOLOGY.
"WITHOUT REGRETS."
EXCEPT FOR ONE.
I WISH AT LONG LAST I COULD'VE TOLD MY SON...MY HEIR...WHAT I TRULY--
IT WILL HAVE TO WAIT, OLD MAN.

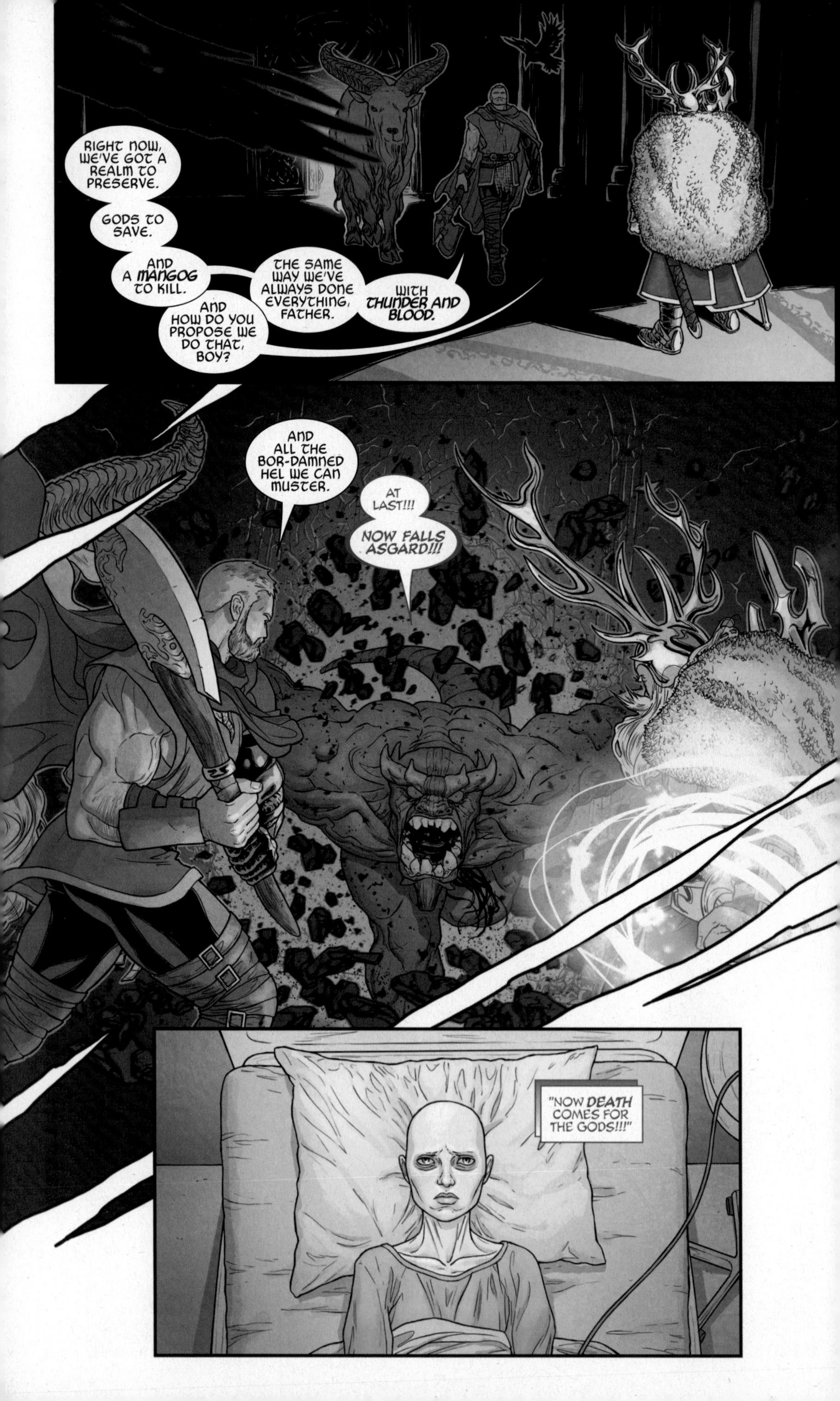
RIGHT NOW, WE'VE GOT A REALM TO PRESERVE.
GODS TO SAVE.
AND A MANGOG TO KILL.
AND HOW DO YOU PROPOSE WE DO THAT, BOY?
THE SAME WAY WE'VE ALWAYS DONE EVERYTHING, FATHER.
WITH THUNDER AND BLOOD.
AND ALL THE BOR-DAMNED HEL WE CAN MUSTER.
AT LAST!!!
NOW FALLS ASGARD!!!
"NOW DEATH COMES FOR THE GODS!!!"

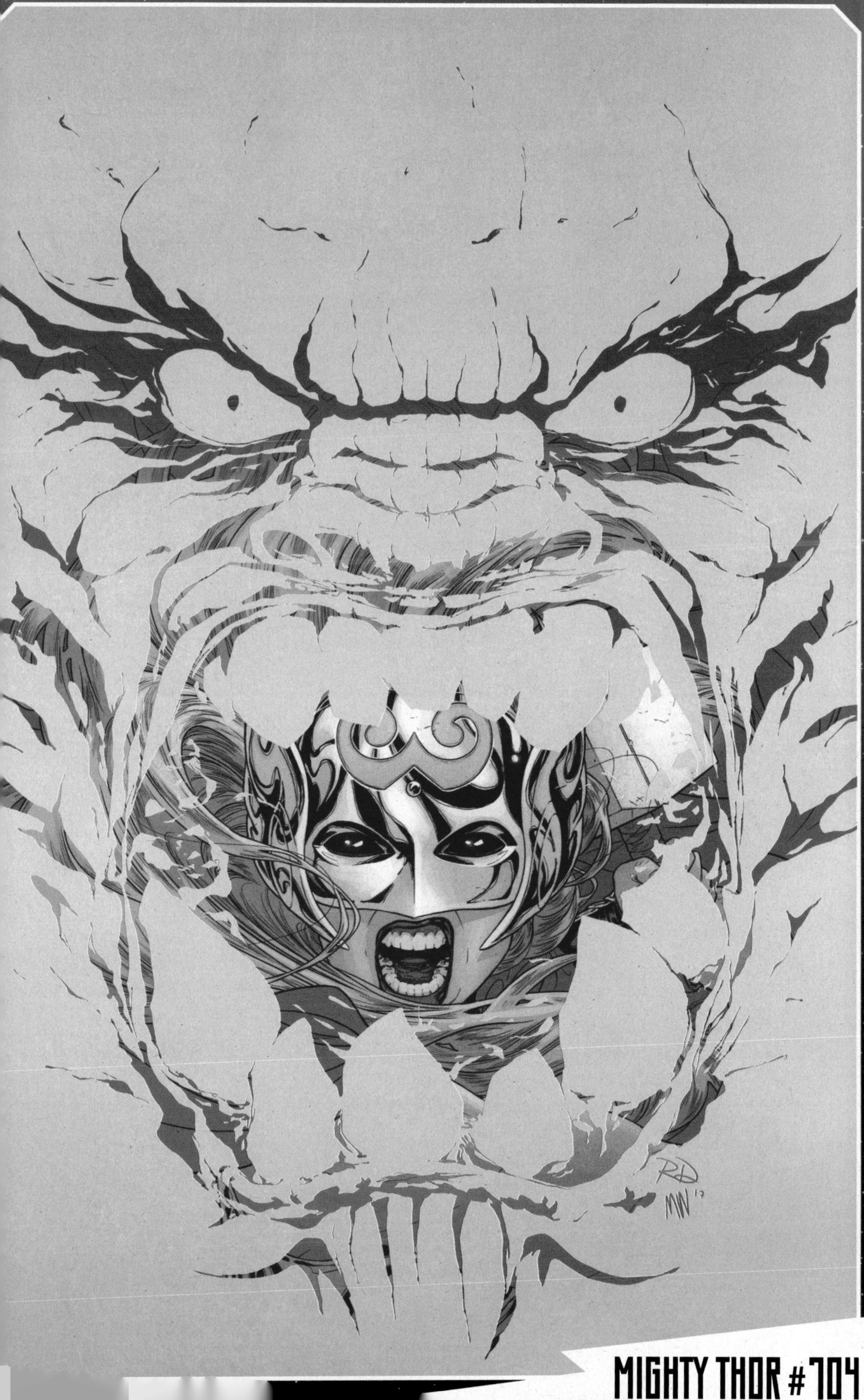

MIGHTY THOR #704

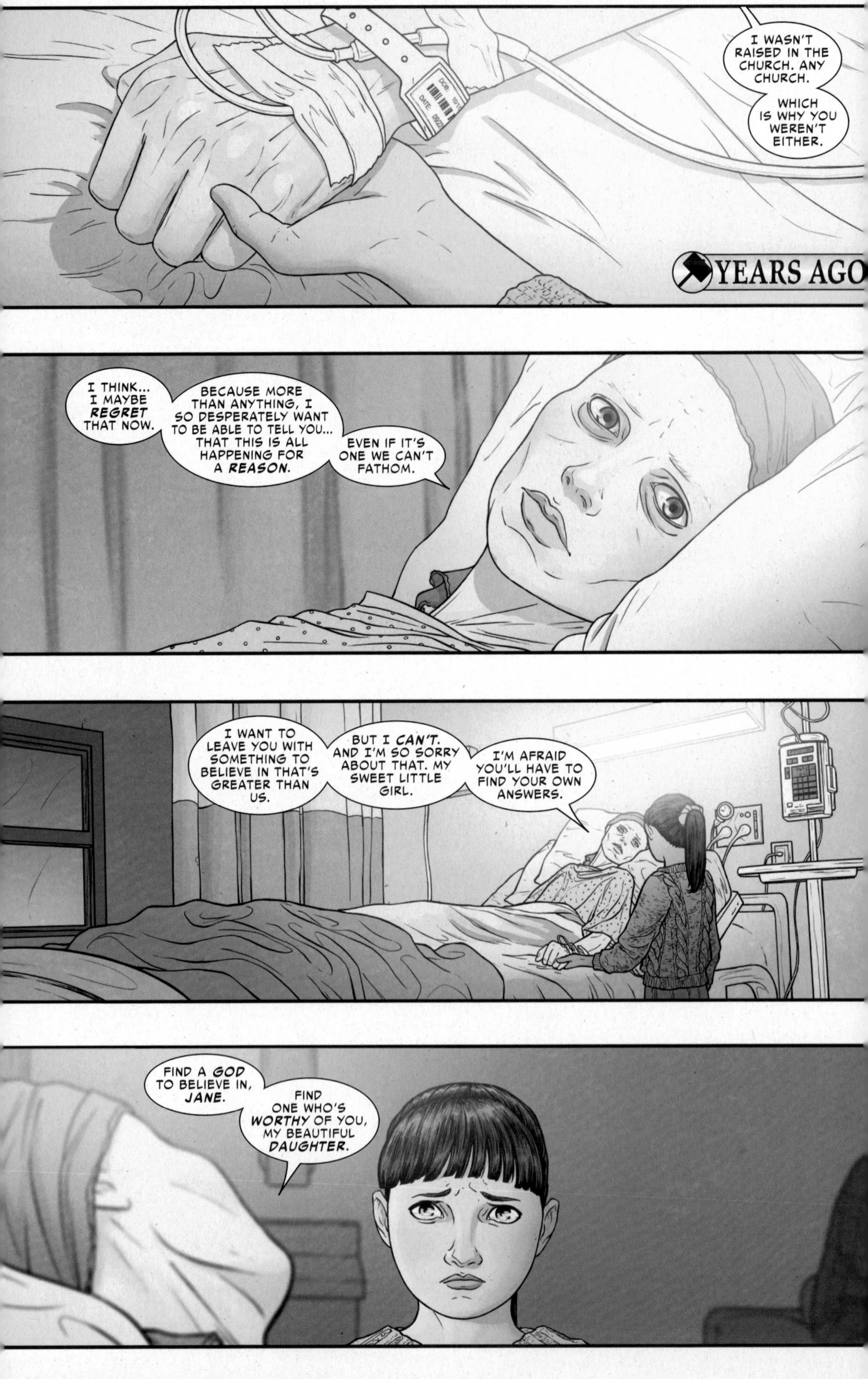
I WASN'T RAISED IN THE CHURCH. ANY CHURCH.
WHICH IS WHY YOU WEREN'T EITHER.
YEARS AGO
I THINK... I MAYBE REGRET THAT NOW.
BECAUSE MORE THAN ANYTHING, I SO DESPERATELY WANT TO BE ABLE TO TELL YOU... THAT THIS IS ALL HAPPENING FOR A REASON.
EVEN IF IT'S ONE WE CAN'T FATHOM.
I WANT TO LEAVE YOU WITH SOMETHING TO BELIEVE IN THAT'S GREATER THAN US.
BUT I CAN'T. AND I'M SO SORRY ABOUT THAT. MY SWEET LITTLE GIRL.
I'M AFRAID YOU'LL HAVE TO FIND YOUR OWN ANSWERS.
FIND A GOD TO BELIEVE IN, JANE.
FIND ONE WHO'S WORTHY OF YOU, MY BEAUTIFUL DAUGHTER.

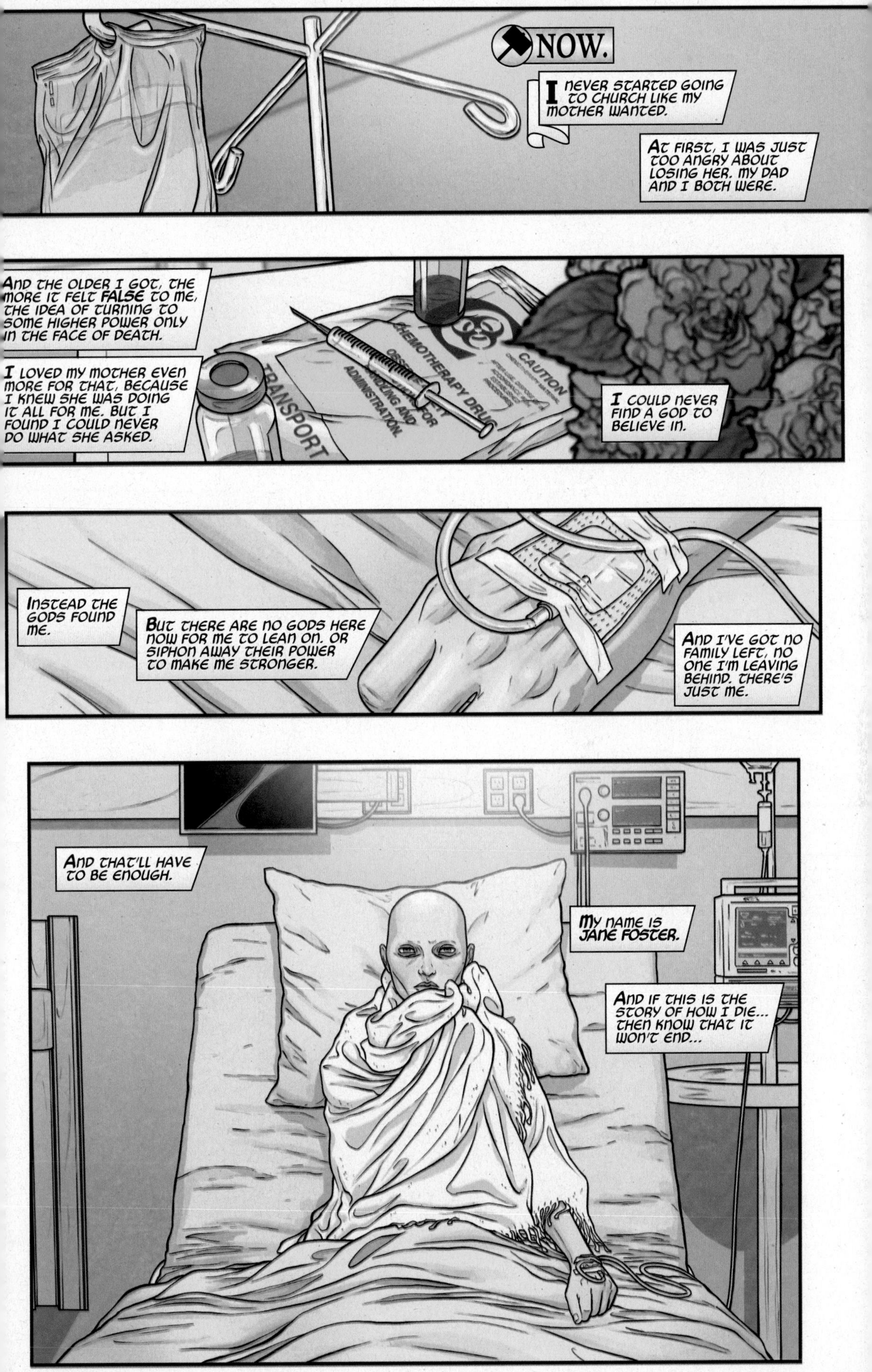
NOW.
I NEVER STARTED GOING TO CHURCH LIKE MY MOTHER WANTED.
AT FIRST, I WAS JUST TOO ANGRY ABOUT LOSING HER. MY DAD AND I BOTH WERE.
AND THE OLDER I GOT, THE MORE IT FELT FALSE TO ME, THE IDEA OF TURNING TO SOME HIGHER POWER ONLY IN THE FACE OF DEATH.
I LOVED MY MOTHER EVEN MORE FOR THAT, BECAUSE I KNEW SHE WAS DOING IT ALL FOR ME. BUT I FOUND I COULD NEVER DO WHAT SHE ASKED.
CAUTION
CHEMOTHERAPY DRUG
TRANSPORT
I COULD NEVER FIND A GOD TO BELIEVE IN.
INSTEAD THE GODS FOUND ME.
BUT THERE ARE NO GODS HERE NOW FOR ME TO LEAN ON. OR SIPHON AWAY THEIR POWER TO MAKE ME STRONGER.
AND I'VE GOT NO FAMILY LEFT, NO ONE I'M LEAVING BEHIND. THERE'S JUST ME.
AND THAT'LL HAVE TO BE ENOUGH.
MY NAME IS JANE FOSTER.
AND IF THIS IS THE STORY OF HOW I DIE... THEN KNOW THAT IT WON'T END...

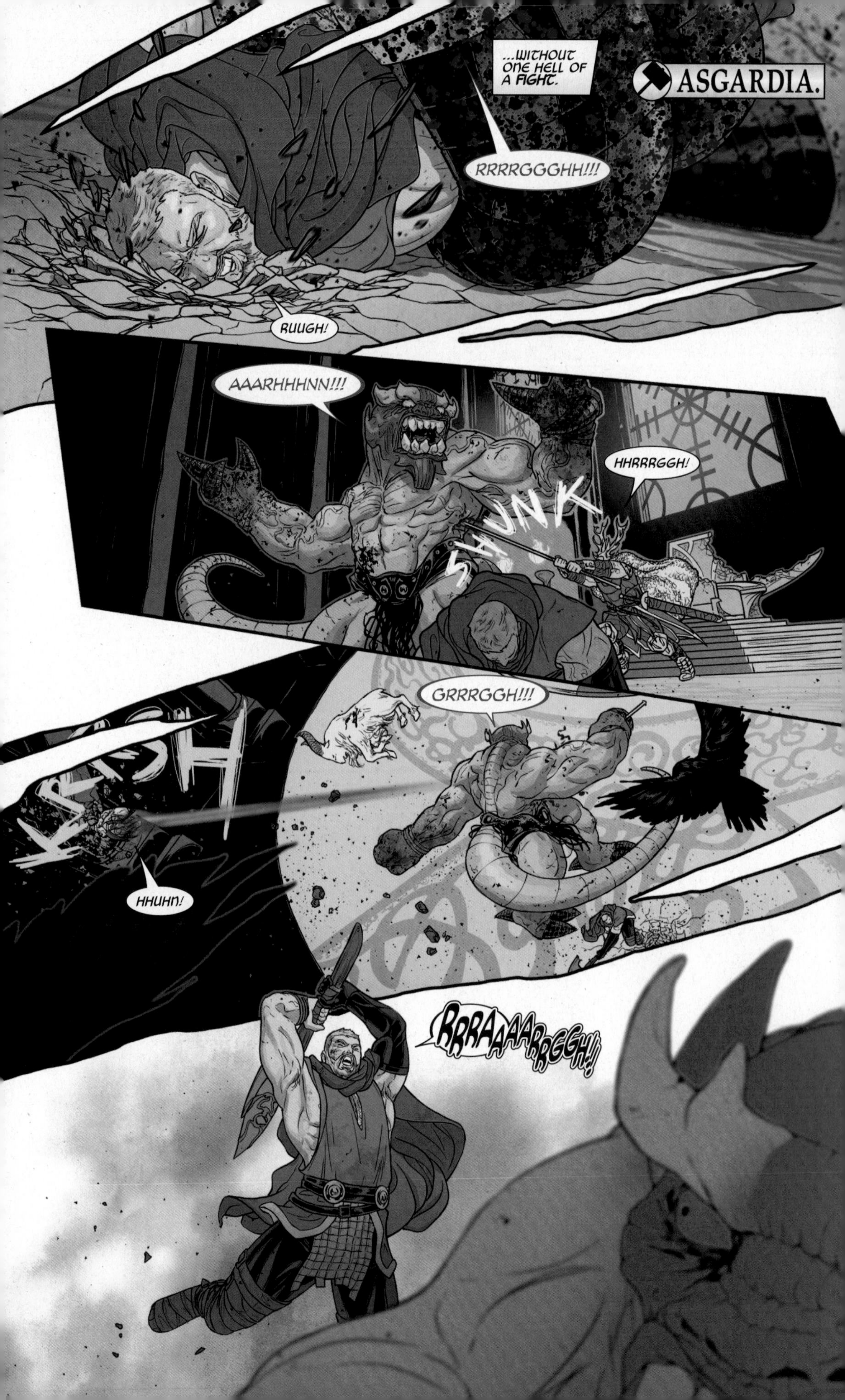

...WITHOUT ONE HELL OF A FIGHT.
ASGARDIA.
RRRRGGGHH!!!
RUUGH!
AAARHHHNN!!!
HHRRRGGH!
SHUNK
GRRRGGH!!!
HHUHN!
RRRAAAARRGGH!!

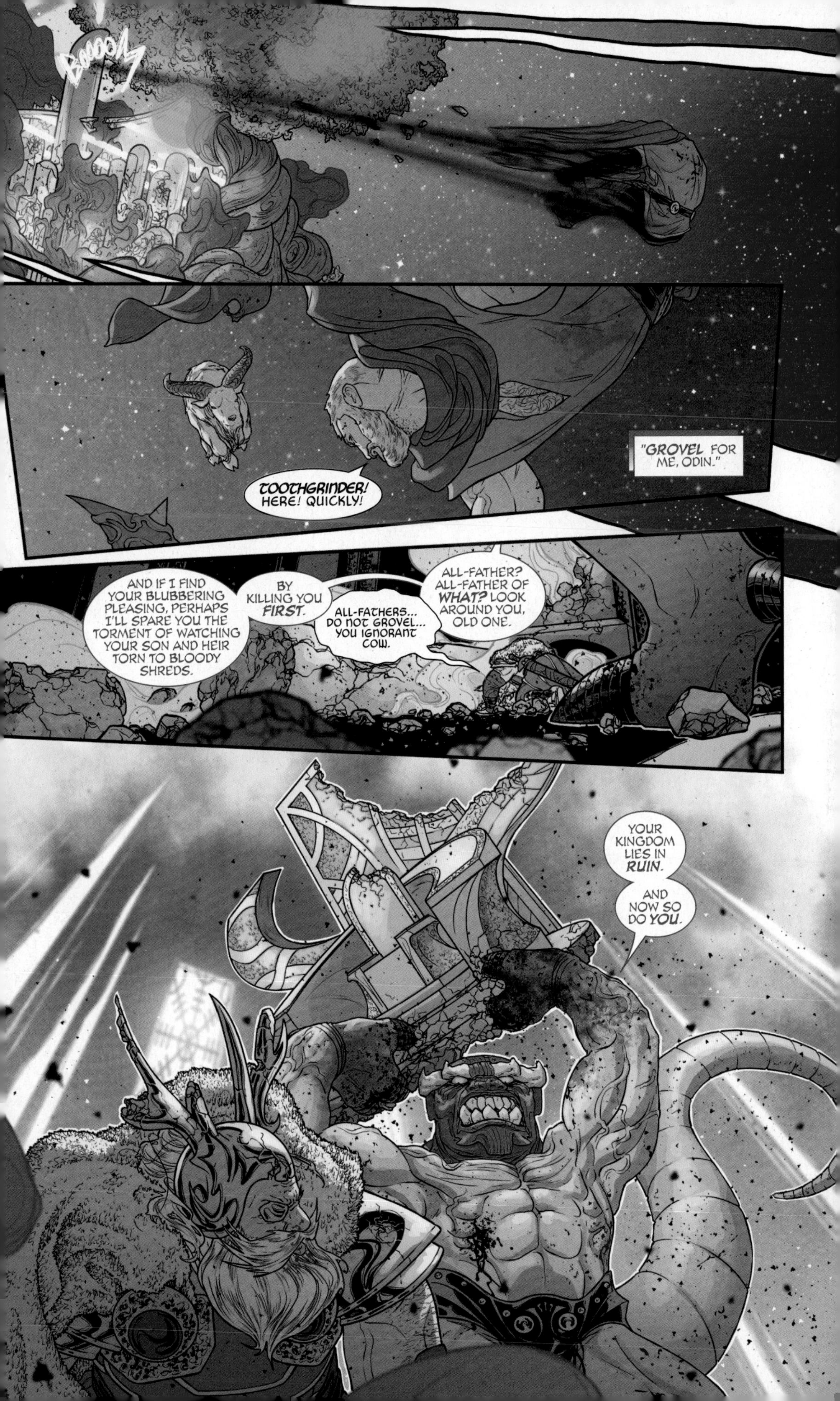
BOOOOM
"GROVEL FOR ME, ODIN."
TOOTHGRINDER! HERE! QUICKLY!
AND IF I FIND YOUR BLUBBERING PLEASING, PERHAPS I'LL SPARE YOU THE TORMENT OF WATCHING YOUR SON AND HEIR TORN TO BLOODY SHREDS.
BY KILLING YOU FIRST.
ALL-FATHERS... DO NOT GROVEL... YOU IGNORANT COW.
ALL-FATHER? ALL-FATHER OF WHAT? LOOK AROUND YOU, OLD ONE.
YOUR KINGDOM LIES IN RUIN.
AND NOW SO DO YOU.

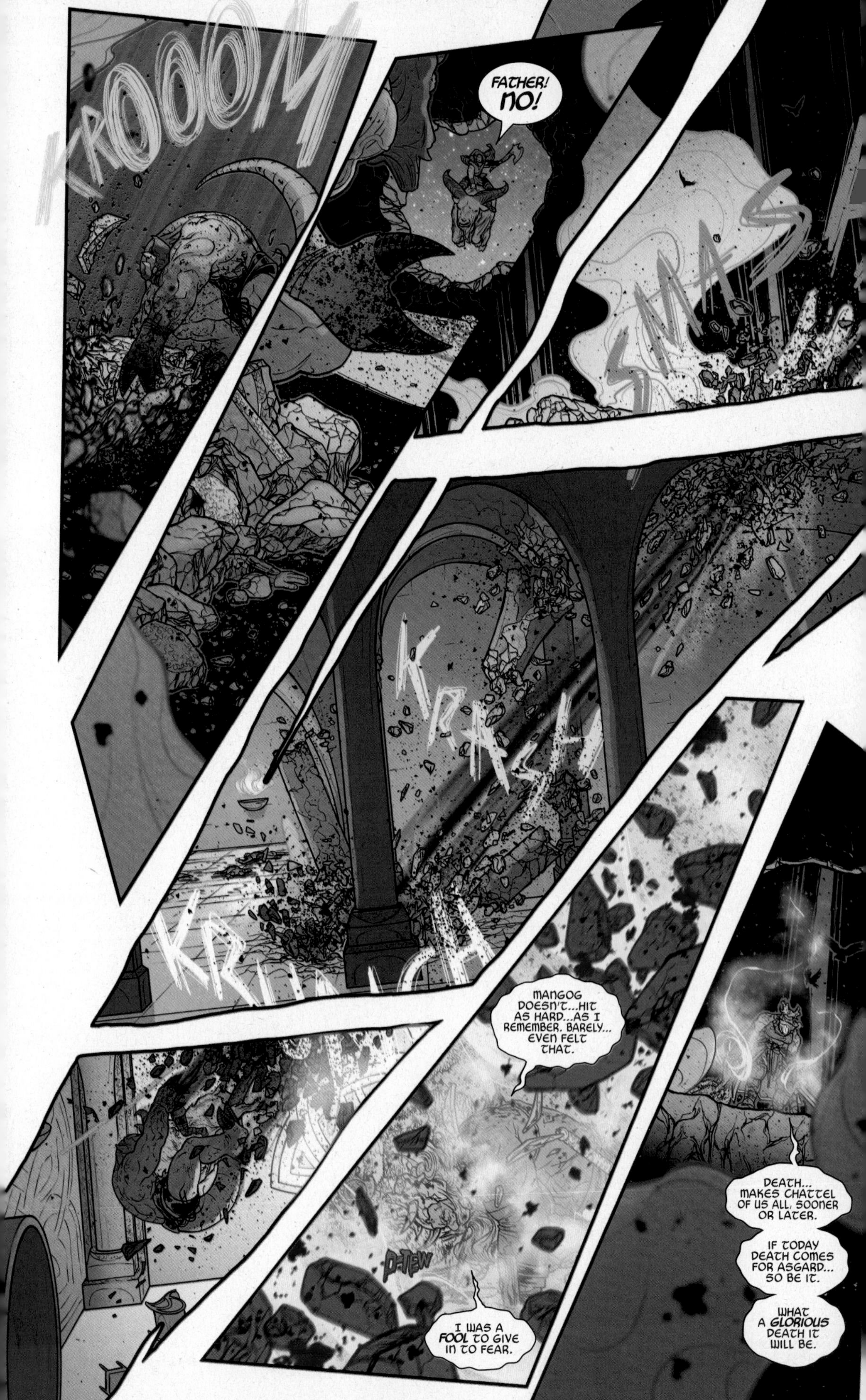
KROOOM
FATHER! NO!
SMASH
KRASH
KRUNCH
MANGOG DOESN'T...HIT AS HARD...AS I REMEMBER. BARELY... EVEN FELT THAT.
DEATH... MAKES CHATTEL OF US ALL, SOONER OR LATER.
IF TODAY DEATH COMES FOR ASGARD... SO BE IT.
WHAT A GLORIOUS DEATH IT WILL BE.
I WAS A FOOL TO GIVE IN TO FEAR.

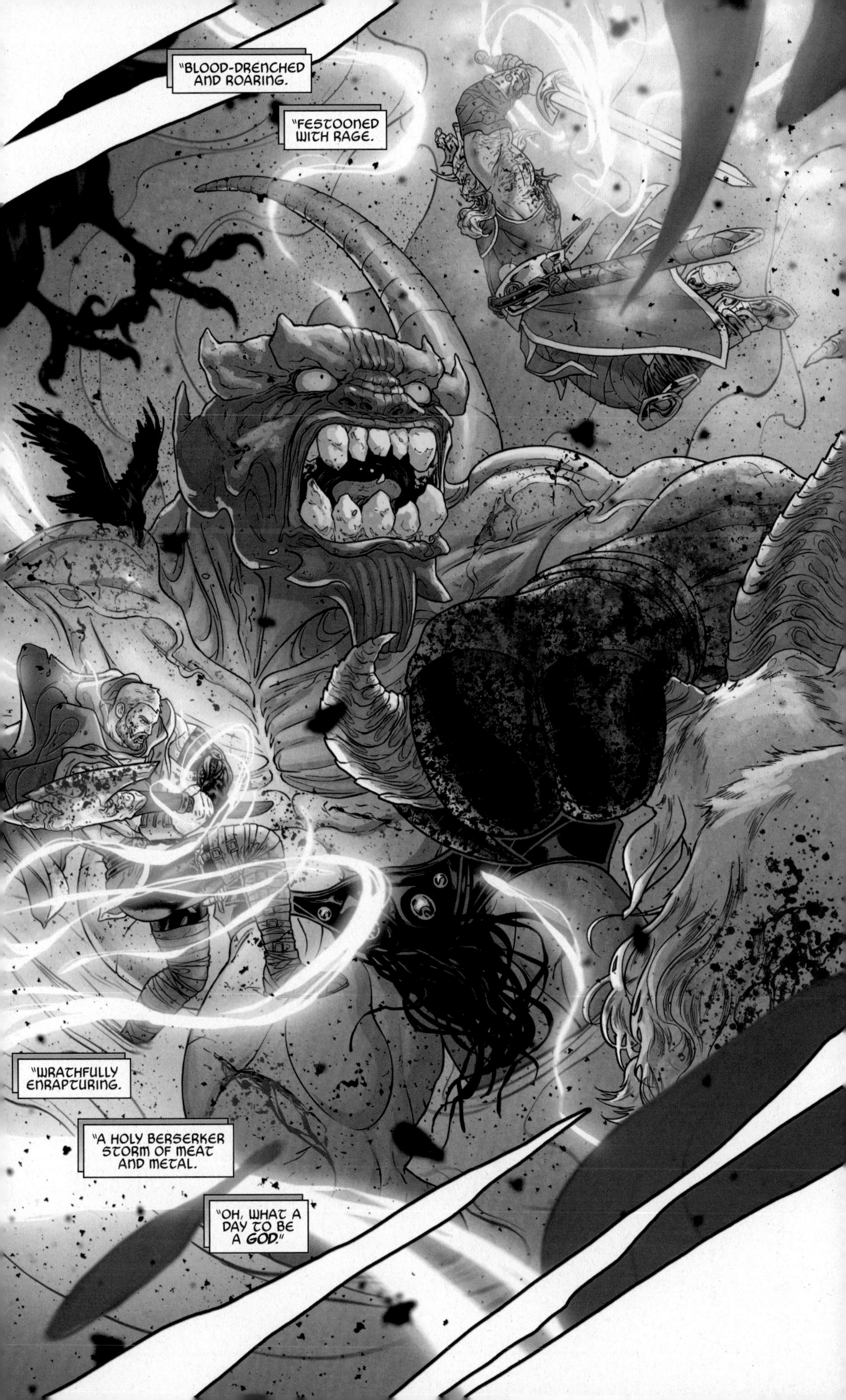
"BLOOD-DRENCHED AND ROARING.
"FESTOONED WITH RAGE.
"WRATHFULLY ENRAPTURING.
"A HOLY BERSERKER STORM OF MEAT AND METAL.
"OH, WHAT A DAY TO BE A GOD."

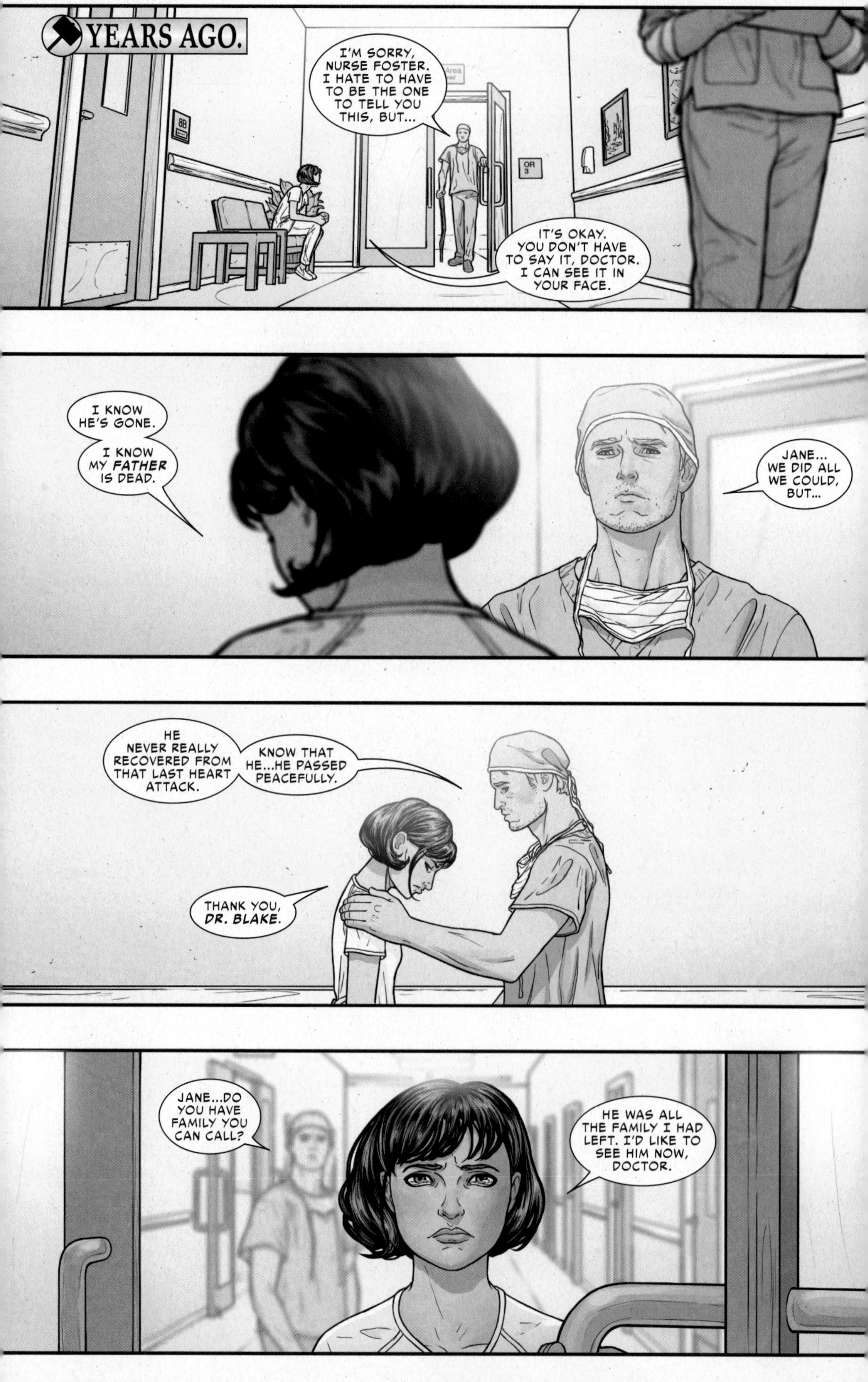
YEARS AGO.
I'M SORRY, NURSE FOSTER. I HATE TO HAVE TO BE THE ONE TO TELL YOU THIS, BUT...
IT'S OKAY. YOU DON'T HAVE TO SAY IT, DOCTOR. I CAN SEE IT IN YOUR FACE.
I KNOW HE'S GONE.
I KNOW MY *FATHER* IS DEAD.
JANE... WE DID ALL WE COULD, BUT...
HE NEVER REALLY RECOVERED FROM THAT LAST HEART ATTACK.
KNOW THAT HE...HE PASSED PEACEFULLY.
THANK YOU, ***DR. BLAKE.***
JANE...DO YOU HAVE FAMILY YOU CAN CALL?
HE WAS ALL THE FAMILY I HAD LEFT. I'D LIKE TO SEE HIM NOW, DOCTOR.

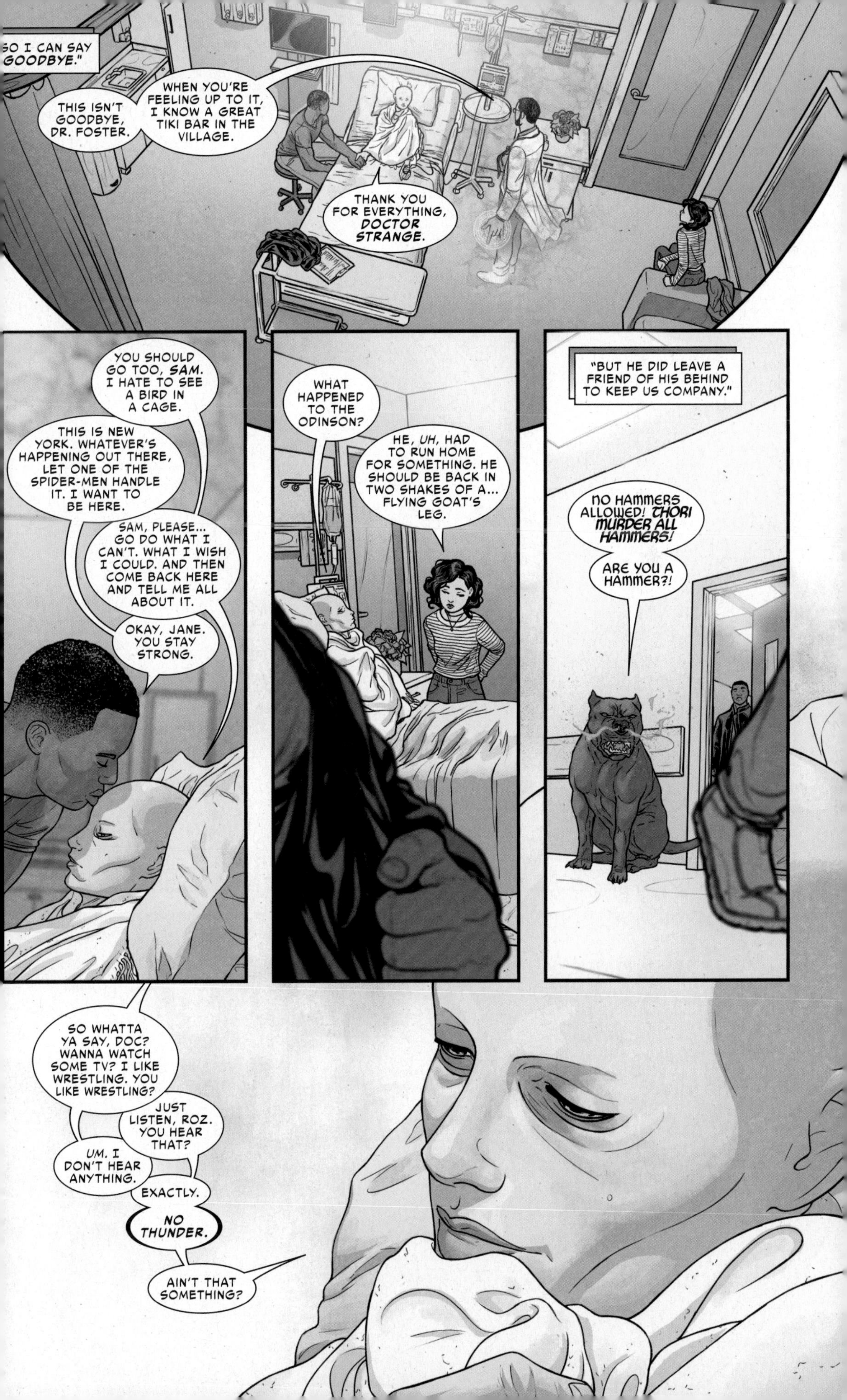

SO I CAN SAY GOODBYE."
THIS ISN'T GOODBYE, DR. FOSTER.
WHEN YOU'RE FEELING UP TO IT, I KNOW A GREAT TIKI BAR IN THE VILLAGE.
THANK YOU FOR EVERYTHING, DOCTOR STRANGE.
YOU SHOULD GO TOO, SAM. I HATE TO SEE A BIRD IN A CAGE.
THIS IS NEW YORK. WHATEVER'S HAPPENING OUT THERE, LET ONE OF THE SPIDER-MEN HANDLE IT. I WANT TO BE HERE.
SAM, PLEASE... GO DO WHAT I CAN'T. WHAT I WISH I COULD. AND THEN COME BACK HERE AND TELL ME ALL ABOUT IT.
OKAY, JANE. YOU STAY STRONG.
WHAT HAPPENED TO THE ODINSON?
HE, UH, HAD TO RUN HOME FOR SOMETHING. HE SHOULD BE BACK IN TWO SHAKES OF A... FLYING GOAT'S LEG.
"BUT HE DID LEAVE A FRIEND OF HIS BEHIND TO KEEP US COMPANY."
NO HAMMERS ALLOWED! THORI MURDER ALL HAMMERS!
ARE YOU A HAMMER?!
SO WHATTA YA SAY, DOC? WANNA WATCH SOME TV? I LIKE WRESTLING. YOU LIKE WRESTLING?
JUST LISTEN, ROZ. YOU HEAR THAT?
UM. I DON'T HEAR ANYTHING.
EXACTLY.
NO THUNDER.
AIN'T THAT SOMETHING?

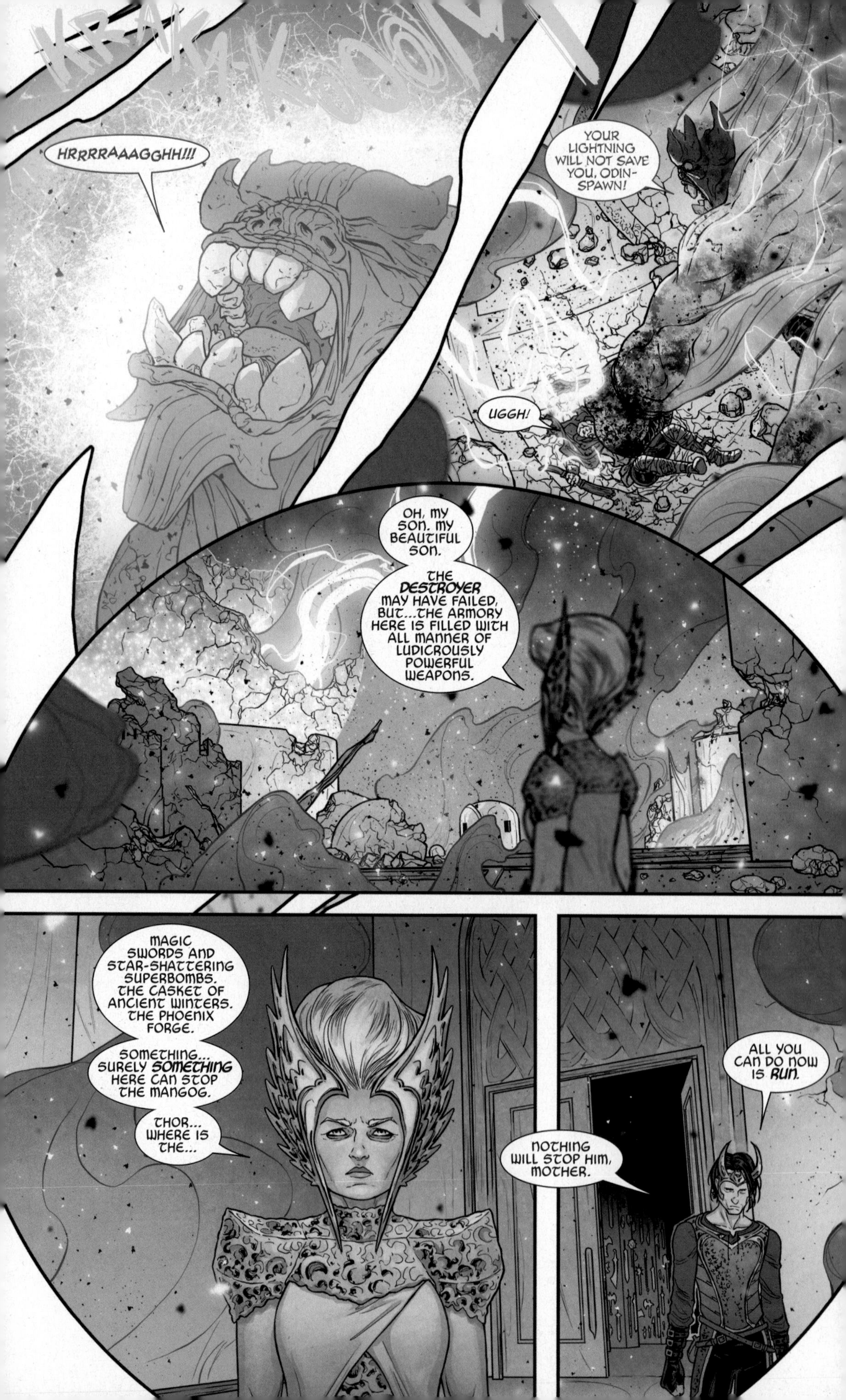
KRAKA-KOOM
HRRRRAAAGGHH!!!
YOUR LIGHTNING WILL NOT SAVE YOU, ODIN-SPAWN!
UGGH!
OH, MY SON. MY BEAUTIFUL SON.
THE DESTROYER MAY HAVE FAILED, BUT...THE ARMORY HERE IS FILLED WITH ALL MANNER OF LUDICROUSLY POWERFUL WEAPONS.
MAGIC SWORDS AND STAR-SHATTERING SUPERBOMBS. THE CASKET OF ANCIENT WINTERS. THE PHOENIX FORGE.
SOMETHING... SURELY SOMETHING HERE CAN STOP THE MANGOG.
THOR... WHERE IS THE...
ALL YOU CAN DO NOW IS RUN.
NOTHING WILL STOP HIM, MOTHER.

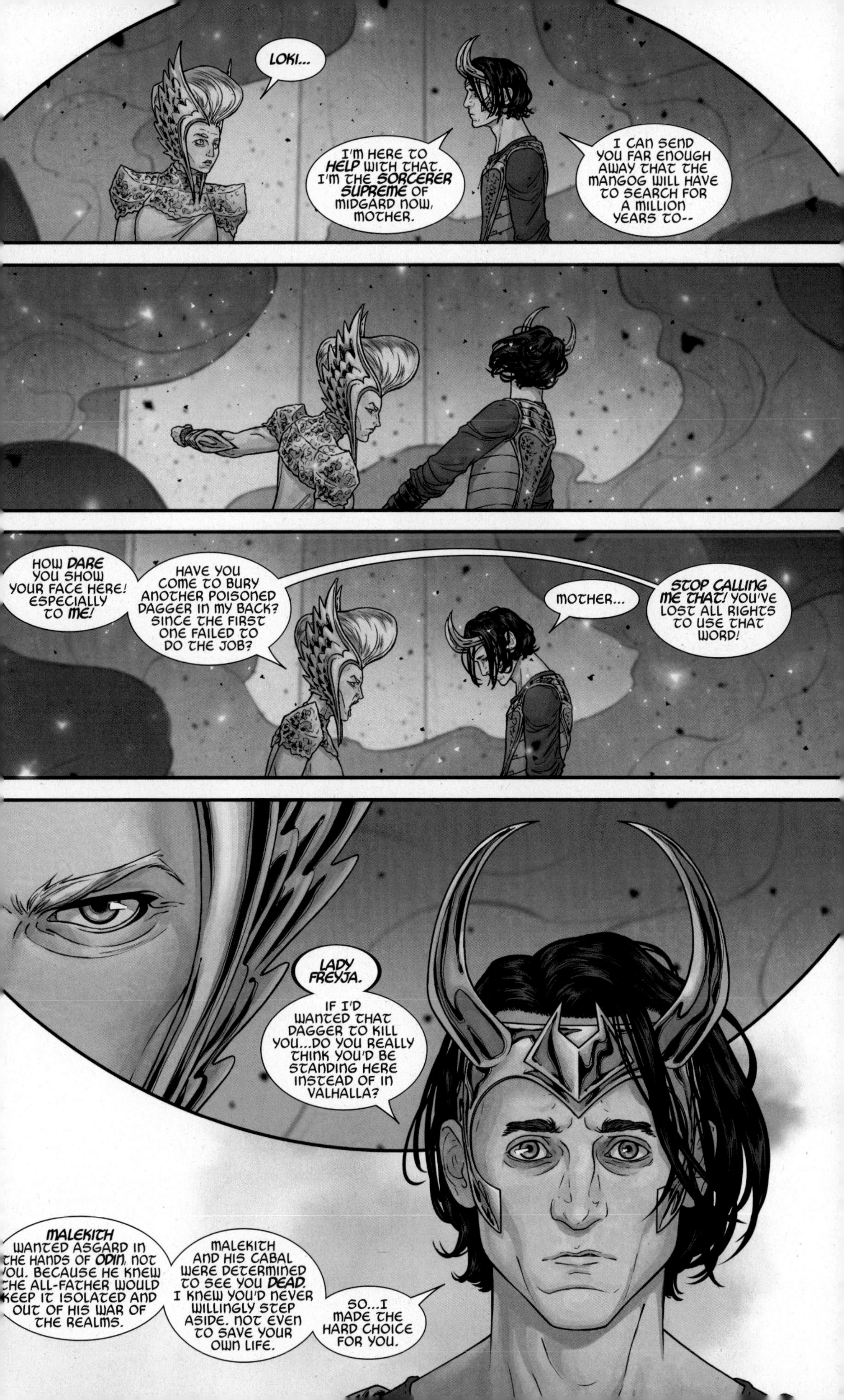
LOKI...
I'M HERE TO HELP WITH THAT. I'M THE SORCERER SUPREME OF MIDGARD NOW, MOTHER.
I CAN SEND YOU FAR ENOUGH AWAY THAT THE MANGOG WILL HAVE TO SEARCH FOR A MILLION YEARS TO--
HOW DARE YOU SHOW YOUR FACE HERE! ESPECIALLY TO ME!
HAVE YOU COME TO BURY ANOTHER POISONED DAGGER IN MY BACK? SINCE THE FIRST ONE FAILED TO DO THE JOB?
MOTHER...
STOP CALLING ME THAT! YOU'VE LOST ALL RIGHTS TO USE THAT WORD!
LADY FREYJA.
IF I'D WANTED THAT DAGGER TO KILL YOU...DO YOU REALLY THINK YOU'D BE STANDING HERE INSTEAD OF IN VALHALLA?
MALEKITH WANTED ASGARD IN THE HANDS OF ODIN, NOT YOU. BECAUSE HE KNEW THE ALL-FATHER WOULD KEEP IT ISOLATED AND OUT OF HIS WAR OF THE REALMS.
MALEKITH AND HIS CABAL WERE DETERMINED TO SEE YOU DEAD. I KNEW YOU'D NEVER WILLINGLY STEP ASIDE. NOT EVEN TO SAVE YOUR OWN LIFE.
SO...I MADE THE HARD CHOICE FOR YOU.

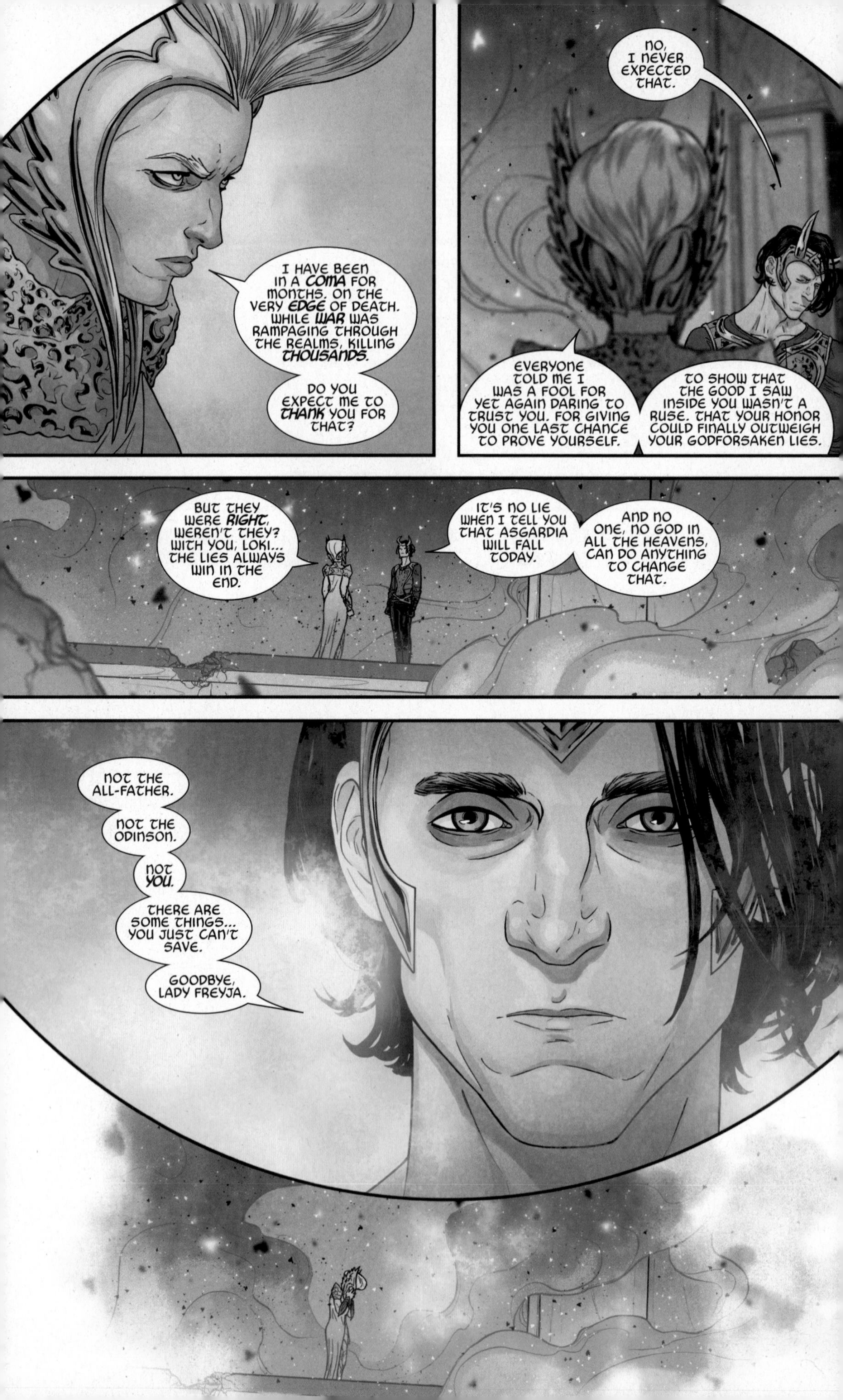
I HAVE BEEN IN A COMA FOR MONTHS. ON THE VERY EDGE OF DEATH. WHILE WAR WAS RAMPAGING THROUGH THE REALMS, KILLING THOUSANDS.
DO YOU EXPECT ME TO THANK YOU FOR THAT?
NO, I NEVER EXPECTED THAT.
EVERYONE TOLD ME I WAS A FOOL FOR YET AGAIN DARING TO TRUST YOU. FOR GIVING YOU ONE LAST CHANCE TO PROVE YOURSELF.
TO SHOW THAT THE GOOD I SAW INSIDE YOU WASN'T A RUSE. THAT YOUR HONOR COULD FINALLY OUTWEIGH YOUR GODFORSAKEN LIES.
BUT THEY WERE RIGHT, WEREN'T THEY? WITH YOU, LOKI... THE LIES ALWAYS WIN IN THE END.
IT'S NO LIE WHEN I TELL YOU THAT ASGARDIA WILL FALL TODAY.
AND NO ONE, NO GOD IN ALL THE HEAVENS, CAN DO ANYTHING TO CHANGE THAT.
NOT THE ALL-FATHER.
NOT THE ODINSON.
NOT YOU.
THERE ARE SOME THINGS... YOU JUST CAN'T SAVE.
GOODBYE, LADY FREYJA.

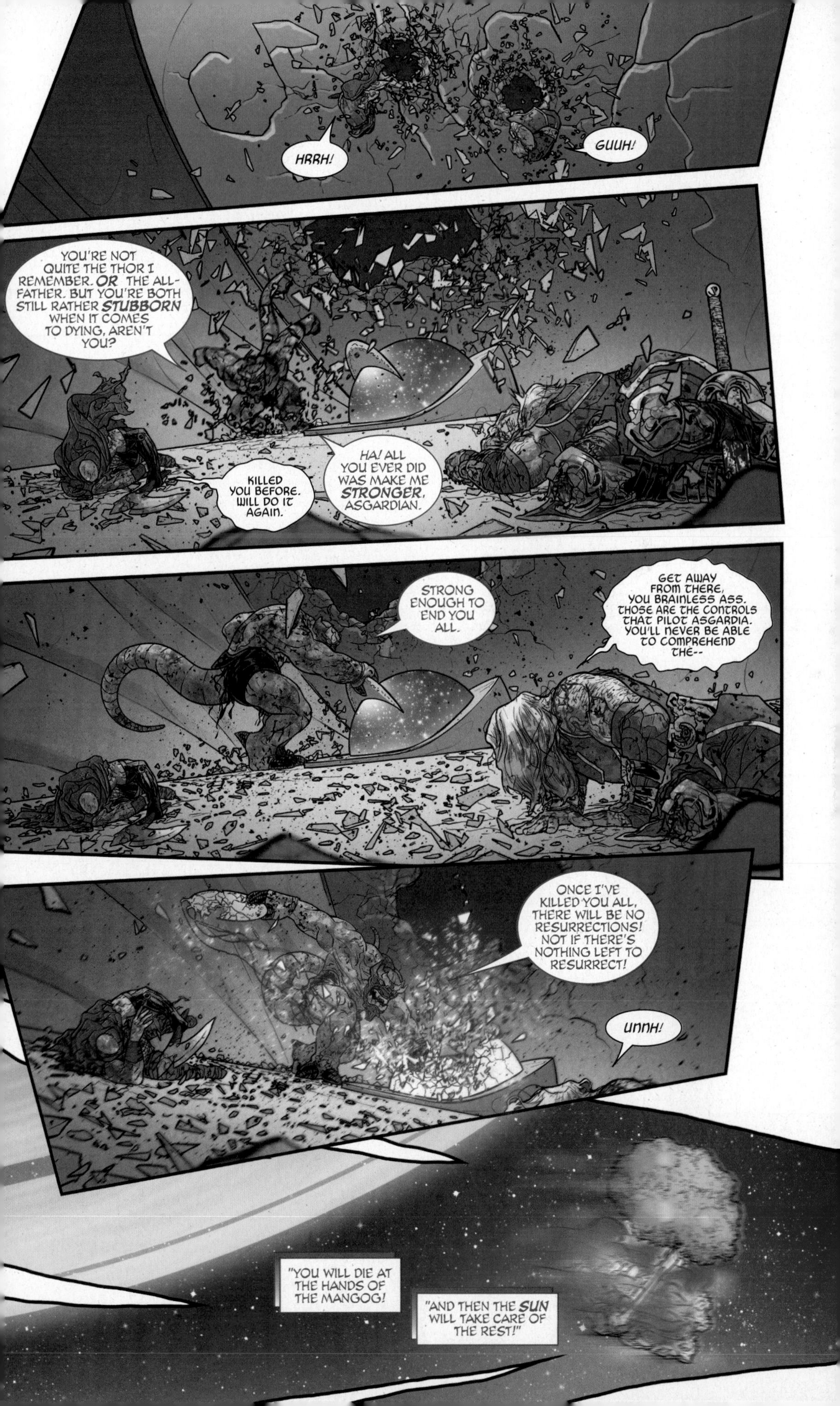

HRRH!
GUUH!
YOU'RE NOT QUITE THE THOR I REMEMBER. OR THE ALL-FATHER. BUT YOU'RE BOTH STILL RATHER STUBBORN WHEN IT COMES TO DYING, AREN'T YOU?
KILLED YOU BEFORE. WILL DO IT AGAIN.
HA! ALL YOU EVER DID WAS MAKE ME STRONGER, ASGARDIAN.
STRONG ENOUGH TO END YOU ALL.
GET AWAY FROM THERE, YOU BRAINLESS ASS. THOSE ARE THE CONTROLS THAT PILOT ASGARDIA. YOU'LL NEVER BE ABLE TO COMPREHEND THE--
ONCE I'VE KILLED YOU ALL, THERE WILL BE NO RESURRECTIONS! NOT IF THERE'S NOTHING LEFT TO RESURRECT!
UNNH!
"YOU WILL DIE AT THE HANDS OF THE MANGOG!
"AND THEN THE SUN WILL TAKE CARE OF THE REST!"

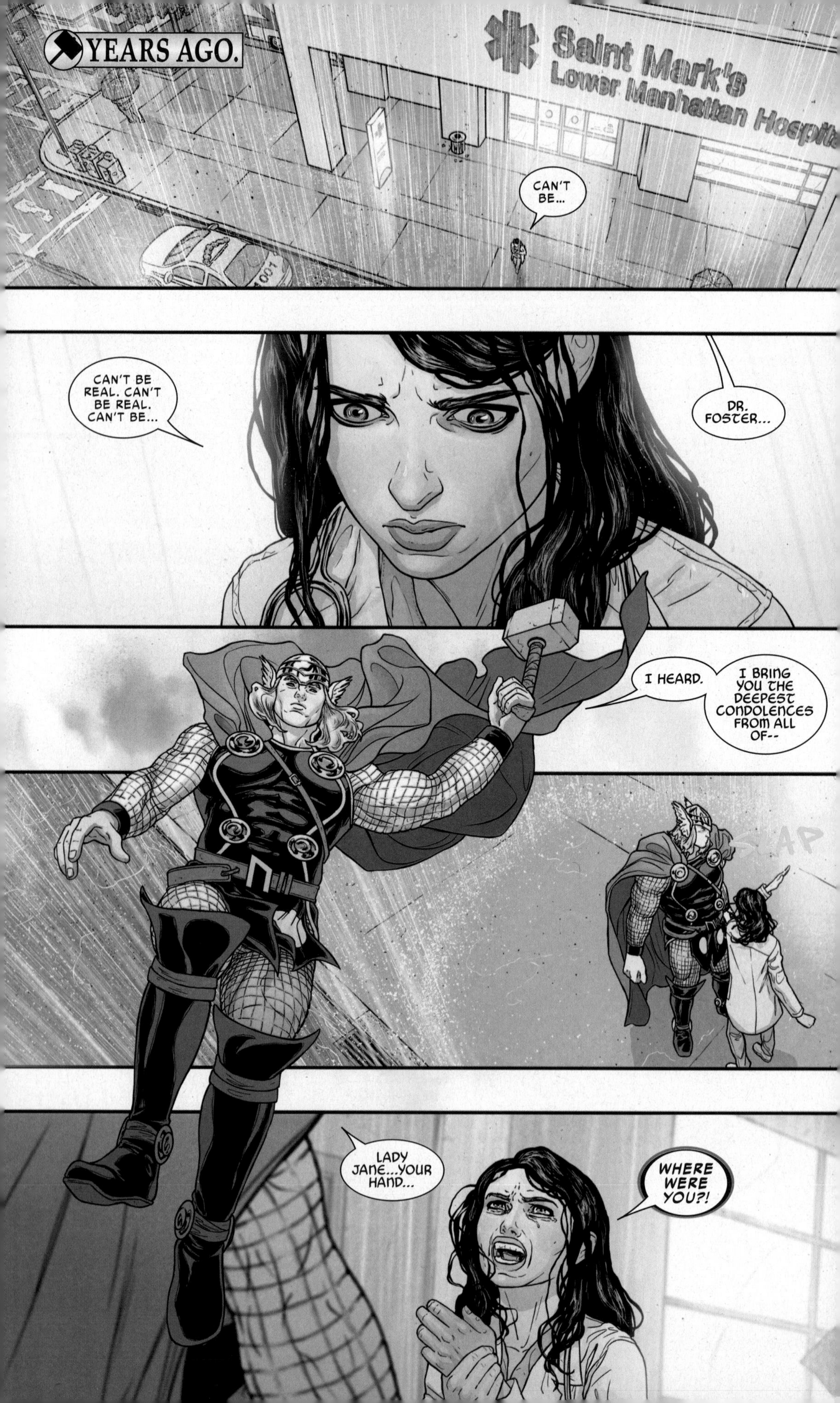
YEARS AGO.
Saint Mark's
Lower Manhattan Hospital
CAN'T BE...
CAN'T BE REAL. CAN'T BE REAL. CAN'T BE...
DR. FOSTER...
I HEARD.
I BRING YOU THE DEEPEST CONDOLENCES FROM ALL OF--
SLAP
LADY JANE...YOUR HAND...
WHERE WERE YOU?!

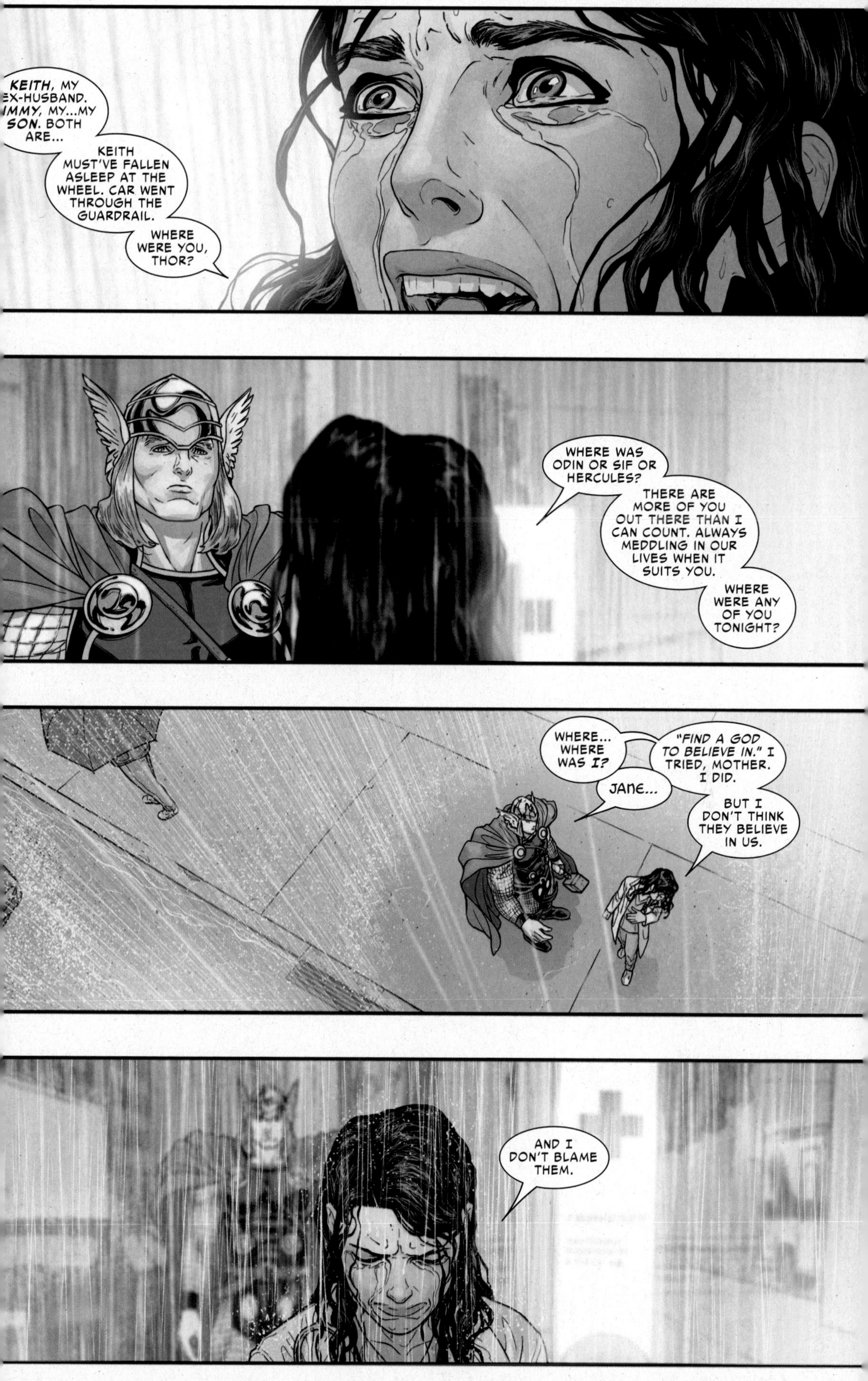
KEITH, MY EX-HUSBAND. JIMMY, MY...MY SON. BOTH ARE...
KEITH MUST'VE FALLEN ASLEEP AT THE WHEEL. CAR WENT THROUGH THE GUARDRAIL.
WHERE WERE YOU, THOR?
WHERE WAS ODIN OR SIF OR HERCULES?
THERE ARE MORE OF YOU OUT THERE THAN I CAN COUNT. ALWAYS MEDDLING IN OUR LIVES WHEN IT SUITS YOU.
WHERE WERE ANY OF YOU TONIGHT?
WHERE... WHERE WAS I?
JANE...
"FIND A GOD TO BELIEVE IN." I TRIED, MOTHER. I DID.
BUT I DON'T THINK THEY BELIEVE IN US.
AND I DON'T BLAME THEM.

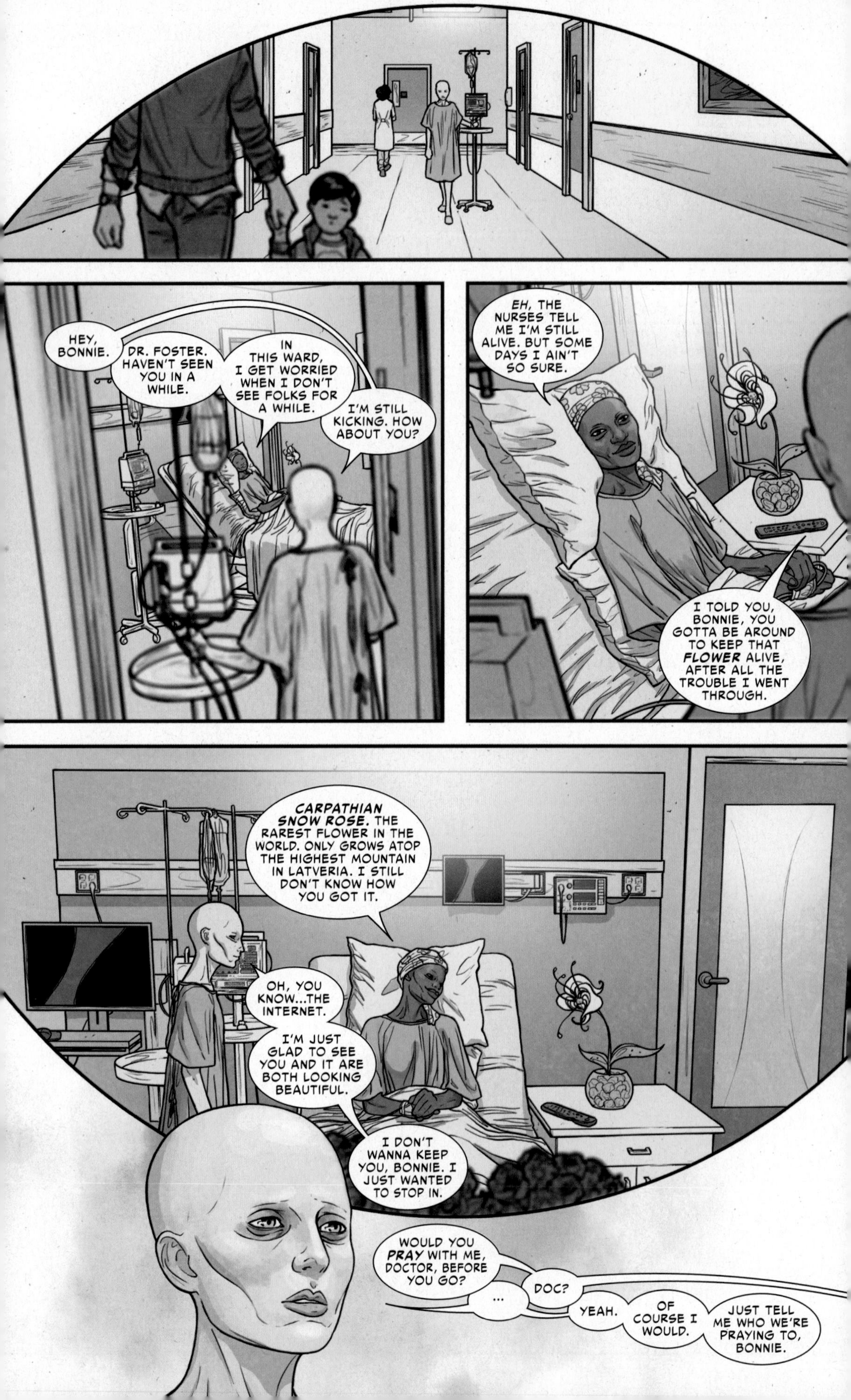
HEY, BONNIE.
DR. FOSTER. HAVEN'T SEEN YOU IN A WHILE.
IN THIS WARD, I GET WORRIED WHEN I DON'T SEE FOLKS FOR A WHILE.
I'M STILL KICKING. HOW ABOUT YOU?
EH, THE NURSES TELL ME I'M STILL ALIVE. BUT SOME DAYS I AIN'T SO SURE.
I TOLD YOU, BONNIE, YOU GOTTA BE AROUND TO KEEP THAT FLOWER ALIVE, AFTER ALL THE TROUBLE I WENT THROUGH.
CARPATHIAN SNOW ROSE. THE RAREST FLOWER IN THE WORLD. ONLY GROWS ATOP THE HIGHEST MOUNTAIN IN LATVERIA. I STILL DON'T KNOW HOW YOU GOT IT.
OH, YOU KNOW...THE INTERNET.
I'M JUST GLAD TO SEE YOU AND IT ARE BOTH LOOKING BEAUTIFUL.
I DON'T WANNA KEEP YOU, BONNIE. I JUST WANTED TO STOP IN.
WOULD YOU PRAY WITH ME, DOCTOR, BEFORE YOU GO?
...
DOC?
YEAH.
OF COURSE I WOULD.
JUST TELL ME WHO WE'RE PRAYING TO, BONNIE.

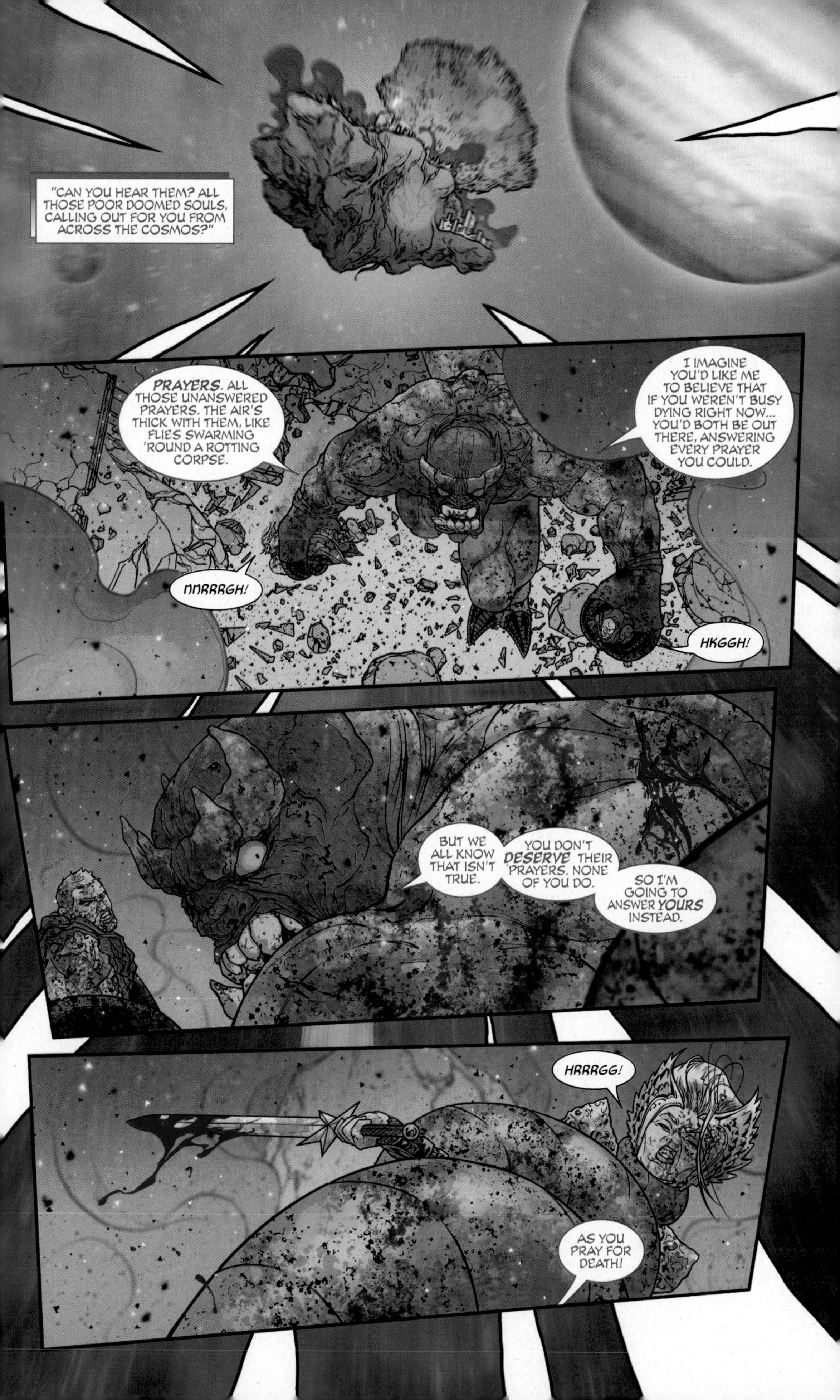
"CAN YOU HEAR THEM? ALL THOSE POOR DOOMED SOULS, CALLING OUT FOR YOU FROM ACROSS THE COSMOS?"
PRAYERS. ALL THOSE UNANSWERED PRAYERS. THE AIR'S THICK WITH THEM, LIKE FLIES SWARMING 'ROUND A ROTTING CORPSE.
I IMAGINE YOU'D LIKE ME TO BELIEVE THAT IF YOU WEREN'T BUSY DYING RIGHT NOW... YOU'D BOTH BE OUT THERE, ANSWERING EVERY PRAYER YOU COULD.
NNRRRGH!
HKGGH!
BUT WE ALL KNOW THAT ISN'T TRUE.
YOU DON'T DESERVE THEIR PRAYERS. NONE OF YOU DO.
SO I'M GOING TO ANSWER YOURS INSTEAD.
HRRRGG!
AS YOU PRAY FOR DEATH!

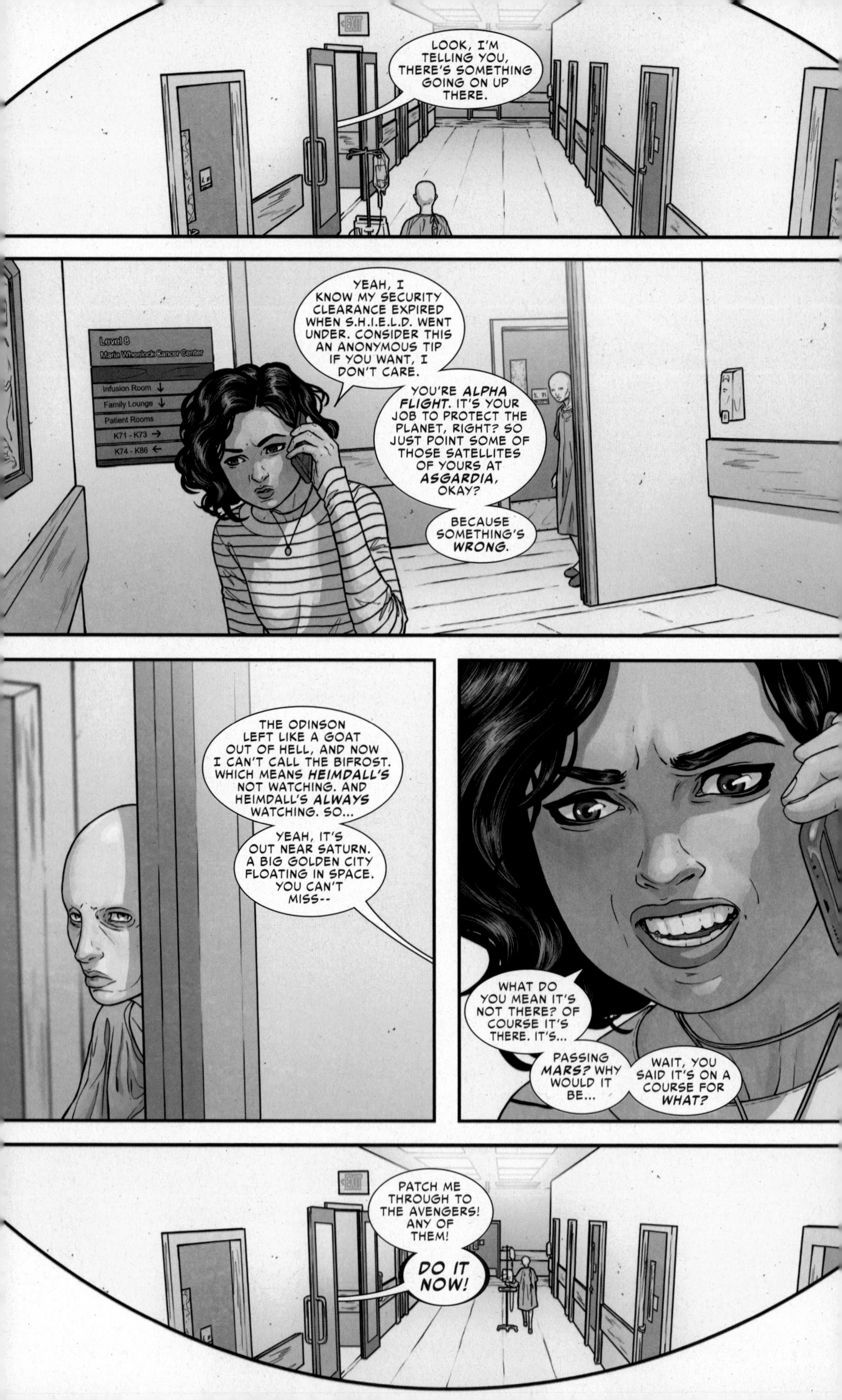

EXIT
LOOK, I'M TELLING YOU, THERE'S SOMETHING GOING ON UP THERE.
Level 8
Maria Wheelock Cancer Center
Infusion Room
Family Lounge
Patient Rooms
K71 - K73
K74 - K86
YEAH, I KNOW MY SECURITY CLEARANCE EXPIRED WHEN S.H.I.E.L.D. WENT UNDER. CONSIDER THIS AN ANONYMOUS TIP IF YOU WANT, I DON'T CARE.
YOU'RE ALPHA FLIGHT. IT'S YOUR JOB TO PROTECT THE PLANET, RIGHT? SO JUST POINT SOME OF THOSE SATELLITES OF YOURS AT ASGARDIA, OKAY?
BECAUSE SOMETHING'S WRONG.
THE ODINSON LEFT LIKE A GOAT OUT OF HELL, AND NOW I CAN'T CALL THE BIFROST. WHICH MEANS HEIMDALL'S NOT WATCHING. AND HEIMDALL'S ALWAYS WATCHING. SO...
YEAH, IT'S OUT NEAR SATURN. A BIG GOLDEN CITY FLOATING IN SPACE. YOU CAN'T MISS--
WHAT DO YOU MEAN IT'S NOT THERE? OF COURSE IT'S THERE. IT'S...
PASSING MARS? WHY WOULD IT BE...
WAIT, YOU SAID IT'S ON A COURSE FOR WHAT?
EXIT
PATCH ME THROUGH TO THE AVENGERS! ANY OF THEM!
DO IT NOW!

RAWF HAMMER!

RAWF RAWF MURDER!

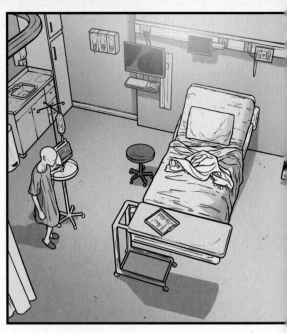

I WOULD'VE BEATEN YOU, YOU LITTLE CANCEROUS SONS OF BITCHES.

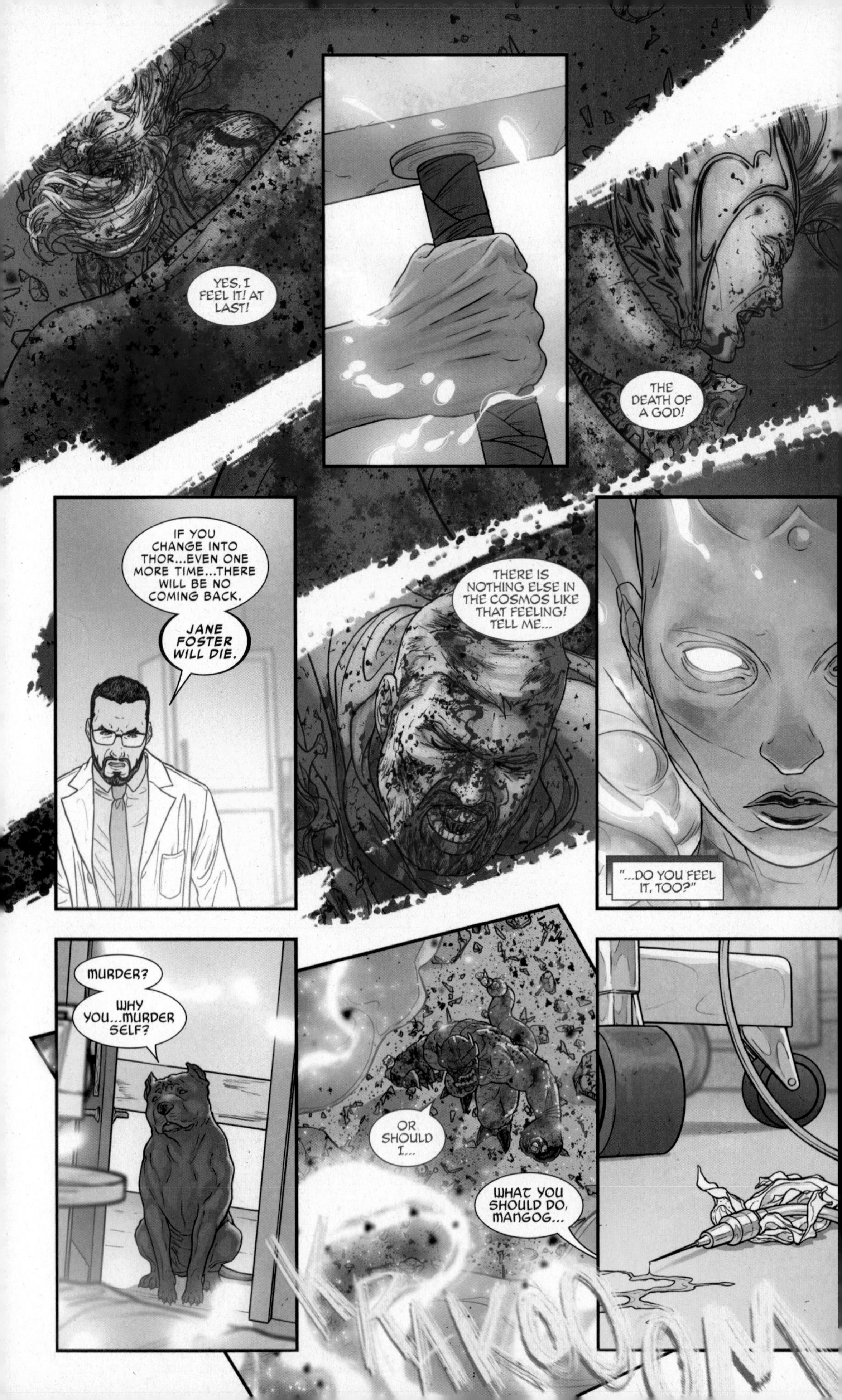
YES, I FEEL IT! AT LAST!
THE DEATH OF A GOD!
IF YOU CHANGE INTO THOR...EVEN ONE MORE TIME...THERE WILL BE NO COMING BACK.
JANE FOSTER WILL DIE.
THERE IS NOTHING ELSE IN THE COSMOS LIKE THAT FEELING! TELL ME...
"...DO YOU FEEL IT, TOO?"
MURDER?
WHY YOU...MURDER SELF?
OR SHOULD I...
WHAT YOU SHOULD DO, MANGOG...
KRAKOOOM

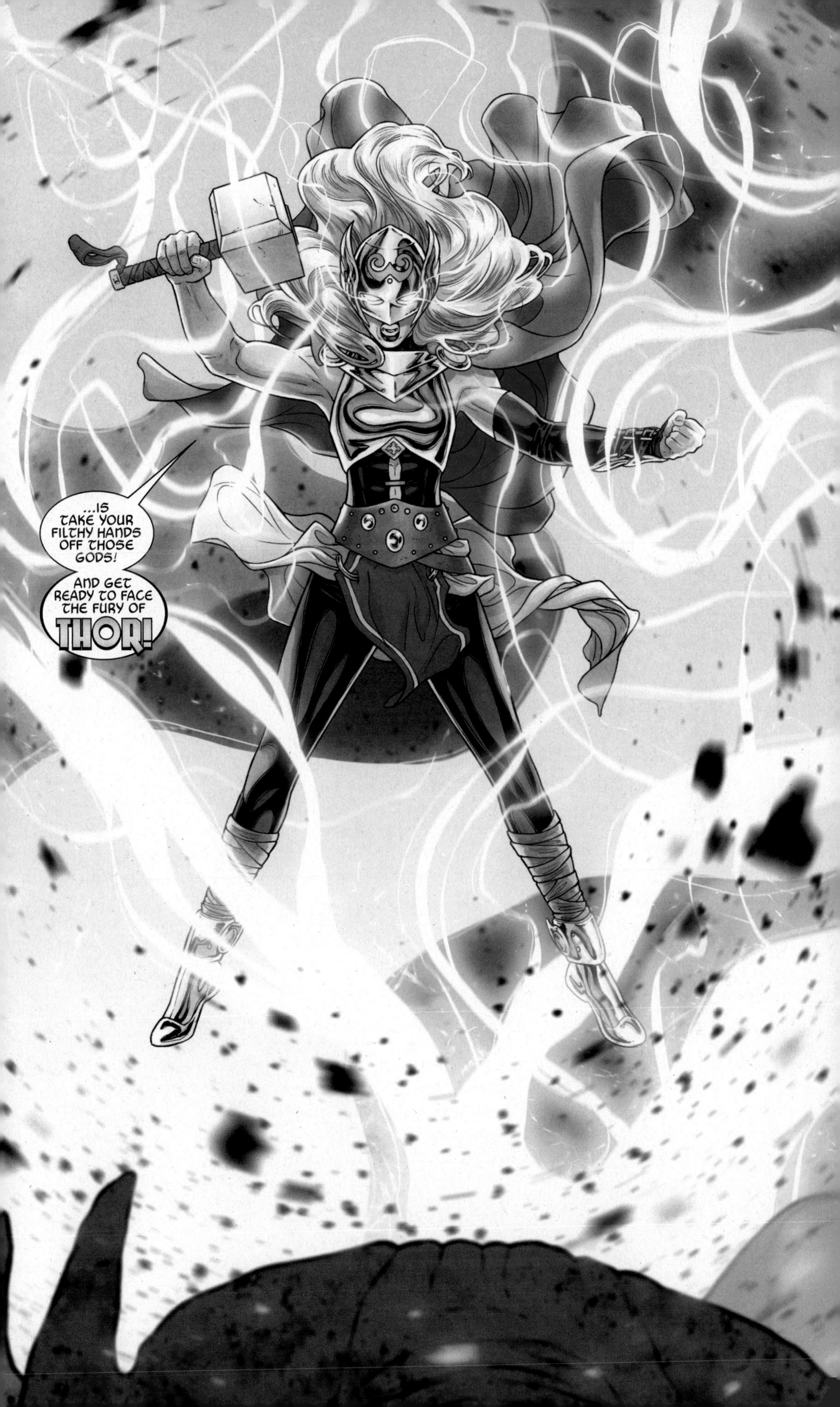
...IS TAKE YOUR FILTHY HANDS OFF THOSE GODS!
AND GET READY TO FACE THE FURY OF THOR!

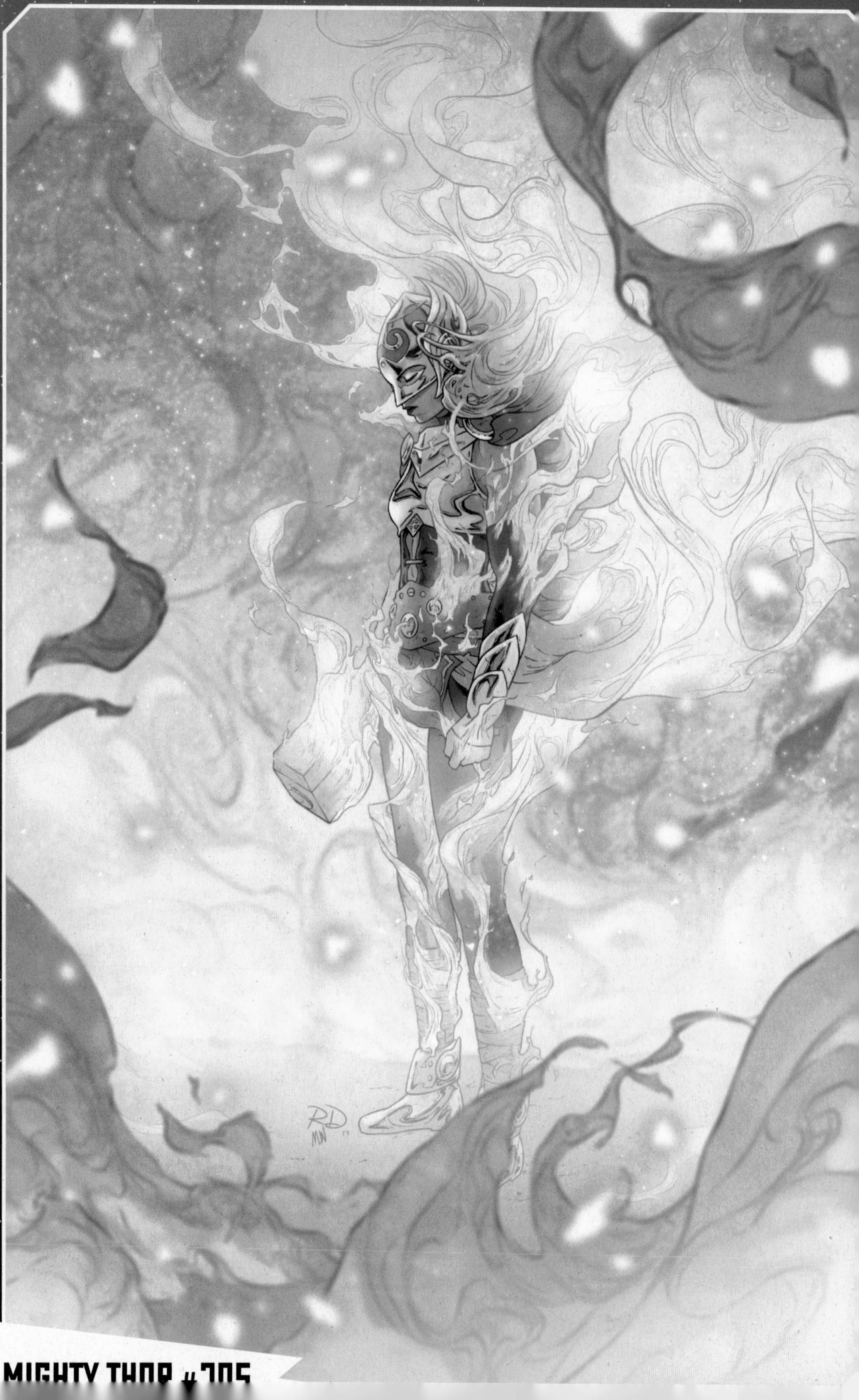
RD
MW '17

MIGHTY THOR #705

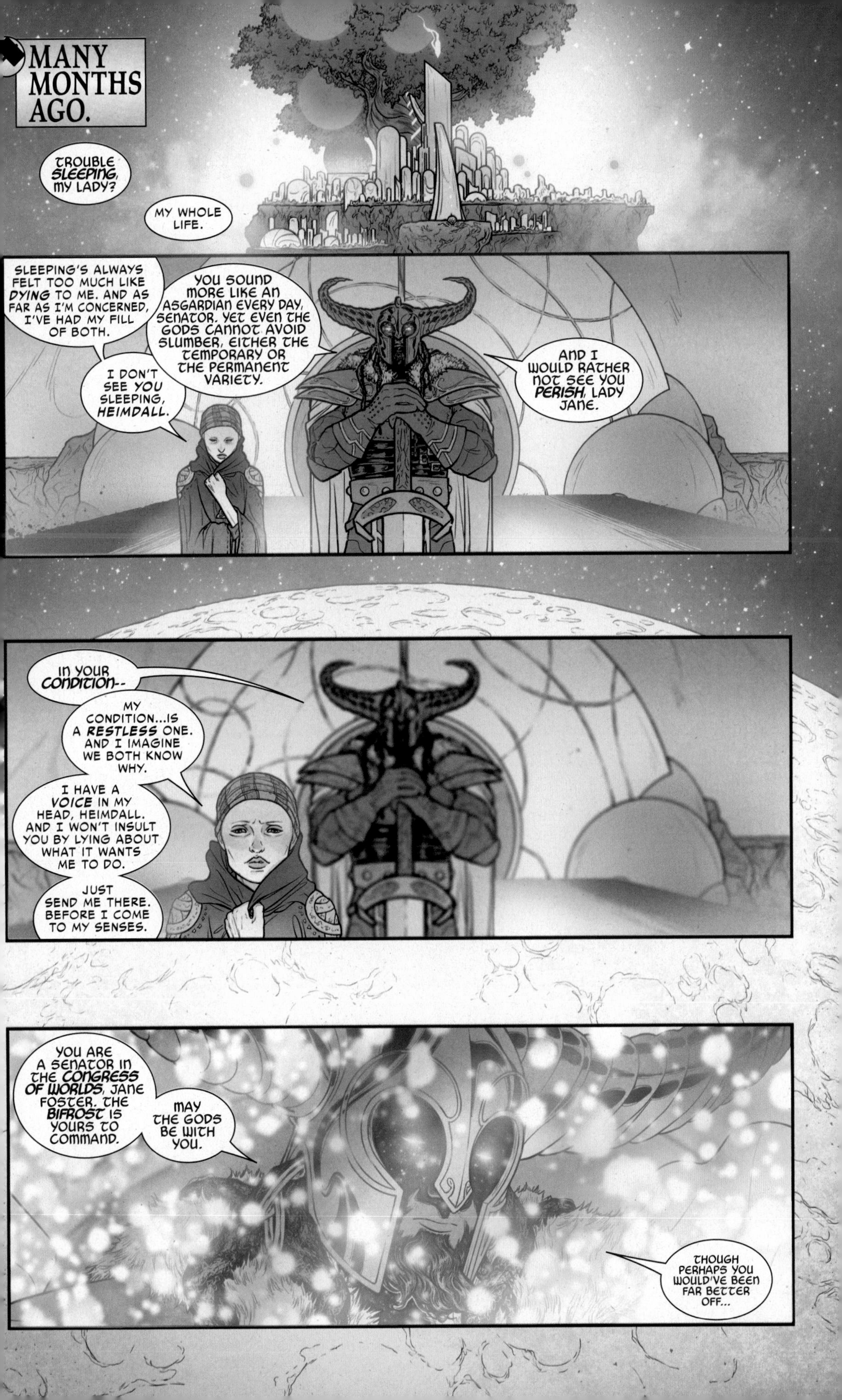
MANY MONTHS AGO.
TROUBLE SLEEPING, MY LADY?
MY WHOLE LIFE.
SLEEPING'S ALWAYS FELT TOO MUCH LIKE DYING TO ME. AND AS FAR AS I'M CONCERNED, I'VE HAD MY FILL OF BOTH.
I DON'T SEE YOU SLEEPING, HEIMDALL.
YOU SOUND MORE LIKE AN ASGARDIAN EVERY DAY, SENATOR. YET EVEN THE GODS CANNOT AVOID SLUMBER, EITHER THE TEMPORARY OR THE PERMANENT VARIETY.
AND I WOULD RATHER NOT SEE YOU PERISH, LADY JANE.
IN YOUR CONDITION--
MY CONDITION...IS A RESTLESS ONE. AND I IMAGINE WE BOTH KNOW WHY.
I HAVE A VOICE IN MY HEAD, HEIMDALL. AND I WON'T INSULT YOU BY LYING ABOUT WHAT IT WANTS ME TO DO.
JUST SEND ME THERE. BEFORE I COME TO MY SENSES.
YOU ARE A SENATOR IN THE CONGRESS OF WORLDS, JANE FOSTER. THE BIFROST IS YOURS TO COMMAND.
MAY THE GODS BE WITH YOU.
THOUGH PERHAPS YOU WOULD'VE BEEN FAR BETTER OFF...

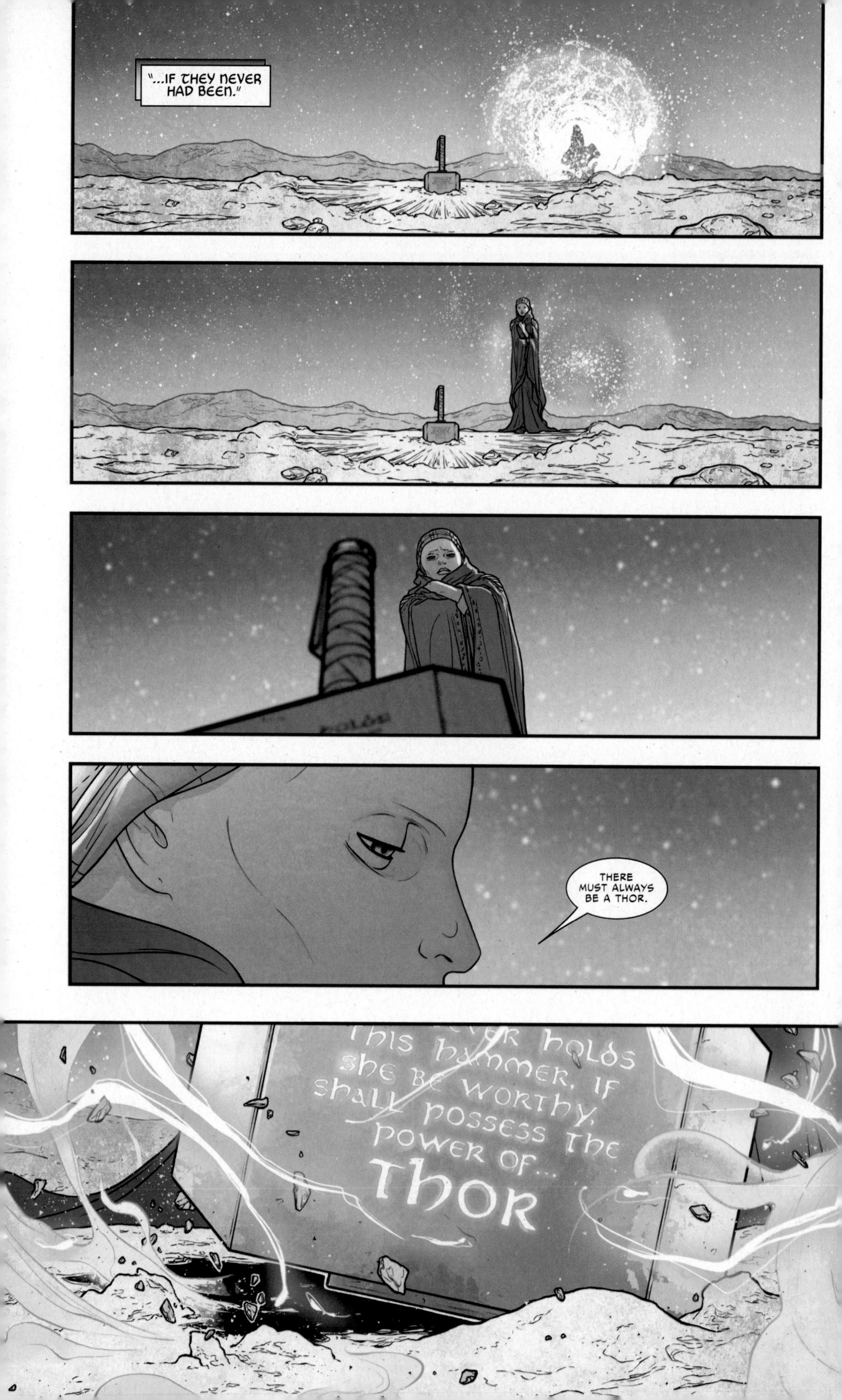
"...IF THEY NEVER HAD BEEN."
THERE MUST ALWAYS BE A THOR.
ever holds
this hammer, if
she be worthy,
shall possess the
power of...
THOR

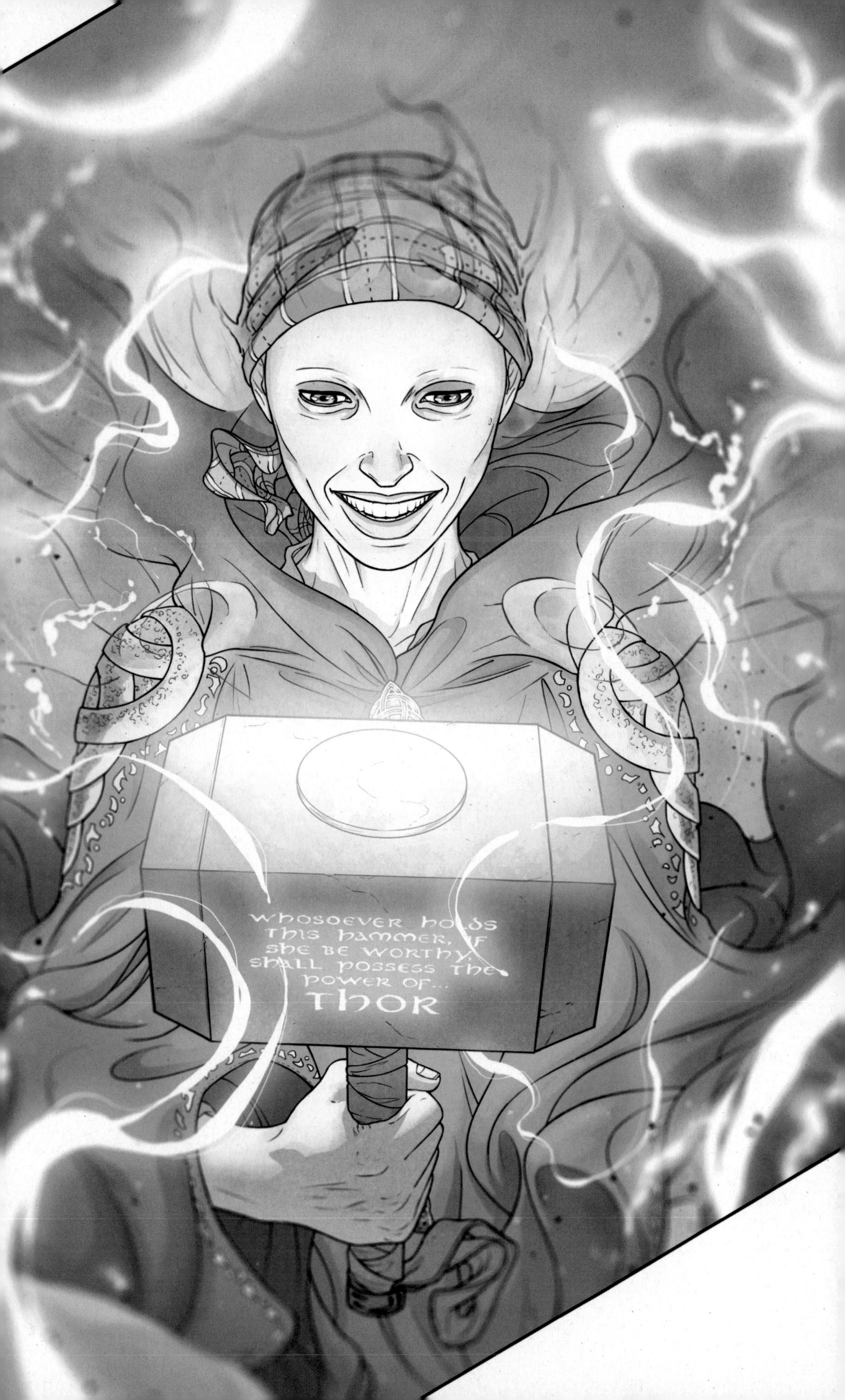
WHOSOEVER HOLDS
THIS HAMMER, IF
SHE BE WORTHY,
SHALL POSSESS THE
POWER OF...
THOR

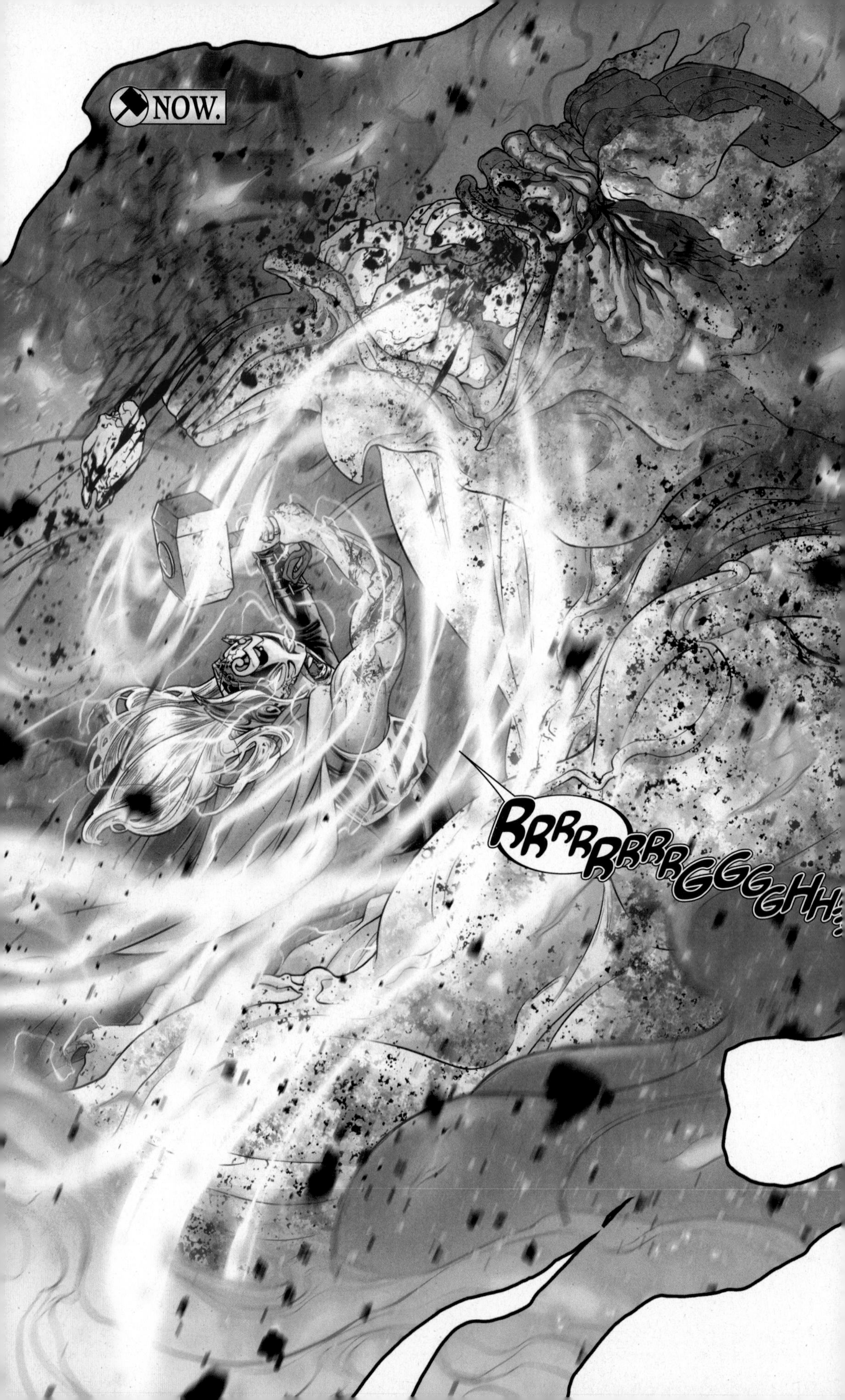
NOW.
RRRRRRRRGGGGHH!

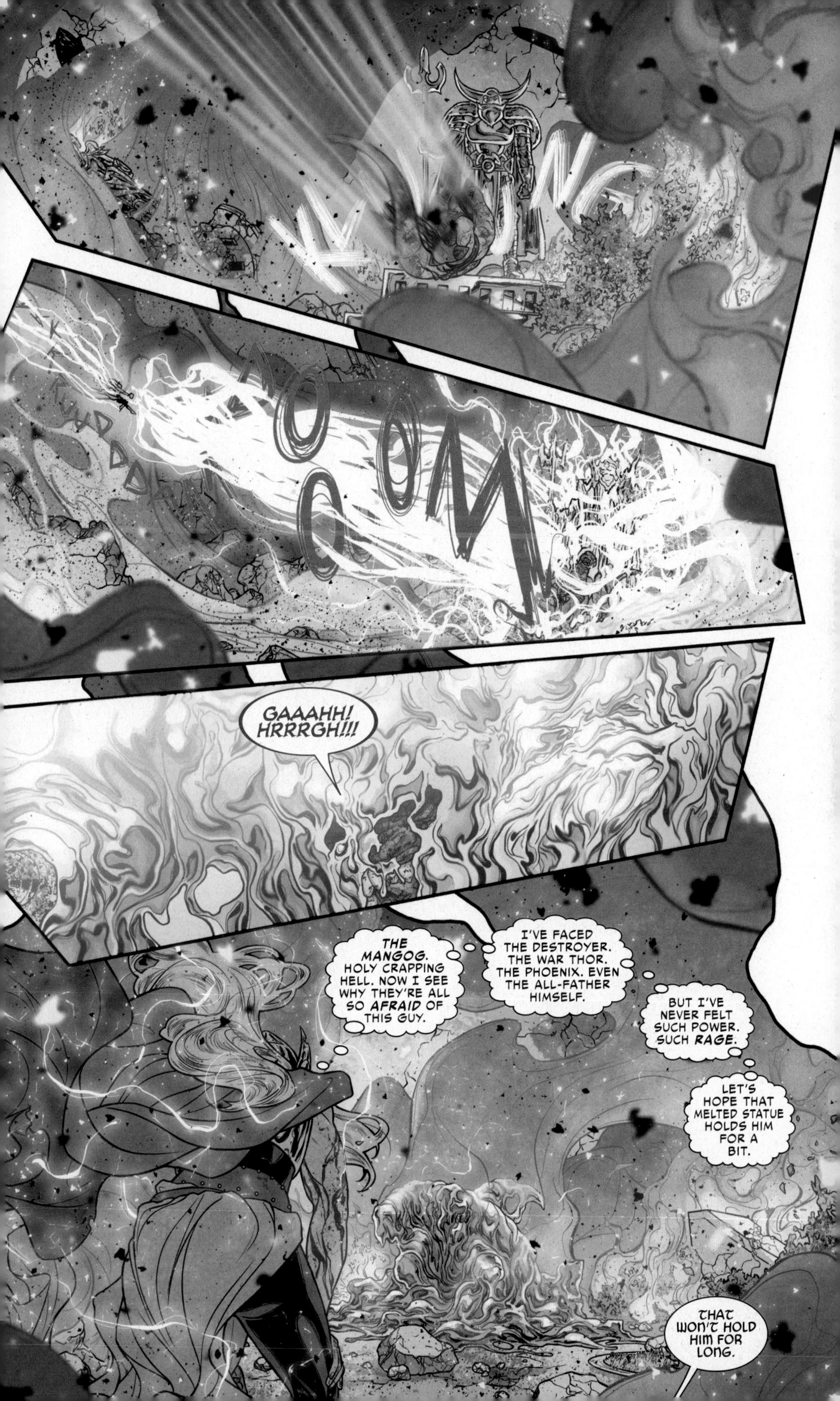
KVUNG
GAAAHH! HRRRGH!!!
THE MANGOG. HOLY CRAPPING HELL. NOW I SEE WHY THEY'RE ALL SO AFRAID OF THIS GUY.
I'VE FACED THE DESTROYER. THE WAR THOR. THE PHOENIX. EVEN THE ALL-FATHER HIMSELF.
BUT I'VE NEVER FELT SUCH POWER. SUCH RAGE.
LET'S HOPE THAT MELTED STATUE HOLDS HIM FOR A BIT.
THAT WON'T HOLD HIM FOR LONG.

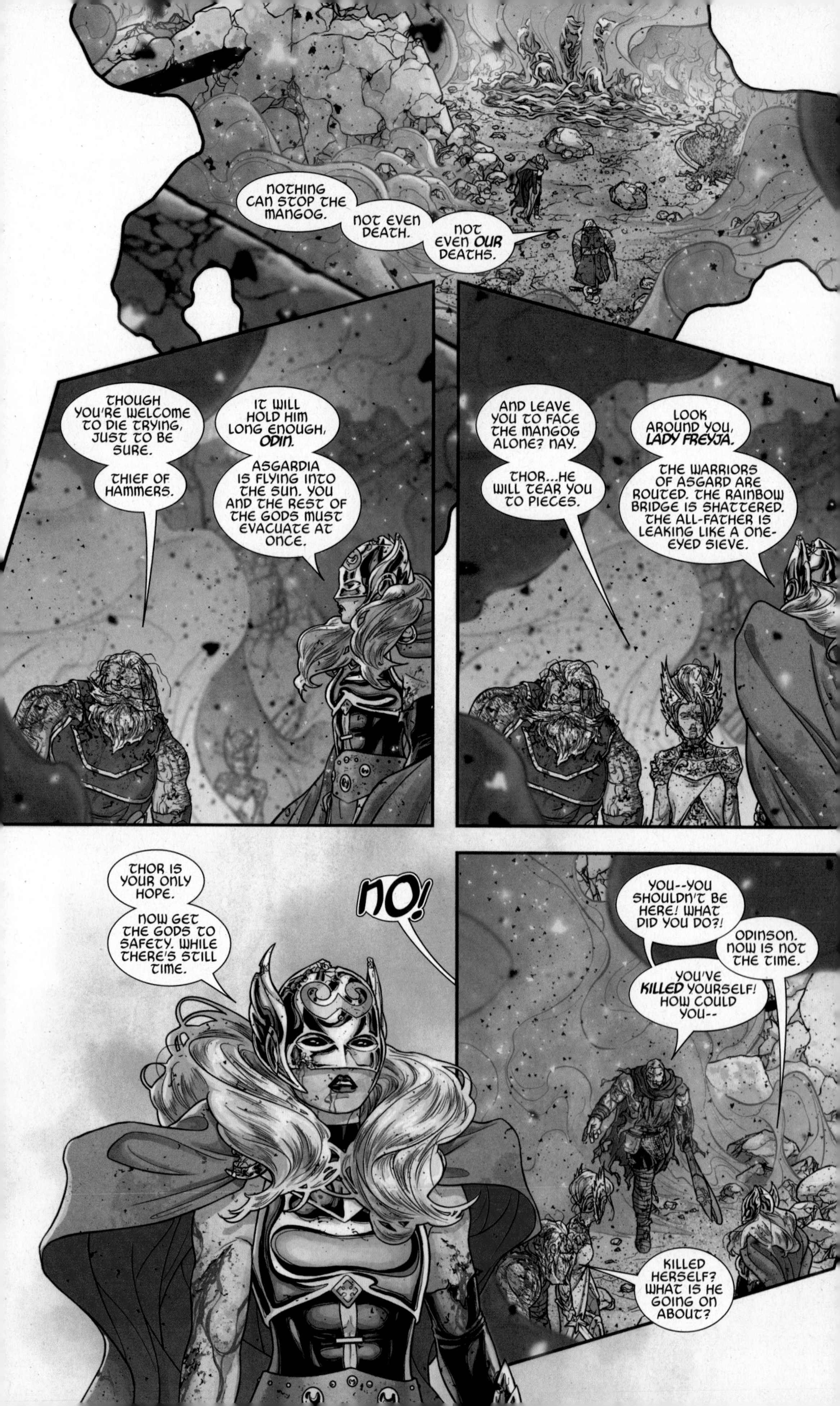
NOTHING CAN STOP THE MANGOG.
NOT EVEN DEATH.
NOT EVEN OUR DEATHS.
THOUGH YOU'RE WELCOME TO DIE TRYING, JUST TO BE SURE.
THIEF OF HAMMERS.
IT WILL HOLD HIM LONG ENOUGH, ODIN.
ASGARDIA IS FLYING INTO THE SUN. YOU AND THE REST OF THE GODS MUST EVACUATE AT ONCE.
AND LEAVE YOU TO FACE THE MANGOG ALONE? NAY.
THOR...HE WILL TEAR YOU TO PIECES.
LOOK AROUND YOU, LADY FREYJA.
THE WARRIORS OF ASGARD ARE ROUTED. THE RAINBOW BRIDGE IS SHATTERED. THE ALL-FATHER IS LEAKING LIKE A ONE-EYED SIEVE.
THOR IS YOUR ONLY HOPE.
NOW GET THE GODS TO SAFETY. WHILE THERE'S STILL TIME.
NO!
YOU--YOU SHOULDN'T BE HERE! WHAT DID YOU DO?!
ODINSON. NOW IS NOT THE TIME.
YOU'VE KILLED YOURSELF! HOW COULD YOU--
KILLED HERSELF? WHAT IS HE GOING ON ABOUT?

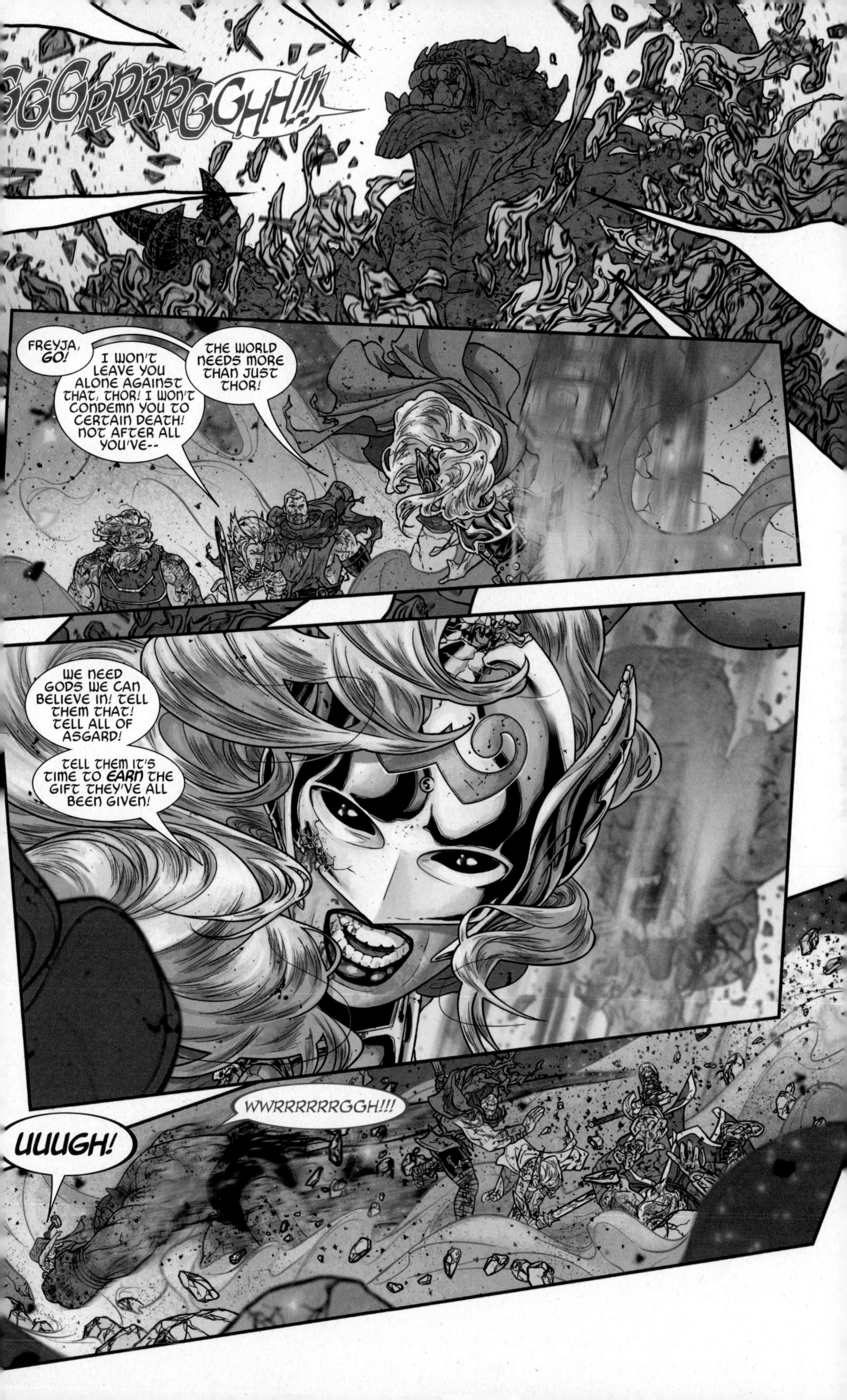
GGGRRRRRGGHH!!!
FREYJA, GO!
I WON'T LEAVE YOU ALONE AGAINST THAT, THOR! I WON'T CONDEMN YOU TO CERTAIN DEATH! NOT AFTER ALL YOU'VE--
THE WORLD NEEDS MORE THAN JUST THOR!
WE NEED GODS WE CAN BELIEVE IN! TELL THEM THAT! TELL ALL OF ASGARD!
TELL THEM IT'S TIME TO EARN THE GIFT THEY'VE ALL BEEN GIVEN!
WWRRRRRRGGH!!!
UUUGH!

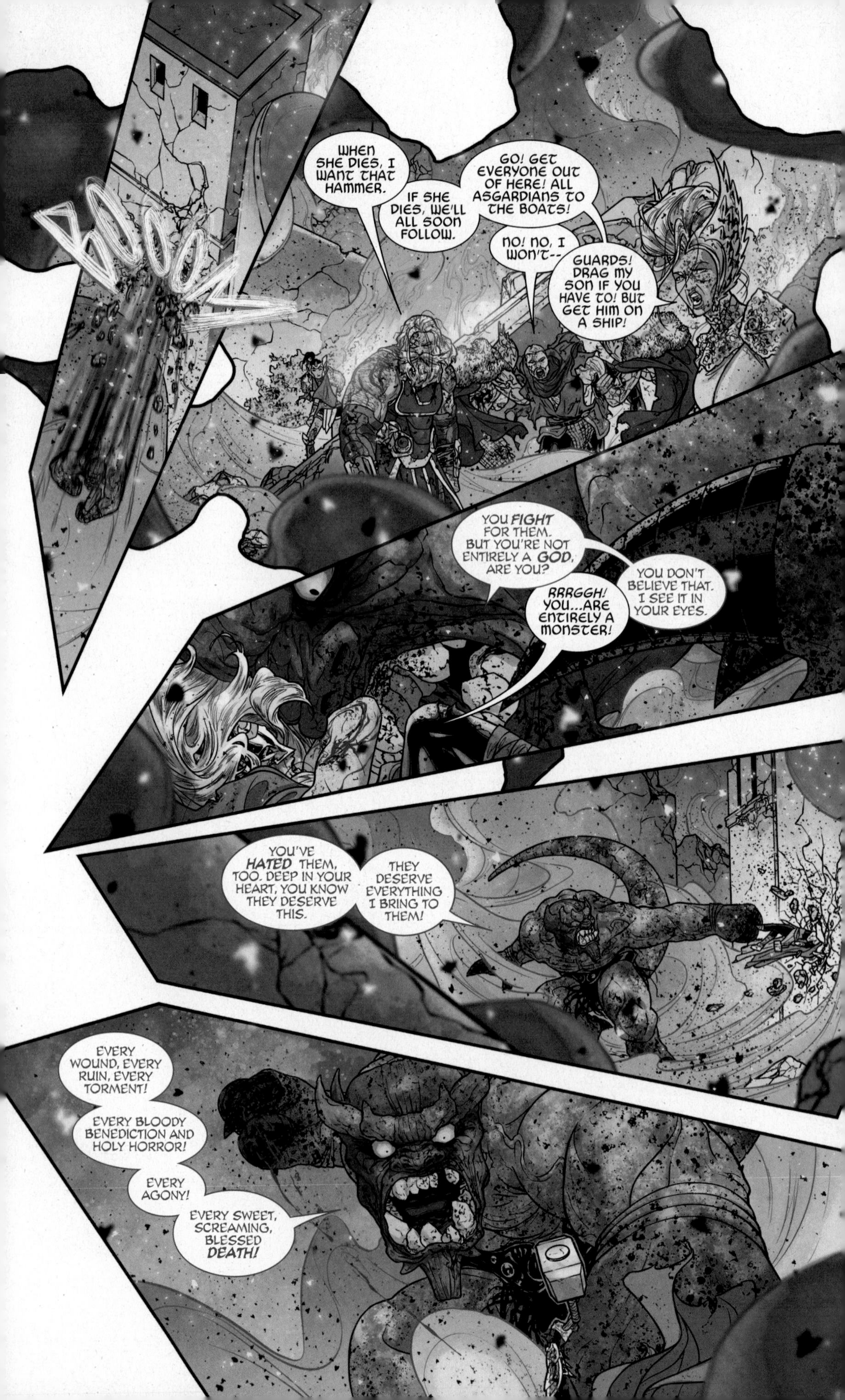
BOOOM
WHEN SHE DIES, I WANT THAT HAMMER.
IF SHE DIES, WE'LL ALL SOON FOLLOW.
GO! GET EVERYONE OUT OF HERE! ALL ASGARDIANS TO THE BOATS!
NO! NO, I WON'T--
GUARDS! DRAG MY SON IF YOU HAVE TO! BUT GET HIM ON A SHIP!
YOU FIGHT FOR THEM. BUT YOU'RE NOT ENTIRELY A GOD, ARE YOU?
RRRGGH! YOU...ARE ENTIRELY A MONSTER!
YOU DON'T BELIEVE THAT. I SEE IT IN YOUR EYES.
YOU'VE HATED THEM, TOO. DEEP IN YOUR HEART, YOU KNOW THEY DESERVE THIS.
THEY DESERVE EVERYTHING I BRING TO THEM!
EVERY WOUND, EVERY RUIN, EVERY TORMENT!
EVERY BLOODY BENEDICTION AND HOLY HORROR!
EVERY AGONY!
EVERY SWEET, SCREAMING, BLESSED DEATH!

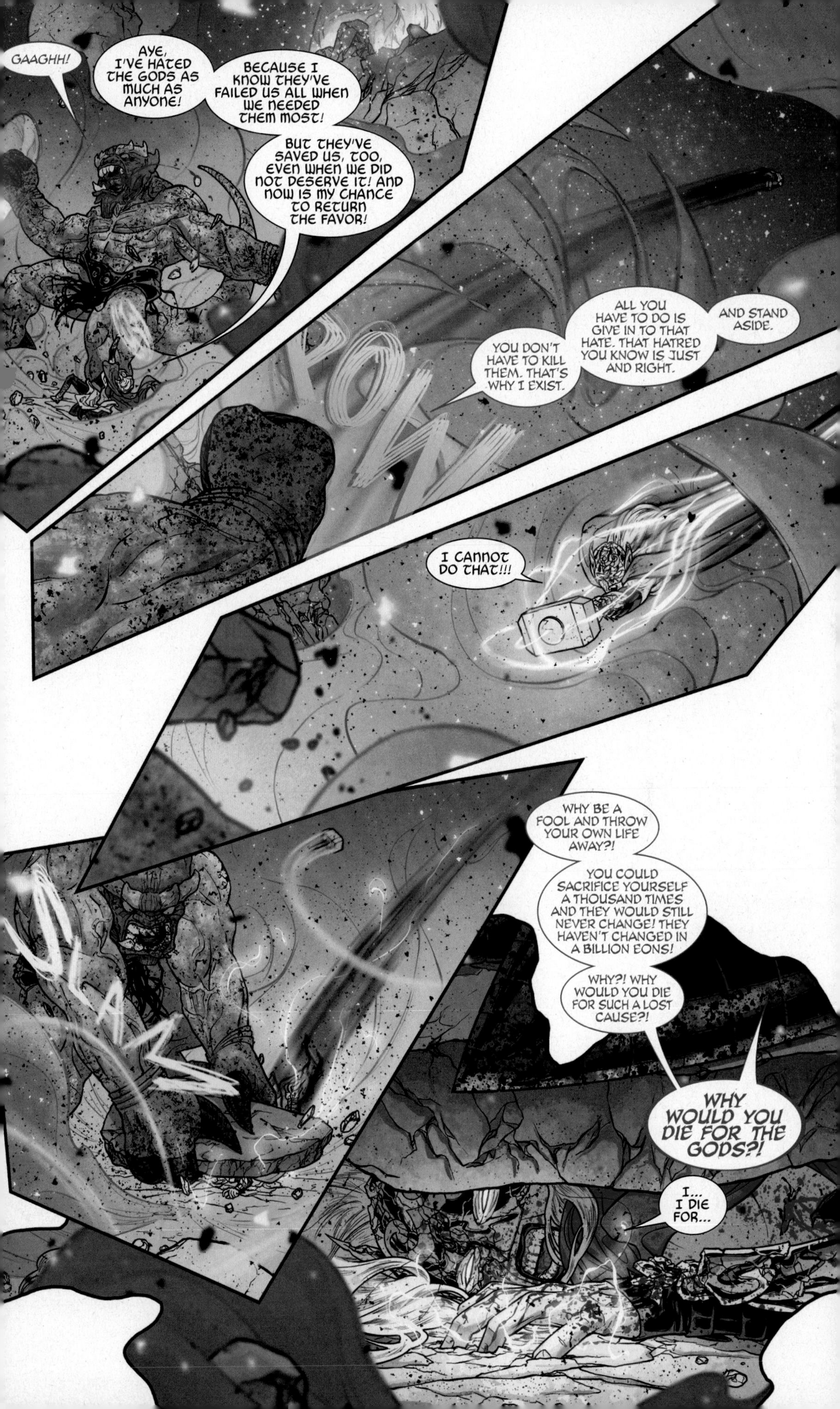
GAAGHH!
AYE, I'VE HATED THE GODS AS MUCH AS ANYONE!
BECAUSE I KNOW THEY'VE FAILED US ALL WHEN WE NEEDED THEM MOST!
BUT THEY'VE SAVED US, TOO, EVEN WHEN WE DID NOT DESERVE IT! AND NOW IS MY CHANCE TO RETURN THE FAVOR!
POW
YOU DON'T HAVE TO KILL THEM. THAT'S WHY I EXIST.
ALL YOU HAVE TO DO IS GIVE IN TO THAT HATE. THAT HATRED YOU KNOW IS JUST AND RIGHT.
AND STAND ASIDE.
I CANNOT DO THAT!!!
SLAM
WHY BE A FOOL AND THROW YOUR OWN LIFE AWAY?!
YOU COULD SACRIFICE YOURSELF A THOUSAND TIMES AND THEY WOULD STILL NEVER CHANGE! THEY HAVEN'T CHANGED IN A BILLION EONS!
WHY?! WHY WOULD YOU DIE FOR SUCH A LOST CAUSE?!
WHY WOULD YOU DIE FOR THE GODS?!
I... I DIE FOR...

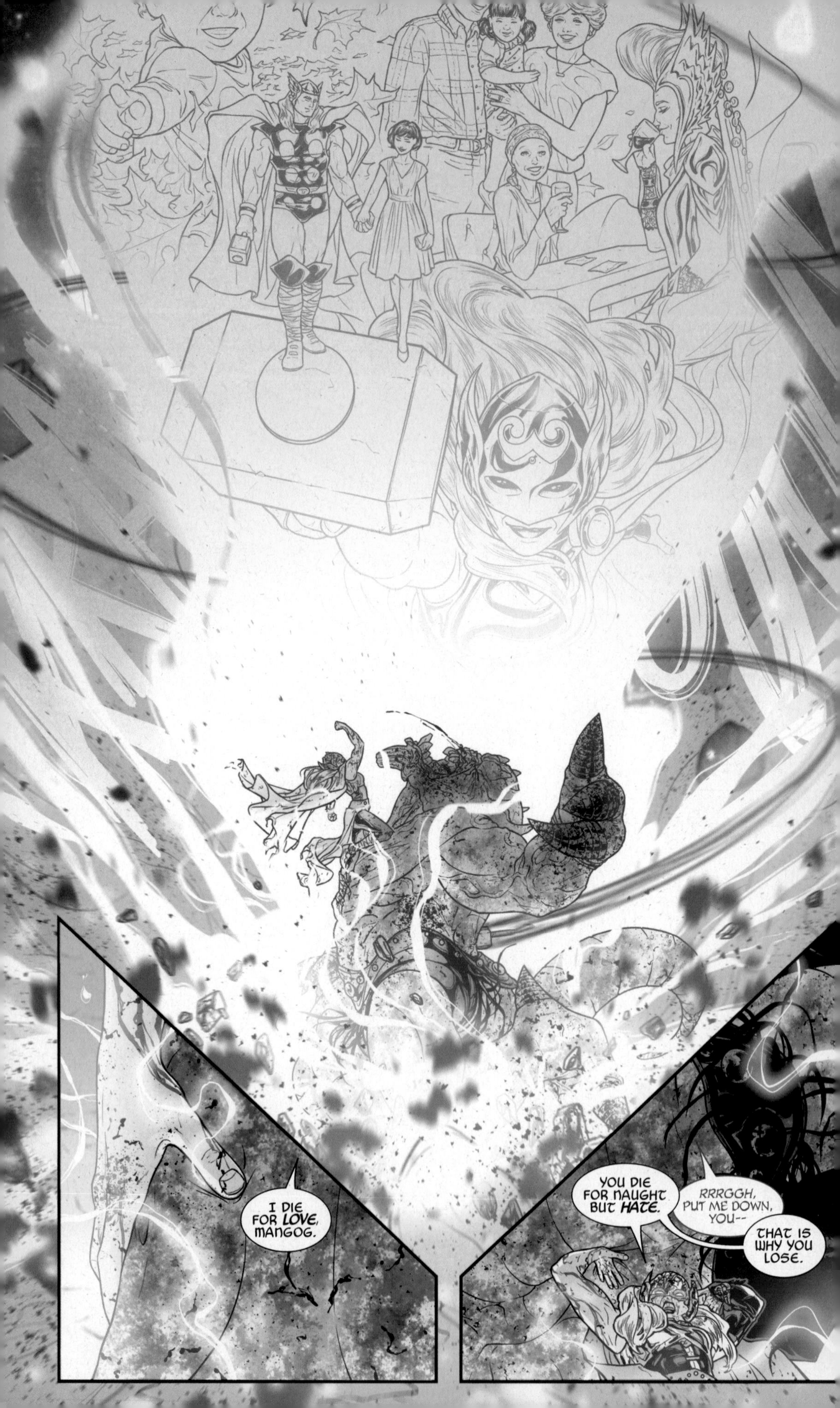
I DIE FOR LOVE, MANGOG.
YOU DIE FOR NAUGHT BUT HATE.
RRRGGH, PUT ME DOWN, YOU--
THAT IS WHY YOU LOSE.

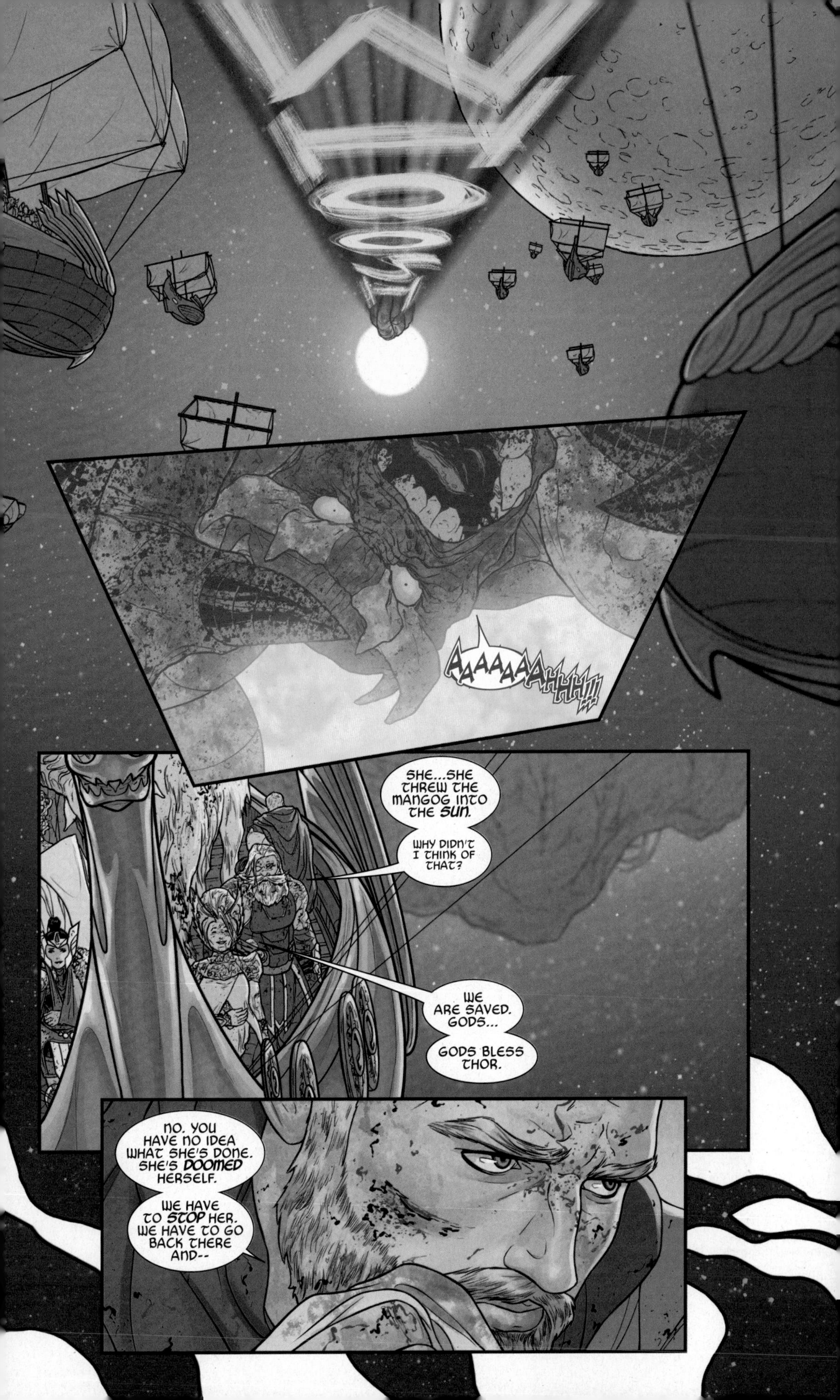
AAAAAAAHHH!!!
SHE...SHE THREW THE MANGOG INTO THE SUN.
WHY DIDN'T I THINK OF THAT?
WE ARE SAVED. GODS...
GODS BLESS THOR.
NO. YOU HAVE NO IDEA WHAT SHE'S DONE. SHE'S DOOMED HERSELF.
WE HAVE TO STOP HER. WE HAVE TO GO BACK THERE AND--

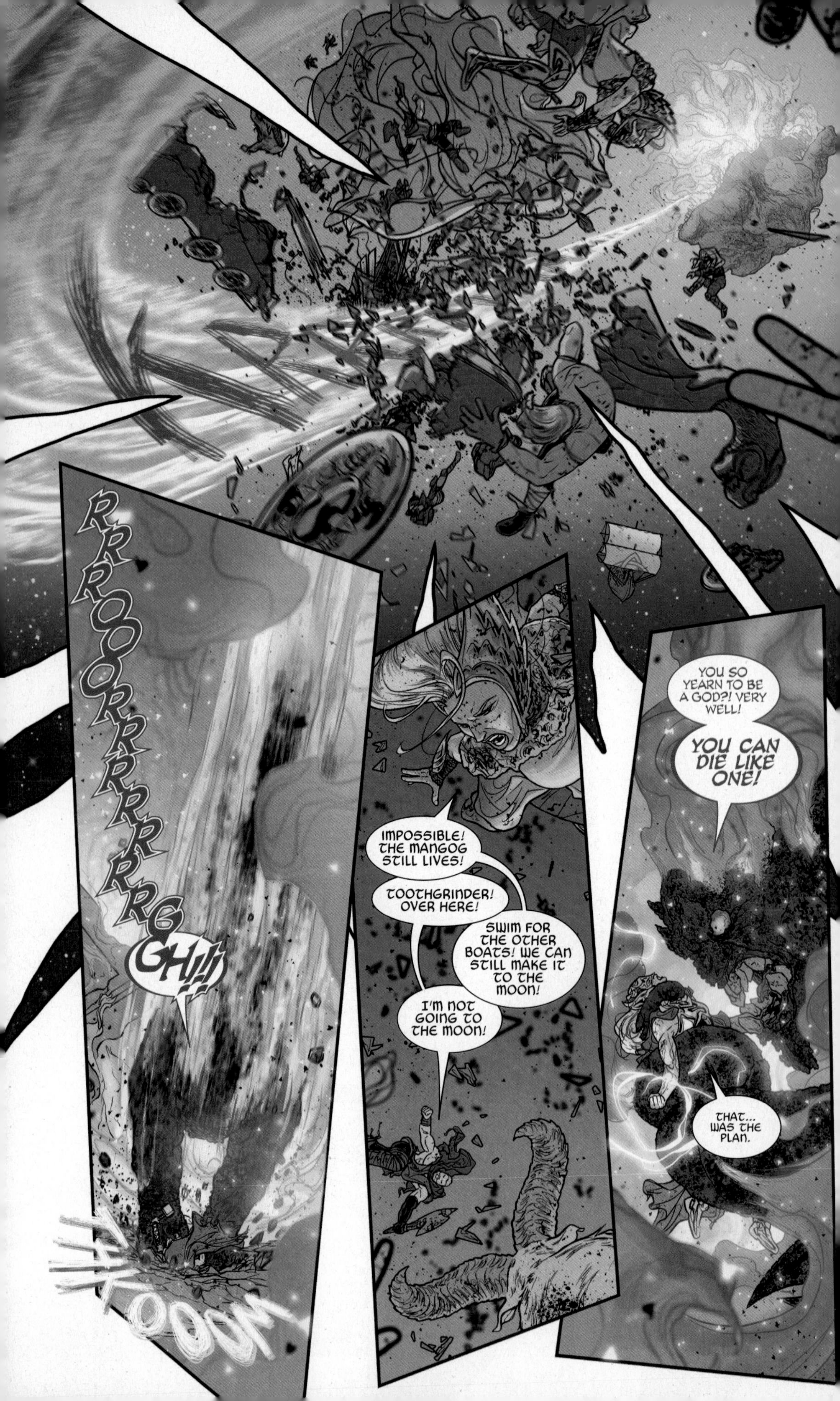
RRRROOOORRRRRRRRRGGH!!!
THOOOM
IMPOSSIBLE! THE MANGOG STILL LIVES!
TOOTHGRINDER! OVER HERE!
SWIM FOR THE OTHER BOATS! WE CAN STILL MAKE IT TO THE MOON!
I'M NOT GOING TO THE MOON!
YOU SO YEARN TO BE A GOD?! VERY WELL!
YOU CAN DIE LIKE ONE!
THAT... WAS THE PLAN.

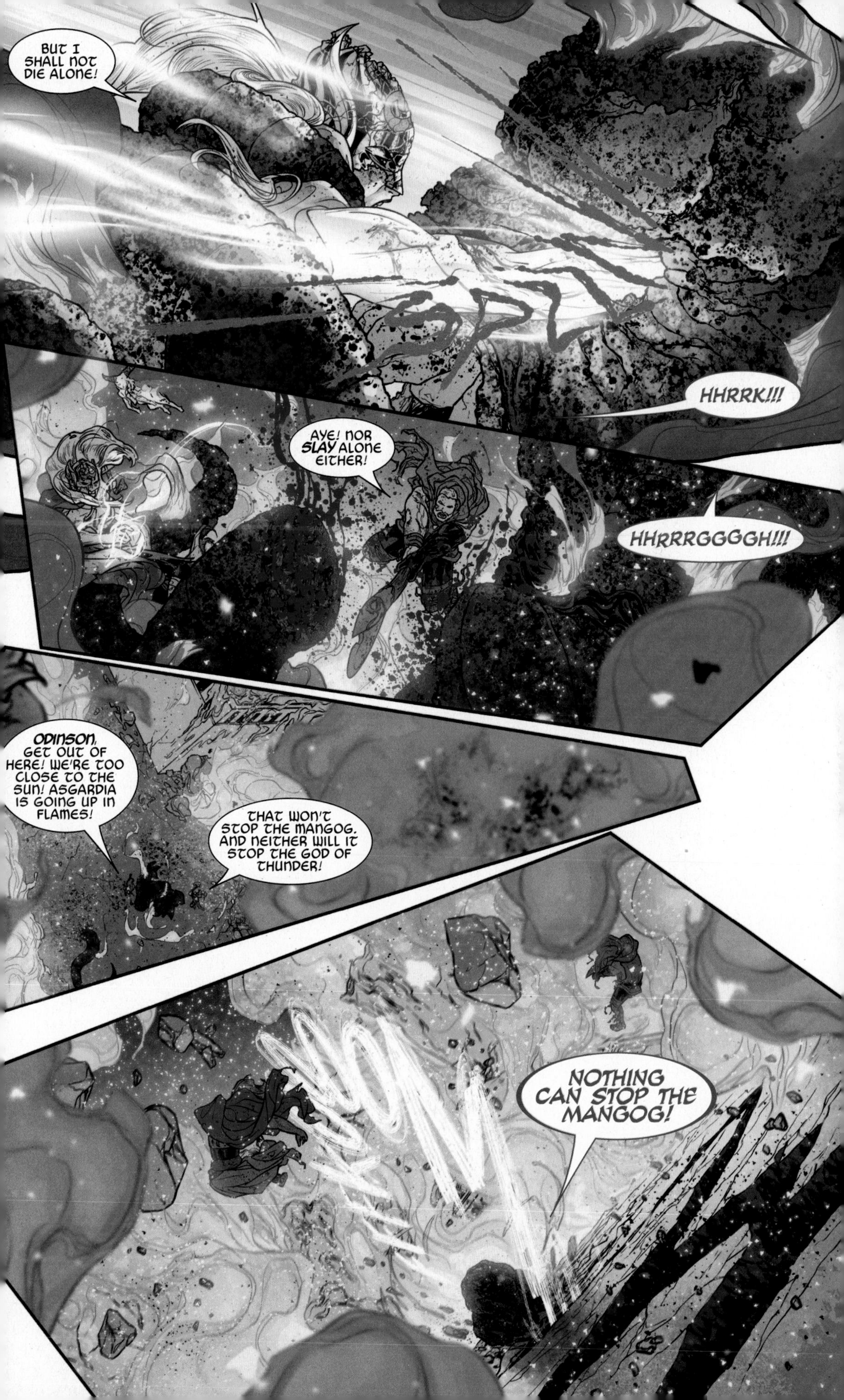
BUT I SHALL NOT DIE ALONE!
HHRRK!!!
AYE! NOR SLAY ALONE EITHER!
HHRRRGGGGH!!!
ODINSON, GET OUT OF HERE! WE'RE TOO CLOSE TO THE SUN! ASGARDIA IS GOING UP IN FLAMES!
THAT WON'T STOP THE MANGOG. AND NEITHER WILL IT STOP THE GOD OF THUNDER!
NOTHING CAN STOP THE MANGOG!

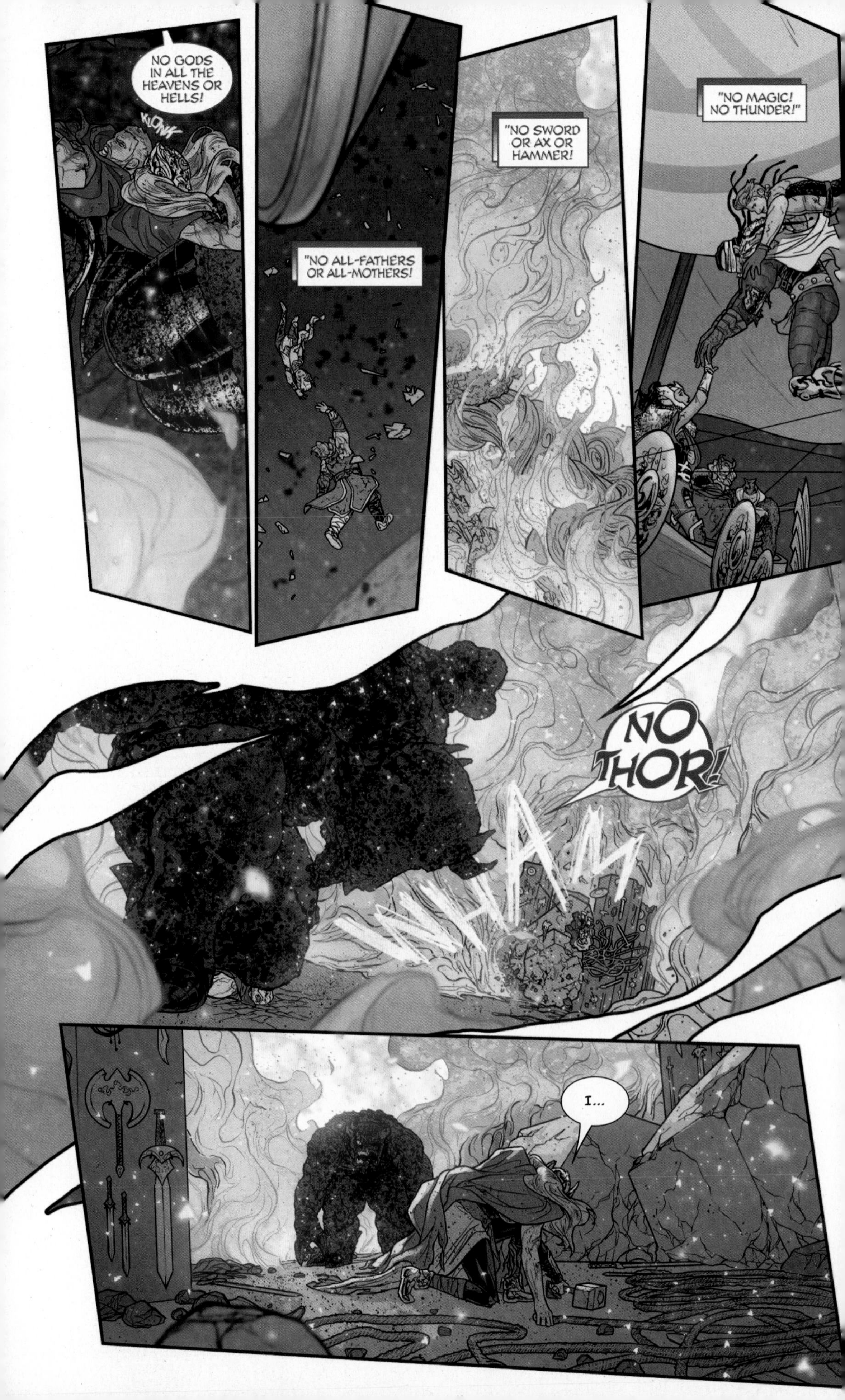
NO GODS IN ALL THE HEAVENS OR HELLS!
KLONK
"NO ALL-FATHERS OR ALL-MOTHERS!
"NO SWORD OR AX OR HAMMER!
"NO MAGIC! NO THUNDER!"
NO THOR!
WHAM
I...

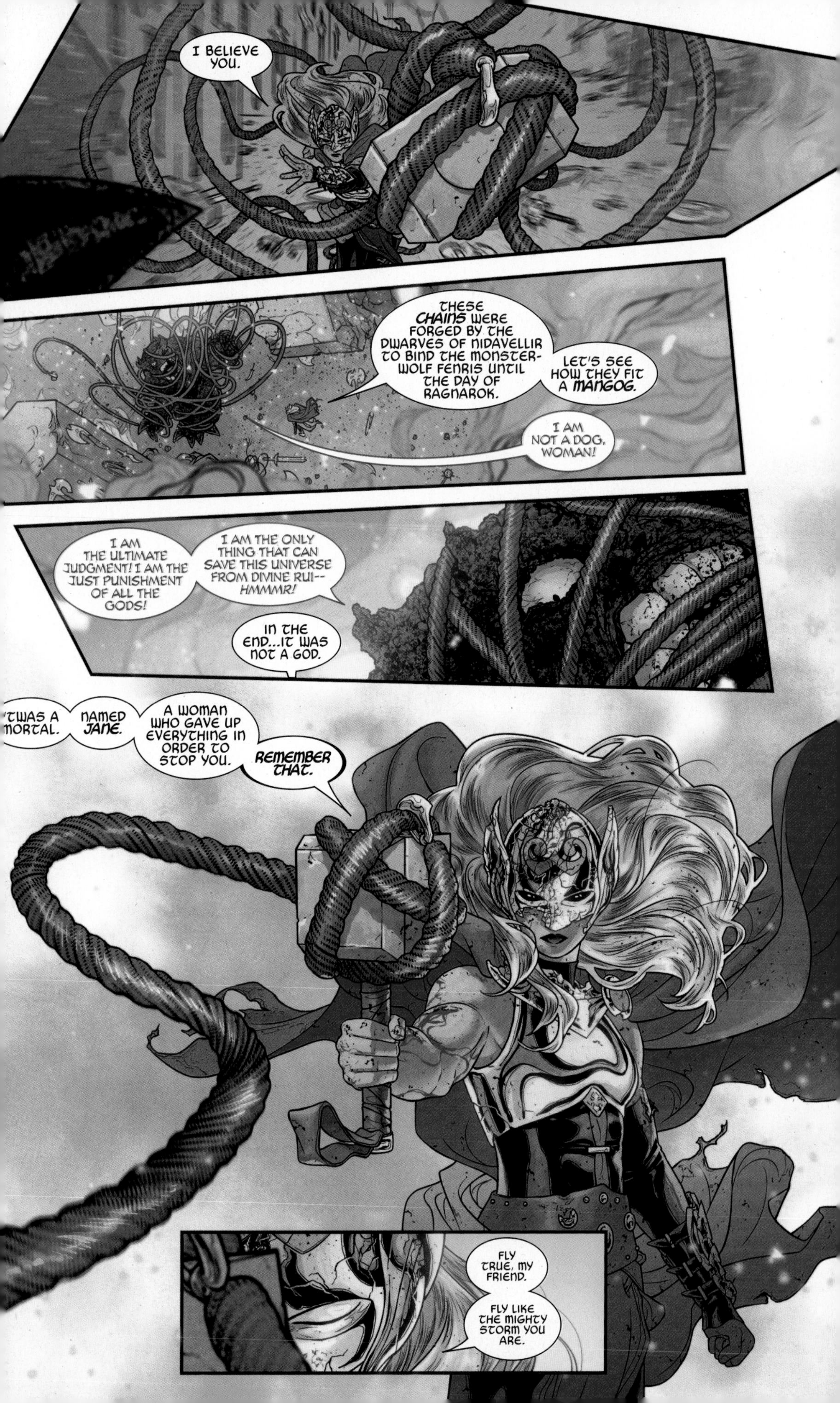

I BELIEVE YOU.
THESE CHAINS WERE FORGED BY THE DWARVES OF NIDAVELLIR TO BIND THE MONSTER-WOLF FENRIS UNTIL THE DAY OF RAGNAROK.
LET'S SEE HOW THEY FIT A MANGOG.
I AM NOT A DOG, WOMAN!
I AM THE ULTIMATE JUDGMENT! I AM THE JUST PUNISHMENT OF ALL THE GODS!
I AM THE ONLY THING THAT CAN SAVE THIS UNIVERSE FROM DIVINE RUI-- HMMMR!
IN THE END...IT WAS NOT A GOD.
'TWAS A MORTAL.
NAMED JANE.
A WOMAN WHO GAVE UP EVERYTHING IN ORDER TO STOP YOU.
REMEMBER THAT.
FLY TRUE, MY FRIEND.
FLY LIKE THE MIGHTY STORM YOU ARE.

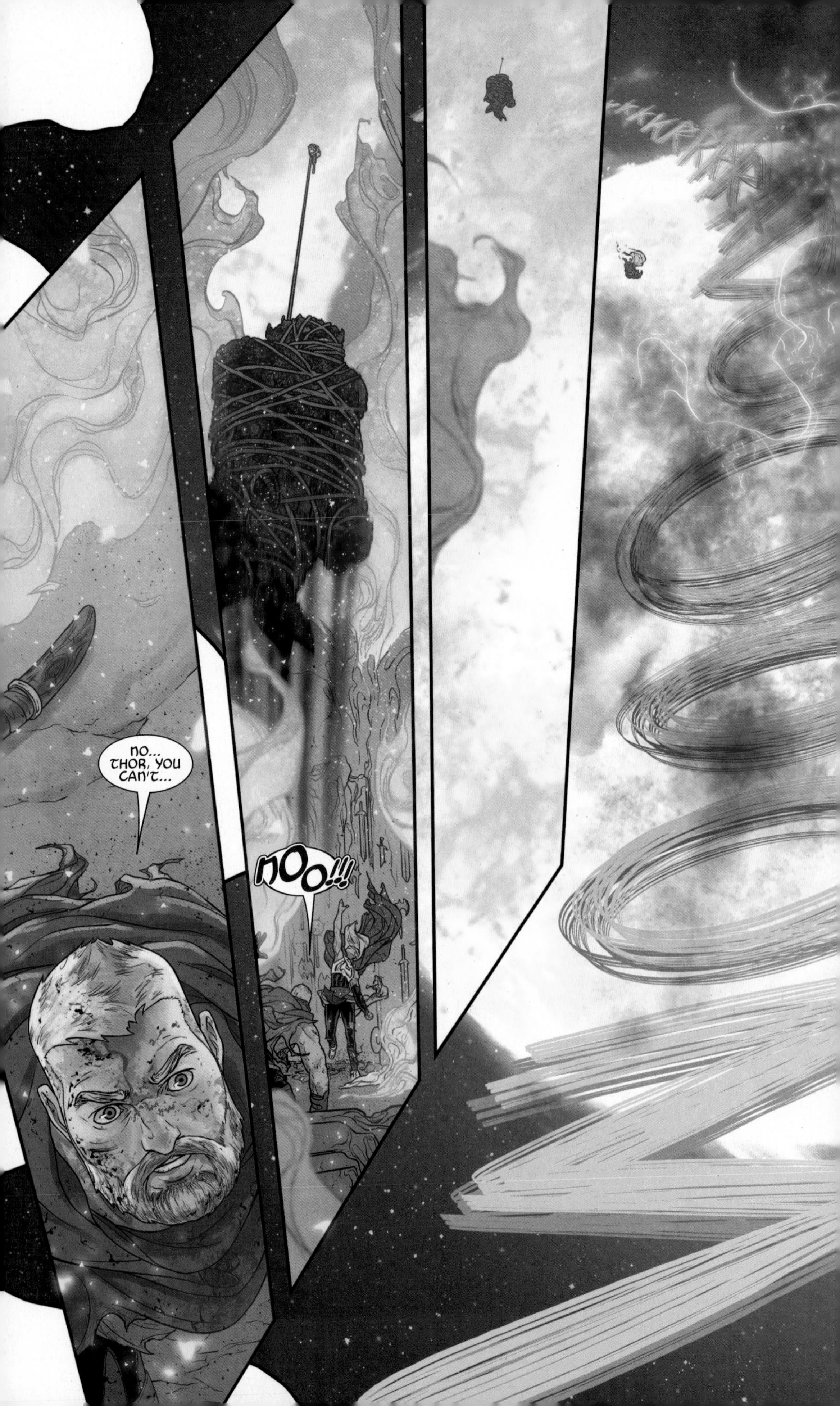
NO... THOR, YOU CAN'T...
NOO!!!

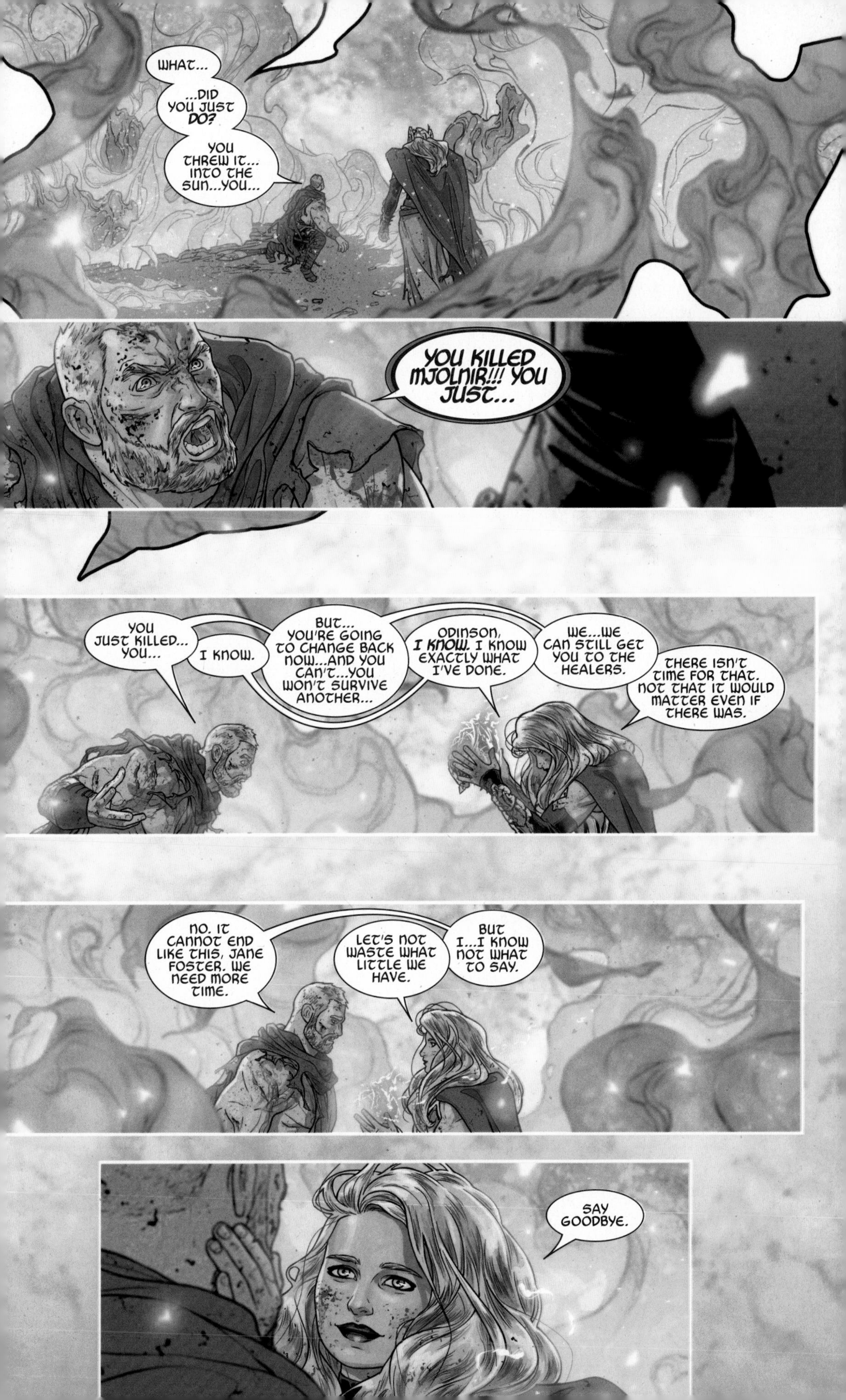

WHAT...
...DID YOU JUST DO?
YOU THREW IT... INTO THE SUN...YOU...
YOU KILLED MJOLNIR!!! YOU JUST...
YOU JUST KILLED... YOU...
I KNOW.
BUT... YOU'RE GOING TO CHANGE BACK NOW...AND YOU CAN'T...YOU WON'T SURVIVE ANOTHER...
ODINSON, I KNOW. I KNOW EXACTLY WHAT I'VE DONE.
WE...WE CAN STILL GET YOU TO THE HEALERS.
THERE ISN'T TIME FOR THAT. NOT THAT IT WOULD MATTER EVEN IF THERE WAS.
NO. IT CANNOT END LIKE THIS, JANE FOSTER. WE NEED MORE TIME.
LET'S NOT WASTE WHAT LITTLE WE HAVE.
BUT I...I KNOW NOT WHAT TO SAY.
SAY GOODBYE.

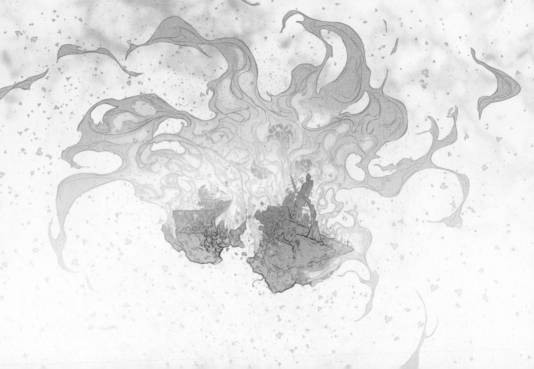

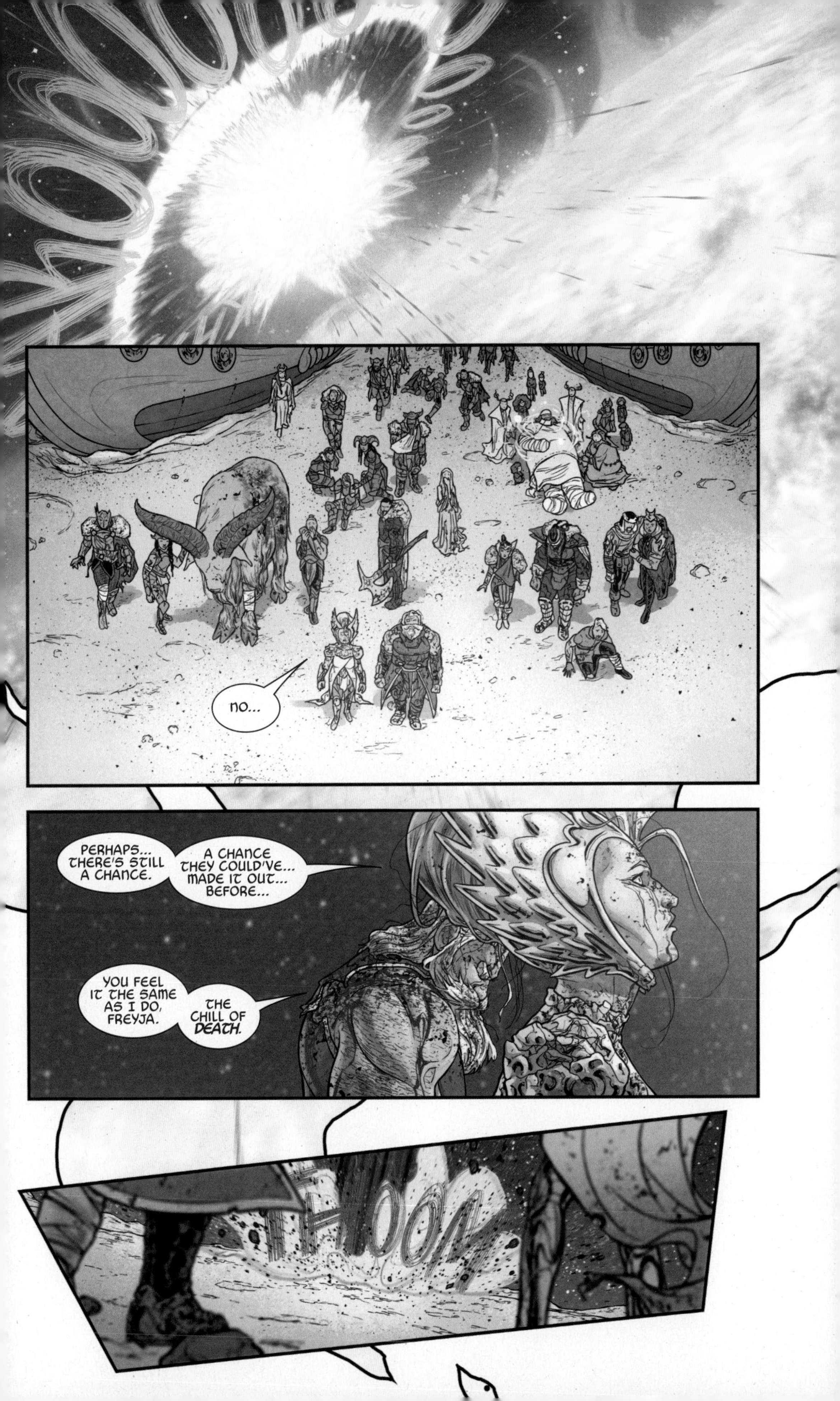
no...
PERHAPS... THERE'S STILL A CHANCE.
A CHANCE THEY COULD'VE... MADE IT OUT... BEFORE...
YOU FEEL IT THE SAME AS I DO, FREYJA.
THE CHILL OF DEATH.
THOOM

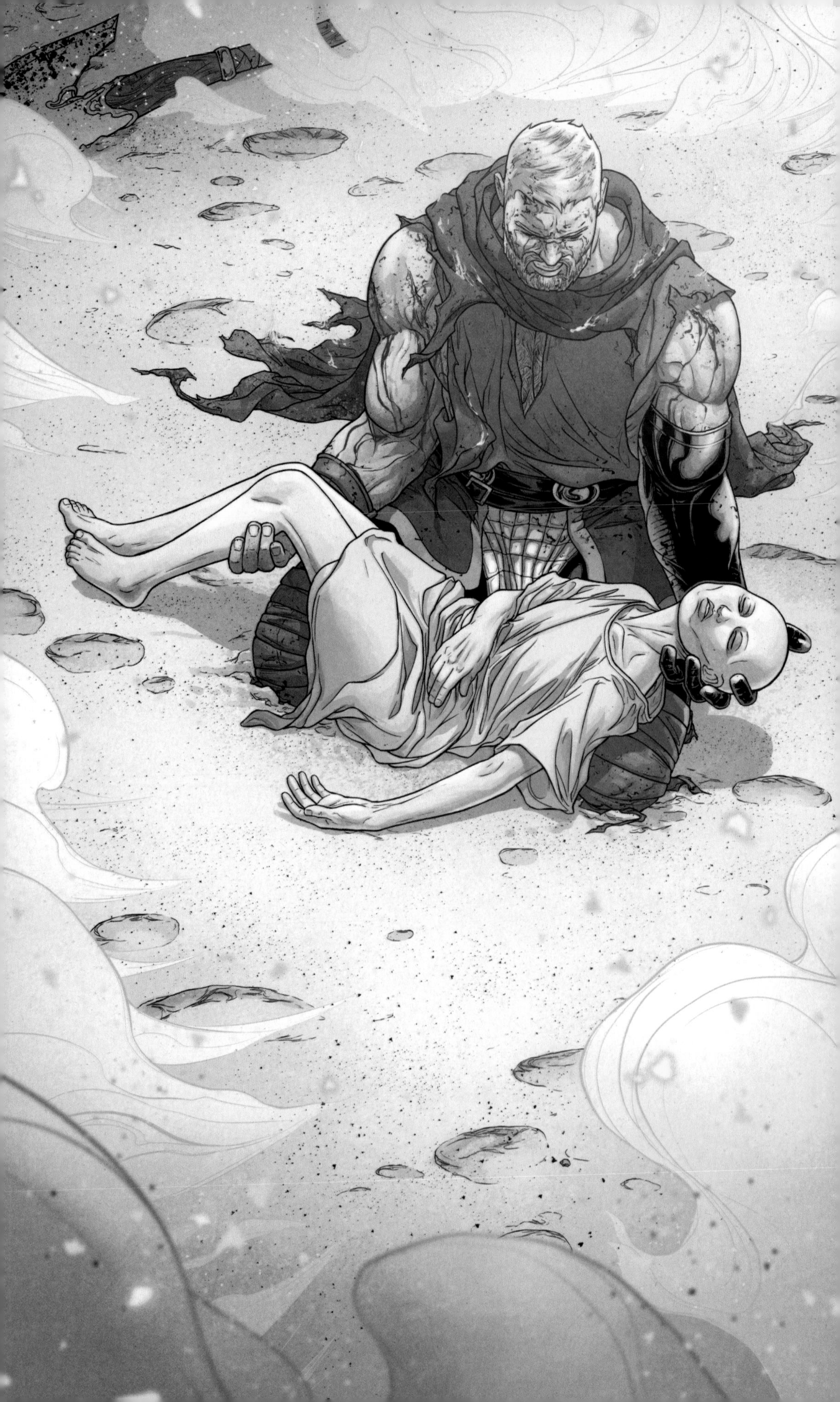

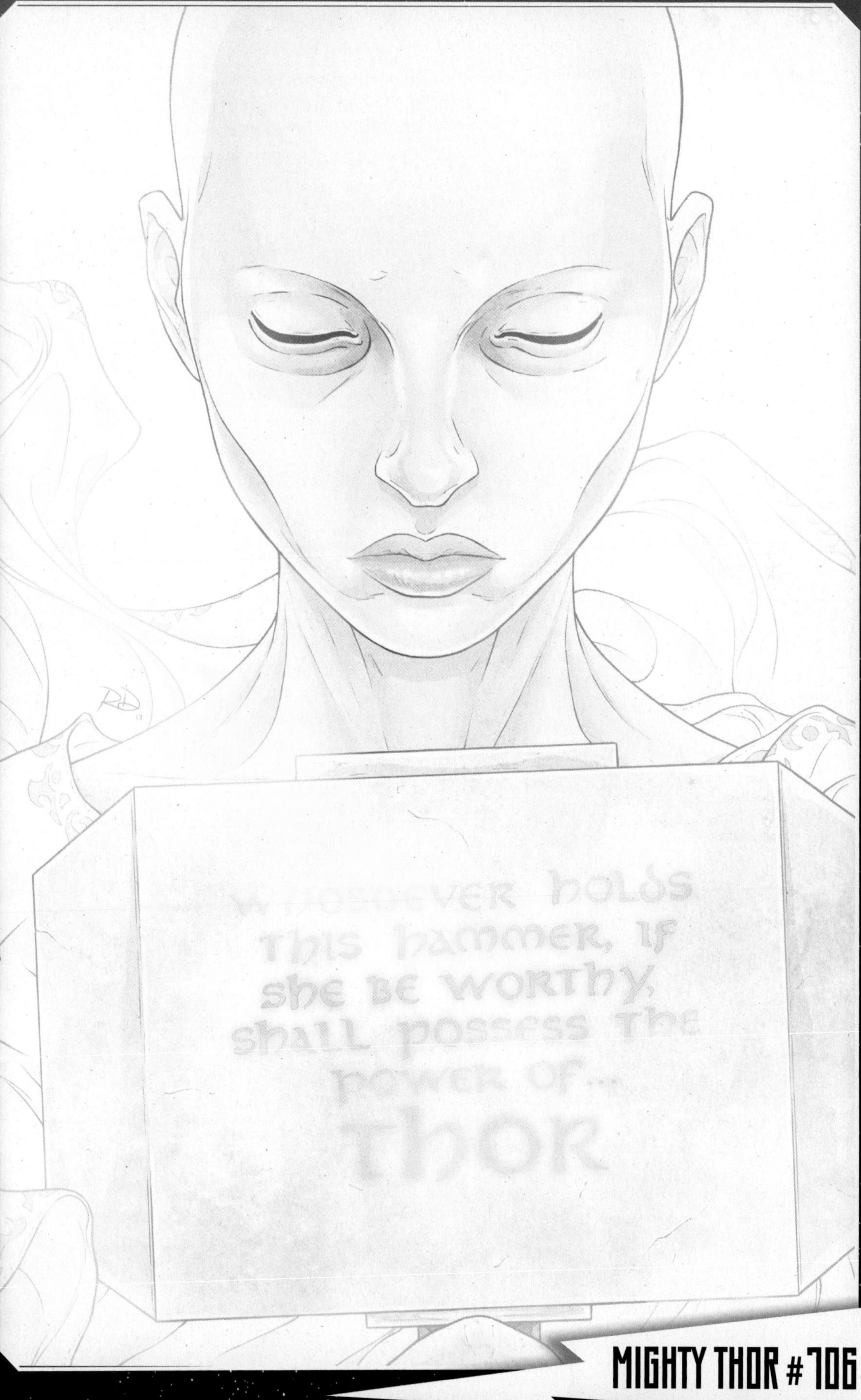
HOLDS
THIS HAMMER, IF
SHE BE WORTHY,
SHALL POSSESS THE
POWER OF...
THOR

MIGHTY THOR #706

NO! THIS CAN'T BE HOW IT ENDS! HEALERS!
WHERE ARE THE BOR-DAMNED HEALERS?!
JANE FOSTER.
JANE FOSTER OF MIDGARD WAS THE NEW THOR. I...HAD NO IDEA.
A MORTAL. A DISEASED ONE AT THAT--
--A SICKLY MORTAL JUST SAVED THE GODS OF ASGARD.
HRRPH.
RGGHH!
RRRRGGGGH!!!
HELP HER! SOMEONE SAVE HER!
HEIMDALL, IS SHE TRULY...
EVEN BLINDED, I CAN SEE THE TRUTH, SIF. I AM AFRAID IT IS TOO LATE, DEAR SISTER.

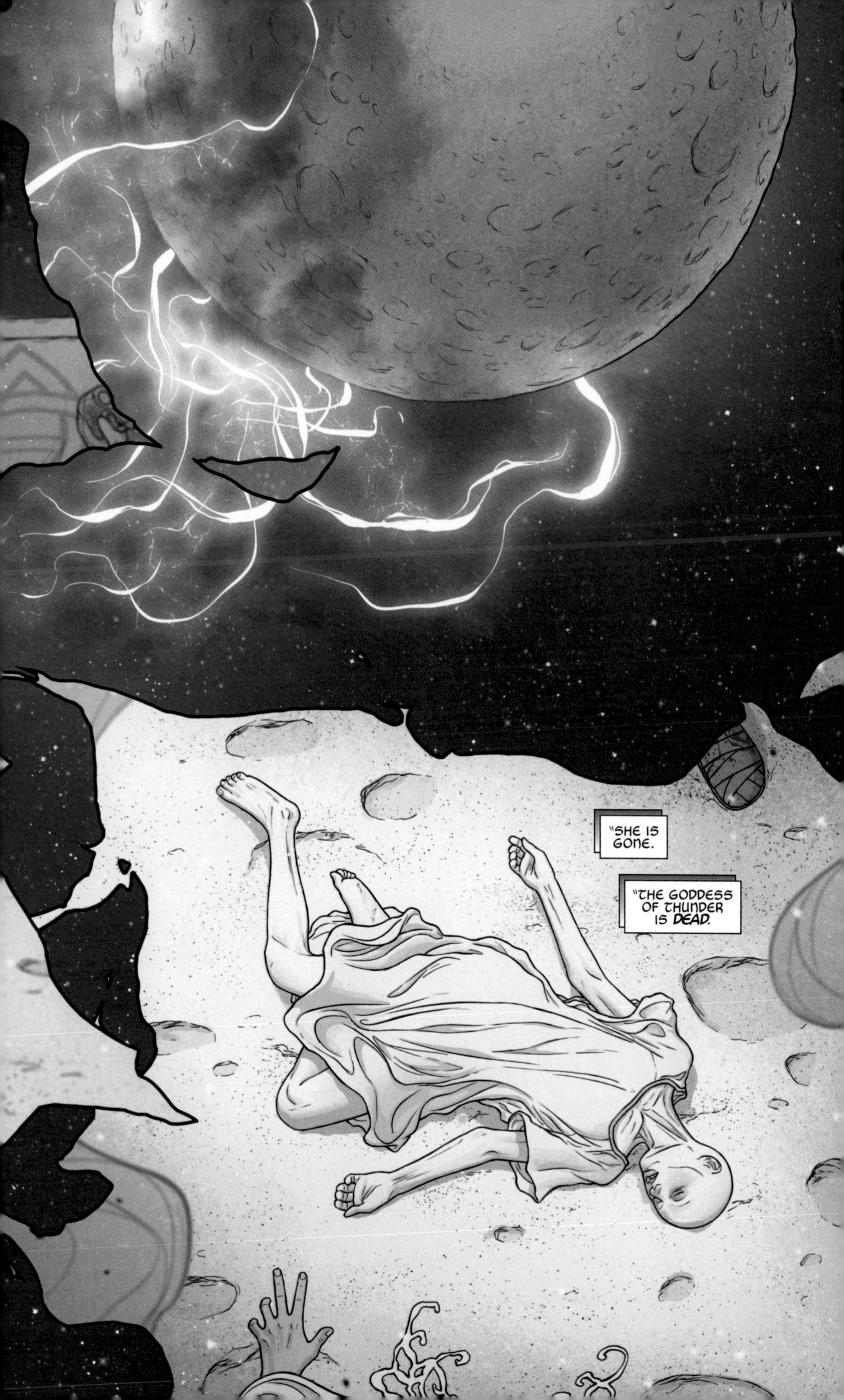
"SHE IS GONE.
"THE GODDESS OF THUNDER IS DEAD.

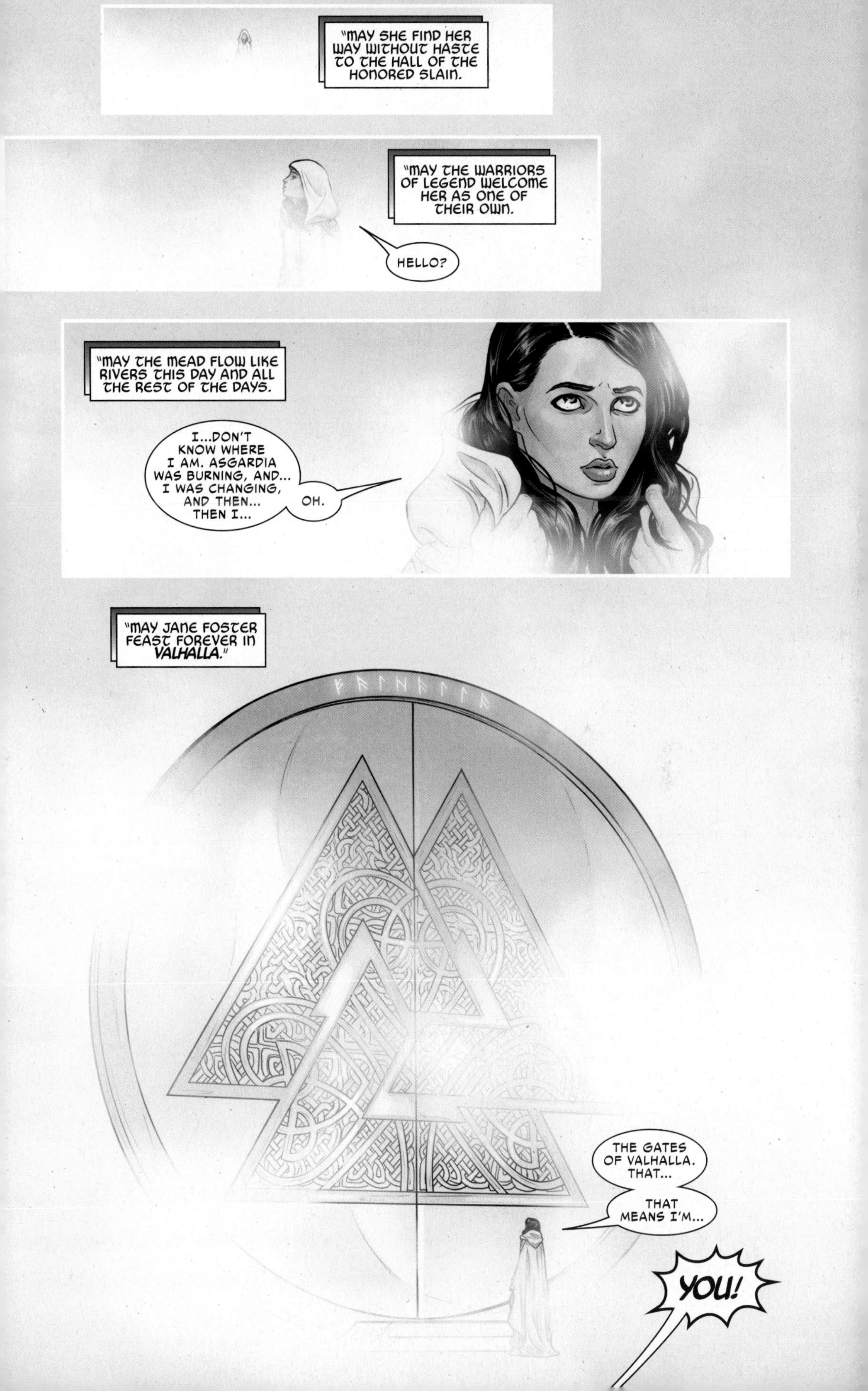
"MAY SHE FIND HER WAY WITHOUT HASTE TO THE HALL OF THE HONORED SLAIN.
"MAY THE WARRIORS OF LEGEND WELCOME HER AS ONE OF THEIR OWN.
HELLO?
"MAY THE MEAD FLOW LIKE RIVERS THIS DAY AND ALL THE REST OF THE DAYS.
I...DON'T KNOW WHERE I AM. ASGARDIA WAS BURNING, AND... I WAS CHANGING, AND THEN... THEN I...
OH.
"MAY JANE FOSTER FEAST FOREVER IN VALHALLA."
THE GATES OF VALHALLA. THAT...
THAT MEANS I'M...
YOU!

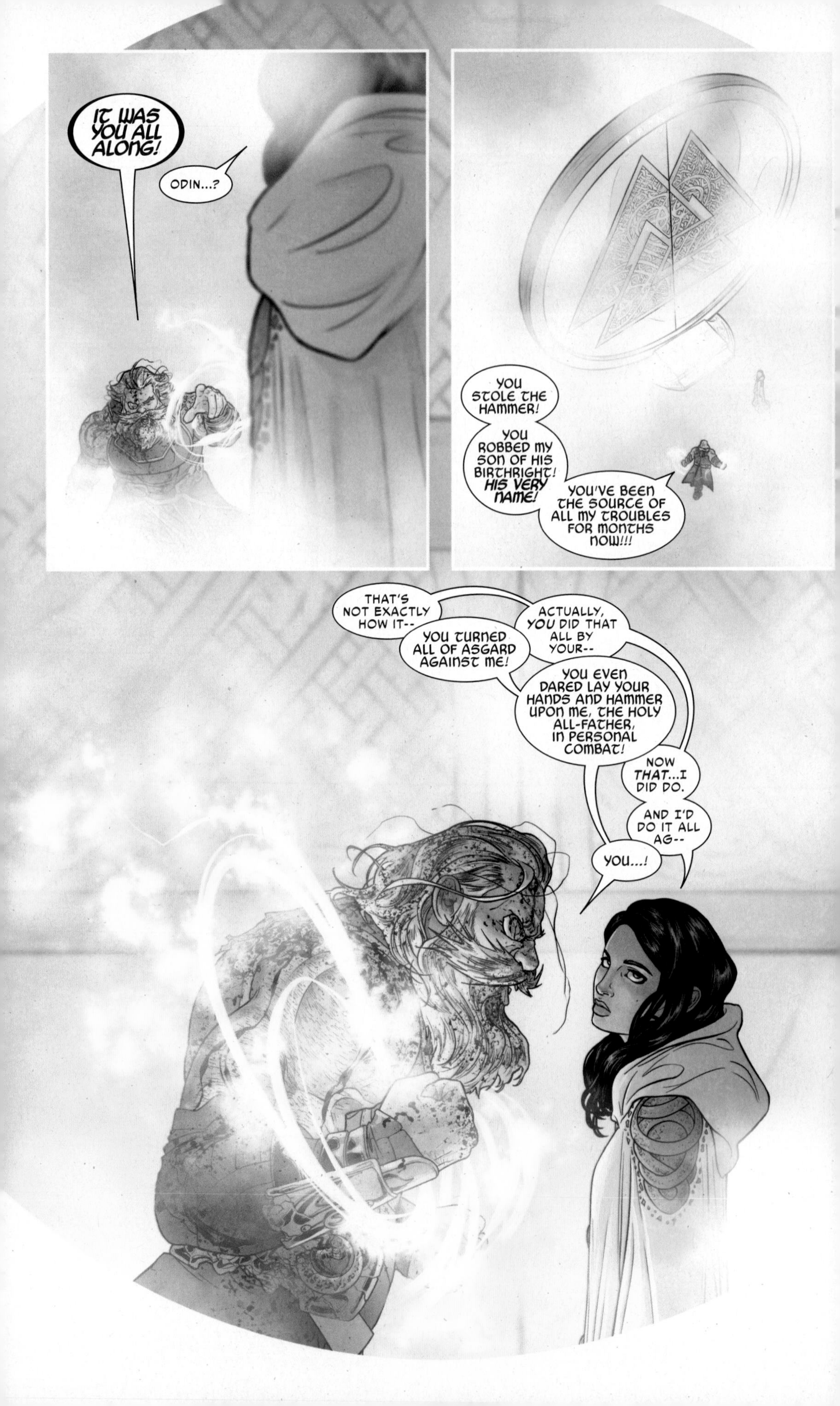
IT WAS YOU ALL ALONG!
ODIN...?
YOU STOLE THE HAMMER!
YOU ROBBED MY SON OF HIS BIRTHRIGHT! HIS VERY NAME!
YOU'VE BEEN THE SOURCE OF ALL MY TROUBLES FOR MONTHS NOW!!!
THAT'S NOT EXACTLY HOW IT--
ACTUALLY, YOU DID THAT ALL BY YOUR--
YOU TURNED ALL OF ASGARD AGAINST ME!
YOU EVEN DARED LAY YOUR HANDS AND HAMMER UPON ME, THE HOLY ALL-FATHER, IN PERSONAL COMBAT!
NOW THAT...I DID DO.
AND I'D DO IT ALL AG--
YOU...!

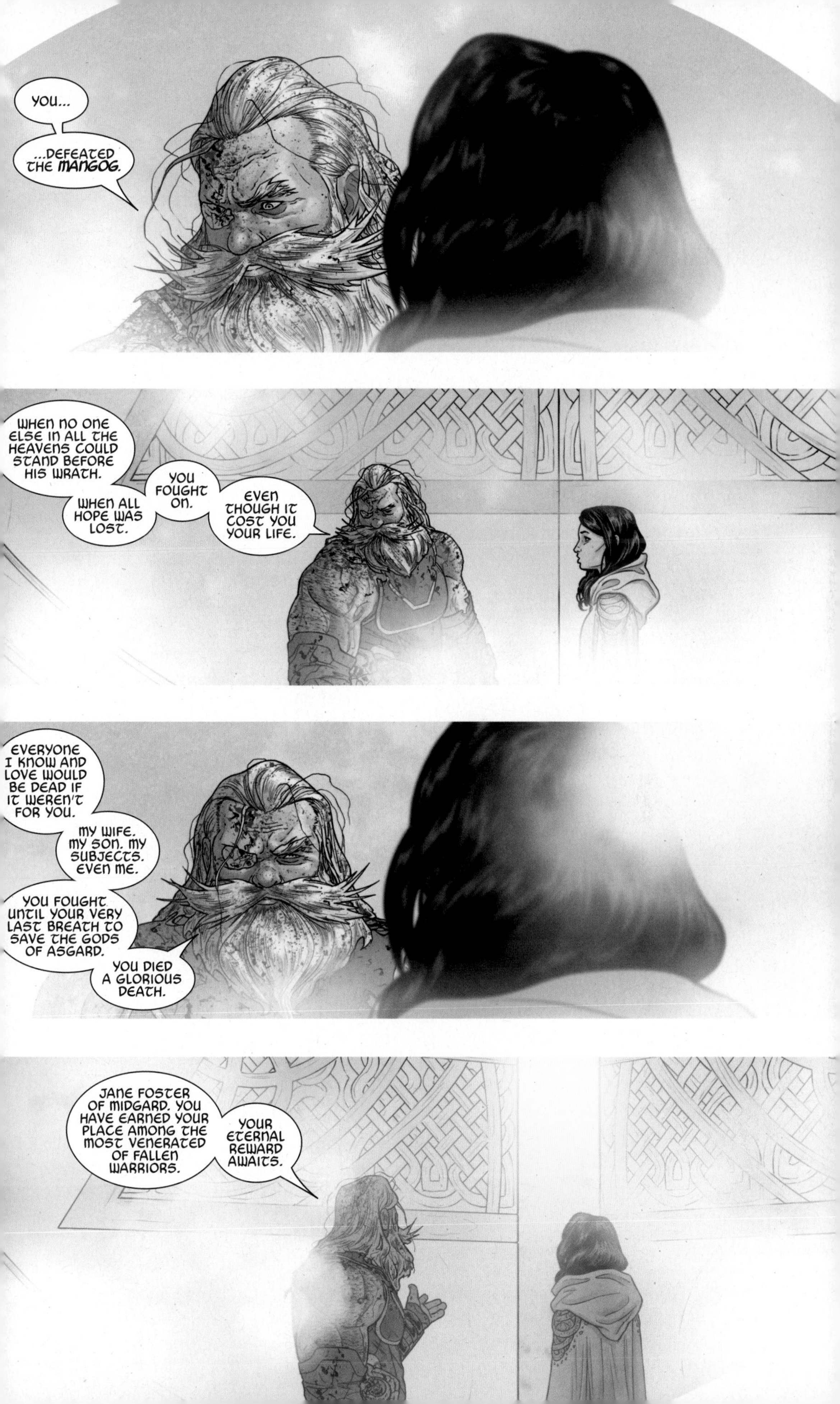
YOU...
...DEFEATED THE MANGOG.
WHEN NO ONE ELSE IN ALL THE HEAVENS COULD STAND BEFORE HIS WRATH.
WHEN ALL HOPE WAS LOST.
YOU FOUGHT ON.
EVEN THOUGH IT COST YOU YOUR LIFE.
EVERYONE I KNOW AND LOVE WOULD BE DEAD IF IT WEREN'T FOR YOU.
MY WIFE. MY SON. MY SUBJECTS. EVEN ME.
YOU FOUGHT UNTIL YOUR VERY LAST BREATH TO SAVE THE GODS OF ASGARD.
YOU DIED A GLORIOUS DEATH.
JANE FOSTER OF MIDGARD. YOU HAVE EARNED YOUR PLACE AMONG THE MOST VENERATED OF FALLEN WARRIORS.
YOUR ETERNAL REWARD AWAITS.

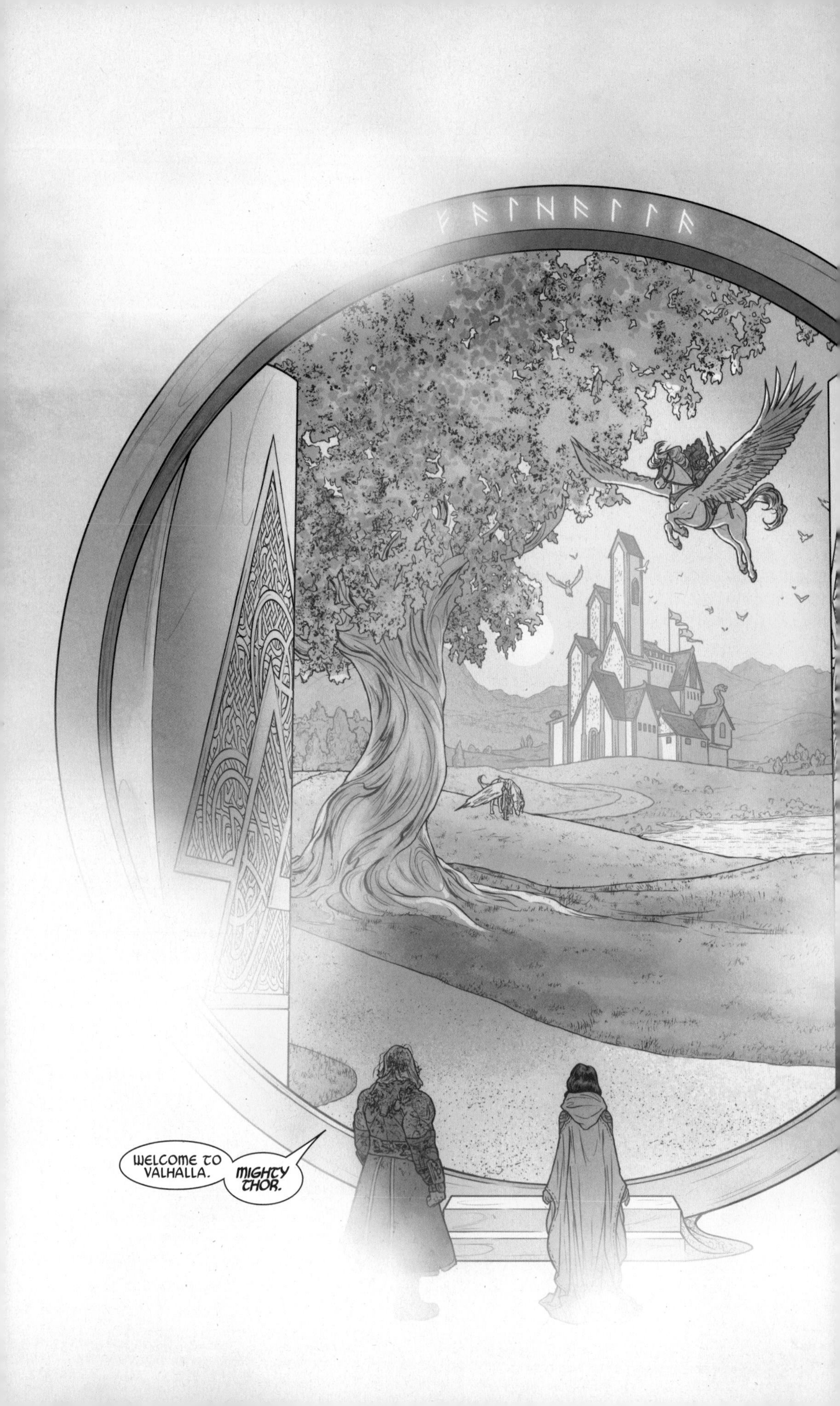
WELCOME TO VALHALLA.
MIGHTY THOR.

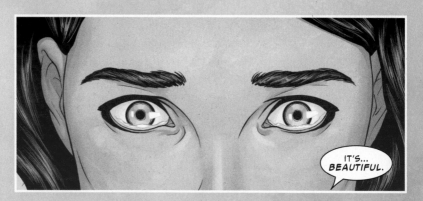

IT'S... BEAUTIFUL.

WHY DO YOU HESITATE? A GREAT FEAST IS ABOUT TO BEGIN, IN YOUR HONOR.

BE NOT AFRAID. YOU HAVE NOTHING MORE TO FEAR FROM ME OR ANYONE ELSE EVER AGAIN.

ALL WHO FALL VALIANTLY IN BATTLE ARE CHILDREN OF ODIN. SO TELL ME...

WHAT TROUBLES THEE, DAUGHTER JANE?

I... I WASN'T READY.

I WASN'T READY TO DIE.

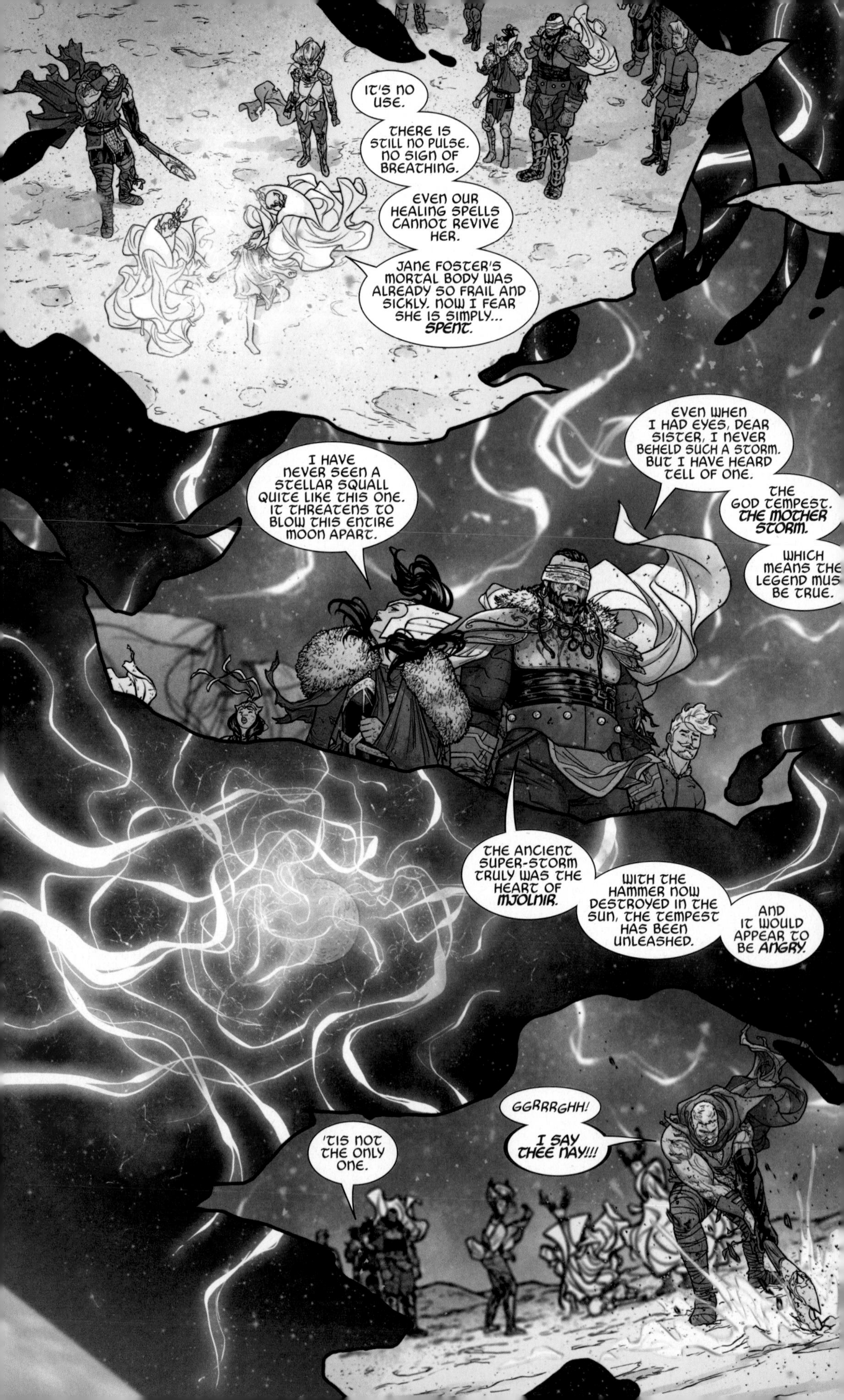
IT'S NO USE.
THERE IS STILL NO PULSE. NO SIGN OF BREATHING.
EVEN OUR HEALING SPELLS CANNOT REVIVE HER.
JANE FOSTER'S MORTAL BODY WAS ALREADY SO FRAIL AND SICKLY. NOW I FEAR SHE IS SIMPLY... SPENT.
I HAVE NEVER SEEN A STELLAR SQUALL QUITE LIKE THIS ONE. IT THREATENS TO BLOW THIS ENTIRE MOON APART.
EVEN WHEN I HAD EYES, DEAR SISTER, I NEVER BEHELD SUCH A STORM. BUT I HAVE HEARD TELL OF ONE.
THE GOD TEMPEST. THE MOTHER STORM.
WHICH MEANS THE LEGEND MUS BE TRUE.
THE ANCIENT SUPER-STORM TRULY WAS THE HEART OF MJOLNIR.
WITH THE HAMMER NOW DESTROYED IN THE SUN, THE TEMPEST HAS BEEN UNLEASHED.
AND IT WOULD APPEAR TO BE ANGRY.
'TIS NOT THE ONLY ONE.
GGRRRGHH!
I SAY THEE NAY!!!

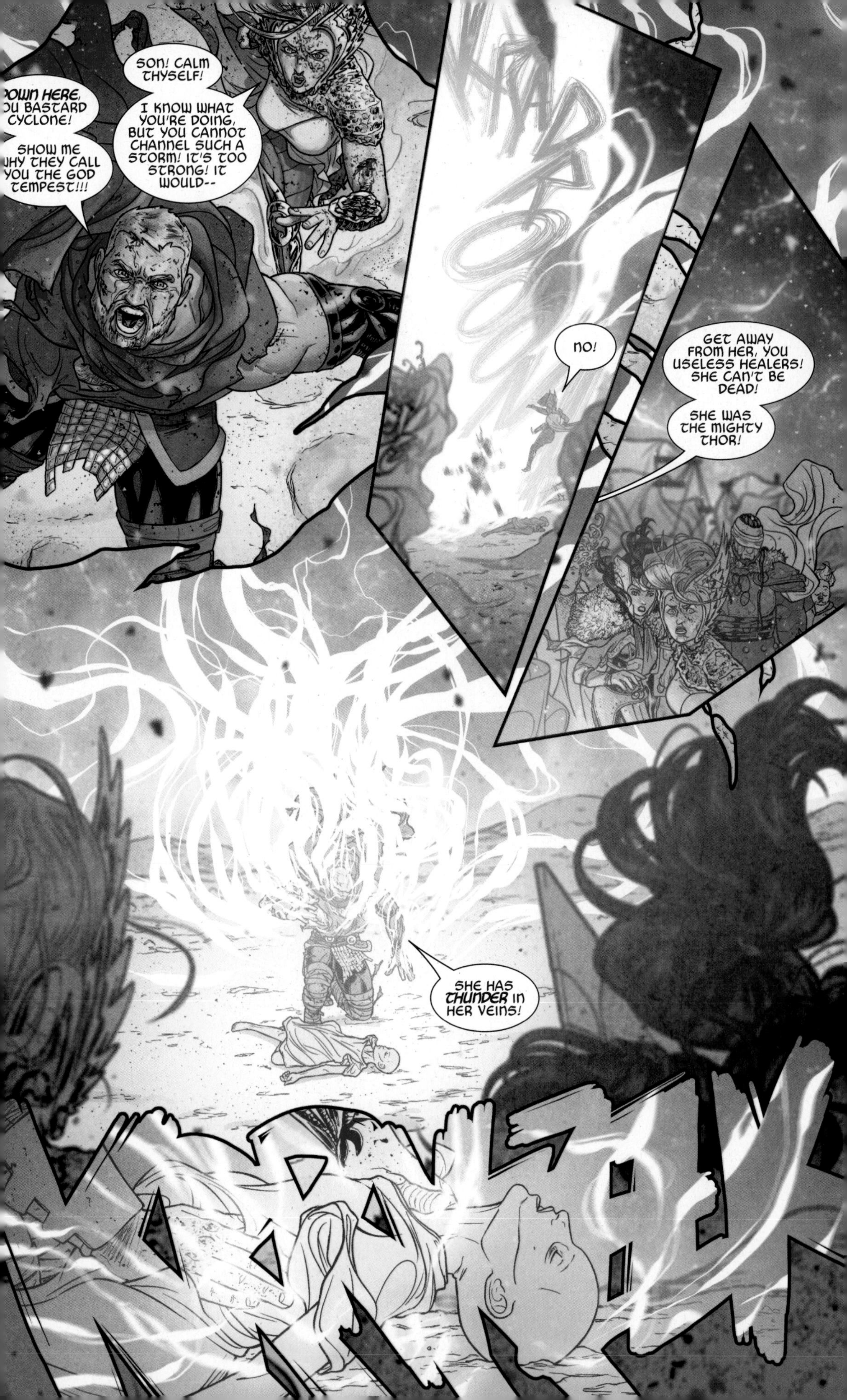
DOWN HERE, YOU BASTARD CYCLONE!
SHOW ME WHY THEY CALL YOU THE GOD TEMPEST!!!
SON! CALM THYSELF!
I KNOW WHAT YOU'RE DOING, BUT YOU CANNOT CHANNEL SUCH A STORM! IT'S TOO STRONG! IT WOULD--
NO!
GET AWAY FROM HER, YOU USELESS HEALERS! SHE CAN'T BE DEAD!
SHE WAS THE MIGHTY THOR!
SHE HAS THUNDER IN HER VEINS!

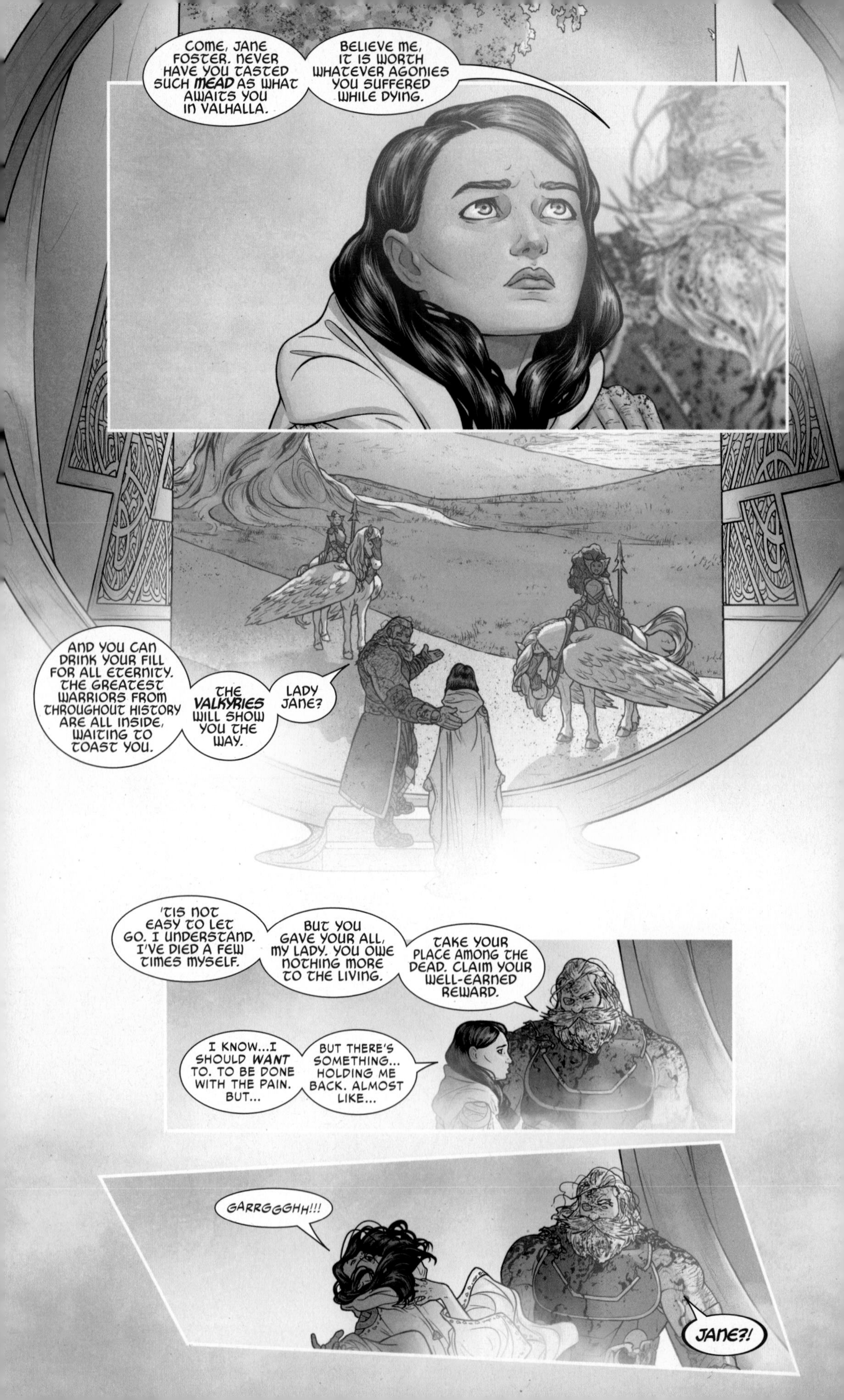
COME, JANE FOSTER. NEVER HAVE YOU TASTED SUCH MEAD AS WHAT AWAITS YOU IN VALHALLA.
BELIEVE ME, IT IS WORTH WHATEVER AGONIES YOU SUFFERED WHILE DYING.
AND YOU CAN DRINK YOUR FILL FOR ALL ETERNITY. THE GREATEST WARRIORS FROM THROUGHOUT HISTORY ARE ALL INSIDE, WAITING TO TOAST YOU.
THE VALKYRIES WILL SHOW YOU THE WAY.
LADY JANE?
'TIS NOT EASY TO LET GO. I UNDERSTAND. I'VE DIED A FEW TIMES MYSELF.
BUT YOU GAVE YOUR ALL, MY LADY. YOU OWE NOTHING MORE TO THE LIVING.
TAKE YOUR PLACE AMONG THE DEAD. CLAIM YOUR WELL-EARNED REWARD.
I KNOW...I SHOULD WANT TO. TO BE DONE WITH THE PAIN. BUT...
BUT THERE'S SOMETHING... HOLDING ME BACK. ALMOST LIKE...
GARRGGGHH!!!
JANE?!

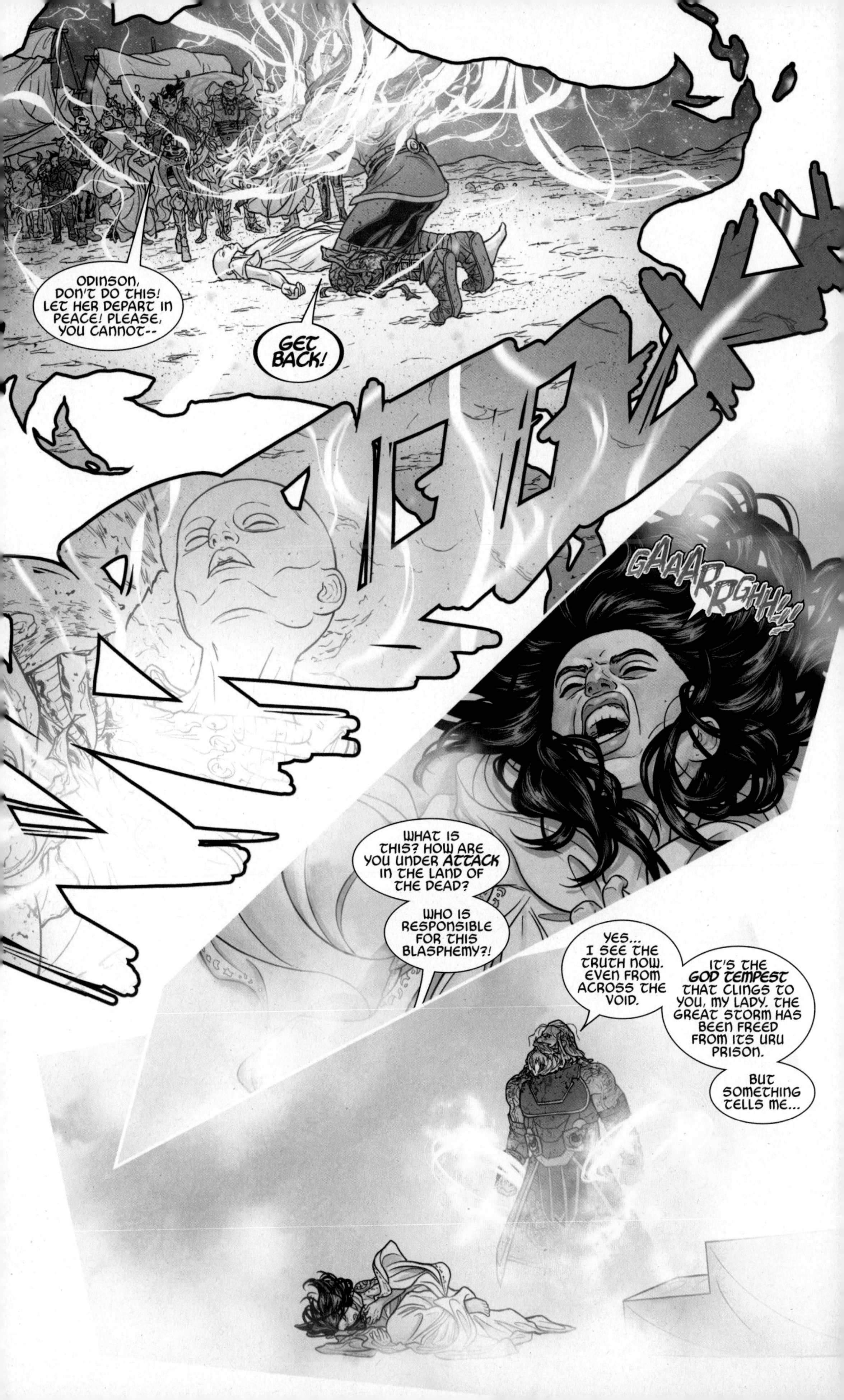
ODINSON, DON'T DO THIS! LET HER DEPART IN PEACE! PLEASE, YOU CANNOT--
GET BACK!
GAAAARRGHHH!!
WHAT IS THIS? HOW ARE YOU UNDER ATTACK IN THE LAND OF THE DEAD?
WHO IS RESPONSIBLE FOR THIS BLASPHEMY?!
YES... I SEE THE TRUTH NOW. EVEN FROM ACROSS THE VOID.
IT'S THE GOD TEMPEST THAT CLINGS TO YOU, MY LADY. THE GREAT STORM HAS BEEN FREED FROM ITS URU PRISON.
BUT SOMETHING TELLS ME...

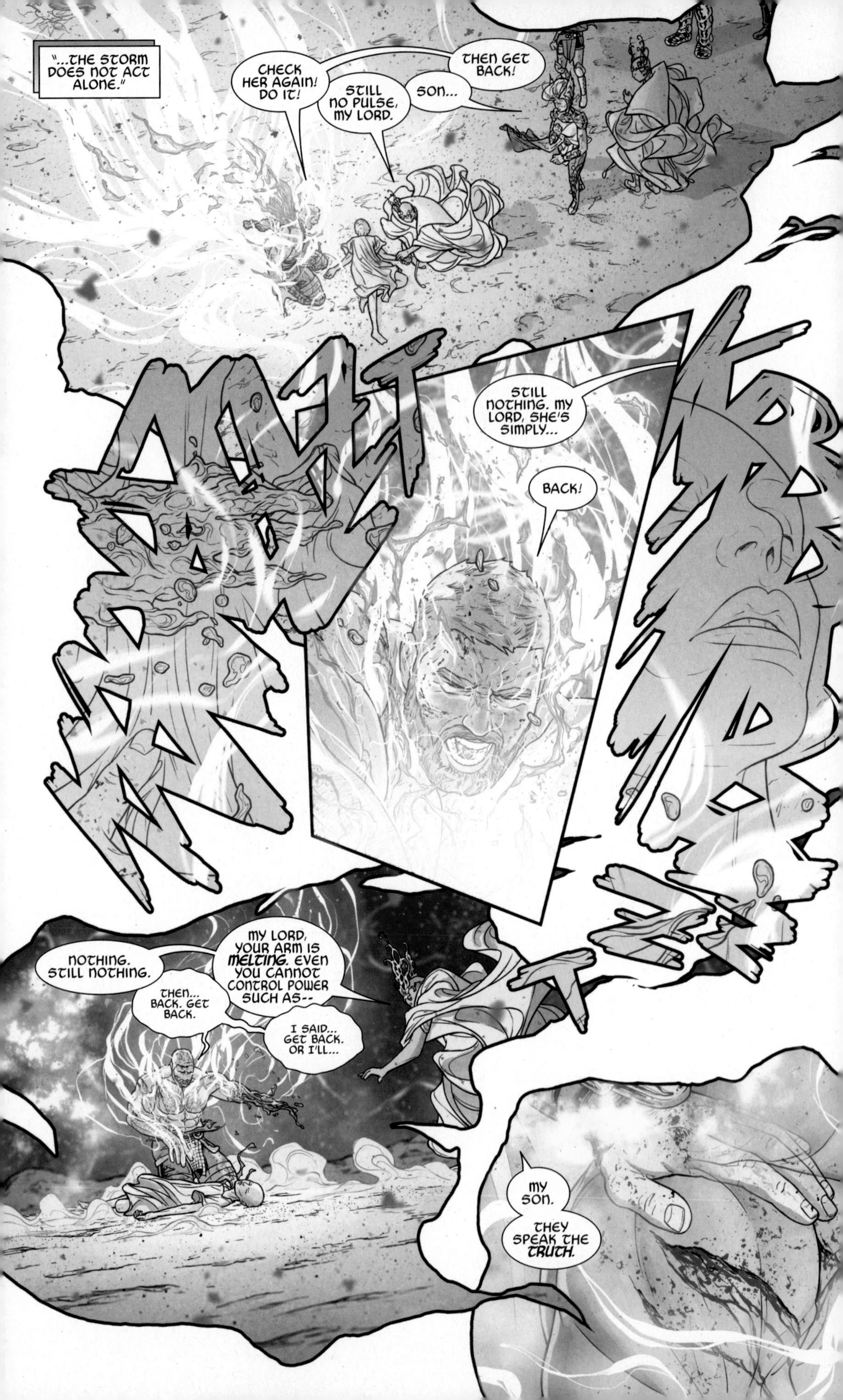
"...THE STORM DOES NOT ACT ALONE."
CHECK HER AGAIN! DO IT!
STILL NO PULSE, MY LORD.
SON...
THEN GET BACK!
STILL NOTHING. MY LORD, SHE'S SIMPLY...
BACK!
NOTHING. STILL NOTHING.
MY LORD, YOUR ARM IS MELTING. EVEN YOU CANNOT CONTROL POWER SUCH AS--
THEN... BACK. GET BACK.
I SAID... GET BACK. OR I'LL...
MY SON.
THEY SPEAK THE TRUTH.

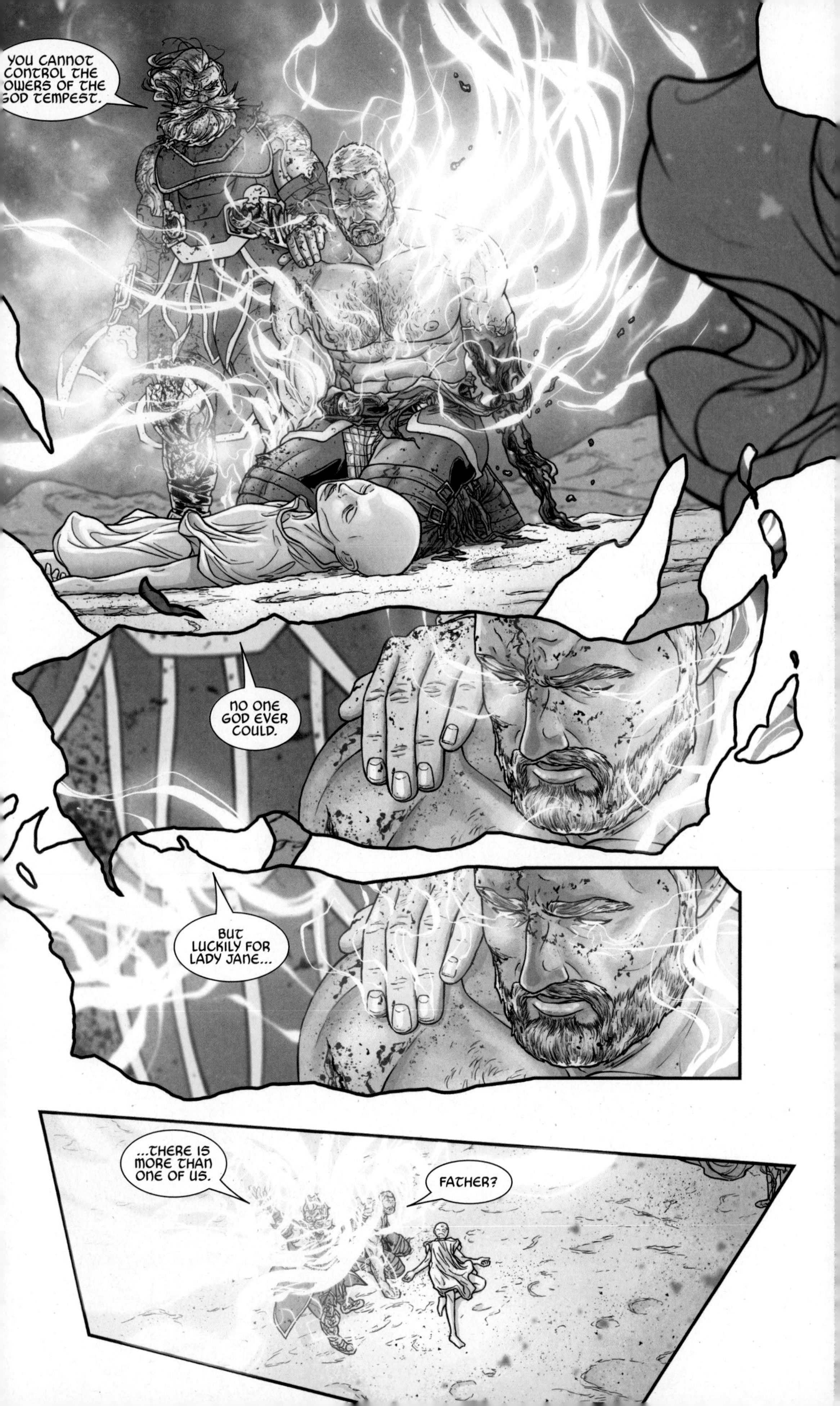
YOU CANNOT CONTROL THE POWERS OF THE GOD TEMPEST.
NO ONE GOD EVER COULD.
BUT LUCKILY FOR LADY JANE...
...THERE IS MORE THAN ONE OF US.
FATHER?

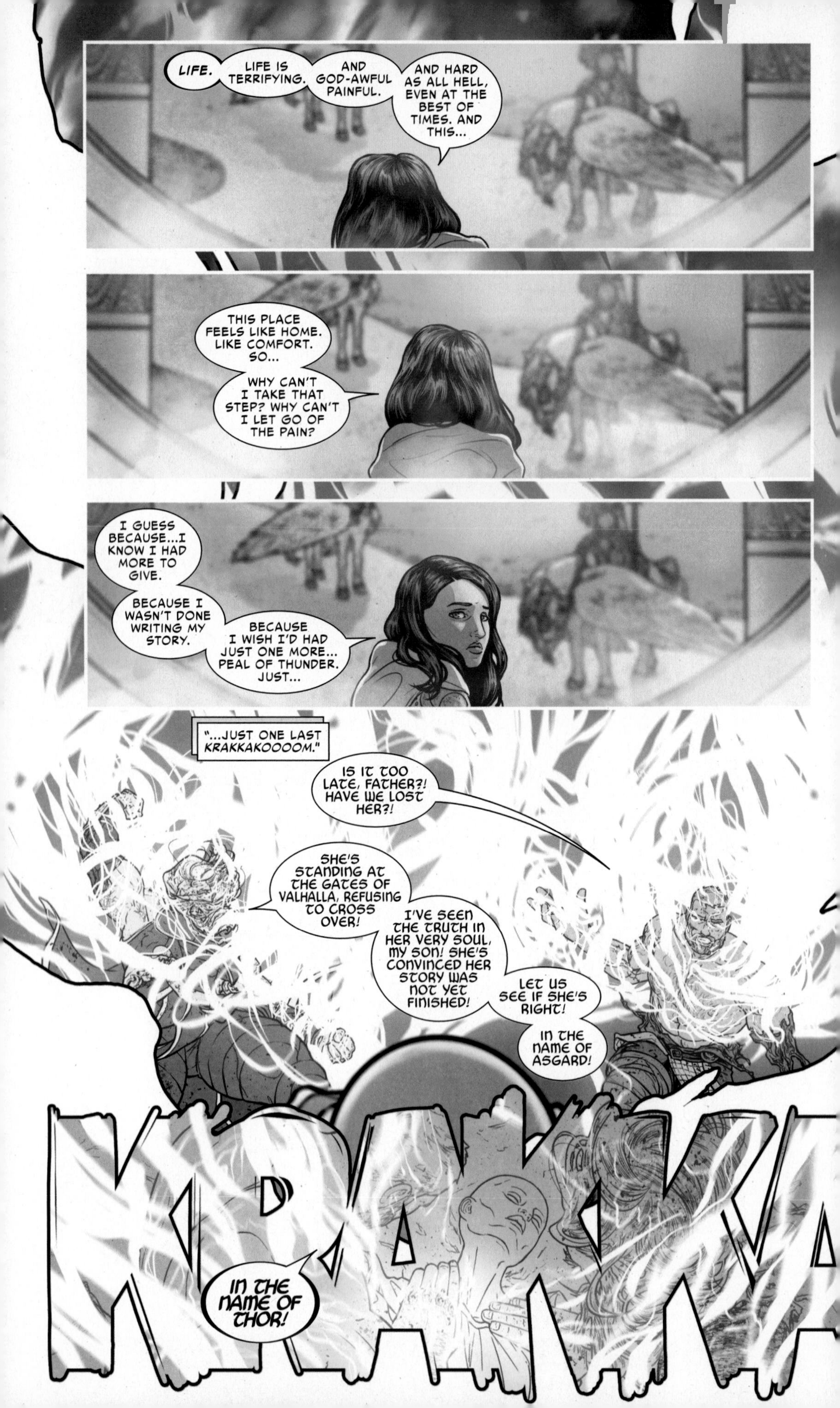

LIFE.
LIFE IS TERRIFYING.
AND GOD-AWFUL PAINFUL.
AND HARD AS ALL HELL, EVEN AT THE BEST OF TIMES. AND THIS...
THIS PLACE FEELS LIKE HOME. LIKE COMFORT. SO...
WHY CAN'T I TAKE THAT STEP? WHY CAN'T I LET GO OF THE PAIN?
I GUESS BECAUSE...I KNOW I HAD MORE TO GIVE.
BECAUSE I WASN'T DONE WRITING MY STORY.
BECAUSE I WISH I'D HAD JUST ONE MORE... PEAL OF THUNDER. JUST...
"...JUST ONE LAST KRAKKAKOOOOM."
IS IT TOO LATE, FATHER?! HAVE WE LOST HER?!
SHE'S STANDING AT THE GATES OF VALHALLA, REFUSING TO CROSS OVER!
I'VE SEEN THE TRUTH IN HER VERY SOUL, MY SON! SHE'S CONVINCED HER STORY WAS NOT YET FINISHED!
LET US SEE IF SHE'S RIGHT!
IN THE NAME OF ASGARD!
IN THE NAME OF THOR!

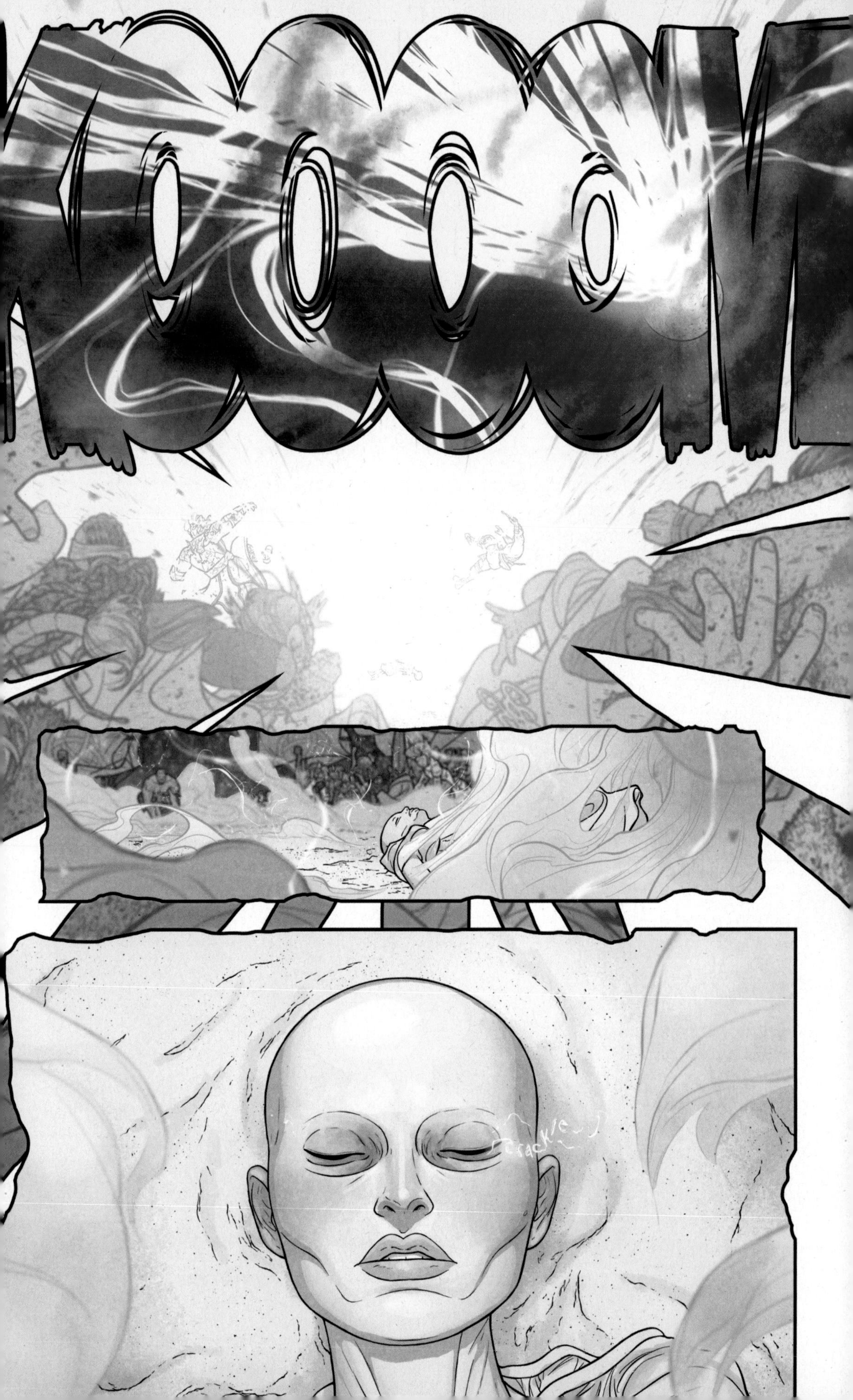
crackle

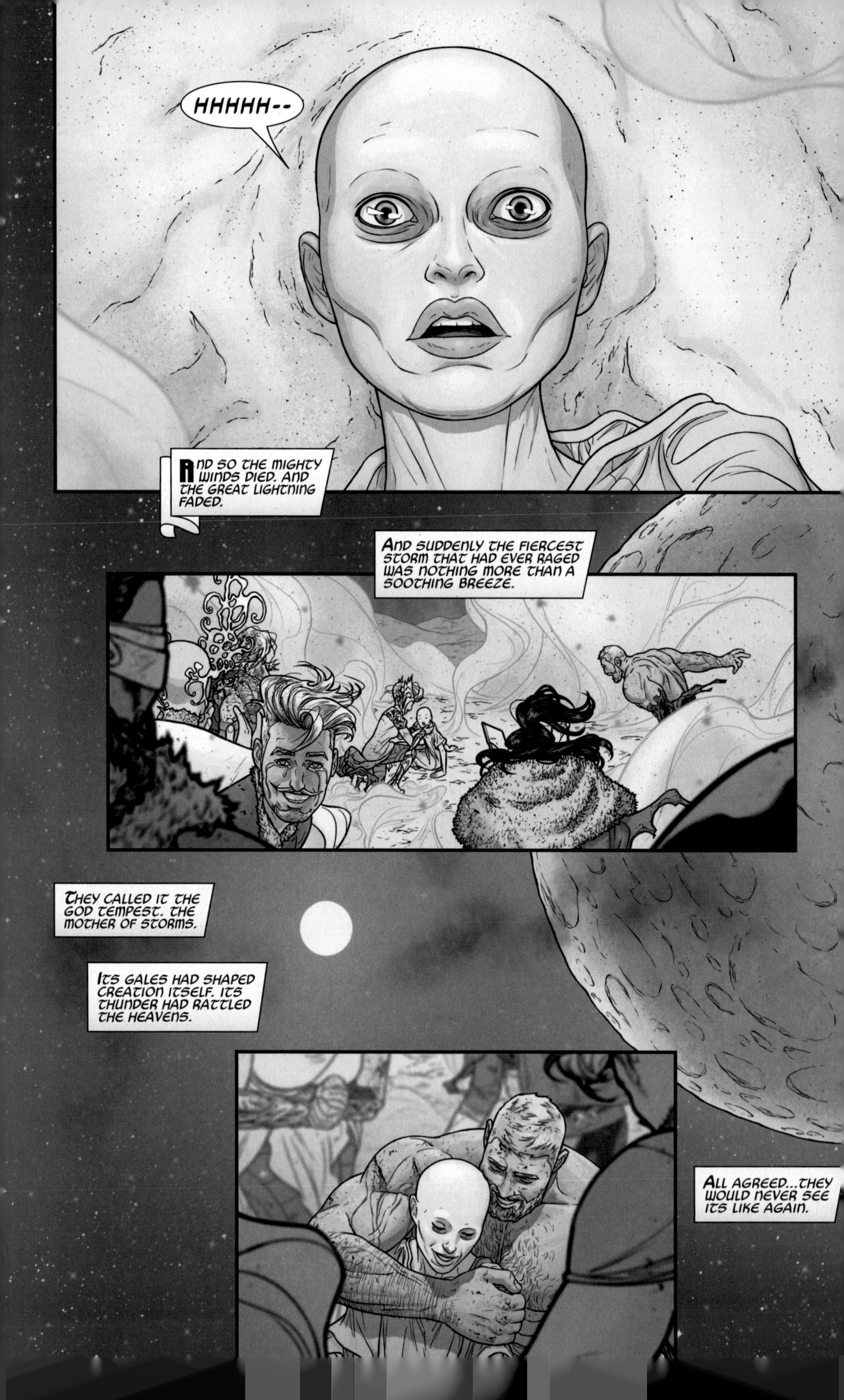
HHHHH--
AND SO THE MIGHTY WINDS DIED. AND THE GREAT LIGHTNING FADED.
AND SUDDENLY THE FIERCEST STORM THAT HAD EVER RAGED WAS NOTHING MORE THAN A SOOTHING BREEZE.
THEY CALLED IT THE GOD TEMPEST. THE MOTHER OF STORMS.
ITS GALES HAD SHAPED CREATION ITSELF. ITS THUNDER HAD RATTLED THE HEAVENS.
ALL AGREED...THEY WOULD NEVER SEE ITS LIKE AGAIN.

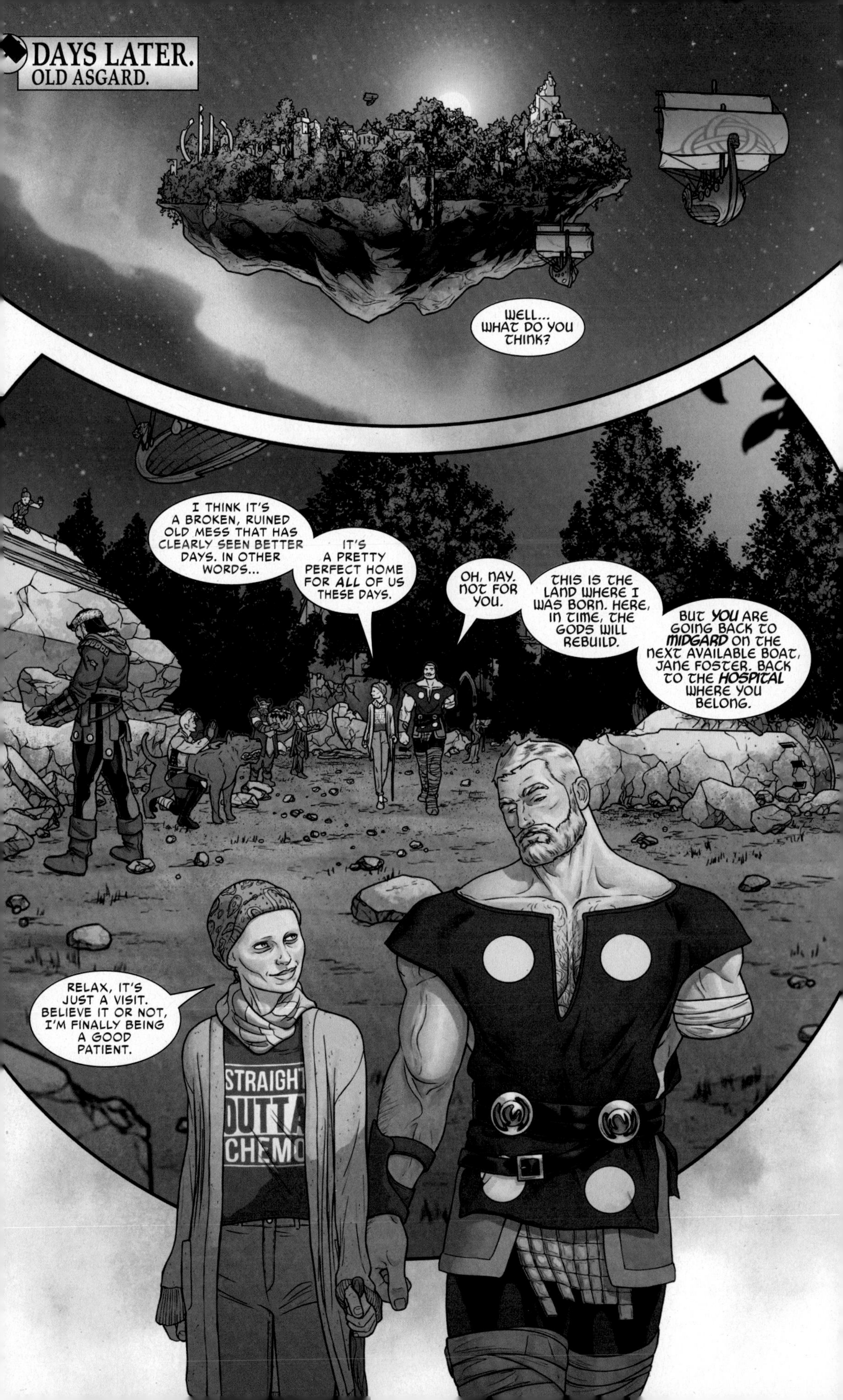
DAYS LATER.
OLD ASGARD.
WELL... WHAT DO YOU THINK?
I THINK IT'S A BROKEN, RUINED OLD MESS THAT HAS CLEARLY SEEN BETTER DAYS. IN OTHER WORDS...
IT'S A PRETTY PERFECT HOME FOR ALL OF US THESE DAYS.
OH, NAY. NOT FOR YOU.
THIS IS THE LAND WHERE I WAS BORN. HERE, IN TIME, THE GODS WILL REBUILD.
BUT YOU ARE GOING BACK TO MIDGARD ON THE NEXT AVAILABLE BOAT, JANE FOSTER. BACK TO THE HOSPITAL WHERE YOU BELONG.
RELAX, IT'S JUST A VISIT. BELIEVE IT OR NOT, I'M FINALLY BEING A GOOD PATIENT.
STRAIGHT OUTTA CHEMO

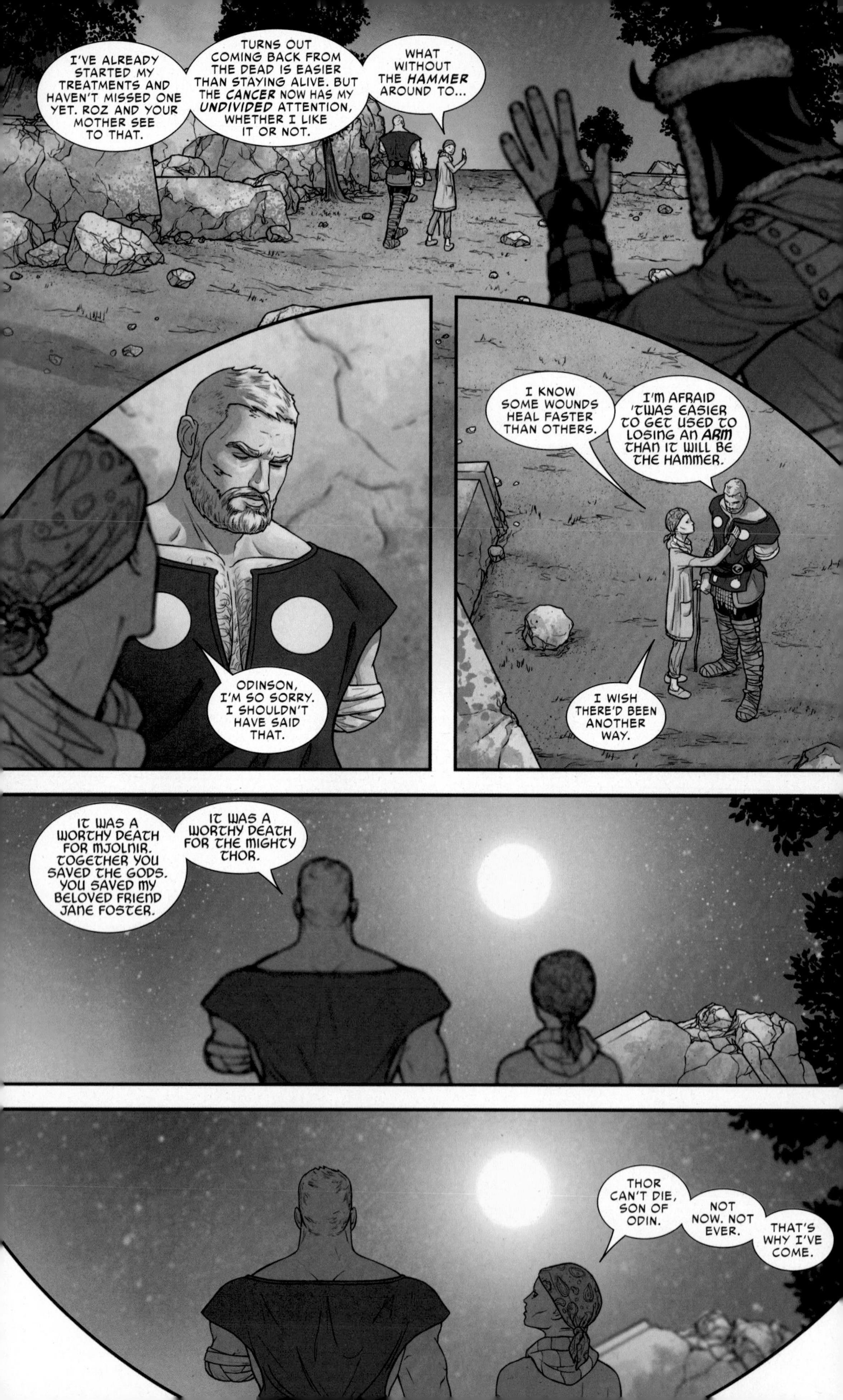
I'VE ALREADY STARTED MY TREATMENTS AND HAVEN'T MISSED ONE YET. ROZ AND YOUR MOTHER SEE TO THAT.
TURNS OUT COMING BACK FROM THE DEAD IS EASIER THAN STAYING ALIVE. BUT THE CANCER NOW HAS MY UNDIVIDED ATTENTION, WHETHER I LIKE IT OR NOT.
WHAT WITHOUT THE HAMMER AROUND TO...
ODINSON, I'M SO SORRY. I SHOULDN'T HAVE SAID THAT.
I KNOW SOME WOUNDS HEAL FASTER THAN OTHERS.
I'M AFRAID 'TWAS EASIER TO GET USED TO LOSING AN ARM THAN IT WILL BE THE HAMMER.
I WISH THERE'D BEEN ANOTHER WAY.
IT WAS A WORTHY DEATH FOR MJOLNIR. TOGETHER YOU SAVED THE GODS. YOU SAVED MY BELOVED FRIEND JANE FOSTER.
IT WAS A WORTHY DEATH FOR THE MIGHTY THOR.
THOR CAN'T DIE, SON OF ODIN.
NOT NOW. NOT EVER.
THAT'S WHY I'VE COME.

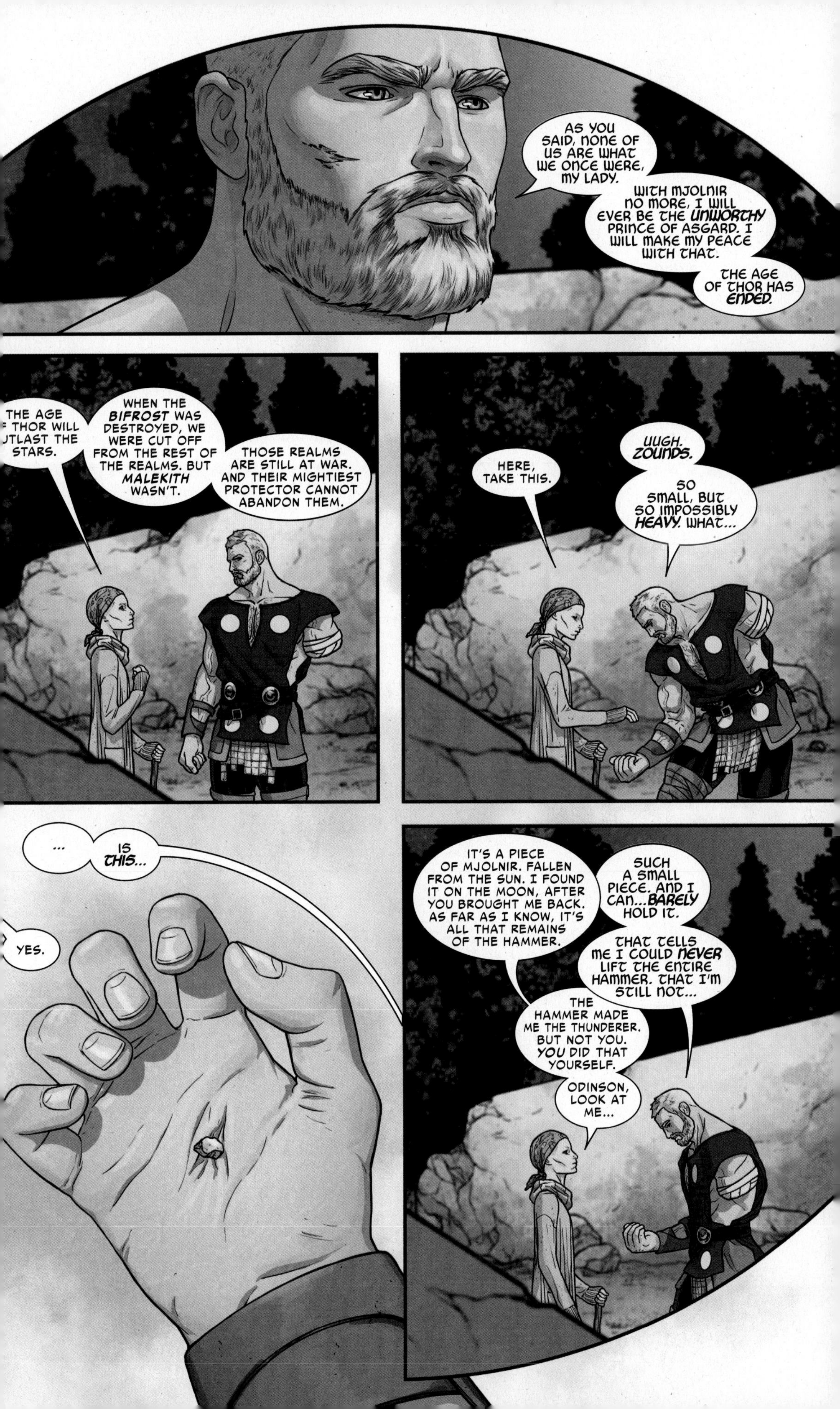
AS YOU SAID, NONE OF US ARE WHAT WE ONCE WERE, MY LADY.
WITH MJOLNIR NO MORE, I WILL EVER BE THE UNWORTHY PRINCE OF ASGARD. I WILL MAKE MY PEACE WITH THAT.
THE AGE OF THOR HAS ENDED.
THE AGE OF THOR WILL OUTLAST THE STARS.
WHEN THE BIFROST WAS DESTROYED, WE WERE CUT OFF FROM THE REST OF THE REALMS. BUT MALEKITH WASN'T.
THOSE REALMS ARE STILL AT WAR. AND THEIR MIGHTIEST PROTECTOR CANNOT ABANDON THEM.
HERE, TAKE THIS.
UUGH. ZOUNDS.
SO SMALL, BUT SO IMPOSSIBLY HEAVY. WHAT...
...
IS THIS...
YES.
IT'S A PIECE OF MJOLNIR. FALLEN FROM THE SUN. I FOUND IT ON THE MOON, AFTER YOU BROUGHT ME BACK. AS FAR AS I KNOW, IT'S ALL THAT REMAINS OF THE HAMMER.
SUCH A SMALL PIECE. AND I CAN...BARELY HOLD IT.
THAT TELLS ME I COULD NEVER LIFT THE ENTIRE HAMMER. THAT I'M STILL NOT...
THE HAMMER MADE ME THE THUNDERER. BUT NOT YOU. YOU DID THAT YOURSELF.
ODINSON, LOOK AT ME...

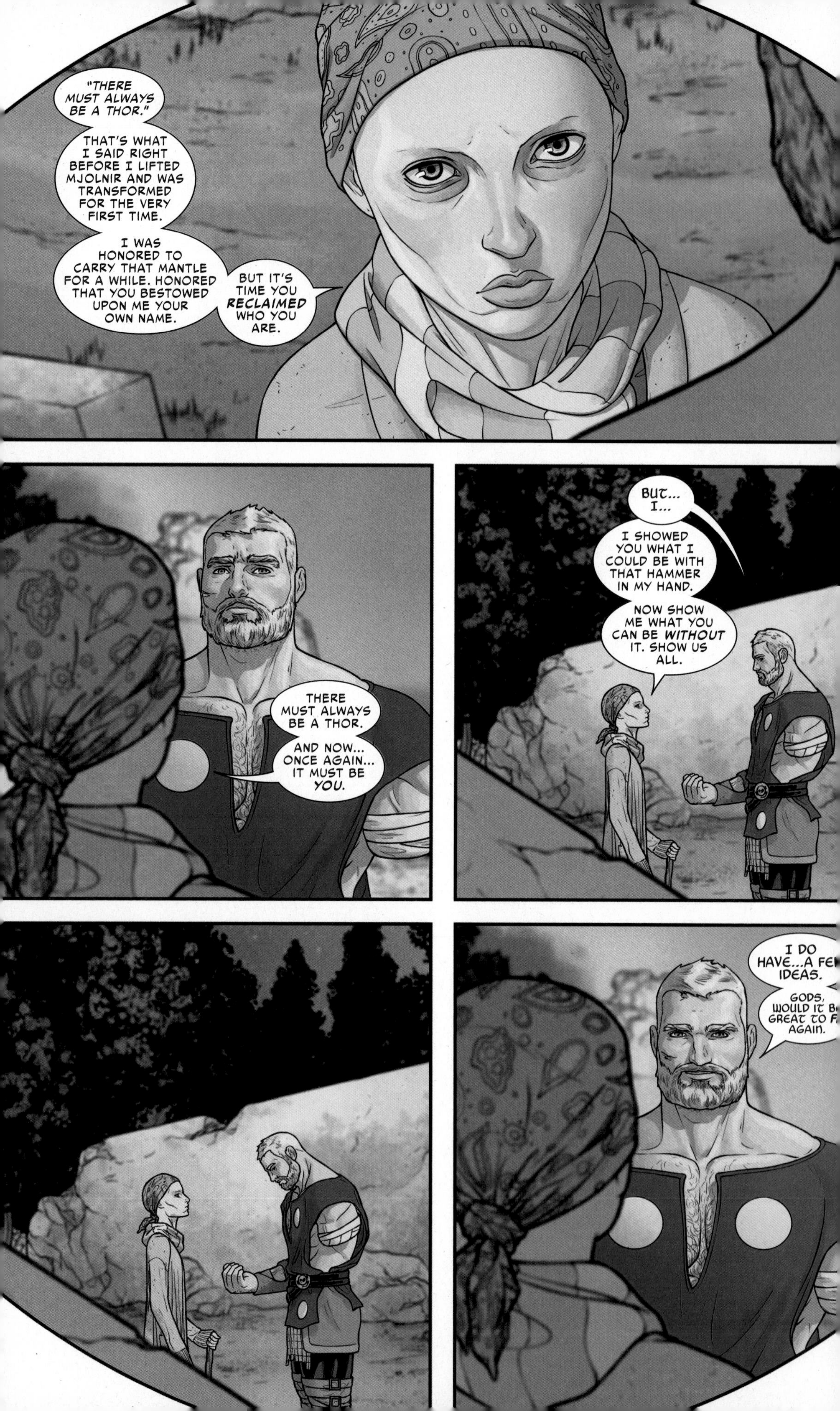

"THERE MUST ALWAYS BE A THOR."
THAT'S WHAT I SAID RIGHT BEFORE I LIFTED MJOLNIR AND WAS TRANSFORMED FOR THE VERY FIRST TIME.
I WAS HONORED TO CARRY THAT MANTLE FOR A WHILE. HONORED THAT YOU BESTOWED UPON ME YOUR OWN NAME.
BUT IT'S TIME YOU RECLAIMED WHO YOU ARE.
THERE MUST ALWAYS BE A THOR.
AND NOW... ONCE AGAIN... IT MUST BE YOU.
BUT... I...
I SHOWED YOU WHAT I COULD BE WITH THAT HAMMER IN MY HAND.
NOW SHOW ME WHAT YOU CAN BE WITHOUT IT. SHOW US ALL.
I DO HAVE...A FE
IDEAS.
GODS, WOULD IT B
GREAT TO F
AGAIN.

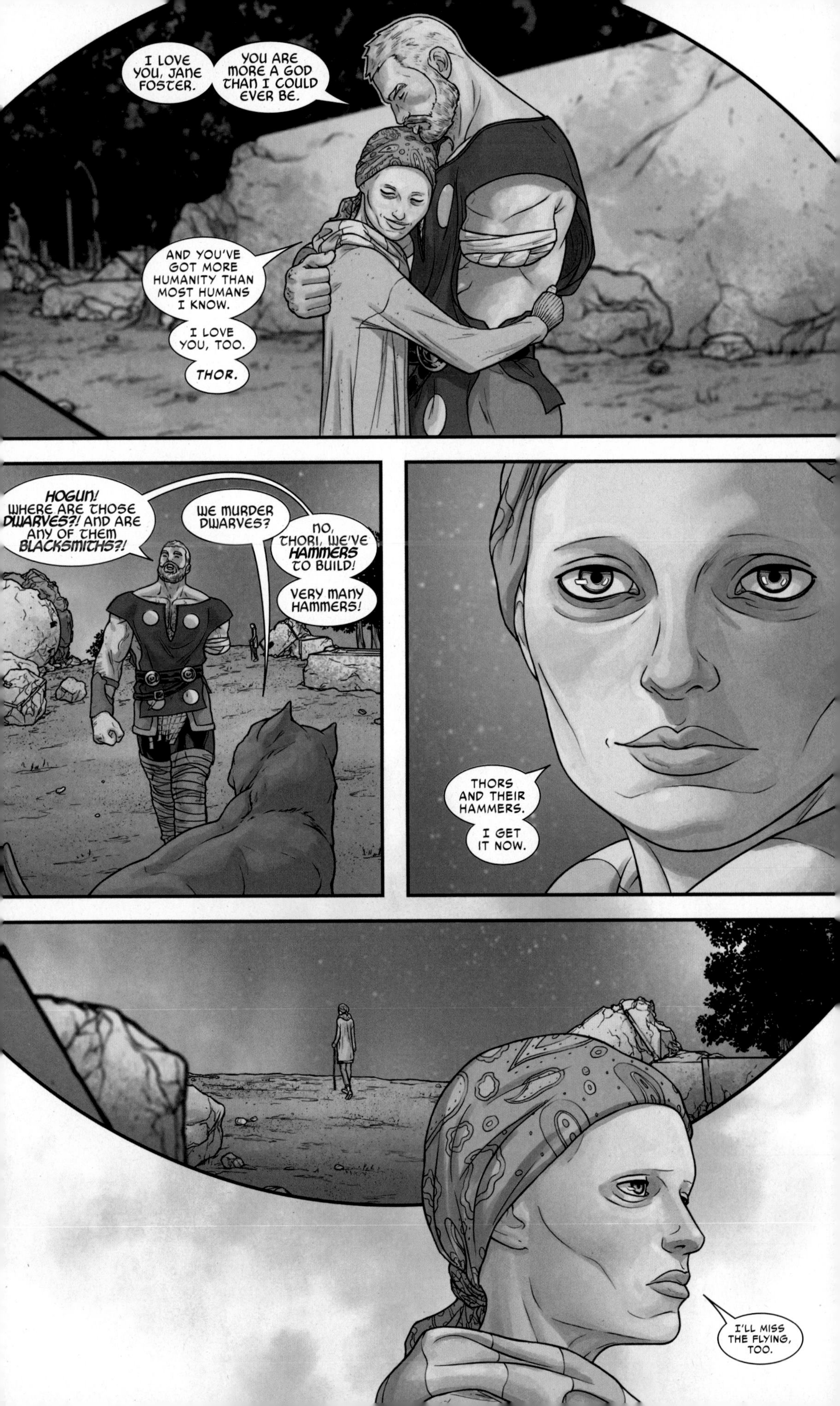
I LOVE YOU, JANE FOSTER.
YOU ARE MORE A GOD THAN I COULD EVER BE.
AND YOU'VE GOT MORE HUMANITY THAN MOST HUMANS I KNOW.
I LOVE YOU, TOO.
THOR.
HOGUN! WHERE ARE THOSE DWARVES?! AND ARE ANY OF THEM BLACKSMITHS?!
WE MURDER DWARVES?
NO, THORI, WE'VE HAMMERS TO BUILD!
VERY MANY HAMMERS!
THORS AND THEIR HAMMERS.
I GET IT NOW.
I'LL MISS THE FLYING, TOO.

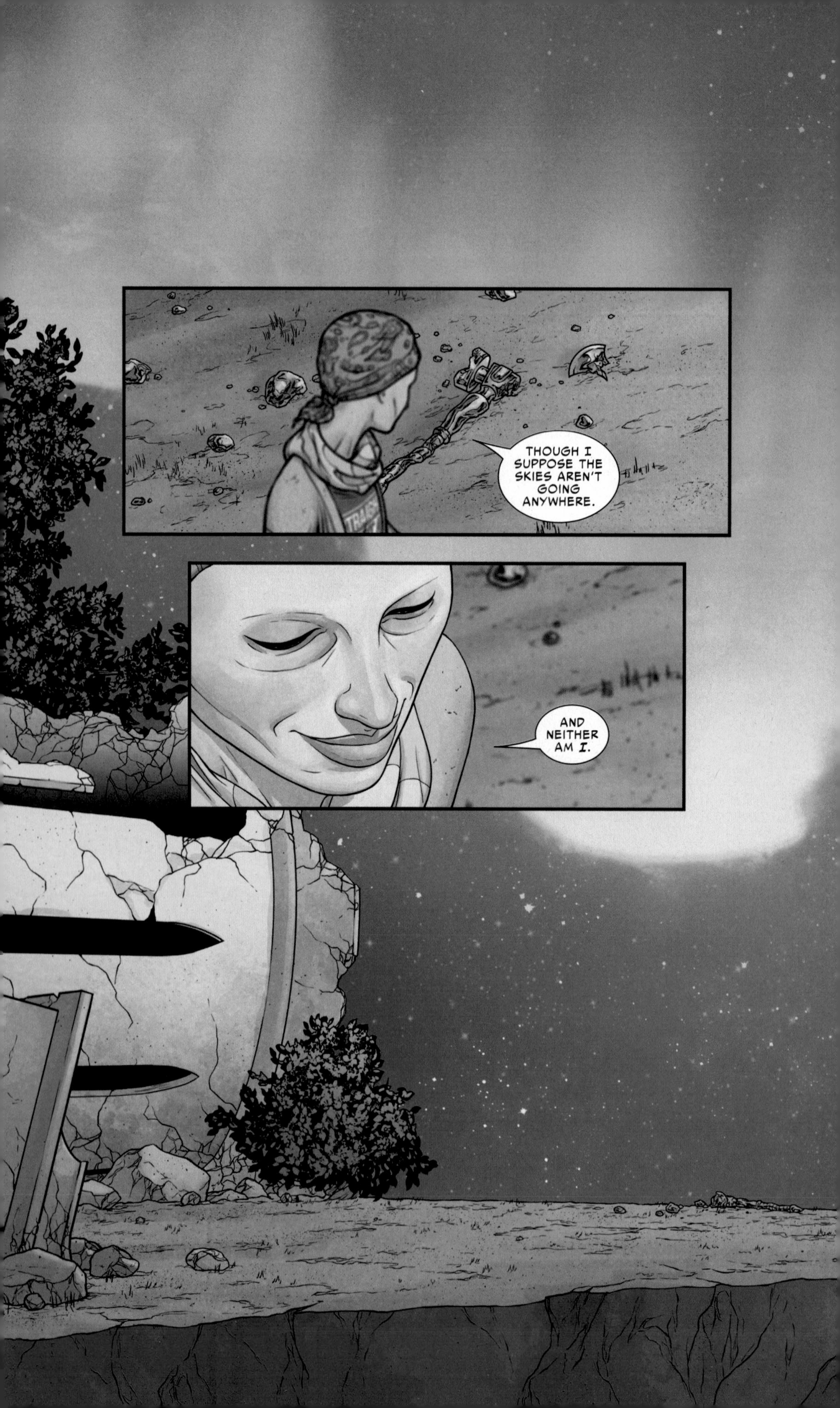
THOUGH I SUPPOSE THE SKIES AREN'T GOING ANYWHERE.
AND NEITHER AM *I*.

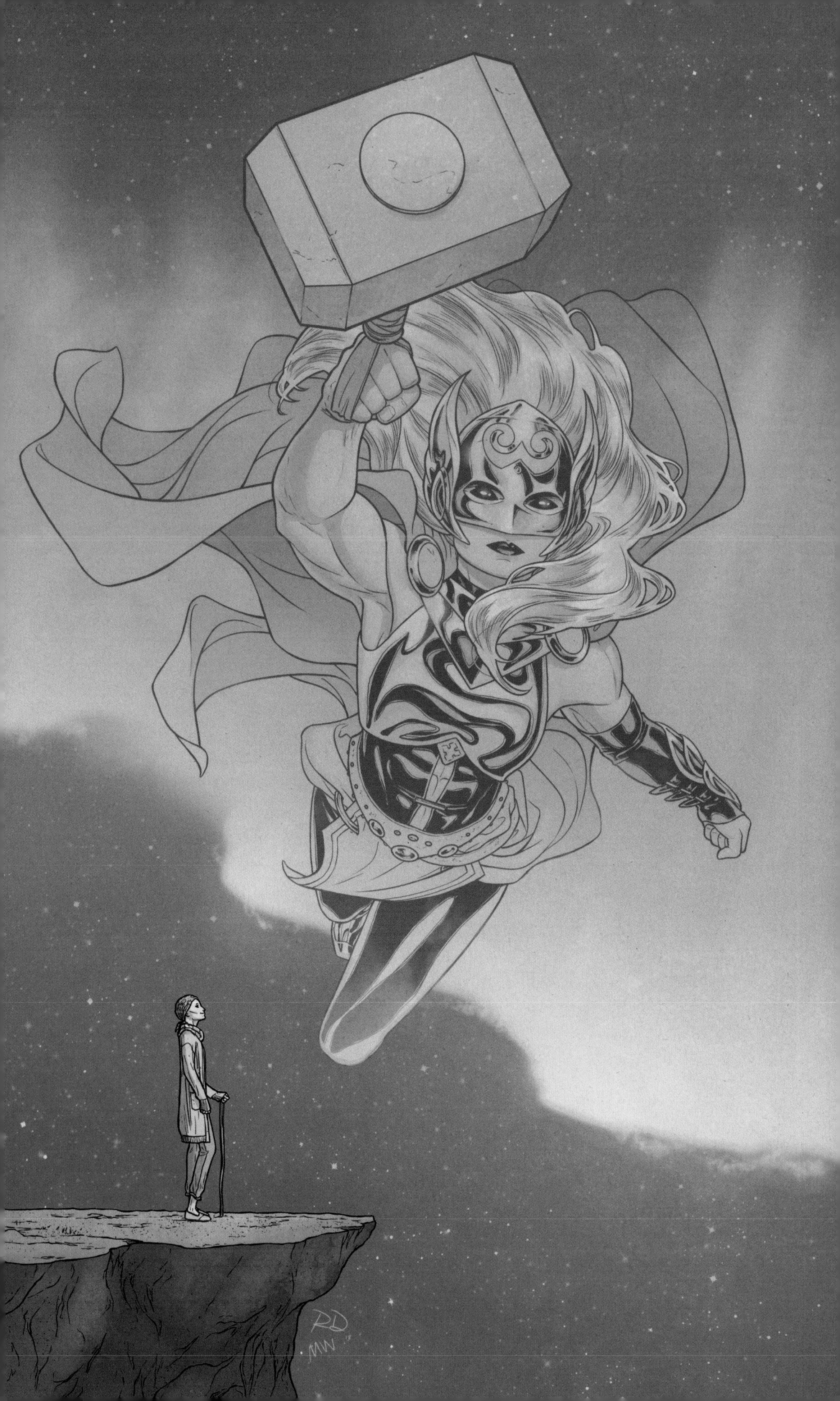

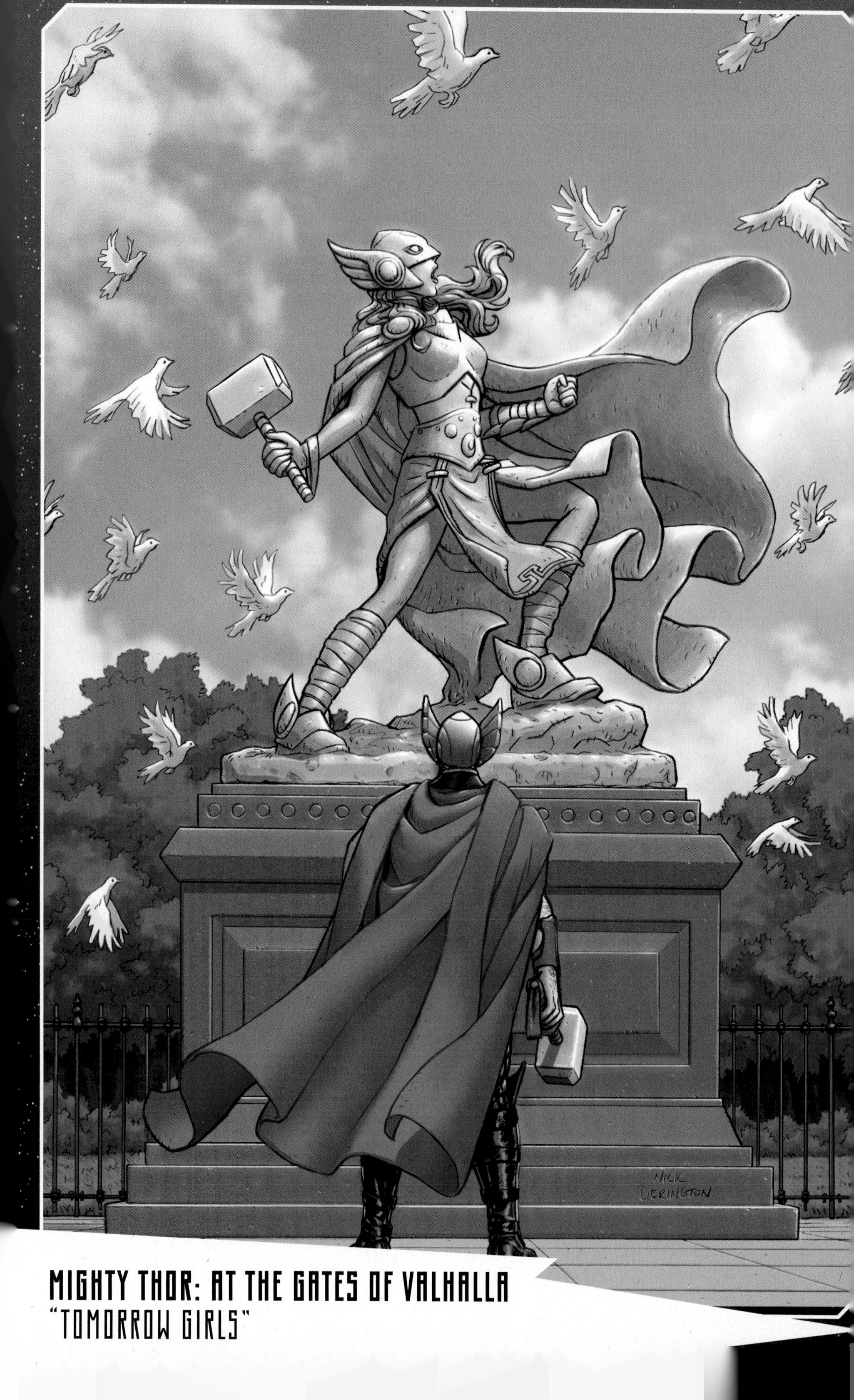
NICK
DERINGTON

MIGHTY THOR: AT THE GATES OF VALHALLA
"TOMORROW GIRLS"

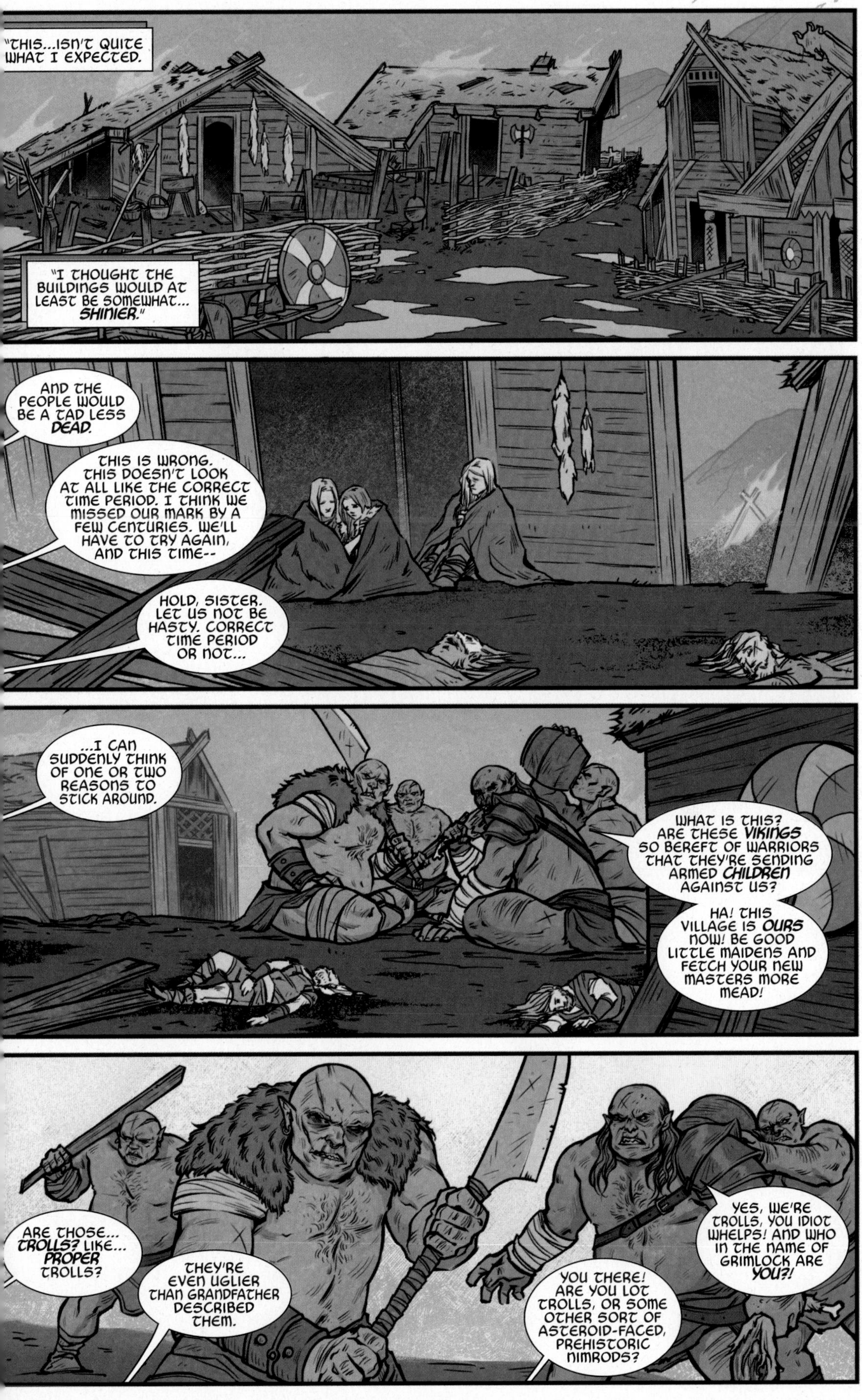
"THIS...ISN'T QUITE WHAT I EXPECTED.
"I THOUGHT THE BUILDINGS WOULD AT LEAST BE SOMEWHAT... SHINIER."
AND THE PEOPLE WOULD BE A TAD LESS DEAD.
THIS IS WRONG. THIS DOESN'T LOOK AT ALL LIKE THE CORRECT TIME PERIOD. I THINK WE MISSED OUR MARK BY A FEW CENTURIES. WE'LL HAVE TO TRY AGAIN, AND THIS TIME--
HOLD, SISTER. LET US NOT BE HASTY. CORRECT TIME PERIOD OR NOT...
...I CAN SUDDENLY THINK OF ONE OR TWO REASONS TO STICK AROUND.
WHAT IS THIS? ARE THESE VIKINGS SO BEREFT OF WARRIORS THAT THEY'RE SENDING ARMED CHILDREN AGAINST US?
HA! THIS VILLAGE IS OURS NOW! BE GOOD LITTLE MAIDENS AND FETCH YOUR NEW MASTERS MORE MEAD!
ARE THOSE... TROLLS? LIKE... PROPER TROLLS?
THEY'RE EVEN UGLIER THAN GRANDFATHER DESCRIBED THEM.
YOU THERE! ARE YOU LOT TROLLS, OR SOME OTHER SORT OF ASTEROID-FACED, PREHISTORIC NIMRODS?
YES, WE'RE TROLLS, YOU IDIOT WHELPS! AND WHO IN THE NAME OF GRIMLOCK ARE YOU?!

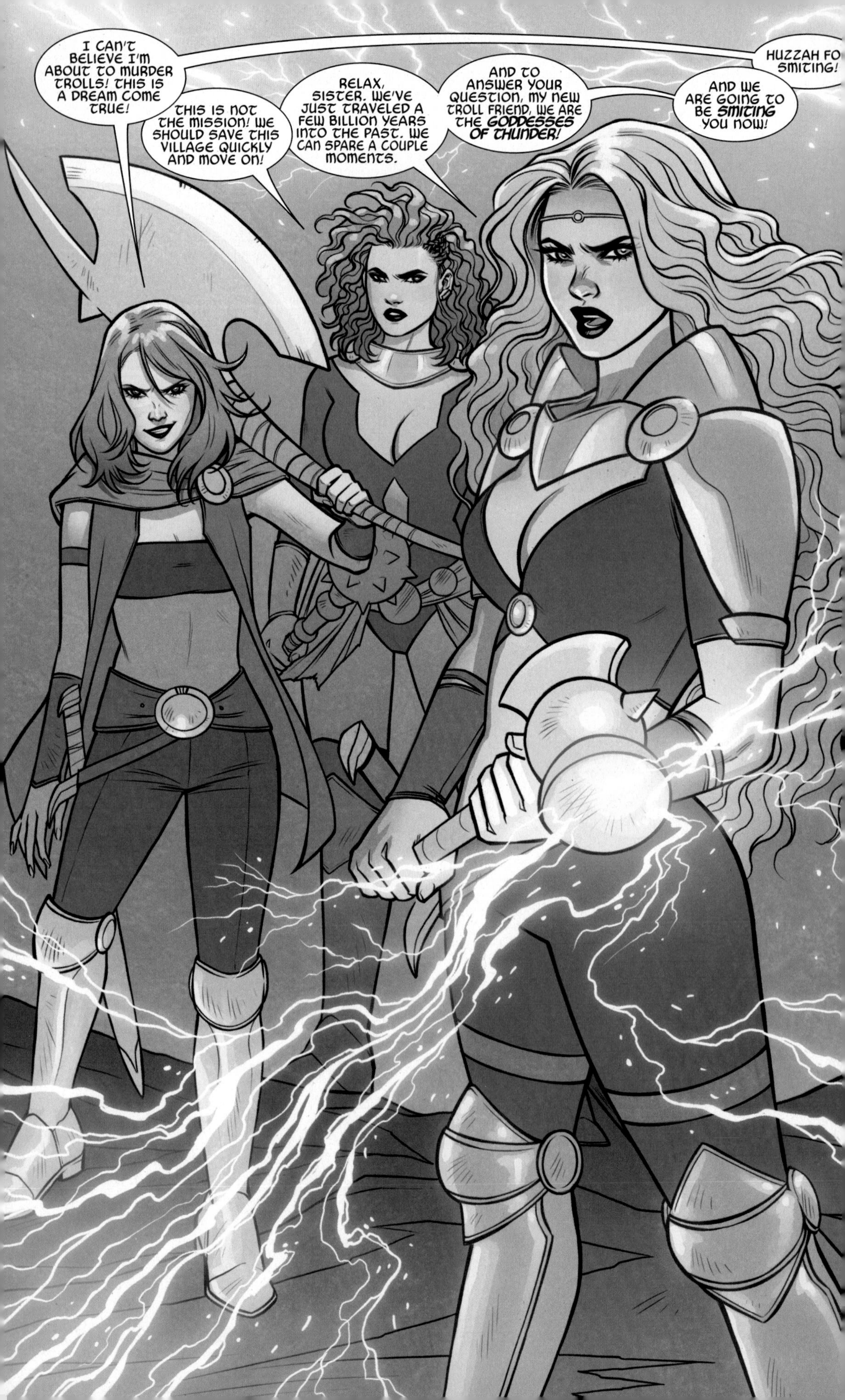
I CAN'T BELIEVE I'M ABOUT TO MURDER TROLLS! THIS IS A DREAM COME TRUE!
THIS IS NOT THE MISSION! WE SHOULD SAVE THIS VILLAGE QUICKLY AND MOVE ON!
RELAX, SISTER. WE'VE JUST TRAVELED A FEW BILLION YEARS INTO THE PAST. WE CAN SPARE A COUPLE MOMENTS.
AND TO ANSWER YOUR QUESTION, MY NEW TROLL FRIEND, WE ARE THE GODDESSES OF THUNDER!
AND WE ARE GOING TO BE SMITING YOU NOW!
HUZZAH FO SMITING!

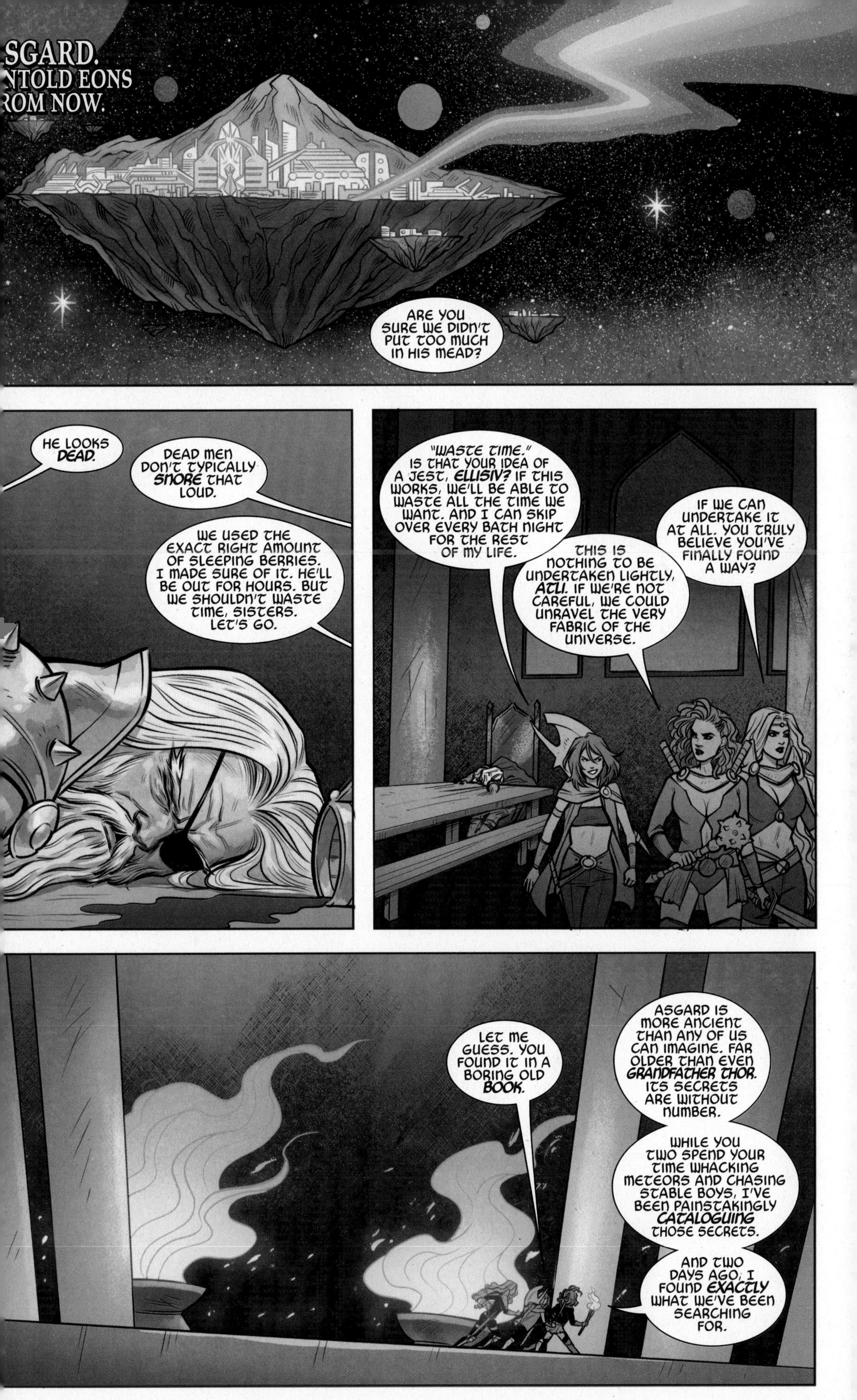

SGARD.
NTOLD EONS
ROM NOW.
ARE YOU SURE WE DIDN'T PUT TOO MUCH IN HIS MEAD?
HE LOOKS DEAD.
DEAD MEN DON'T TYPICALLY SNORE THAT LOUD.
WE USED THE EXACT RIGHT AMOUNT OF SLEEPING BERRIES. I MADE SURE OF IT. HE'LL BE OUT FOR HOURS. BUT WE SHOULDN'T WASTE TIME, SISTERS. LET'S GO.
"WASTE TIME." IS THAT YOUR IDEA OF A JEST, ELLISIV? IF THIS WORKS, WE'LL BE ABLE TO WASTE ALL THE TIME WE WANT. AND I CAN SKIP OVER EVERY BATH NIGHT FOR THE REST OF MY LIFE.
THIS IS NOTHING TO BE UNDERTAKEN LIGHTLY, ATLI. IF WE'RE NOT CAREFUL, WE COULD UNRAVEL THE VERY FABRIC OF THE UNIVERSE.
IF WE CAN UNDERTAKE IT AT ALL. YOU TRULY BELIEVE YOU'VE FINALLY FOUND A WAY?
LET ME GUESS. YOU FOUND IT IN A BORING OLD BOOK.
ASGARD IS MORE ANCIENT THAN ANY OF US CAN IMAGINE. FAR OLDER THAN EVEN GRANDFATHER THOR. ITS SECRETS ARE WITHOUT NUMBER.
WHILE YOU TWO SPEND YOUR TIME WHACKING METEORS AND CHASING STABLE BOYS, I'VE BEEN PAINSTAKINGLY CATALOGUING THOSE SECRETS.
AND TWO DAYS AGO, I FOUND EXACTLY WHAT WE'VE BEEN SEARCHING FOR.

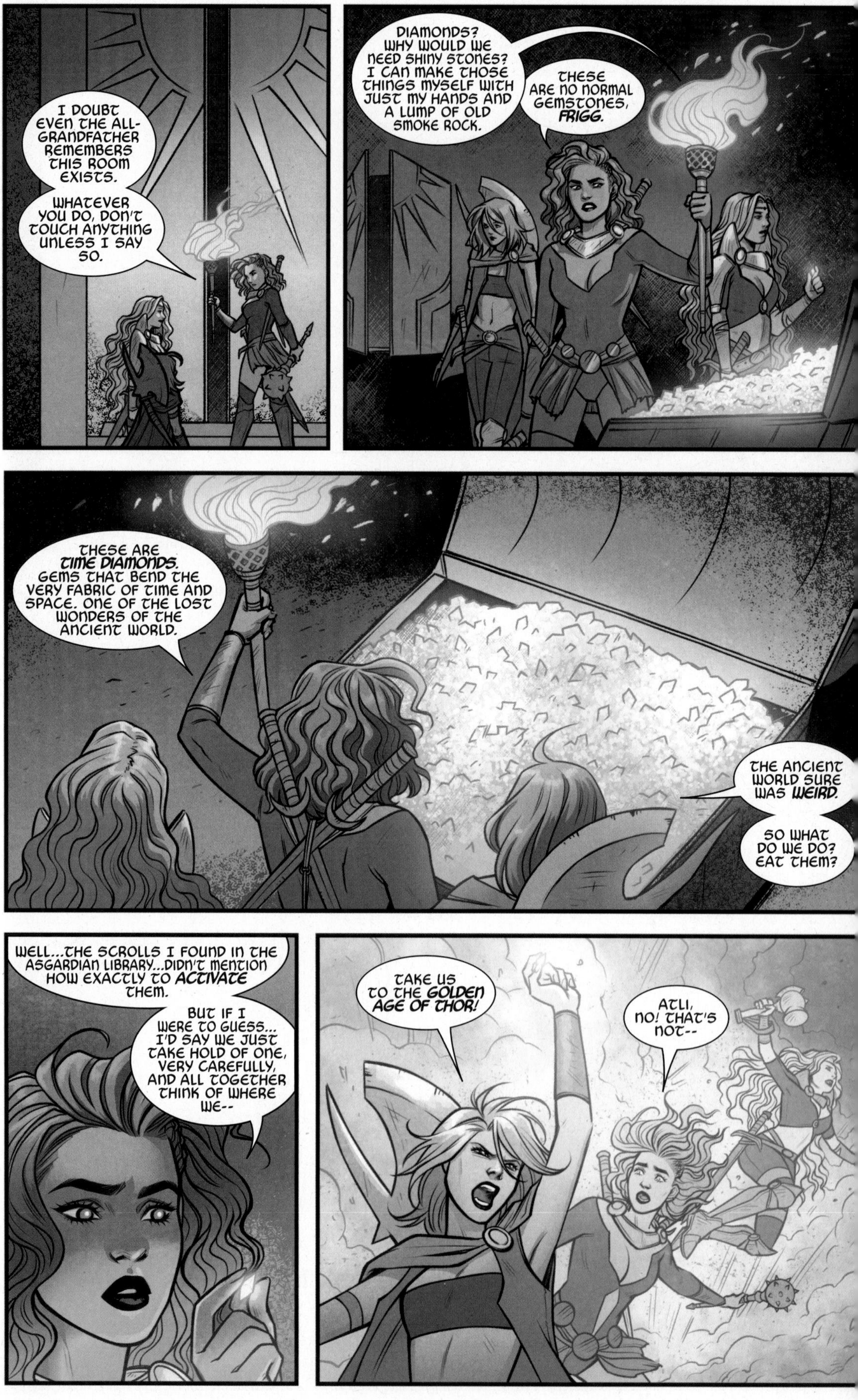
I DOUBT EVEN THE ALL-GRANDFATHER REMEMBERS THIS ROOM EXISTS.
WHATEVER YOU DO, DON'T TOUCH ANYTHING UNLESS I SAY SO.
DIAMONDS? WHY WOULD WE NEED SHINY STONES? I CAN MAKE THOSE THINGS MYSELF WITH JUST MY HANDS AND A LUMP OF OLD SMOKE ROCK.
THESE ARE NO NORMAL GEMSTONES, FRIGG.
THESE ARE TIME DIAMONDS. GEMS THAT BEND THE VERY FABRIC OF TIME AND SPACE. ONE OF THE LOST WONDERS OF THE ANCIENT WORLD.
THE ANCIENT WORLD SURE WAS WEIRD.
SO WHAT DO WE DO? EAT THEM?
WELL...THE SCROLLS I FOUND IN THE ASGARDIAN LIBRARY...DIDN'T MENTION HOW EXACTLY TO ACTIVATE THEM.
BUT IF I WERE TO GUESS... I'D SAY WE JUST TAKE HOLD OF ONE, VERY CAREFULLY, AND ALL TOGETHER THINK OF WHERE WE--
TAKE US TO THE GOLDEN AGE OF THOR!
ATLI, NO! THAT'S NOT--

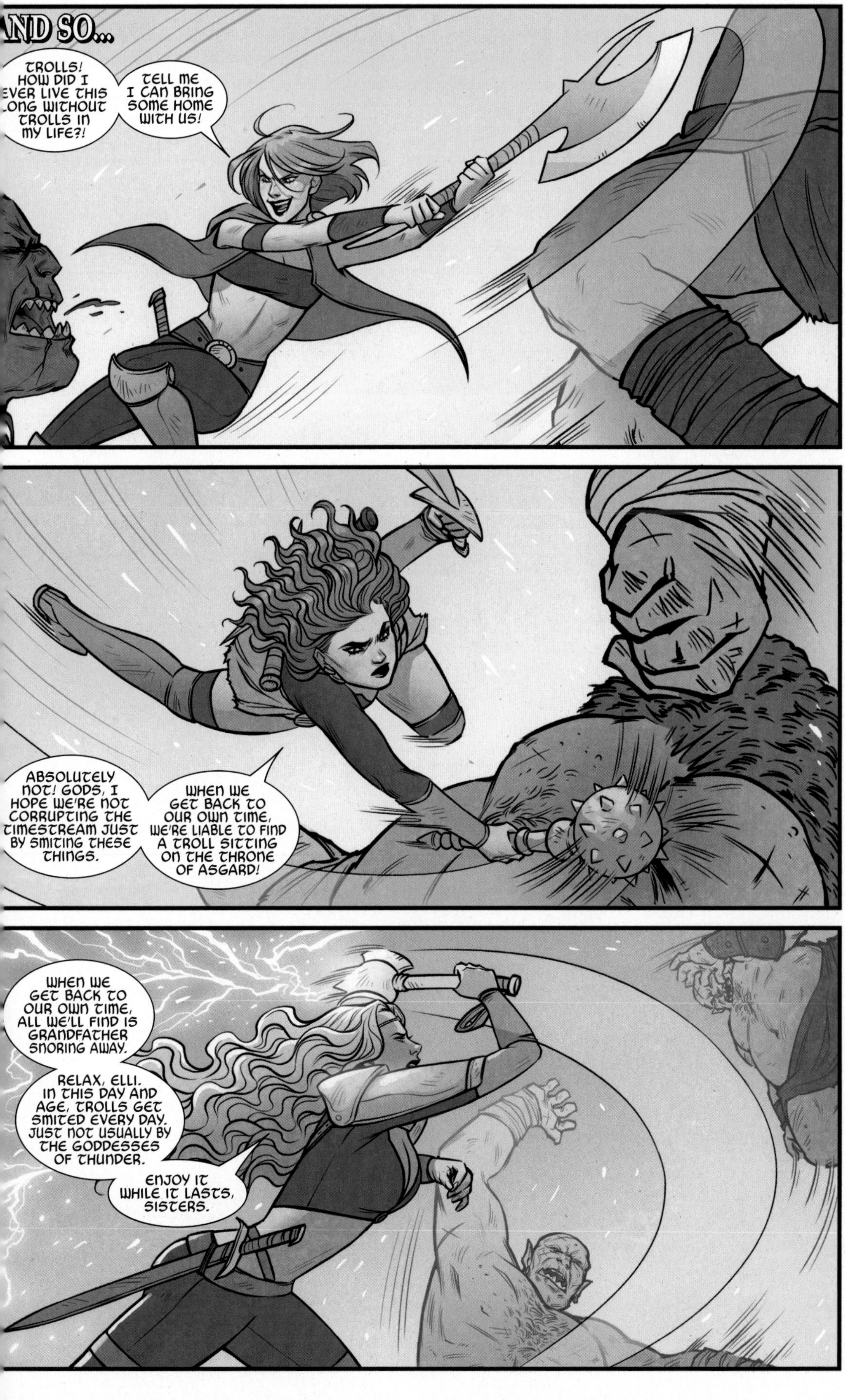
AND SO...
TROLLS! HOW DID I EVER LIVE THIS LONG WITHOUT TROLLS IN MY LIFE?!
TELL ME I CAN BRING SOME HOME WITH US!
ABSOLUTELY NOT! GODS, I HOPE WE'RE NOT CORRUPTING THE TIMESTREAM JUST BY SMITING THESE THINGS.
WHEN WE GET BACK TO OUR OWN TIME, WE'RE LIABLE TO FIND A TROLL SITTING ON THE THRONE OF ASGARD!
WHEN WE GET BACK TO OUR OWN TIME, ALL WE'LL FIND IS GRANDFATHER SNORING AWAY.
RELAX, ELLI. IN THIS DAY AND AGE, TROLLS GET SMITED EVERY DAY. JUST NOT USUALLY BY THE GODDESSES OF THUNDER.
ENJOY IT WHILE IT LASTS, SISTERS.

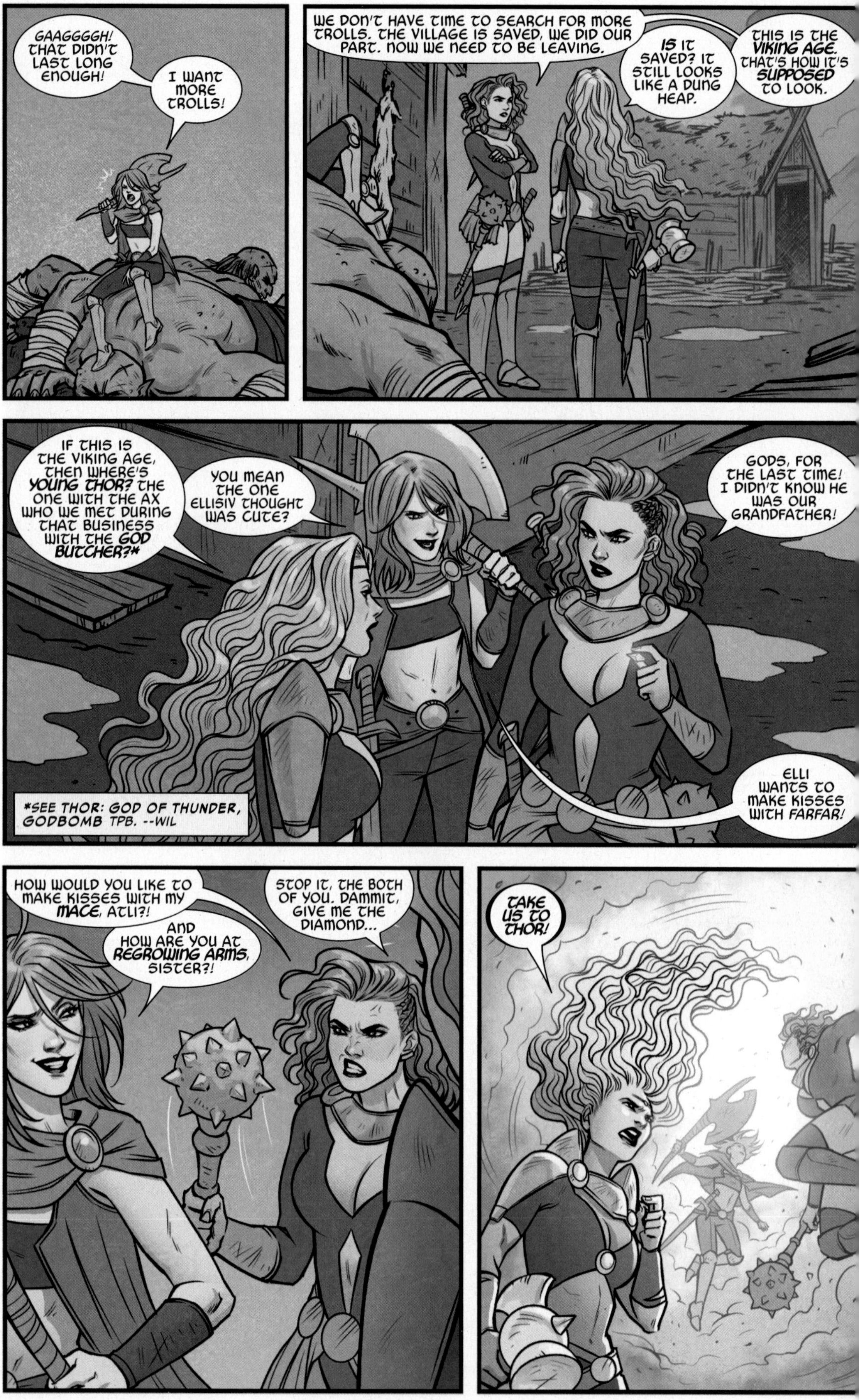
GAAGGGGH! THAT DIDN'T LAST LONG ENOUGH!
I WANT MORE TROLLS!
WE DON'T HAVE TIME TO SEARCH FOR MORE TROLLS. THE VILLAGE IS SAVED, WE DID OUR PART. NOW WE NEED TO BE LEAVING.
IS IT SAVED? IT STILL LOOKS LIKE A DUNG HEAP.
THIS IS THE VIKING AGE. THAT'S HOW IT'S SUPPOSED TO LOOK.
IF THIS IS THE VIKING AGE, THEN WHERE'S YOUNG THOR? THE ONE WITH THE AX WHO WE MET DURING THAT BUSINESS WITH THE GOD BUTCHER?*
YOU MEAN THE ONE ELLISIV THOUGHT WAS CUTE?
GODS, FOR THE LAST TIME! I DIDN'T KNOW HE WAS OUR GRANDFATHER!
*SEE THOR: GOD OF THUNDER, GODBOMB TPB. --WIL
ELLI WANTS TO MAKE KISSES WITH FARFAR!
HOW WOULD YOU LIKE TO MAKE KISSES WITH MY MACE, ATLI?!
AND HOW ARE YOU AT REGROWING ARMS, SISTER?!
STOP IT, THE BOTH OF YOU. DAMMIT, GIVE ME THE DIAMOND...
TAKE US TO THOR!

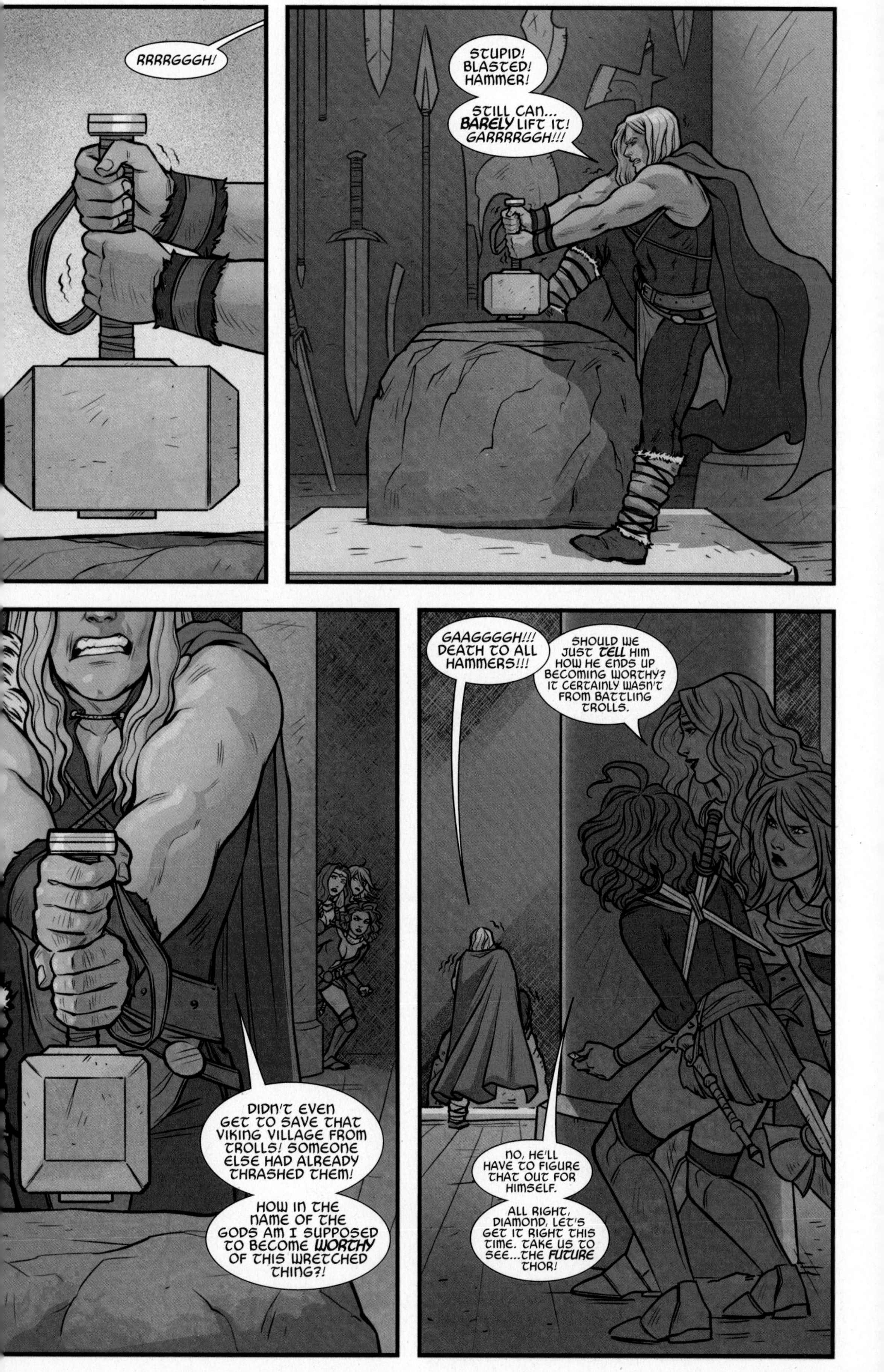

RRRRGGGH!
STUPID! BLASTED! HAMMER!
STILL CAN... BARELY LIFT IT! GARRRRGGH!!!
DIDN'T EVEN GET TO SAVE THAT VIKING VILLAGE FROM TROLLS! SOMEONE ELSE HAD ALREADY THRASHED THEM!
HOW IN THE NAME OF THE GODS AM I SUPPOSED TO BECOME WORTHY OF THIS WRETCHED THING?!
GAAGGGGH!!! DEATH TO ALL HAMMERS!!!
SHOULD WE JUST TELL HIM HOW HE ENDS UP BECOMING WORTHY? IT CERTAINLY WASN'T FROM BATTLING TROLLS.
NO, HE'LL HAVE TO FIGURE THAT OUT FOR HIMSELF.
ALL RIGHT, DIAMOND, LET'S GET IT RIGHT THIS TIME. TAKE US TO SEE...THE FUTURE THOR!

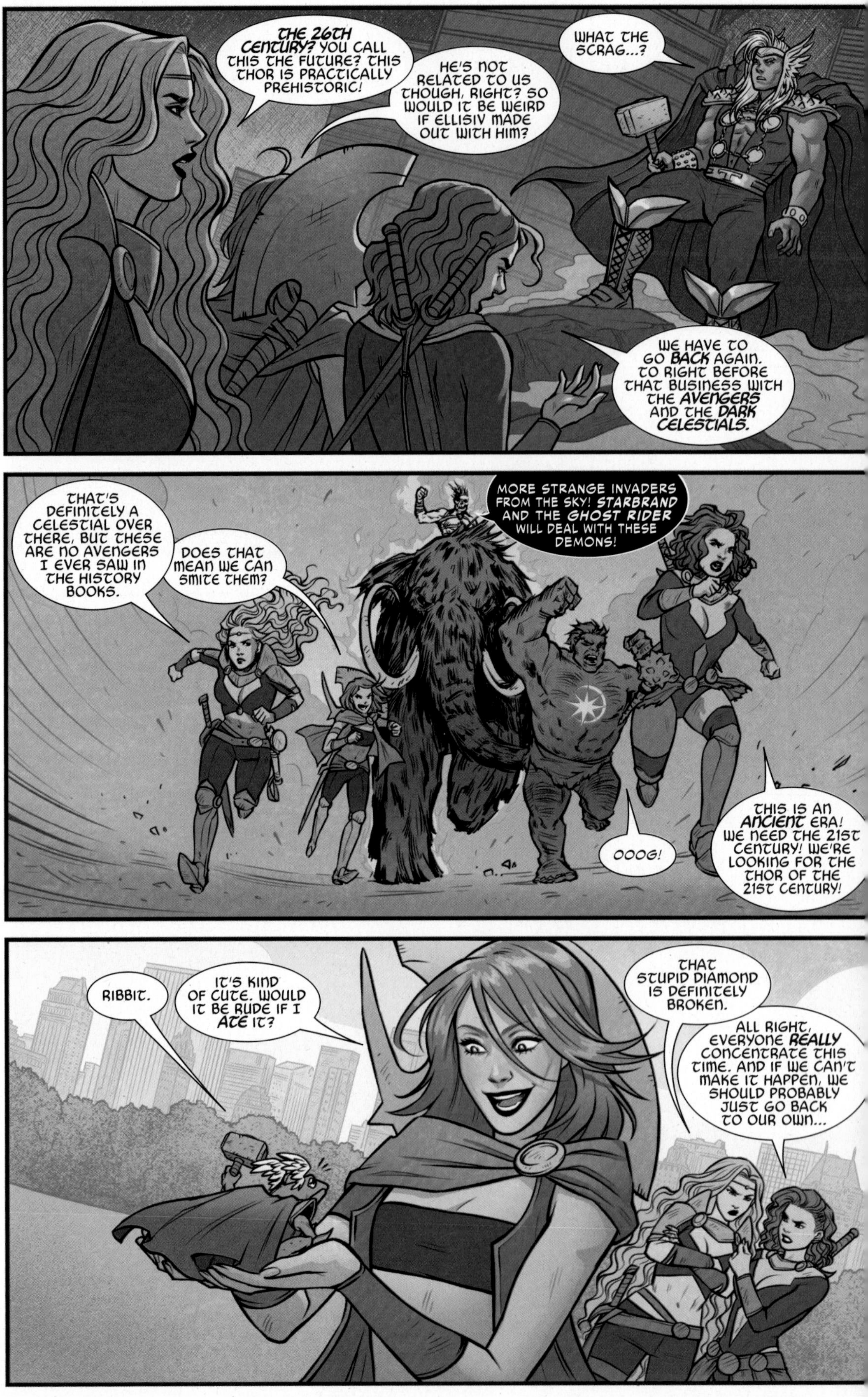
THE 26TH CENTURY? YOU CALL THIS THE FUTURE? THIS THOR IS PRACTICALLY PREHISTORIC!
HE'S NOT RELATED TO US THOUGH, RIGHT? SO WOULD IT BE WEIRD IF ELLISIV MADE OUT WITH HIM?
WHAT THE SCRAG...?
WE HAVE TO GO BACK AGAIN. TO RIGHT BEFORE THAT BUSINESS WITH THE AVENGERS AND THE DARK CELESTIALS.
THAT'S DEFINITELY A CELESTIAL OVER THERE, BUT THESE ARE NO AVENGERS I EVER SAW IN THE HISTORY BOOKS.
DOES THAT MEAN WE CAN SMITE THEM?
MORE STRANGE INVADERS FROM THE SKY! STARBRAND AND THE GHOST RIDER WILL DEAL WITH THESE DEMONS!
OOOG!
THIS IS AN ANCIENT ERA! WE NEED THE 21ST CENTURY! WE'RE LOOKING FOR THE THOR OF THE 21ST CENTURY!
RIBBIT.
IT'S KIND OF CUTE. WOULD IT BE RUDE IF I ATE IT?
THAT STUPID DIAMOND IS DEFINITELY BROKEN.
ALL RIGHT, EVERYONE REALLY CONCENTRATE THIS TIME. AND IF WE CAN'T MAKE IT HAPPEN, WE SHOULD PROBABLY JUST GO BACK TO OUR OWN...

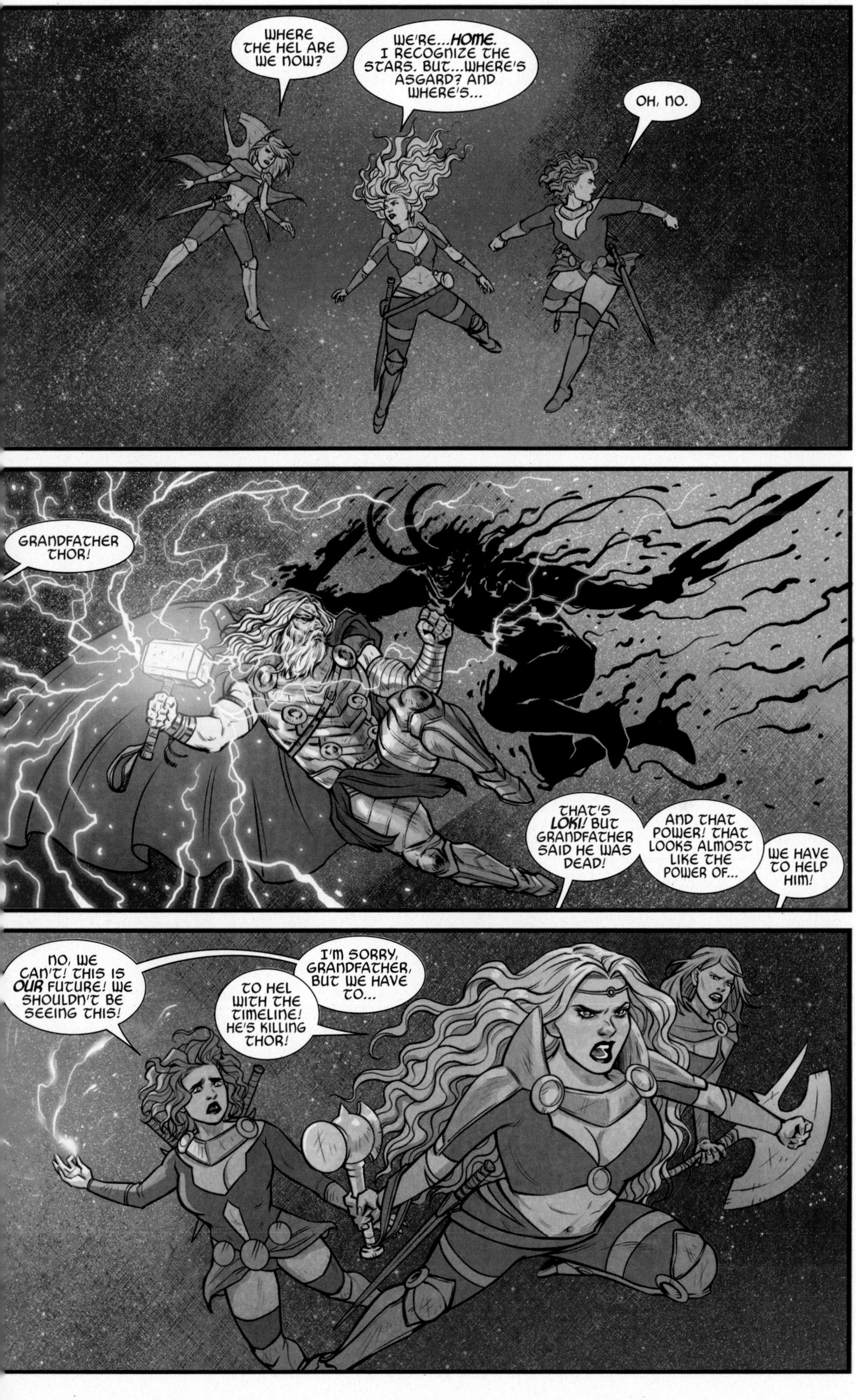
WHERE THE HEL ARE WE NOW?
WE'RE...HOME. I RECOGNIZE THE STARS. BUT...WHERE'S ASGARD? AND WHERE'S...
OH, NO.
GRANDFATHER THOR!
THAT'S LOKI! BUT GRANDFATHER SAID HE WAS DEAD!
AND THAT POWER! THAT LOOKS ALMOST LIKE THE POWER OF...
WE HAVE TO HELP HIM!
NO, WE CAN'T! THIS IS OUR FUTURE! WE SHOULDN'T BE SEEING THIS!
I'M SORRY, GRANDFATHER, BUT WE HAVE TO...
TO HEL WITH THE TIMELINE! HE'S KILLING THOR!

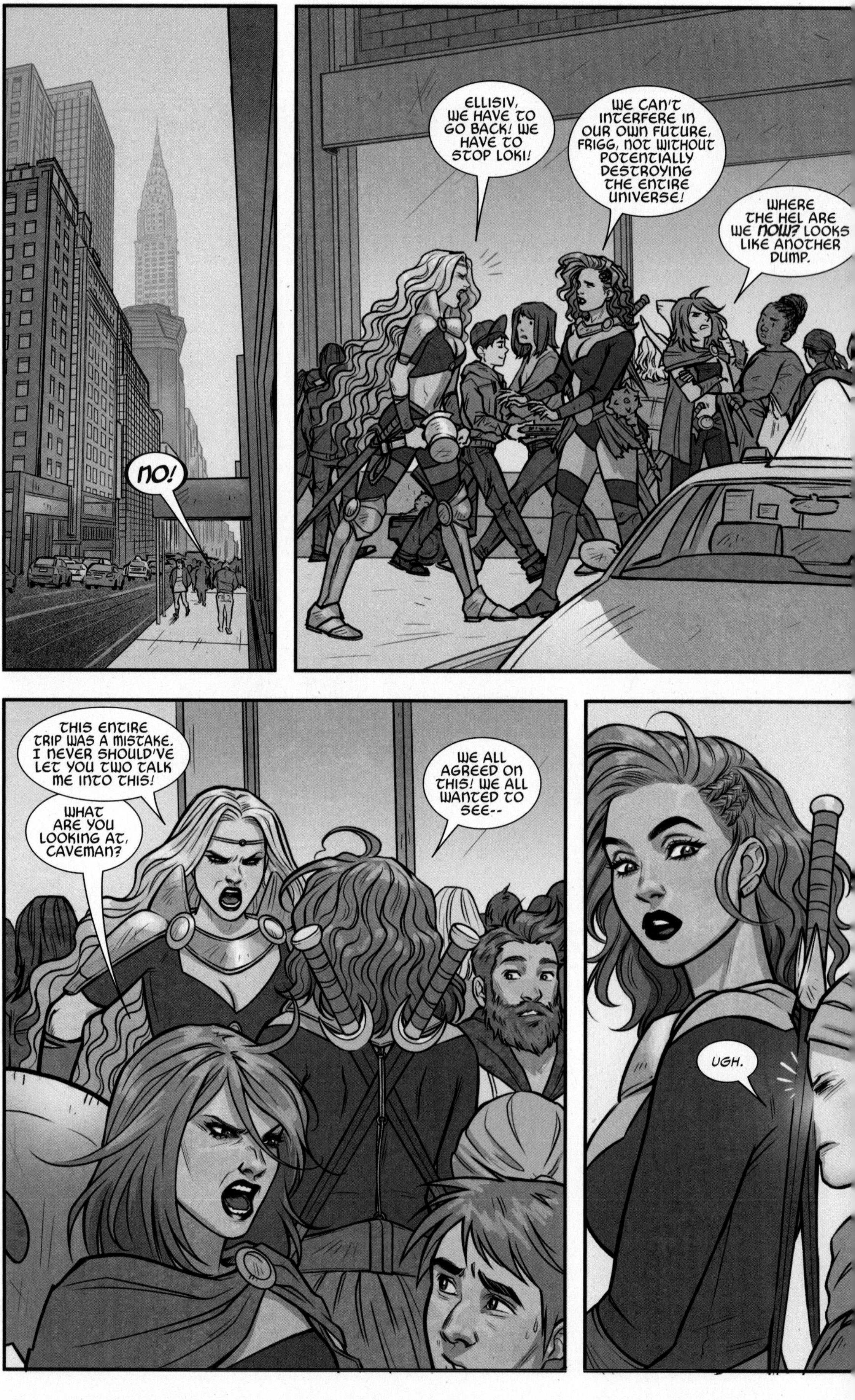
NO!
ELLISIV, WE HAVE TO GO BACK! WE HAVE TO STOP LOKI!
WE CAN'T INTERFERE IN OUR OWN FUTURE, FRIGG, NOT WITHOUT POTENTIALLY DESTROYING THE ENTIRE UNIVERSE!
WHERE THE HEL ARE WE NOW? LOOKS LIKE ANOTHER DUMP.
THIS ENTIRE TRIP WAS A MISTAKE. I NEVER SHOULD'VE LET YOU TWO TALK ME INTO THIS!
WHAT ARE YOU LOOKING AT, CAVEMAN?
WE ALL AGREED ON THIS! WE ALL WANTED TO SEE--
UGH.

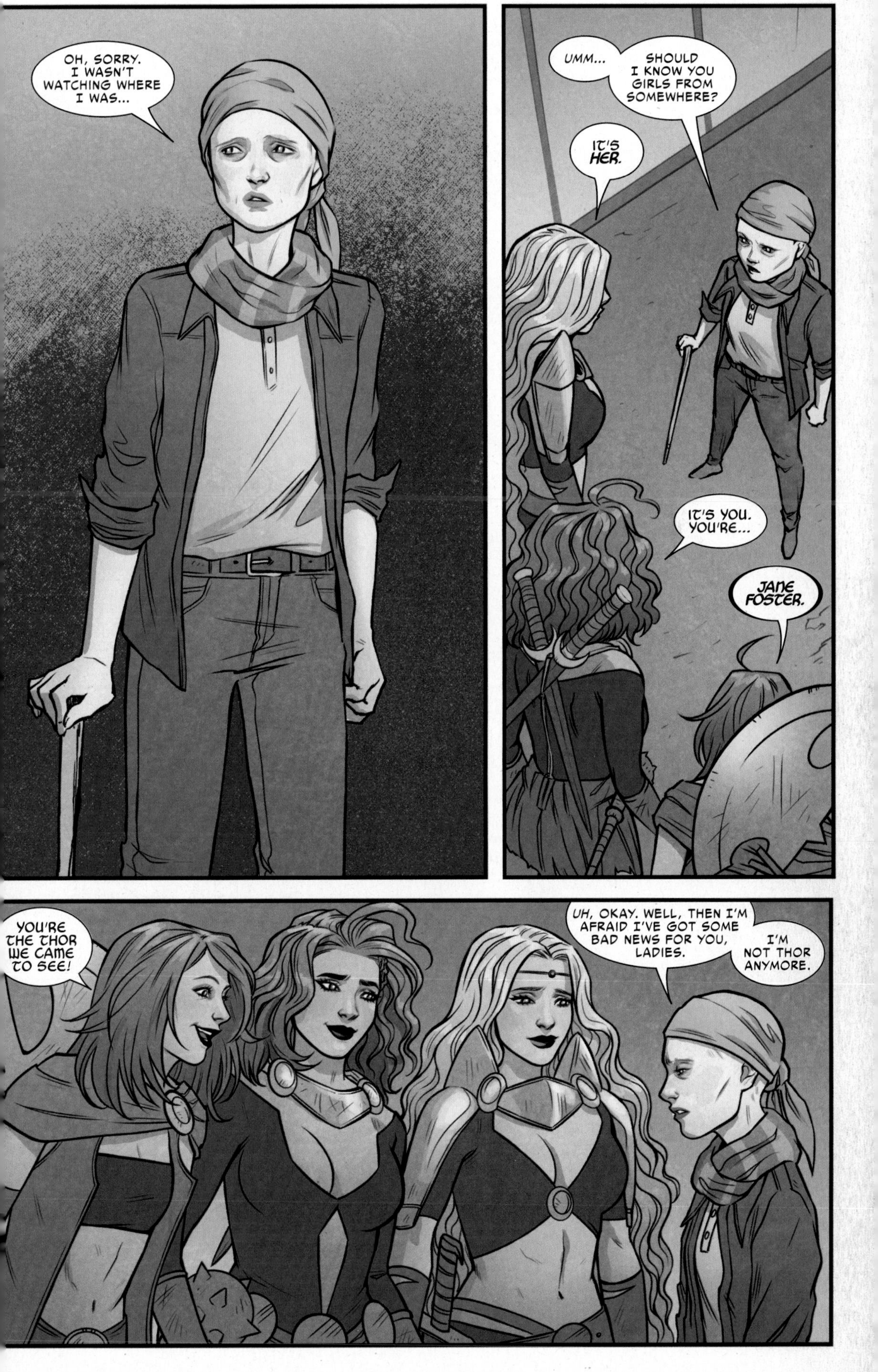
OH, SORRY. I WASN'T WATCHING WHERE I WAS...
UMM...
SHOULD I KNOW YOU GIRLS FROM SOMEWHERE?
IT'S HER.
IT'S YOU. YOU'RE...
JANE FOSTER.
YOU'RE THE THOR WE CAME TO SEE!
UH, OKAY. WELL, THEN I'M AFRAID I'VE GOT SOME BAD NEWS FOR YOU, LADIES.
I'M NOT THOR ANYMORE.

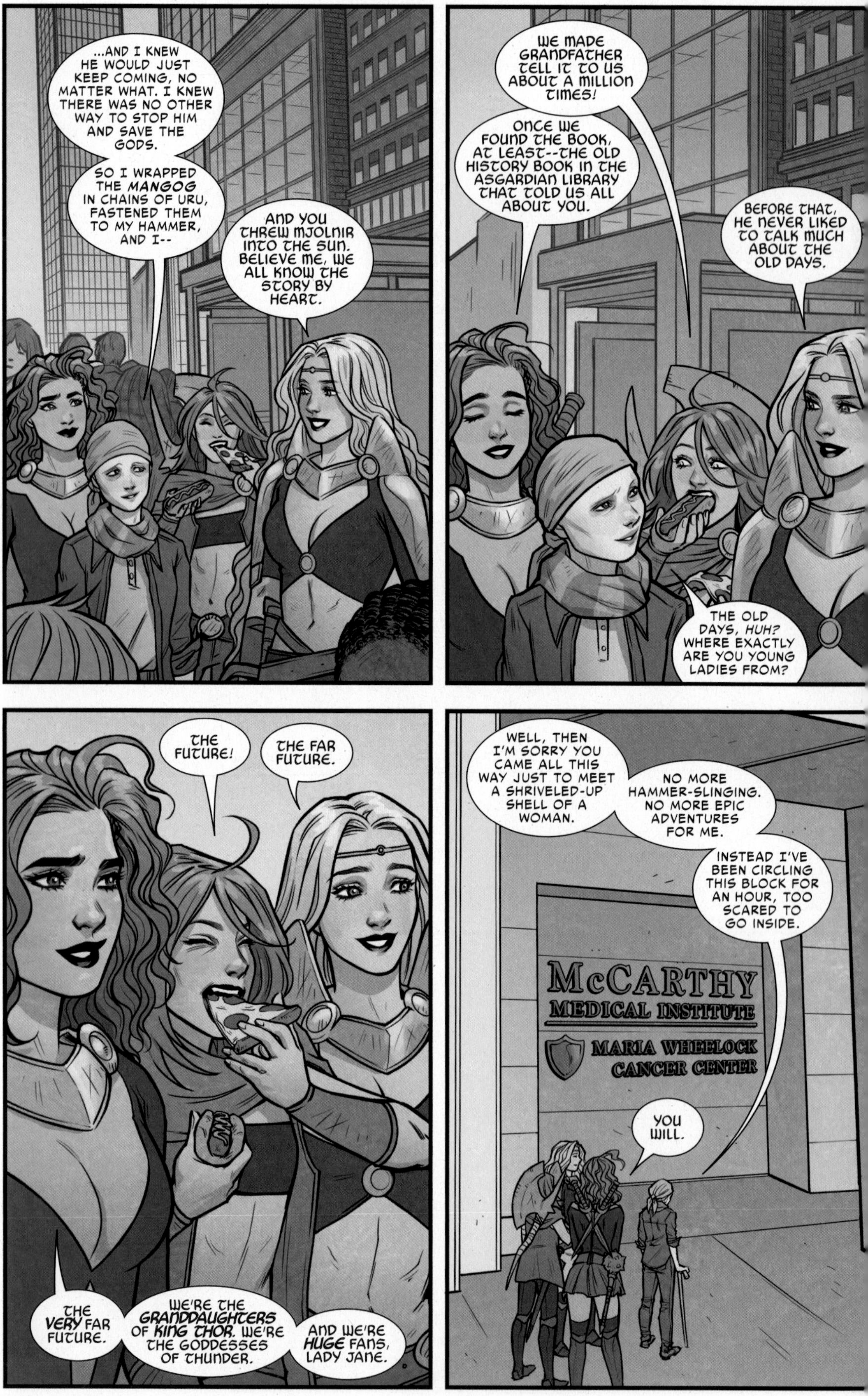
...AND I KNEW HE WOULD JUST KEEP COMING, NO MATTER WHAT. I KNEW THERE WAS NO OTHER WAY TO STOP HIM AND SAVE THE GODS.
SO I WRAPPED THE *MANGOG* IN CHAINS OF URU, FASTENED THEM TO MY HAMMER, AND I--
AND YOU THREW MJOLNIR INTO THE SUN. BELIEVE ME, WE ALL KNOW THE STORY BY HEART.
WE MADE GRANDFATHER TELL IT TO US ABOUT A MILLION TIMES!
ONCE WE FOUND THE BOOK, AT LEAST--THE OLD HISTORY BOOK IN THE ASGARDIAN LIBRARY THAT TOLD US ALL ABOUT YOU.
BEFORE THAT, HE NEVER LIKED TO TALK MUCH ABOUT THE OLD DAYS.
THE OLD DAYS, *HUH?* WHERE EXACTLY ARE YOU YOUNG LADIES FROM?
THE FUTURE!
THE FAR FUTURE.
THE *VERY* FAR FUTURE.
WE'RE THE *GRANDDAUGHTERS* OF *KING THOR.* WE'RE THE GODDESSES OF THUNDER.
AND WE'RE *HUGE* FANS, LADY JANE.
WELL, THEN I'M SORRY YOU CAME ALL THIS WAY JUST TO MEET A SHRIVELED-UP SHELL OF A WOMAN.
NO MORE HAMMER-SLINGING. NO MORE EPIC ADVENTURES FOR ME.
INSTEAD I'VE BEEN CIRCLING THIS BLOCK FOR AN HOUR, TOO SCARED TO GO INSIDE.
McCARTHY MEDICAL INSTITUTE
MARIA WHEELOCK CANCER CENTER
YOU WILL.

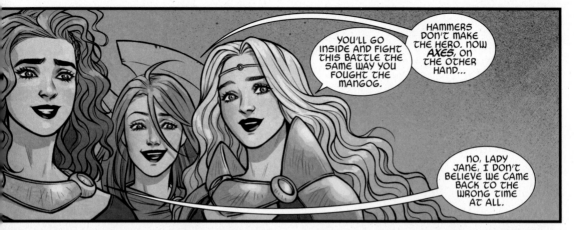

HAMMERS DON'T MAKE THE HERO. NOW *AXES*, ON THE OTHER HAND...

YOU'LL GO INSIDE AND FIGHT THIS BATTLE THE SAME WAY YOU FOUGHT THE MANGOG.

NO, LADY JANE, I DON'T BELIEVE WE CAME BACK TO THE WRONG TIME AT ALL.

I THINK YOU'RE *EXACTLY* THE WOMAN WE WANTED TO MEET.

THANK YOU, LADIES.

THANK *YOU*. WE LEARNED HOW TO BE GODDESSES OF THUNDER BY READING ABOUT YOU.

IS IT TRUE WHAT THEY SAY YOU DID TO THE KING OF THE FROST GIANTS?

IS IT TRUE YOU PUNCHED ODIN THROUGH THREE PLANETS WHEN YOU GUYS FOUGHT?

SHHH, SHE HASN'T DONE THAT YET.

I DON'T WANNA KNOW ABOUT THE FUTURE, GIRLS.

I'VE GOT MY HANDS FULL WITH *TODAY*.

BUT BEFORE I TAKE THIS NEXT STEP, HOW ABOUT YOU THUNDER GODDESSES DO ME JUST *ONE* LITTLE FAVOR?

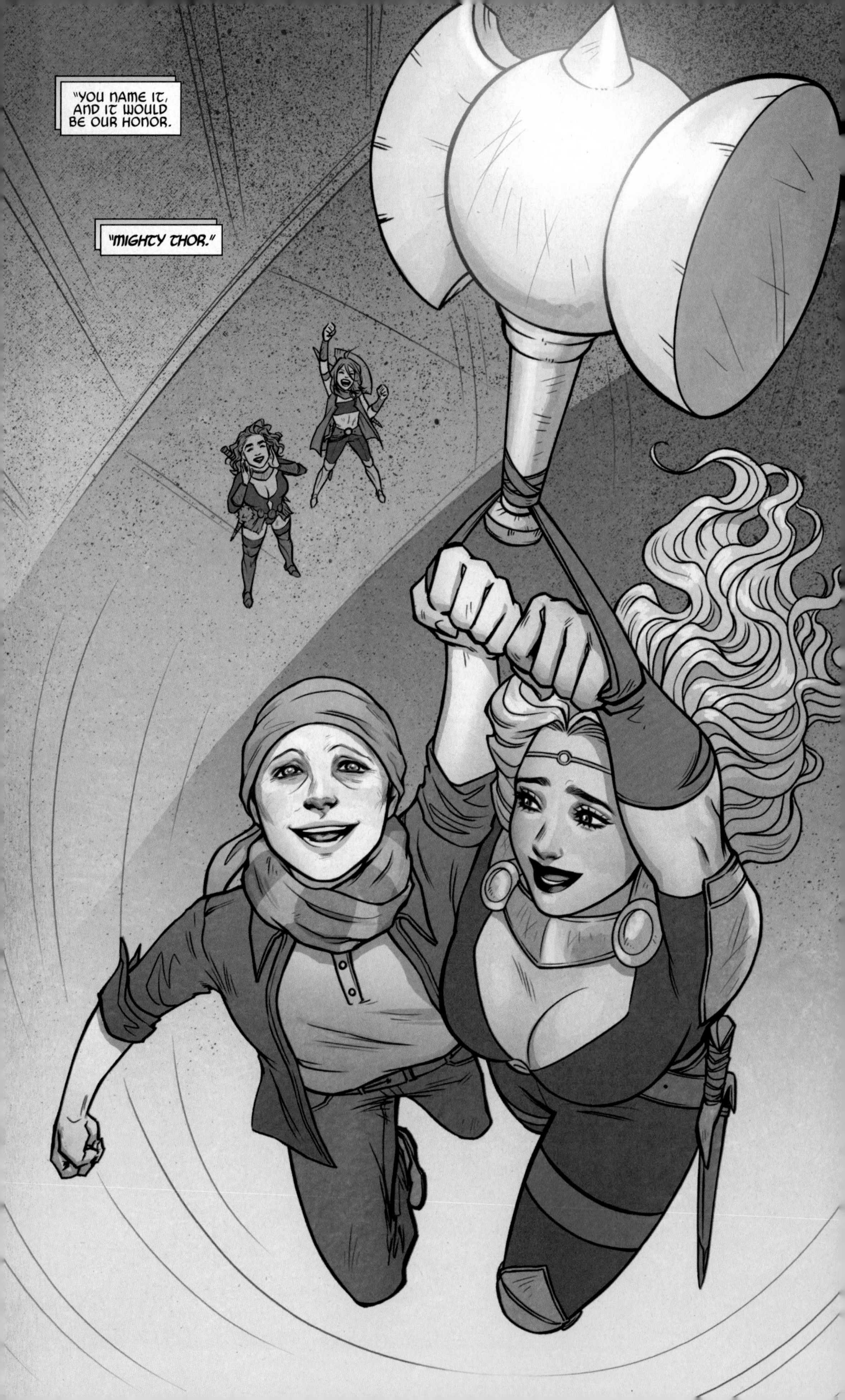
"YOU NAME IT, AND IT WOULD BE OUR HONOR.
"MIGHTY THOR."

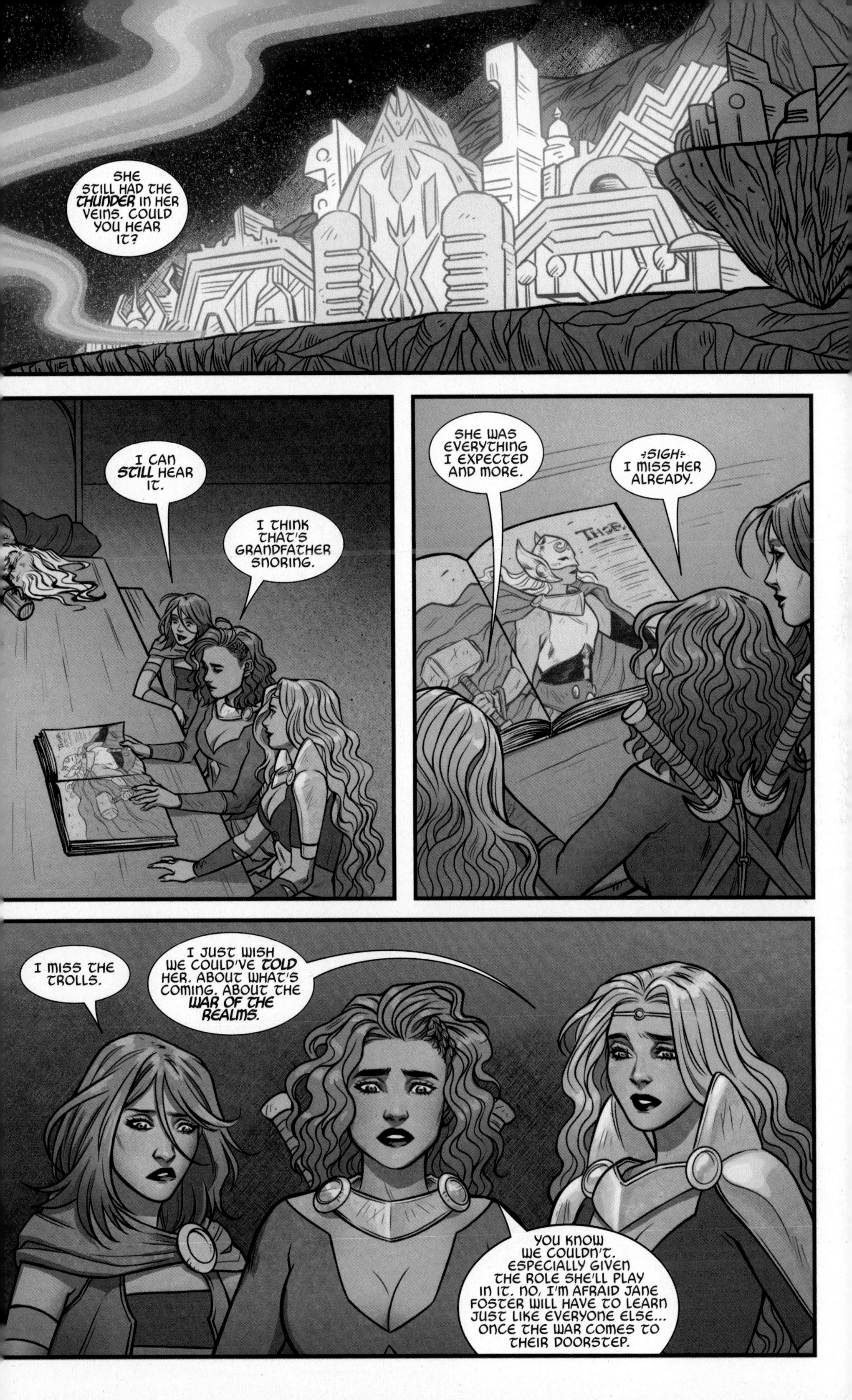
SHE STILL HAD THE THUNDER IN HER VEINS. COULD YOU HEAR IT?
I CAN STILL HEAR IT.
I THINK THAT'S GRANDFATHER SNORING.
SHE WAS EVERYTHING I EXPECTED AND MORE.
-SIGH- I MISS HER ALREADY.
I MISS THE TROLLS.
I JUST WISH WE COULD'VE TOLD HER. ABOUT WHAT'S COMING. ABOUT THE WAR OF THE REALMS.
YOU KNOW WE COULDN'T. ESPECIALLY GIVEN THE ROLE SHE'LL PLAY IN IT. NO, I'M AFRAID JANE FOSTER WILL HAVE TO LEARN JUST LIKE EVERYONE ELSE... ONCE THE WAR COMES TO THEIR DOORSTEP.

Malekith the Accursed has been defeated, his armies driven from Midgard and his allies scattered. Thor has been named the new All-Father. The War of the Realms is over. Now its major players must contend with what's left behind.

Jane Foster took up the hammer of the War Thor and helped turn the tide of the war. But after one last mighty blow, the hammer broke apart — and attached itself to Jane. The former goddess of thunder...is about to become something else entirely.

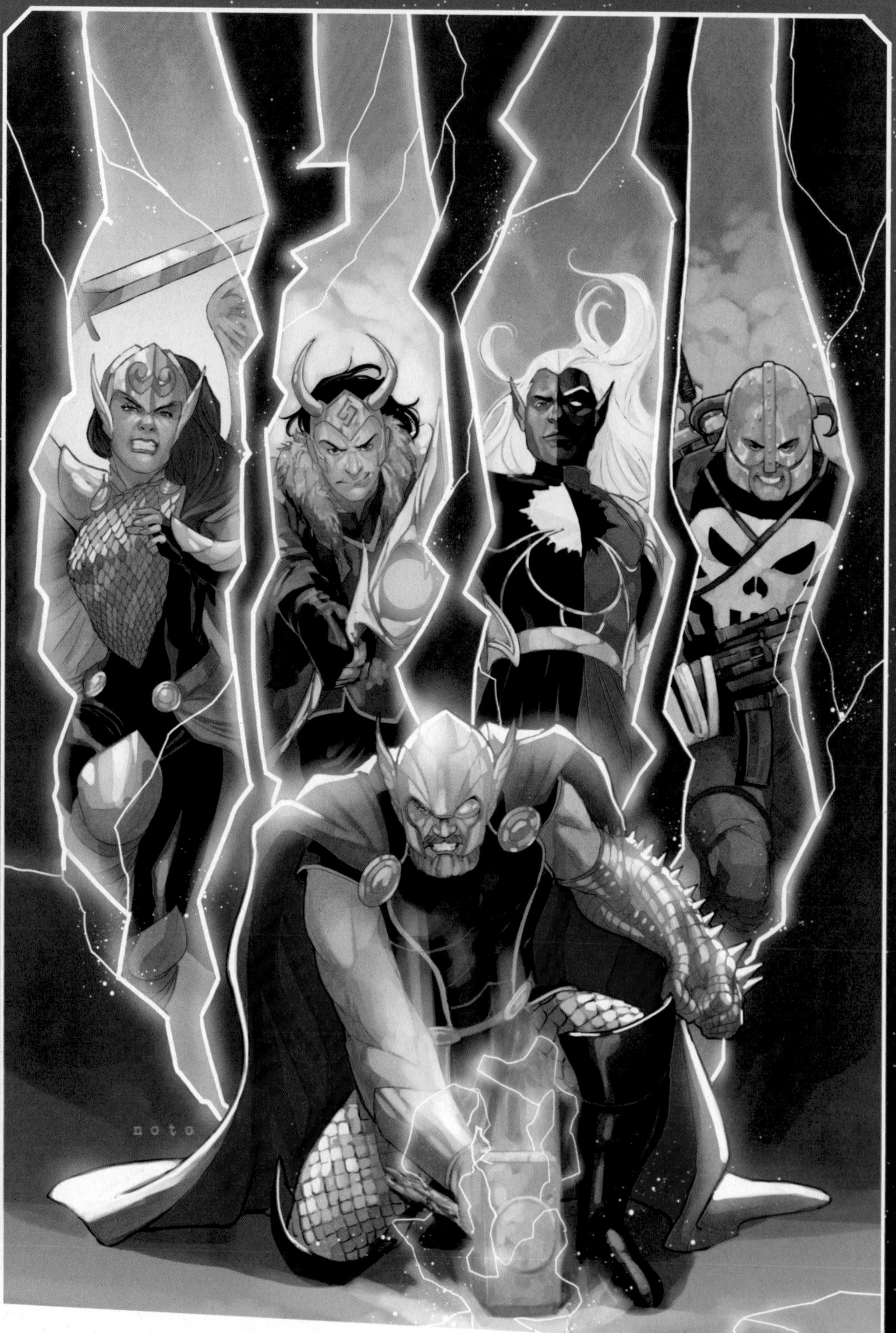
noto

WAR OF THE REALMS OMEGA
"GOD AND THE DEVIL WALK INTO A CHURCH"

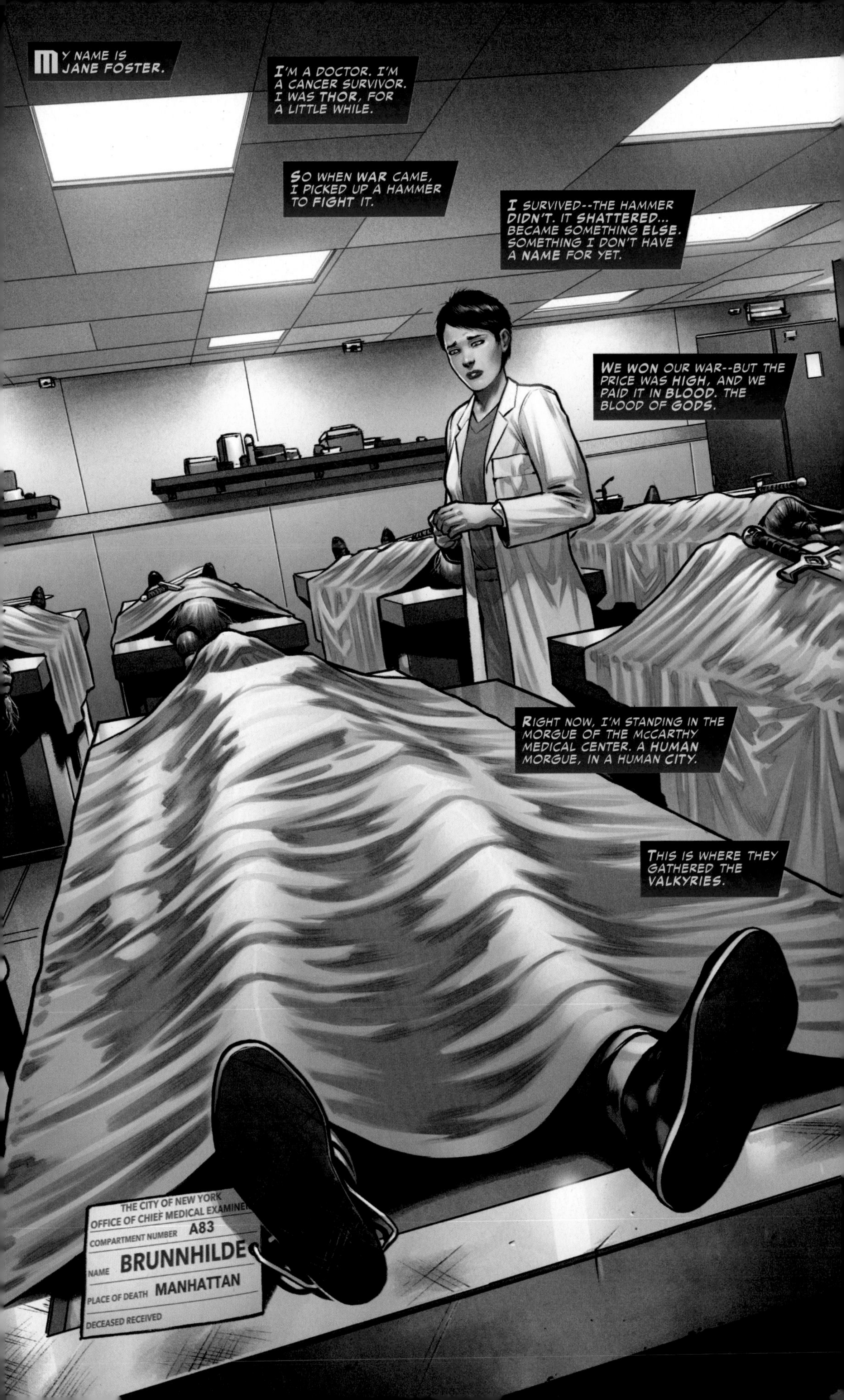
MY NAME IS JANE FOSTER.
I'M A DOCTOR. I'M A CANCER SURVIVOR. I WAS THOR, FOR A LITTLE WHILE.
SO WHEN WAR CAME, I PICKED UP A HAMMER TO FIGHT IT.
I SURVIVED--THE HAMMER DIDN'T. IT SHATTERED... BECAME SOMETHING ELSE. SOMETHING I DON'T HAVE A NAME FOR YET.
WE WON OUR WAR--BUT THE PRICE WAS HIGH, AND WE PAID IT IN BLOOD. THE BLOOD OF GODS.
RIGHT NOW, I'M STANDING IN THE MORGUE OF THE McCARTHY MEDICAL CENTER. A HUMAN MORGUE, IN A HUMAN CITY.
THIS IS WHERE THEY GATHERED THE VALKYRIES.
THE CITY OF NEW YORK
OFFICE OF CHIEF MEDICAL EXAMINER
COMPARTMENT NUMBER A83
NAME BRUNNHILDE
PLACE OF DEATH MANHATTAN
DECEASED RECEIVED

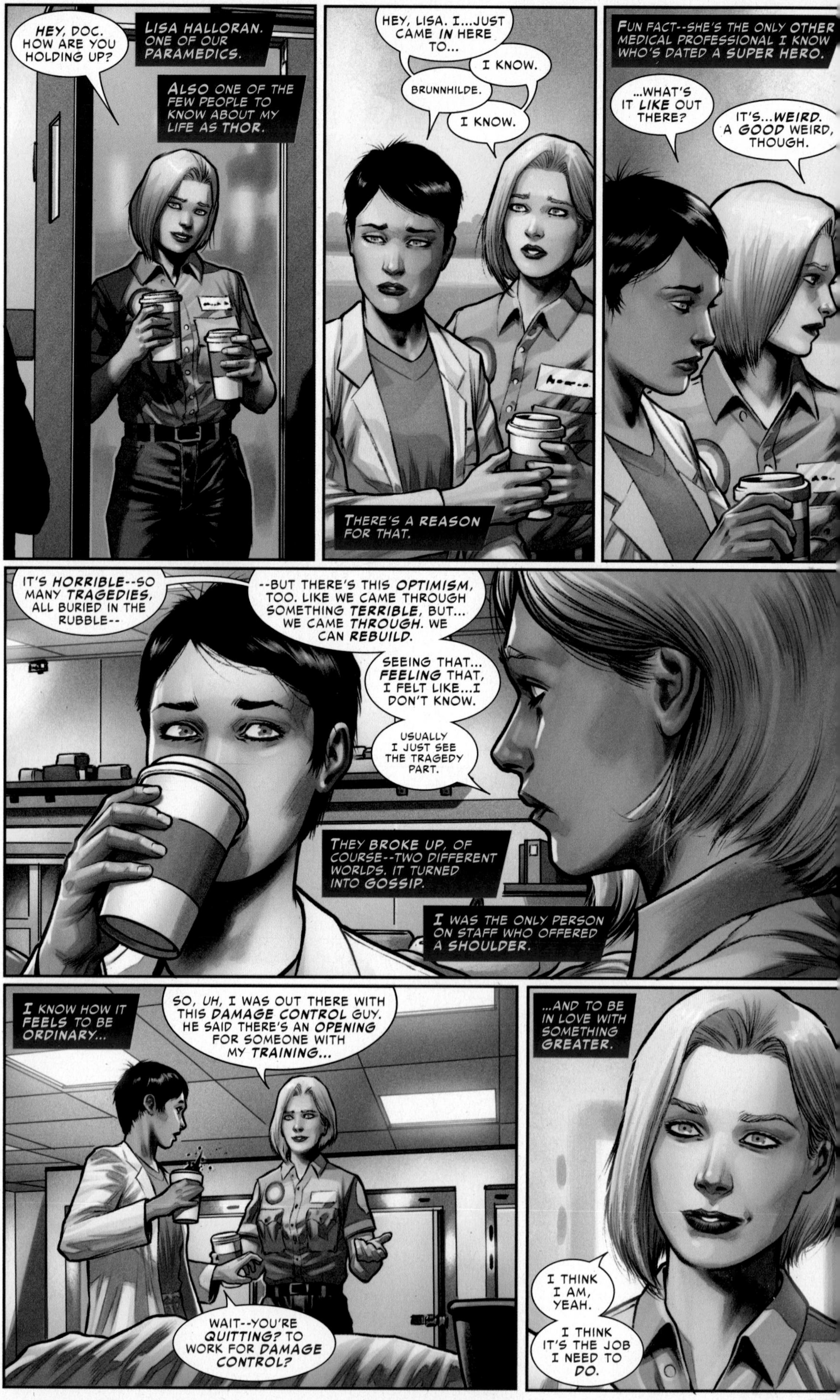
HEY, DOC. HOW ARE YOU HOLDING UP?
LISA HALLORAN. ONE OF OUR PARAMEDICS.
ALSO ONE OF THE FEW PEOPLE TO KNOW ABOUT MY LIFE AS THOR.
HEY, LISA. I...JUST CAME IN HERE TO...
I KNOW.
BRUNNHILDE.
I KNOW.
THERE'S A REASON FOR THAT.
FUN FACT--SHE'S THE ONLY OTHER MEDICAL PROFESSIONAL I KNOW WHO'S DATED A SUPER HERO.
...WHAT'S IT LIKE OUT THERE?
IT'S...WEIRD. A GOOD WEIRD, THOUGH.
IT'S HORRIBLE--SO MANY TRAGEDIES, ALL BURIED IN THE RUBBLE--
--BUT THERE'S THIS OPTIMISM, TOO. LIKE WE CAME THROUGH SOMETHING TERRIBLE, BUT... WE CAME THROUGH. WE CAN REBUILD.
SEEING THAT... FEELING THAT, I FELT LIKE...I DON'T KNOW.
USUALLY I JUST SEE THE TRAGEDY PART.
THEY BROKE UP, OF COURSE--TWO DIFFERENT WORLDS. IT TURNED INTO GOSSIP.
I WAS THE ONLY PERSON ON STAFF WHO OFFERED A SHOULDER.
I KNOW HOW IT FEELS TO BE ORDINARY...
SO, UH, I WAS OUT THERE WITH THIS DAMAGE CONTROL GUY. HE SAID THERE'S AN OPENING FOR SOMEONE WITH MY TRAINING...
WAIT--YOU'RE QUITTING? TO WORK FOR DAMAGE CONTROL?
...AND TO BE IN LOVE WITH SOMETHING GREATER.
I THINK I AM, YEAH.
I THINK IT'S THE JOB I NEED TO DO.

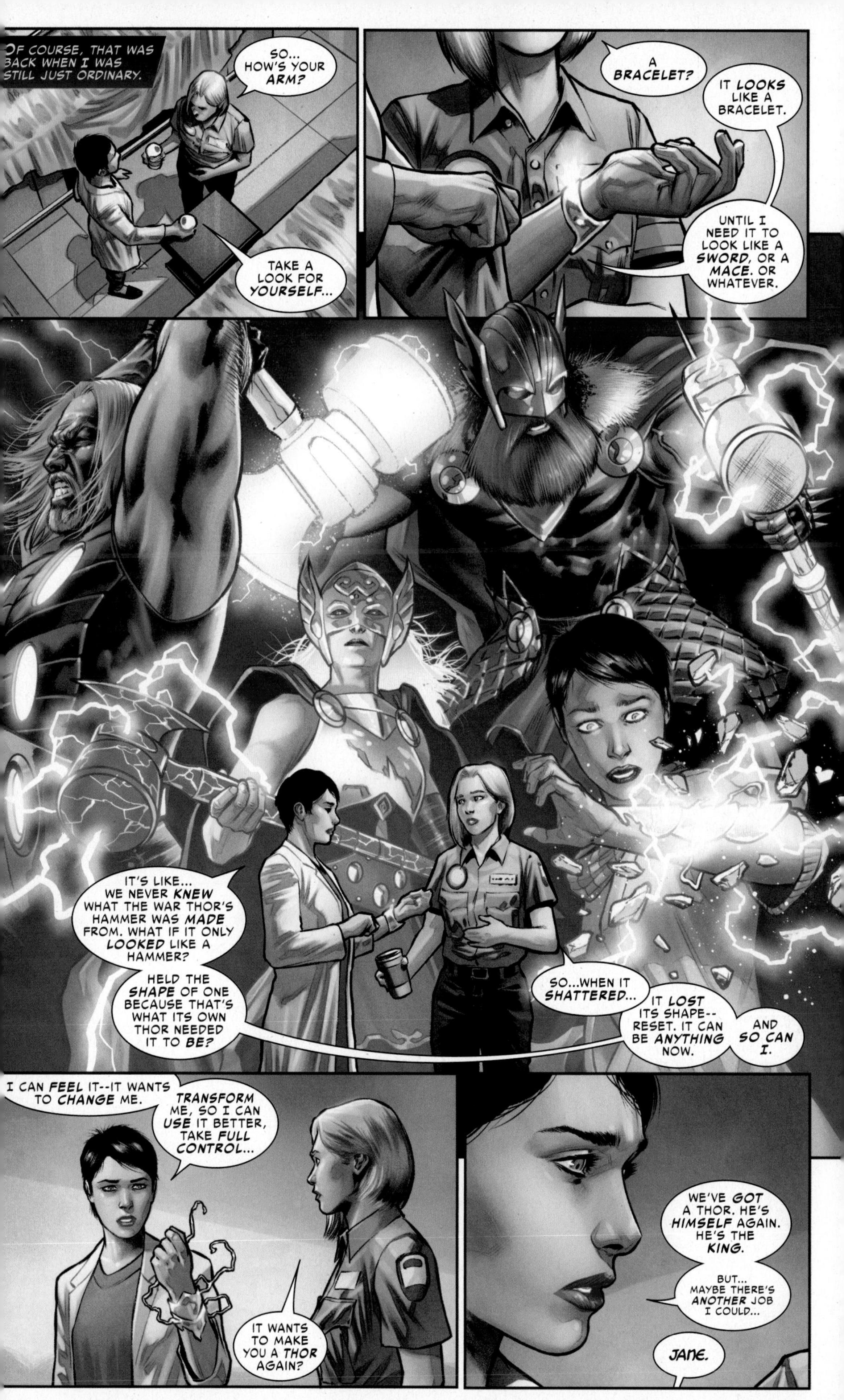
OF COURSE, THAT WAS BACK WHEN I WAS STILL JUST ORDINARY.
SO... HOW'S YOUR ARM?
TAKE A LOOK FOR YOURSELF...
A BRACELET?
IT LOOKS LIKE A BRACELET.
UNTIL I NEED IT TO LOOK LIKE A SWORD, OR A MACE. OR WHATEVER.
IT'S LIKE... WE NEVER KNEW WHAT THE WAR THOR'S HAMMER WAS MADE FROM. WHAT IF IT ONLY LOOKED LIKE A HAMMER?
HELD THE SHAPE OF ONE BECAUSE THAT'S WHAT ITS OWN THOR NEEDED IT TO BE?
SO...WHEN IT SHATTERED...
IT LOST ITS SHAPE-- RESET. IT CAN BE ANYTHING NOW.
AND SO CAN I.
I CAN FEEL IT--IT WANTS TO CHANGE ME.
TRANSFORM ME, SO I CAN USE IT BETTER, TAKE FULL CONTROL...
IT WANTS TO MAKE YOU A THOR AGAIN?
WE'VE GOT A THOR. HE'S HIMSELF AGAIN. HE'S THE KING.
BUT... MAYBE THERE'S ANOTHER JOB I COULD...
JANE.

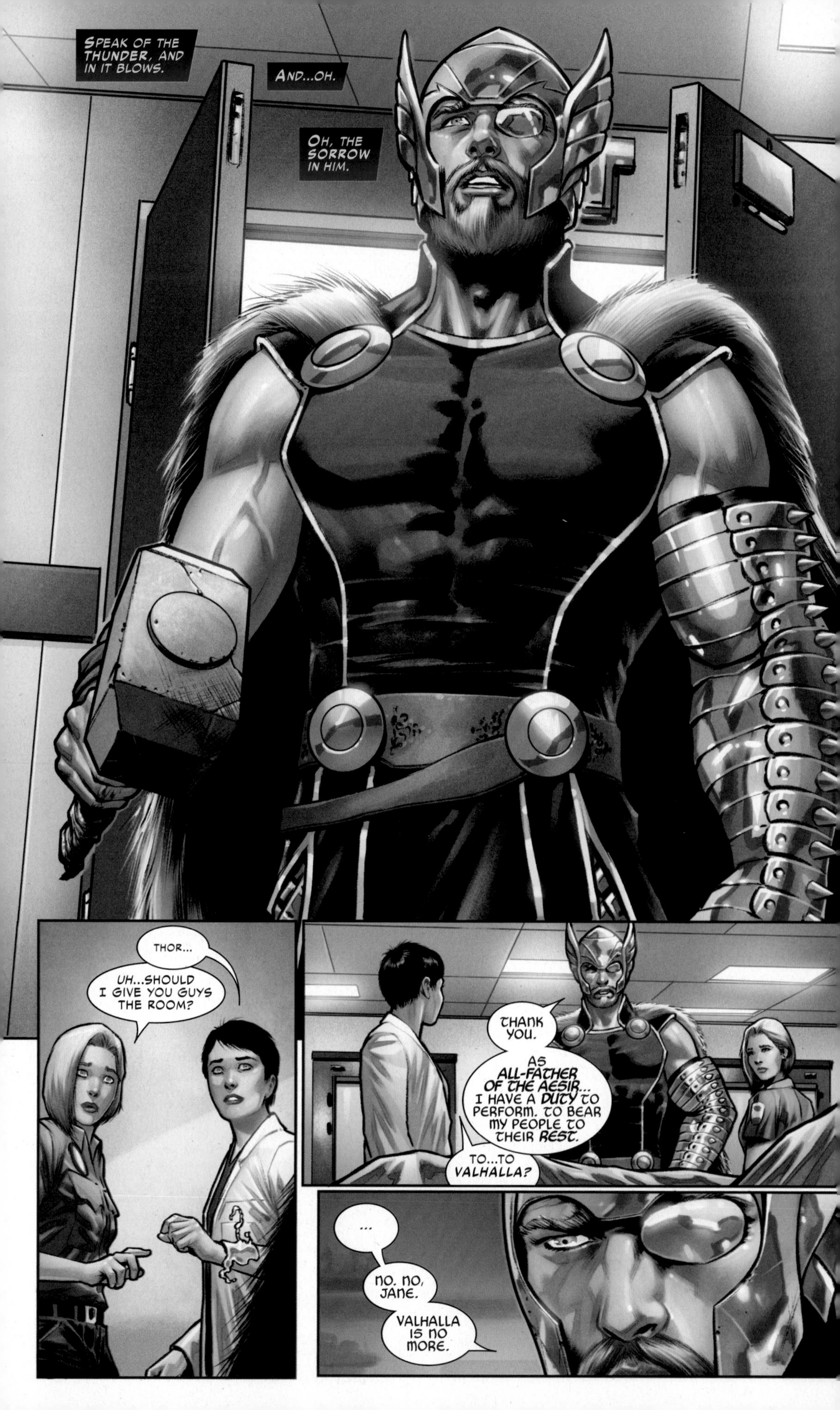

SPEAK OF THE THUNDER, AND IN IT BLOWS.
AND...OH.
OH, THE SORROW IN HIM.
THOR...
UH...SHOULD I GIVE YOU GUYS THE ROOM?
THANK YOU.
AS ALL-FATHER OF THE AESIR... I HAVE A DUTY TO PERFORM. TO BEAR MY PEOPLE TO THEIR REST.
TO...TO VALHALLA?
...
NO. NO, JANE.
VALHALLA IS NO MORE.

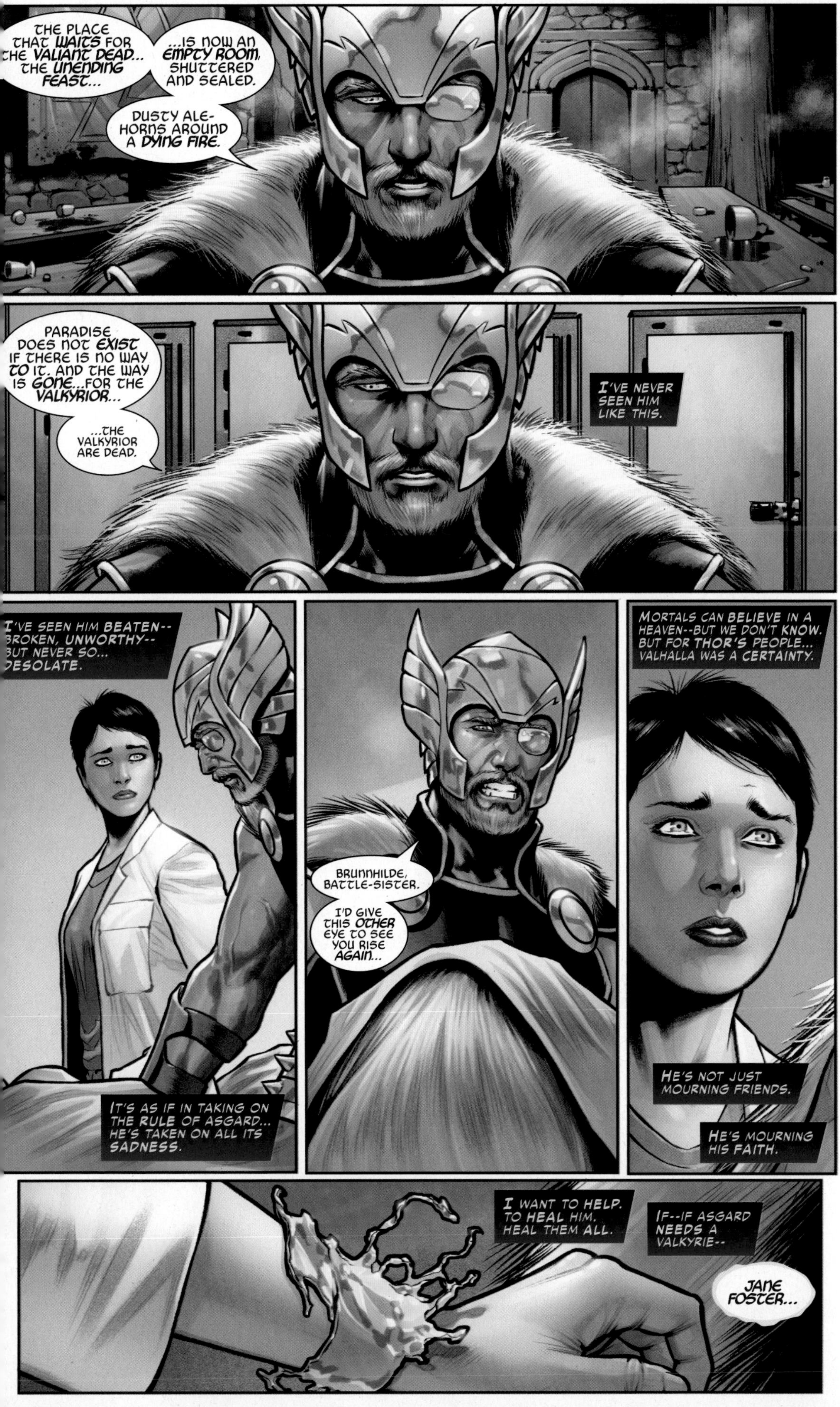

THE PLACE THAT WAITS FOR THE VALIANT DEAD... THE UNENDING FEAST...
...IS NOW AN EMPTY ROOM, SHUTTERED AND SEALED.
DUSTY ALE-HORNS AROUND A DYING FIRE.
PARADISE DOES NOT EXIST IF THERE IS NO WAY TO IT. AND THE WAY IS GONE...FOR THE VALKYRIOR...
...THE VALKYRIOR ARE DEAD.
I'VE NEVER SEEN HIM LIKE THIS.
I'VE SEEN HIM BEATEN--BROKEN, UNWORTHY--BUT NEVER SO... DESOLATE.
IT'S AS IF IN TAKING ON THE RULE OF ASGARD... HE'S TAKEN ON ALL ITS SADNESS.
BRUNNHILDE, BATTLE-SISTER.
I'D GIVE THIS OTHER EYE TO SEE YOU RISE AGAIN...
MORTALS CAN BELIEVE IN A HEAVEN--BUT WE DON'T KNOW. BUT FOR THOR'S PEOPLE... VALHALLA WAS A CERTAINTY.
HE'S NOT JUST MOURNING FRIENDS.
HE'S MOURNING HIS FAITH.
I WANT TO HELP. TO HEAL HIM. HEAL THEM ALL.
IF--IF ASGARD NEEDS A VALKYRIE--
JANE FOSTER...

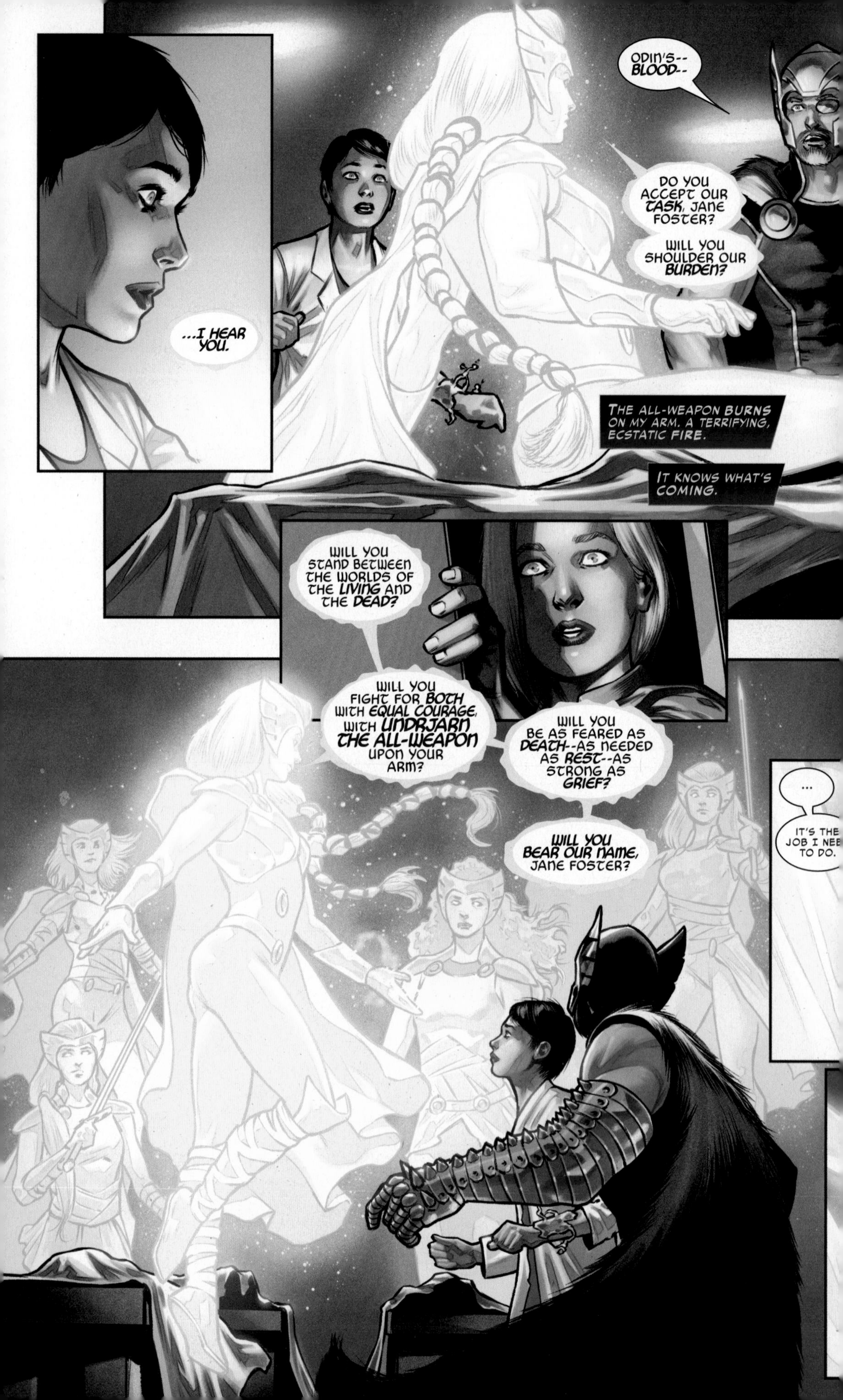

...I HEAR YOU.
ODIN'S-- BLOOD--
DO YOU ACCEPT OUR TASK, JANE FOSTER?
WILL YOU SHOULDER OUR BURDEN?
THE ALL-WEAPON BURNS ON MY ARM. A TERRIFYING, ECSTATIC FIRE.
IT KNOWS WHAT'S COMING.
WILL YOU STAND BETWEEN THE WORLDS OF THE LIVING AND THE DEAD?
WILL YOU FIGHT FOR BOTH WITH EQUAL COURAGE, WITH UNDRJARN THE ALL-WEAPON UPON YOUR ARM?
WILL YOU BE AS FEARED AS DEATH--AS NEEDED AS REST--AS STRONG AS GRIEF?
WILL YOU BEAR OUR NAME, JANE FOSTER?
...

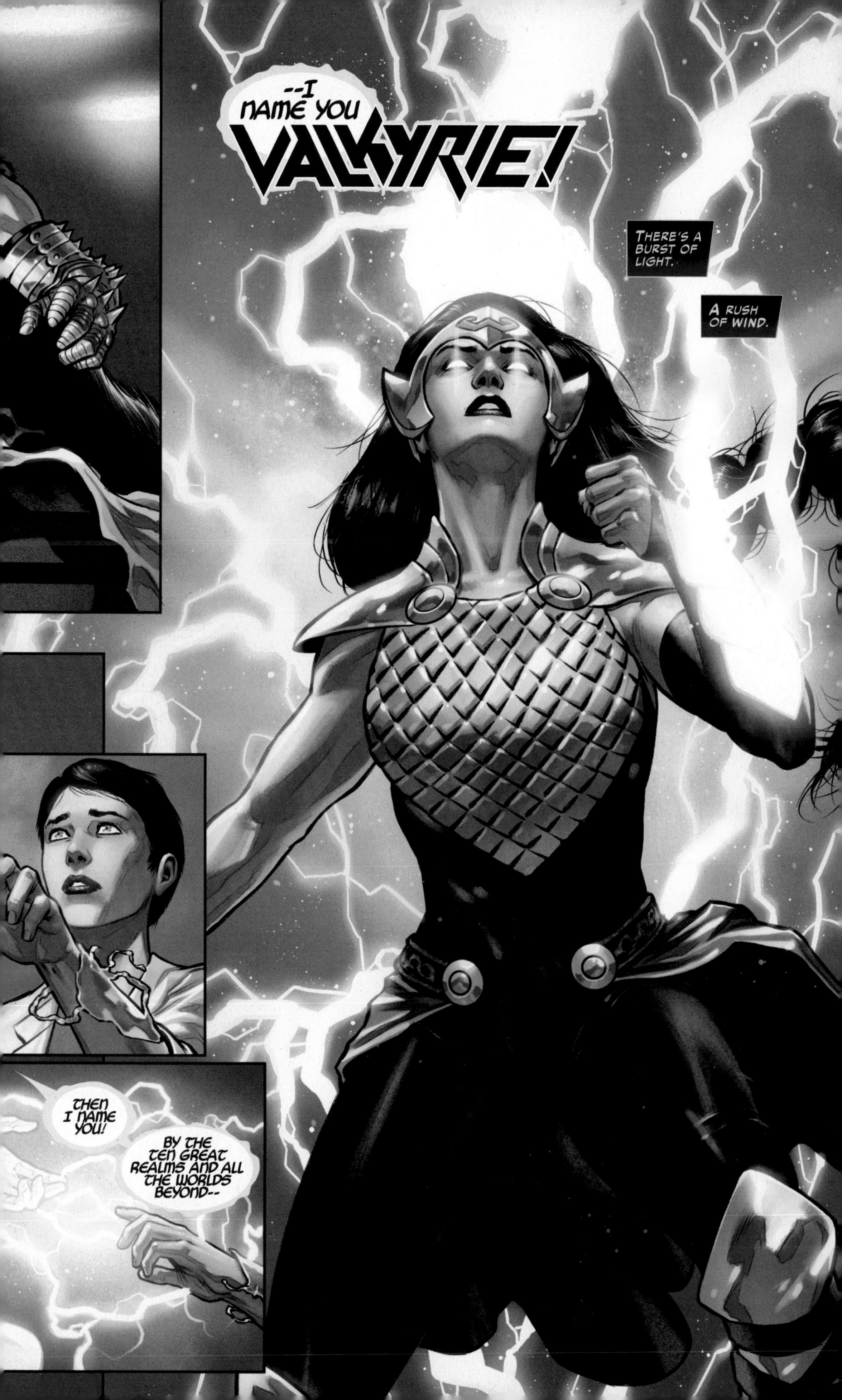
--I NAME YOU VALKYRIE!
THERE'S A BURST OF LIGHT.
A RUSH OF WIND.
THEN I NAME YOU!
BY THE TEN GREAT REALMS AND ALL THE WORLDS BEYOND--

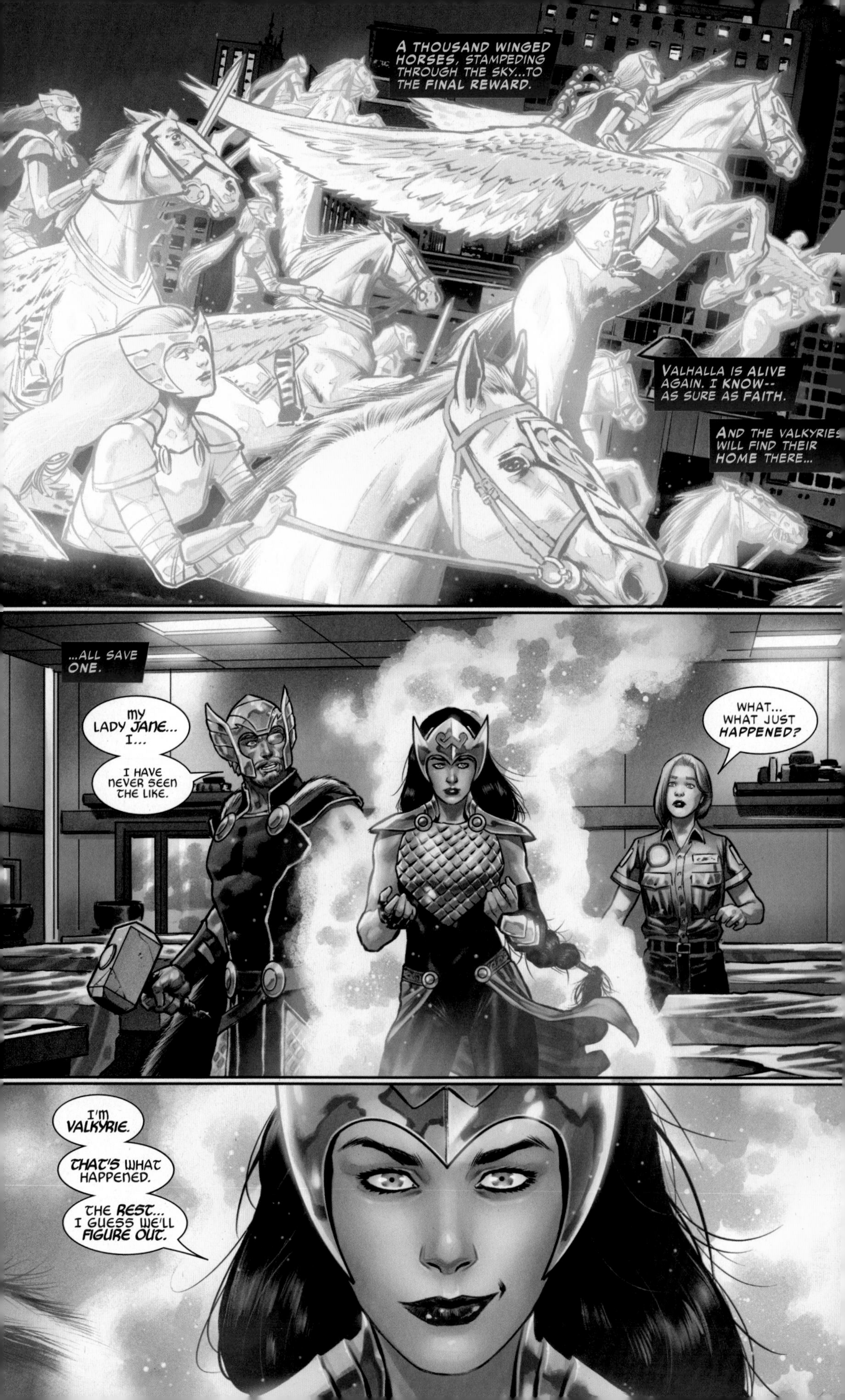
A THOUSAND WINGED HORSES, STAMPEDING THROUGH THE SKY...TO THE FINAL REWARD.
VALHALLA IS ALIVE AGAIN. I KNOW-- AS SURE AS FAITH.
AND THE VALKYRIES WILL FIND THEIR HOME THERE...
...ALL SAVE ONE.
MY LADY JANE... I...
I HAVE NEVER SEEN THE LIKE.
WHAT... WHAT JUST HAPPENED?
I'M VALKYRIE.
THAT'S WHAT HAPPENED.
THE REST... I GUESS WE'LL FIGURE OUT.

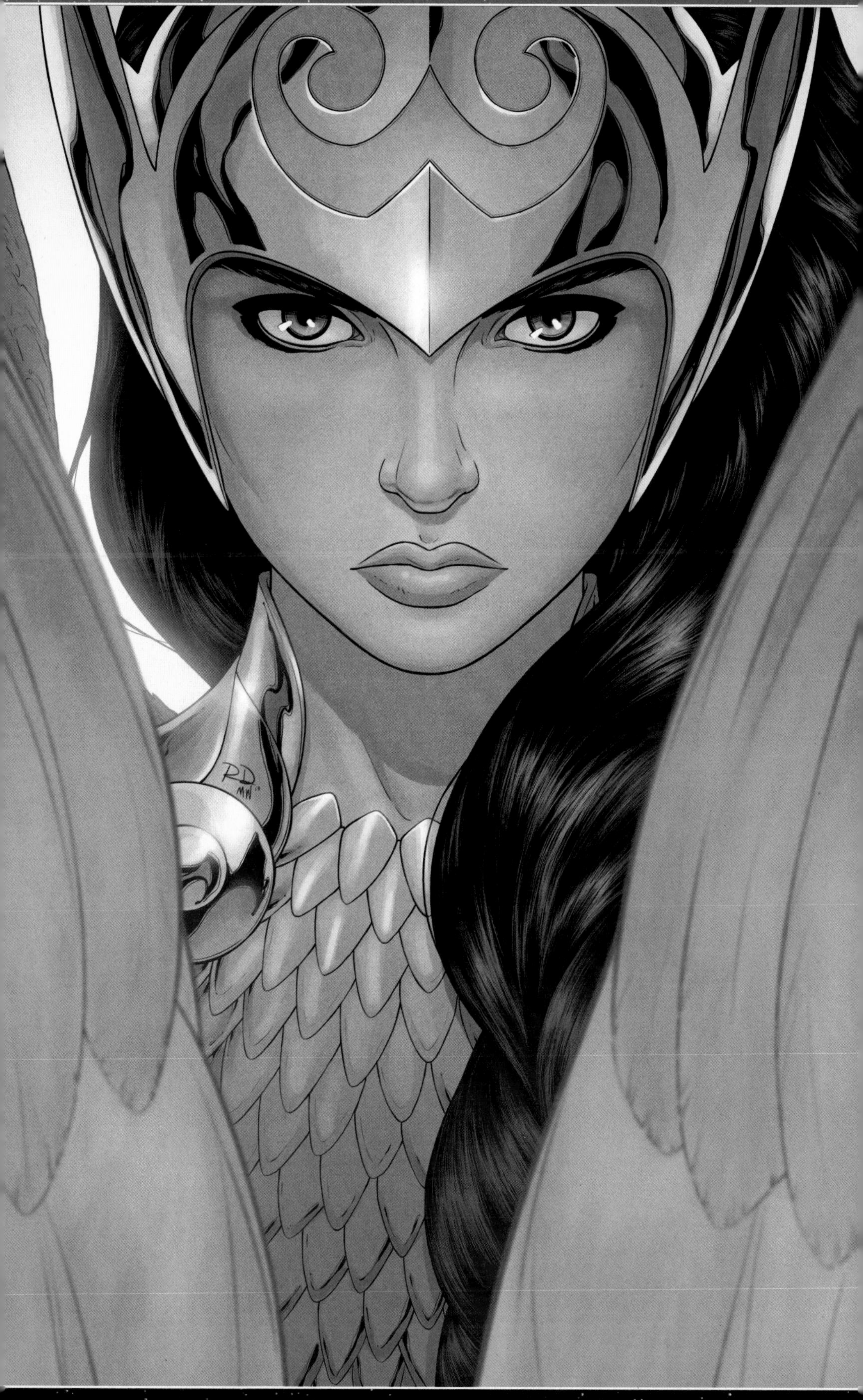

VALKYRIE: JANE FOSTER #1 VARIANT BY RUSSELL DAUTERMAN & MATTHEW WILSON

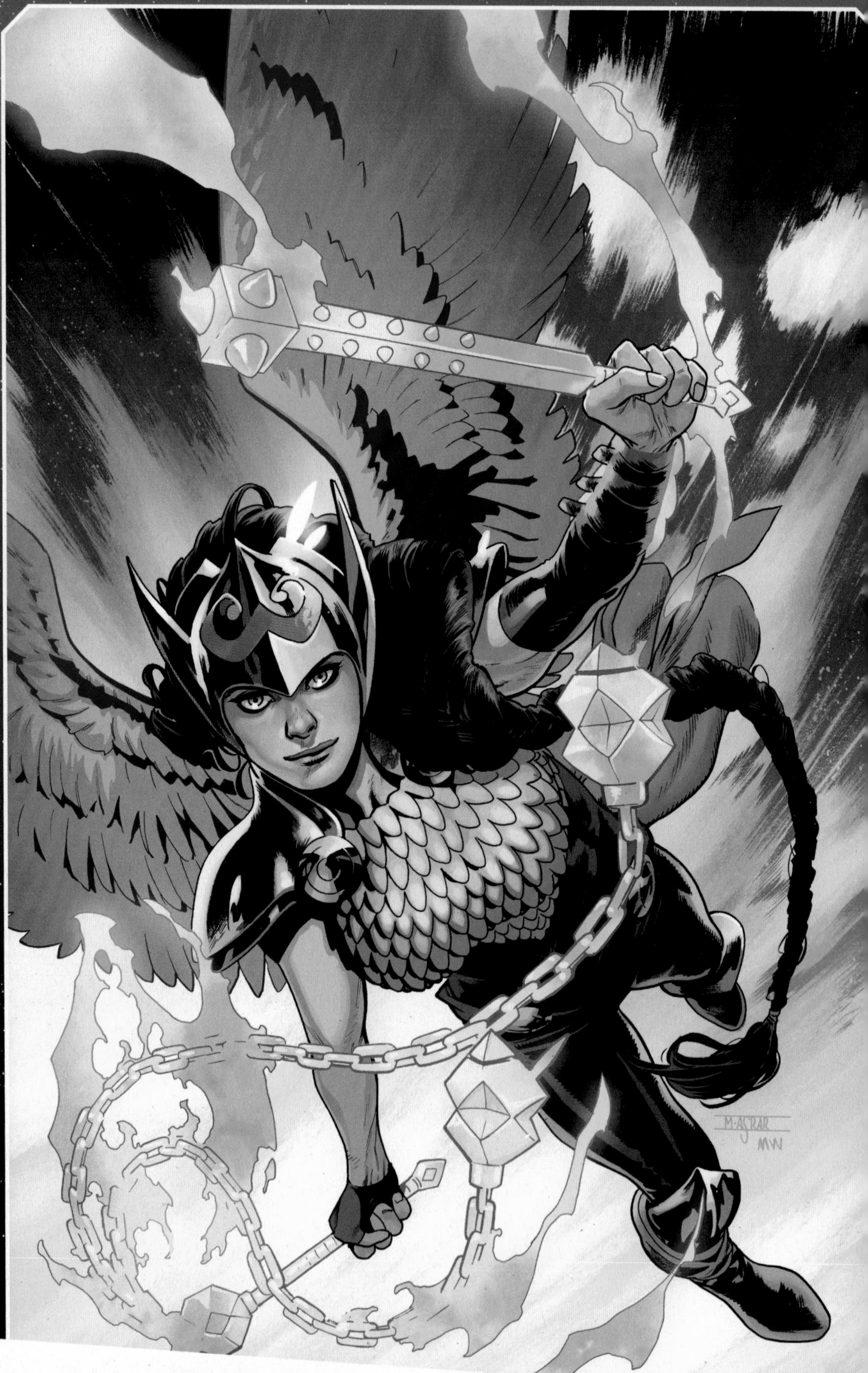

VALKYRIE: JANE FOSTER #1

MY NAME IS JANE FOSTER. I'M A DOCTOR. I'M A CANCER URVIVOR. FOR A WHILE, I WAS SUPER HERO.
I HAD A MAGIC HAMMER AND A HERO NAME, AND I FOUGHT THE GOOD FIGHT AND STARED DEATH IN THE FACE.
AND LIFE WAS TERRIFYING AND EXHILARATING AND JOYOUS AND HEARTBREAKING.
BUT I WAS JUST HOLDING THE HAMMER FOR A FRIEND. THE NAME TOO. EVENTUALLY I HAD TO LET THEM BOTH GO. AND FOR A WHILE AFTER THAT, LIFE WAS JUST...LIFE.
AND WHEN YOU'VE STARED DEATH IN THE FACE, LIFE IS ENOUGH. AND WHEN YOU'VE STARED DEATH IN THE FACE...IT'S NOT.
I NEEDED MORE.
ANYWAY--THERE WAS A WAR. I WAS CALLED. I ANSWERED.
I'M JANE FOSTER. I'M THE LAST OF THE VALKYRIES. I'M BACK...
...AND LIFE IS GOOD.

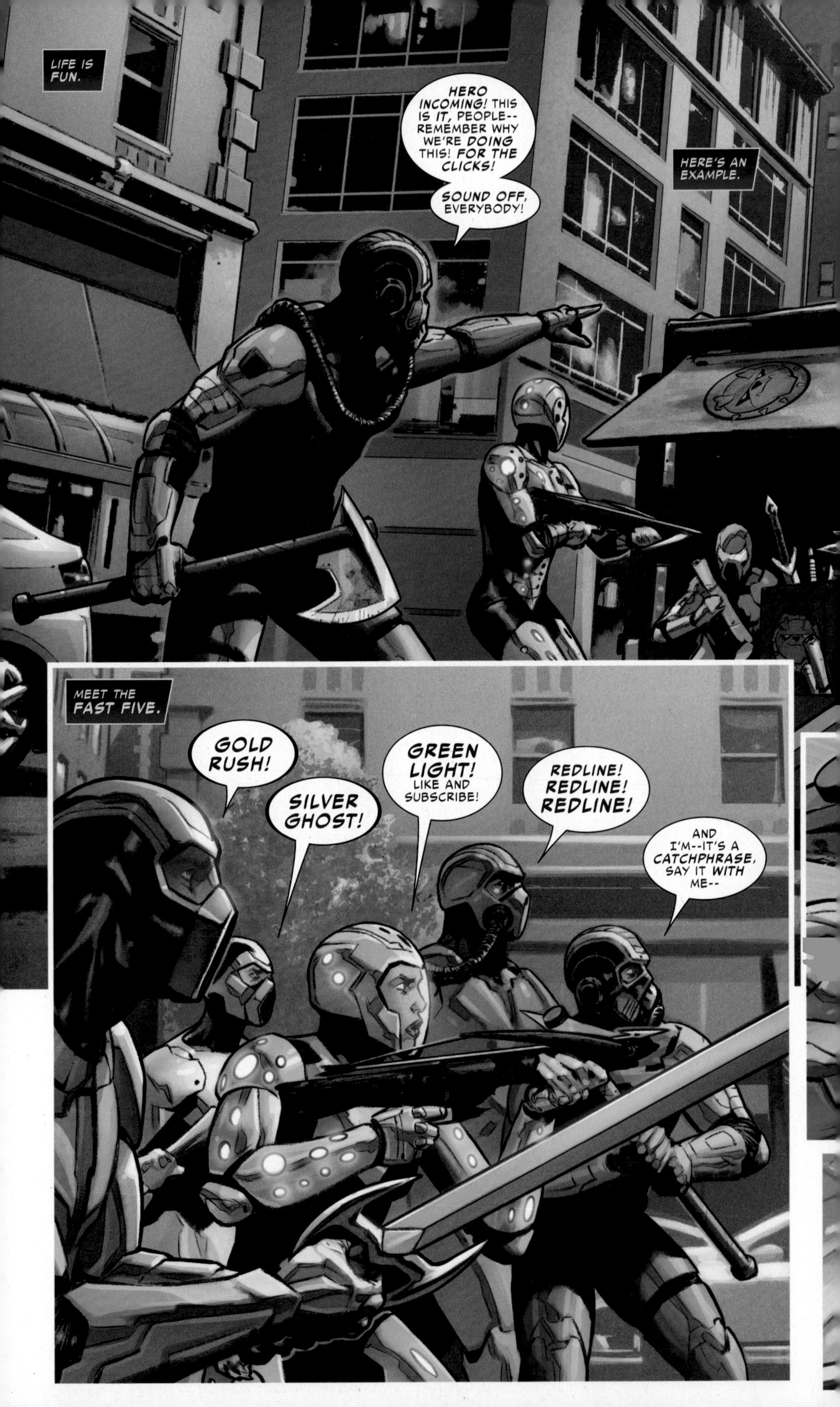
LIFE IS FUN.
HERO INCOMING! THIS IS IT, PEOPLE-- REMEMBER WHY WE'RE DOING THIS! FOR THE CLICKS!
SOUND OFF, EVERYBODY!
HERE'S AN EXAMPLE.
MEET THE FAST FIVE.
GOLD RUSH!
SILVER GHOST!
GREEN LIGHT! LIKE AND SUBSCRIBE!
REDLINE! REDLINE! REDLINE!
AND I'M--IT'S A CATCHPHRASE, SAY IT WITH ME--

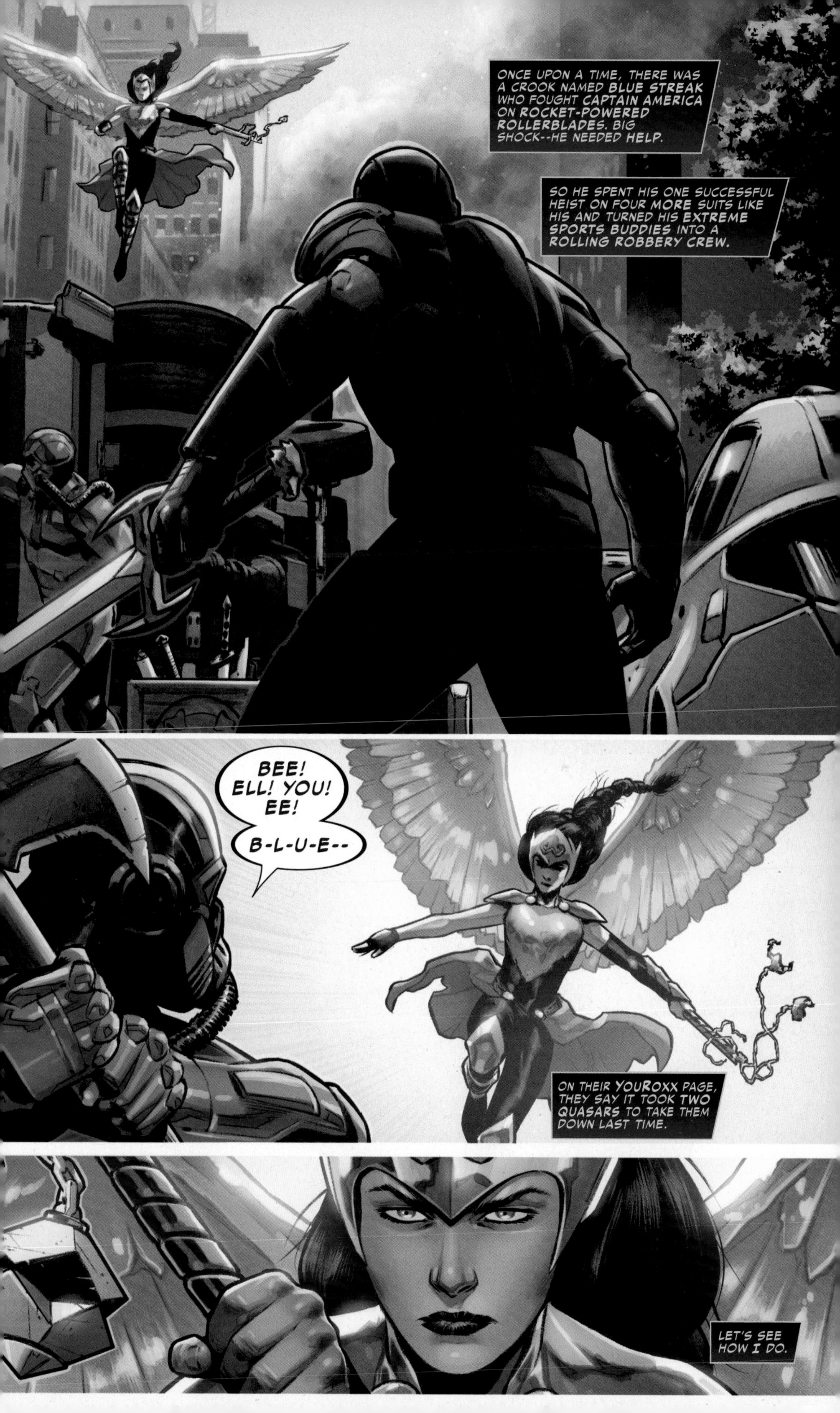
ONCE UPON A TIME, THERE WAS A CROOK NAMED BLUE STREAK WHO FOUGHT CAPTAIN AMERICA ON ROCKET-POWERED ROLLERBLADES. BIG SHOCK--HE NEEDED HELP.
SO HE SPENT HIS ONE SUCCESSFUL HEIST ON FOUR MORE SUITS LIKE HIS AND TURNED HIS EXTREME SPORTS BUDDIES INTO A ROLLING ROBBERY CREW.
BEE! ELL! YOU! EE!
B-L-U-E--
ON THEIR YOUROXX PAGE, THEY SAY IT TOOK TWO QUASARS TO TAKE THEM DOWN LAST TIME.
LET'S SEE HOW I DO.

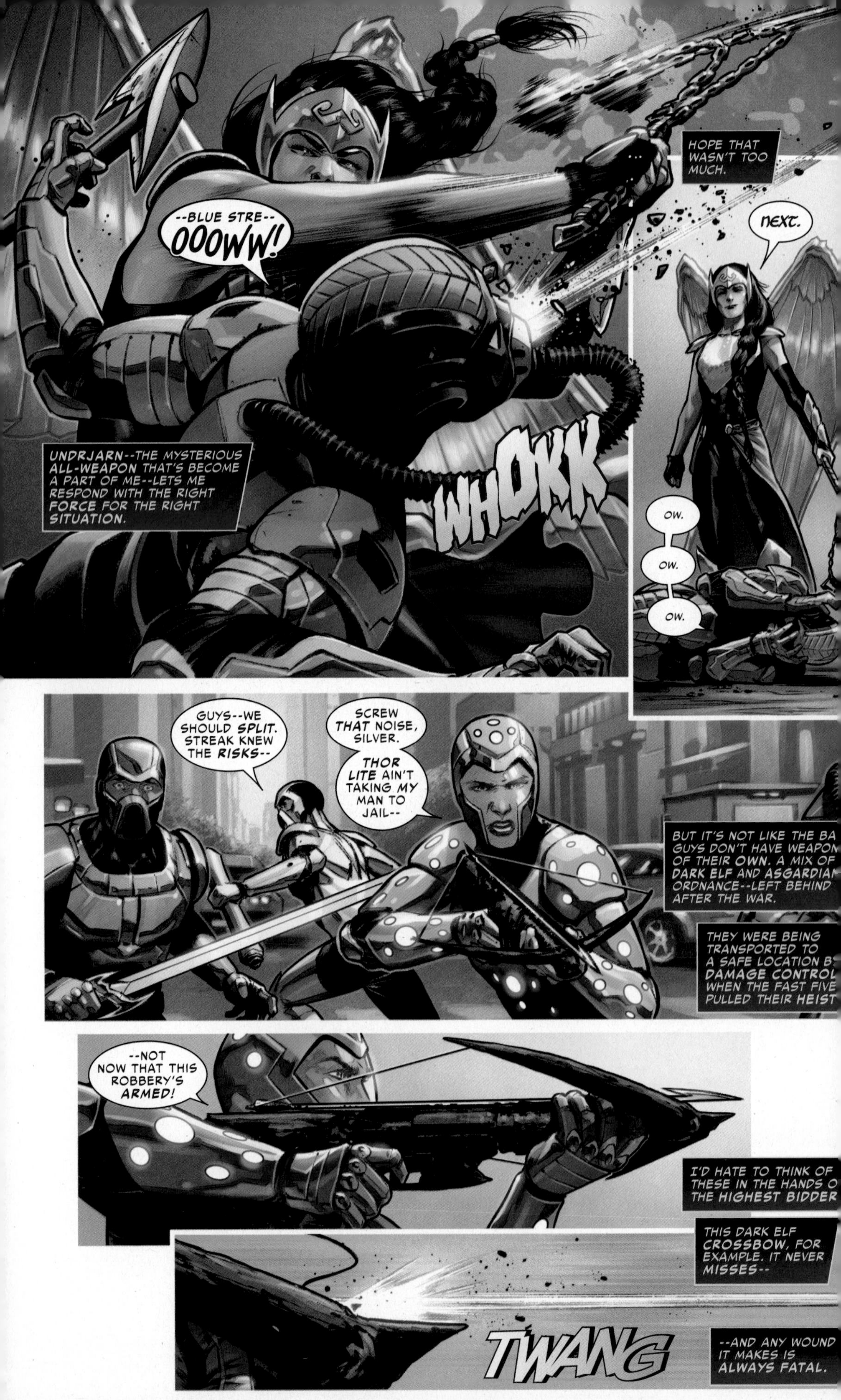
--BLUE STRE--
OOOWW!
UNDRJARN--THE MYSTERIOUS ALL-WEAPON THAT'S BECOME A PART OF ME--LETS ME RESPOND WITH THE RIGHT FORCE FOR THE RIGHT SITUATION.
WHOKK
HOPE THAT WASN'T TOO MUCH.
NEXT.
OW.
OW.
OW.
GUYS--WE SHOULD SPLIT. STREAK KNEW THE RISKS--
SCREW THAT NOISE, SILVER.
THOR LITE AIN'T TAKING MY MAN TO JAIL--
BUT IT'S NOT LIKE THE BA GUYS DON'T HAVE WEAPON OF THEIR OWN. A MIX OF DARK ELF AND ASGARDIA ORDNANCE--LEFT BEHIND AFTER THE WAR.
THEY WERE BEING TRANSPORTED TO A SAFE LOCATION B DAMAGE CONTROL WHEN THE FAST FIVE PULLED THEIR HEIST
--NOT NOW THAT THIS ROBBERY'S ARMED!
I'D HATE TO THINK OF THESE IN THE HANDS O THE HIGHEST BIDDER
THIS DARK ELF CROSSBOW, FOR EXAMPLE. IT NEVER MISSES--
TWANG
--AND ANY WOUND IT MAKES IS ALWAYS FATAL.

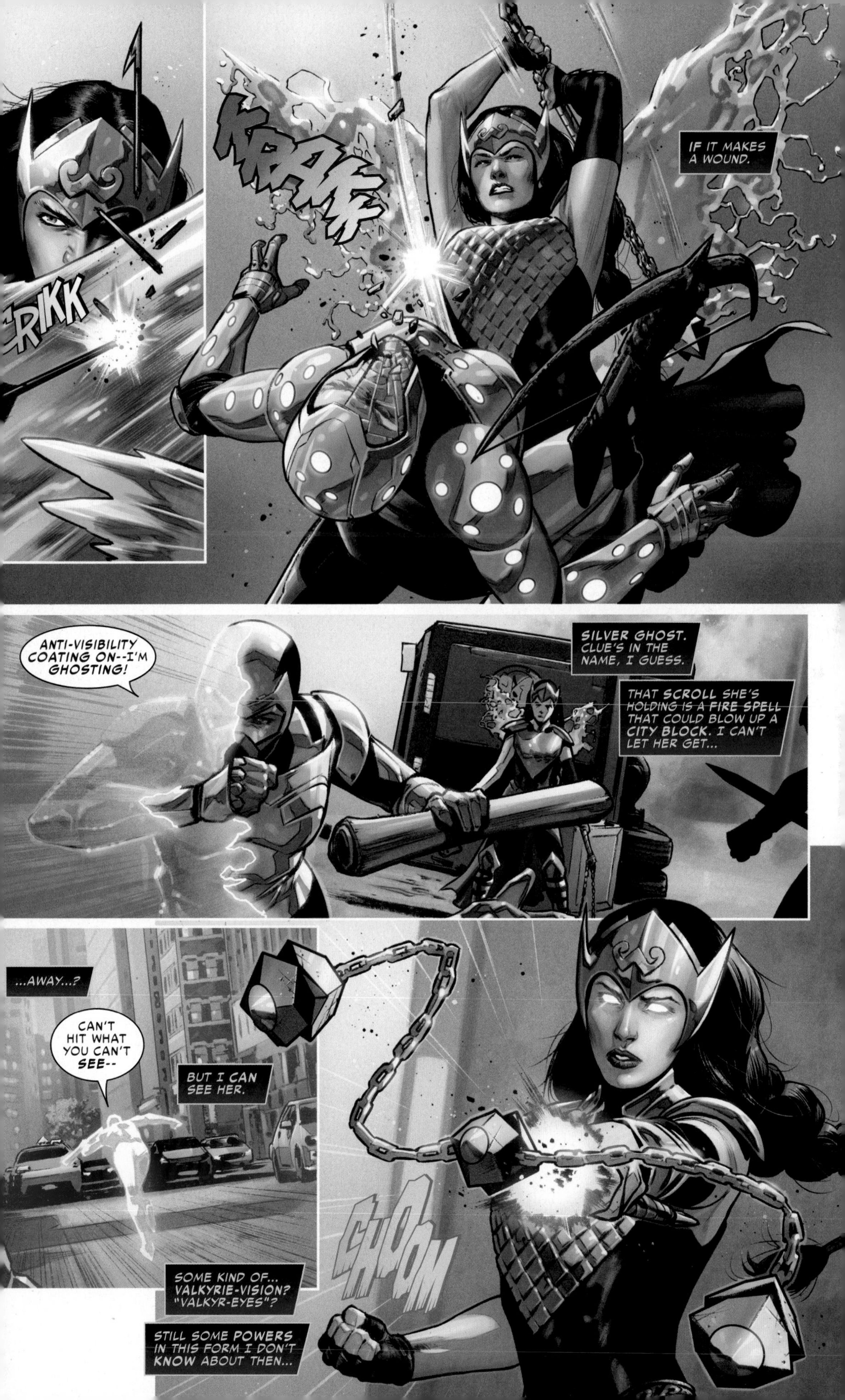
RIKK
IF IT MAKES A WOUND.
ANTI-VISIBILITY COATING ON--I'M GHOSTING!
SILVER GHOST. CLUE'S IN THE NAME, I GUESS.
THAT SCROLL SHE'S HOLDING IS A FIRE SPELL THAT COULD BLOW UP A CITY BLOCK. I CAN'T LET HER GET...
...AWAY...?
CAN'T HIT WHAT YOU CAN'T SEE--
BUT I CAN SEE HER.
SOME KIND OF... VALKYRIE-VISION? "VALKYR-EYES"?
STILL SOME POWERS IN THIS FORM I DON'T KNOW ABOUT THEN...
CHOOM

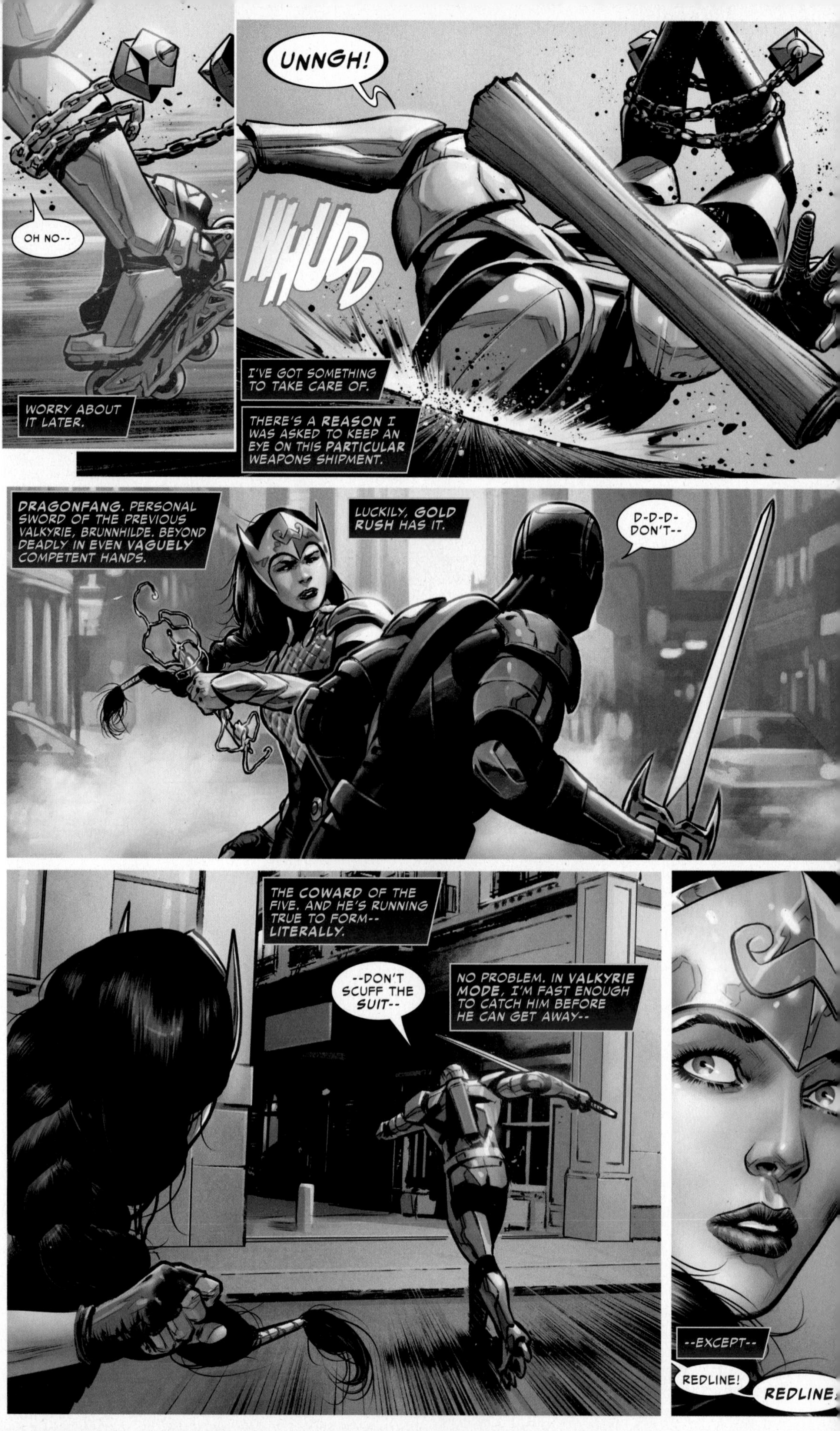
OH NO--
WORRY ABOUT IT LATER.
UNNGH!
WHUDD
I'VE GOT SOMETHING TO TAKE CARE OF.
THERE'S A REASON I WAS ASKED TO KEEP AN EYE ON THIS PARTICULAR WEAPONS SHIPMENT.
DRAGONFANG. PERSONAL SWORD OF THE PREVIOUS VALKYRIE, BRUNNHILDE. BEYOND DEADLY IN EVEN VAGUELY COMPETENT HANDS.
LUCKILY, GOLD RUSH HAS IT.
D-D-D-DON'T--
THE COWARD OF THE FIVE. AND HE'S RUNNING TRUE TO FORM--LITERALLY.
--DON'T SCUFF THE SUIT--
NO PROBLEM. IN VALKYRIE MODE, I'M FAST ENOUGH TO CATCH HIM BEFORE HE CAN GET AWAY--
--EXCEPT--
REDLINE!
REDLINE!

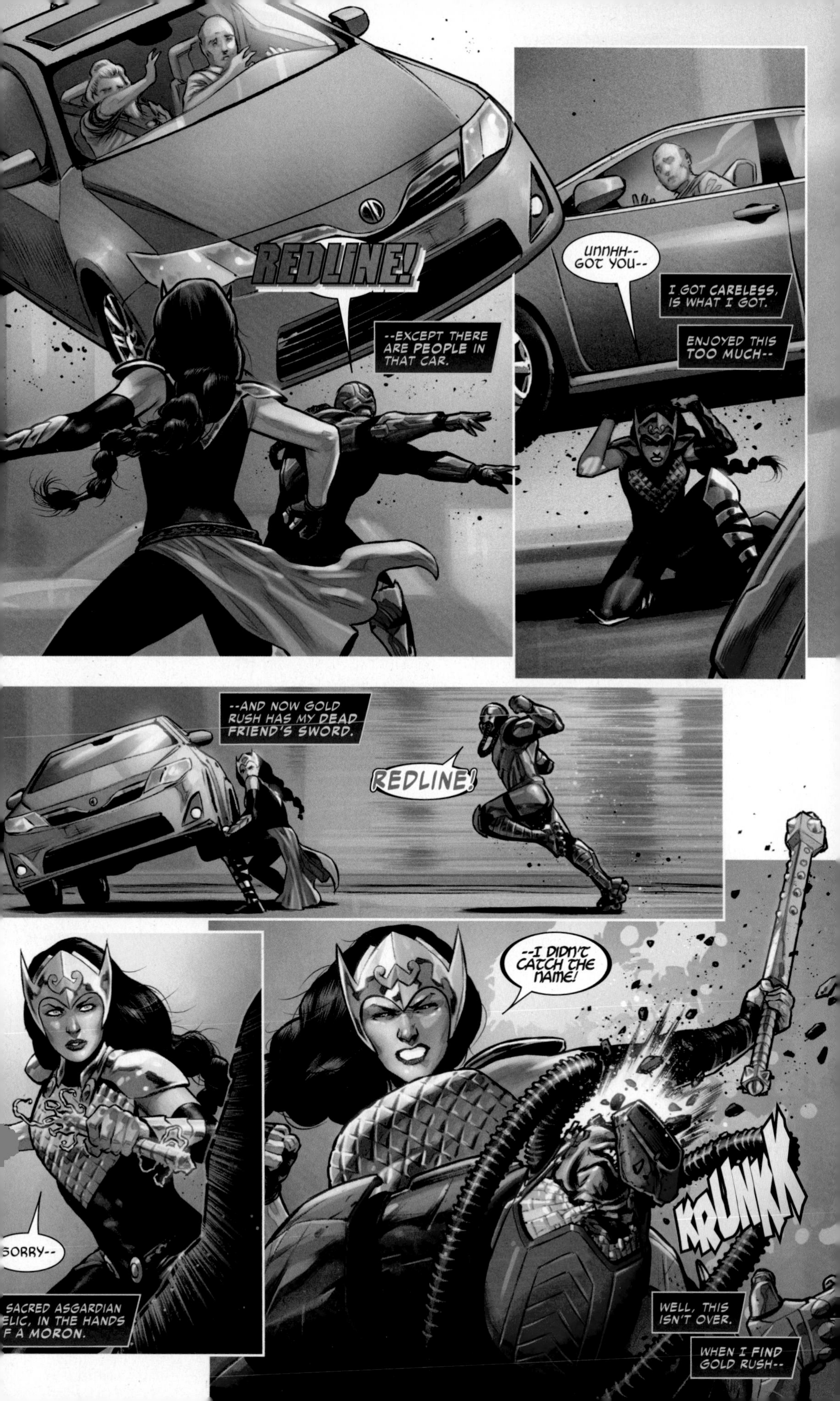
REDLINE!
--EXCEPT THERE ARE PEOPLE IN THAT CAR.
UNNHH-- GOT YOU--
I GOT CARELESS, IS WHAT I GOT.
ENJOYED THIS TOO MUCH--
--AND NOW GOLD RUSH HAS MY DEAD FRIEND'S SWORD.
REDLINE!
SORRY--
SACRED ASGARDIAN ELIC, IN THE HANDS F A MORON.
--I DIDN'T CATCH THE NAME!
KRUNKK
WELL, THIS ISN'T OVER.
WHEN I FIND GOLD RUSH--

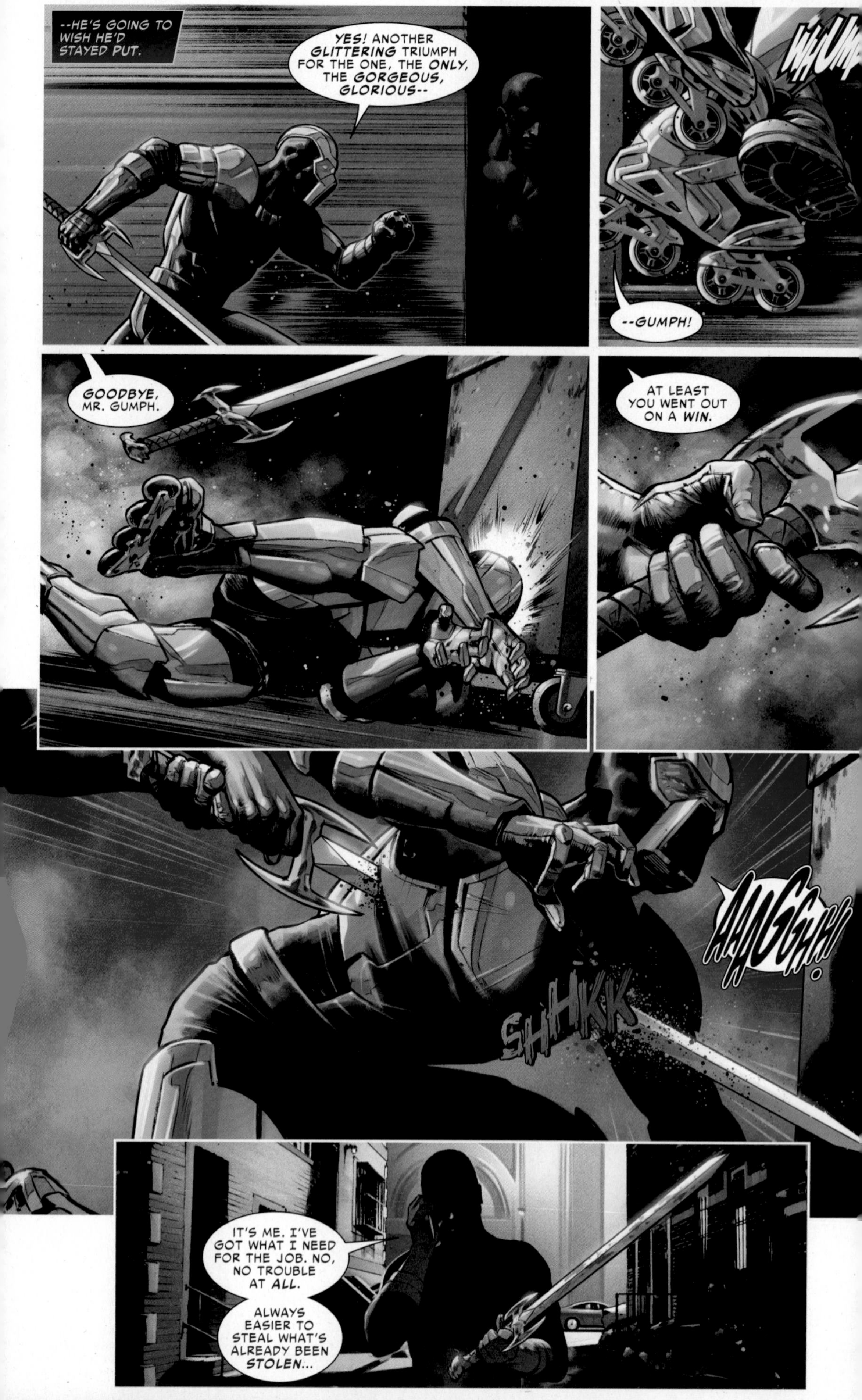
--HE'S GOING TO WISH HE'D STAYED PUT.
YES! ANOTHER GLITTERING TRIUMPH FOR THE ONE, THE ONLY, THE GORGEOUS, GLORIOUS--
WHUMP
--GUMPH!
GOODBYE, MR. GUMPH.
AT LEAST YOU WENT OUT ON A WIN.
AAAGGH!!
SHHKK
IT'S ME. I'VE GOT WHAT I NEED FOR THE JOB. NO, NO TROUBLE AT ALL.
ALWAYS EASIER TO STEAL WHAT'S ALREADY BEEN STOLEN...

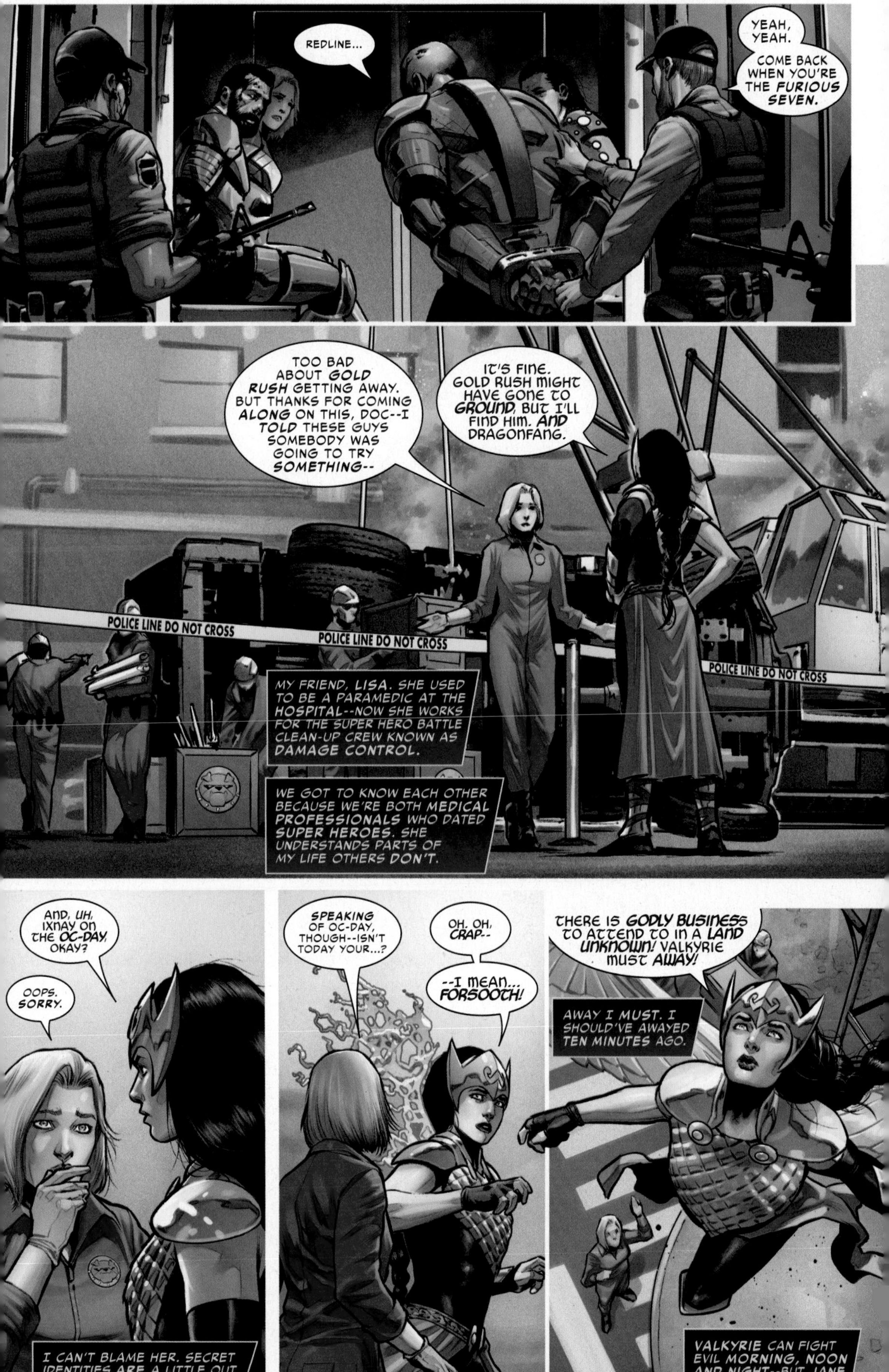
REDLINE...
YEAH, YEAH.
COME BACK WHEN YOU'RE THE FURIOUS SEVEN.
TOO BAD ABOUT GOLD RUSH GETTING AWAY. BUT THANKS FOR COMING ALONG ON THIS, DOC--I TOLD THESE GUYS SOMEBODY WAS GOING TO TRY SOMETHING--
IT'S FINE. GOLD RUSH MIGHT HAVE GONE TO GROUND, BUT I'LL FIND HIM. AND DRAGONFANG.
POLICE LINE DO NOT CROSS
POLICE LINE DO NOT CROSS
POLICE LINE DO NOT CROSS
MY FRIEND, LISA. SHE USED TO BE A PARAMEDIC AT THE HOSPITAL--NOW SHE WORKS FOR THE SUPER HERO BATTLE CLEAN-UP CREW KNOWN AS DAMAGE CONTROL.
WE GOT TO KNOW EACH OTHER BECAUSE WE'RE BOTH MEDICAL PROFESSIONALS WHO DATED SUPER HEROES. SHE UNDERSTANDS PARTS OF MY LIFE OTHERS DON'T.
AND, UH, IXNAY ON THE OC-DAY, OKAY?
OOPS. SORRY.
I CAN'T BLAME HER. SECRET IDENTITIES ARE A LITTLE OUT OF FASHION THESE DAYS...
SPEAKING OF OC-DAY, THOUGH--ISN'T TODAY YOUR...?
OH. OH, CRAP--
--I MEAN... FORSOOTH!
THERE IS GODLY BUSINESS TO ATTEND TO IN A LAND UNKNOWN! VALKYRIE MUST AWAY!
AWAY I MUST. I SHOULD'VE AWAYED TEN MINUTES AGO.
VALKYRIE CAN FIGHT EVIL MORNING, NOON AND NIGHT--BUT JANE FOSTER HAS A LIFE. AND SHE'S LATE...

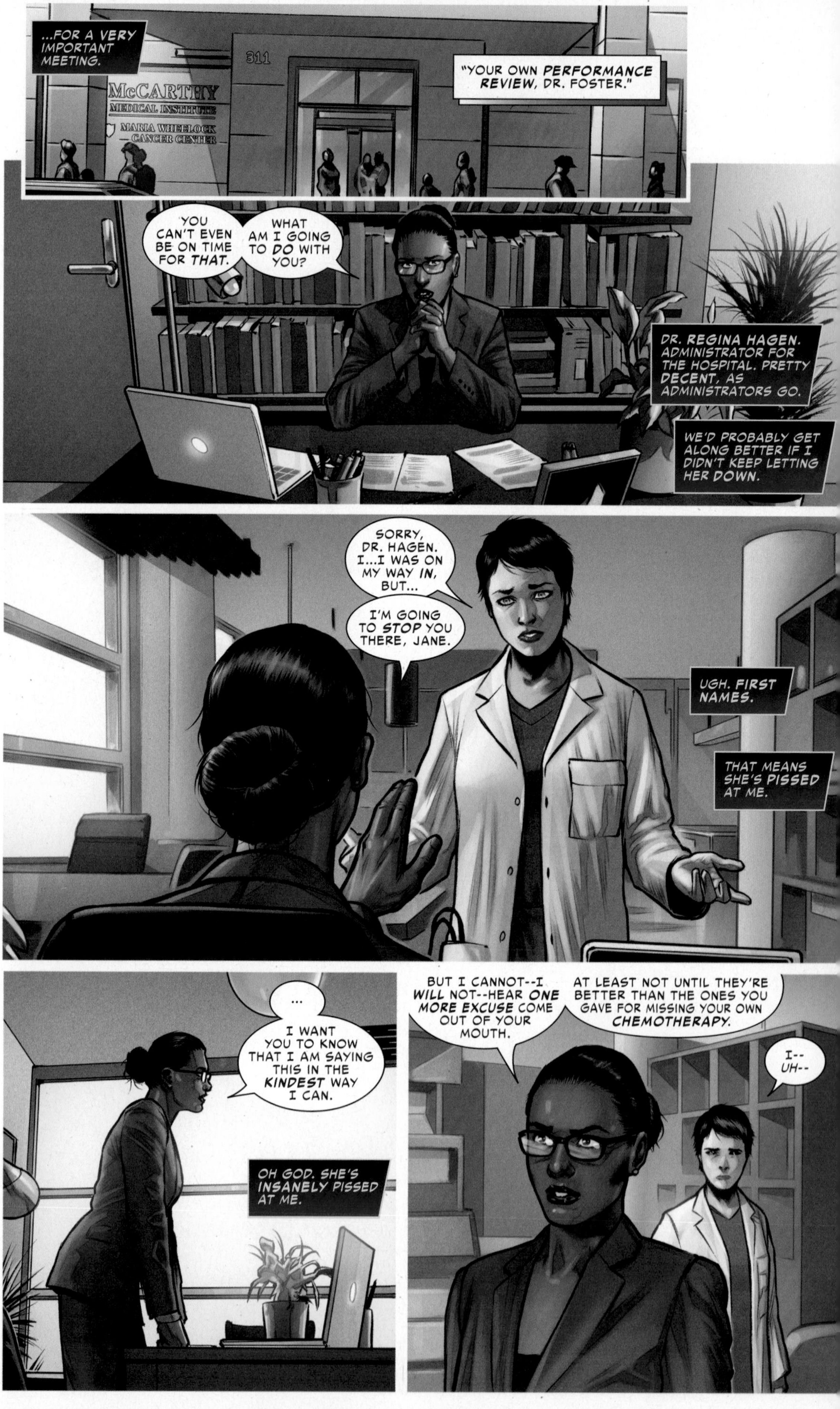
...FOR A VERY IMPORTANT MEETING.
311
McCARTHY MEDICAL INSTITUTE
MARIA WHEELOCK CANCER CENTER
"YOUR OWN PERFORMANCE REVIEW, DR. FOSTER."
YOU CAN'T EVEN BE ON TIME FOR THAT.
WHAT AM I GOING TO DO WITH YOU?
DR. REGINA HAGEN. ADMINISTRATOR FOR THE HOSPITAL. PRETTY DECENT, AS ADMINISTRATORS GO.
WE'D PROBABLY GET ALONG BETTER IF I DIDN'T KEEP LETTING HER DOWN.
SORRY, DR. HAGEN. I...I WAS ON MY WAY IN, BUT...
I'M GOING TO STOP YOU THERE, JANE.
UGH. FIRST NAMES.
THAT MEANS SHE'S PISSED AT ME.
...
I WANT YOU TO KNOW THAT I AM SAYING THIS IN THE KINDEST WAY I CAN.
OH GOD. SHE'S INSANELY PISSED AT ME.
BUT I CANNOT--I WILL NOT--HEAR ONE MORE EXCUSE COME OUT OF YOUR MOUTH.
AT LEAST NOT UNTIL THEY'RE BETTER THAN THE ONES YOU GAVE FOR MISSING YOUR OWN CHEMOTHERAPY.
I-- UH--

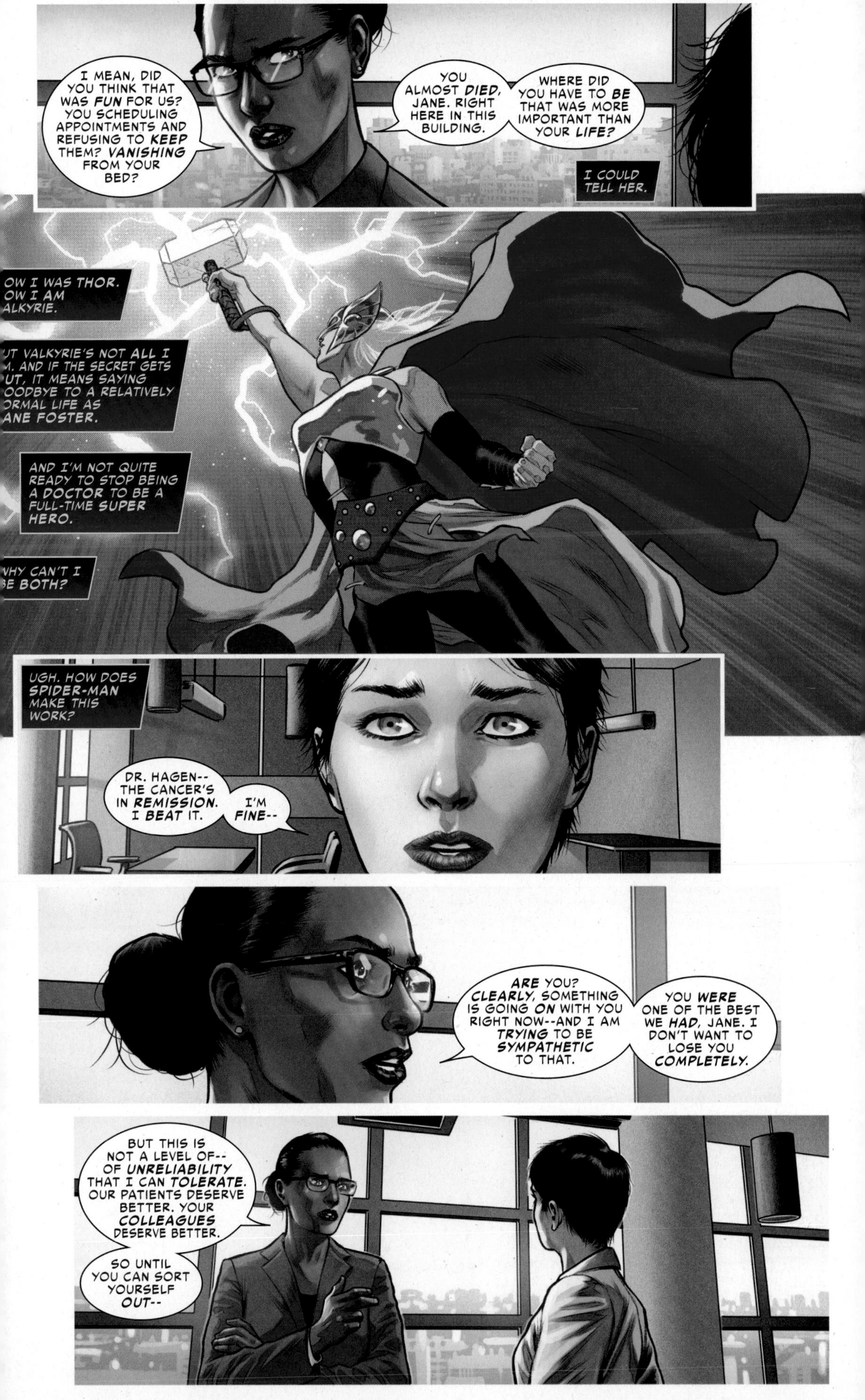

I MEAN, DID YOU THINK THAT WAS FUN FOR US? YOU SCHEDULING APPOINTMENTS AND REFUSING TO KEEP THEM? VANISHING FROM YOUR BED?
YOU ALMOST DIED, JANE. RIGHT HERE IN THIS BUILDING.
WHERE DID YOU HAVE TO BE THAT WAS MORE IMPORTANT THAN YOUR LIFE?
I COULD TELL HER.
OW I WAS THOR. OW I AM ALKYRIE.
UT VALKYRIE'S NOT ALL I M. AND IF THE SECRET GETS UT, IT MEANS SAYING OODBYE TO A RELATIVELY ORMAL LIFE AS ANE FOSTER.
AND I'M NOT QUITE READY TO STOP BEING A DOCTOR TO BE A FULL-TIME SUPER HERO.
WHY CAN'T I E BOTH?
UGH. HOW DOES SPIDER-MAN MAKE THIS WORK?
DR. HAGEN-- THE CANCER'S IN REMISSION. I BEAT IT.
I'M FINE--
ARE YOU? CLEARLY, SOMETHING IS GOING ON WITH YOU RIGHT NOW--AND I AM TRYING TO BE SYMPATHETIC TO THAT.
YOU WERE ONE OF THE BEST WE HAD, JANE. I DON'T WANT TO LOSE YOU COMPLETELY.
BUT THIS IS NOT A LEVEL OF-- OF UNRELIABILITY THAT I CAN TOLERATE. OUR PATIENTS DESERVE BETTER. YOUR COLLEAGUES DESERVE BETTER.
SO UNTIL YOU CAN SORT YOURSELF OUT--

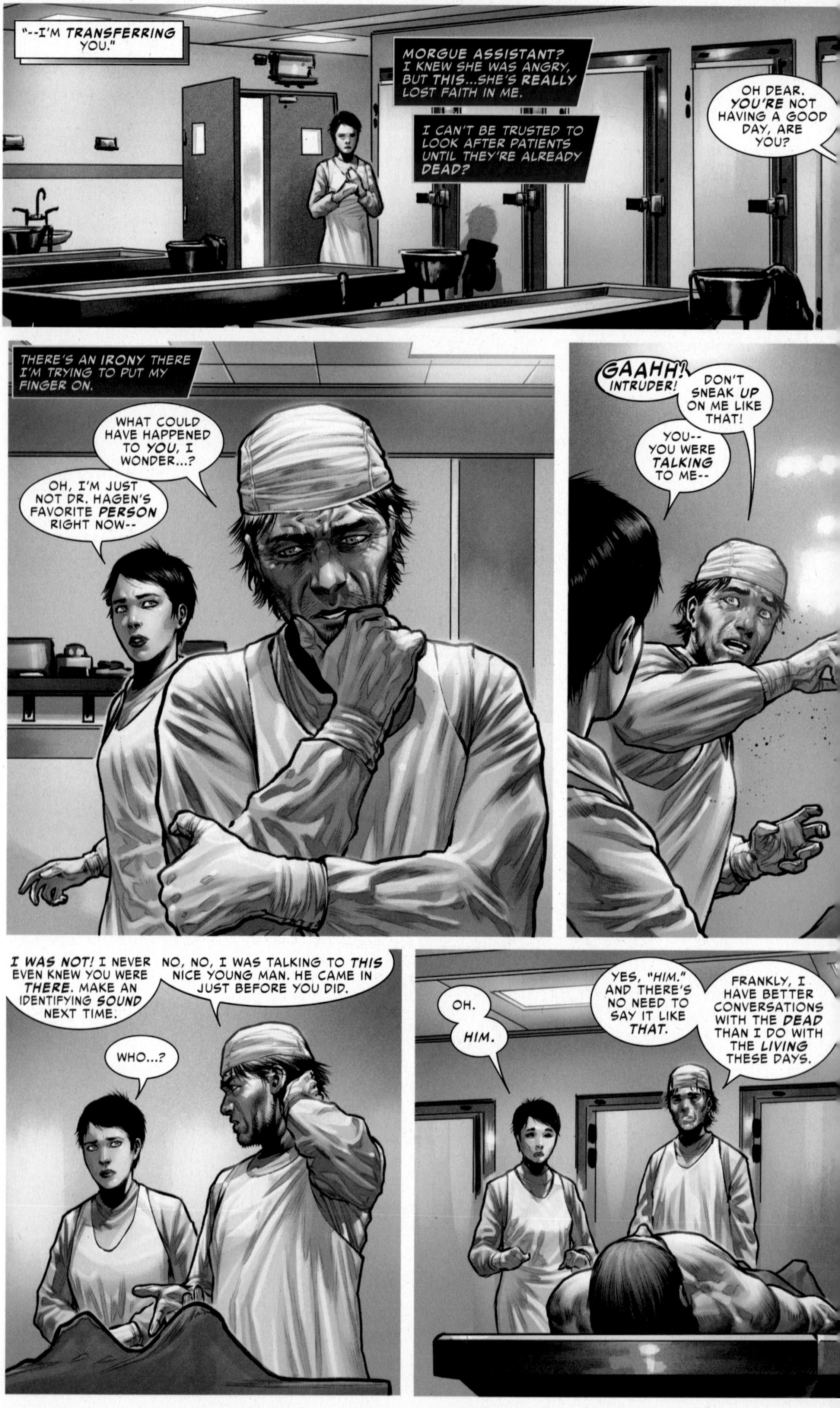
"--I'M TRANSFERRING YOU."
MORGUE ASSISTANT? I KNEW SHE WAS ANGRY, BUT THIS...SHE'S REALLY LOST FAITH IN ME.
I CAN'T BE TRUSTED TO LOOK AFTER PATIENTS UNTIL THEY'RE ALREADY DEAD?
OH DEAR. YOU'RE NOT HAVING A GOOD DAY, ARE YOU?
THERE'S AN IRONY THERE I'M TRYING TO PUT MY FINGER ON.
WHAT COULD HAVE HAPPENED TO YOU, I WONDER...?
OH, I'M JUST NOT DR. HAGEN'S FAVORITE PERSON RIGHT NOW--
GAAHH?! INTRUDER!
DON'T SNEAK UP ON ME LIKE THAT!
YOU-- YOU WERE TALKING TO ME--
I WAS NOT! I NEVER EVEN KNEW YOU WERE THERE. MAKE AN IDENTIFYING SOUND NEXT TIME.
NO, NO, I WAS TALKING TO THIS NICE YOUNG MAN. HE CAME IN JUST BEFORE YOU DID.
WHO...?
OH.
HIM.
YES, "HIM." AND THERE'S NO NEED TO SAY IT LIKE THAT.
FRANKLY, I HAVE BETTER CONVERSATIONS WITH THE DEAD THAN I DO WITH THE LIVING THESE DAYS.

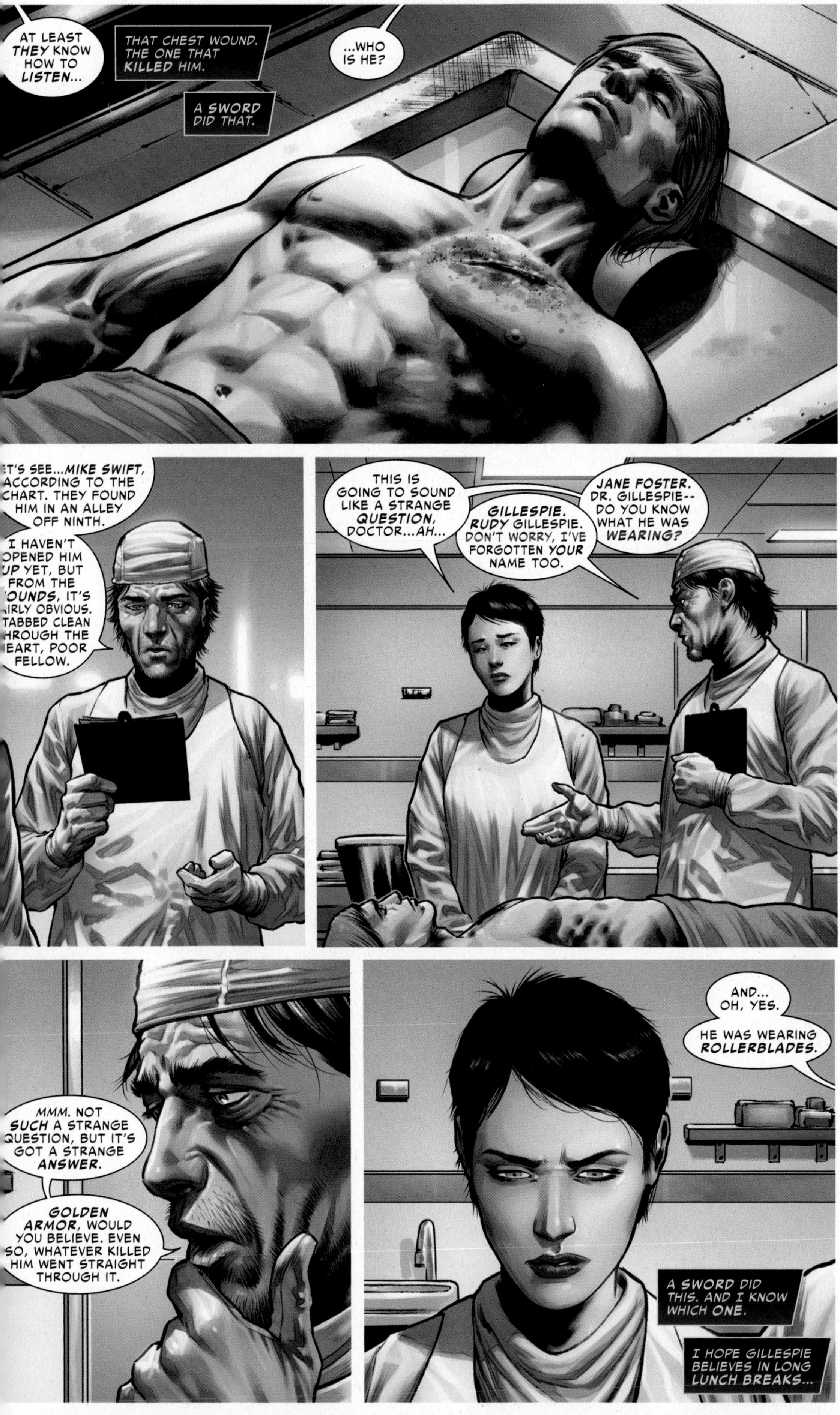

AT LEAST THEY KNOW HOW TO LISTEN...
THAT CHEST WOUND. THE ONE THAT KILLED HIM.
A SWORD DID THAT.
...WHO IS HE?
T'S SEE...MIKE SWIFT, ACCORDING TO THE CHART. THEY FOUND HIM IN AN ALLEY OFF NINTH.
I HAVEN'T OPENED HIM UP YET, BUT FROM THE OUNDS, IT'S IRLY OBVIOUS. TABBED CLEAN HROUGH THE EART, POOR FELLOW.
THIS IS GOING TO SOUND LIKE A STRANGE QUESTION, DOCTOR...AH...
GILLESPIE. RUDY GILLESPIE. DON'T WORRY, I'VE FORGOTTEN YOUR NAME TOO.
JANE FOSTER. DR. GILLESPIE-- DO YOU KNOW WHAT HE WAS WEARING?
MMM. NOT SUCH A STRANGE QUESTION, BUT IT'S GOT A STRANGE ANSWER.
GOLDEN ARMOR, WOULD YOU BELIEVE. EVEN SO, WHATEVER KILLED HIM WENT STRAIGHT THROUGH IT.
AND... OH, YES.
HE WAS WEARING ROLLERBLADES.
A SWORD DID THIS. AND I KNOW WHICH ONE.
I HOPE GILLESPIE BELIEVES IN LONG LUNCH BREAKS...

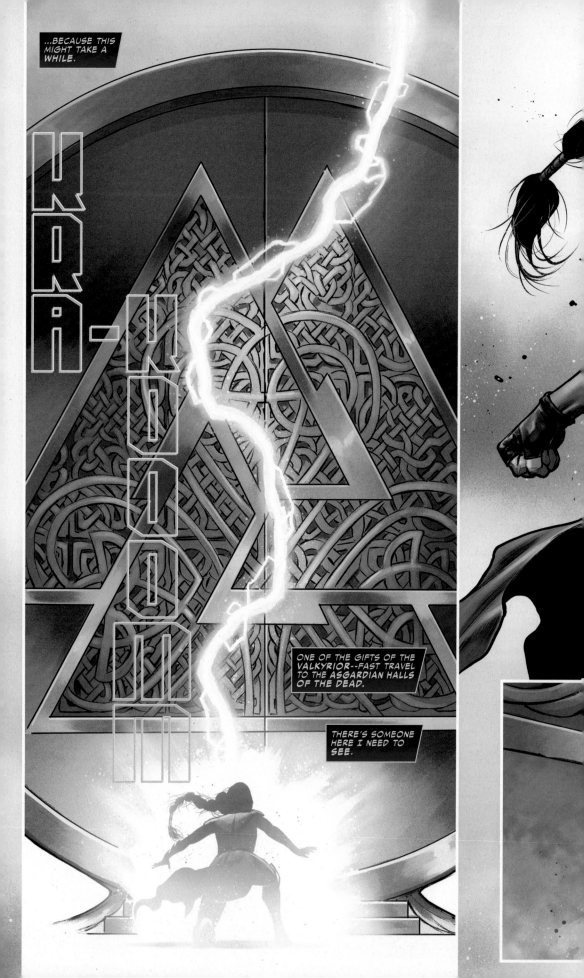

...BECAUSE THIS MIGHT TAKE A WHILE.

ONE OF THE GIFTS OF THE VALKYRIOR--FAST TRAVEL TO THE ASGARDIAN HALLS OF THE DEAD.

THERE'S SOMEONE HERE I NEED TO SEE.

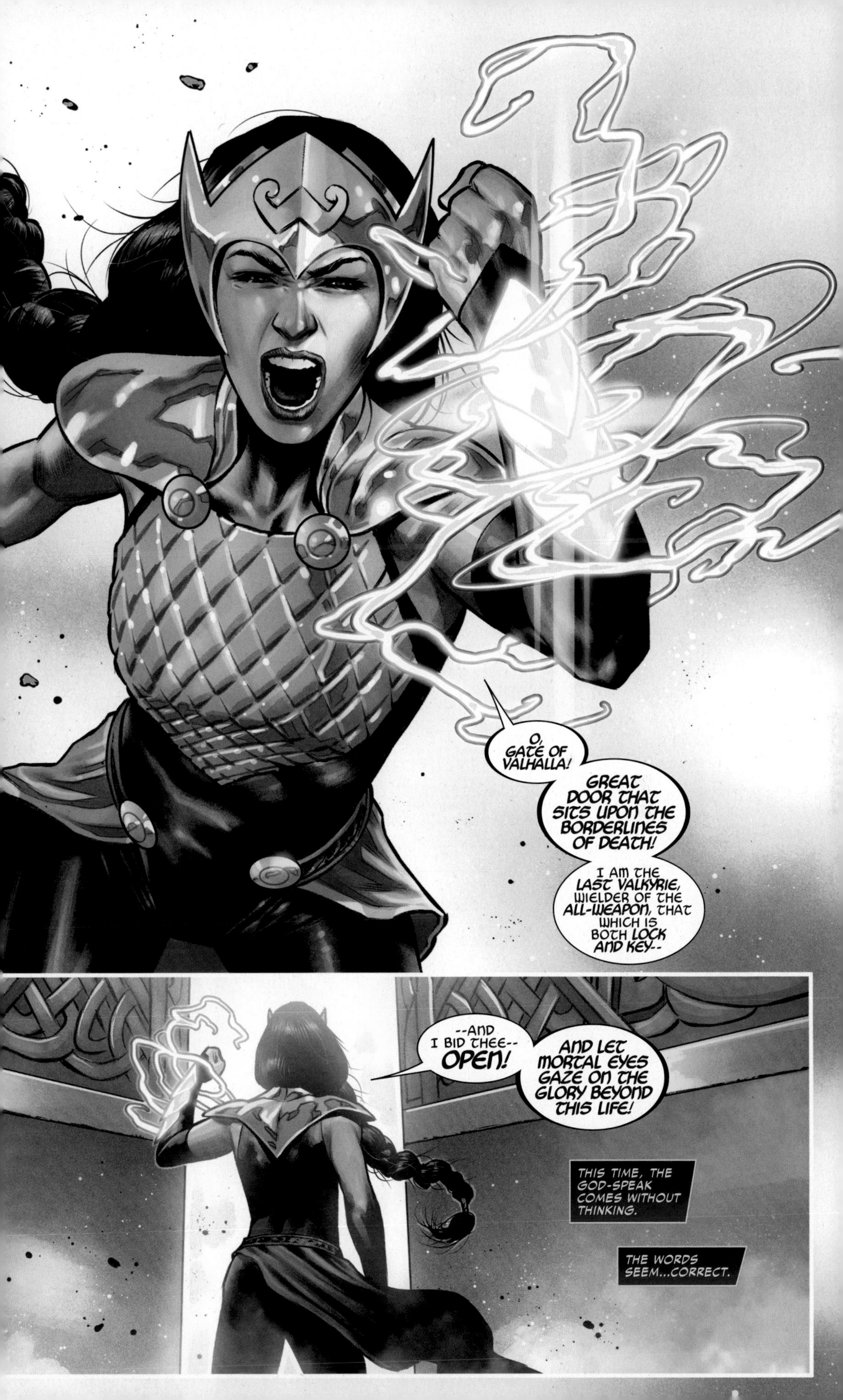
O, GATE OF VALHALLA!
GREAT DOOR THAT SITS UPON THE BORDERLINES OF DEATH!
I AM THE LAST VALKYRIE, WIELDER OF THE ALL-WEAPON, THAT WHICH IS BOTH LOCK AND KEY--
--AND I BID THEE-- OPEN!
AND LET MORTAL EYES GAZE ON THE GLORY BEYOND THIS LIFE!
THIS TIME, THE GOD-SPEAK COMES WITHOUT THINKING.
THE WORDS SEEM...CORRECT.

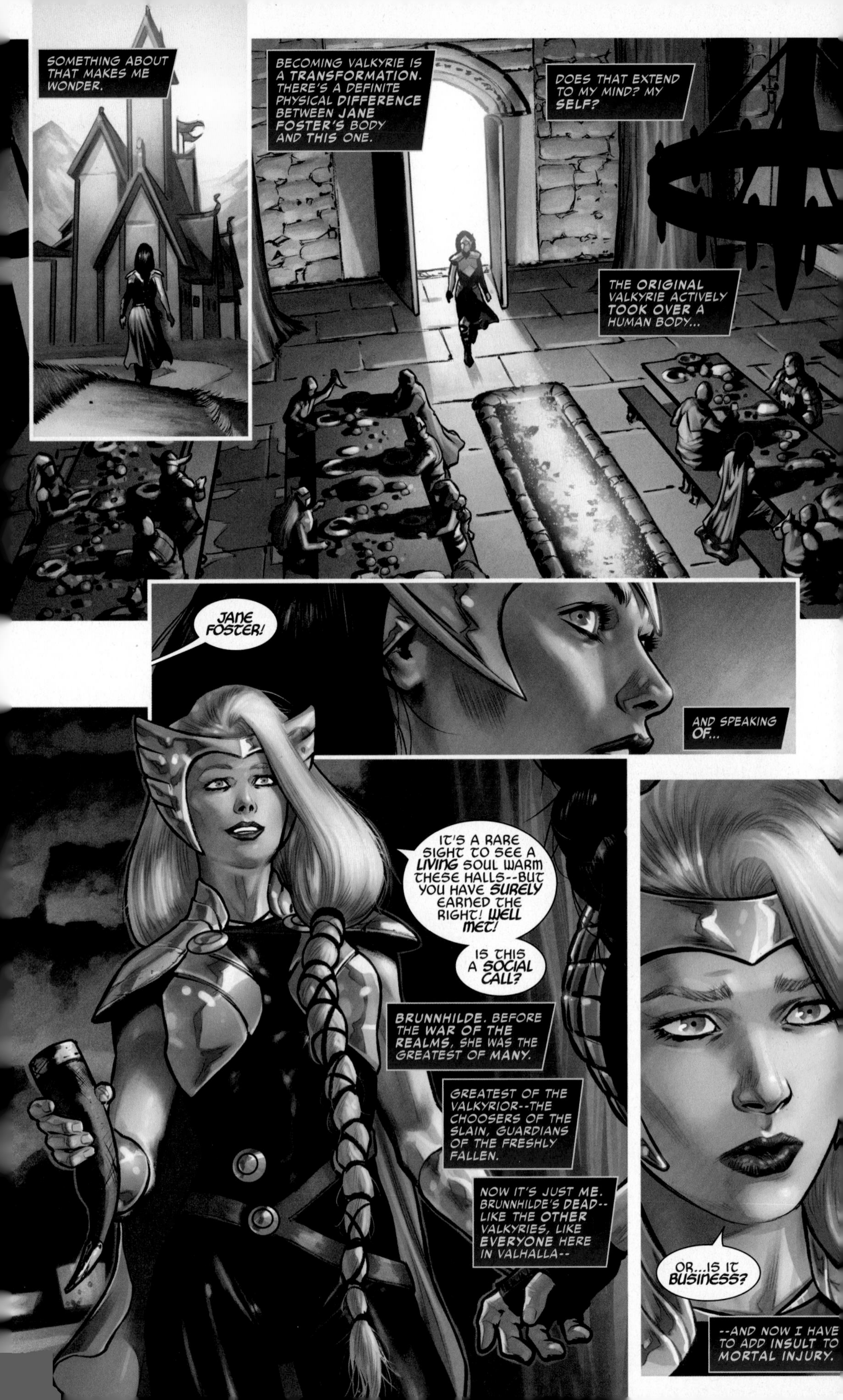
SOMETHING ABOUT THAT MAKES ME WONDER.
BECOMING VALKYRIE IS A TRANSFORMATION. THERE'S A DEFINITE PHYSICAL DIFFERENCE BETWEEN JANE FOSTER'S BODY AND THIS ONE.
DOES THAT EXTEND TO MY MIND? MY SELF?
THE ORIGINAL VALKYRIE ACTIVELY TOOK OVER A HUMAN BODY...
JANE FOSTER!
AND SPEAKING OF...
IT'S A RARE SIGHT TO SEE A LIVING SOUL WARM THESE HALLS--BUT YOU HAVE SURELY EARNED THE RIGHT! WELL MET!
IS THIS A SOCIAL CALL?
BRUNNHILDE. BEFORE THE WAR OF THE REALMS, SHE WAS THE GREATEST OF MANY.
GREATEST OF THE VALKYRIOR--THE CHOOSERS OF THE SLAIN, GUARDIANS OF THE FRESHLY FALLEN.
NOW IT'S JUST ME. BRUNNHILDE'S DEAD--LIKE THE OTHER VALKYRIES, LIKE EVERYONE HERE IN VALHALLA--
OR...IS IT BUSINESS?
--AND NOW I HAVE TO ADD INSULT TO MORTAL INJURY.

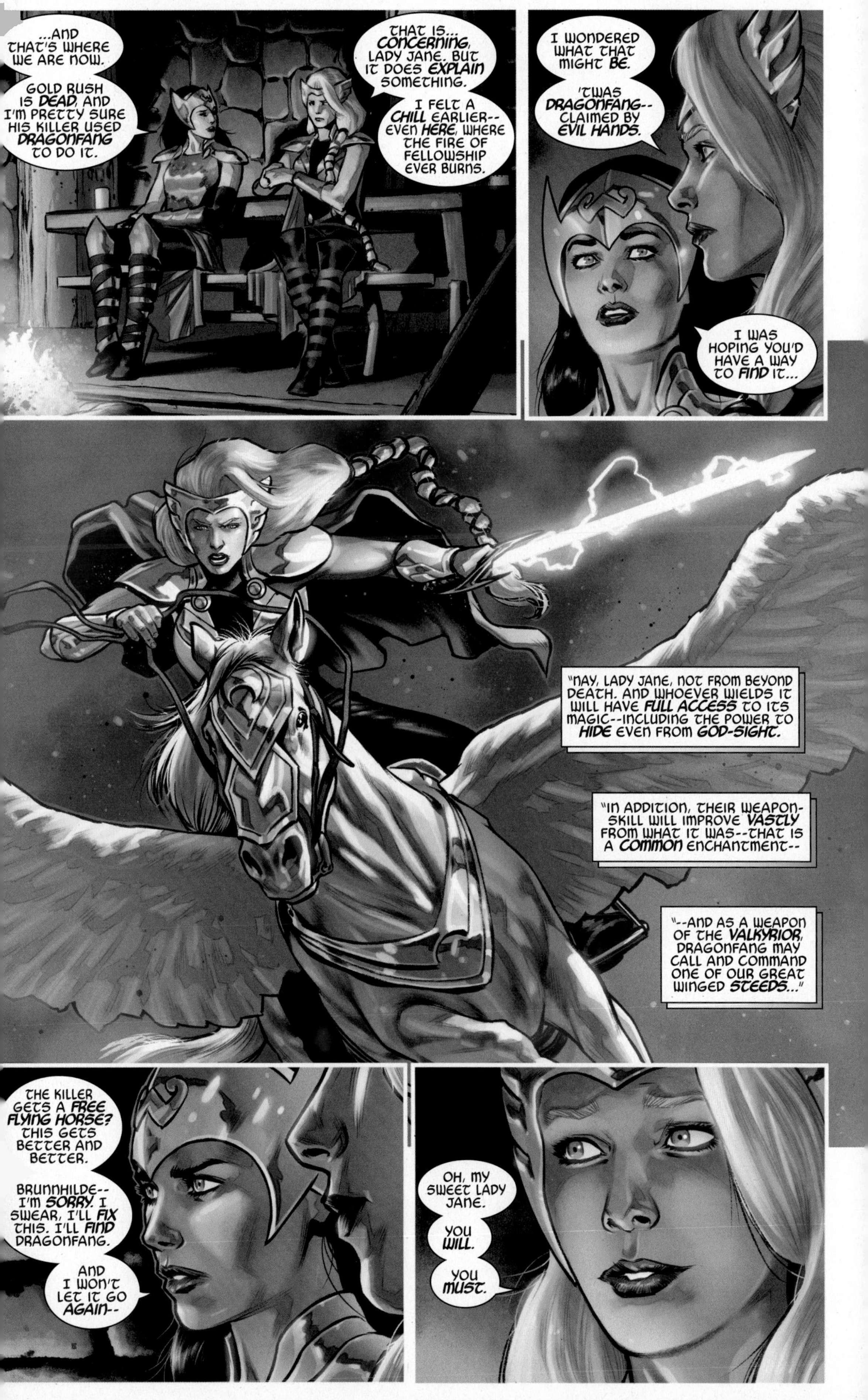
...AND THAT'S WHERE WE ARE NOW.
GOLD RUSH IS DEAD, AND I'M PRETTY SURE HIS KILLER USED DRAGONFANG TO DO IT.
THAT IS... CONCERNING, LADY JANE. BUT IT DOES EXPLAIN SOMETHING.
I FELT A CHILL EARLIER--EVEN HERE, WHERE THE FIRE OF FELLOWSHIP EVER BURNS.
I WONDERED WHAT THAT MIGHT BE.
'TWAS DRAGONFANG--CLAIMED BY EVIL HANDS.
I WAS HOPING YOU'D HAVE A WAY TO FIND IT...
"NAY, LADY JANE, NOT FROM BEYOND DEATH. AND WHOEVER WIELDS IT WILL HAVE FULL ACCESS TO ITS MAGIC--INCLUDING THE POWER TO HIDE EVEN FROM GOD-SIGHT.
"IN ADDITION, THEIR WEAPON-SKILL WILL IMPROVE VASTLY FROM WHAT IT WAS--THAT IS A COMMON ENCHANTMENT--
"--AND AS A WEAPON OF THE VALKYRIOR, DRAGONFANG MAY CALL AND COMMAND ONE OF OUR GREAT WINGED STEEDS..."
THE KILLER GETS A FREE FLYING HORSE? THIS GETS BETTER AND BETTER.
BRUNNHILDE--I'M SORRY. I SWEAR, I'LL FIX THIS. I'LL FIND DRAGONFANG.
AND I WON'T LET IT GO AGAIN--
OH, MY SWEET LADY JANE.
YOU WILL.
YOU MUST.

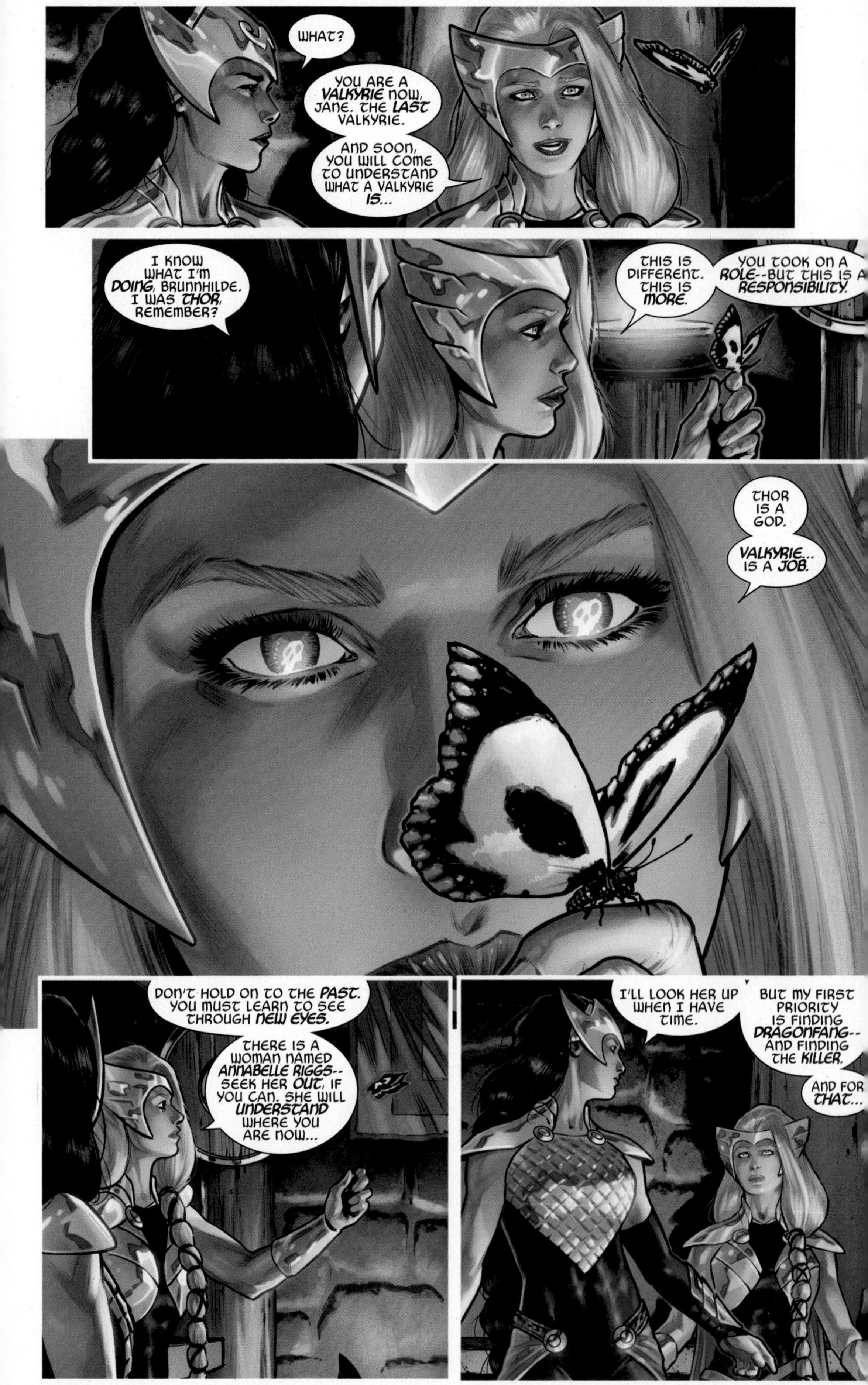
WHAT?
YOU ARE A VALKYRIE NOW, JANE. THE LAST VALKYRIE.
AND SOON, YOU WILL COME TO UNDERSTAND WHAT A VALKYRIE IS...
I KNOW WHAT I'M DOING, BRUNNHILDE. I WAS THOR, REMEMBER?
THIS IS DIFFERENT. THIS IS MORE.
YOU TOOK ON A ROLE--BUT THIS IS A RESPONSIBILITY.
THOR IS A GOD.
VALKYRIE... IS A JOB.
DON'T HOLD ON TO THE PAST. YOU MUST LEARN TO SEE THROUGH NEW EYES.
THERE IS A WOMAN NAMED ANNABELLE RIGGS--SEEK HER OUT, IF YOU CAN. SHE WILL UNDERSTAND WHERE YOU ARE NOW...
I'LL LOOK HER UP WHEN I HAVE TIME.
BUT MY FIRST PRIORITY IS FINDING DRAGONFANG--AND FINDING THE KILLER.
AND FOR THAT...

"...I'M GOING TO NEED A SPECIALIST'S HELP."

HMM. IT MAKES *SENSE*, LADY JANE.

TO FIND WHAT *HIDES* FROM THE SIGHT OF *GODS*--YOU NEED THE SERVICES OF THE *GOD OF SEEING*...

...HEIMDALL OF THE AESIR.

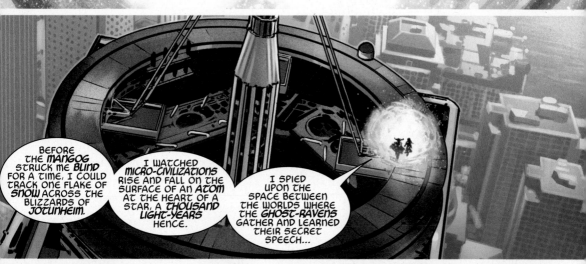

BEFORE THE *MANGOG* STRUCK ME *BLIND* FOR A TIME, I COULD TRACK ONE FLAKE OF *SNOW* ACROSS THE BLIZZARDS OF *JOTUNHEIM*.

I WATCHED *MICRO-CIVILIZATIONS* RISE AND FALL ON THE SURFACE OF AN *ATOM* AT THE HEART OF A STAR, A *THOUSAND LIGHT-YEARS* HENCE.

I SPIED UPON THE SPACE BETWEEN THE WORLDS WHERE THE *GHOST-RAVENS* GATHER AND LEARNED THEIR *SECRET SPEECH*...

LOOKING PAST THE HIDING-MAGICS OF *DRAGONFANG* WILL BE A *FINE* TEST OF HOW FAR THESE EYES HAVE *HEALED*.

THANKS, HEIMDALL. I *APPRECIATE* IT.

CAN I... DO ANYTHING TO *HELP*?

WELL, OF *COURSE!* YOU ARE *VALKYRIE*, ARE YOU NOT?

YOU CAN SEE WHAT I *CAN'T*.

...WHAT?

WHAT DID BRUNNHILDE SAY? "SEE THROUGH NEW EYES."

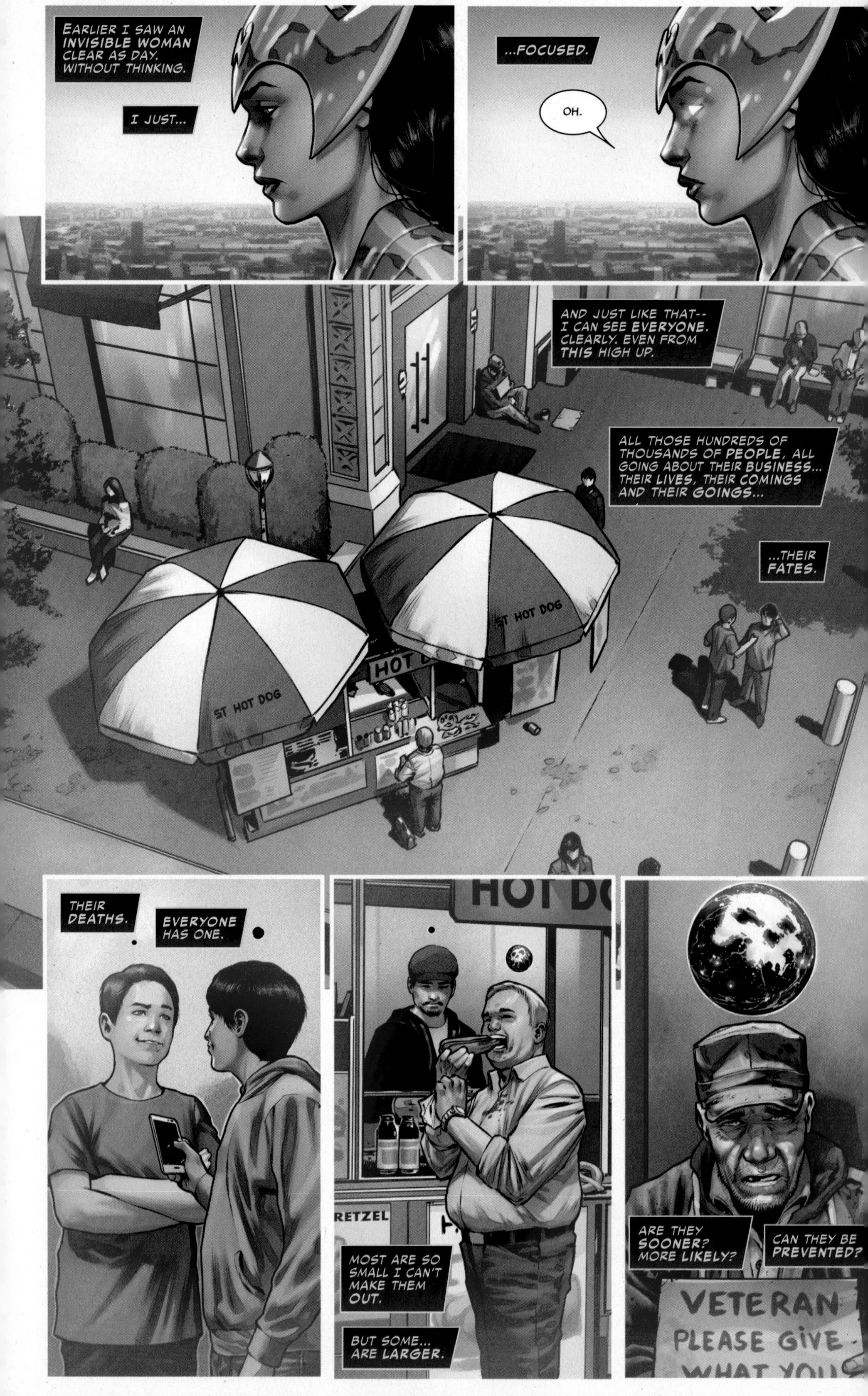
EARLIER I SAW AN INVISIBLE WOMAN CLEAR AS DAY. WITHOUT THINKING.
I JUST...
...FOCUSED.
OH.
AND JUST LIKE THAT-- I CAN SEE EVERYONE. CLEARLY. EVEN FROM THIS HIGH UP.
ALL THOSE HUNDREDS OF THOUSANDS OF PEOPLE, ALL GOING ABOUT THEIR BUSINESS... THEIR LIVES, THEIR COMINGS AND THEIR GOINGS...
...THEIR FATES.
ST HOT DOG
ST HOT DOG
HOT
THEIR DEATHS.
EVERYONE HAS ONE.
HOT D
RETZEL
MOST ARE SO SMALL I CAN'T MAKE THEM OUT.
BUT SOME... ARE LARGER.
ARE THEY SOONER? MORE LIKELY?
CAN THEY BE PREVENTED?
VETERAN
PLEASE GIVE

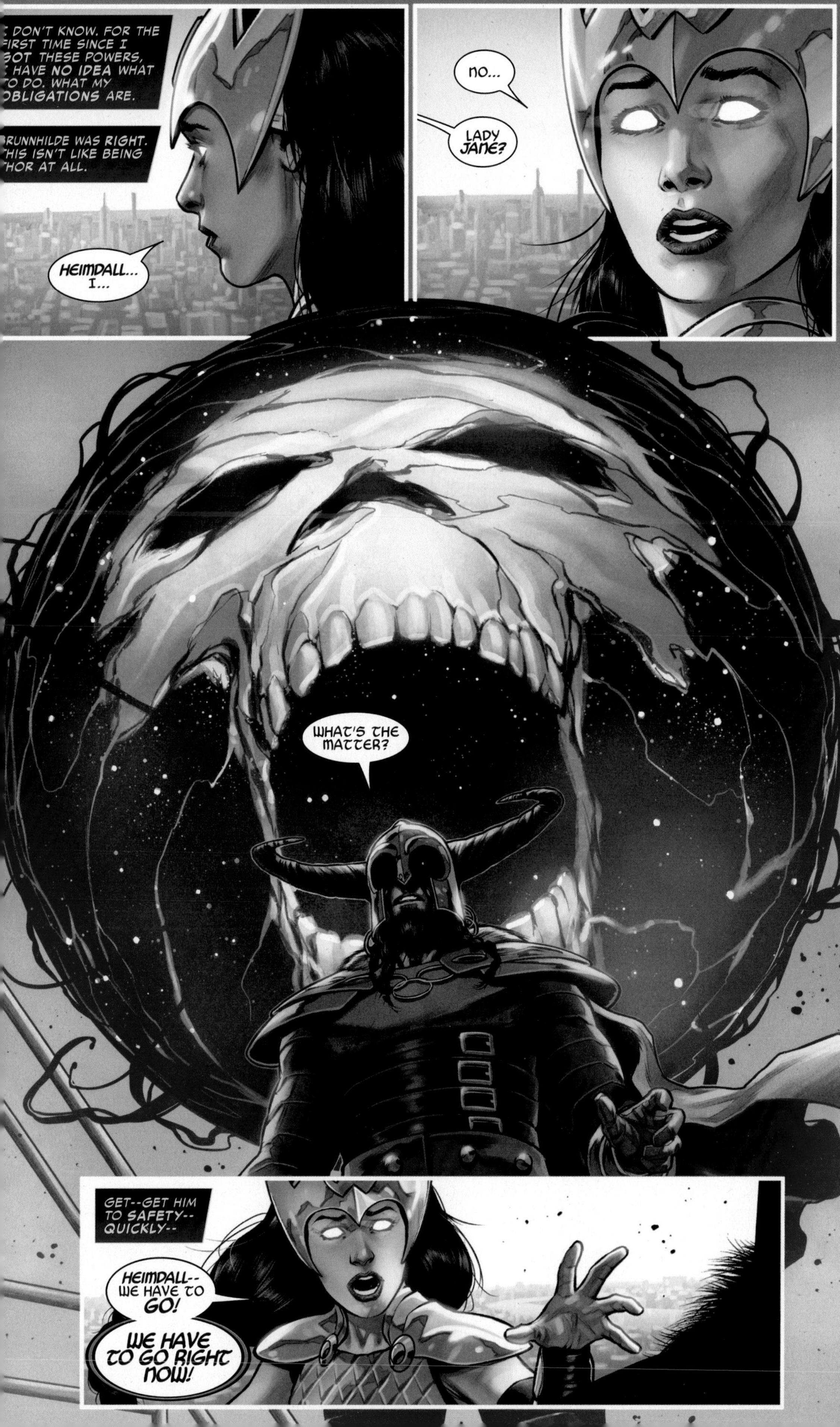

I DON'T KNOW. FOR THE FIRST TIME SINCE I GOT THESE POWERS, I HAVE NO IDEA WHAT TO DO. WHAT MY OBLIGATIONS ARE.
BRUNNHILDE WAS RIGHT. THIS ISN'T LIKE BEING THOR AT ALL.
HEIMDALL... I...
no...
LADY JANE?
WHAT'S THE MATTER?
GET--GET HIM TO SAFETY--QUICKLY--
HEIMDALL--WE HAVE TO GO!
WE HAVE TO GO RIGHT NOW!

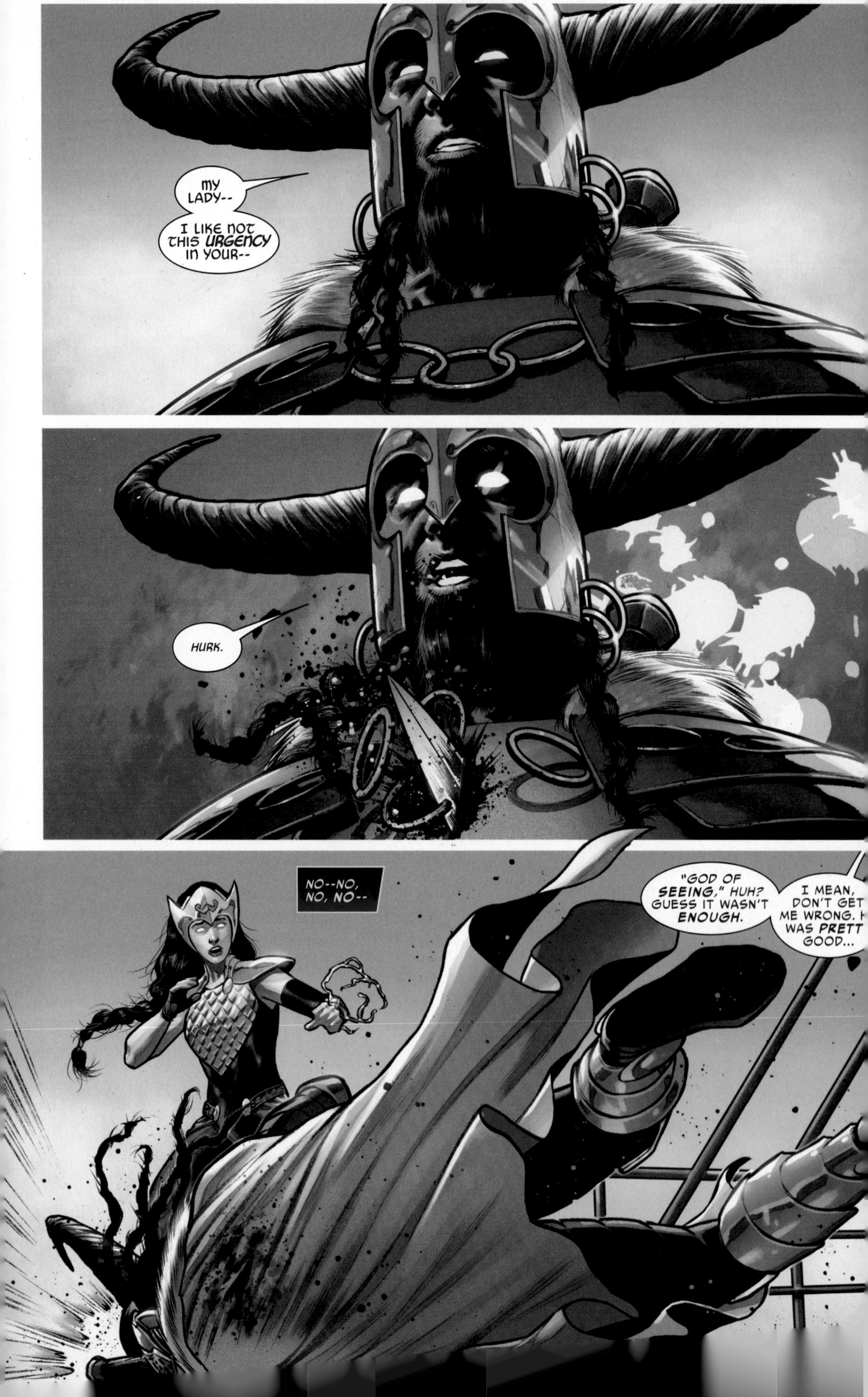
MY LADY--
I LIKE NOT THIS URGENCY IN YOUR--
HURK.
NO--NO, NO, NO--
"GOD OF SEEING," HUH? GUESS IT WASN'T ENOUGH.
I MEAN, DON'T GET ME WRONG. H WAS PRETT GOOD...

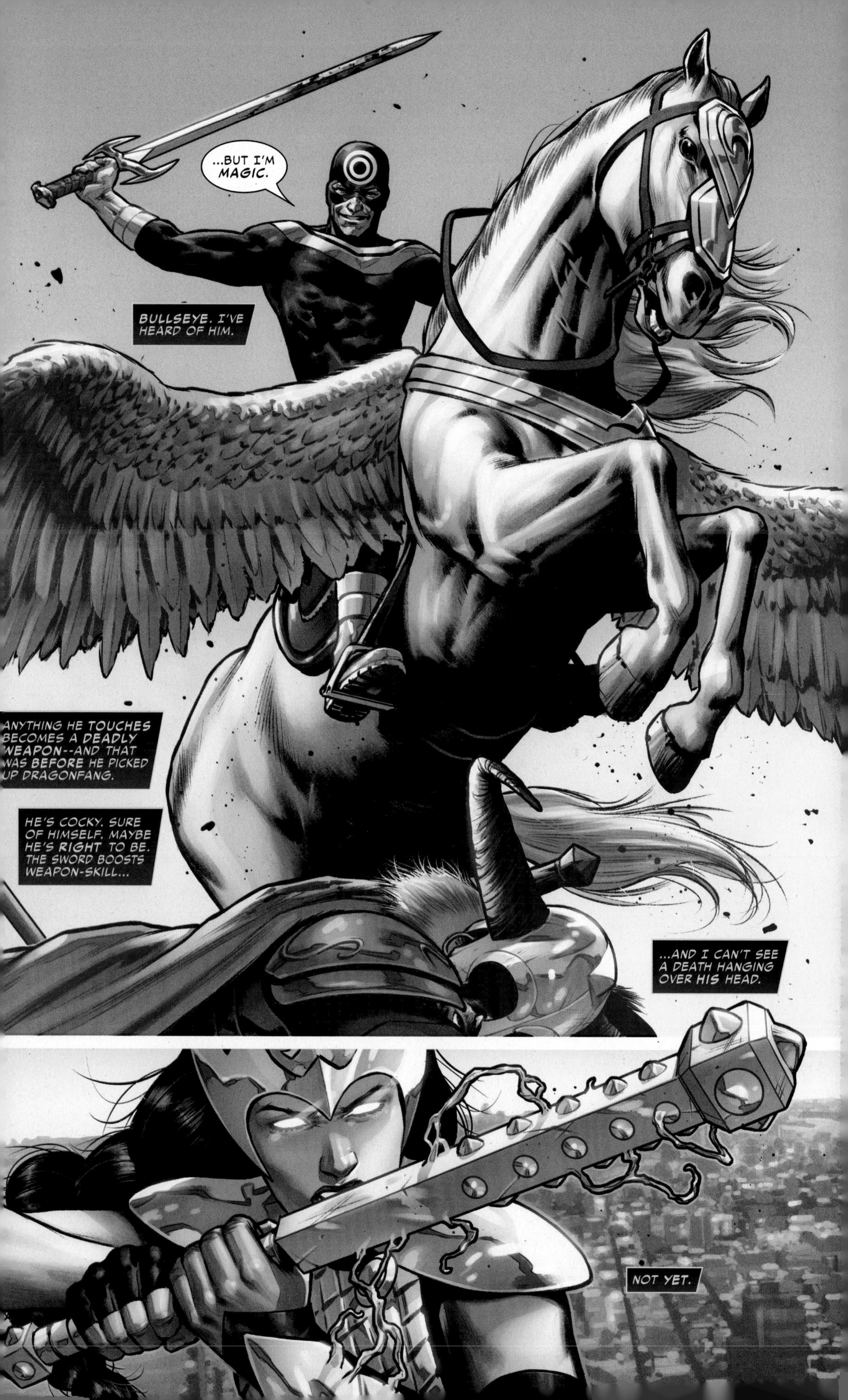

...BUT I'M MAGIC.
BULLSEYE. I'VE HEARD OF HIM.
ANYTHING HE TOUCHES BECOMES A DEADLY WEAPON--AND THAT WAS BEFORE HE PICKED UP DRAGONFANG.
HE'S COCKY. SURE OF HIMSELF. MAYBE HE'S RIGHT TO BE. THE SWORD BOOSTS WEAPON-SKILL...
...AND I CAN'T SEE A DEATH HANGING OVER HIS HEAD.
NOT YET.

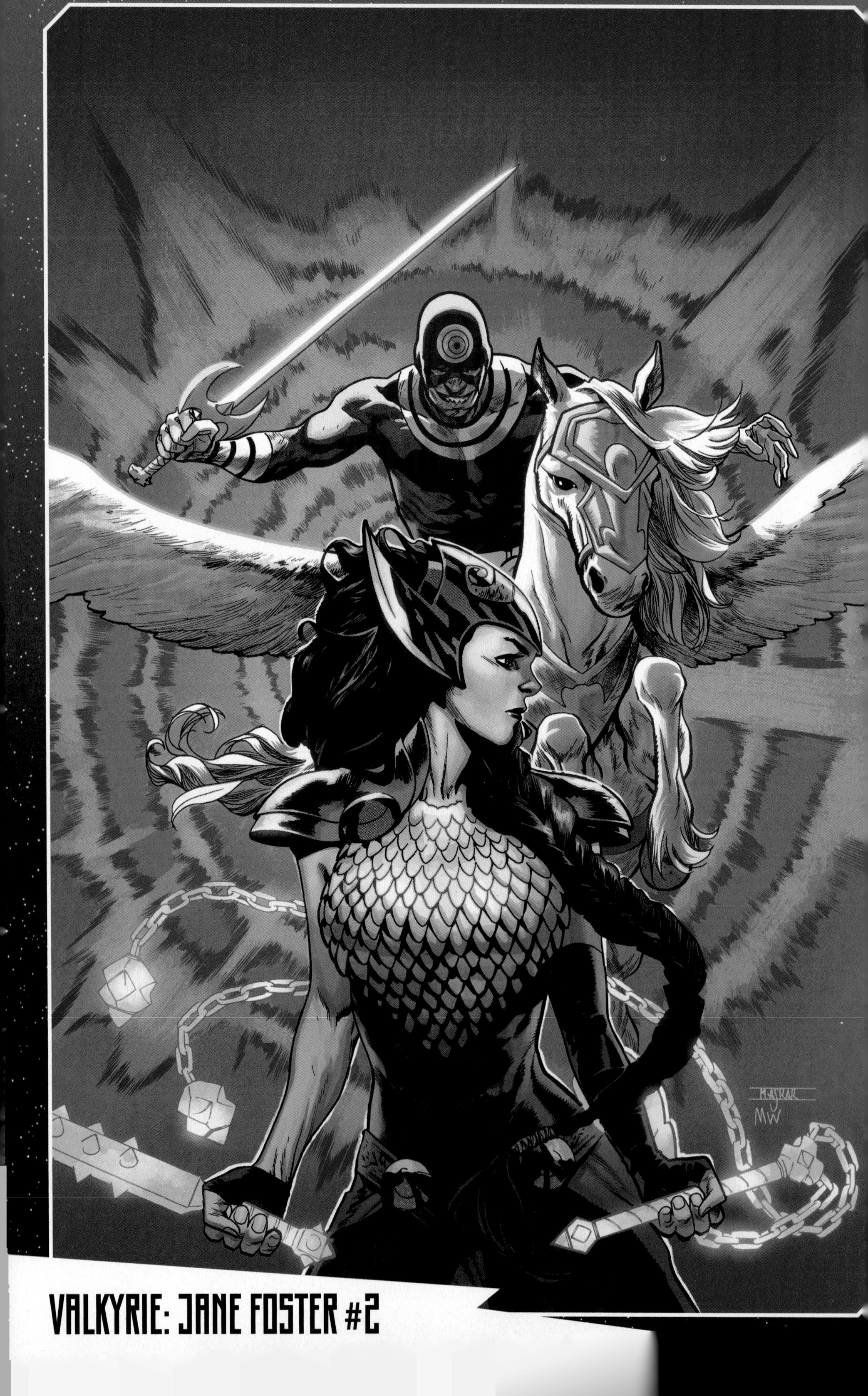

VALKYRIE: JANE FOSTER #2

MY NAME IS JANE FOSTER.

I'M A DOCTOR--WELL, A MORGUE ASSISTANT, BUT THAT'S TEMPORARY. I'M ALSO THE WARRIOR WHO FIGHTS FOR THE LIVING AND THE DEAD.

I'M THE VALKYRIE.

HIS NAME IS HEIMDALL.

HE'S AN ASGARDIAN GOD. A FEW SECONDS AGO, I SAW DEATH HANGING OVER HIS HEAD AND TRIED TO GET HIM TO SAFETY.

THEN DEATH MADE HIS ENTRANCE.

HIS NAME IS BULLSEYE.

HE'S A MURDERER. HE STABBED HEIMDALL THROUGH THE CHEST. HE TURNS WHATEVER HE'S HOLDING INTO A DEADLY WEAPON.

RIGHT NOW, HE'S HOLDING THE DEADLIEST WEAPON I KNOW OF.

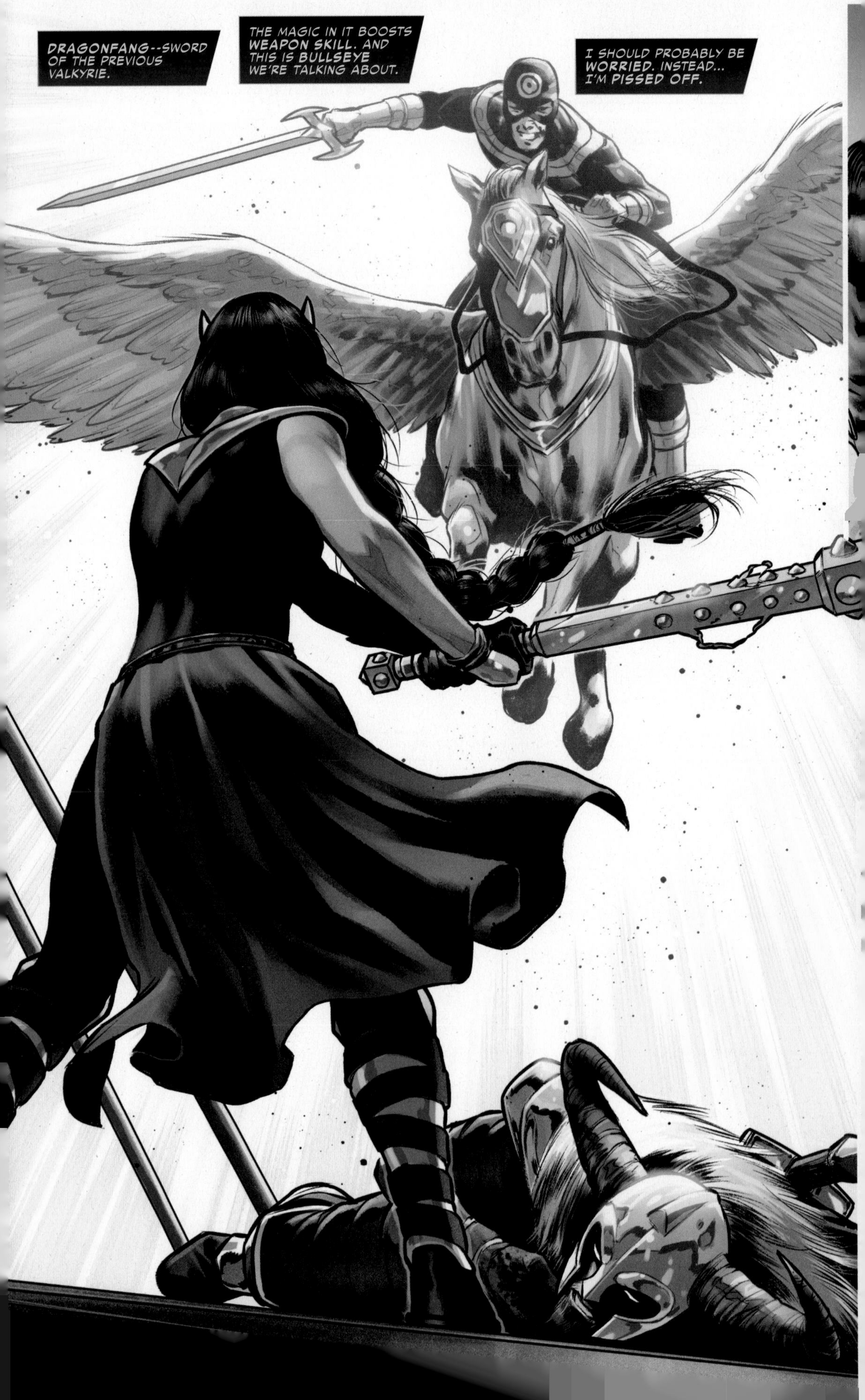
DRAGONFANG--SWORD OF THE PREVIOUS VALKYRIE.
THE MAGIC IN IT BOOSTS WEAPON SKILL. AND THIS IS BULLSEYE WE'RE TALKING ABOUT.
I SHOULD PROBABLY BE WORRIED. INSTEAD... I'M PISSED OFF.

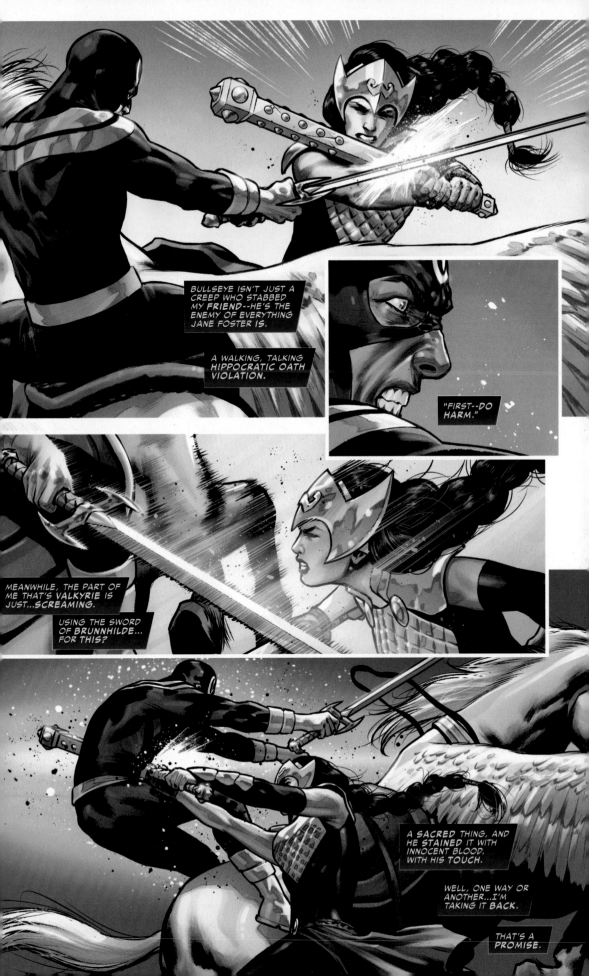

BULLSEYE ISN'T JUST A CREEP WHO STABBED MY FRIEND--HE'S THE ENEMY OF EVERYTHING JANE FOSTER IS.

A WALKING, TALKING HIPPOCRATIC OATH VIOLATION.

"FIRST--DO HARM."

MEANWHILE, THE PART OF ME THAT'S VALKYRIE IS JUST...SCREAMING.

USING THE SWORD OF BRUNNHILDE... FOR THIS?

A SACRED THING, AND HE STAINED IT WITH INNOCENT BLOOD. WITH HIS TOUCH.

WELL, ONE WAY OR ANOTHER...I'M TAKING IT BACK.

THAT'S A PROMISE.

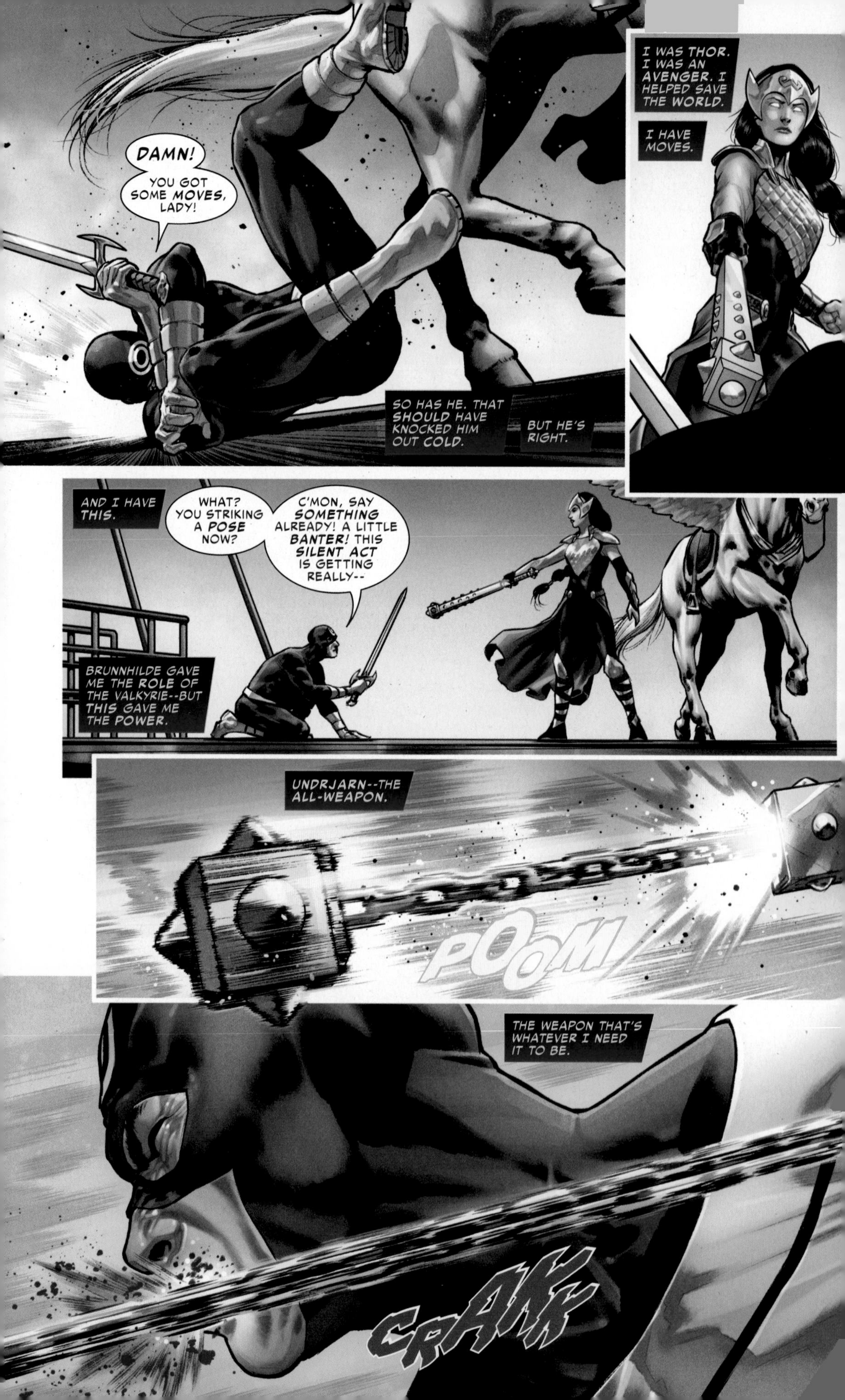

DAMN!
YOU GOT SOME MOVES, LADY!
I WAS THOR. I WAS AN AVENGER. I HELPED SAVE THE WORLD.
I HAVE MOVES.
SO HAS HE. THAT SHOULD HAVE KNOCKED HIM OUT COLD.
BUT HE'S RIGHT.
AND I HAVE THIS.
WHAT? YOU STRIKING A POSE NOW?
C'MON, SAY SOMETHING ALREADY! A LITTLE BANTER! THIS SILENT ACT IS GETTING REALLY--
BRUNNHILDE GAVE ME THE ROLE OF THE VALKYRIE--BUT THIS GAVE ME THE POWER.
UNDRJARN--THE ALL-WEAPON.
POOOM
THE WEAPON THAT'S WHATEVER I NEED IT TO BE.
CRAAK

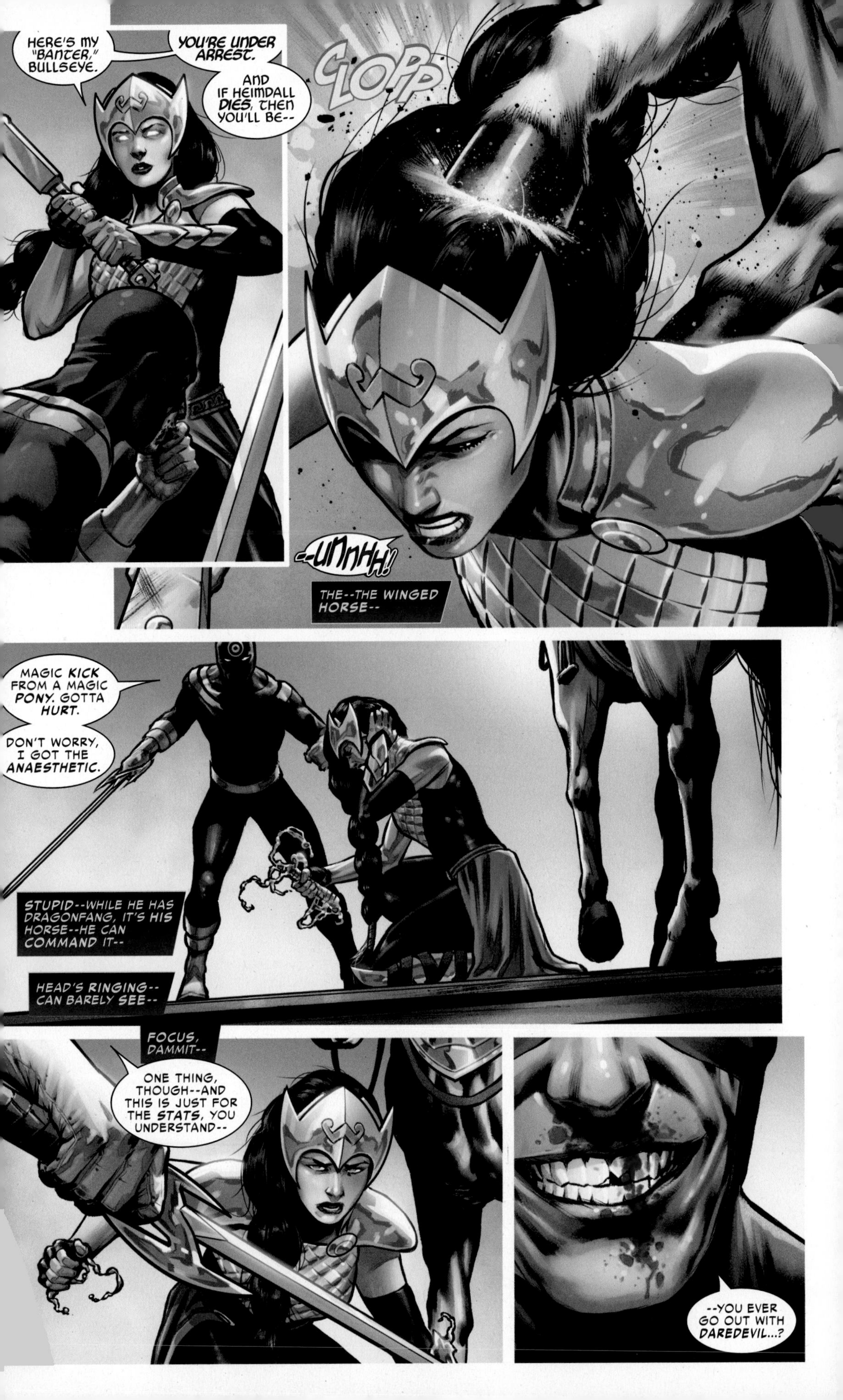
HERE'S MY "BANTER," BULLSEYE.
YOU'RE UNDER ARREST.
AND IF HEIMDALL DIES, THEN YOU'LL BE--
CLOPP
--UNNHH!
THE--THE WINGED HORSE--
MAGIC KICK FROM A MAGIC PONY. GOTTA HURT.
DON'T WORRY, I GOT THE ANAESTHETIC.
STUPID--WHILE HE HAS DRAGONFANG, IT'S HIS HORSE--HE CAN COMMAND IT--
HEAD'S RINGING--CAN BARELY SEE--
FOCUS, DAMMIT--
ONE THING, THOUGH--AND THIS IS JUST FOR THE STATS, YOU UNDERSTAND--
--YOU EVER GO OUT WITH DAREDEVIL...?

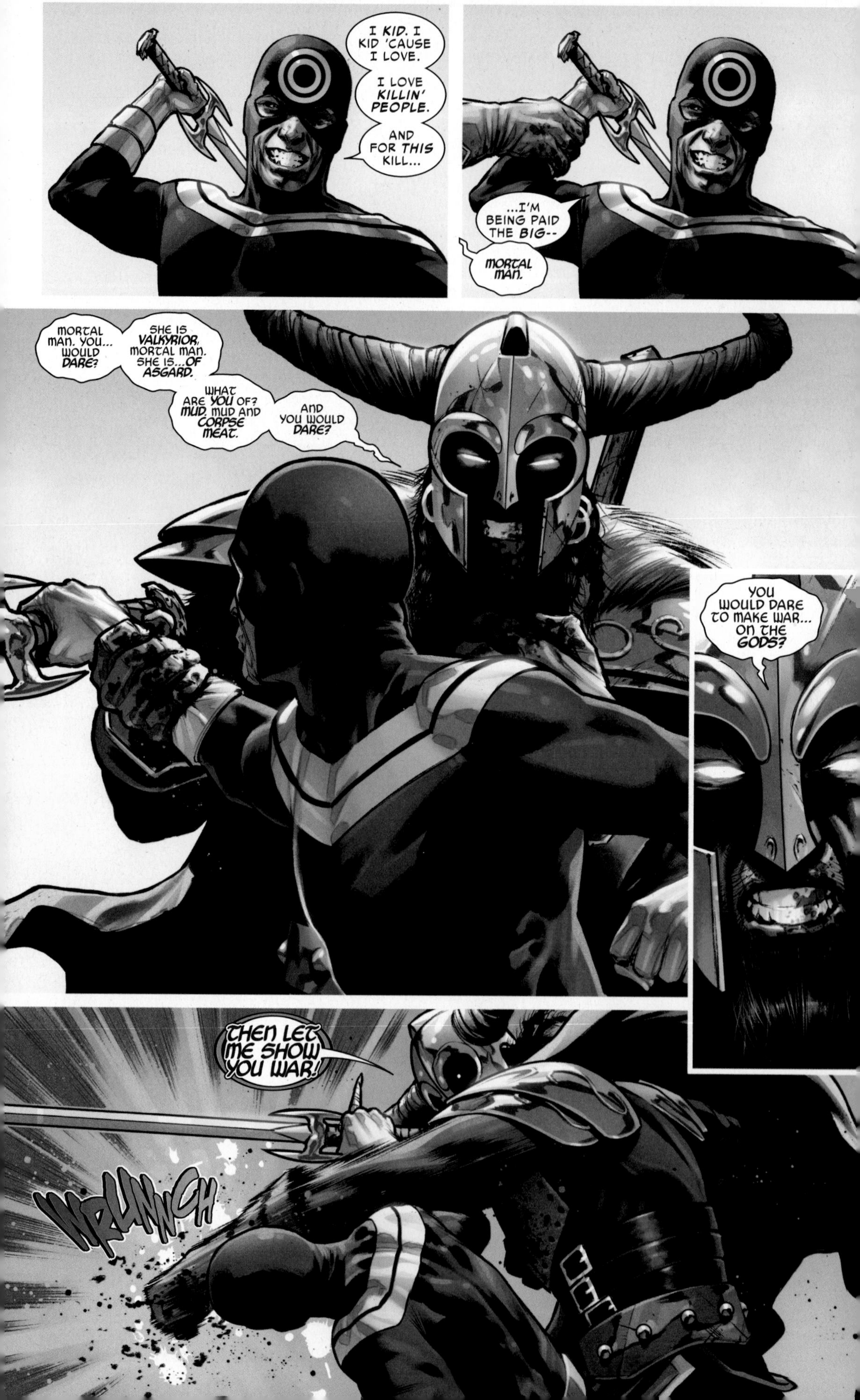

I KID. I KID 'CAUSE I LOVE.
I LOVE KILLIN' PEOPLE.
AND FOR THIS KILL...
...I'M BEING PAID THE BIG--
MORTAL MAN.
MORTAL MAN. YOU... WOULD DARE?
SHE IS VALKYRIOR, MORTAL MAN. SHE IS...OF ASGARD.
WHAT ARE YOU OF? MUD. MUD AND CORPSE MEAT.
AND YOU WOULD DARE?
YOU WOULD DARE TO MAKE WAR... ON THE GODS?
THEN LET ME SHOW YOU WAR!
WRUNNCH

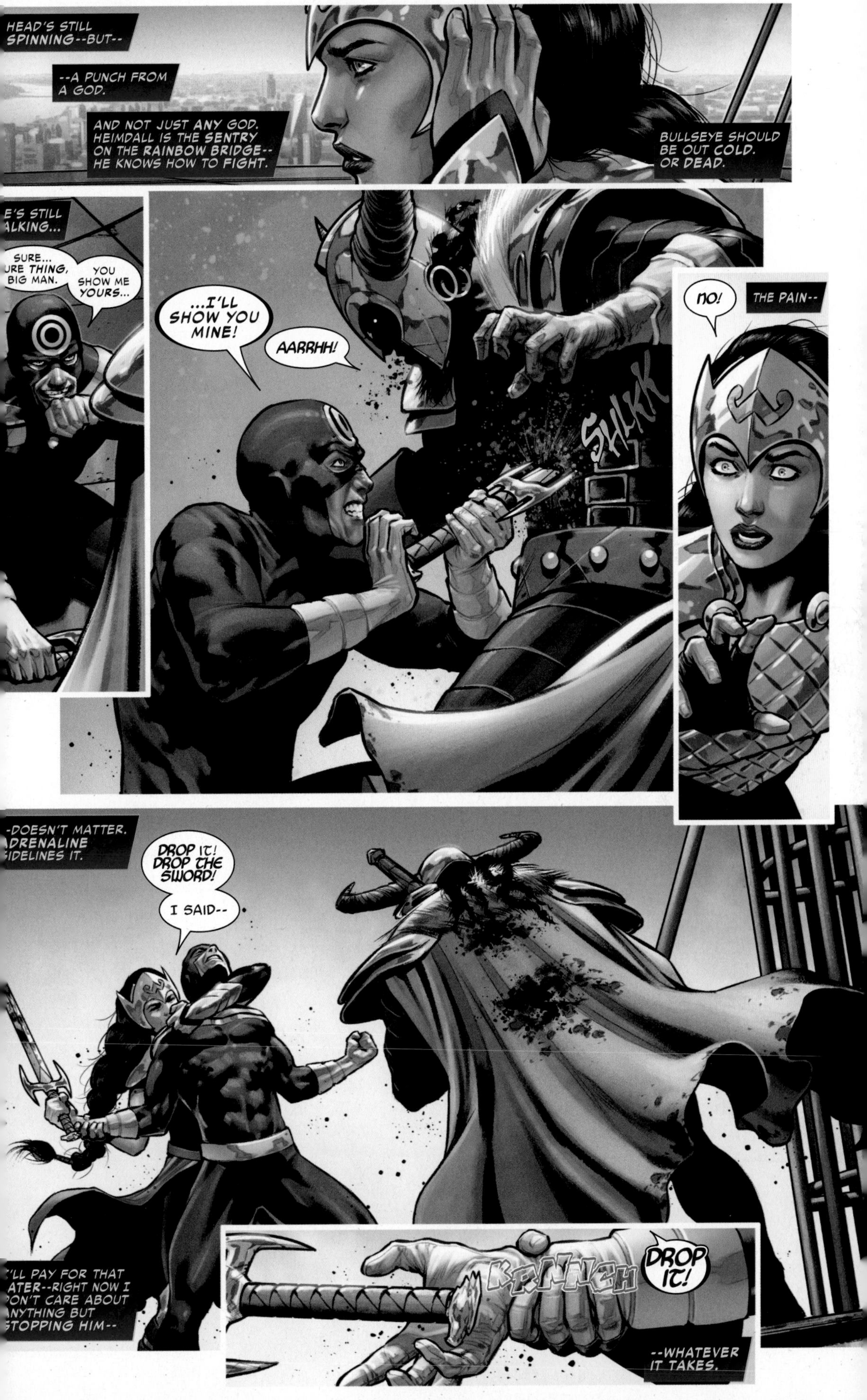

HEAD'S STILL SPINNING--BUT--
--A PUNCH FROM A GOD.
AND NOT JUST ANY GOD. HEIMDALL IS THE SENTRY ON THE RAINBOW BRIDGE--HE KNOWS HOW TO FIGHT.
BULLSEYE SHOULD BE OUT COLD. OR DEAD.
E'S STILL ALKING...
SURE... URE THING, BIG MAN.
YOU SHOW ME YOURS...
...I'LL SHOW YOU MINE!
AARRHH!
SHLKK
NO!
THE PAIN--
-DOESN'T MATTER. DRENALINE IDELINES IT.
DROP IT! DROP THE SWORD!
I SAID--
'LL PAY FOR THAT ATER--RIGHT NOW I ON'T CARE ABOUT NYTHING BUT TOPPING HIM--
DROP IT!
--WHATEVER IT TAKES.

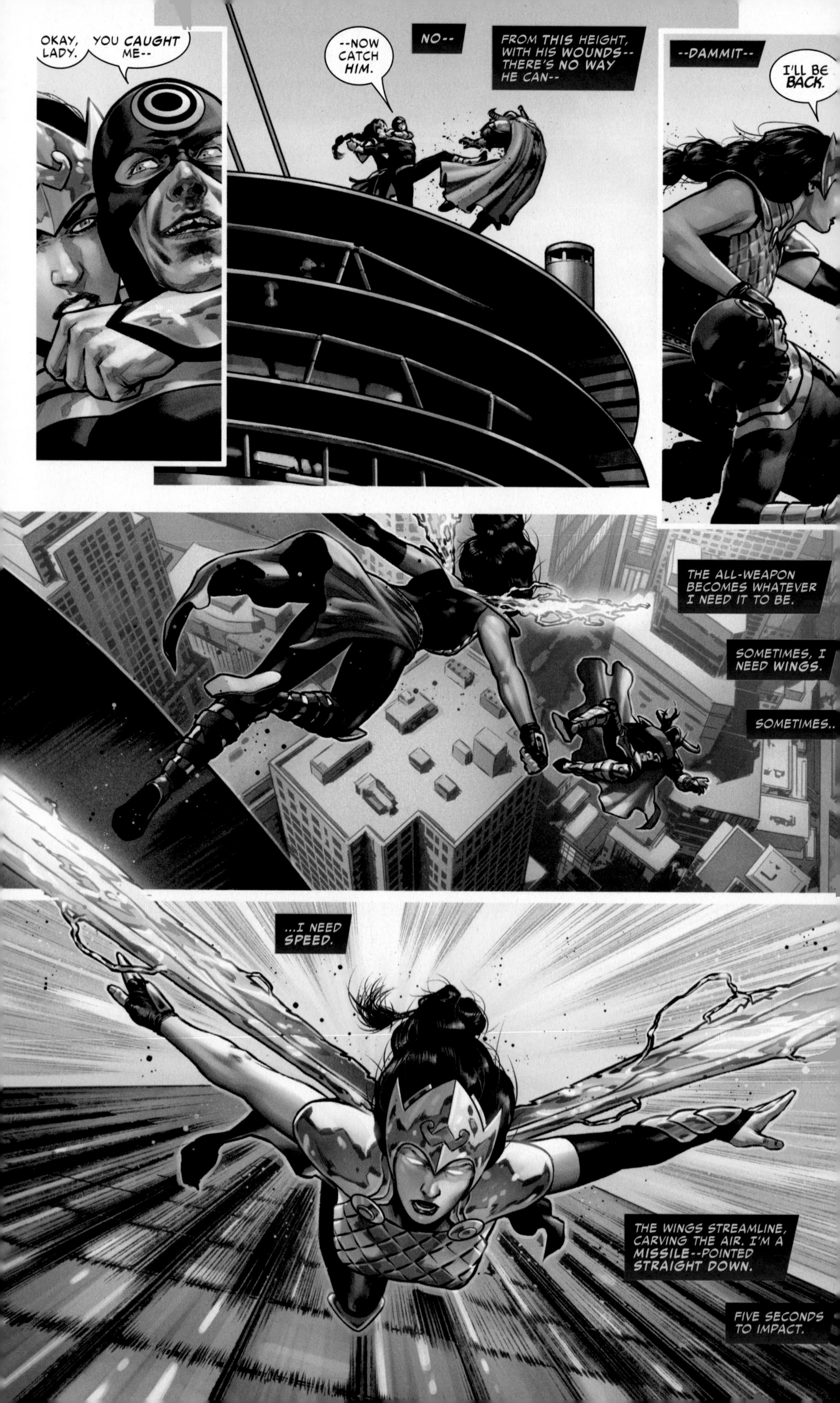

OKAY, LADY.
YOU CAUGHT ME--
--NOW CATCH HIM.
NO--
FROM THIS HEIGHT, WITH HIS WOUNDS-- THERE'S NO WAY HE CAN--
--DAMMIT--
I'LL BE BACK.
THE ALL-WEAPON BECOMES WHATEVER I NEED IT TO BE.
SOMETIMES, I NEED WINGS.
SOMETIMES...
...I NEED SPEED.
THE WINGS STREAMLINE, CARVING THE AIR. I'M A MISSILE--POINTED STRAIGHT DOWN.
FIVE SECONDS TO IMPACT.

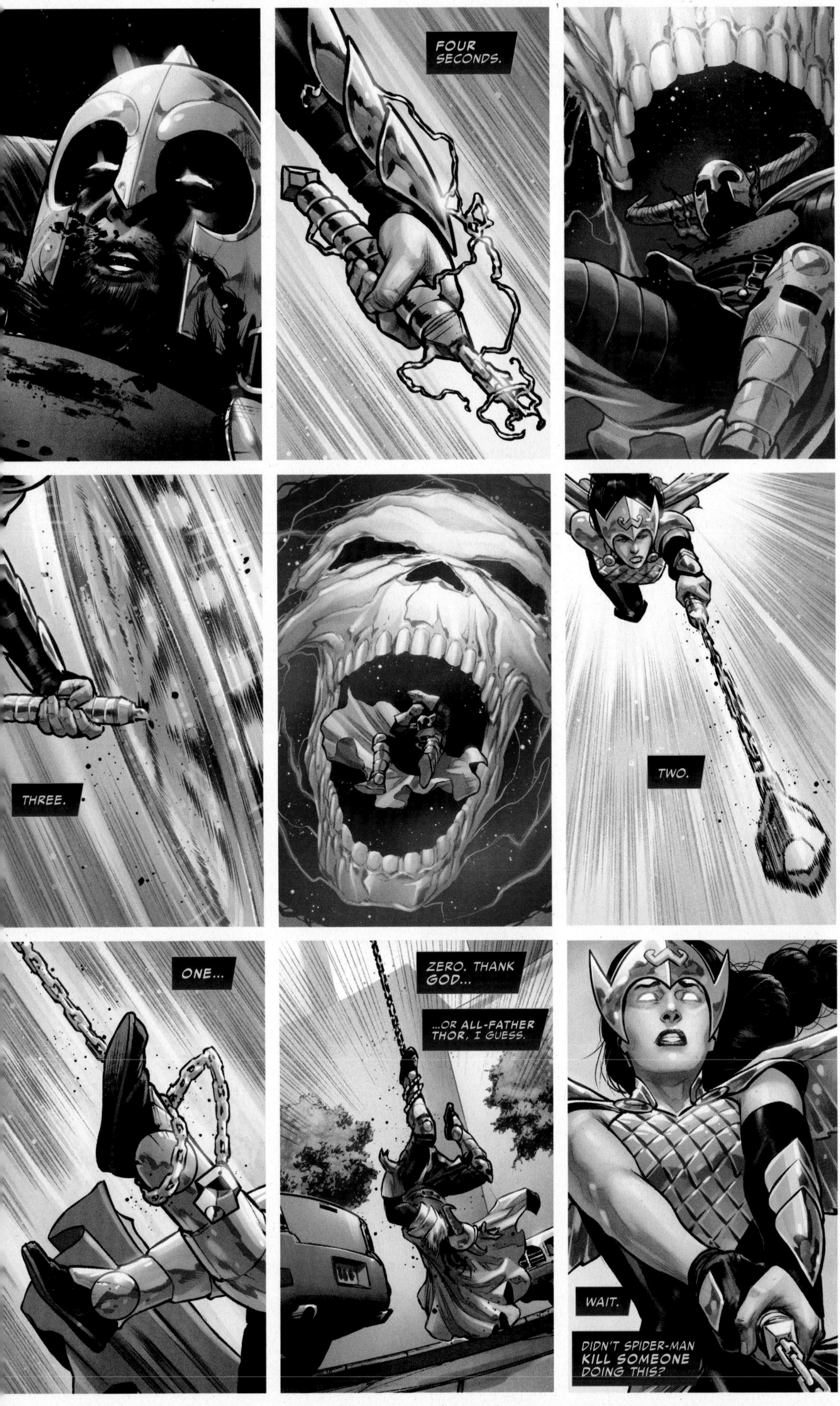
FOUR SECONDS.
THREE.
TWO.
ONE...
ZERO. THANK GOD...
...OR ALL-FATHER THOR, I GUESS.
WAIT.
DIDN'T SPIDER-MAN KILL SOMEONE DOING THIS?

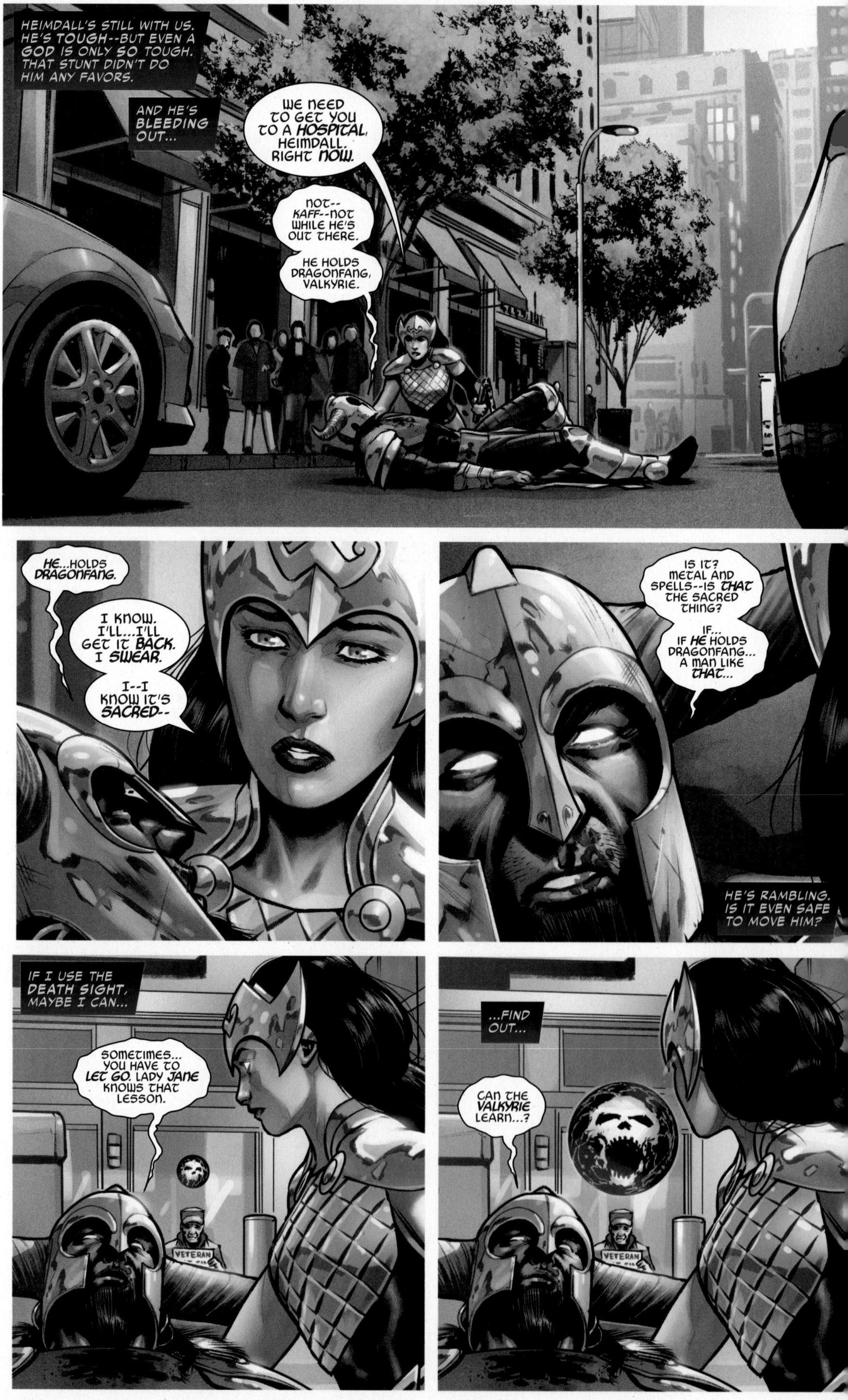
HEIMDALL'S STILL WITH US. HE'S TOUGH--BUT EVEN A GOD IS ONLY SO TOUGH. THAT STUNT DIDN'T DO HIM ANY FAVORS.
AND HE'S BLEEDING OUT...
WE NEED TO GET YOU TO A HOSPITAL, HEIMDALL. RIGHT NOW.
NOT-- KAFF--NOT WHILE HE'S OUT THERE.
HE HOLDS DRAGONFANG, VALKYRIE.
HE...HOLDS DRAGONFANG.
I KNOW. I'LL...I'LL GET IT BACK. I SWEAR.
I--I KNOW IT'S SACRED--
IS IT? METAL AND SPELLS--IS THAT THE SACRED THING?
IF... IF HE HOLDS DRAGONFANG... A MAN LIKE THAT...
HE'S RAMBLING. IS IT EVEN SAFE TO MOVE HIM?
IF I USE THE DEATH SIGHT, MAYBE I CAN...
SOMETIMES... YOU HAVE TO LET GO. LADY JANE KNOWS THAT LESSON.
VETERAN
...FIND OUT...
CAN THE VALKYRIE LEARN...?
VETERAN

I'M LEARNING THE RULES AS I GO.

RULE ONE: DEATH IS OVER EVERYONE'S HEAD.

PFFT. ALWAYS SOME CAPED CRAP...

VETERAN PLEASE G

BUT WHEN IT'S A BIG DEATH...

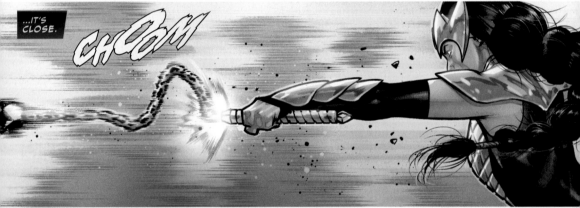

...IT'S CLOSE.

CHOOM

YAAAHH!

WH-WHAT THE HELL--

VETERAN PLEASE GIVE WHAT YOU CAN.

SHLINNGGG

HE'S CLOSE.

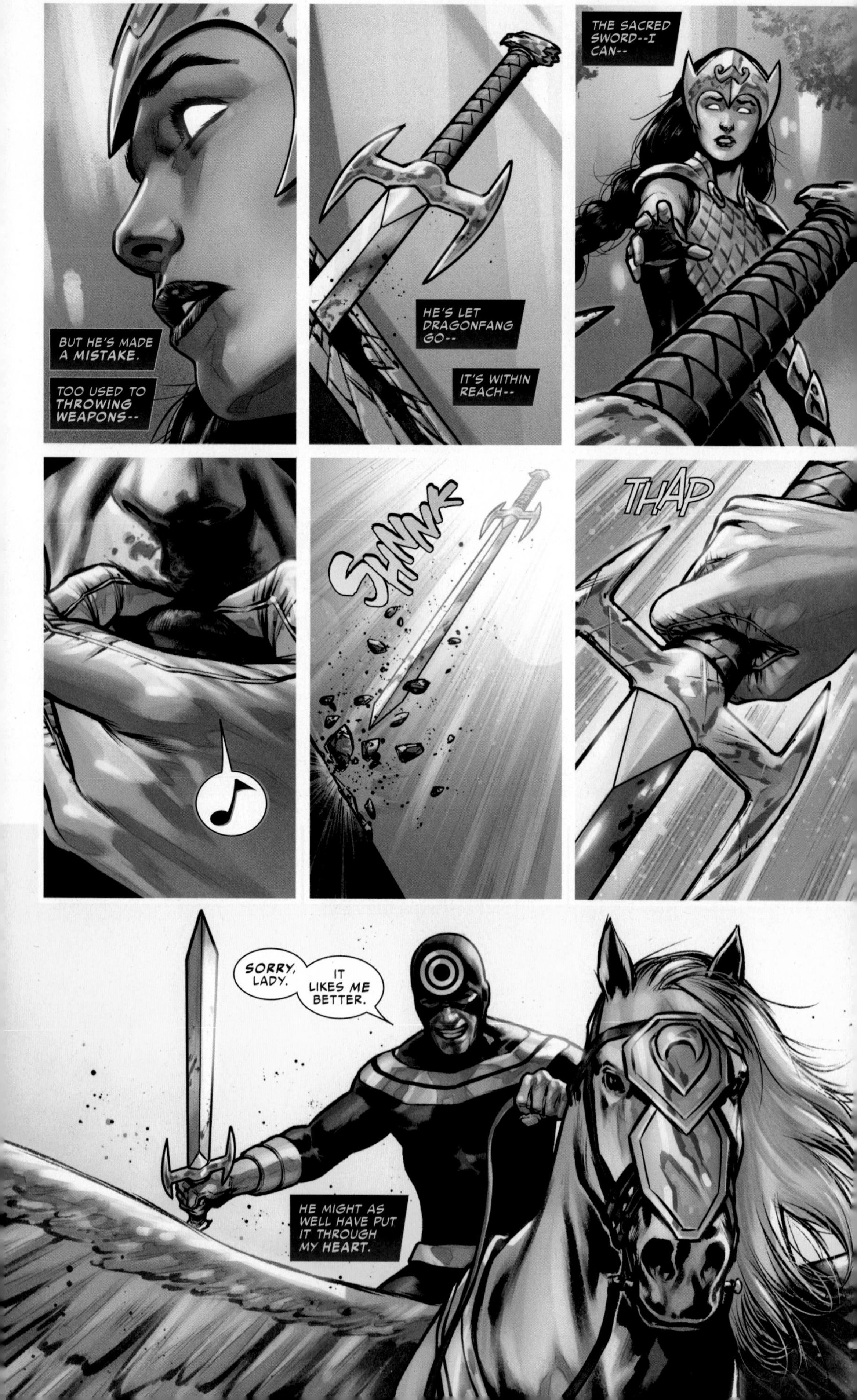
BUT HE'S MADE A MISTAKE.
TOO USED TO THROWING WEAPONS--
HE'S LET DRAGONFANG GO--
IT'S WITHIN REACH--
THE SACRED SWORD--I CAN--
SHNNK
THAP
SORRY, LADY.
IT LIKES ME BETTER.
HE MIGHT AS WELL HAVE PUT IT THROUGH MY HEART.

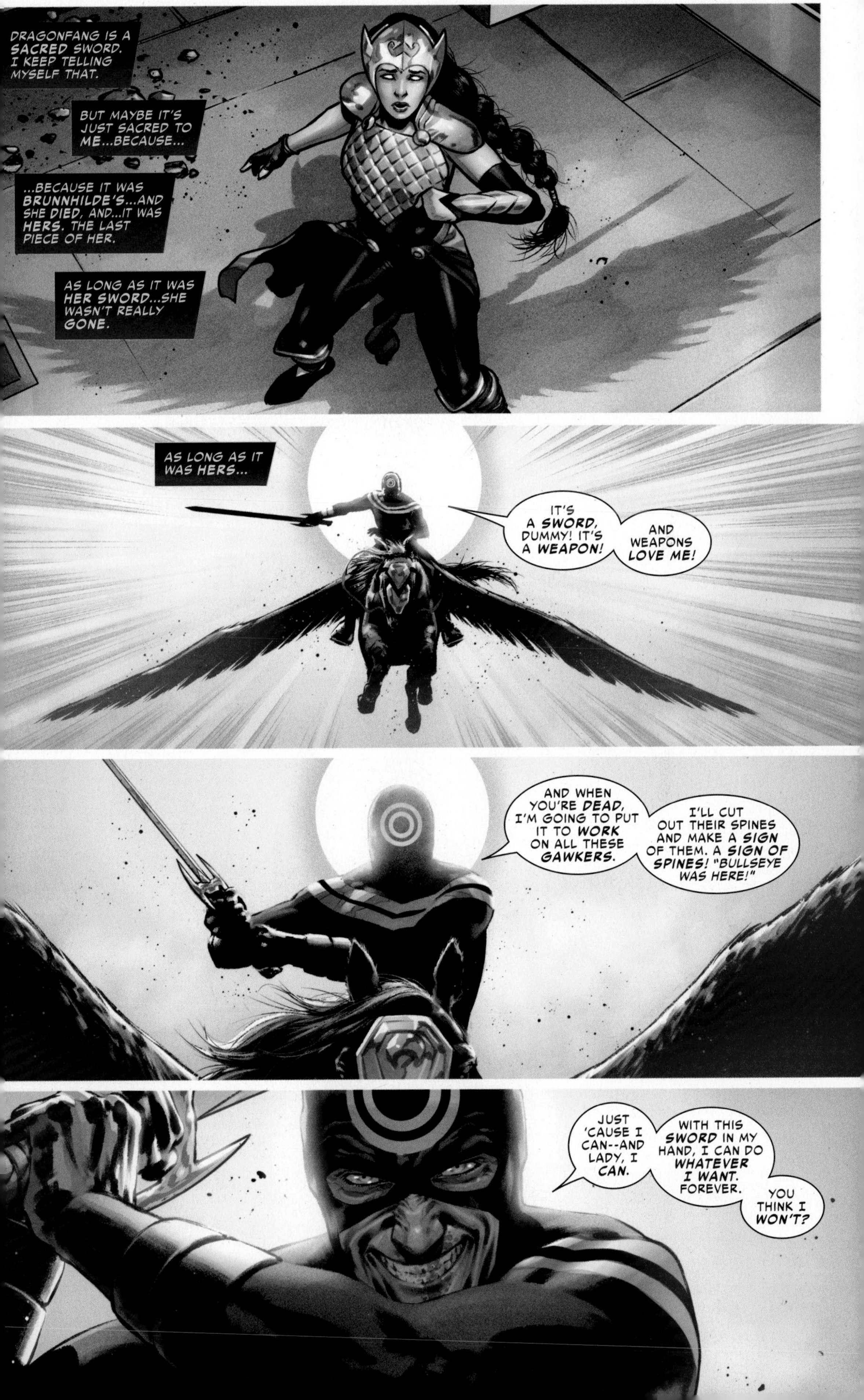
DRAGONFANG IS A SACRED SWORD. I KEEP TELLING MYSELF THAT.
BUT MAYBE IT'S JUST SACRED TO ME...BECAUSE...
...BECAUSE IT WAS BRUNNHILDE'S...AND SHE DIED, AND...IT WAS HERS. THE LAST PIECE OF HER.
AS LONG AS IT WAS HER SWORD...SHE WASN'T REALLY GONE.
AS LONG AS IT WAS HERS...
IT'S A SWORD, DUMMY! IT'S A WEAPON!
AND WEAPONS LOVE ME!
AND WHEN YOU'RE DEAD, I'M GOING TO PUT IT TO WORK ON ALL THESE GAWKERS.
I'LL CUT OUT THEIR SPINES AND MAKE A SIGN OF THEM. A SIGN OF SPINES! "BULLSEYE WAS HERE!"
JUST 'CAUSE I CAN--AND LADY, I CAN.
WITH THIS SWORD IN MY HAND, I CAN DO WHATEVER I WANT. FOREVER.
YOU THINK I WON'T?

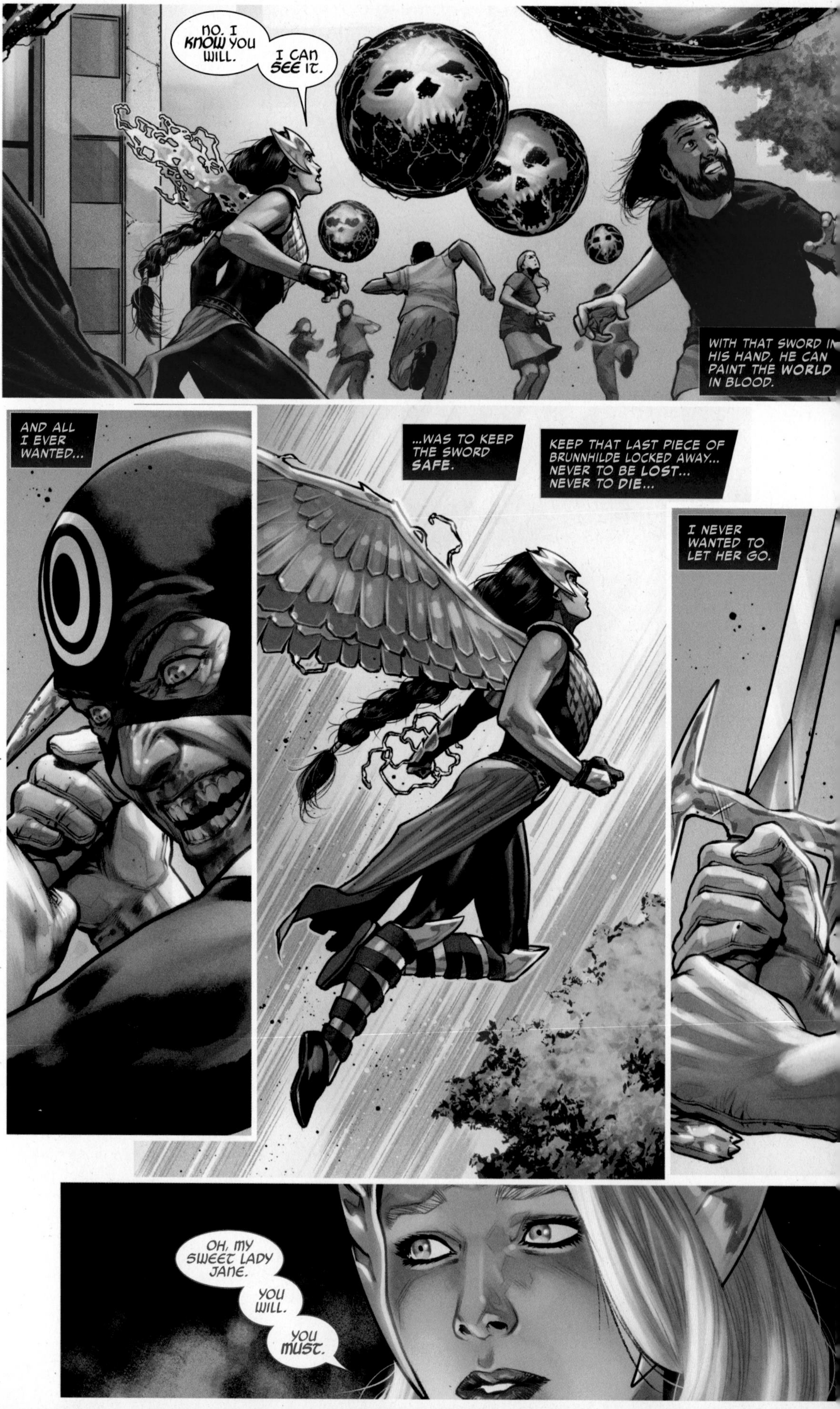
NO. I KNOW YOU WILL.
I CAN SEE IT.
WITH THAT SWORD IN HIS HAND, HE CAN PAINT THE WORLD IN BLOOD.
AND ALL I EVER WANTED...
...WAS TO KEEP THE SWORD SAFE.
KEEP THAT LAST PIECE OF BRUNNHILDE LOCKED AWAY... NEVER TO BE LOST... NEVER TO DIE...
I NEVER WANTED TO LET HER GO.
OH, MY SWEET LADY JANE.
YOU WILL.
YOU MUST.

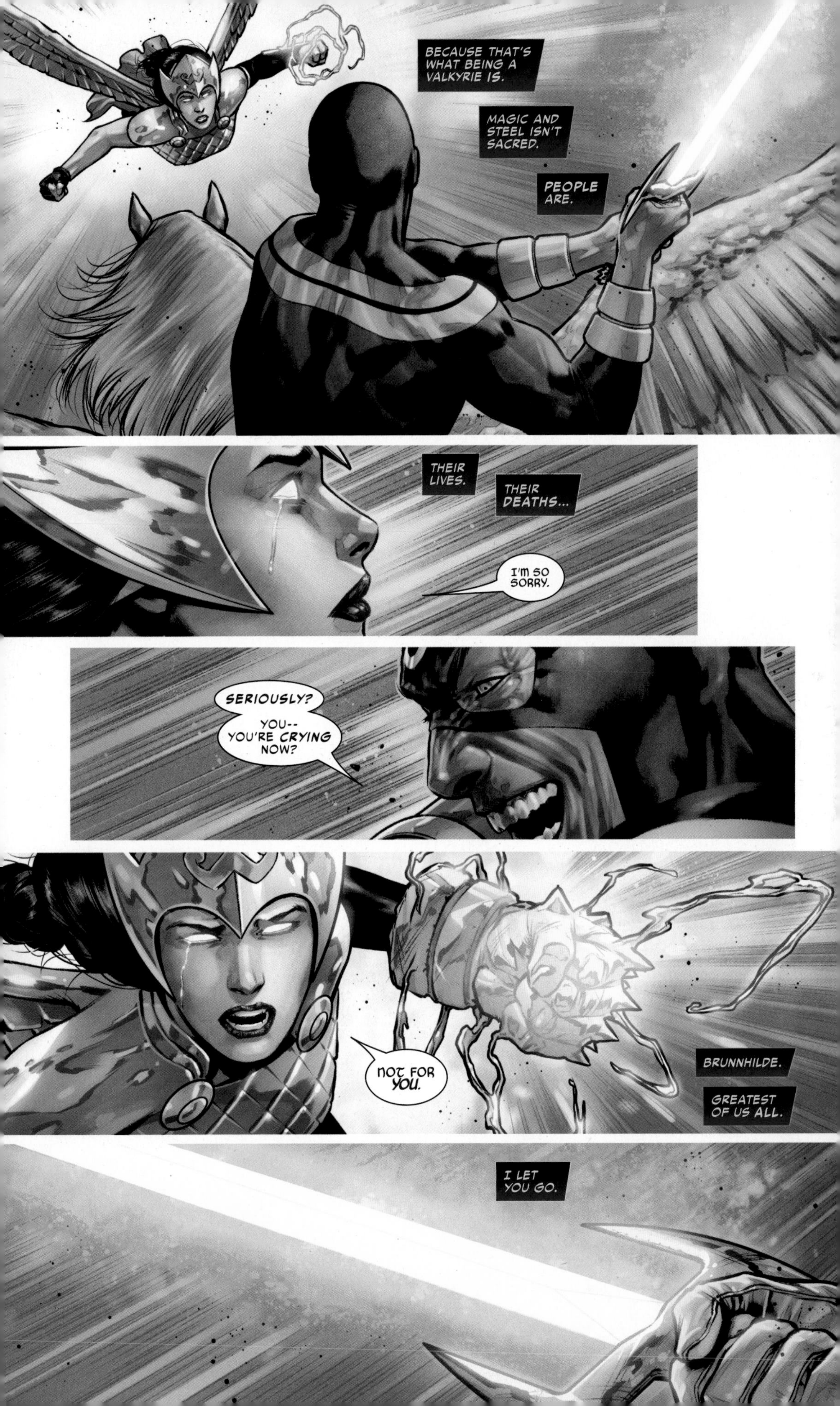
BECAUSE THAT'S WHAT BEING A VALKYRIE IS.
MAGIC AND STEEL ISN'T SACRED.
PEOPLE ARE.
THEIR LIVES.
THEIR DEATHS...
I'M SO SORRY.
SERIOUSLY? YOU-- YOU'RE CRYING NOW?
NOT FOR YOU.
BRUNNHILDE.
GREATEST OF US ALL.
I LET YOU GO.

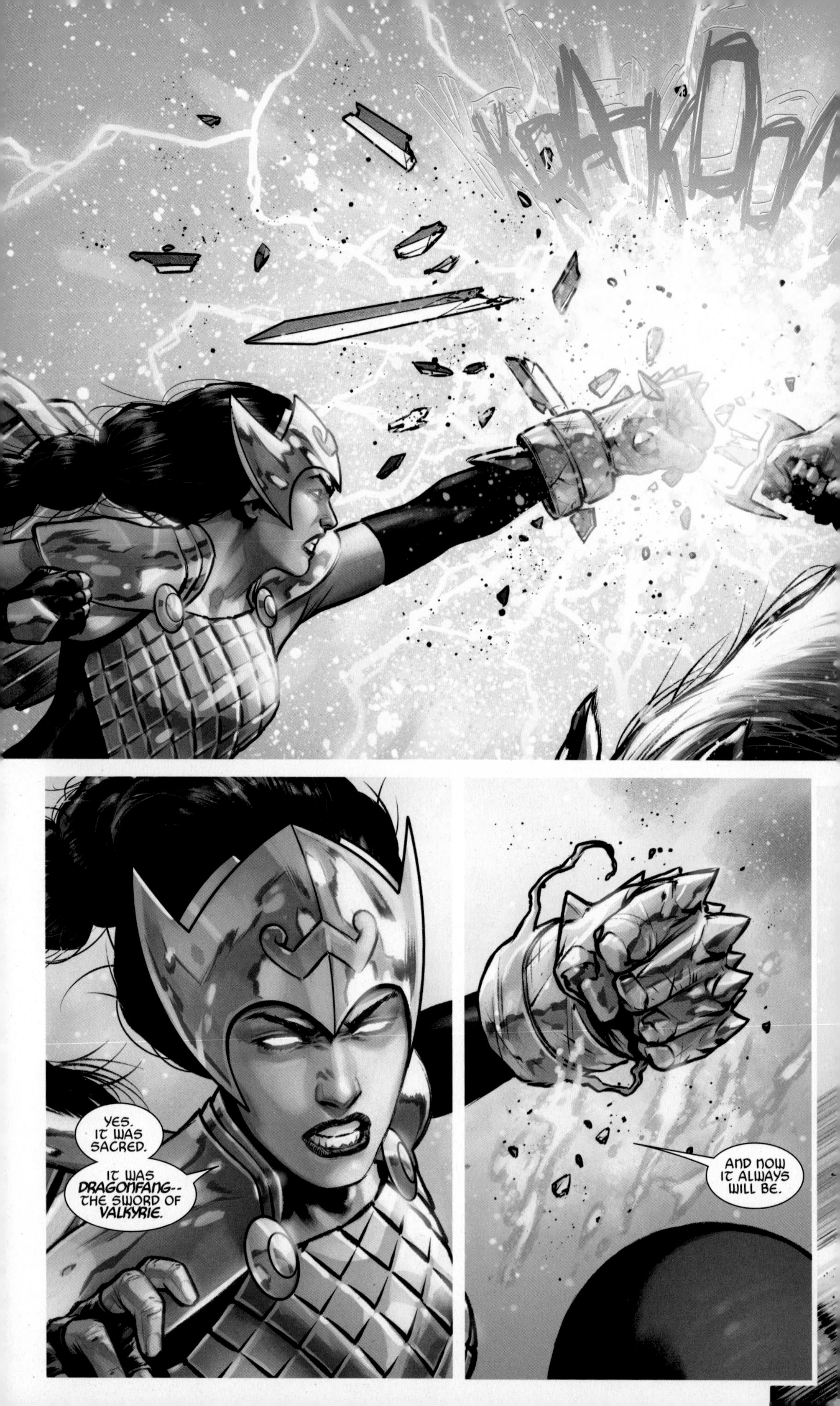

KRAKOOM
YES. IT WAS SACRED.
IT WAS DRAGONFANG-- THE SWORD OF VALKYRIE.
AND NOW IT ALWAYS WILL BE.

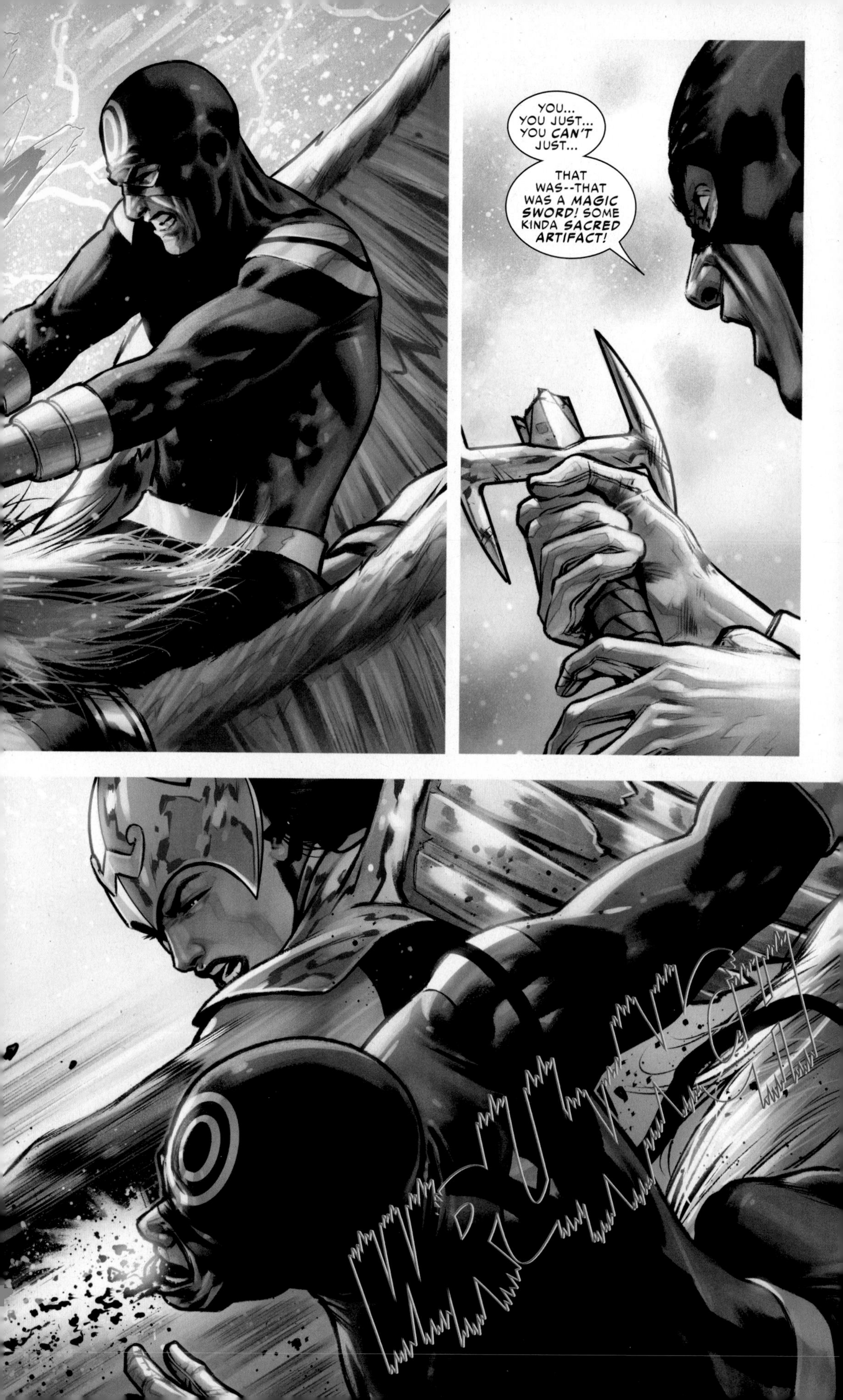
YOU... YOU JUST... YOU CAN'T JUST...
THAT WAS--THAT WAS A MAGIC SWORD! SOME KINDA SACRED ARTIFACT!

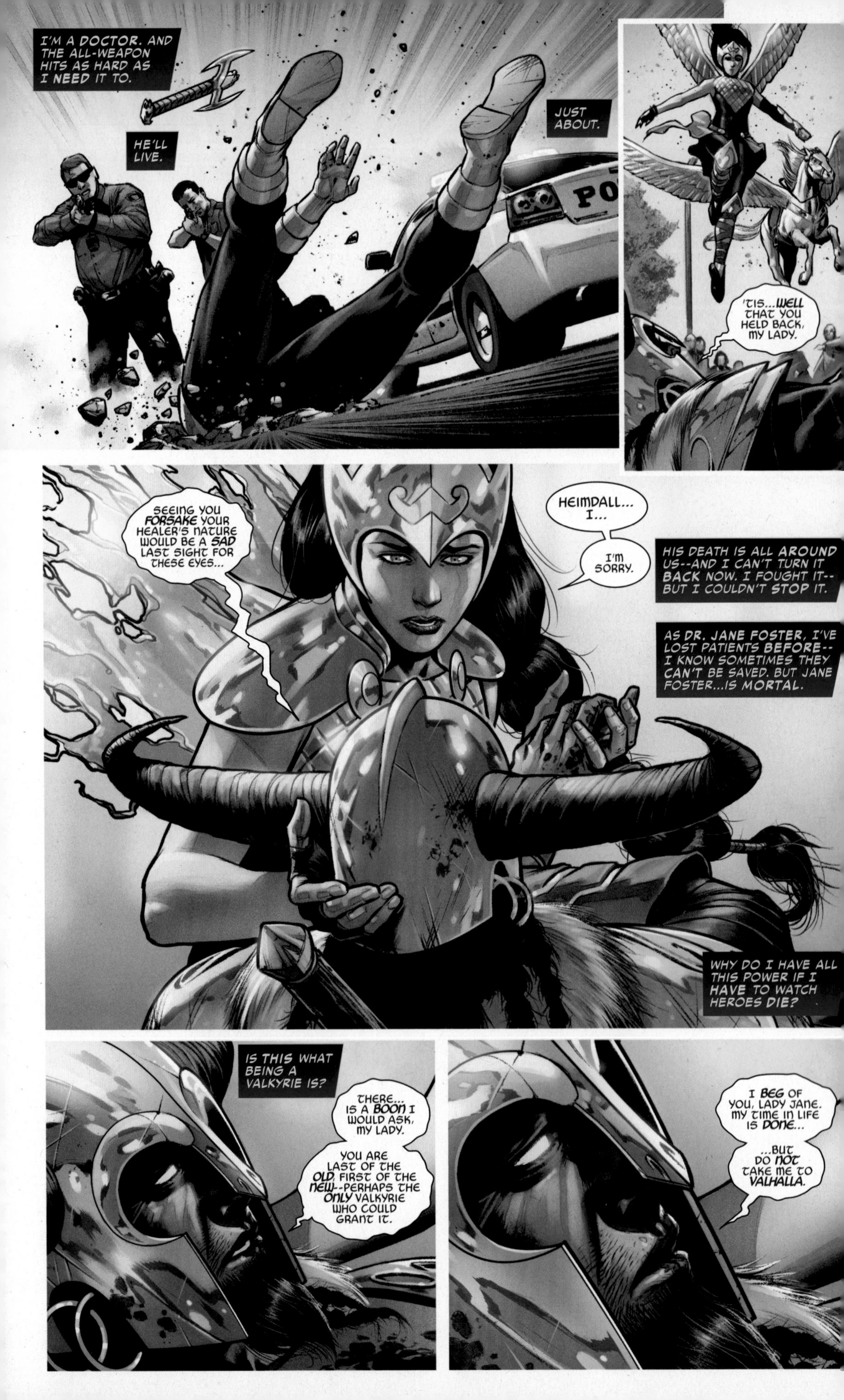
I'M A DOCTOR. AND THE ALL-WEAPON HITS AS HARD AS I NEED IT TO.
HE'LL LIVE.
JUST ABOUT.
PO
'TIS...WELL THAT YOU HELD BACK, MY LADY.
SEEING YOU FORSAKE YOUR HEALER'S NATURE WOULD BE A SAD LAST SIGHT FOR THESE EYES...
HEIMDALL... I...
I'M SORRY.
HIS DEATH IS ALL AROUND US--AND I CAN'T TURN IT BACK NOW. I FOUGHT IT--BUT I COULDN'T STOP IT.
AS DR. JANE FOSTER, I'VE LOST PATIENTS BEFORE--I KNOW SOMETIMES THEY CAN'T BE SAVED. BUT JANE FOSTER...IS MORTAL.
WHY DO I HAVE ALL THIS POWER IF I HAVE TO WATCH HEROES DIE?
IS THIS WHAT BEING A VALKYRIE IS?
THERE... IS A BOON I WOULD ASK, MY LADY.
YOU ARE LAST OF THE OLD, FIRST OF THE NEW--PERHAPS THE ONLY VALKYRIE WHO COULD GRANT IT.
I BEG OF YOU, LADY JANE. MY TIME IN LIFE IS DONE...
...BUT DO NOT TAKE ME TO VALHALLA.

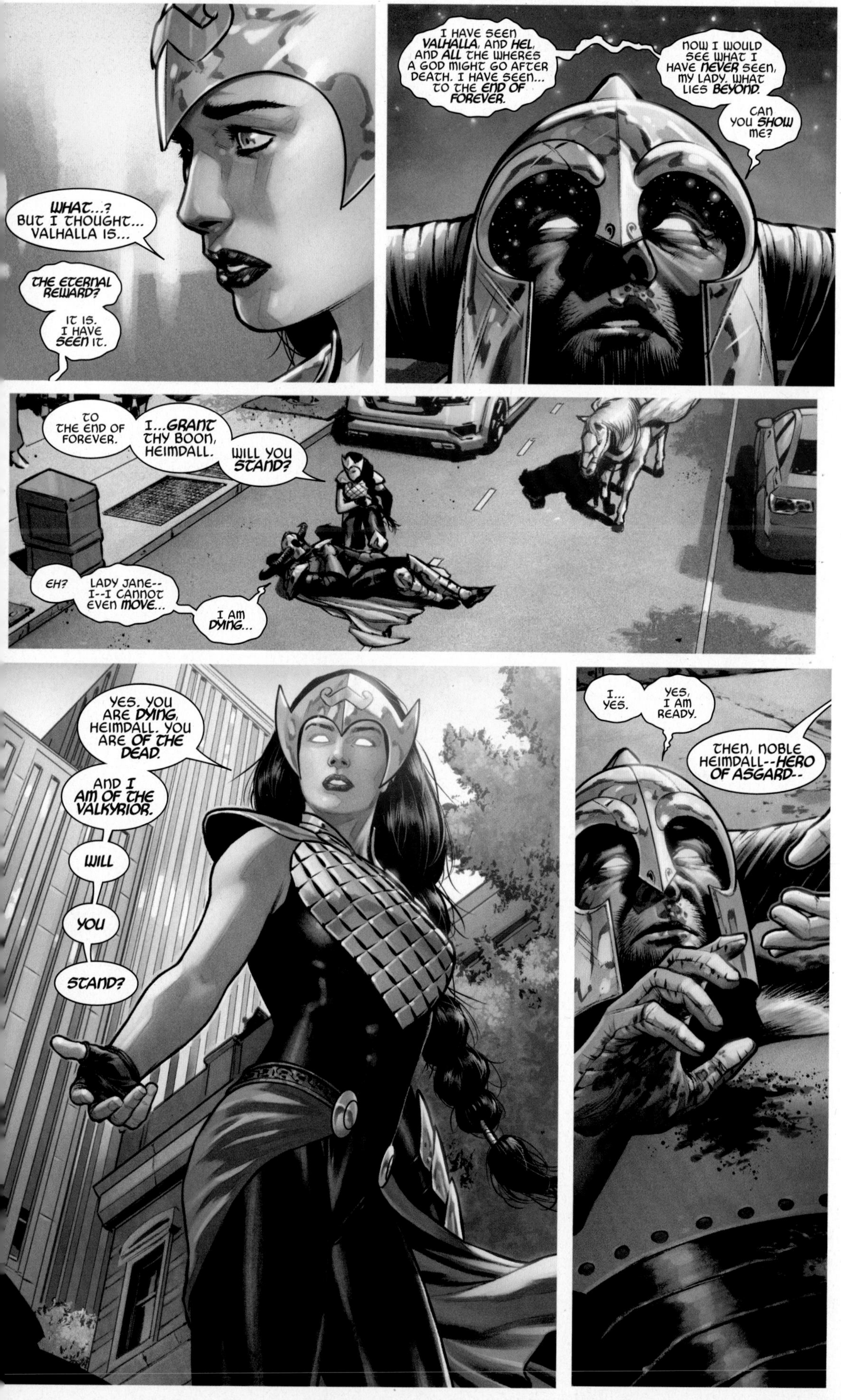

WHAT...? BUT I THOUGHT... VALHALLA IS...
THE ETERNAL REWARD?
IT IS. I HAVE SEEN IT.
I HAVE SEEN VALHALLA, AND HEL, AND ALL THE WHERES A GOD MIGHT GO AFTER DEATH. I HAVE SEEN... TO THE END OF FOREVER.
NOW I WOULD SEE WHAT I HAVE NEVER SEEN, MY LADY. WHAT LIES BEYOND.
CAN YOU SHOW ME?
TO THE END OF FOREVER.
I...GRANT THY BOON, HEIMDALL.
WILL YOU STAND?
EH?
LADY JANE-- I--I CANNOT EVEN MOVE...
I AM DYING...
YES. YOU ARE DYING, HEIMDALL. YOU ARE OF THE DEAD.
AND I AM OF THE VALKYRIOR.
WILL
YOU
STAND?
I... YES.
YES, I AM READY.
THEN, NOBLE HEIMDALL--HERO OF ASGARD--

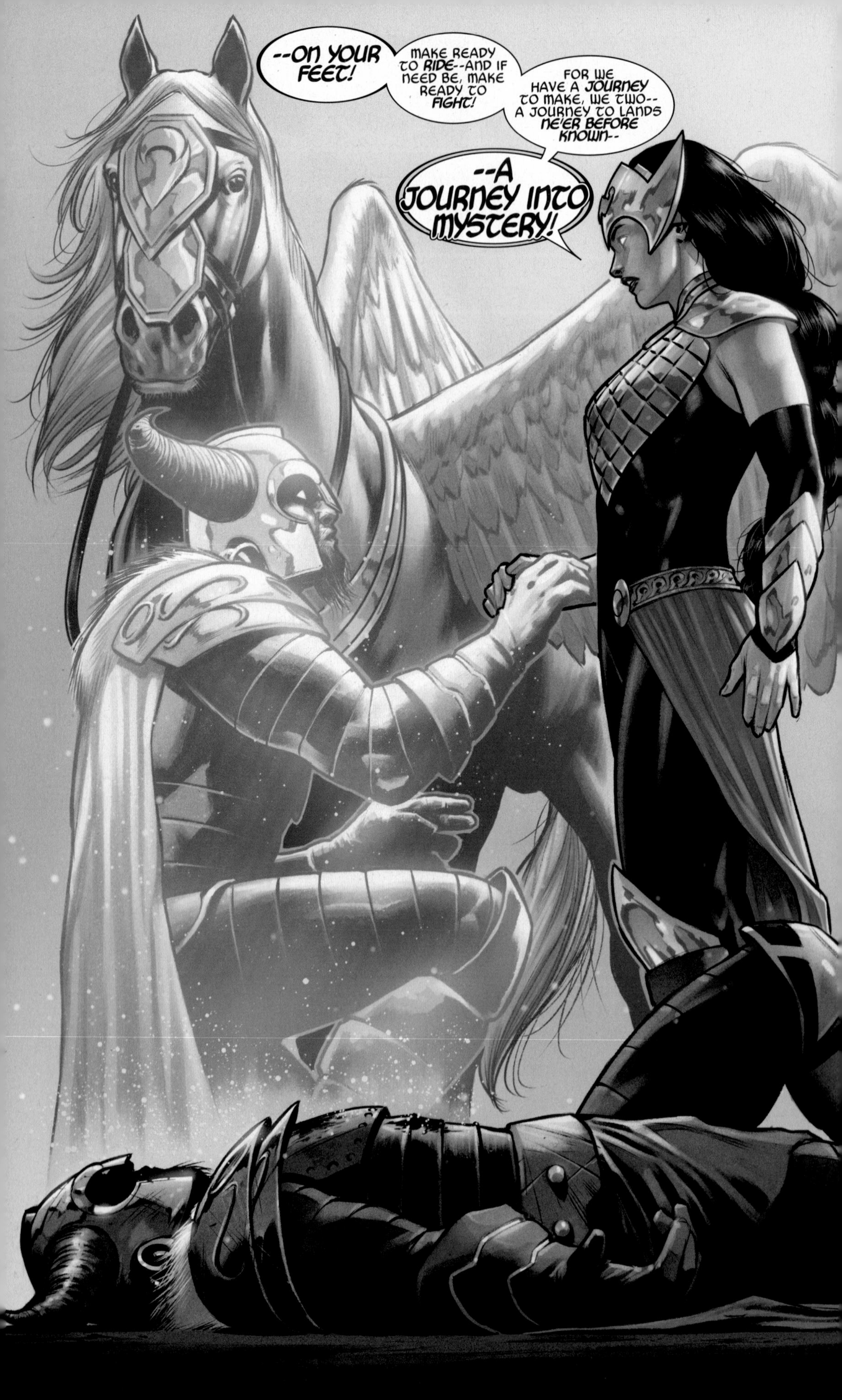
--ON YOUR FEET!
MAKE READY TO RIDE--AND IF NEED BE, MAKE READY TO FIGHT!
FOR WE HAVE A JOURNEY TO MAKE, WE TWO-- A JOURNEY TO LANDS NE'ER BEFORE KNOWN--
--A JOURNEY INTO MYSTERY!

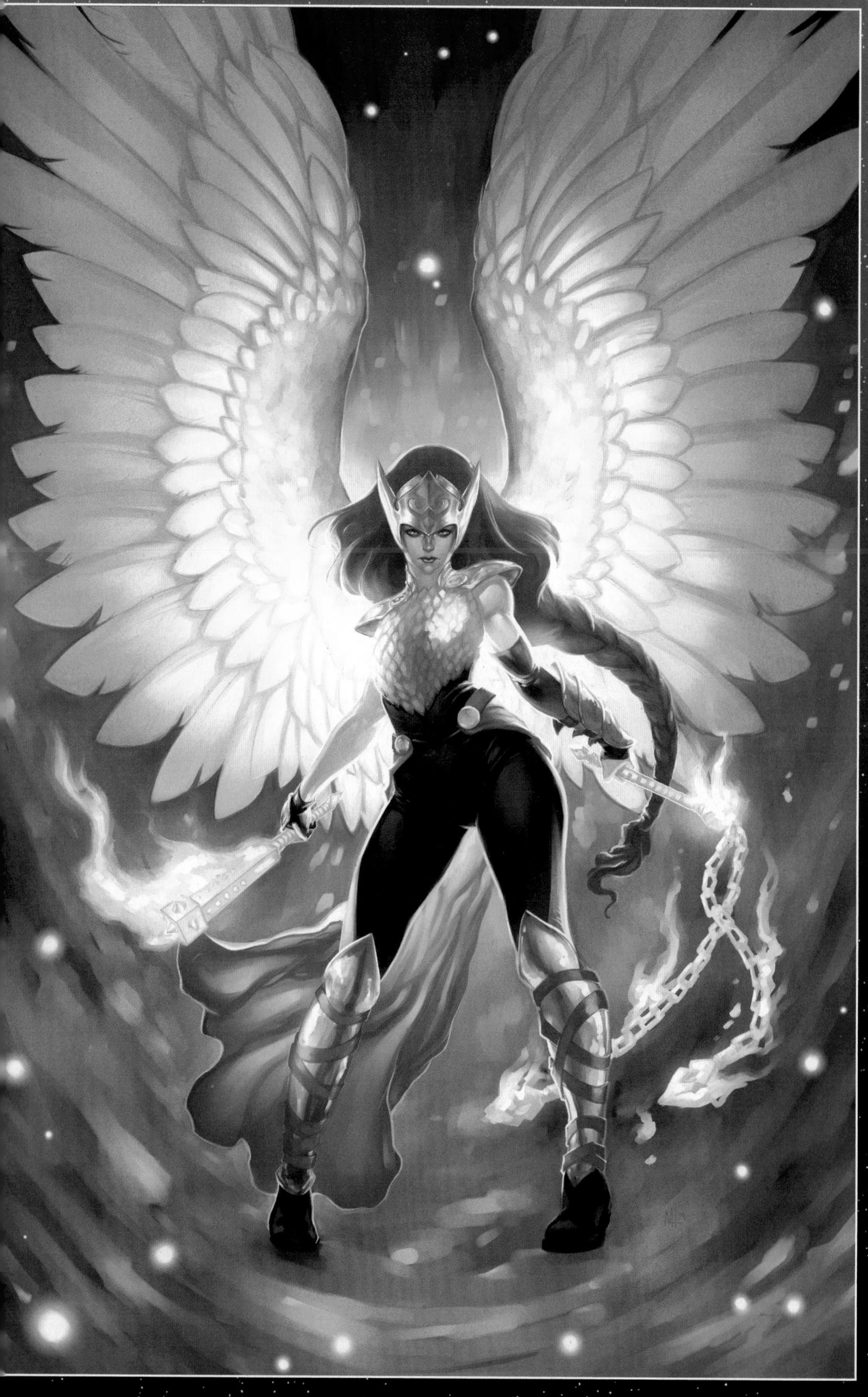

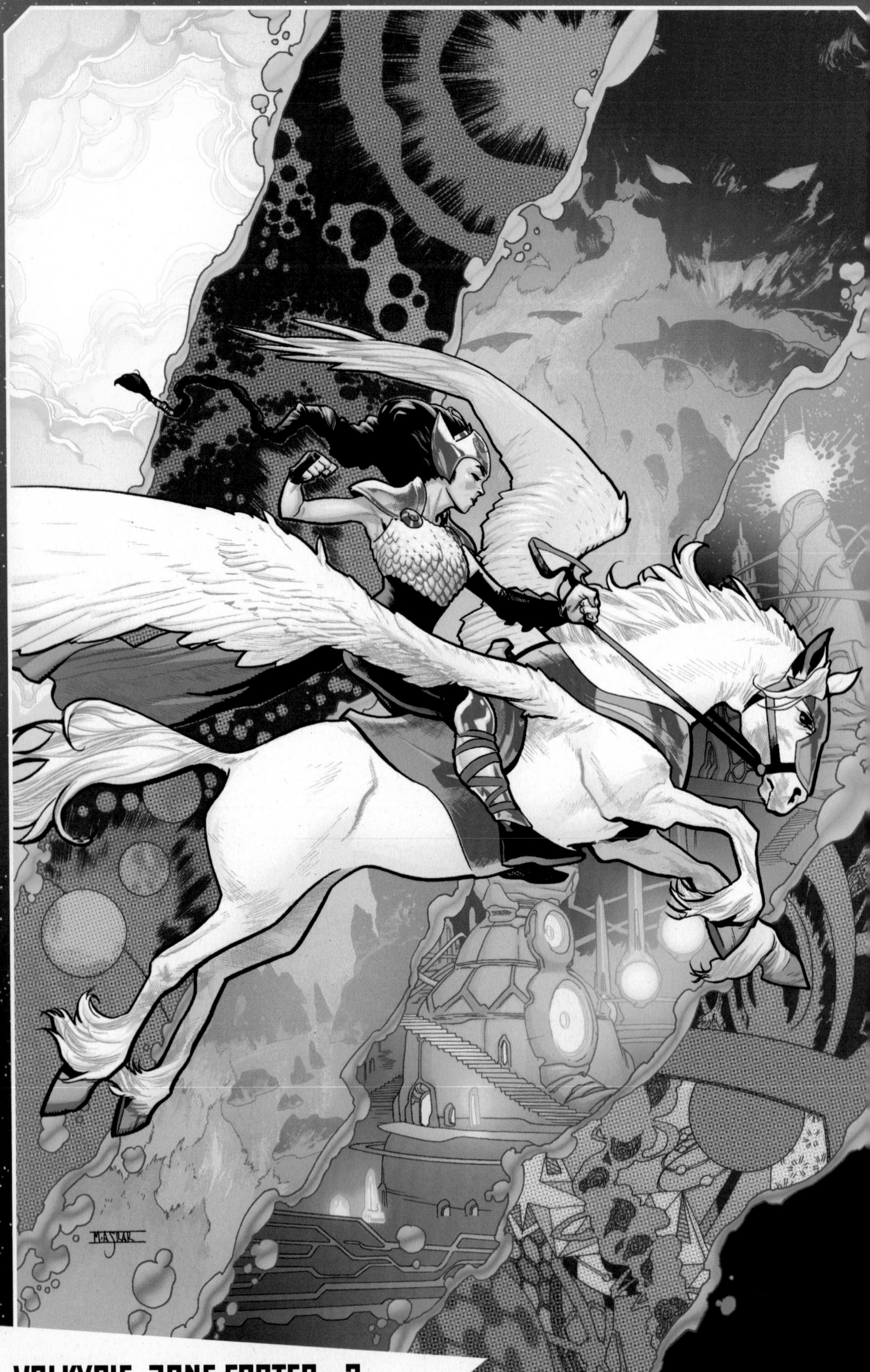
M. ASRAR

VALKYRIE: JANE FOSTER #3

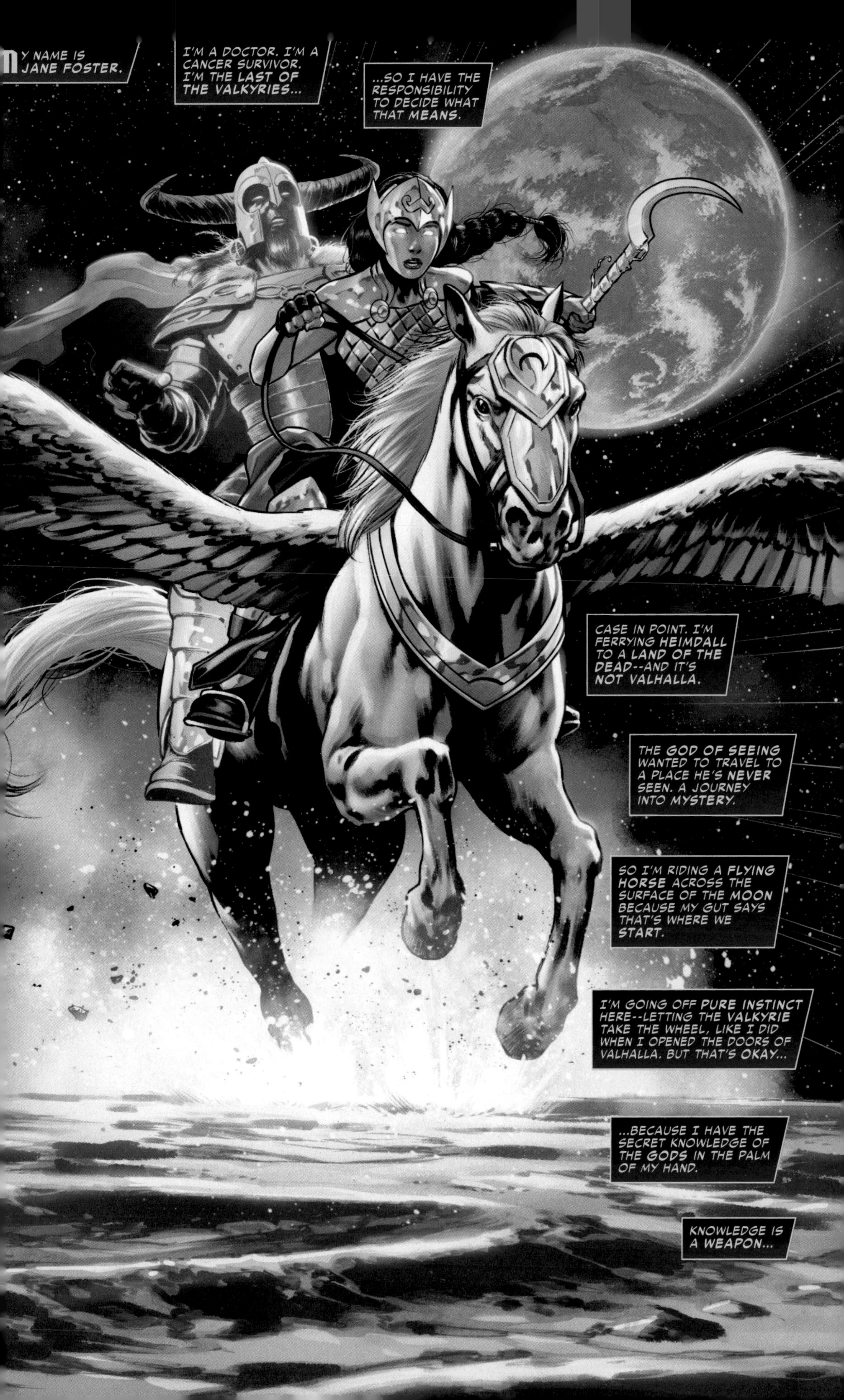
MY NAME IS JANE FOSTER.
I'M A DOCTOR. I'M A CANCER SURVIVOR. I'M THE LAST OF THE VALKYRIES...
...SO I HAVE THE RESPONSIBILITY TO DECIDE WHAT THAT MEANS.
CASE IN POINT. I'M FERRYING HEIMDALL TO A LAND OF THE DEAD--AND IT'S NOT VALHALLA.
THE GOD OF SEEING WANTED TO TRAVEL TO A PLACE HE'S NEVER SEEN. A JOURNEY INTO MYSTERY.
SO I'M RIDING A FLYING HORSE ACROSS THE SURFACE OF THE MOON BECAUSE MY GUT SAYS THAT'S WHERE WE START.
I'M GOING OFF PURE INSTINCT HERE--LETTING THE VALKYRIE TAKE THE WHEEL, LIKE I DID WHEN I OPENED THE DOORS OF VALHALLA. BUT THAT'S OKAY...
...BECAUSE I HAVE THE SECRET KNOWLEDGE OF THE GODS IN THE PALM OF MY HAND.
KNOWLEDGE IS A WEAPON...

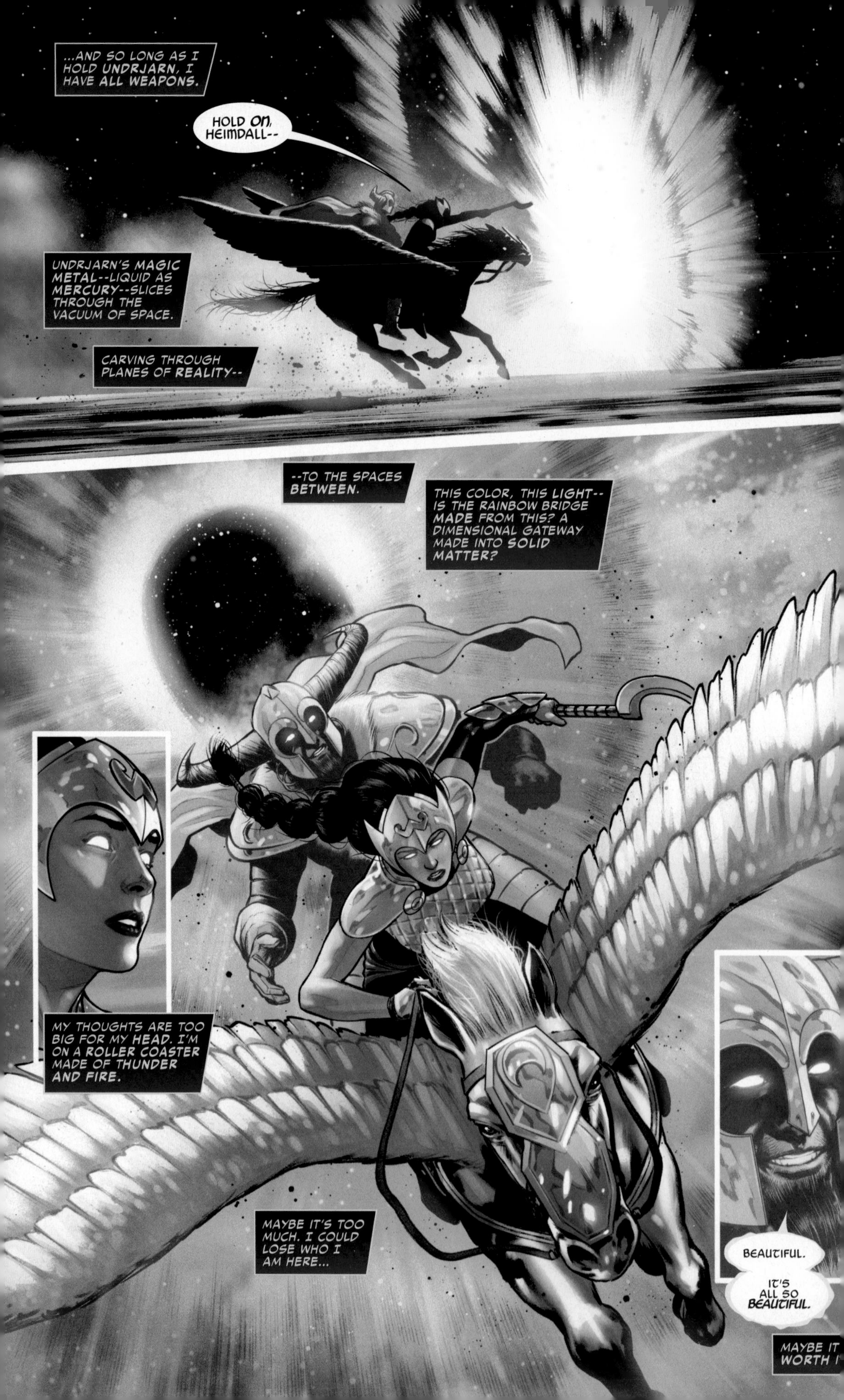
...AND SO LONG AS I HOLD UNDRJARN, I HAVE ALL WEAPONS.
HOLD ON, HEIMDALL--
UNDRJARN'S MAGIC METAL--LIQUID AS MERCURY--SLICES THROUGH THE VACUUM OF SPACE.
CARVING THROUGH PLANES OF REALITY--
--TO THE SPACES BETWEEN.
THIS COLOR, THIS LIGHT--IS THE RAINBOW BRIDGE MADE FROM THIS? A DIMENSIONAL GATEWAY MADE INTO SOLID MATTER?
MY THOUGHTS ARE TOO BIG FOR MY HEAD. I'M ON A ROLLER COASTER MADE OF THUNDER AND FIRE.
MAYBE IT'S TOO MUCH. I COULD LOSE WHO I AM HERE...
BEAUTIFUL.
IT'S ALL SO BEAUTIFUL.
MAYBE IT WORTH I

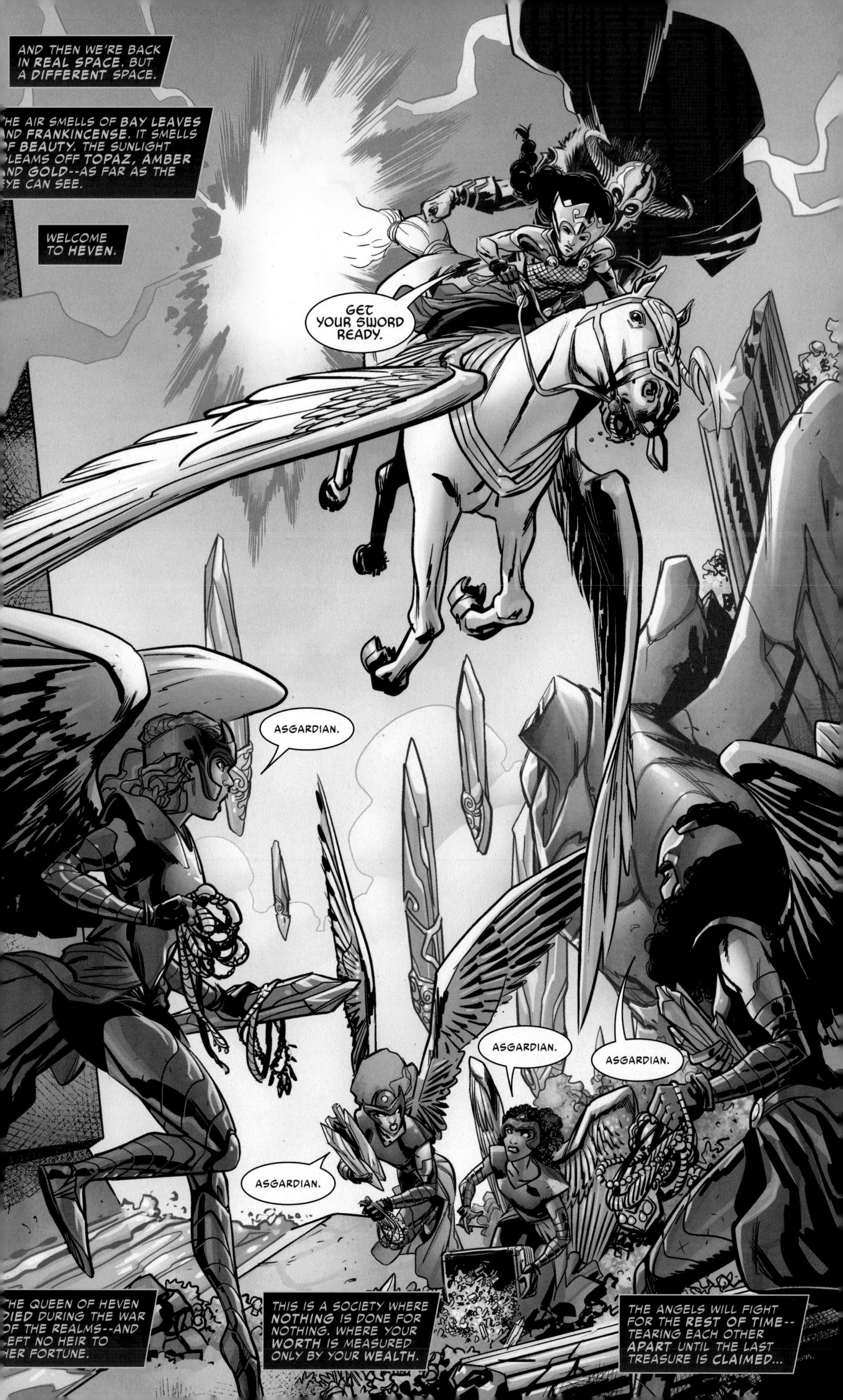

AND THEN WE'RE BACK IN REAL SPACE. BUT A DIFFERENT SPACE.
HE AIR SMELLS OF BAY LEAVES ND FRANKINCENSE. IT SMELLS F BEAUTY. THE SUNLIGHT LEAMS OFF TOPAZ, AMBER ND GOLD--AS FAR AS THE YE CAN SEE.
WELCOME TO HEVEN.
GET YOUR SWORD READY.
ASGARDIAN.
ASGARDIAN.
ASGARDIAN.
ASGARDIAN.
HE QUEEN OF HEVEN DIED DURING THE WAR OF THE REALMS--AND EFT NO HEIR TO HER FORTUNE.
THIS IS A SOCIETY WHERE NOTHING IS DONE FOR NOTHING. WHERE YOUR WORTH IS MEASURED ONLY BY YOUR WEALTH.
THE ANGELS WILL FIGHT FOR THE REST OF TIME--TEARING EACH OTHER APART UNTIL THE LAST TREASURE IS CLAIMED...

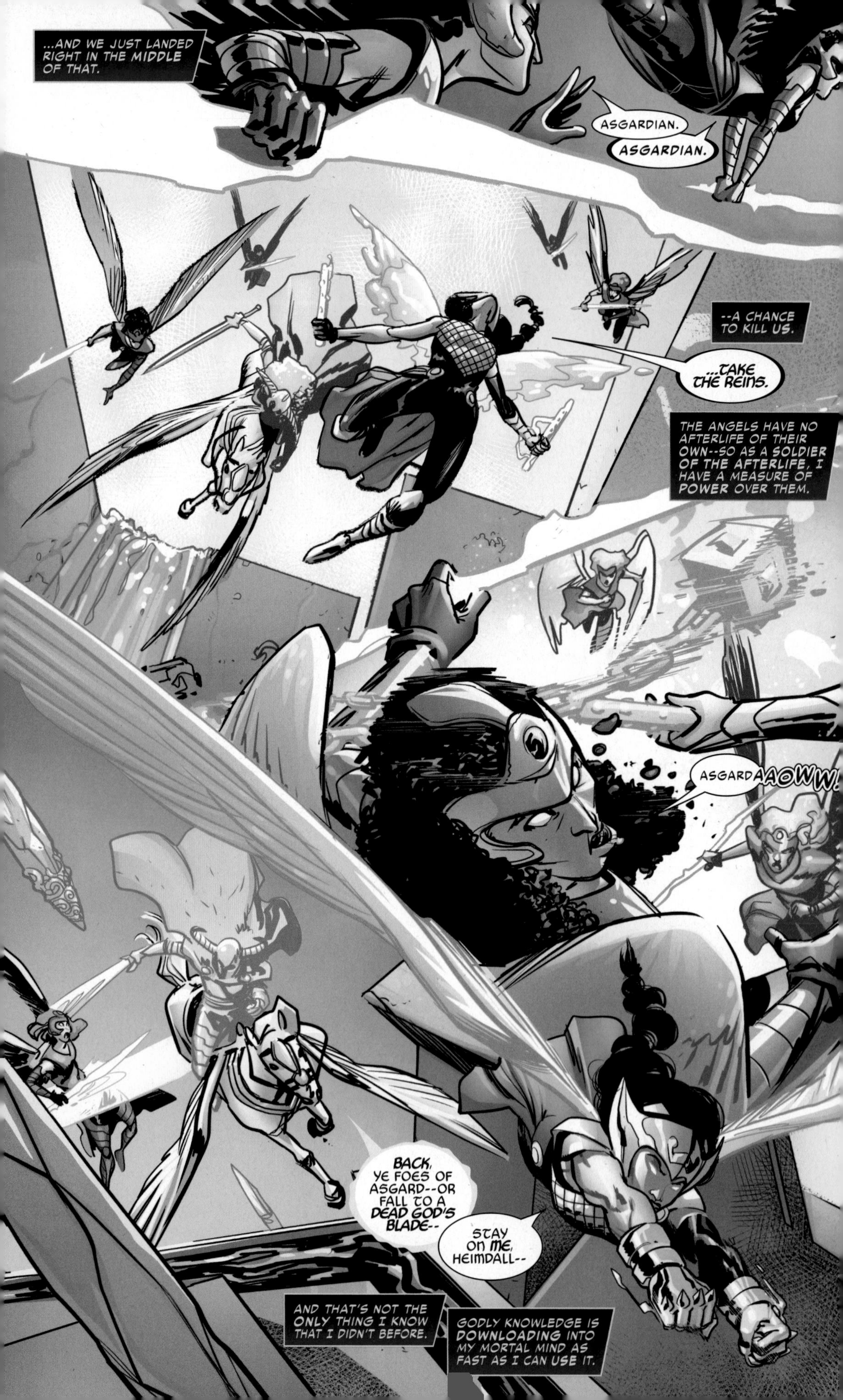
...AND WE JUST LANDED RIGHT IN THE MIDDLE OF THAT.
ASGARDIAN.
ASGARDIAN.
--A CHANCE TO KILL US.
...TAKE THE REINS.
THE ANGELS HAVE NO AFTERLIFE OF THEIR OWN--SO AS A SOLDIER OF THE AFTERLIFE, I HAVE A MEASURE OF POWER OVER THEM.
ASGARDAAOWW!
BACK, YE FOES OF ASGARD--OR FALL TO A DEAD GOD'S BLADE--
STAY ON ME, HEIMDALL--
AND THAT'S NOT THE ONLY THING I KNOW THAT I DIDN'T BEFORE.
GODLY KNOWLEDGE IS DOWNLOADING INTO MY MORTAL MIND AS FAST AS I CAN USE IT.

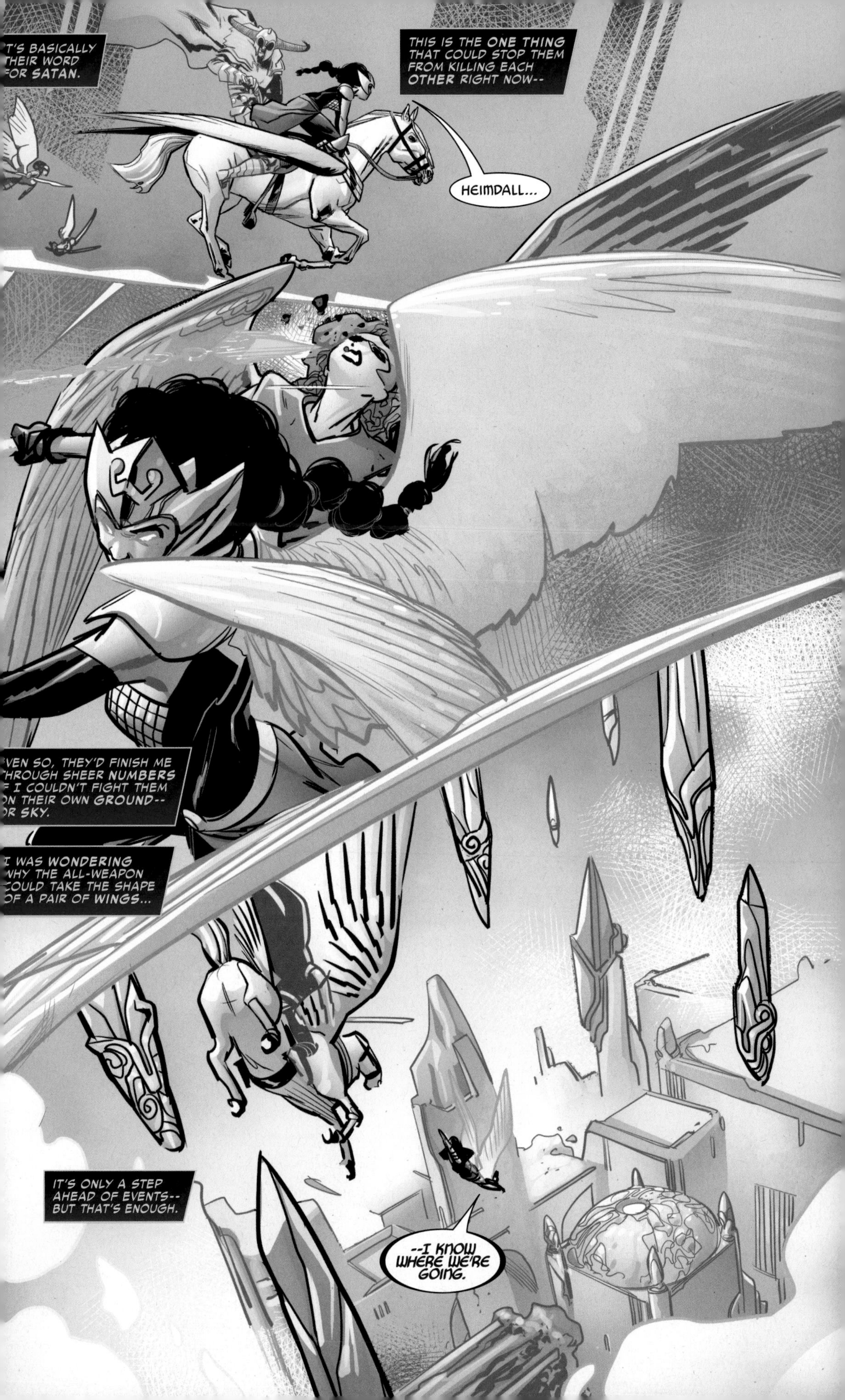
T'S BASICALLY THEIR WORD FOR SATAN.
THIS IS THE ONE THING THAT COULD STOP THEM FROM KILLING EACH OTHER RIGHT NOW--
HEIMDALL...
VEN SO, THEY'D FINISH ME THROUGH SHEER NUMBERS F I COULDN'T FIGHT THEM ON THEIR OWN GROUND-- OR SKY.
I WAS WONDERING WHY THE ALL-WEAPON COULD TAKE THE SHAPE OF A PAIR OF WINGS...
IT'S ONLY A STEP AHEAD OF EVENTS-- BUT THAT'S ENOUGH.
--I KNOW WHERE WE'RE GOING.

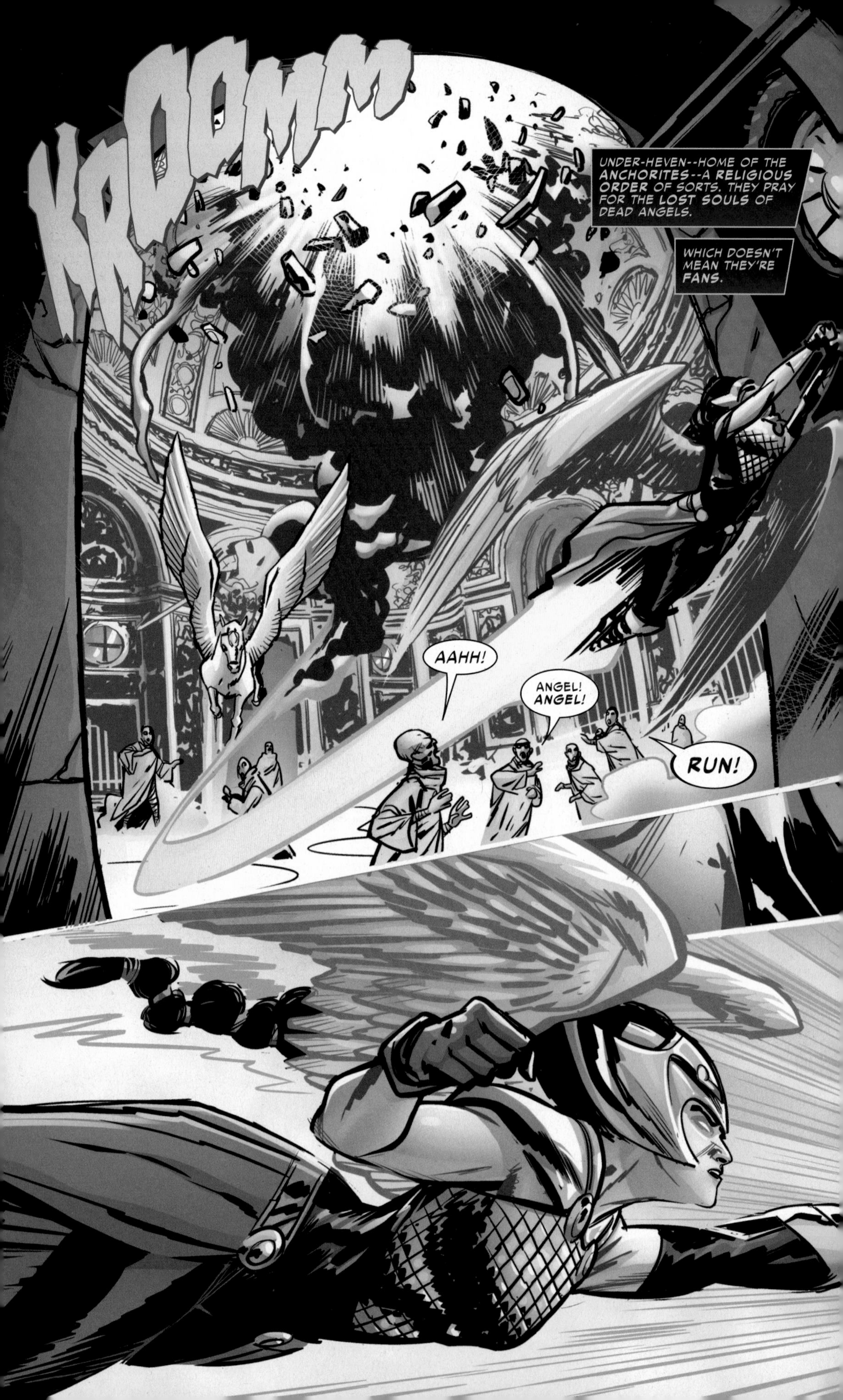
KROOMM
UNDER-HEVEN--HOME OF THE ANCHORITES--A RELIGIOUS ORDER OF SORTS. THEY PRAY FOR THE LOST SOULS OF DEAD ANGELS.
WHICH DOESN'T MEAN THEY'RE FANS.
AAHH!
ANGEL! ANGEL!
RUN!

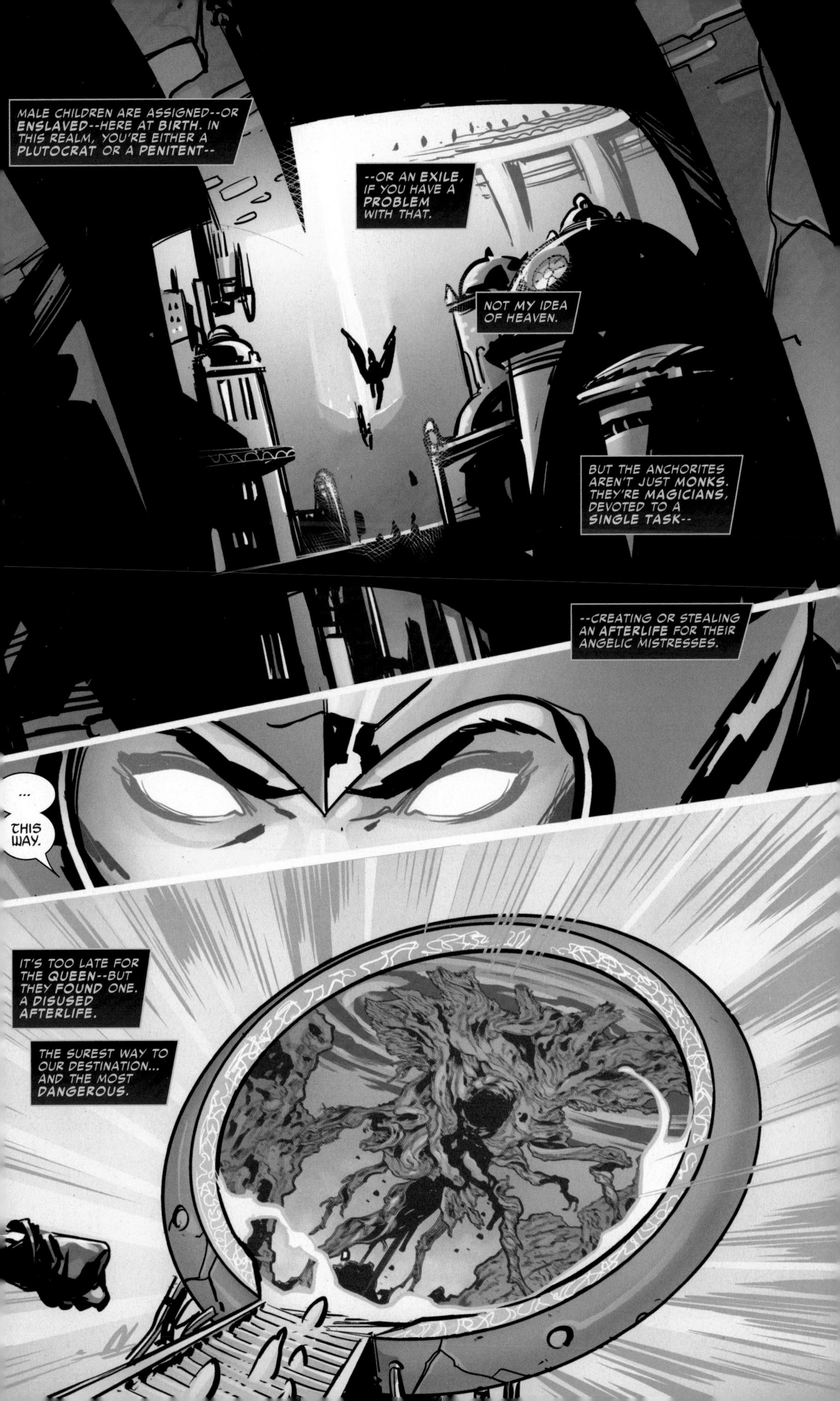

MALE CHILDREN ARE ASSIGNED--OR ENSLAVED--HERE AT BIRTH. IN THIS REALM, YOU'RE EITHER A PLUTOCRAT OR A PENITENT--
--OR AN EXILE, IF YOU HAVE A PROBLEM WITH THAT.
NOT MY IDEA OF HEAVEN.
BUT THE ANCHORITES AREN'T JUST MONKS. THEY'RE MAGICIANS, DEVOTED TO A SINGLE TASK--
--CREATING OR STEALING AN AFTERLIFE FOR THEIR ANGELIC MISTRESSES.
... THIS WAY.
IT'S TOO LATE FOR THE QUEEN--BUT THEY FOUND ONE. A DISUSED AFTERLIFE.
THE SUREST WAY TO OUR DESTINATION... AND THE MOST DANGEROUS.

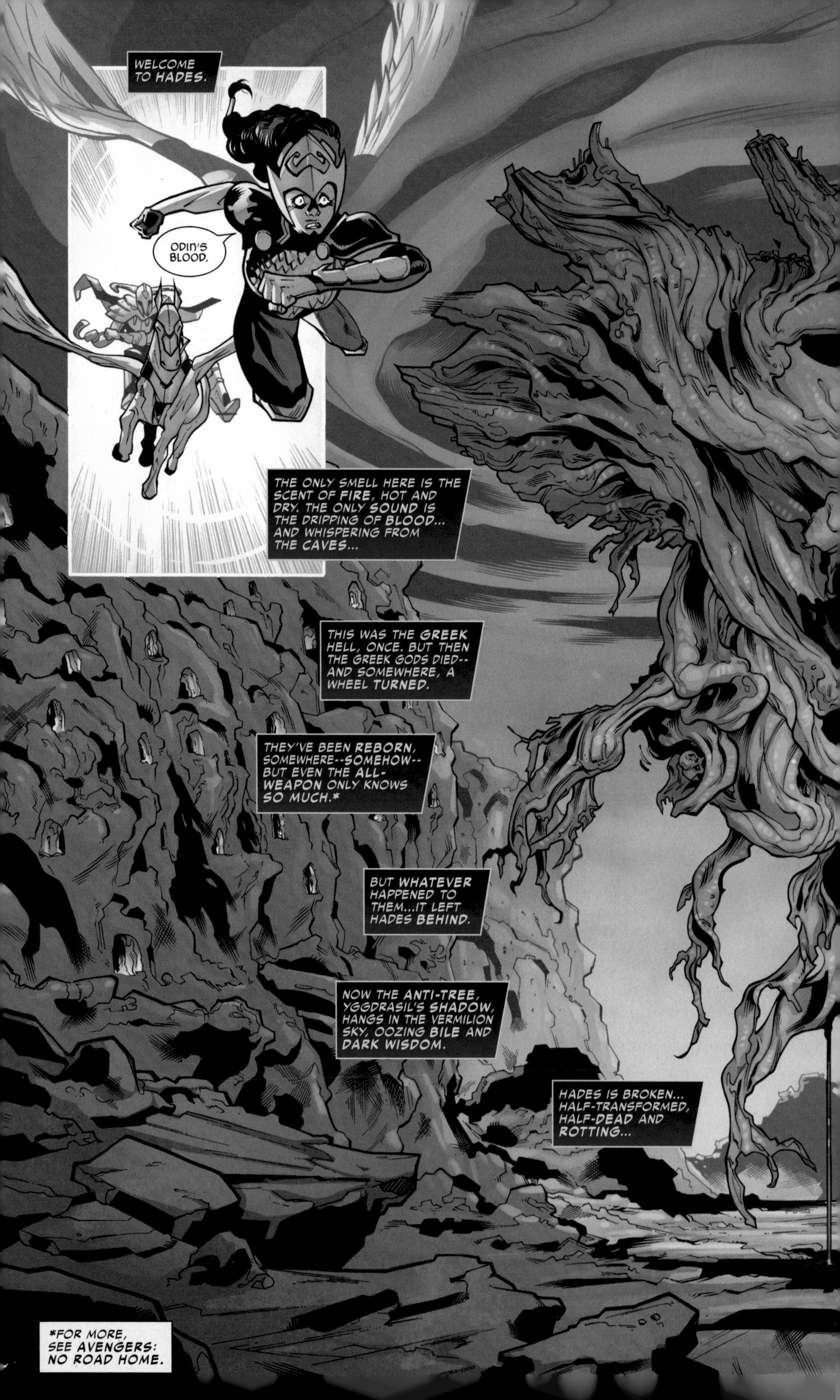
WELCOME TO HADES.
ODIN'S BLOOD.
THE ONLY SMELL HERE IS THE SCENT OF FIRE, HOT AND DRY. THE ONLY SOUND IS THE DRIPPING OF BLOOD... AND WHISPERING FROM THE CAVES...
THIS WAS THE GREEK HELL, ONCE. BUT THEN THE GREEK GODS DIED-- AND SOMEWHERE, A WHEEL TURNED.
THEY'VE BEEN REBORN, SOMEWHERE--SOMEHOW-- BUT EVEN THE ALL-WEAPON ONLY KNOWS SO MUCH.*
BUT WHATEVER HAPPENED TO THEM...IT LEFT HADES BEHIND.
NOW THE ANTI-TREE, YGGDRASIL'S SHADOW, HANGS IN THE VERMILION SKY, OOZING BILE AND DARK WISDOM.
HADES IS BROKEN... HALF-TRANSFORMED, HALF-DEAD AND ROTTING...
*FOR MORE, SEE AVENGERS: NO ROAD HOME.

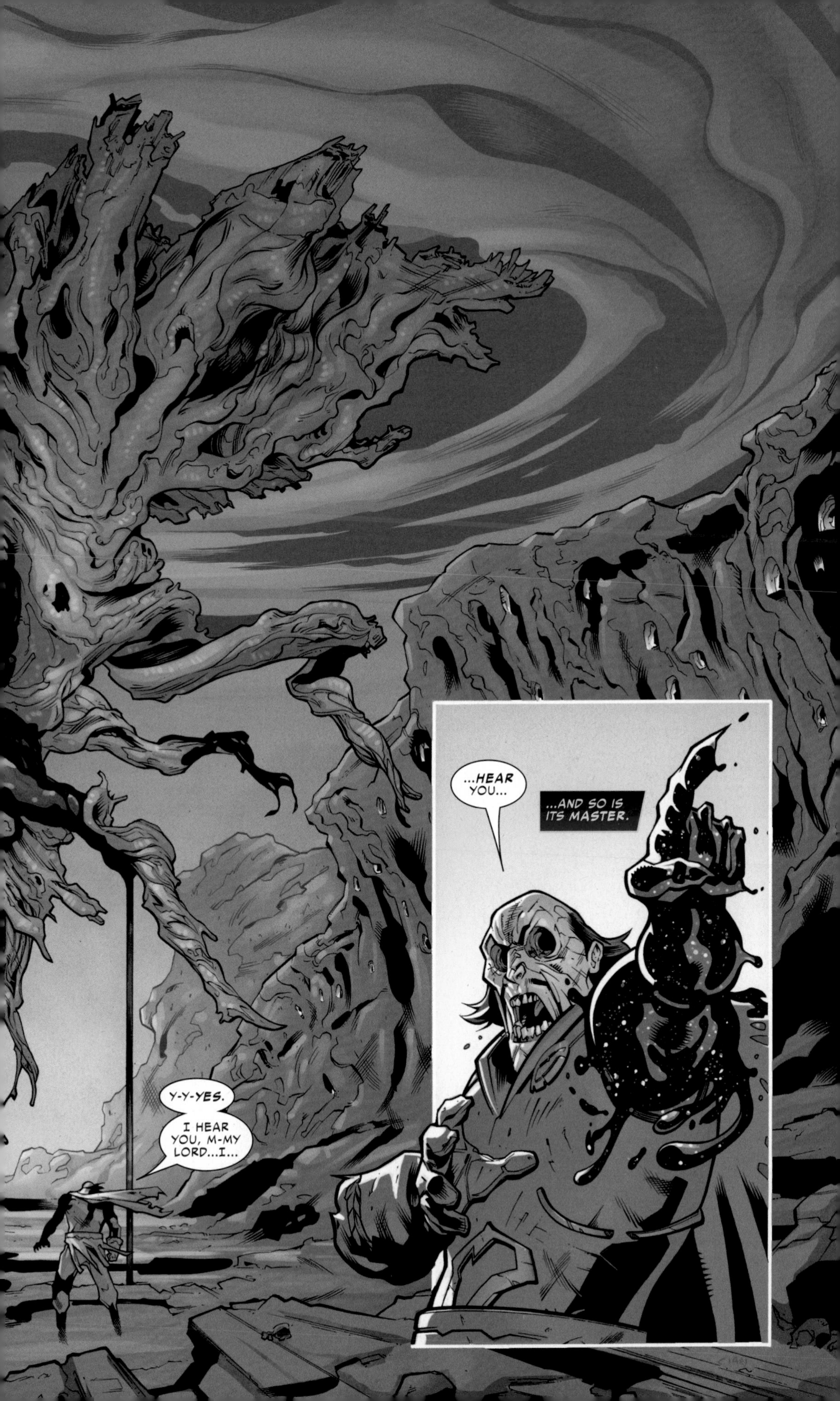

...HEAR YOU...
...AND SO IS ITS MASTER.
Y-Y-YES.
I HEAR YOU, M-MY LORD...I...

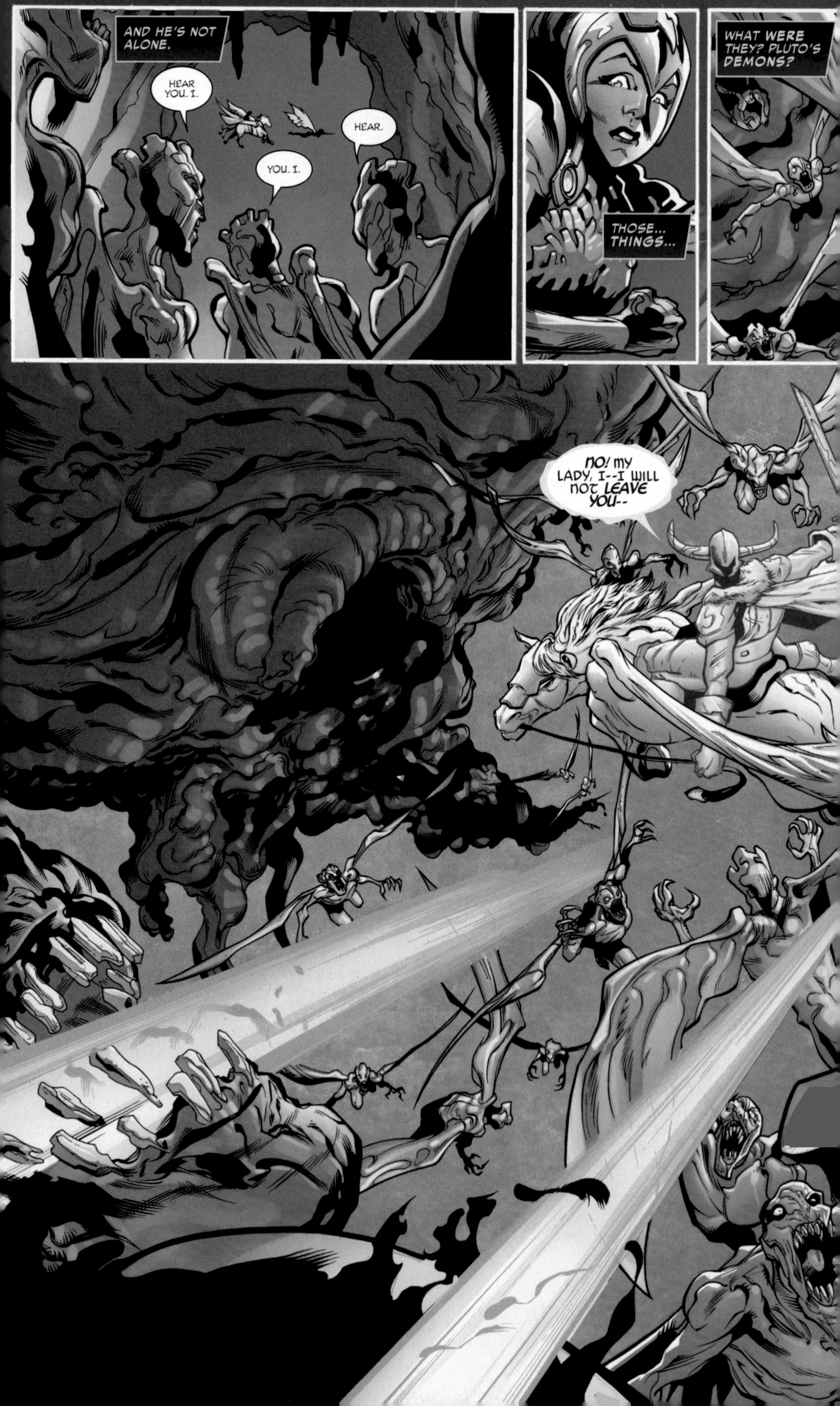
AND HE'S NOT ALONE.
HEAR YOU. I.
HEAR.
YOU. I.
THOSE... THINGS...
WHAT WERE THEY? PLUTO'S DEMONS?
NO! MY LADY, I--I WILL NOT LEAVE YOU--

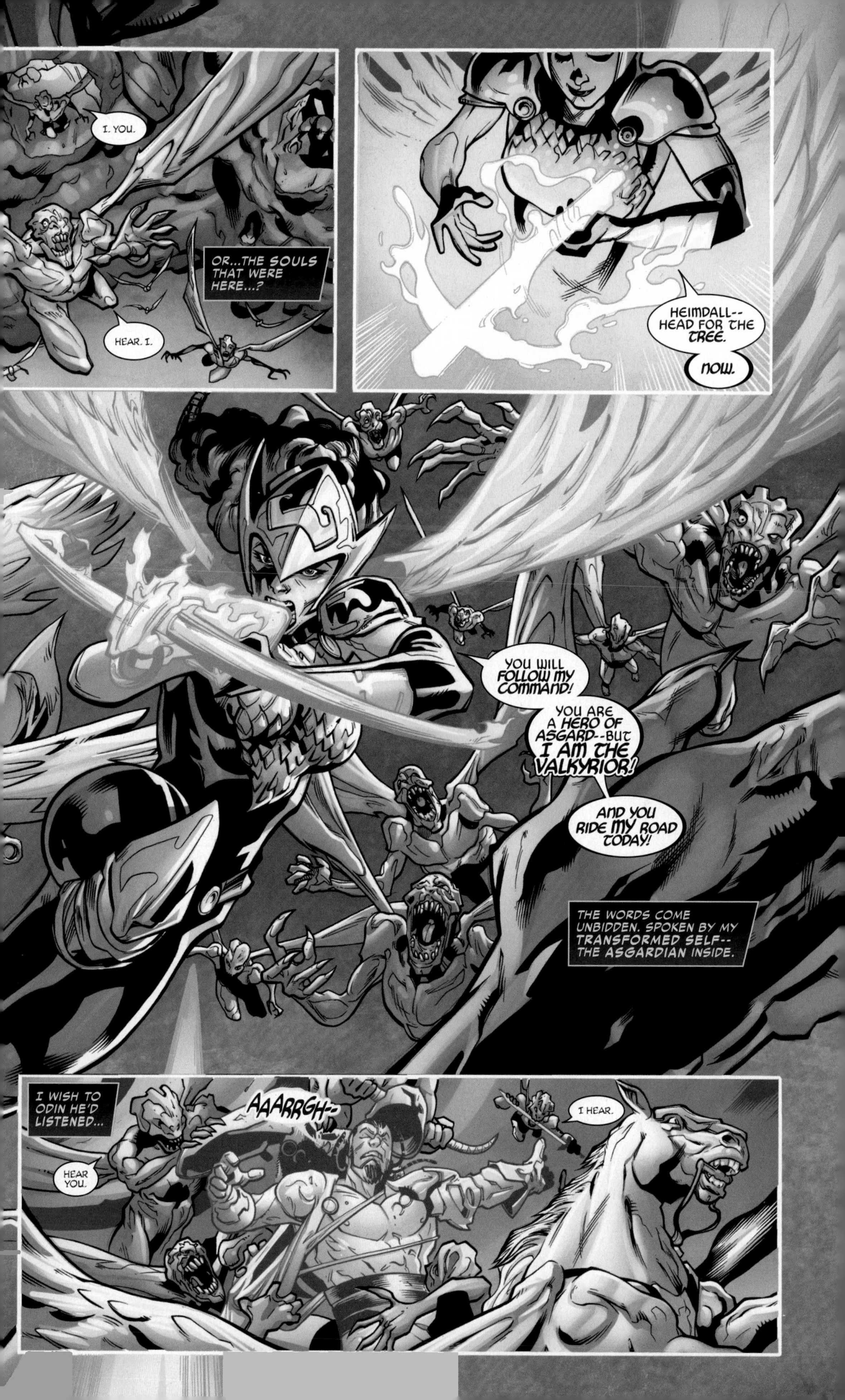
I. YOU.
OR...THE SOULS THAT WERE HERE...?
HEAR. I.
HEIMDALL-- HEAD FOR THE TREE.
NOW.
YOU WILL FOLLOW MY COMMAND!
YOU ARE A HERO OF ASGARD--BUT I AM THE VALKYRIOR!
AND YOU RIDE MY ROAD TODAY!
THE WORDS COME UNBIDDEN. SPOKEN BY MY TRANSFORMED SELF-- THE ASGARDIAN INSIDE.
I WISH TO ODIN HE'D LISTENED...
AAARRGH--
I HEAR.
HEAR YOU.

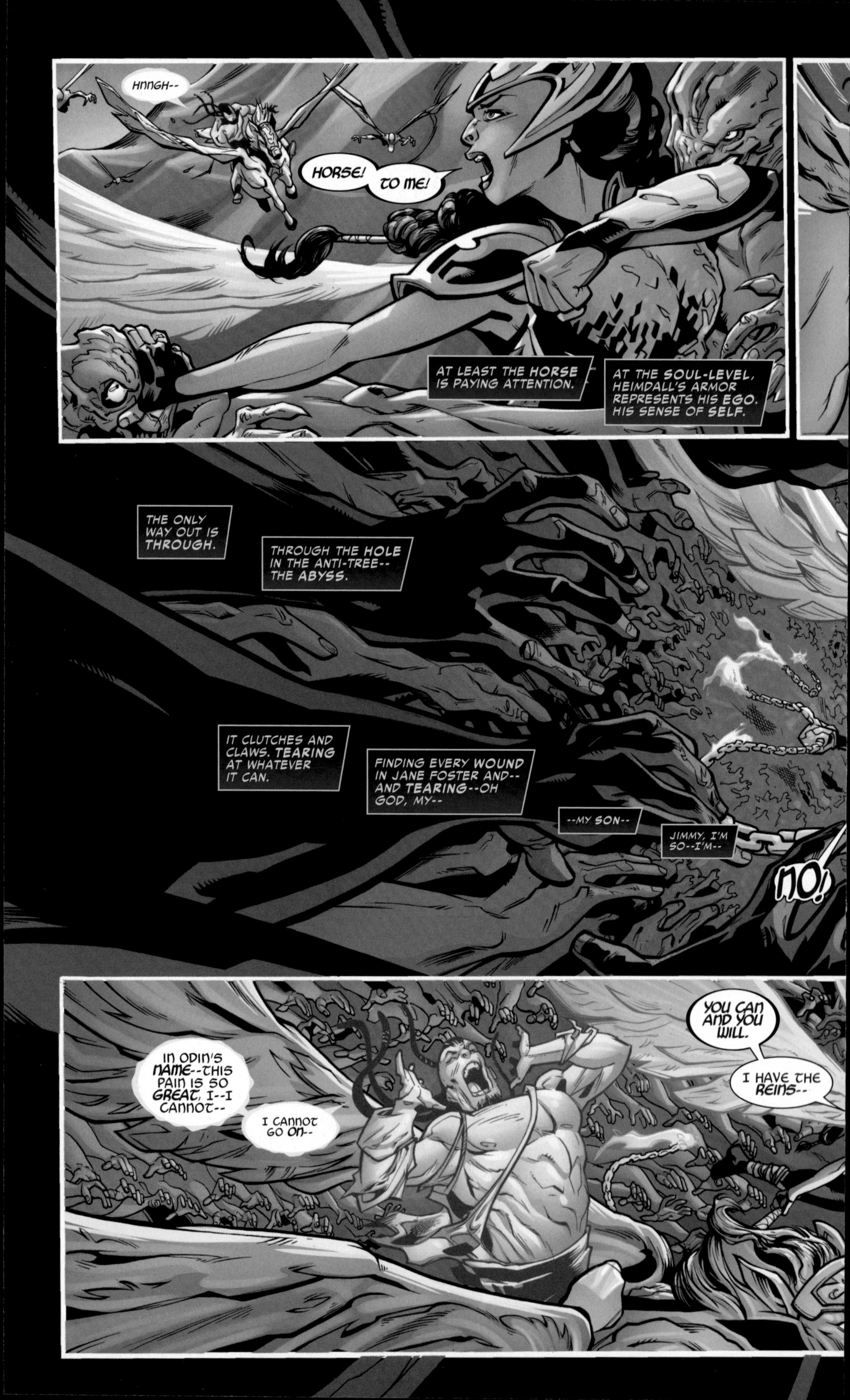
HNNGH--
HORSE!
TO ME!
AT LEAST THE HORSE IS PAYING ATTENTION.
AT THE SOUL-LEVEL, HEIMDALL'S ARMOR REPRESENTS HIS EGO. HIS SENSE OF SELF.
THE ONLY WAY OUT IS THROUGH.
THROUGH THE HOLE IN THE ANTI-TREE-- THE ABYSS.
IT CLUTCHES AND CLAWS. TEARING AT WHATEVER IT CAN.
FINDING EVERY WOUND IN JANE FOSTER AND-- AND TEARING--OH GOD, MY--
--MY SON--
JIMMY, I'M SO--I'M--
NO!
IN ODIN'S NAME--THIS PAIN IS SO GREAT, I--I CANNOT--
I CANNOT GO ON--
YOU CAN AND YOU WILL.
I HAVE THE REINS--

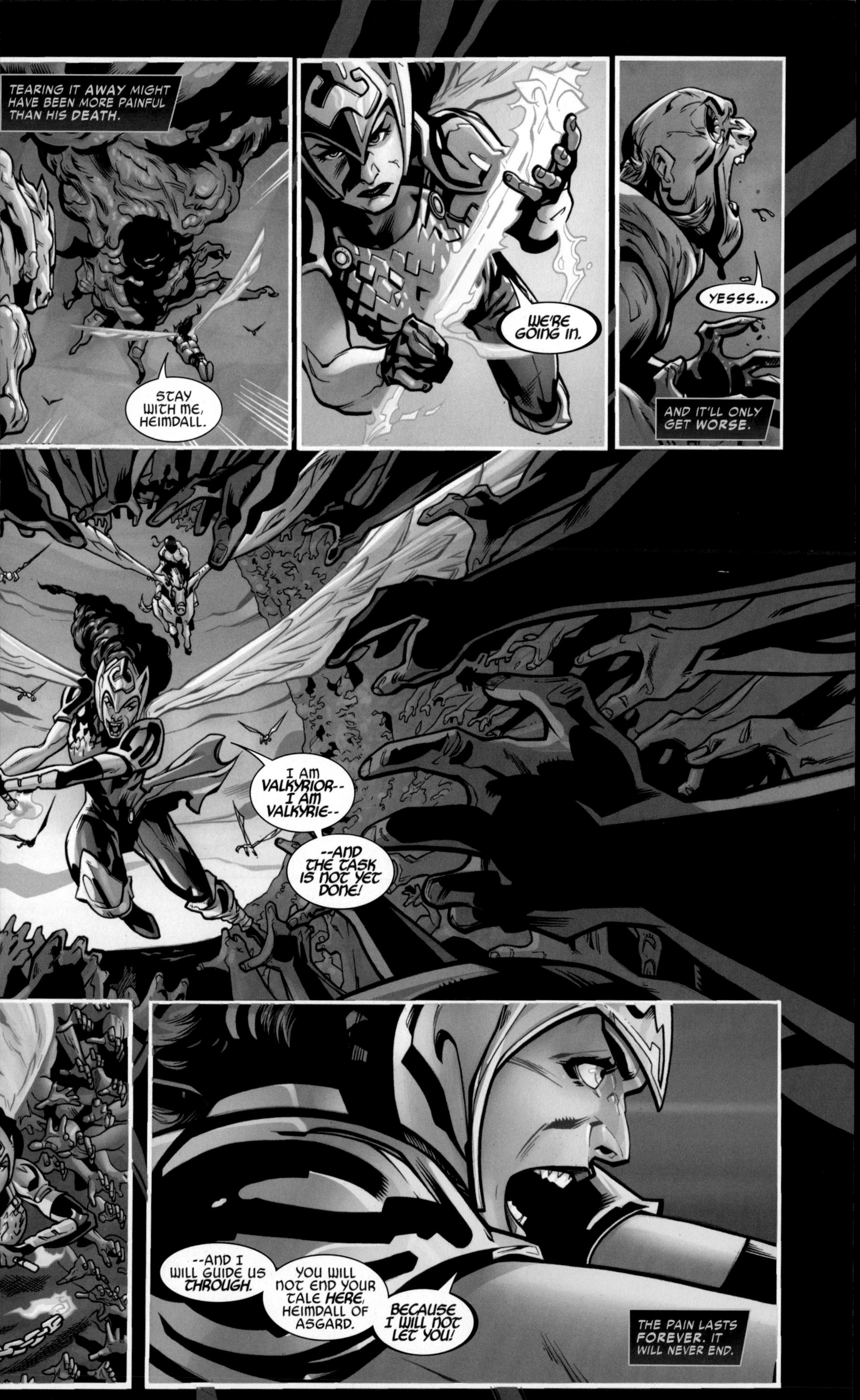
TEARING IT AWAY MIGHT HAVE BEEN MORE PAINFUL THAN HIS DEATH.
STAY WITH ME, HEIMDALL.
WE'RE GOING IN.
YESSS...
AND IT'LL ONLY GET WORSE.
I AM VALKYRIOR-- I AM VALKYRIE--
--AND THE TASK IS NOT YET DONE!
--AND I WILL GUIDE US THROUGH.
YOU WILL NOT END YOUR TALE HERE, HEIMDALL OF ASGARD.
BECAUSE I WILL NOT LET YOU!
THE PAIN LASTS FOREVER. IT WILL NEVER END.

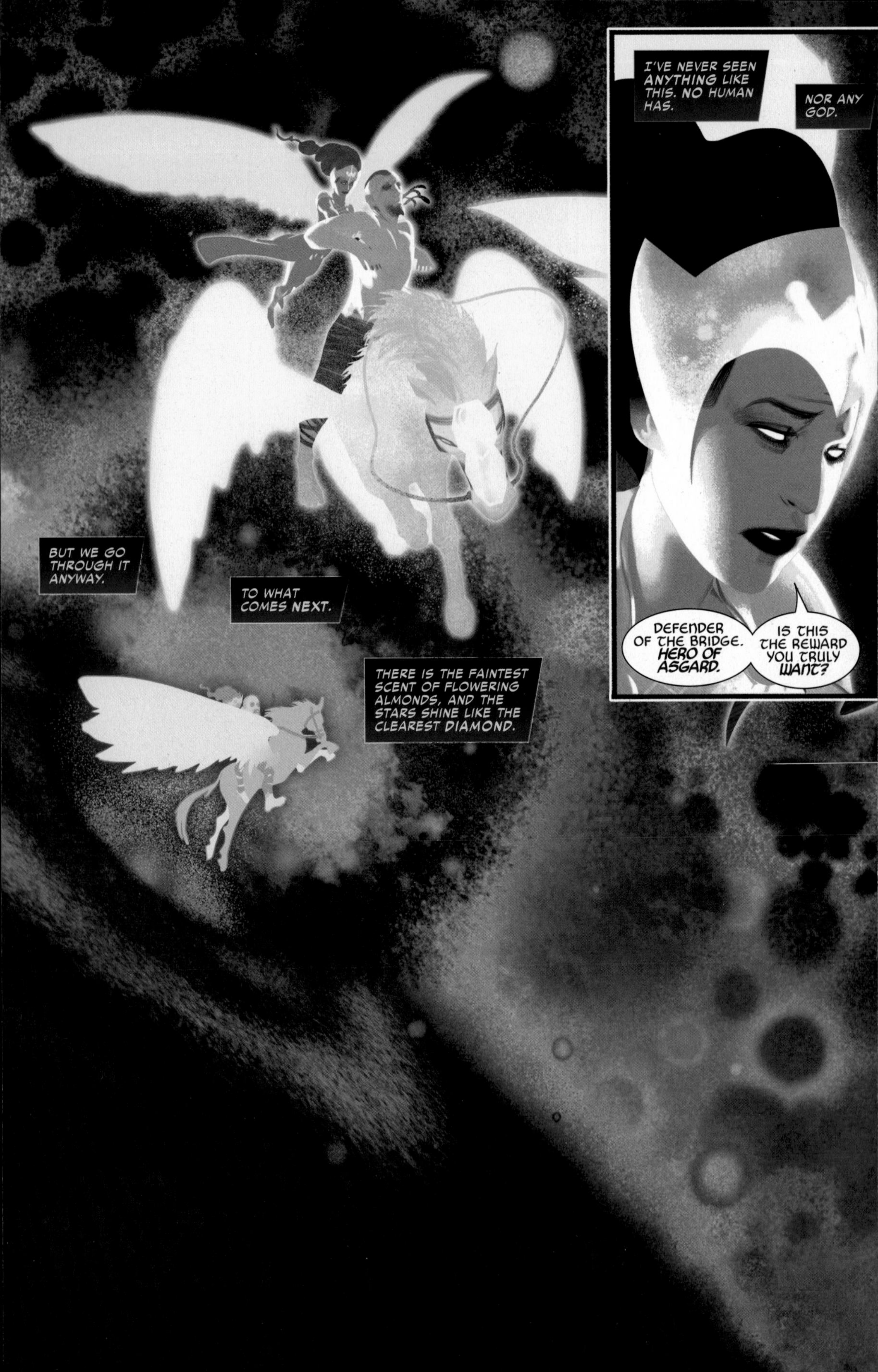
I'VE NEVER SEEN ANYTHING LIKE THIS. NO HUMAN HAS.
NOR ANY GOD.
BUT WE GO THROUGH IT ANYWAY.
TO WHAT COMES NEXT.
DEFENDER OF THE BRIDGE. HERO OF ASGARD.
IS THIS THE REWARD YOU TRULY WANT?
THERE IS THE FAINTEST SCENT OF FLOWERING ALMONDS, AND THE STARS SHINE LIKE THE CLEAREST DIAMOND.

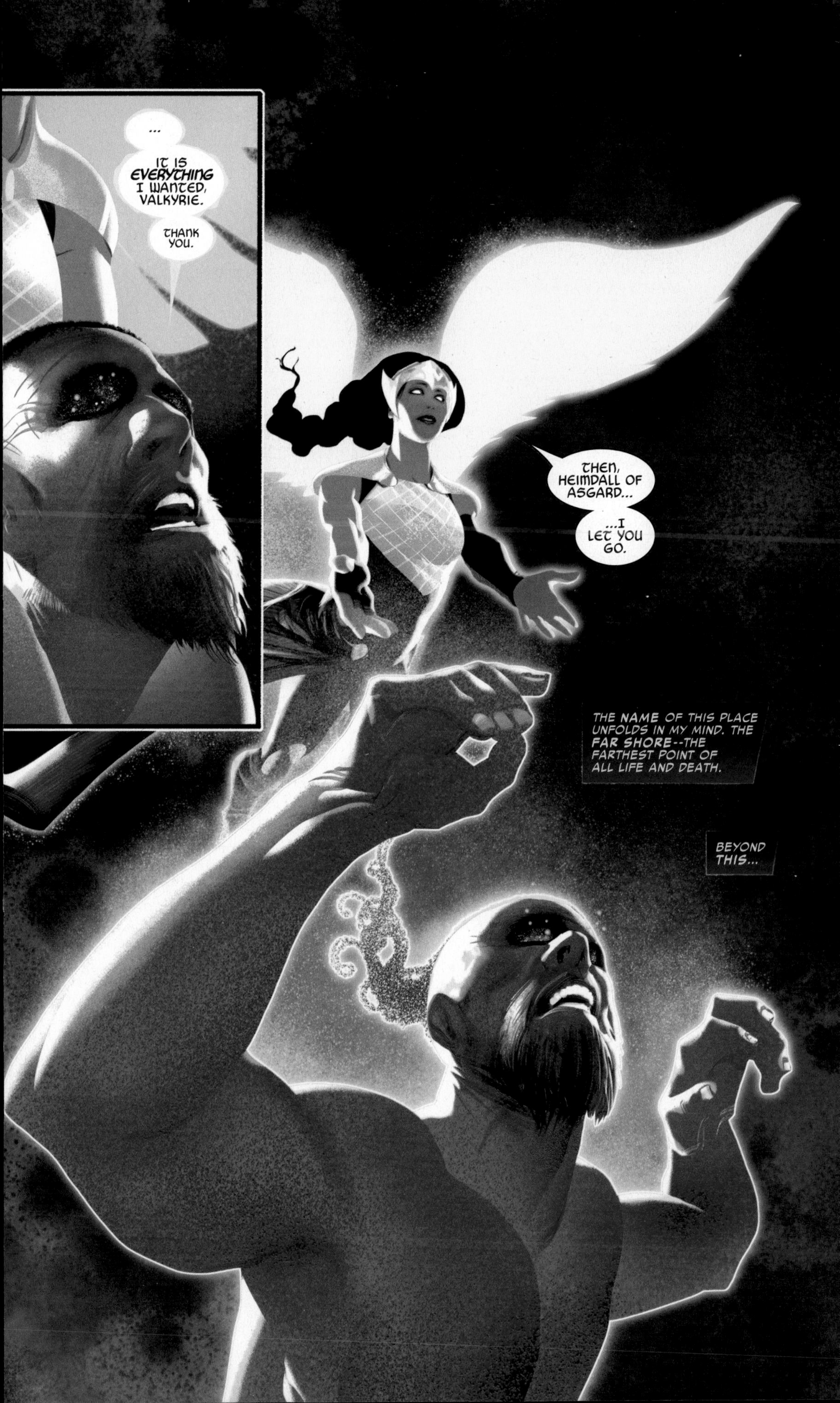
...
IT IS **EVERYTHING** I WANTED, VALKYRIE.
THANK YOU.
THEN, HEIMDALL OF ASGARD...
...I LET YOU GO.
THE **NAME** OF THIS PLACE UNFOLDS IN MY MIND. THE **FAR SHORE**--THE FARTHEST POINT OF ALL LIFE AND DEATH.
BEYOND **THIS**...

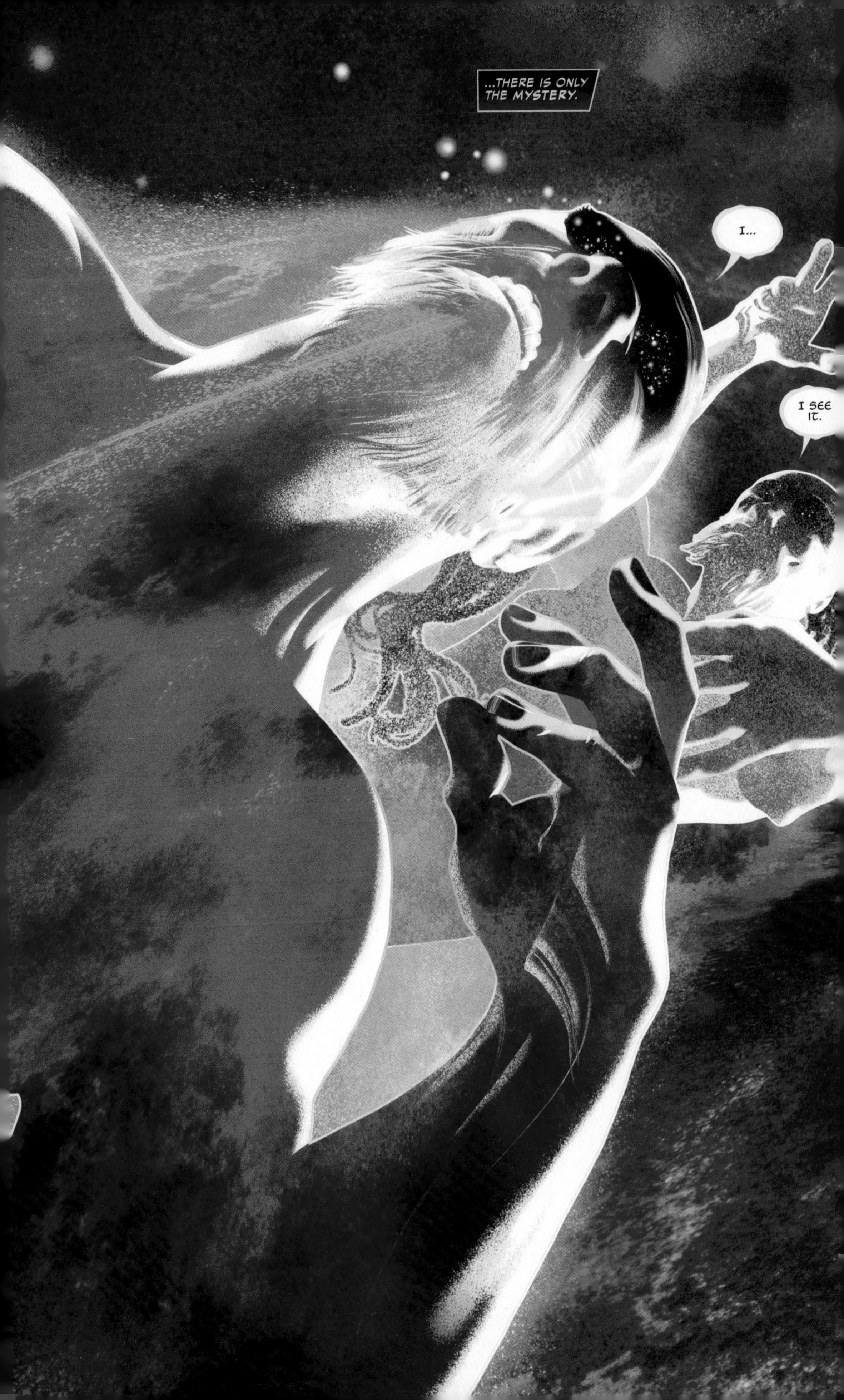
...THERE IS ONLY THE MYSTERY.
I...
I SEE IT.

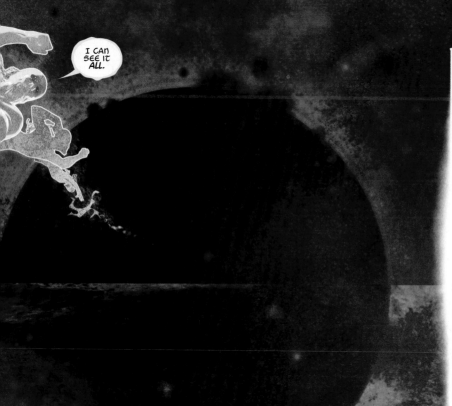

I CAN SEE IT ALL.

I DON'T SEE WHAT HAPPENS NEXT. I'M NOT PERMITTED TO.

AS HEIMDALL CROSSES TO THE FINAL ADVENTURE, THERE IS A FLASH OF BRILLIANT WHITE LIGHT SO BRIGHT IT BLINDS ME--

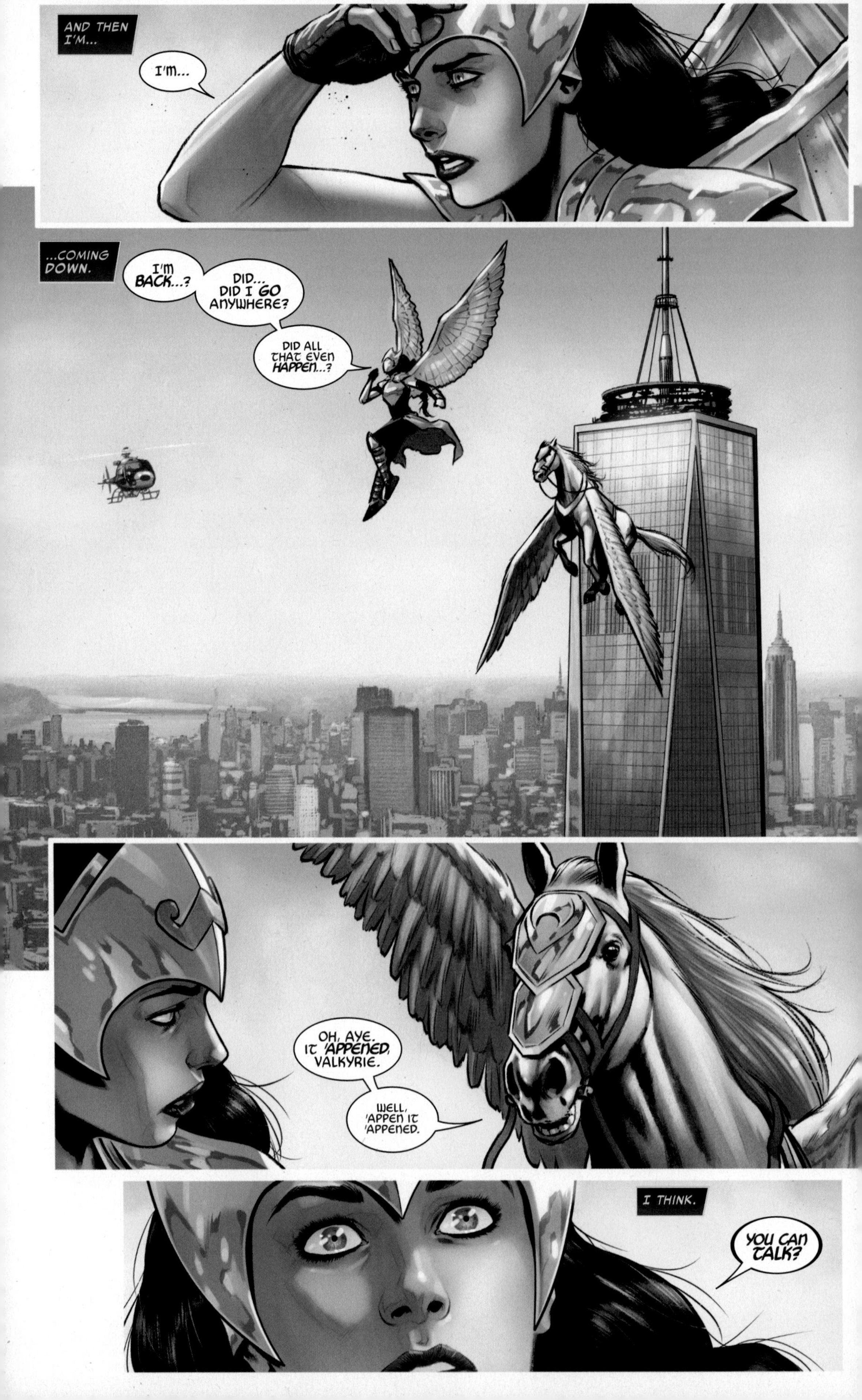
AND THEN I'M...
I'M...
...COMING DOWN.
I'M BACK...?
DID... DID I GO ANYWHERE?
DID ALL THAT EVEN HAPPEN...?
OH, AYE. IT 'APPENED, VALKYRIE.
WELL, 'APPEN IT 'APPENED.
I THINK.
YOU CAN TALK?

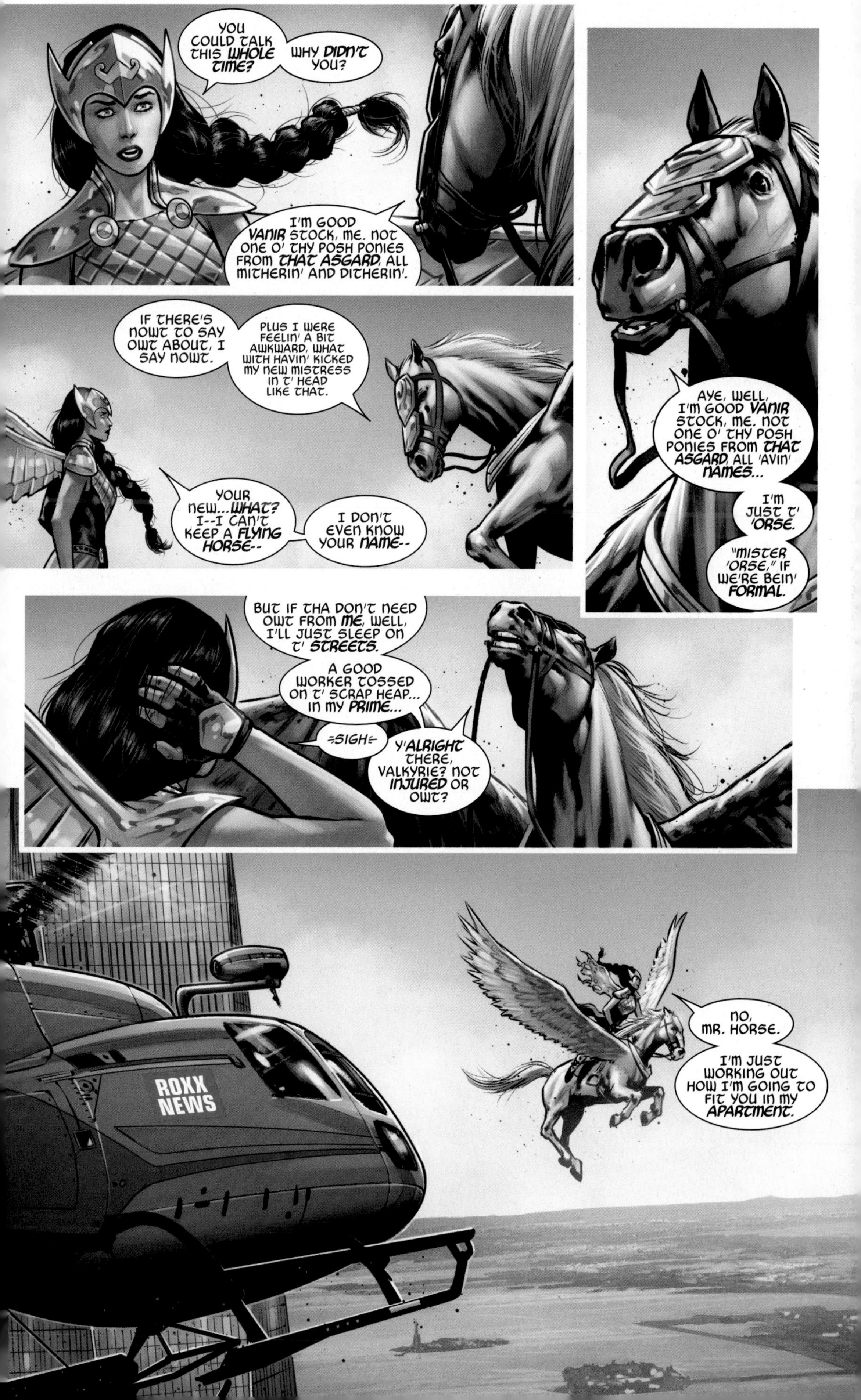

YOU COULD TALK THIS WHOLE TIME?
WHY DIDN'T YOU?
I'M GOOD VANIR STOCK, ME. NOT ONE O' THY POSH PONIES FROM THAT ASGARD, ALL MITHERIN' AND DITHERIN'.
AYE, WELL, I'M GOOD VANIR STOCK, ME. NOT ONE O' THY POSH PONIES FROM THAT ASGARD, ALL 'AVIN' NAMES...
I'M JUST T' 'ORSE.
"MISTER 'ORSE," IF WE'RE BEIN' FORMAL.
IF THERE'S NOWT TO SAY OWT ABOUT, I SAY NOWT.
PLUS I WERE FEELIN' A BIT AWKWARD, WHAT WITH HAVIN' KICKED MY NEW MISTRESS IN T' HEAD LIKE THAT.
YOUR NEW...WHAT? I--I CAN'T KEEP A FLYING HORSE--
I DON'T EVEN KNOW YOUR NAME--
BUT IF THA DON'T NEED OWT FROM ME, WELL, I'LL JUST SLEEP ON T' STREETS.
A GOOD WORKER TOSSED ON T' SCRAP HEAP... IN MY PRIME...
=SIGH=
Y'ALRIGHT THERE, VALKYRIE? NOT INJURED OR OWT?
ROXX NEWS
NO, MR. HORSE.
I'M JUST WORKING OUT HOW I'M GOING TO FIT YOU IN MY APARTMENT.

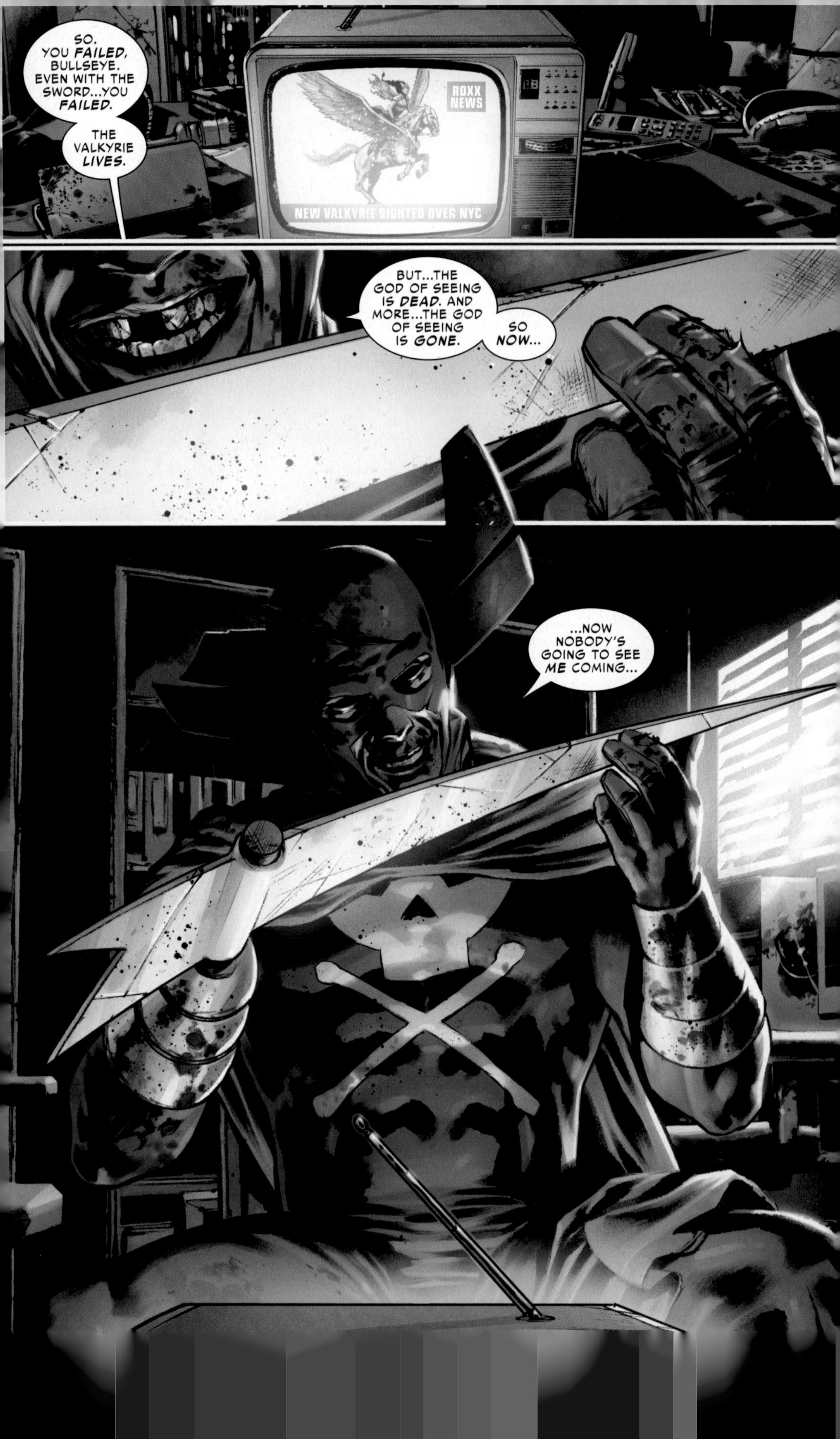
SO. YOU FAILED, BULLSEYE. EVEN WITH THE SWORD...YOU FAILED.
THE VALKYRIE LIVES.
ROXX NEWS
NEW VALKYRIE SIGHTED OVER NYC
BUT...THE GOD OF SEEING IS DEAD. AND MORE...THE GOD OF SEEING IS GONE.
SO NOW...
...NOW NOBODY'S GOING TO SEE ME COMING...

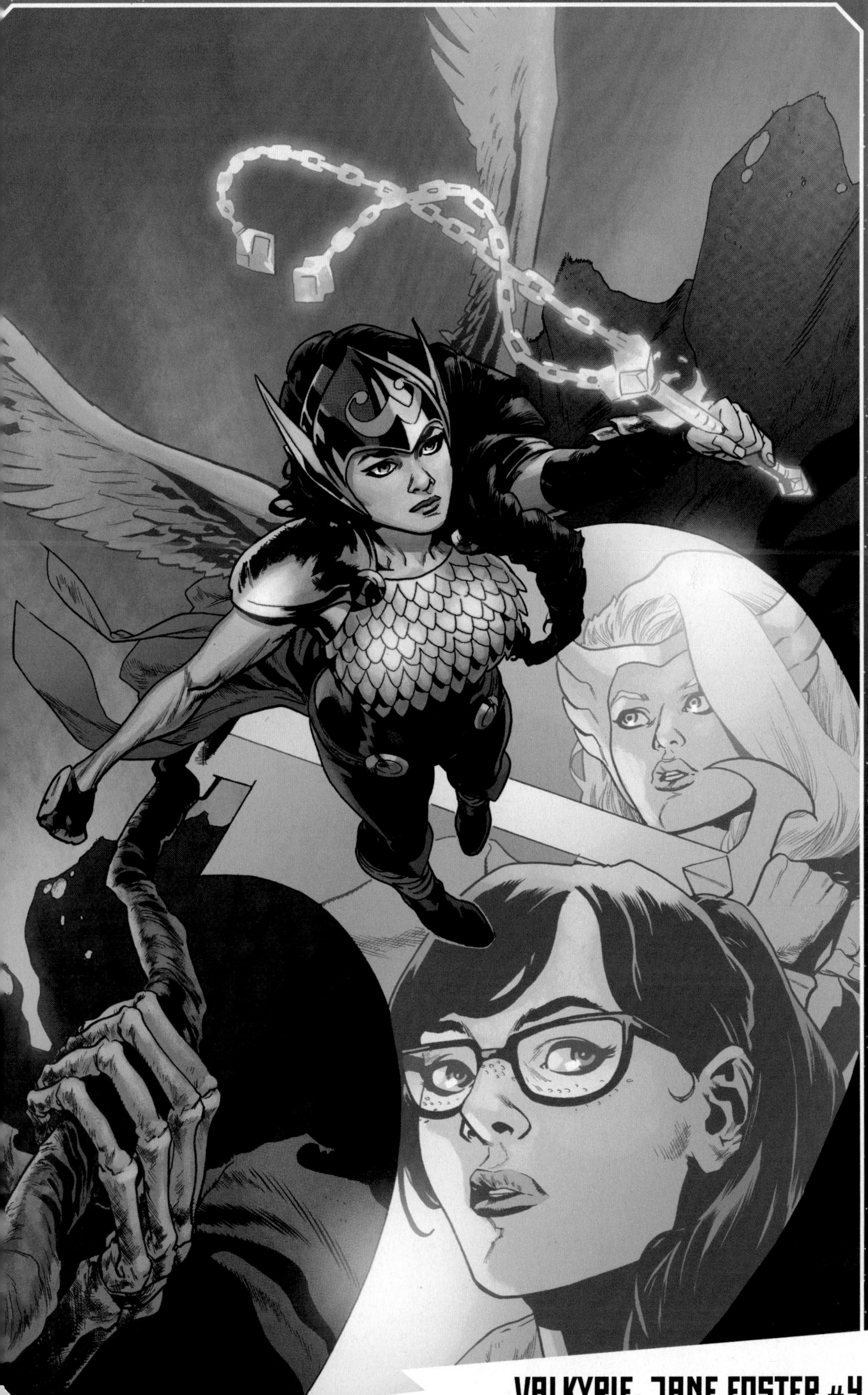

VALKYRIE: JANE FOSTER #4

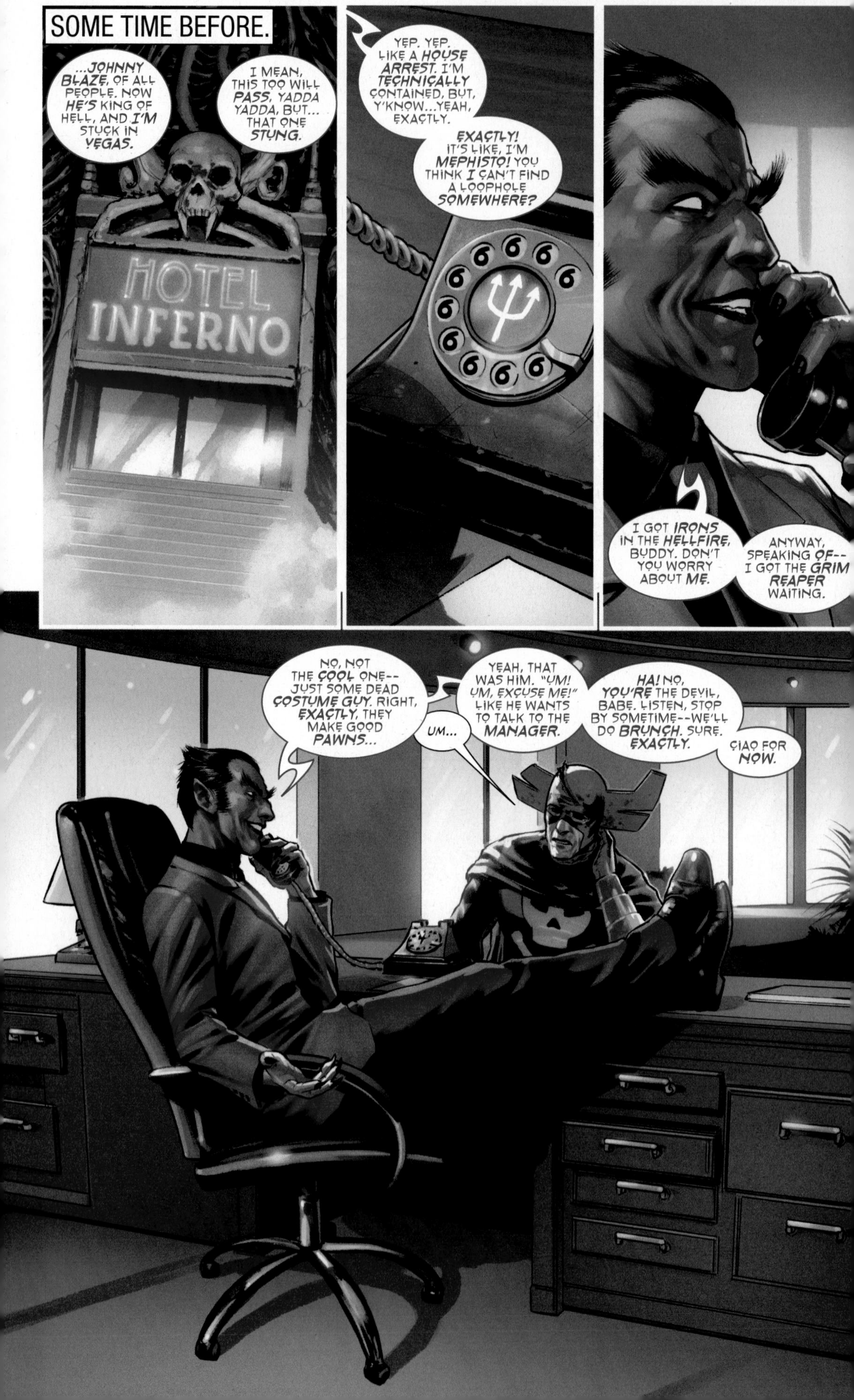

SOME TIME BEFORE.
...JOHNNY BLAZE, OF ALL PEOPLE. NOW HE'S KING OF HELL, AND I'M STUCK IN VEGAS.
I MEAN, THIS TOO WILL PASS, YADDA YADDA, BUT... THAT ONE STUNG.
HOTEL INFERNO
YEP. YEP. LIKE A HOUSE ARREST. I'M TECHNICALLY CONTAINED, BUT, Y'KNOW...YEAH, EXACTLY.
EXACTLY! IT'S LIKE, I'M MEPHISTO! YOU THINK I CAN'T FIND A LOOPHOLE SOMEWHERE?
I GOT IRONS IN THE HELLFIRE, BUDDY. DON'T YOU WORRY ABOUT ME.
ANYWAY, SPEAKING OF-- I GOT THE GRIM REAPER WAITING.
NO, NOT THE COOL ONE-- JUST SOME DEAD COSTUME GUY. RIGHT, EXACTLY, THEY MAKE GOOD PAWNS...
UM...
YEAH, THAT WAS HIM. "UM! UM, EXCUSE ME!" LIKE HE WANTS TO TALK TO THE MANAGER.
HA! NO, YOU'RE THE DEVIL, BABE. LISTEN, STOP BY SOMETIME--WE'LL DO BRUNCH. SURE. EXACTLY.
CIAO FOR NOW.

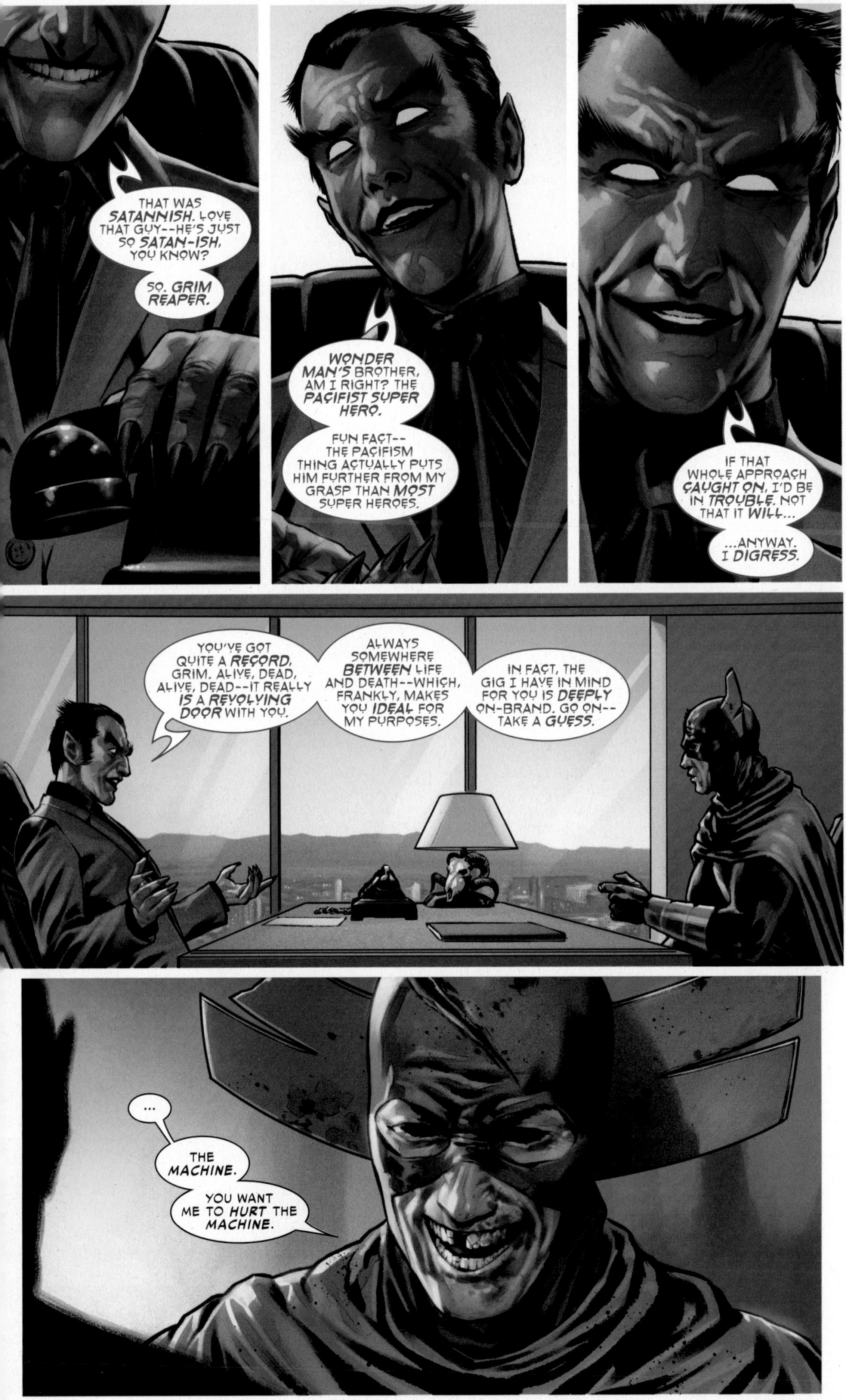

THAT WAS SATANNISH. LOVE THAT GUY--HE'S JUST SO SATAN-ISH, YOU KNOW?
SO. GRIM REAPER.
WONDER MAN'S BROTHER, AM I RIGHT? THE PACIFIST SUPER HERO.
FUN FACT-- THE PACIFISM THING ACTUALLY PUTS HIM FURTHER FROM MY GRASP THAN MOST SUPER HEROES.
IF THAT WHOLE APPROACH CAUGHT ON, I'D BE IN TROUBLE. NOT THAT IT WILL...
...ANYWAY. I DIGRESS.
YOU'VE GOT QUITE A RECORD, GRIM. ALIVE, DEAD, ALIVE, DEAD--IT REALLY IS A REVOLVING DOOR WITH YOU.
ALWAYS SOMEWHERE BETWEEN LIFE AND DEATH--WHICH, FRANKLY, MAKES YOU IDEAL FOR MY PURPOSES.
IN FACT, THE GIG I HAVE IN MIND FOR YOU IS DEEPLY ON-BRAND. GO ON-- TAKE A GUESS.
...
THE MACHINE.
YOU WANT ME TO HURT THE MACHINE.

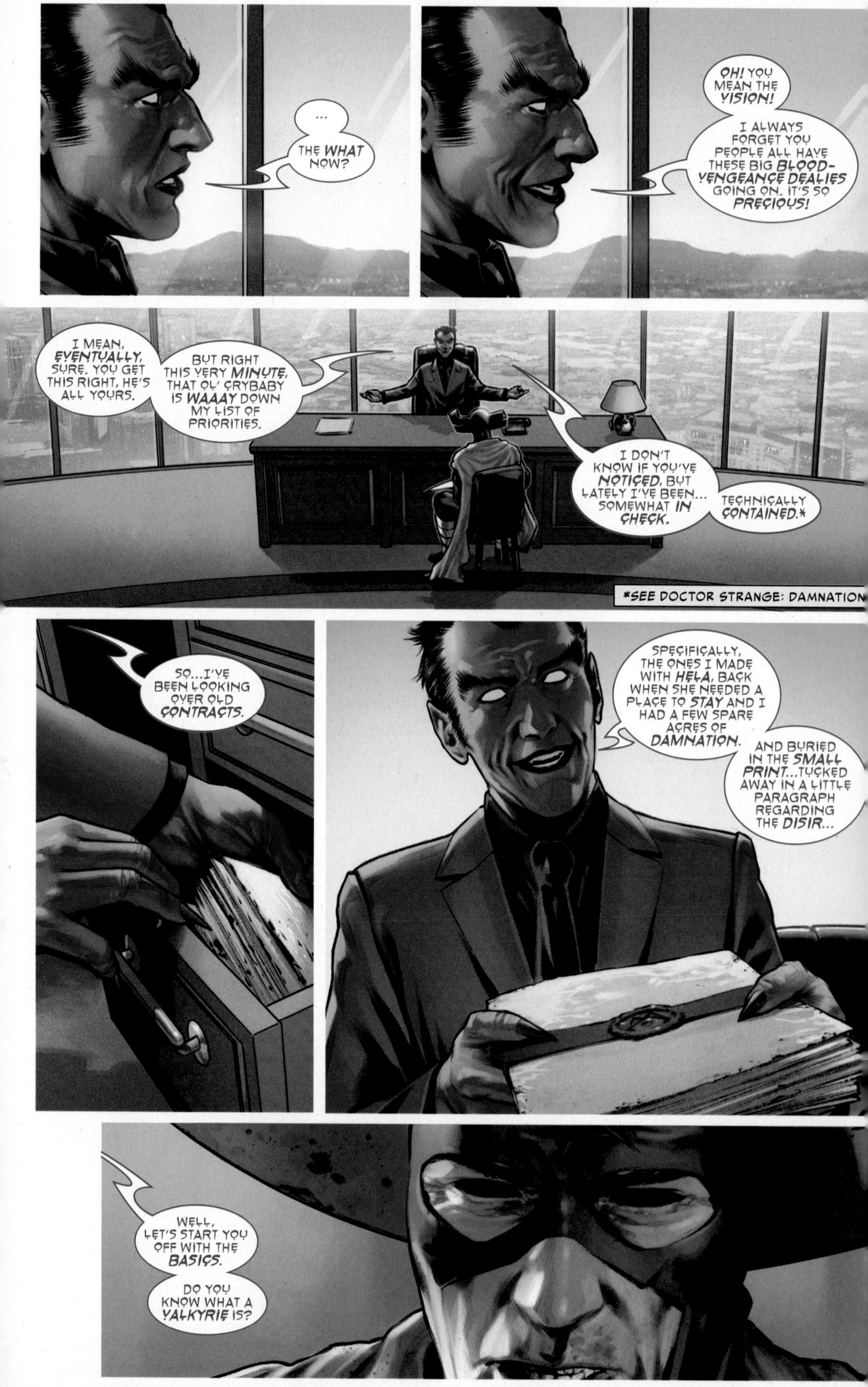
...
THE WHAT NOW?
OH! YOU MEAN THE VISION!
I ALWAYS FORGET YOU PEOPLE ALL HAVE THESE BIG BLOOD-VENGEANCE DEALIES GOING ON. IT'S SO PRECIOUS!
I MEAN, EVENTUALLY, SURE. YOU GET THIS RIGHT, HE'S ALL YOURS.
BUT RIGHT THIS VERY MINUTE, THAT OL' CRYBABY IS WAAAY DOWN MY LIST OF PRIORITIES.
I DON'T KNOW IF YOU'VE NOTICED, BUT LATELY I'VE BEEN... SOMEWHAT IN CHECK.
TECHNICALLY CONTAINED.*
*SEE DOCTOR STRANGE: DAMNATION
SO...I'VE BEEN LOOKING OVER OLD CONTRACTS.
SPECIFICALLY, THE ONES I MADE WITH HELA, BACK WHEN SHE NEEDED A PLACE TO STAY AND I HAD A FEW SPARE ACRES OF DAMNATION.
AND BURIED IN THE SMALL PRINT...TUCKED AWAY IN A LITTLE PARAGRAPH REGARDING THE DISIR...
WELL, LET'S START YOU OFF WITH THE BASICS.
DO YOU KNOW WHAT A VALKYRIE IS?

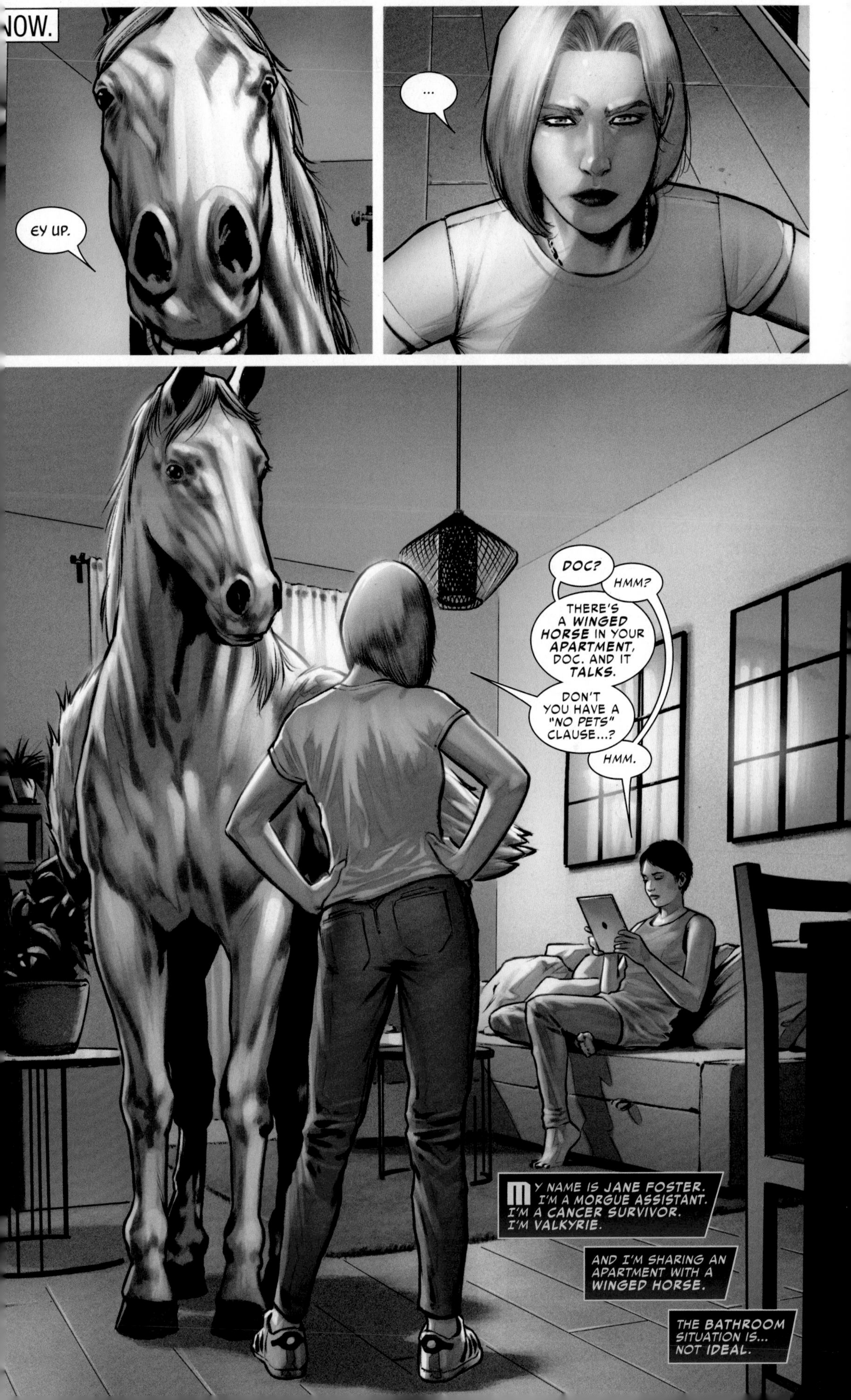
NOW.
EY UP.
...
DOC?
HMM?
THERE'S A WINGED HORSE IN YOUR APARTMENT, DOC. AND IT TALKS.
DON'T YOU HAVE A "NO PETS" CLAUSE...?
HMM.
MY NAME IS JANE FOSTER. I'M A MORGUE ASSISTANT. I'M A CANCER SURVIVOR. I'M VALKYRIE.
AND I'M SHARING AN APARTMENT WITH A WINGED HORSE.
THE BATHROOM SITUATION IS... NOT IDEAL.

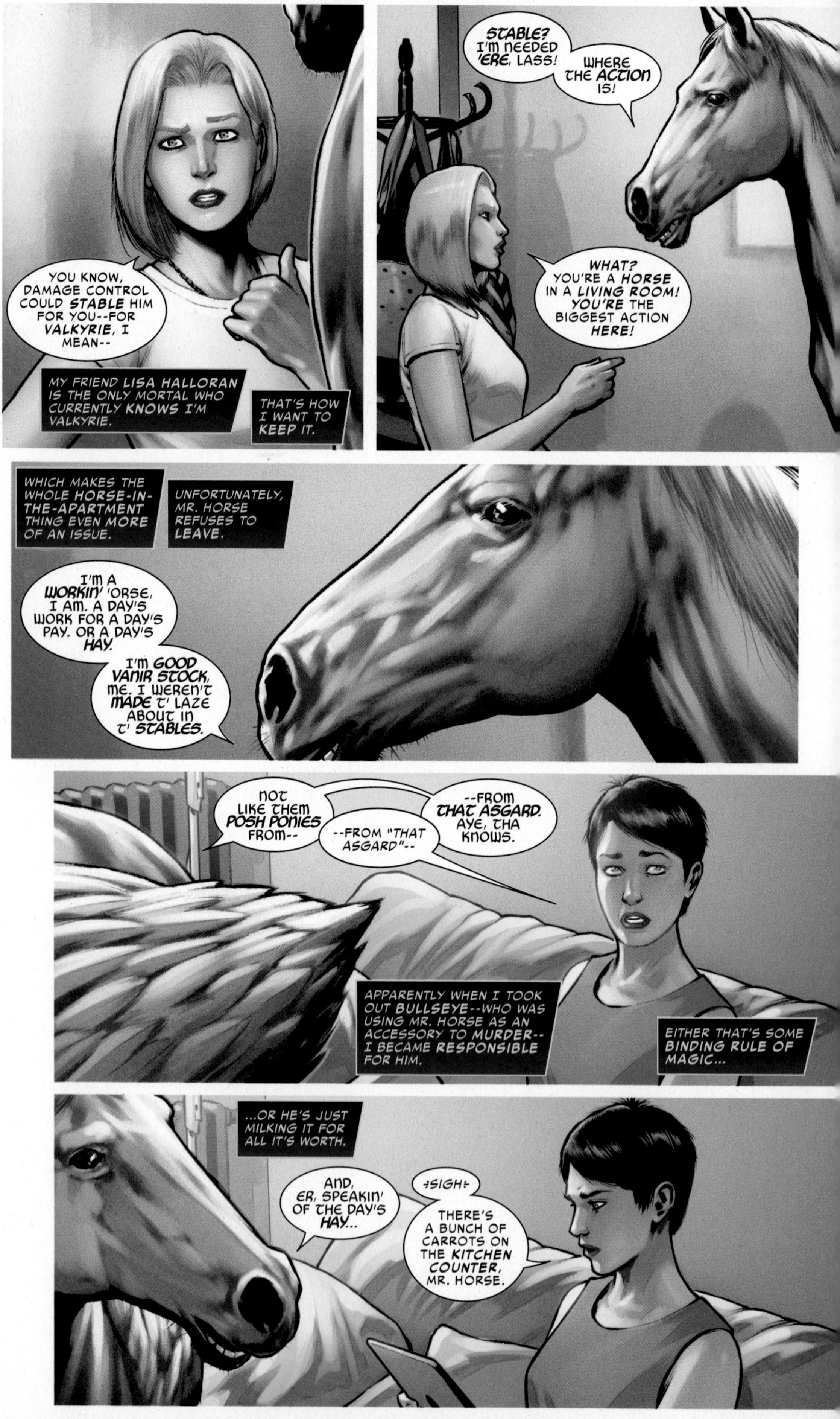

YOU KNOW, DAMAGE CONTROL COULD STABLE HIM FOR YOU--FOR VALKYRIE, I MEAN--
MY FRIEND LISA HALLORAN IS THE ONLY MORTAL WHO CURRENTLY KNOWS I'M VALKYRIE.
THAT'S HOW I WANT TO KEEP IT.
STABLE? I'M NEEDED 'ERE, LASS!
WHERE THE ACTION IS!
WHAT? YOU'RE A HORSE IN A LIVING ROOM! YOU'RE THE BIGGEST ACTION HERE!
WHICH MAKES THE WHOLE HORSE-IN-THE-APARTMENT THING EVEN MORE OF AN ISSUE.
UNFORTUNATELY, MR. HORSE REFUSES TO LEAVE.
I'M A WORKIN' 'ORSE, I AM. A DAY'S WORK FOR A DAY'S PAY. OR A DAY'S HAY.
I'M GOOD VANIR STOCK, ME. I WEREN'T MADE T' LAZE ABOUT IN T' STABLES.
NOT LIKE THEM POSH PONIES FROM--
--FROM "THAT ASGARD"--
--FROM THAT ASGARD. AYE, THA KNOWS.
APPARENTLY WHEN I TOOK OUT BULLSEYE--WHO WAS USING MR. HORSE AS AN ACCESSORY TO MURDER--I BECAME RESPONSIBLE FOR HIM.
EITHER THAT'S SOME BINDING RULE OF MAGIC...
...OR HE'S JUST MILKING IT FOR ALL IT'S WORTH.
AND, ER, SPEAKIN' OF THE DAY'S HAY...
SIGH
THERE'S A BUNCH OF CARROTS ON THE KITCHEN COUNTER, MR. HORSE.

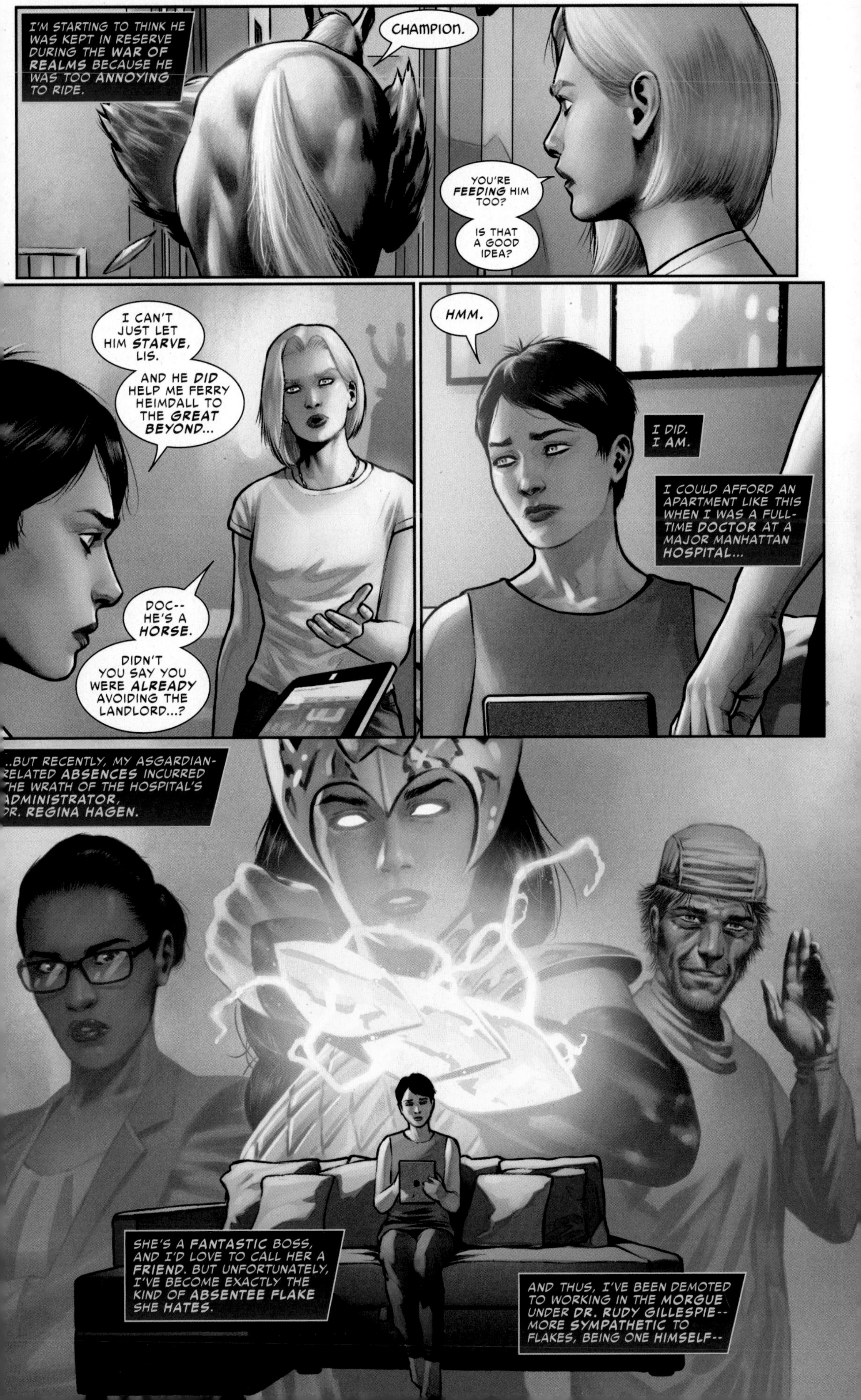
I'M STARTING TO THINK HE WAS KEPT IN RESERVE DURING THE WAR OF REALMS BECAUSE HE WAS TOO ANNOYING TO RIDE.
CHAMPION.
YOU'RE FEEDING HIM TOO?
IS THAT A GOOD IDEA?
I CAN'T JUST LET HIM STARVE, LIS.
AND HE DID HELP ME FERRY HEIMDALL TO THE GREAT BEYOND...
DOC-- HE'S A HORSE.
DIDN'T YOU SAY YOU WERE ALREADY AVOIDING THE LANDLORD...?
HMM.
I DID. I AM.
I COULD AFFORD AN APARTMENT LIKE THIS WHEN I WAS A FULL-TIME DOCTOR AT A MAJOR MANHATTAN HOSPITAL...
..BUT RECENTLY, MY ASGARDIAN-RELATED ABSENCES INCURRED THE WRATH OF THE HOSPITAL'S ADMINISTRATOR, DR. REGINA HAGEN.
SHE'S A FANTASTIC BOSS, AND I'D LOVE TO CALL HER A FRIEND. BUT UNFORTUNATELY, I'VE BECOME EXACTLY THE KIND OF ABSENTEE FLAKE SHE HATES.
AND THUS, I'VE BEEN DEMOTED TO WORKING IN THE MORGUE UNDER DR. RUDY GILLESPIE-- MORE SYMPATHETIC TO FLAKES, BEING ONE HIMSELF--

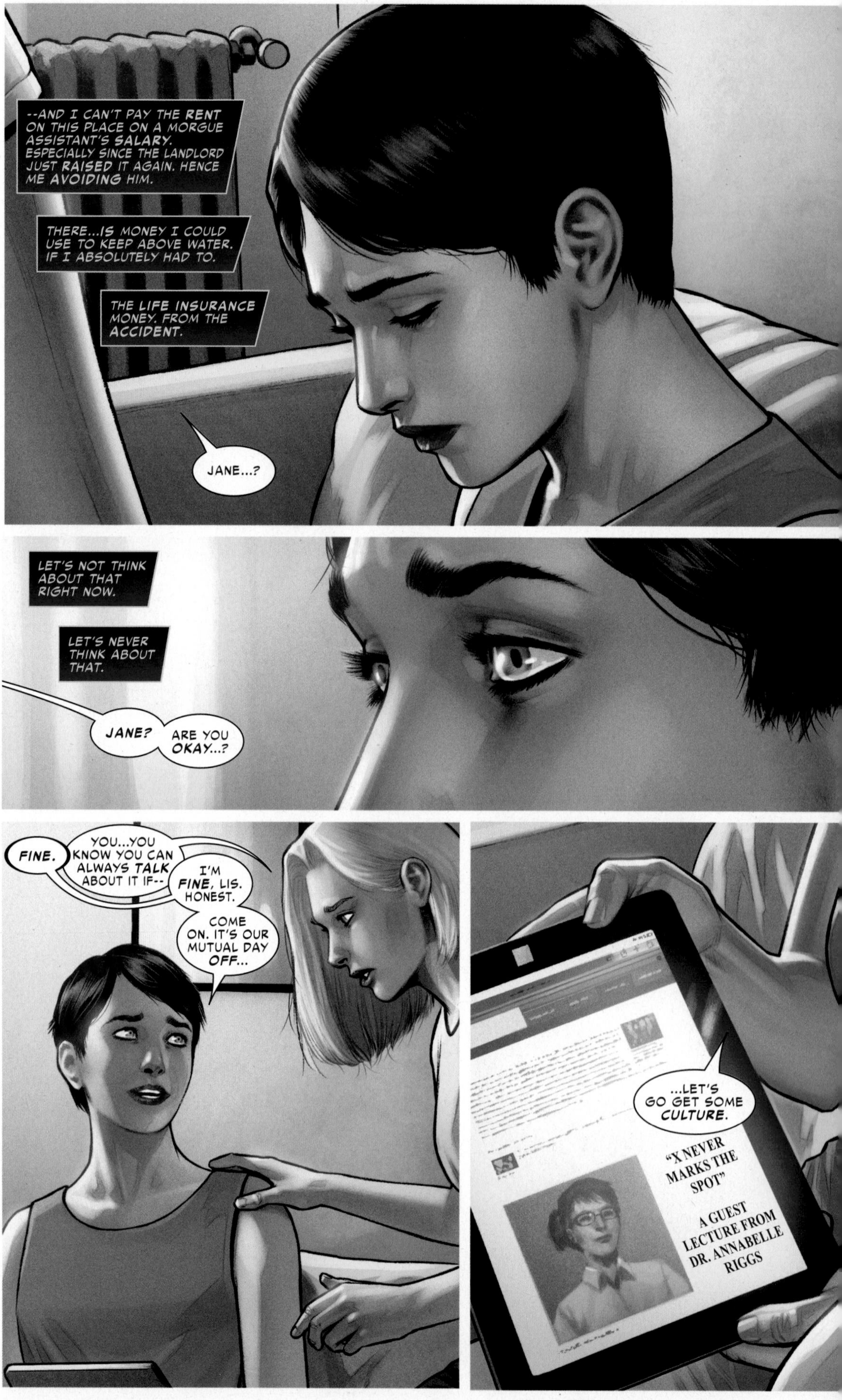
--AND I CAN'T PAY THE RENT ON THIS PLACE ON A MORGUE ASSISTANT'S SALARY. ESPECIALLY SINCE THE LANDLORD JUST RAISED IT AGAIN. HENCE ME AVOIDING HIM.
THERE...IS MONEY I COULD USE TO KEEP ABOVE WATER. IF I ABSOLUTELY HAD TO.
THE LIFE INSURANCE MONEY. FROM THE ACCIDENT.
JANE...?
LET'S NOT THINK ABOUT THAT RIGHT NOW.
LET'S NEVER THINK ABOUT THAT.
JANE?
ARE YOU OKAY...?
FINE.
YOU...YOU KNOW YOU CAN ALWAYS TALK ABOUT IT IF--
I'M FINE, LIS. HONEST.
COME ON. IT'S OUR MUTUAL DAY OFF...
...LET'S GO GET SOME CULTURE.
"X NEVER MARKS THE SPOT"
A GUEST LECTURE FROM DR. ANNABELLE RIGGS

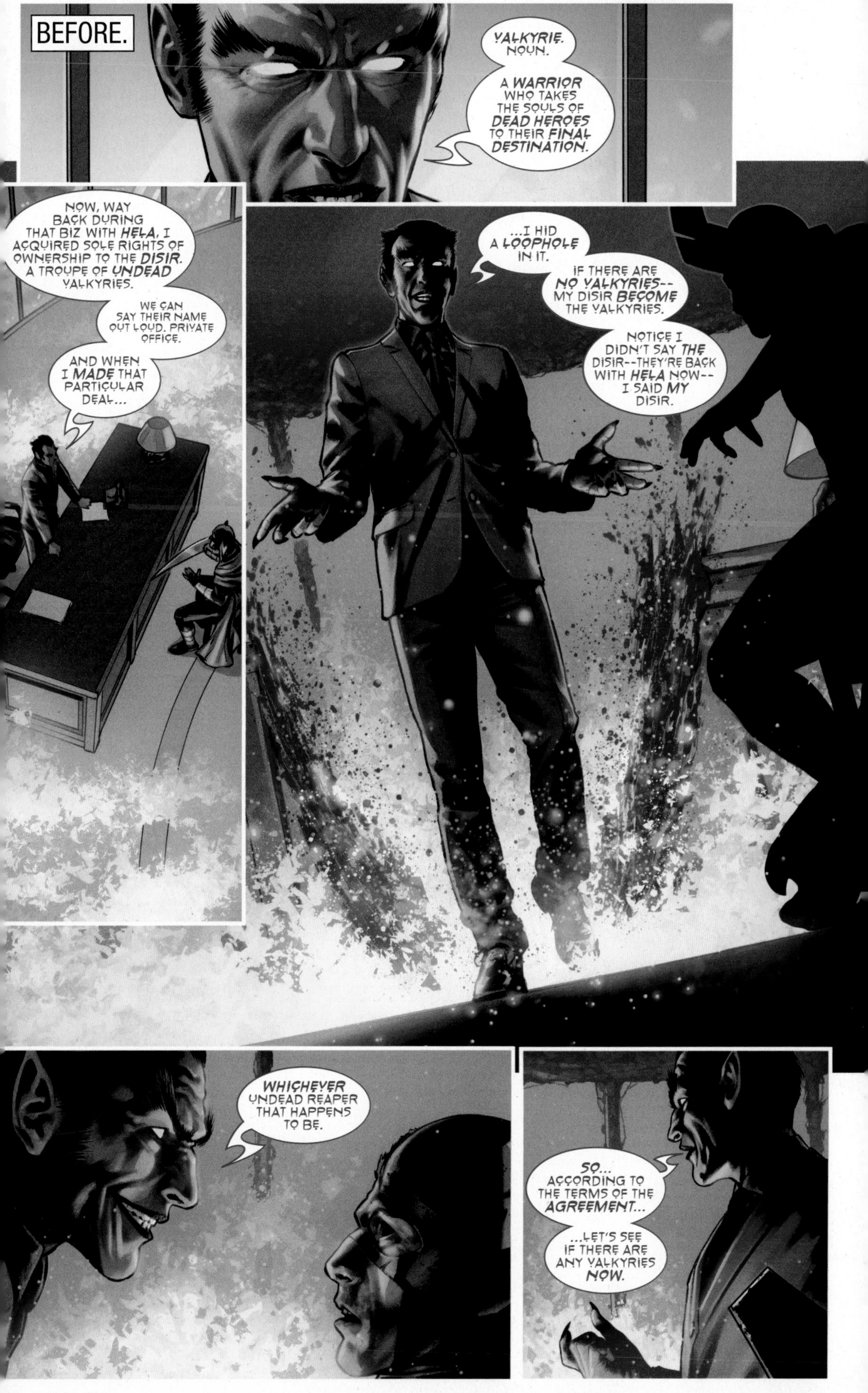
BEFORE.
VALKYRIE. NOUN.
A WARRIOR WHO TAKES THE SOULS OF DEAD HEROES TO THEIR FINAL DESTINATION.
NOW, WAY BACK DURING THAT BIZ WITH HELA, I ACQUIRED SOLE RIGHTS OF OWNERSHIP TO THE DISIR. A TROUPE OF UNDEAD VALKYRIES.
WE CAN SAY THEIR NAME OUT LOUD. PRIVATE OFFICE.
AND WHEN I MADE THAT PARTICULAR DEAL...
...I HID A LOOPHOLE IN IT.
IF THERE ARE NO VALKYRIES-- MY DISIR BECOME THE VALKYRIES.
NOTICE I DIDN'T SAY THE DISIR--THEY'RE BACK WITH HELA NOW-- I SAID MY DISIR.
WHICHEVER UNDEAD REAPER THAT HAPPENS TO BE.
SO... ACCORDING TO THE TERMS OF THE AGREEMENT...
...LET'S SEE IF THERE ARE ANY VALKYRIES NOW.

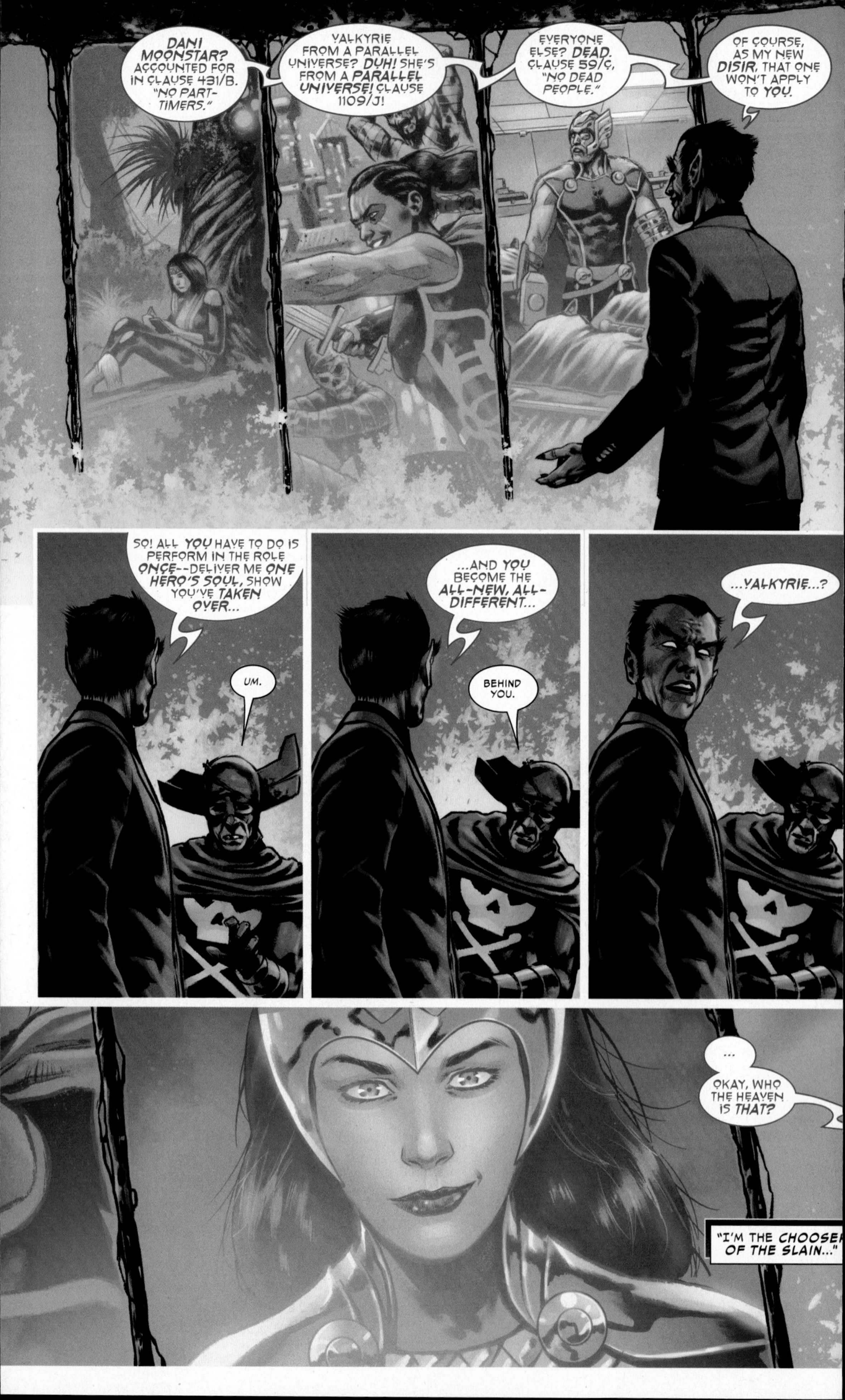
DANI MOONSTAR? ACCOUNTED FOR IN CLAUSE 431/B. "NO PART-TIMERS."
VALKYRIE FROM A PARALLEL UNIVERSE? DUH! SHE'S FROM A PARALLEL UNIVERSE! CLAUSE 1109/J!
EVERYONE ELSE? DEAD. CLAUSE 59/C, "NO DEAD PEOPLE."
OF COURSE, AS MY NEW DISIR, THAT ONE WON'T APPLY TO YOU.
SO! ALL YOU HAVE TO DO IS PERFORM IN THE ROLE ONCE--DELIVER ME ONE HERO'S SOUL, SHOW YOU'VE TAKEN OVER...
UM.
...AND YOU BECOME THE ALL-NEW, ALL-DIFFERENT...
BEHIND YOU.
...VALKYRIE...?
...
OKAY, WHO THE HEAVEN IS THAT?
"I'M THE CHOOSER OF THE SLAIN..."

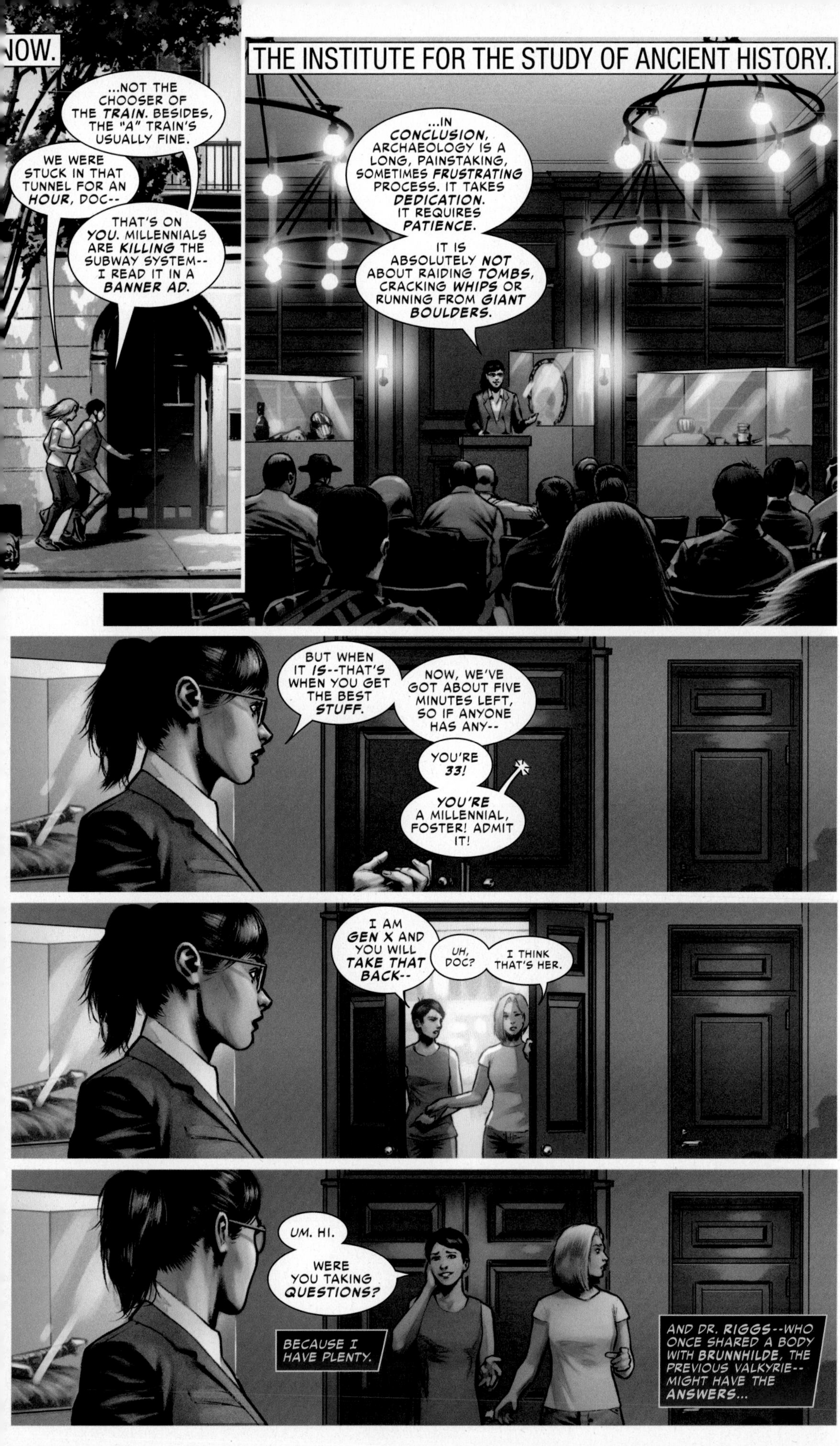
NOW.
...NOT THE CHOOSER OF THE TRAIN. BESIDES, THE "A" TRAIN'S USUALLY FINE.
WE WERE STUCK IN THAT TUNNEL FOR AN HOUR, DOC--
THAT'S ON YOU. MILLENNIALS ARE KILLING THE SUBWAY SYSTEM-- I READ IT IN A BANNER AD.
THE INSTITUTE FOR THE STUDY OF ANCIENT HISTORY.
...IN CONCLUSION, ARCHAEOLOGY IS A LONG, PAINSTAKING, SOMETIMES FRUSTRATING PROCESS. IT TAKES DEDICATION. IT REQUIRES PATIENCE.
IT IS ABSOLUTELY NOT ABOUT RAIDING TOMBS, CRACKING WHIPS OR RUNNING FROM GIANT BOULDERS.
BUT WHEN IT IS--THAT'S WHEN YOU GET THE BEST STUFF.
NOW, WE'VE GOT ABOUT FIVE MINUTES LEFT, SO IF ANYONE HAS ANY--
YOU'RE 33!
YOU'RE A MILLENNIAL, FOSTER! ADMIT IT!
I AM GEN X AND YOU WILL TAKE THAT BACK--
UH, DOC?
I THINK THAT'S HER.
UM. HI.
WERE YOU TAKING QUESTIONS?
BECAUSE I HAVE PLENTY.
AND DR. RIGGS--WHO ONCE SHARED A BODY WITH BRUNNHILDE, THE PREVIOUS VALKYRIE--MIGHT HAVE THE ANSWERS...

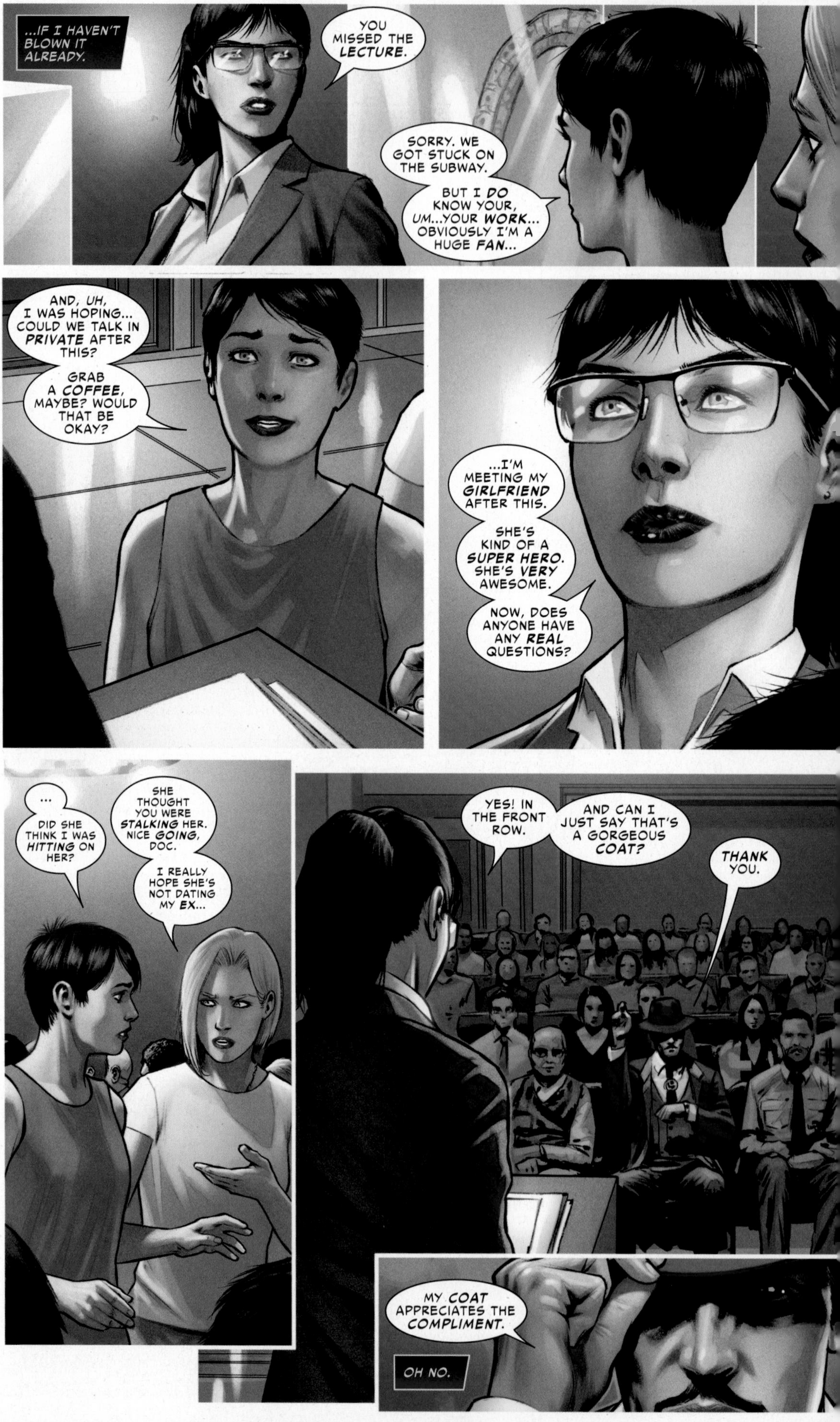
...IF I HAVEN'T BLOWN IT ALREADY.
YOU MISSED THE LECTURE.
SORRY. WE GOT STUCK ON THE SUBWAY.
BUT I DO KNOW YOUR, UM...YOUR WORK... OBVIOUSLY I'M A HUGE FAN...
AND, UH, I WAS HOPING... COULD WE TALK IN PRIVATE AFTER THIS?
GRAB A COFFEE, MAYBE? WOULD THAT BE OKAY?
...I'M MEETING MY GIRLFRIEND AFTER THIS.
SHE'S KIND OF A SUPER HERO. SHE'S VERY AWESOME.
NOW, DOES ANYONE HAVE ANY REAL QUESTIONS?
...
DID SHE THINK I WAS HITTING ON HER?
SHE THOUGHT YOU WERE STALKING HER. NICE GOING, DOC.
I REALLY HOPE SHE'S NOT DATING MY EX...
YES! IN THE FRONT ROW.
AND CAN I JUST SAY THAT'S A GORGEOUS COAT?
THANK YOU.
MY COAT APPRECIATES THE COMPLIMENT.
OH NO.

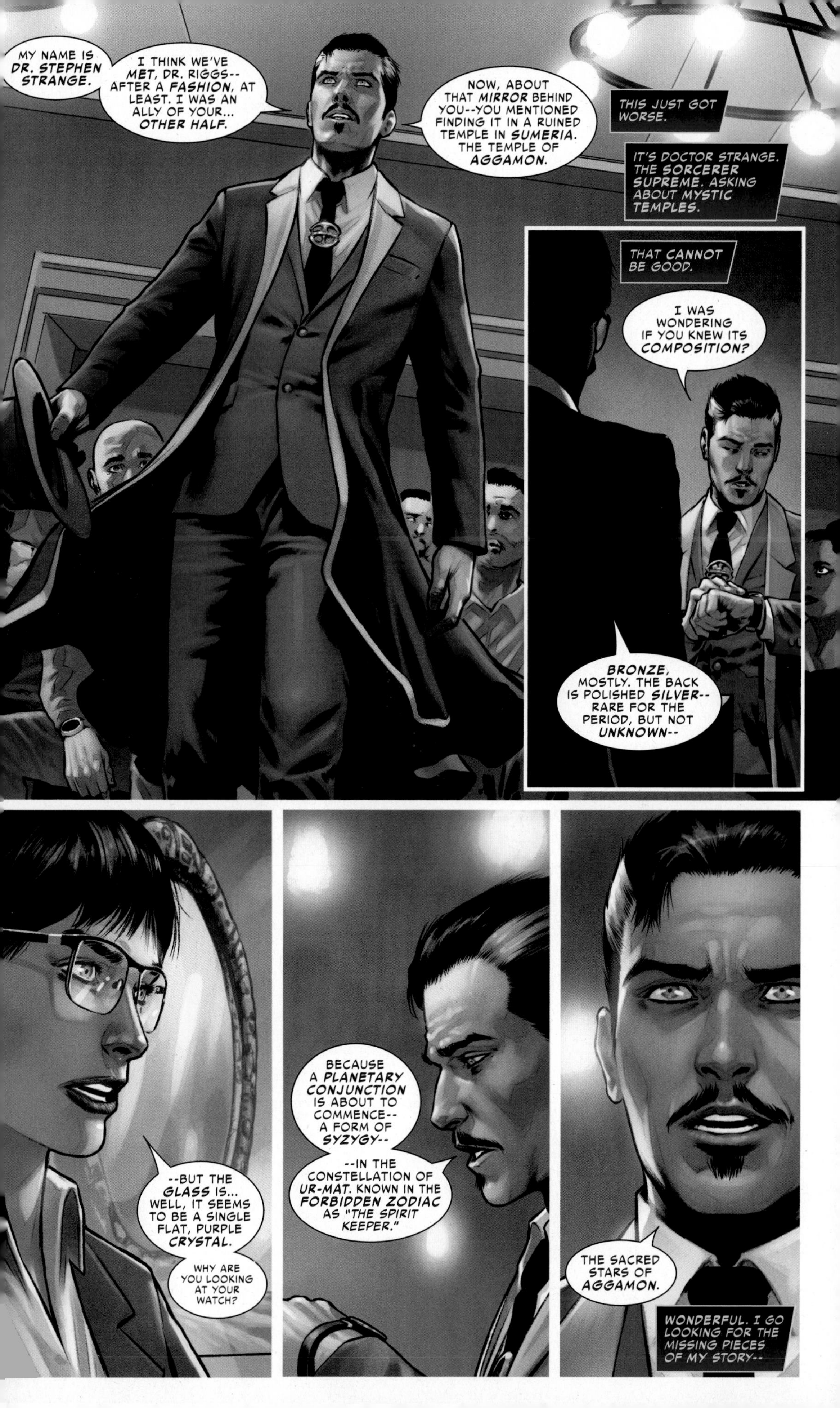
MY NAME IS DR. STEPHEN STRANGE.
I THINK WE'VE MET, DR. RIGGS--AFTER A FASHION, AT LEAST. I WAS AN ALLY OF YOUR... OTHER HALF.
NOW, ABOUT THAT MIRROR BEHIND YOU--YOU MENTIONED FINDING IT IN A RUINED TEMPLE IN SUMERIA. THE TEMPLE OF AGGAMON.
THIS JUST GOT WORSE.
IT'S DOCTOR STRANGE. THE SORCERER SUPREME. ASKING ABOUT MYSTIC TEMPLES.
THAT CANNOT BE GOOD.
I WAS WONDERING IF YOU KNEW ITS COMPOSITION?
BRONZE, MOSTLY. THE BACK IS POLISHED SILVER--RARE FOR THE PERIOD, BUT NOT UNKNOWN--
--BUT THE GLASS IS... WELL, IT SEEMS TO BE A SINGLE FLAT, PURPLE CRYSTAL.
WHY ARE YOU LOOKING AT YOUR WATCH?
BECAUSE A PLANETARY CONJUNCTION IS ABOUT TO COMMENCE--A FORM OF SYZYGY--
--IN THE CONSTELLATION OF UR-MAT. KNOWN IN THE FORBIDDEN ZODIAC AS "THE SPIRIT KEEPER."
THE SACRED STARS OF AGGAMON.
WONDERFUL. I GO LOOKING FOR THE MISSING PIECES OF MY STORY--

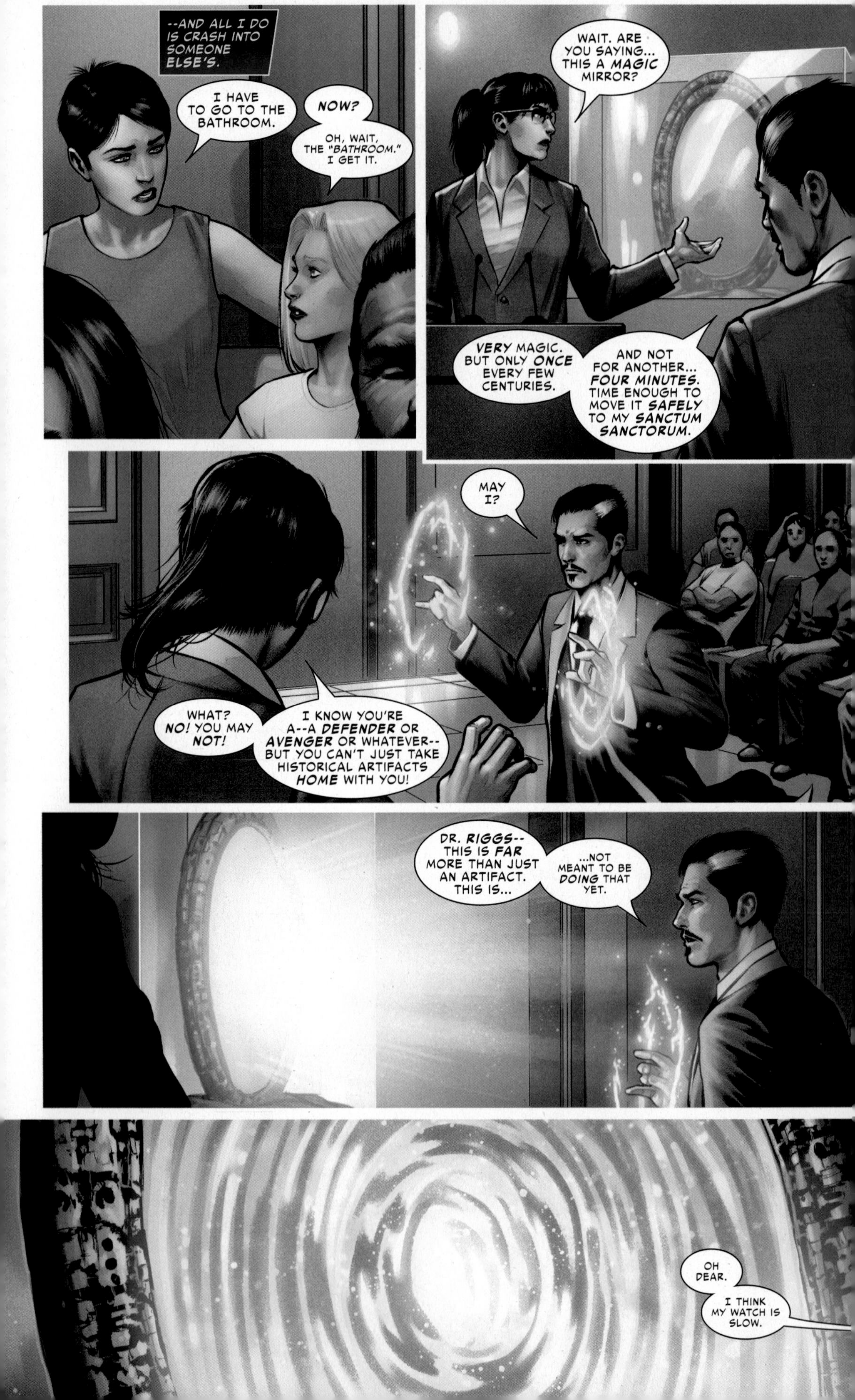
--AND ALL I DO IS CRASH INTO SOMEONE ELSE'S.
I HAVE TO GO TO THE BATHROOM.
NOW?
OH, WAIT, THE "BATHROOM." I GET IT.
WAIT. ARE YOU SAYING... THIS A MAGIC MIRROR?
VERY MAGIC. BUT ONLY ONCE EVERY FEW CENTURIES.
AND NOT FOR ANOTHER... FOUR MINUTES. TIME ENOUGH TO MOVE IT SAFELY TO MY SANCTUM SANCTORUM.
MAY I?
WHAT? NO! YOU MAY NOT!
I KNOW YOU'RE A--A DEFENDER OR AVENGER OR WHATEVER-- BUT YOU CAN'T JUST TAKE HISTORICAL ARTIFACTS HOME WITH YOU!
DR. RIGGS-- THIS IS FAR MORE THAN JUST AN ARTIFACT. THIS IS...
...NOT MEANT TO BE DOING THAT YET.
OH DEAR.
I THINK MY WATCH IS SLOW.

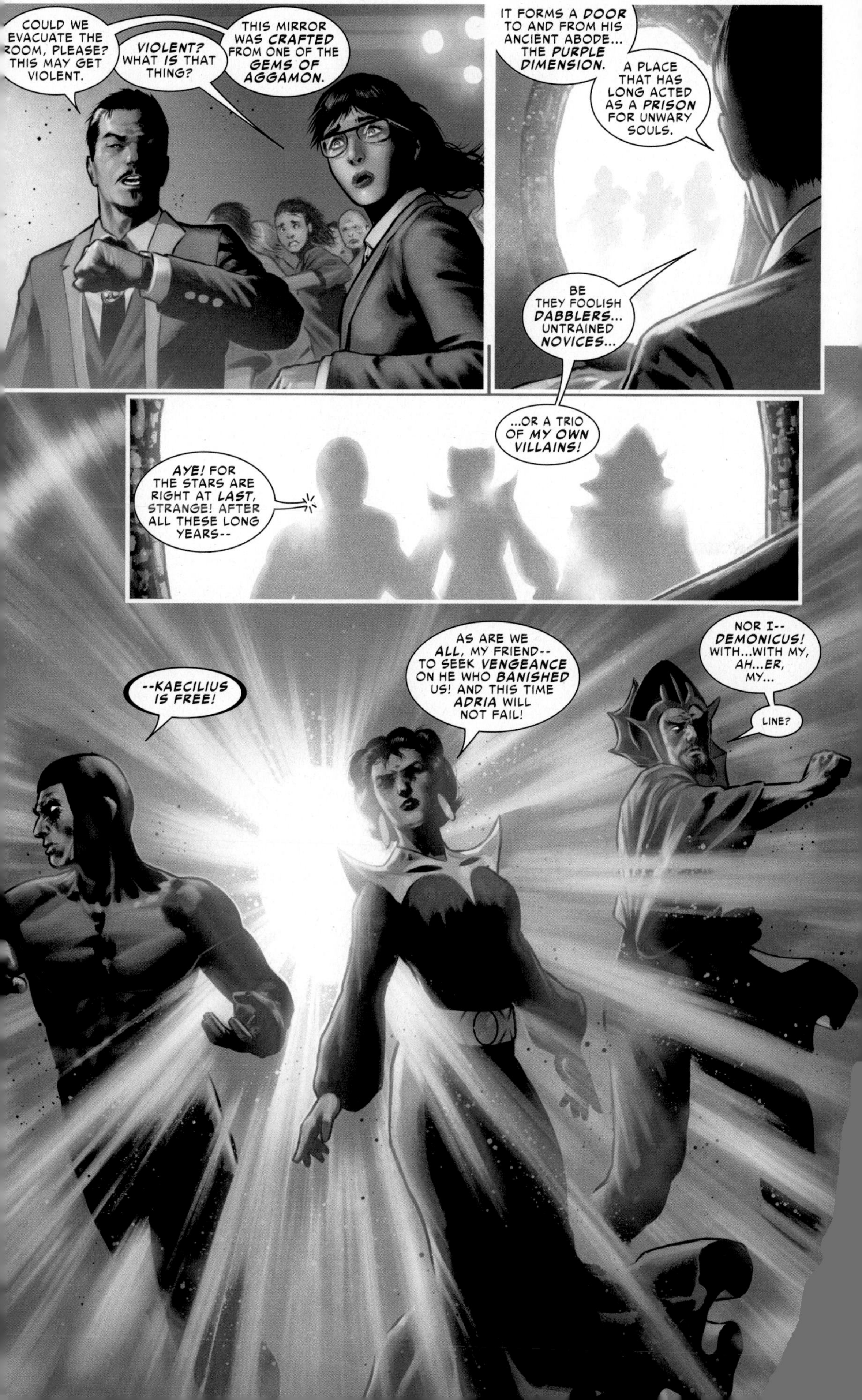
COULD WE EVACUATE THE ROOM, PLEASE? THIS MAY GET VIOLENT.
VIOLENT? WHAT IS THAT THING?
THIS MIRROR WAS CRAFTED FROM ONE OF THE GEMS OF AGGAMON.
IT FORMS A DOOR TO AND FROM HIS ANCIENT ABODE... THE PURPLE DIMENSION.
A PLACE THAT HAS LONG ACTED AS A PRISON FOR UNWARY SOULS.
BE THEY FOOLISH DABBLERS... UNTRAINED NOVICES...
...OR A TRIO OF MY OWN VILLAINS!
AYE! FOR THE STARS ARE RIGHT AT LAST, STRANGE! AFTER ALL THESE LONG YEARS--
--KAECILIUS IS FREE!
AS ARE WE ALL, MY FRIEND-- TO SEEK VENGEANCE ON HE WHO BANISHED US! AND THIS TIME ADRIA WILL NOT FAIL!
NOR I-- DEMONICUS! WITH...WITH MY, AH...ER, MY...
LINE?

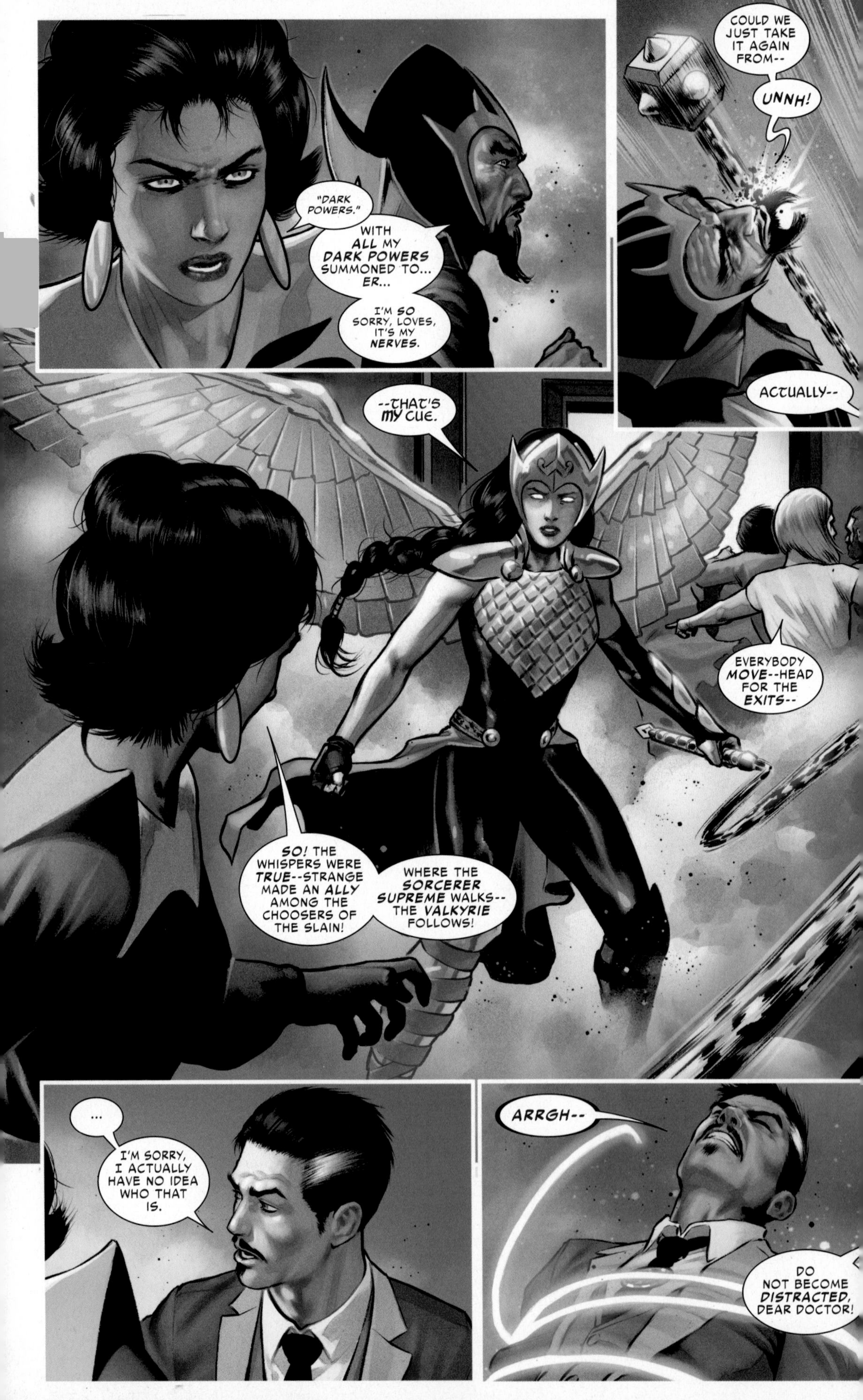
"DARK POWERS."
WITH ALL MY DARK POWERS SUMMONED TO... ER...
I'M SO SORRY, LOVES, IT'S MY NERVES.
COULD WE JUST TAKE IT AGAIN FROM--
UNNH!
ACTUALLY--
--THAT'S MY CUE.
EVERYBODY MOVE--HEAD FOR THE EXITS--
SO! THE WHISPERS WERE TRUE--STRANGE MADE AN ALLY AMONG THE CHOOSERS OF THE SLAIN!
WHERE THE SORCERER SUPREME WALKS--THE VALKYRIE FOLLOWS!
...
I'M SORRY, I ACTUALLY HAVE NO IDEA WHO THAT IS.
ARRGH--
DO NOT BECOME DISTRACTED, DEAR DOCTOR!

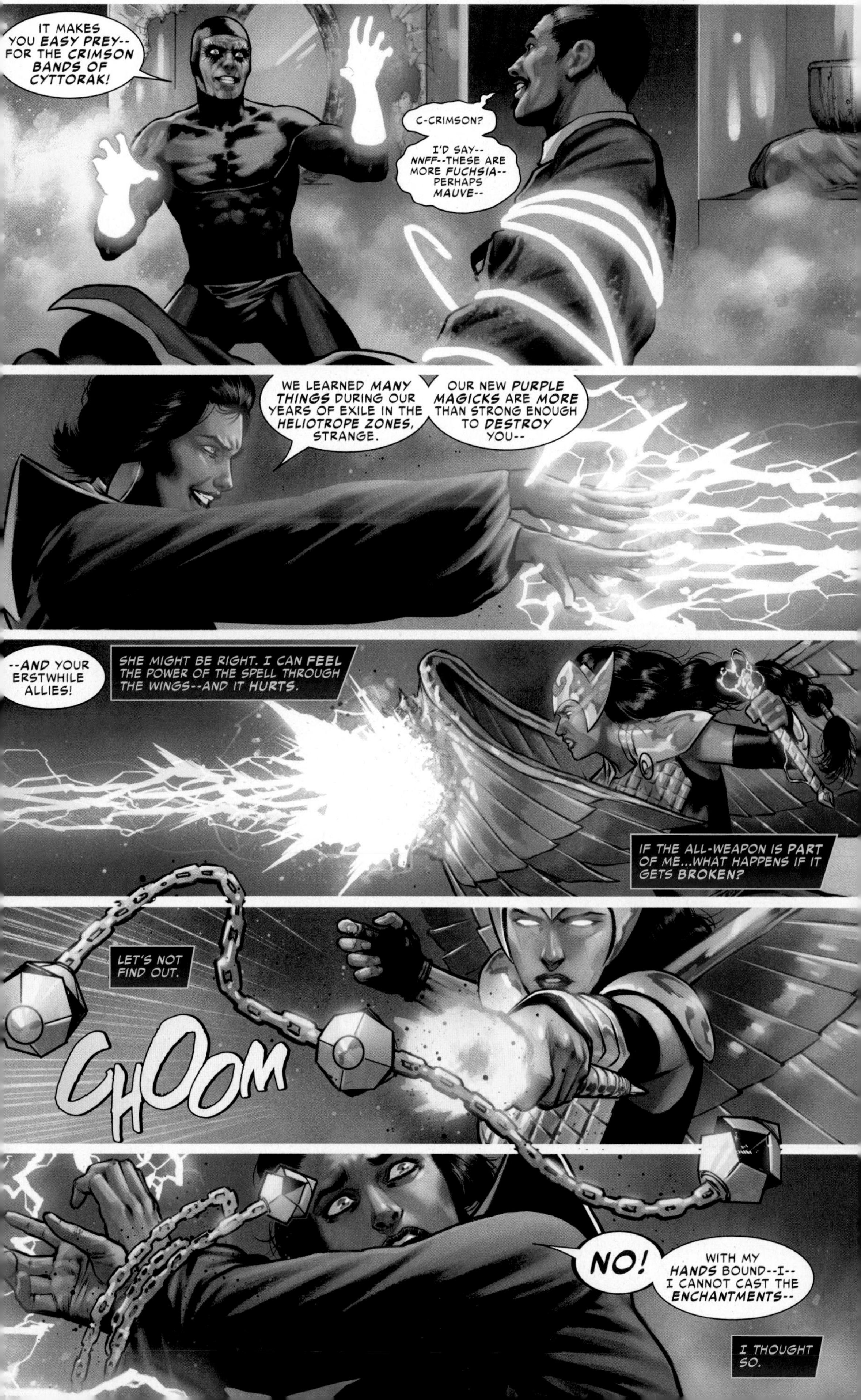
IT MAKES YOU EASY PREY-- FOR THE CRIMSON BANDS OF CYTTORAK!
C-CRIMSON?
I'D SAY-- NNFF--THESE ARE MORE FUCHSIA-- PERHAPS MAUVE--
WE LEARNED MANY THINGS DURING OUR YEARS OF EXILE IN THE HELIOTROPE ZONES, STRANGE.
OUR NEW PURPLE MAGICKS ARE MORE THAN STRONG ENOUGH TO DESTROY YOU--
--AND YOUR ERSTWHILE ALLIES!
SHE MIGHT BE RIGHT. I CAN FEEL THE POWER OF THE SPELL THROUGH THE WINGS--AND IT HURTS.
IF THE ALL-WEAPON IS PART OF ME...WHAT HAPPENS IF IT GETS BROKEN?
LET'S NOT FIND OUT.
CHOOM
NO!
WITH MY HANDS BOUND--I-- I CANNOT CAST THE ENCHANTMENTS--
I THOUGHT SO.

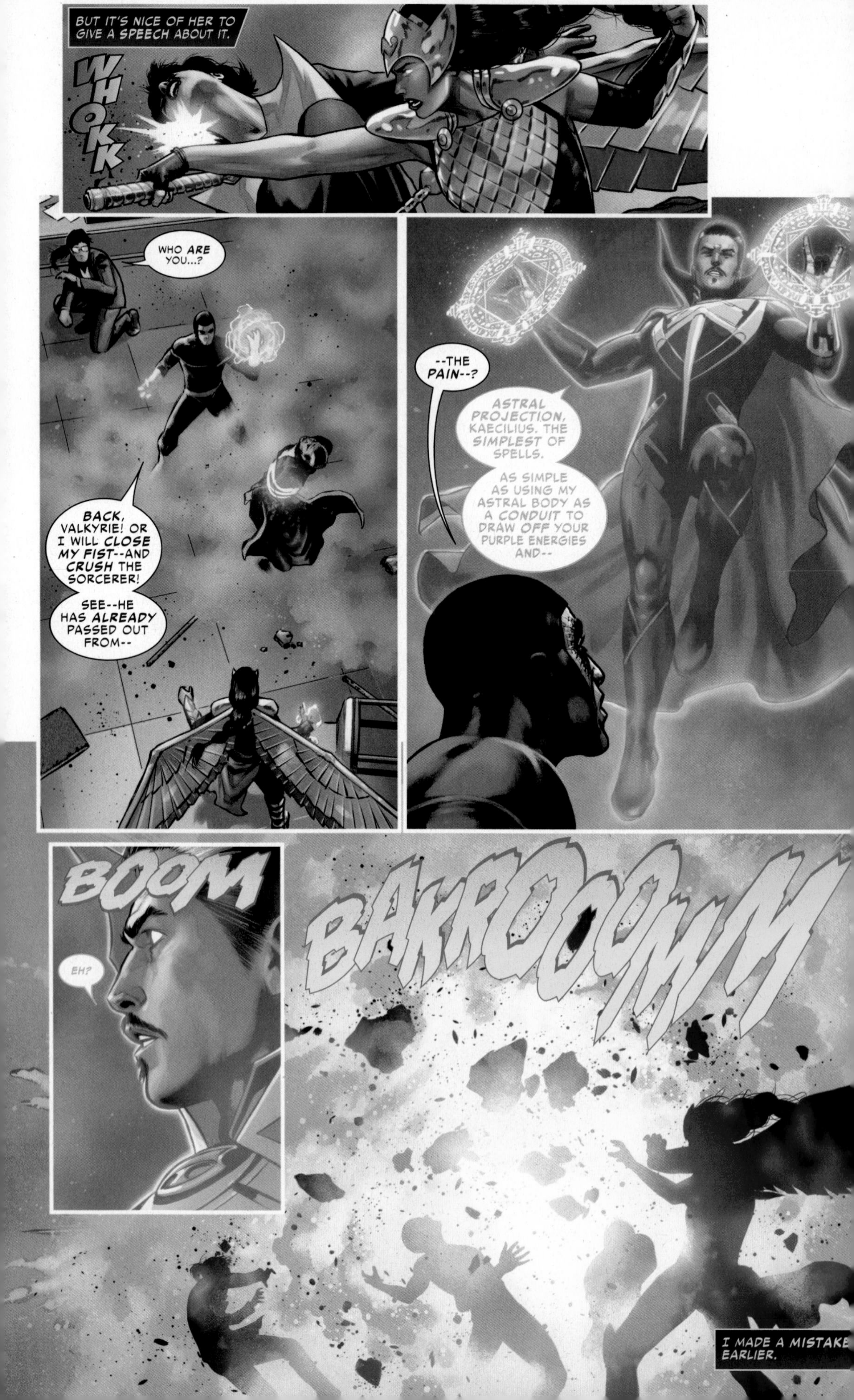

BUT IT'S NICE OF HER TO GIVE A SPEECH ABOUT IT.
WHOKK
WHO ARE YOU...?
BACK, VALKYRIE! OR I WILL CLOSE MY FIST--AND CRUSH THE SORCERER!
SEE--HE HAS ALREADY PASSED OUT FROM--
--THE PAIN--?
ASTRAL PROJECTION, KAECILIUS. THE SIMPLEST OF SPELLS.
AS SIMPLE AS USING MY ASTRAL BODY AS A CONDUIT TO DRAW OFF YOUR PURPLE ENERGIES AND--
BOOM
EH?
BAKROOOMM
I MADE A MISTAKE EARLIER.

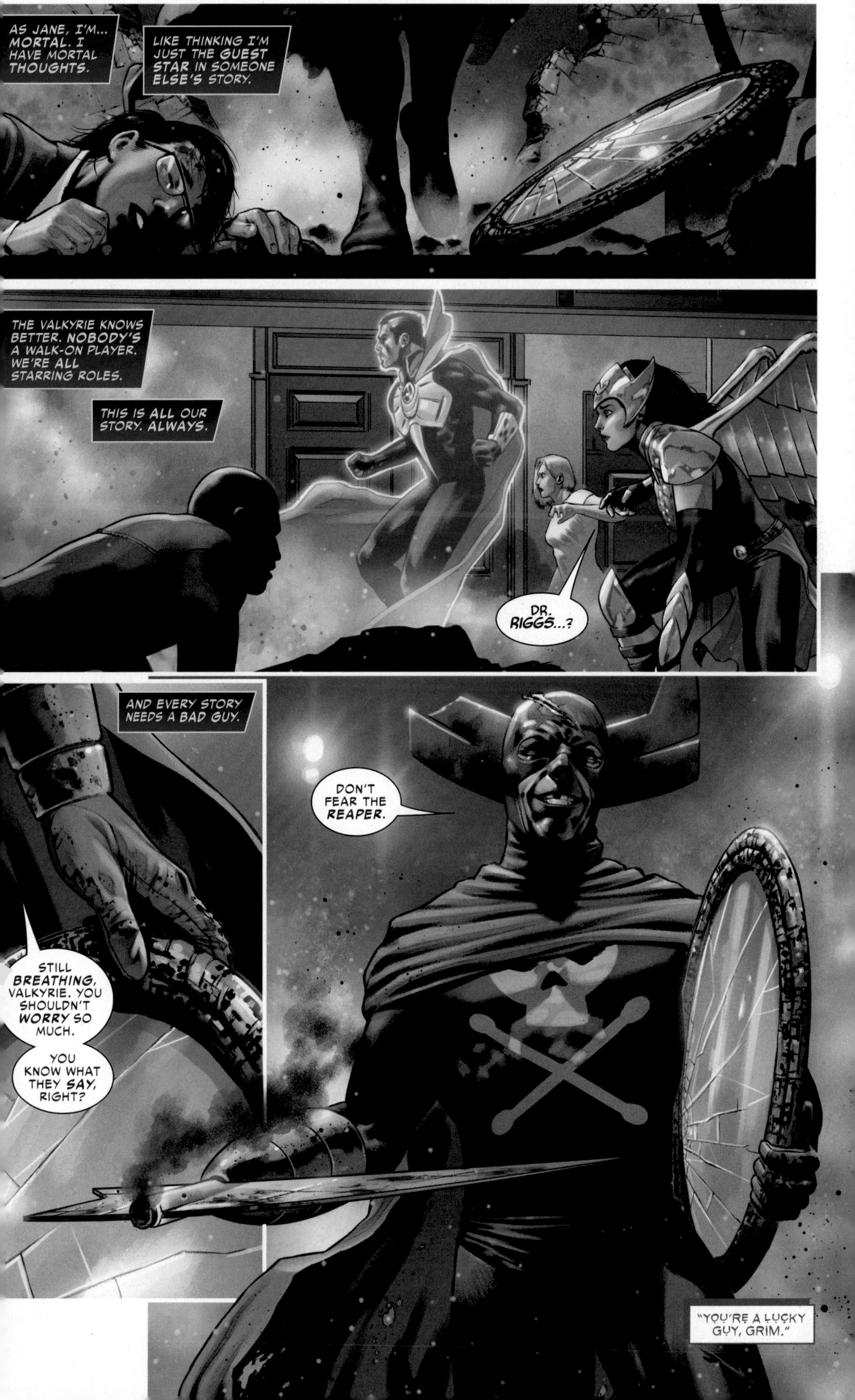
AS JANE, I'M... MORTAL. I HAVE MORTAL THOUGHTS.
LIKE THINKING I'M JUST THE GUEST STAR IN SOMEONE ELSE'S STORY.
THE VALKYRIE KNOWS BETTER. NOBODY'S A WALK-ON PLAYER. WE'RE ALL STARRING ROLES.
THIS IS ALL OUR STORY. ALWAYS.
DR. RIGGS...?
AND EVERY STORY NEEDS A BAD GUY.
STILL BREATHING, VALKYRIE. YOU SHOULDN'T WORRY SO MUCH.
YOU KNOW WHAT THEY SAY, RIGHT?
DON'T FEAR THE REAPER.
"YOU'RE A LUCKY GUY, GRIM."

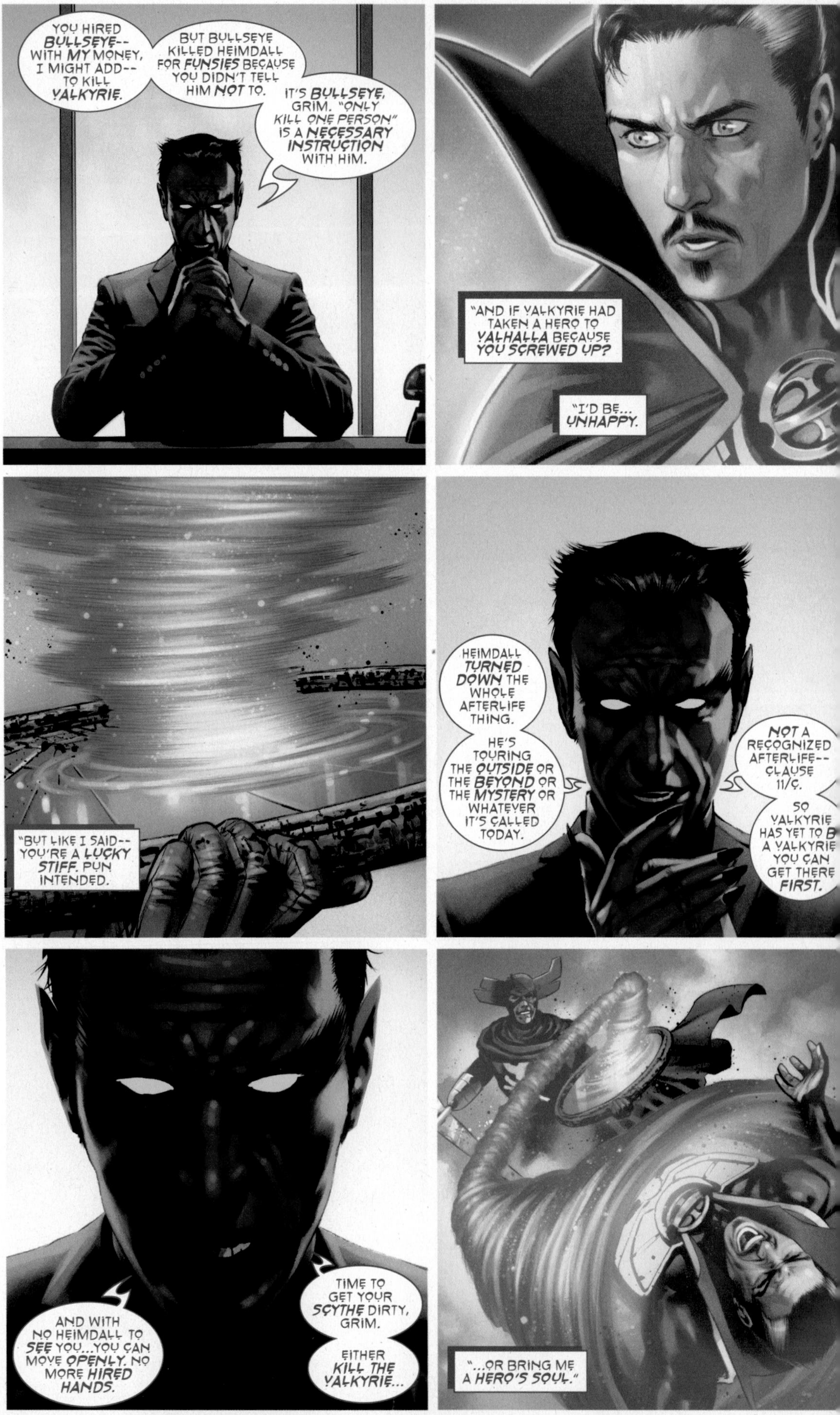
YOU HIRED BULLSEYE-- WITH MY MONEY, I MIGHT ADD-- TO KILL VALKYRIE.
BUT BULLSEYE KILLED HEIMDALL FOR FUNSIES BECAUSE YOU DIDN'T TELL HIM NOT TO.
IT'S BULLSEYE, GRIM. "ONLY KILL ONE PERSON" IS A NECESSARY INSTRUCTION WITH HIM.
"AND IF VALKYRIE HAD TAKEN A HERO TO VALHALLA BECAUSE YOU SCREWED UP?
"I'D BE... UNHAPPY.
"BUT LIKE I SAID-- YOU'RE A LUCKY STIFF. PUN INTENDED.
HEIMDALL TURNED DOWN THE WHOLE AFTERLIFE THING.
HE'S TOURING THE OUTSIDE OR THE BEYOND OR THE MYSTERY OR WHATEVER IT'S CALLED TODAY.
NOT A RECOGNIZED AFTERLIFE-- CLAUSE 11/C.
SO VALKYRIE HAS YET TO B A VALKYRIE YOU CAN GET THERE FIRST.
AND WITH NO HEIMDALL TO SEE YOU...YOU CAN MOVE OPENLY. NO MORE HIRED HANDS.
TIME TO GET YOUR SCYTHE DIRTY, GRIM.
EITHER KILL THE VALKYRIE...
"...OR BRING ME A HERO'S SOUL."

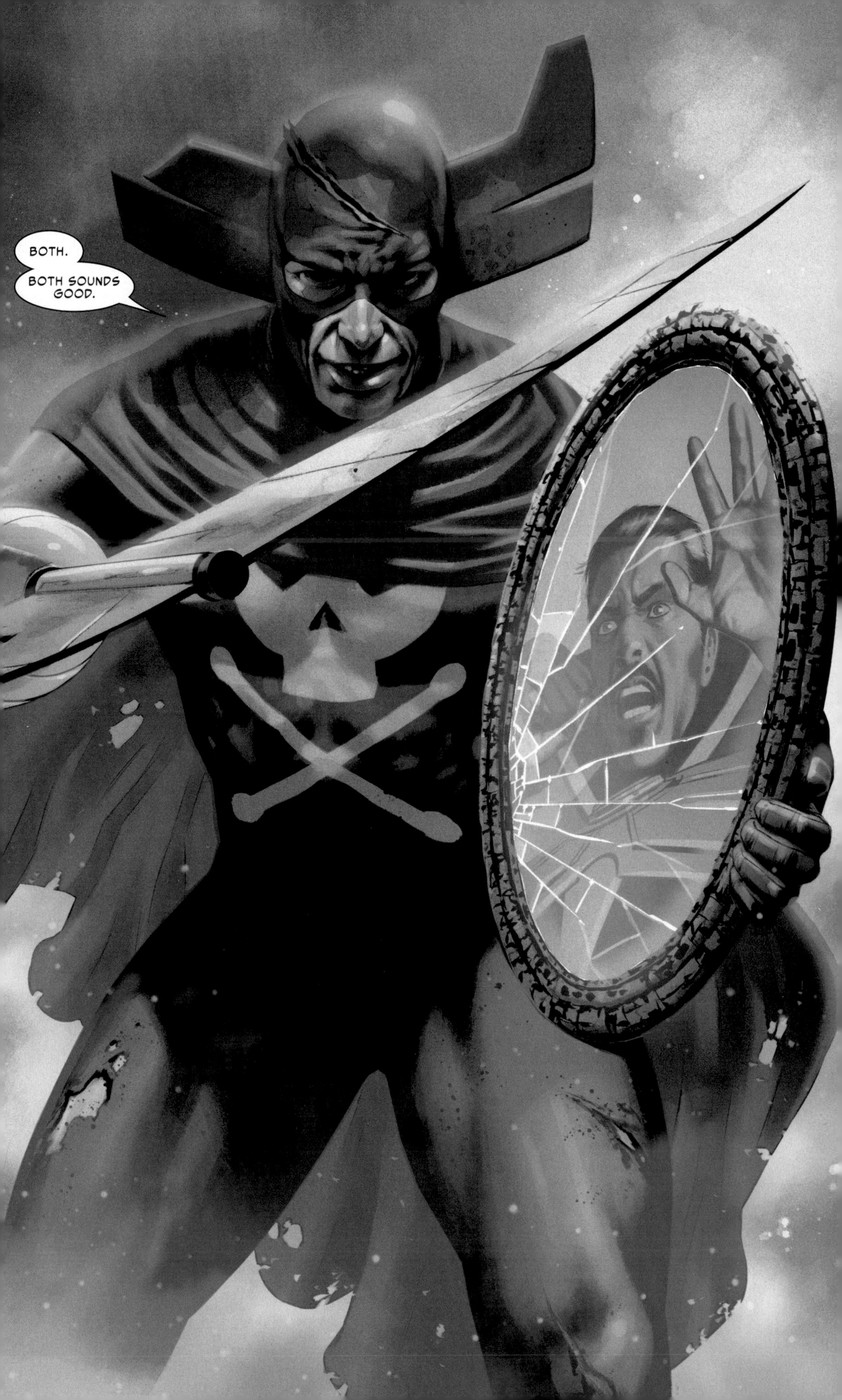
BOTH.
BOTH SOUNDS GOOD.

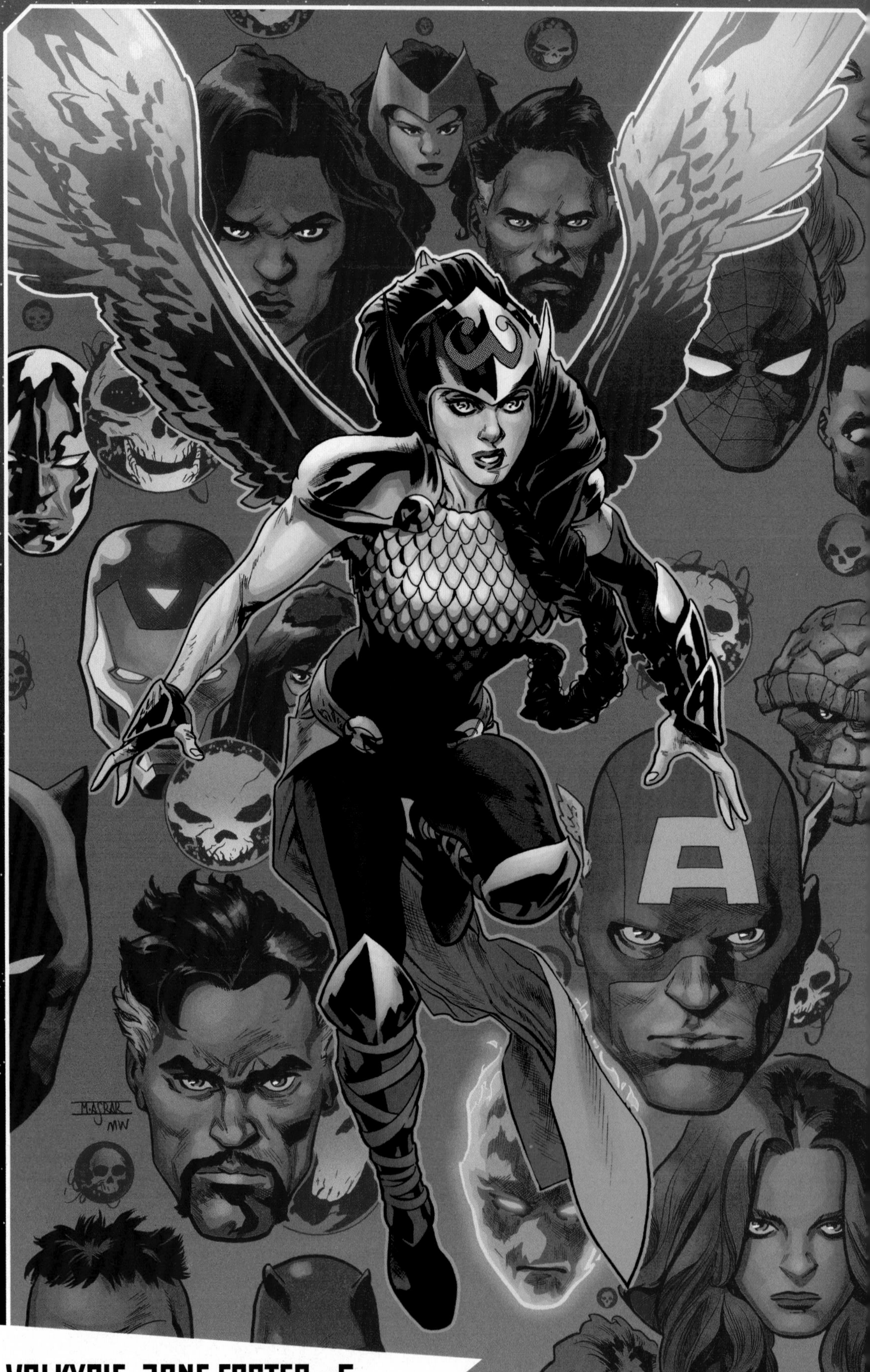
M.ASRAR
MW

VALKYRIE: JANE FOSTER #5

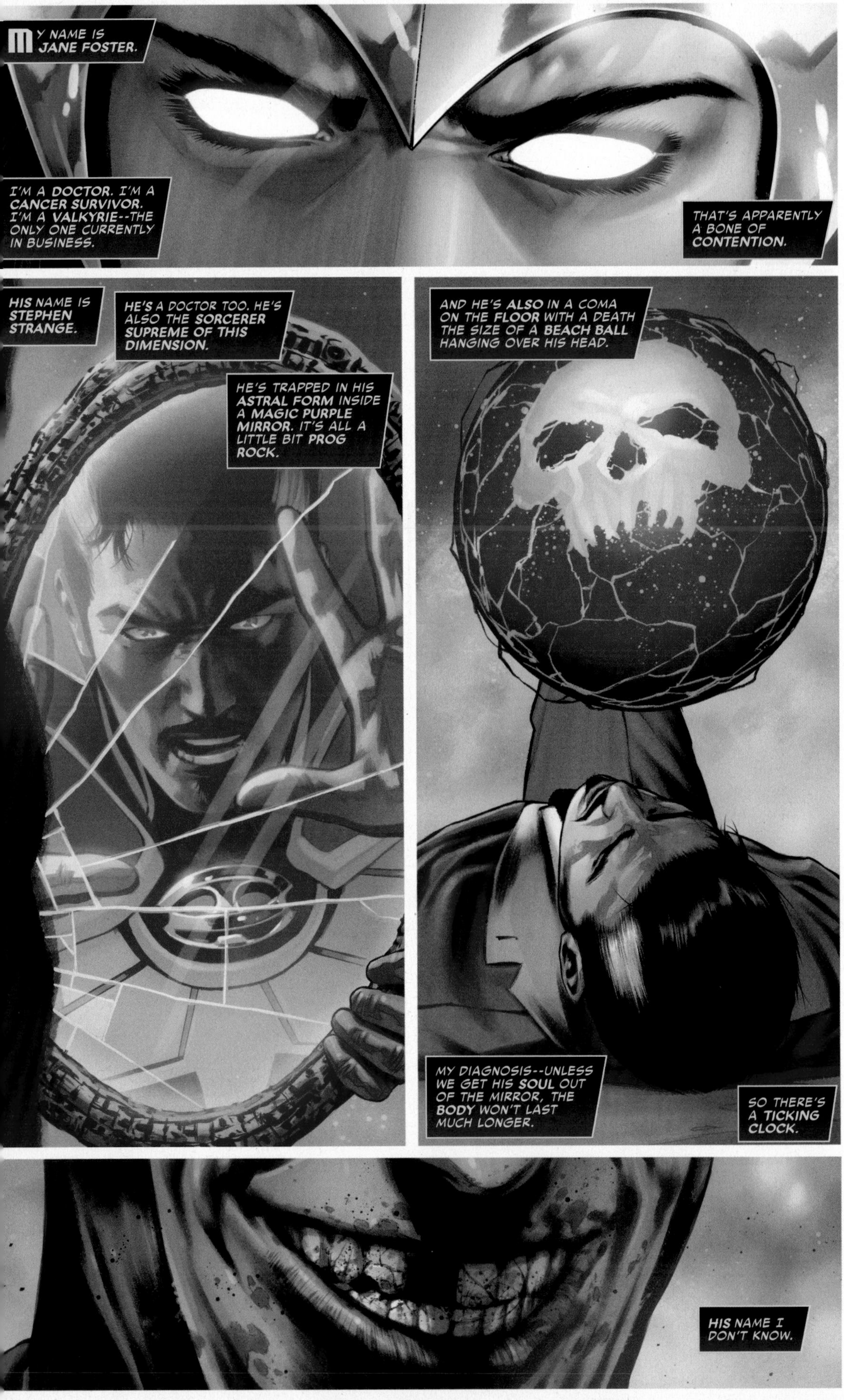
MY NAME IS JANE FOSTER.
I'M A DOCTOR. I'M A CANCER SURVIVOR. I'M A VALKYRIE--THE ONLY ONE CURRENTLY IN BUSINESS.
THAT'S APPARENTLY A BONE OF CONTENTION.
HIS NAME IS STEPHEN STRANGE.
HE'S A DOCTOR TOO. HE'S ALSO THE SORCERER SUPREME OF THIS DIMENSION.
HE'S TRAPPED IN HIS ASTRAL FORM INSIDE A MAGIC PURPLE MIRROR. IT'S ALL A LITTLE BIT PROG ROCK.
AND HE'S ALSO IN A COMA ON THE FLOOR WITH A DEATH THE SIZE OF A BEACH BALL HANGING OVER HIS HEAD.
MY DIAGNOSIS--UNLESS WE GET HIS SOUL OUT OF THE MIRROR, THE BODY WON'T LAST MUCH LONGER.
SO THERE'S A TICKING CLOCK.
HIS NAME I DON'T KNOW.

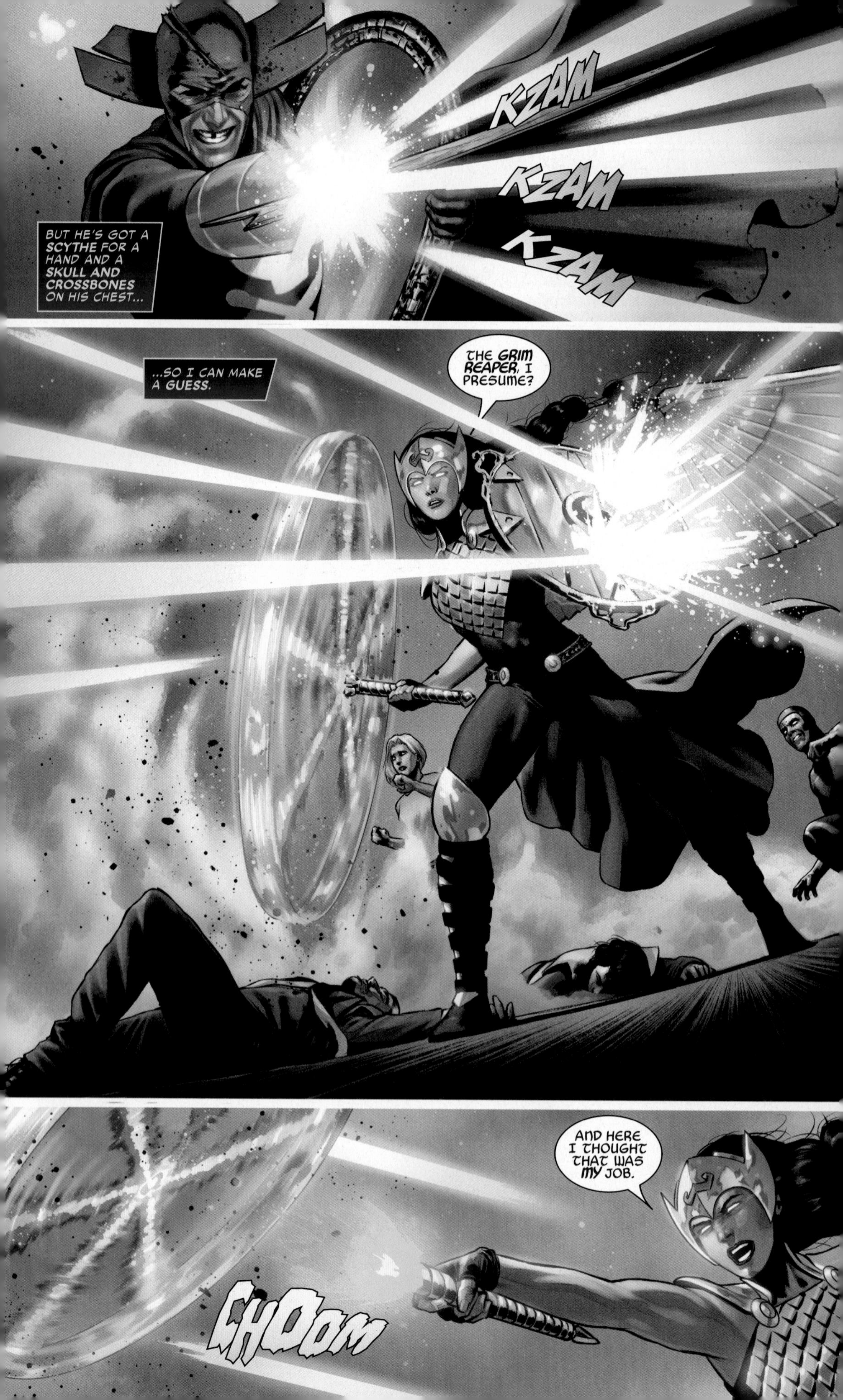
BUT HE'S GOT A SCYTHE FOR A HAND AND A SKULL AND CROSSBONES ON HIS CHEST...
KZAM
KZAM
KZAM
...SO I CAN MAKE A GUESS.
THE GRIM REAPER, I PRESUME?
AND HERE I THOUGHT THAT WAS MY JOB.
CHOOM

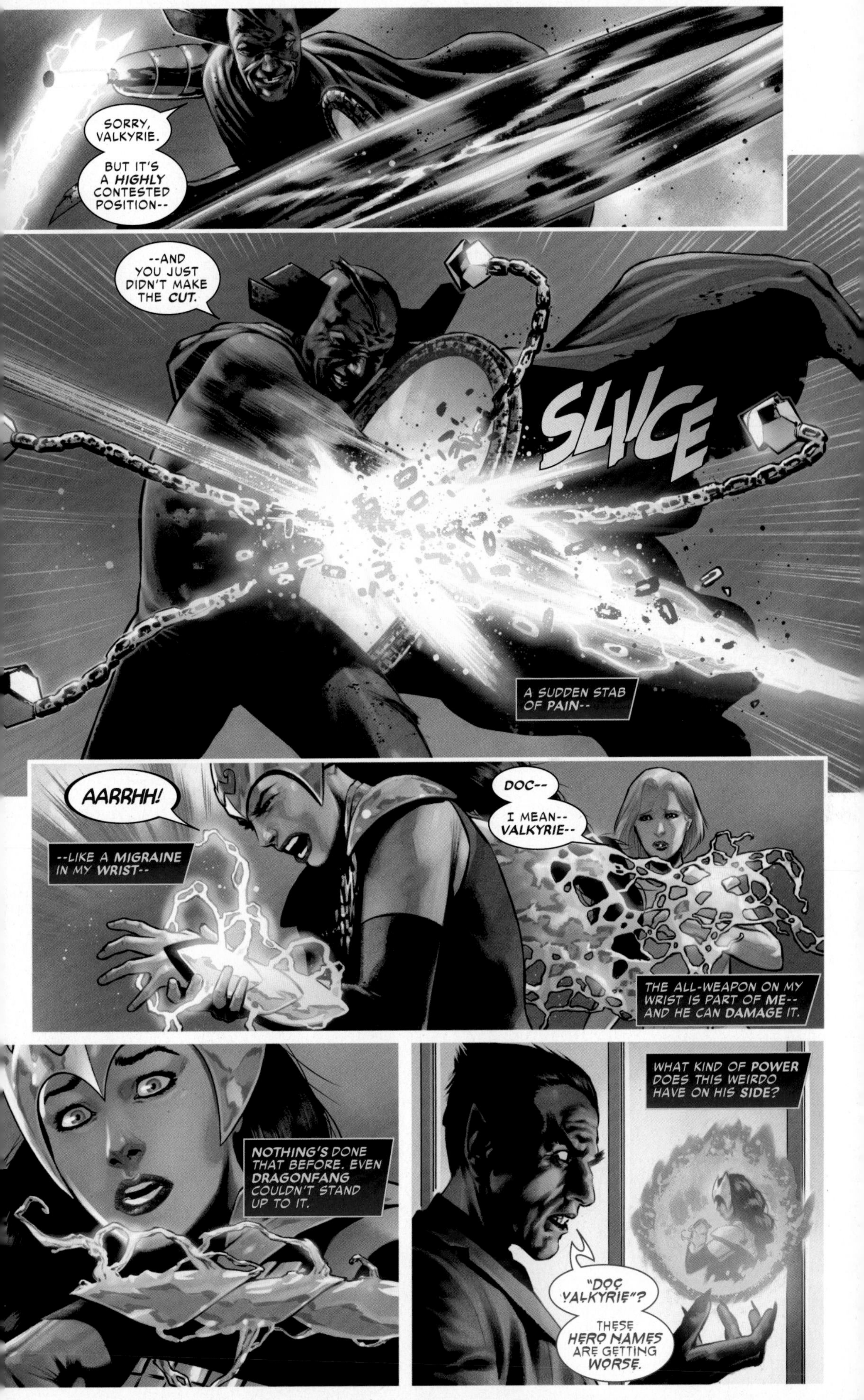
SORRY, VALKYRIE.
BUT IT'S A HIGHLY CONTESTED POSITION--
--AND YOU JUST DIDN'T MAKE THE CUT.
SLICE
A SUDDEN STAB OF PAIN--
AARRHH!
--LIKE A MIGRAINE IN MY WRIST--
DOC--
I MEAN-- VALKYRIE--
THE ALL-WEAPON ON MY WRIST IS PART OF ME-- AND HE CAN DAMAGE IT.
NOTHING'S DONE THAT BEFORE. EVEN DRAGONFANG COULDN'T STAND UP TO IT.
WHAT KIND OF POWER DOES THIS WEIRDO HAVE ON HIS SIDE?
"DOC VALKYRIE"?
THESE HERO NAMES ARE GETTING WORSE.

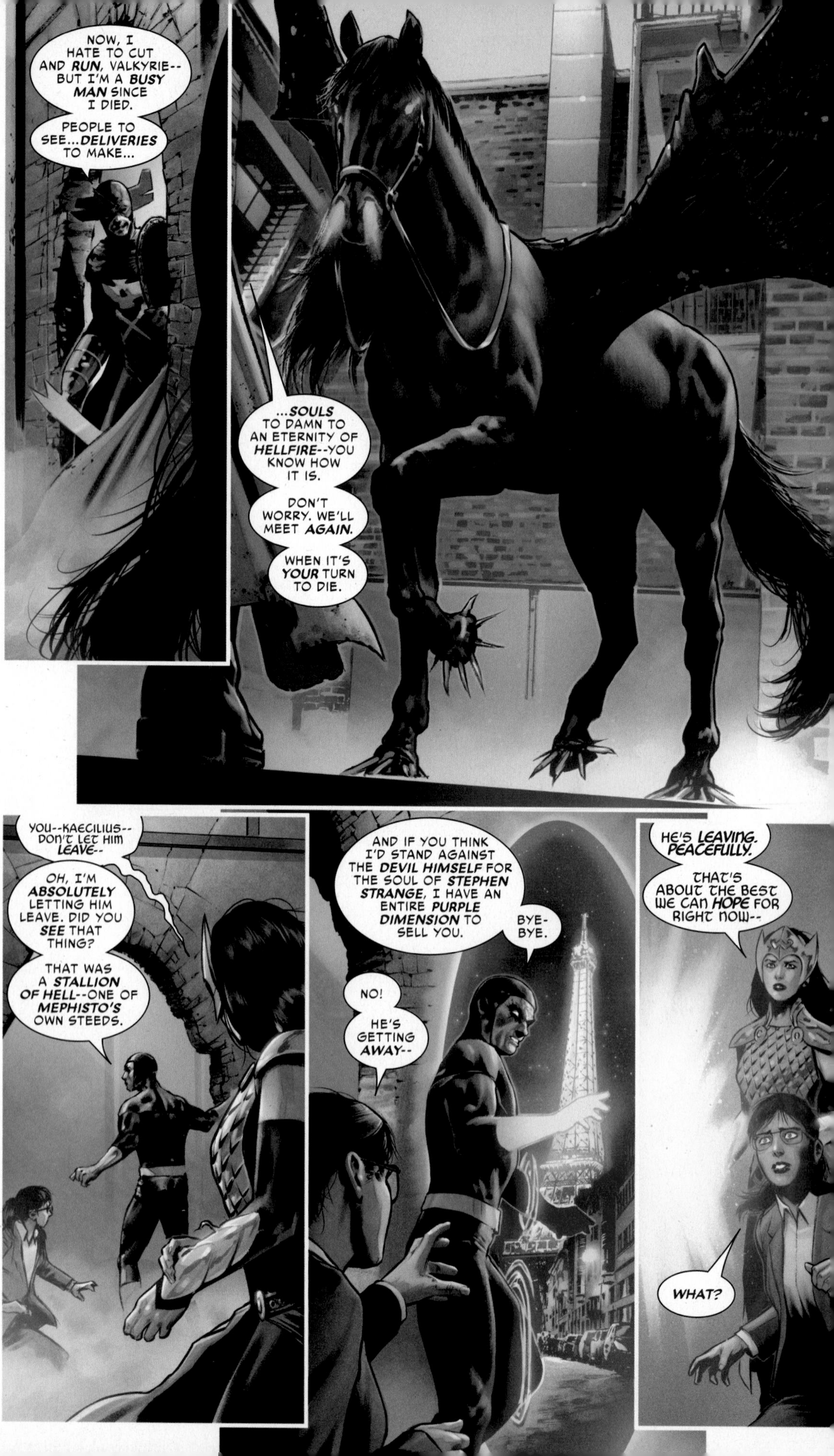
NOW, I HATE TO CUT AND RUN, VALKYRIE-- BUT I'M A BUSY MAN SINCE I DIED.
PEOPLE TO SEE...DELIVERIES TO MAKE...
...SOULS TO DAMN TO AN ETERNITY OF HELLFIRE--YOU KNOW HOW IT IS.
DON'T WORRY. WE'LL MEET AGAIN.
WHEN IT'S YOUR TURN TO DIE.
YOU--KAECILIUS-- DON'T LET HIM LEAVE--
OH, I'M ABSOLUTELY LETTING HIM LEAVE. DID YOU SEE THAT THING?
THAT WAS A STALLION OF HELL--ONE OF MEPHISTO'S OWN STEEDS.
AND IF YOU THINK I'D STAND AGAINST THE DEVIL HIMSELF FOR THE SOUL OF STEPHEN STRANGE, I HAVE AN ENTIRE PURPLE DIMENSION TO SELL YOU.
BYE-BYE.
NO!
HE'S GETTING AWAY--
HE'S LEAVING. PEACEFULLY.
THAT'S ABOUT THE BEST WE CAN HOPE FOR RIGHT NOW--
WHAT?

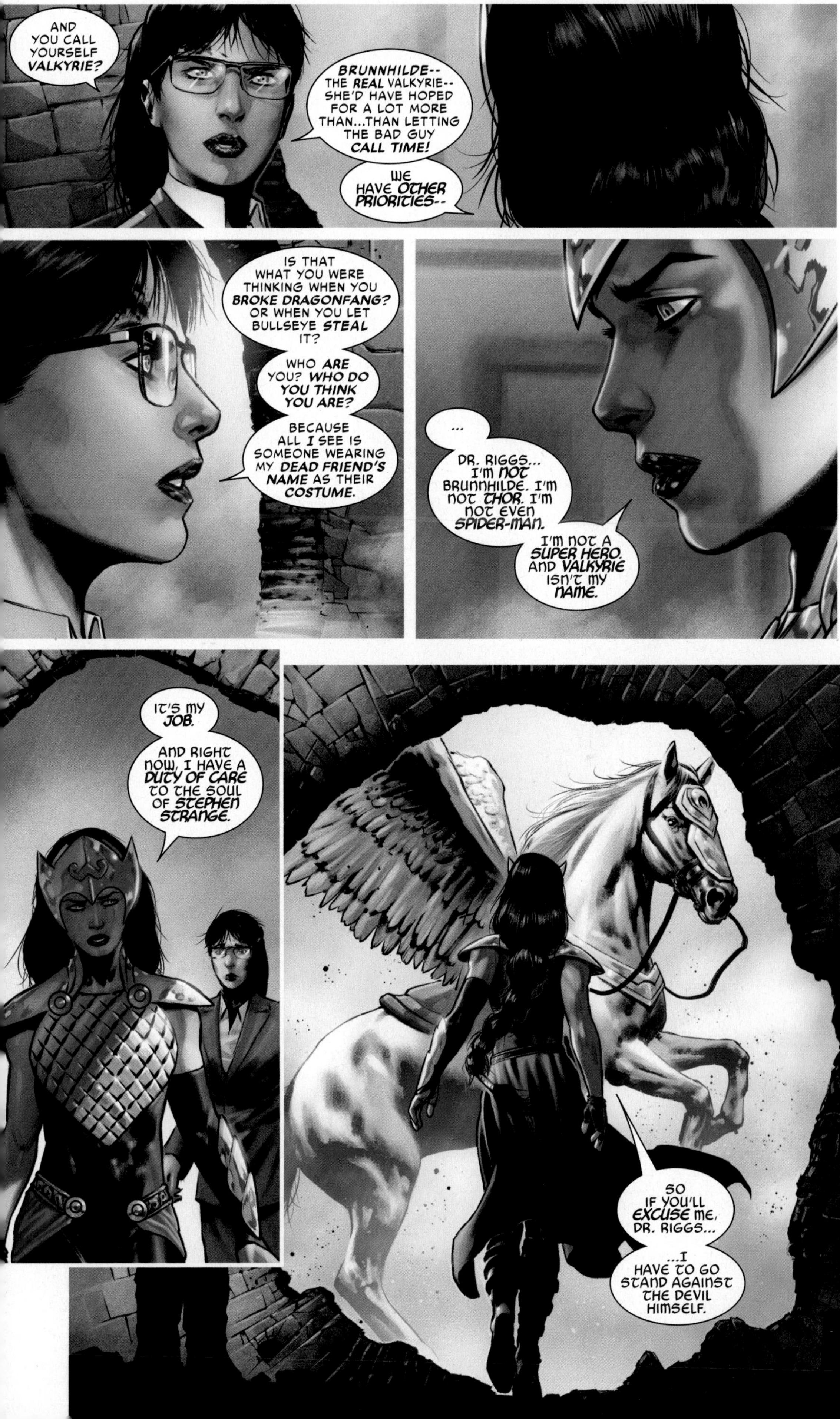
AND YOU CALL YOURSELF VALKYRIE?
BRUNNHILDE-- THE REAL VALKYRIE-- SHE'D HAVE HOPED FOR A LOT MORE THAN...THAN LETTING THE BAD GUY CALL TIME!
WE HAVE OTHER PRIORITIES--
IS THAT WHAT YOU WERE THINKING WHEN YOU BROKE DRAGONFANG? OR WHEN YOU LET BULLSEYE STEAL IT?
WHO ARE YOU? WHO DO YOU THINK YOU ARE?
BECAUSE ALL I SEE IS SOMEONE WEARING MY DEAD FRIEND'S NAME AS THEIR COSTUME.
...
DR. RIGGS... I'M NOT BRUNNHILDE. I'M NOT THOR. I'M NOT EVEN SPIDER-MAN.
I'M NOT A SUPER HERO. AND VALKYRIE ISN'T MY NAME.
IT'S MY JOB.
AND RIGHT NOW, I HAVE A DUTY OF CARE TO THE SOUL OF STEPHEN STRANGE.
SO IF YOU'LL EXCUSE ME, DR. RIGGS...
...I HAVE TO GO STAND AGAINST THE DEVIL HIMSELF.

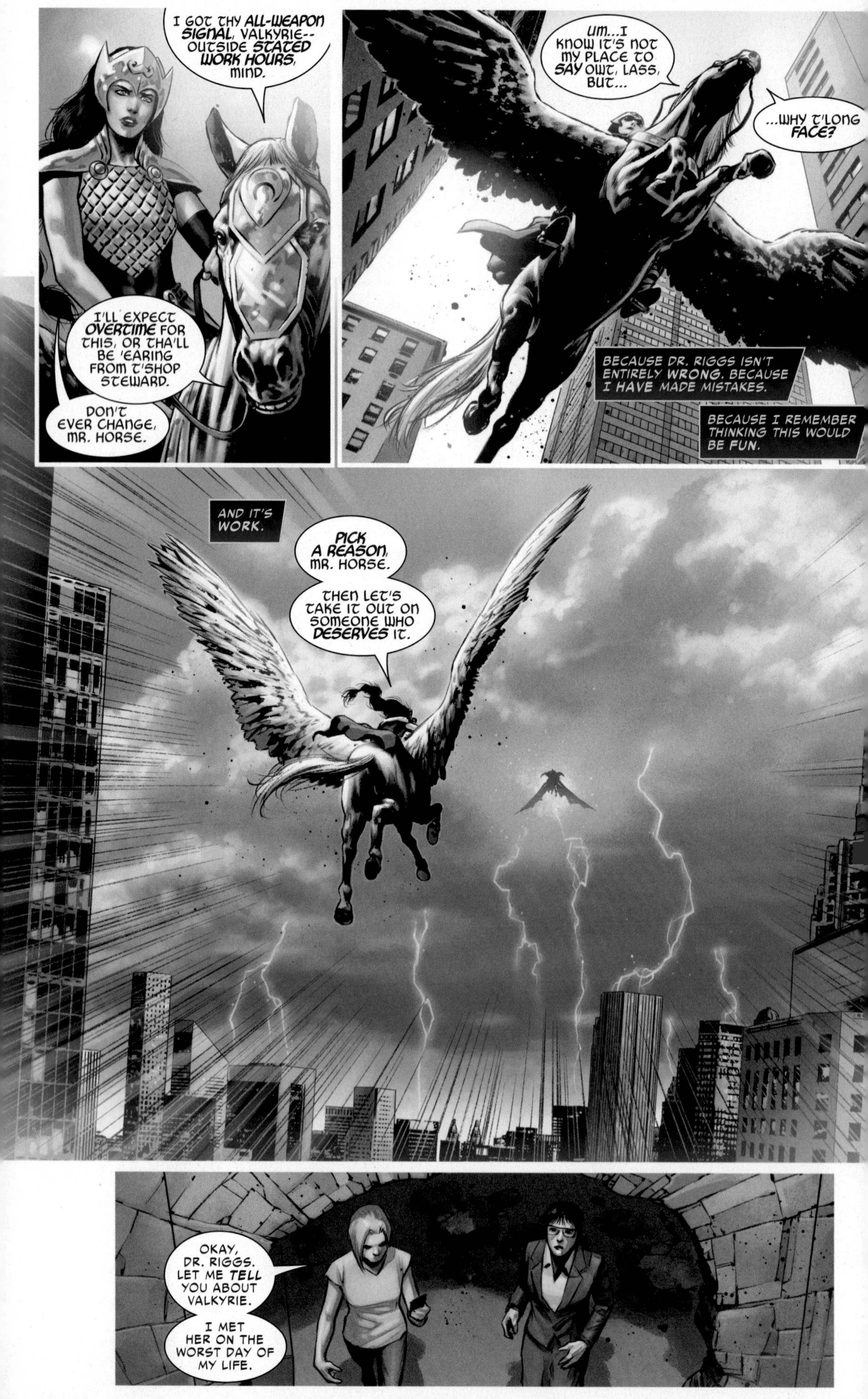
I GOT THY ALL-WEAPON SIGNAL, VALKYRIE--OUTSIDE STATED WORK HOURS, MIND.
I'LL EXPECT OVERTIME FOR THIS, OR THA'LL BE 'EARING FROM T'SHOP STEWARD.
DON'T EVER CHANGE, MR. HORSE.
UM...I KNOW IT'S NOT MY PLACE TO SAY OWT, LASS, BUT...
...WHY T'LONG FACE?
BECAUSE DR. RIGGS ISN'T ENTIRELY WRONG. BECAUSE I HAVE MADE MISTAKES.
BECAUSE I REMEMBER THINKING THIS WOULD BE FUN.
AND IT'S WORK.
PICK A REASON, MR. HORSE.
THEN LET'S TAKE IT OUT ON SOMEONE WHO DESERVES IT.
OKAY, DR. RIGGS. LET ME TELL YOU ABOUT VALKYRIE.
I MET HER ON THE WORST DAY OF MY LIFE.

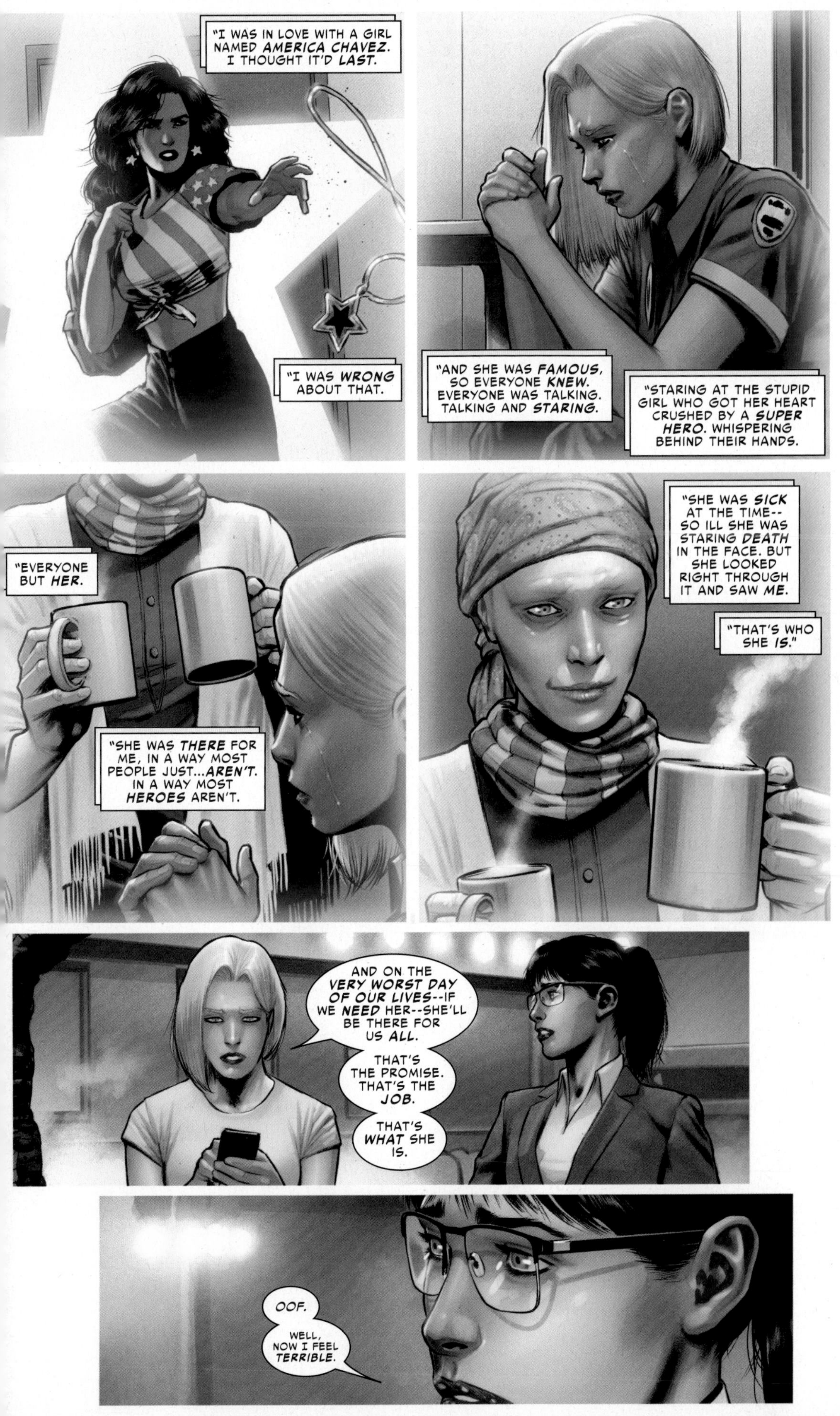
"I WAS IN LOVE WITH A GIRL NAMED AMERICA CHAVEZ. I THOUGHT IT'D LAST.
"I WAS WRONG ABOUT THAT.
"AND SHE WAS FAMOUS, SO EVERYONE KNEW. EVERYONE WAS TALKING. TALKING AND STARING.
"STARING AT THE STUPID GIRL WHO GOT HER HEART CRUSHED BY A SUPER HERO. WHISPERING BEHIND THEIR HANDS.
"EVERYONE BUT HER.
"SHE WAS THERE FOR ME, IN A WAY MOST PEOPLE JUST...AREN'T. IN A WAY MOST HEROES AREN'T.
"SHE WAS SICK AT THE TIME-- SO ILL SHE WAS STARING DEATH IN THE FACE. BUT SHE LOOKED RIGHT THROUGH IT AND SAW ME.
"THAT'S WHO SHE IS."
AND ON THE VERY WORST DAY OF OUR LIVES--IF WE NEED HER--SHE'LL BE THERE FOR US ALL.
THAT'S THE PROMISE. THAT'S THE JOB.
THAT'S WHAT SHE IS.
OOF.
WELL, NOW I FEEL TERRIBLE.

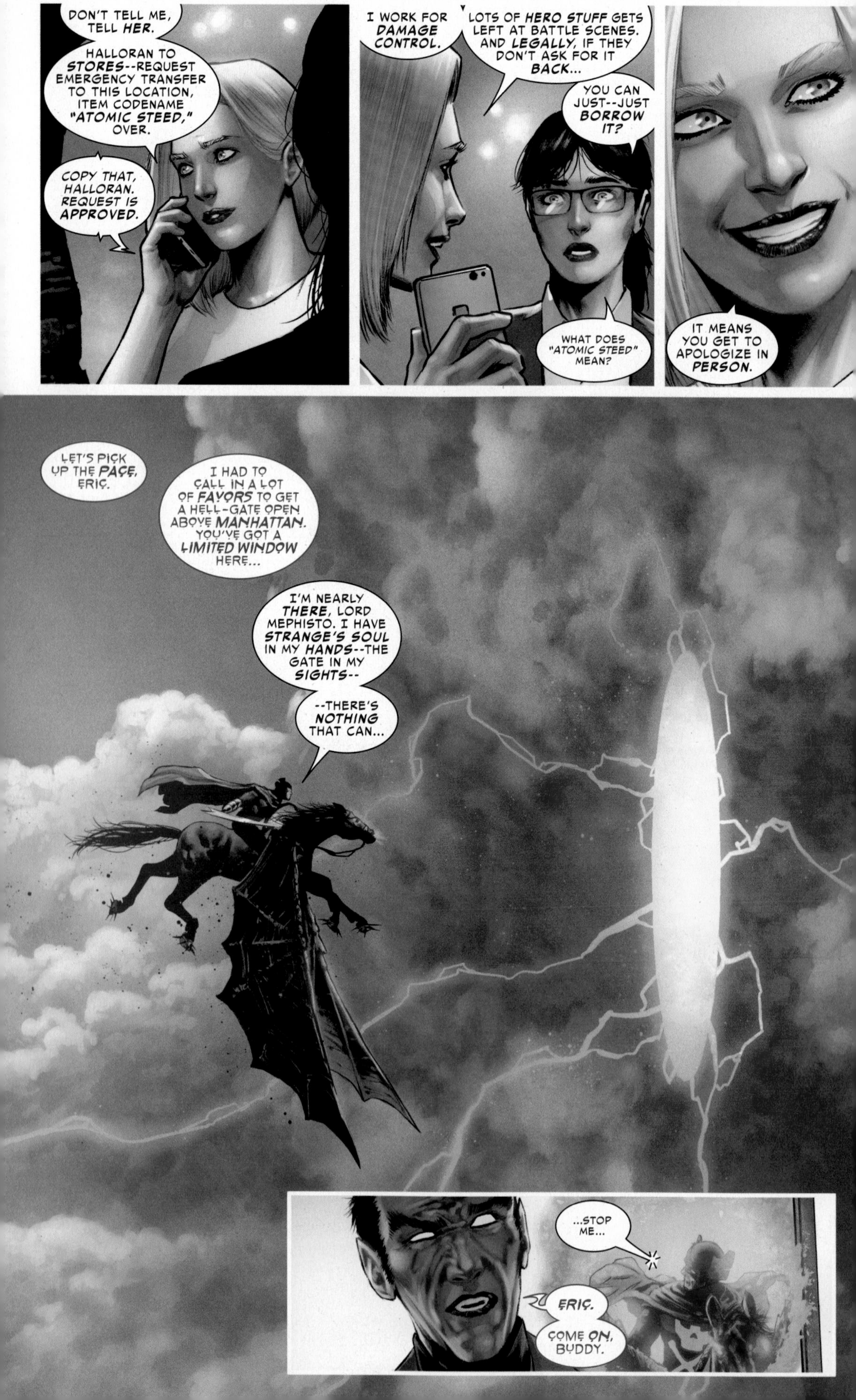

DON'T TELL ME, TELL HER.
HALLORAN TO STORES--REQUEST EMERGENCY TRANSFER TO THIS LOCATION, ITEM CODENAME "ATOMIC STEED," OVER.
COPY THAT, HALLORAN. REQUEST IS APPROVED.
I WORK FOR DAMAGE CONTROL.
LOTS OF HERO STUFF GETS LEFT AT BATTLE SCENES. AND LEGALLY, IF THEY DON'T ASK FOR IT BACK...
YOU CAN JUST--JUST BORROW IT?
WHAT DOES "ATOMIC STEED" MEAN?
IT MEANS YOU GET TO APOLOGIZE IN PERSON.
LET'S PICK UP THE PACE, ERIC.
I HAD TO CALL IN A LOT OF FAVORS TO GET A HELL-GATE OPEN ABOVE MANHATTAN. YOU'VE GOT A LIMITED WINDOW HERE...
I'M NEARLY THERE, LORD MEPHISTO. I HAVE STRANGE'S SOUL IN MY HANDS--THE GATE IN MY SIGHTS--
--THERE'S NOTHING THAT CAN...
...STOP ME...
ERIC.
COME ON, BUDDY.

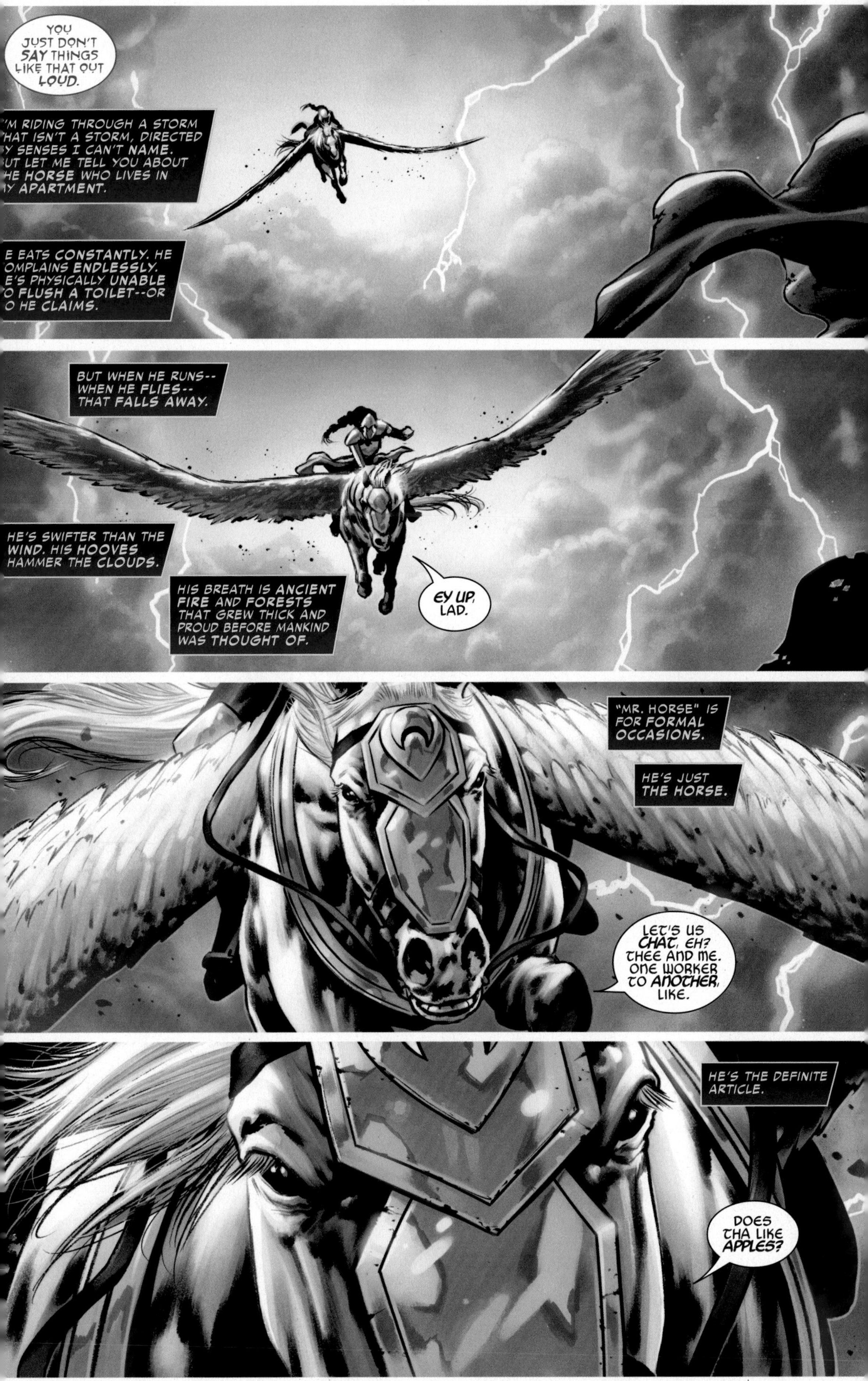
YOU JUST DON'T SAY THINGS LIKE THAT OUT LOUD.
I'M RIDING THROUGH A STORM THAT ISN'T A STORM, DIRECTED BY SENSES I CAN'T NAME. BUT LET ME TELL YOU ABOUT THE HORSE WHO LIVES IN MY APARTMENT.
HE EATS CONSTANTLY. HE COMPLAINS ENDLESSLY. HE'S PHYSICALLY UNABLE TO FLUSH A TOILET--OR SO HE CLAIMS.
BUT WHEN HE RUNS-- WHEN HE FLIES-- THAT FALLS AWAY.
HE'S SWIFTER THAN THE WIND. HIS HOOVES HAMMER THE CLOUDS.
HIS BREATH IS ANCIENT FIRE AND FORESTS THAT GREW THICK AND PROUD BEFORE MANKIND WAS THOUGHT OF.
EY UP, LAD.
"MR. HORSE" IS FOR FORMAL OCCASIONS.
HE'S JUST THE HORSE.
LET'S US CHAT, EH? THEE AND ME. ONE WORKER TO ANOTHER, LIKE.
HE'S THE DEFINITE ARTICLE.
DOES THA LIKE APPLES?

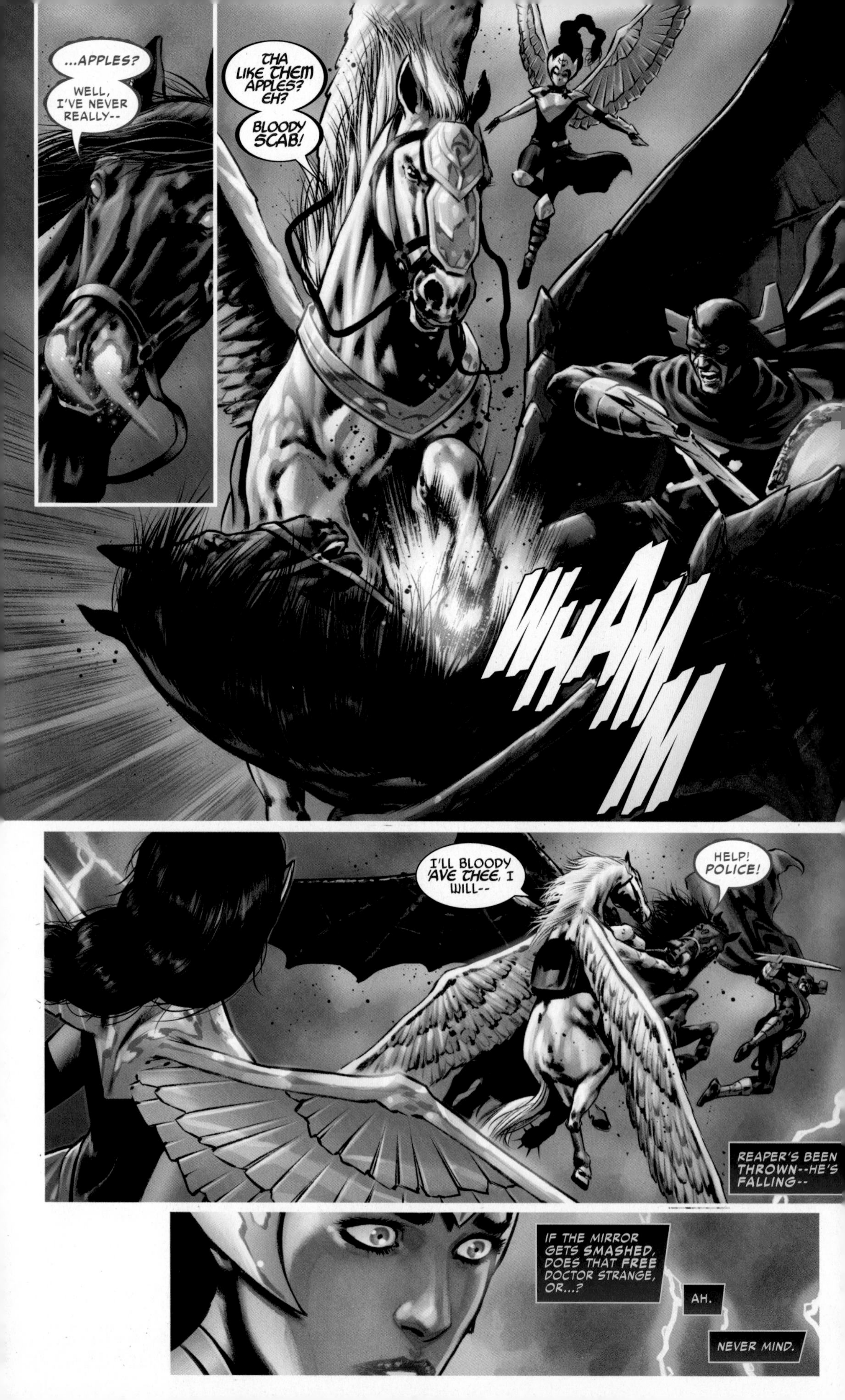
...APPLES?
WELL, I'VE NEVER REALLY--
THA LIKE THEM APPLES? EH?
BLOODY SCAB!
WHAMM
I'LL BLOODY 'AVE THEE, I WILL--
HELP! POLICE!
REAPER'S BEEN THROWN--HE'S FALLING--
IF THE MIRROR GETS SMASHED, DOES THAT FREE DOCTOR STRANGE, OR...?
AH.
NEVER MIND.

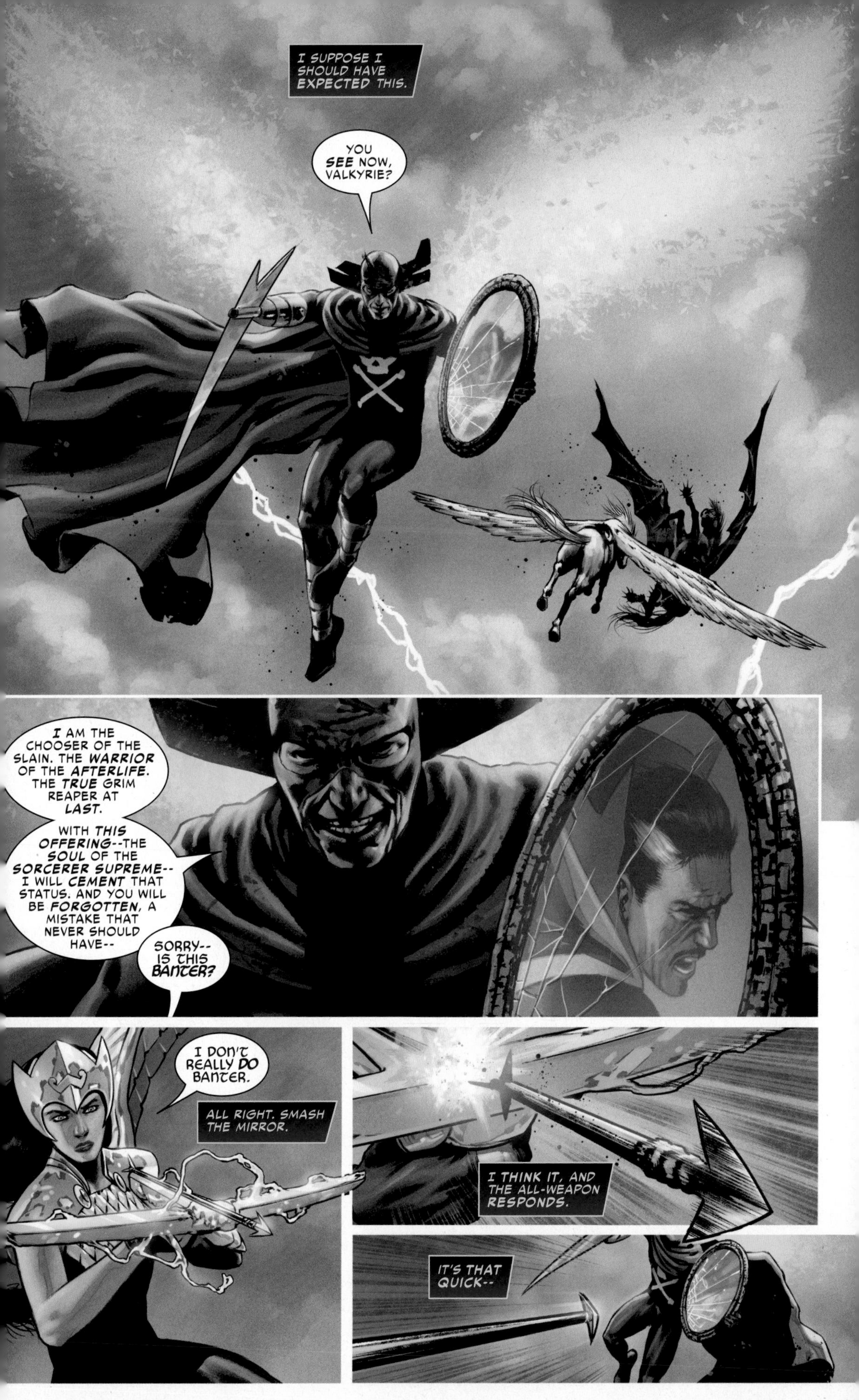
I SUPPOSE I SHOULD HAVE EXPECTED THIS.
YOU SEE NOW, VALKYRIE?
I AM THE CHOOSER OF THE SLAIN. THE WARRIOR OF THE AFTERLIFE. THE TRUE GRIM REAPER AT LAST.
WITH THIS OFFERING--THE SOUL OF THE SORCERER SUPREME--I WILL CEMENT THAT STATUS. AND YOU WILL BE FORGOTTEN, A MISTAKE THAT NEVER SHOULD HAVE--
SORRY--IS THIS BANTER?
I DON'T REALLY DO BANTER.
ALL RIGHT. SMASH THE MIRROR.
I THINK IT, AND THE ALL-WEAPON RESPONDS.
IT'S THAT QUICK--

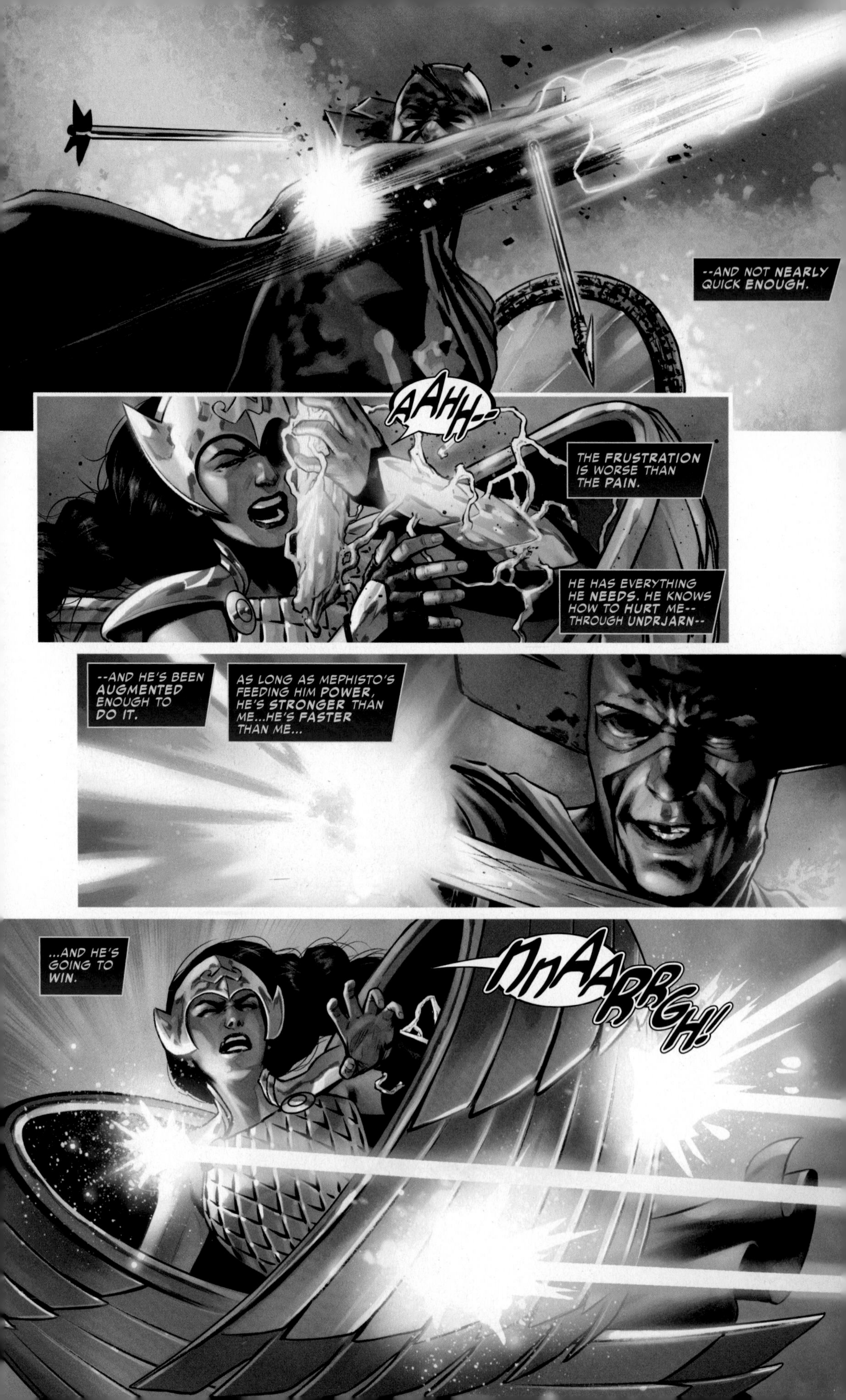
--AND NOT NEARLY QUICK ENOUGH.
AAHH--
THE FRUSTRATION IS WORSE THAN THE PAIN.
HE HAS EVERYTHING HE NEEDS. HE KNOWS HOW TO HURT ME-- THROUGH UNDRJARN--
--AND HE'S BEEN AUGMENTED ENOUGH TO DO IT.
AS LONG AS MEPHISTO'S FEEDING HIM POWER, HE'S STRONGER THAN ME...HE'S FASTER THAN ME...
...AND HE'S GOING TO WIN.
NNAARRGH!

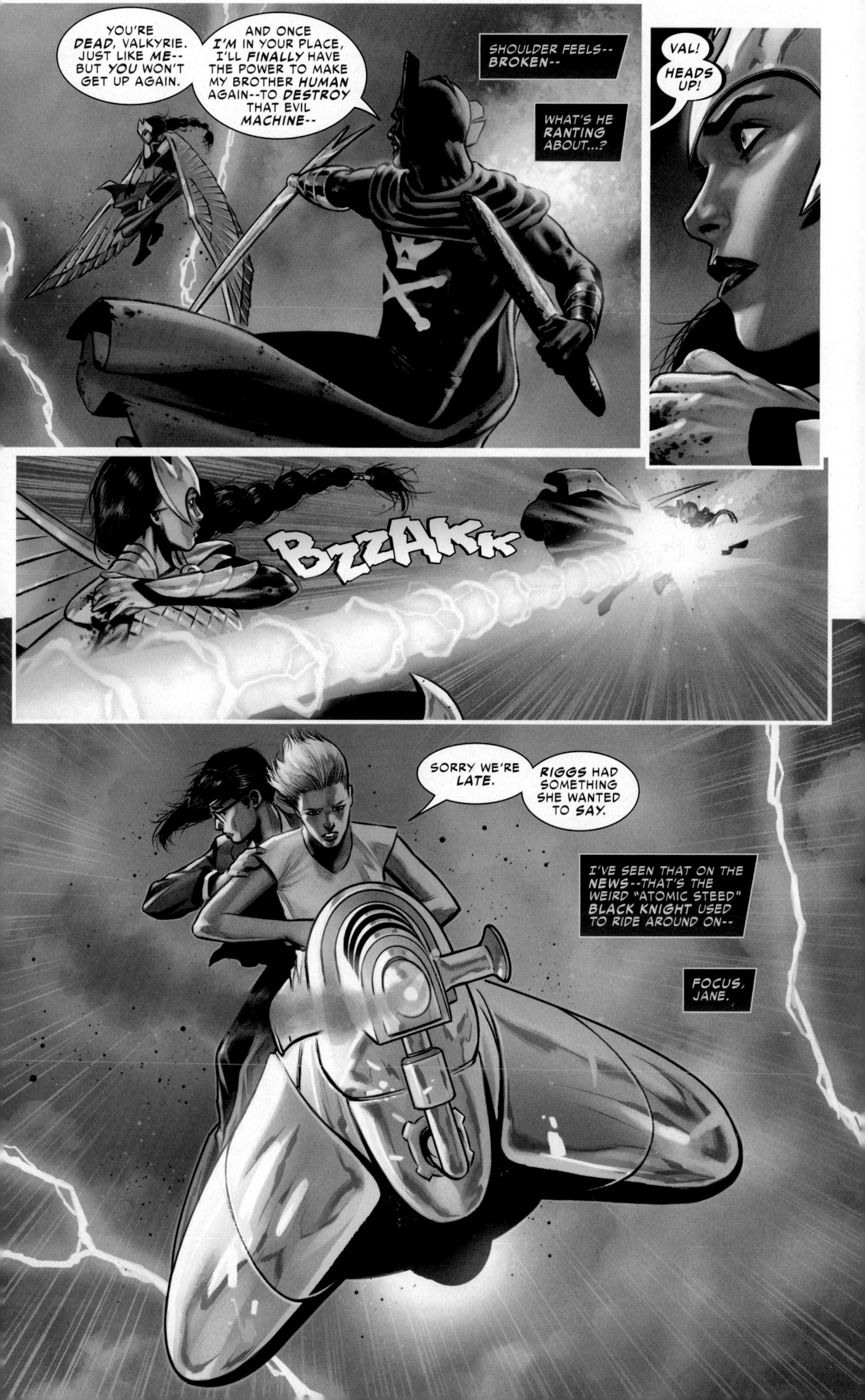
YOU'RE DEAD, VALKYRIE. JUST LIKE ME--BUT YOU WON'T GET UP AGAIN.
AND ONCE I'M IN YOUR PLACE, I'LL FINALLY HAVE THE POWER TO MAKE MY BROTHER HUMAN AGAIN--TO DESTROY THAT EVIL MACHINE--
SHOULDER FEELS--BROKEN--
WHAT'S HE RANTING ABOUT...?
VAL!
HEADS UP!
BZZAKK
SORRY WE'RE LATE.
RIGGS HAD SOMETHING SHE WANTED TO SAY.
I'VE SEEN THAT ON THE NEWS--THAT'S THE WEIRD "ATOMIC STEED" BLACK KNIGHT USED TO RIDE AROUND ON--
FOCUS, JANE.

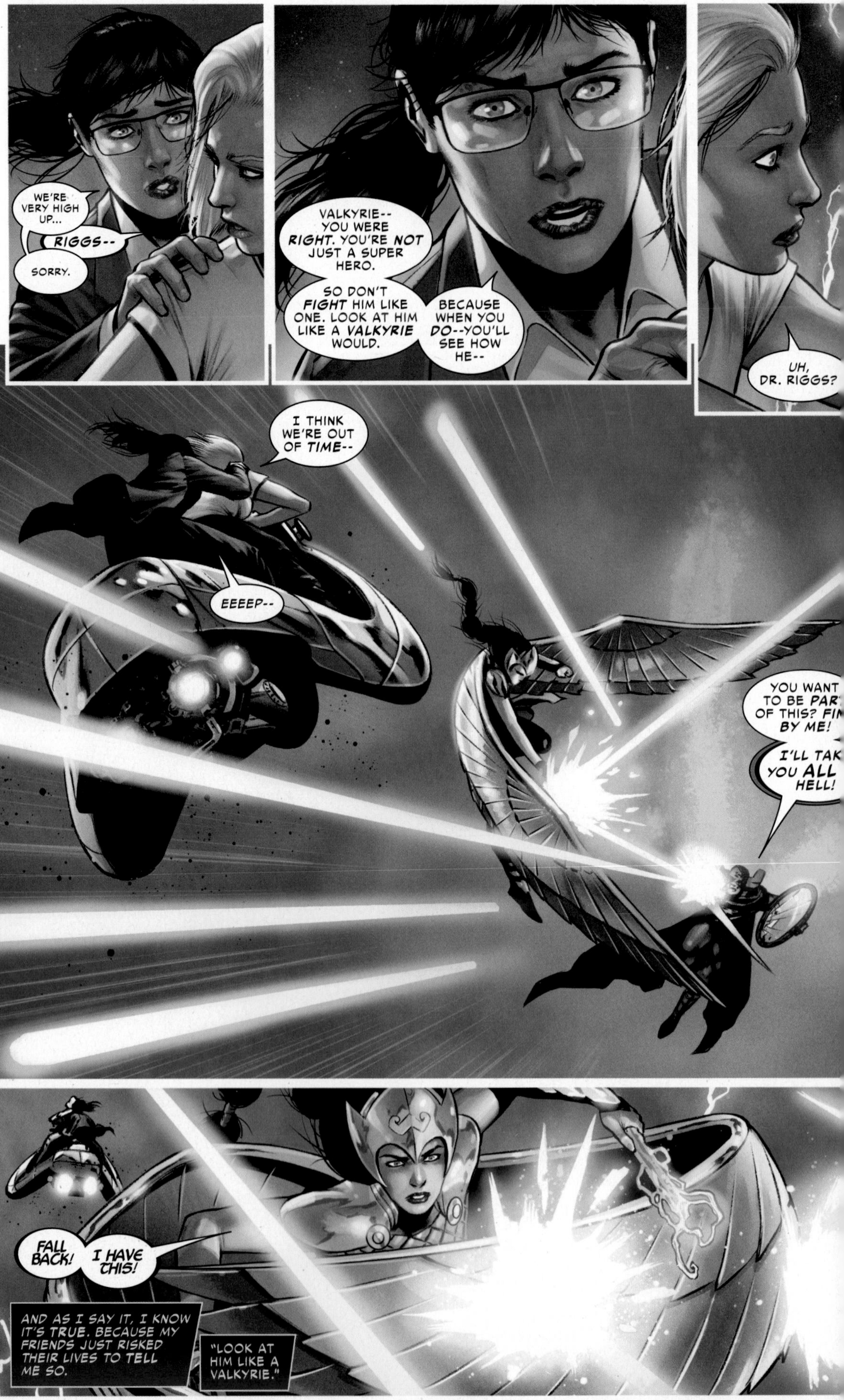
WE'RE VERY HIGH UP...
RIGGS--
SORRY.
VALKYRIE-- YOU WERE RIGHT. YOU'RE NOT JUST A SUPER HERO.
SO DON'T FIGHT HIM LIKE ONE. LOOK AT HIM LIKE A VALKYRIE WOULD.
BECAUSE WHEN YOU DO--YOU'LL SEE HOW HE--
UH, DR. RIGGS?
I THINK WE'RE OUT OF TIME--
EEEEP--
YOU WANT TO BE PAR OF THIS? FIN BY ME!
I'LL TAK YOU ALL HELL!
FALL BACK!
I HAVE THIS!
AND AS I SAY IT, I KNOW IT'S TRUE. BECAUSE MY FRIENDS JUST RISKED THEIR LIVES TO TELL ME SO.
"LOOK AT HIM LIKE A VALKYRIE."

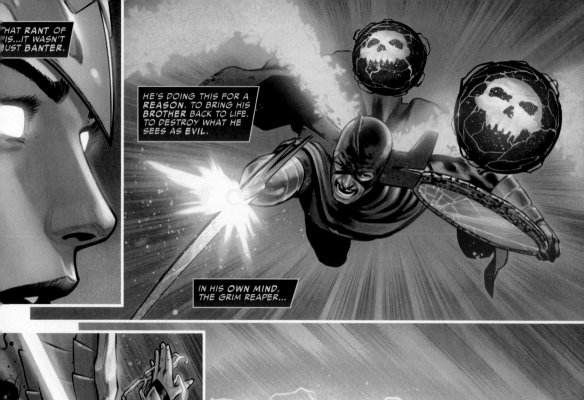

HAT RANT OF
IS...IT WASN'T
UST BANTER.

HE'S DOING THIS FOR A
REASON. TO BRING HIS
BROTHER BACK TO LIFE.
TO DESTROY WHAT HE
SEES AS EVIL.

IN HIS OWN MIND,
THE GRIM REAPER...

...IS A
HERO.

A DEAD
HERO.

AND I KNOW
WHERE DEAD
HEROES GO.

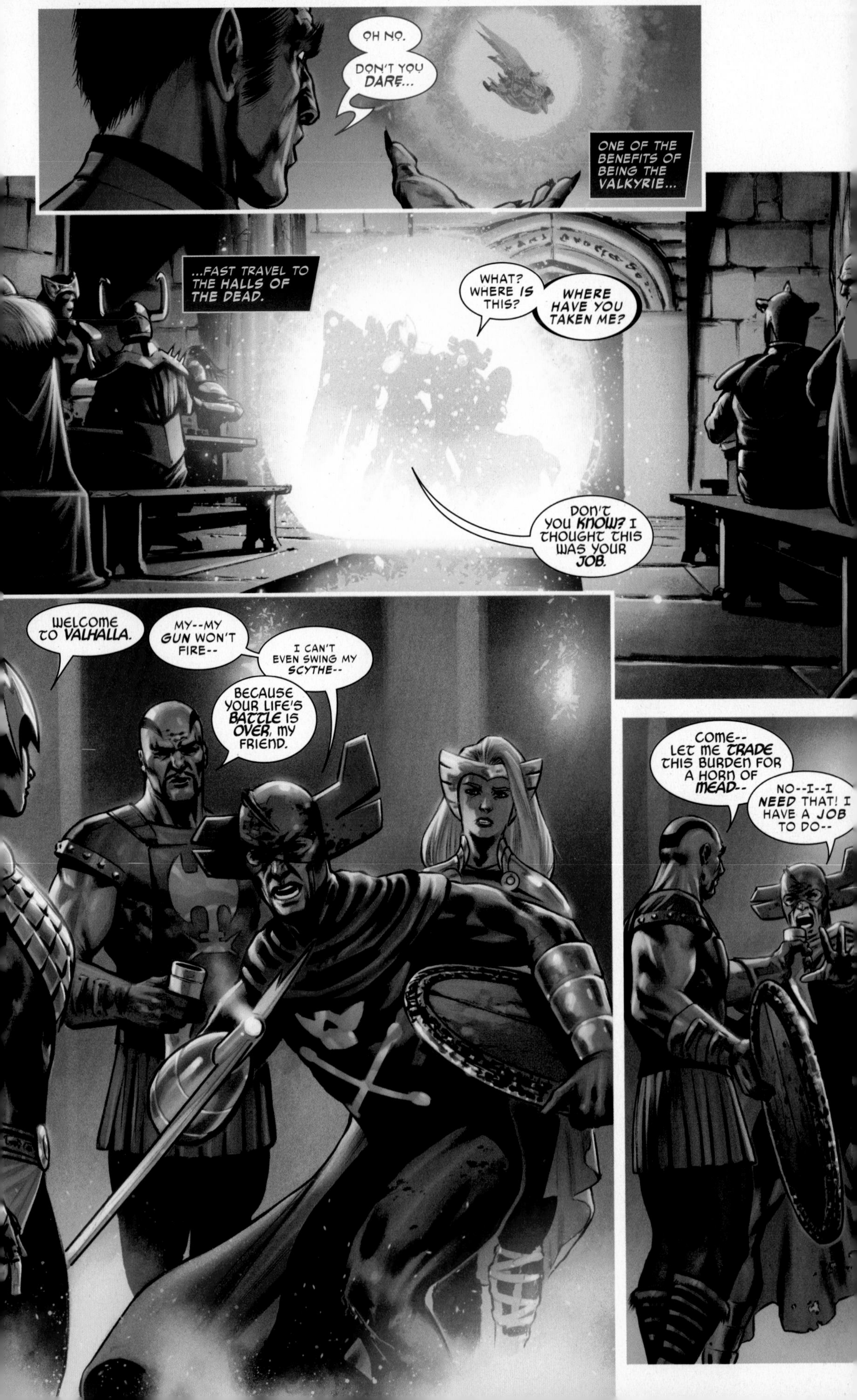

OH NO.
DON'T YOU DARE...
ONE OF THE BENEFITS OF BEING THE VALKYRIE...
...FAST TRAVEL TO THE HALLS OF THE DEAD.
WHAT? WHERE IS THIS?
WHERE HAVE YOU TAKEN ME?
DON'T YOU KNOW? I THOUGHT THIS WAS YOUR JOB.
WELCOME TO VALHALLA.
MY--MY GUN WON'T FIRE--
I CAN'T EVEN SWING MY SCYTHE--
BECAUSE YOUR LIFE'S BATTLE IS OVER, MY FRIEND.
COME-- LET ME TRADE THIS BURDEN FOR A HORN OF MEAD--
NO--I--I NEED THAT! I HAVE A JOB TO DO--

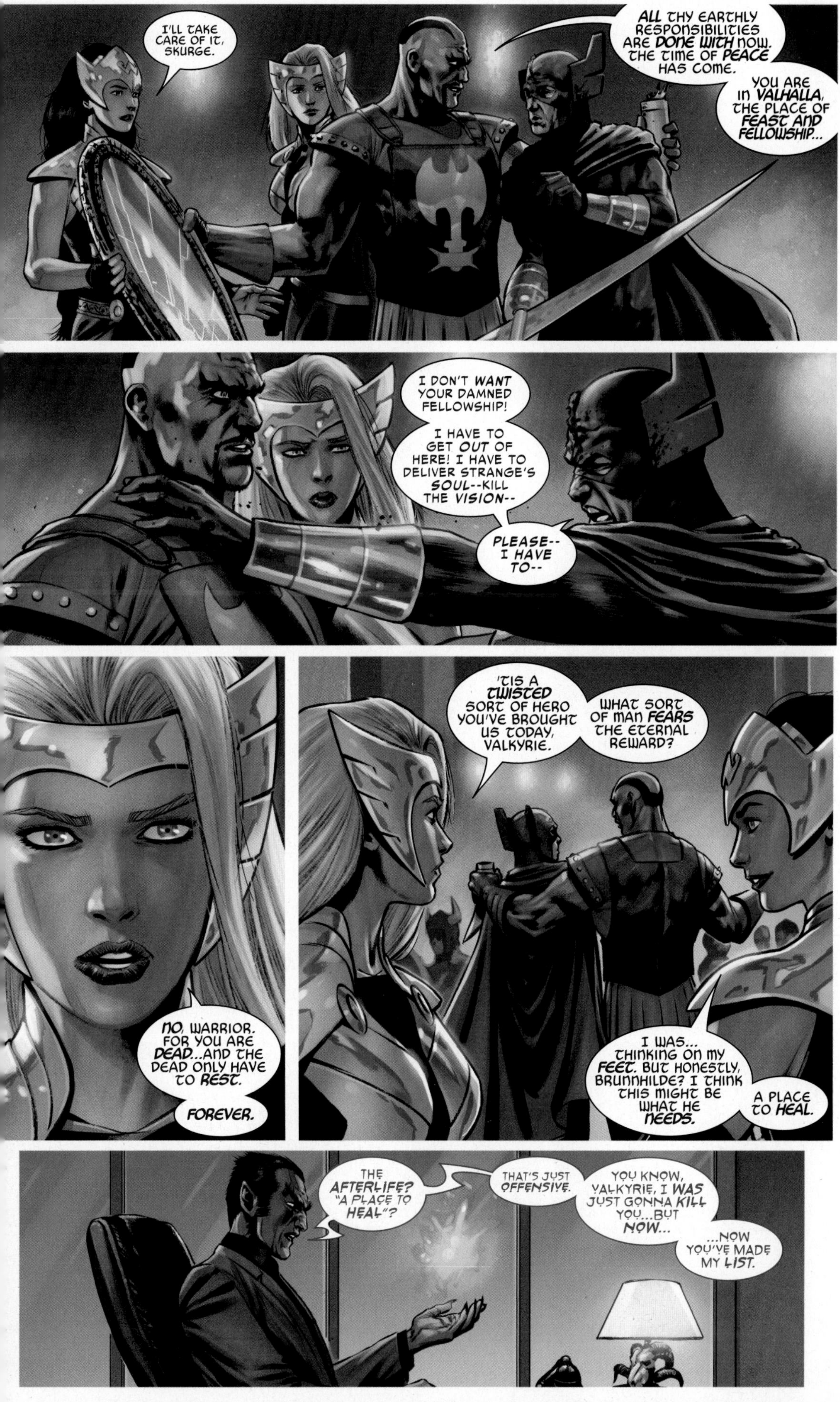
I'LL TAKE CARE OF IT, SKURGE.
ALL THY EARTHLY RESPONSIBILITIES ARE DONE WITH NOW. THE TIME OF PEACE HAS COME.
YOU ARE IN VALHALLA, THE PLACE OF FEAST AND FELLOWSHIP...
I DON'T WANT YOUR DAMNED FELLOWSHIP!
I HAVE TO GET OUT OF HERE! I HAVE TO DELIVER STRANGE'S SOUL--KILL THE VISION--
PLEASE-- I HAVE TO--
NO, WARRIOR. FOR YOU ARE DEAD...AND THE DEAD ONLY HAVE TO REST.
FOREVER.
'TIS A TWISTED SORT OF HERO YOU'VE BROUGHT US TODAY, VALKYRIE.
WHAT SORT OF MAN FEARS THE ETERNAL REWARD?
I WAS... THINKING ON MY FEET. BUT HONESTLY, BRUNNHILDE? I THINK THIS MIGHT BE WHAT HE NEEDS.
A PLACE TO HEAL.
THE AFTERLIFE? "A PLACE TO HEAL"?
THAT'S JUST OFFENSIVE.
YOU KNOW, VALKYRIE, I WAS JUST GONNA KILL YOU...BUT NOW...
...NOW YOU'VE MADE MY LIST.

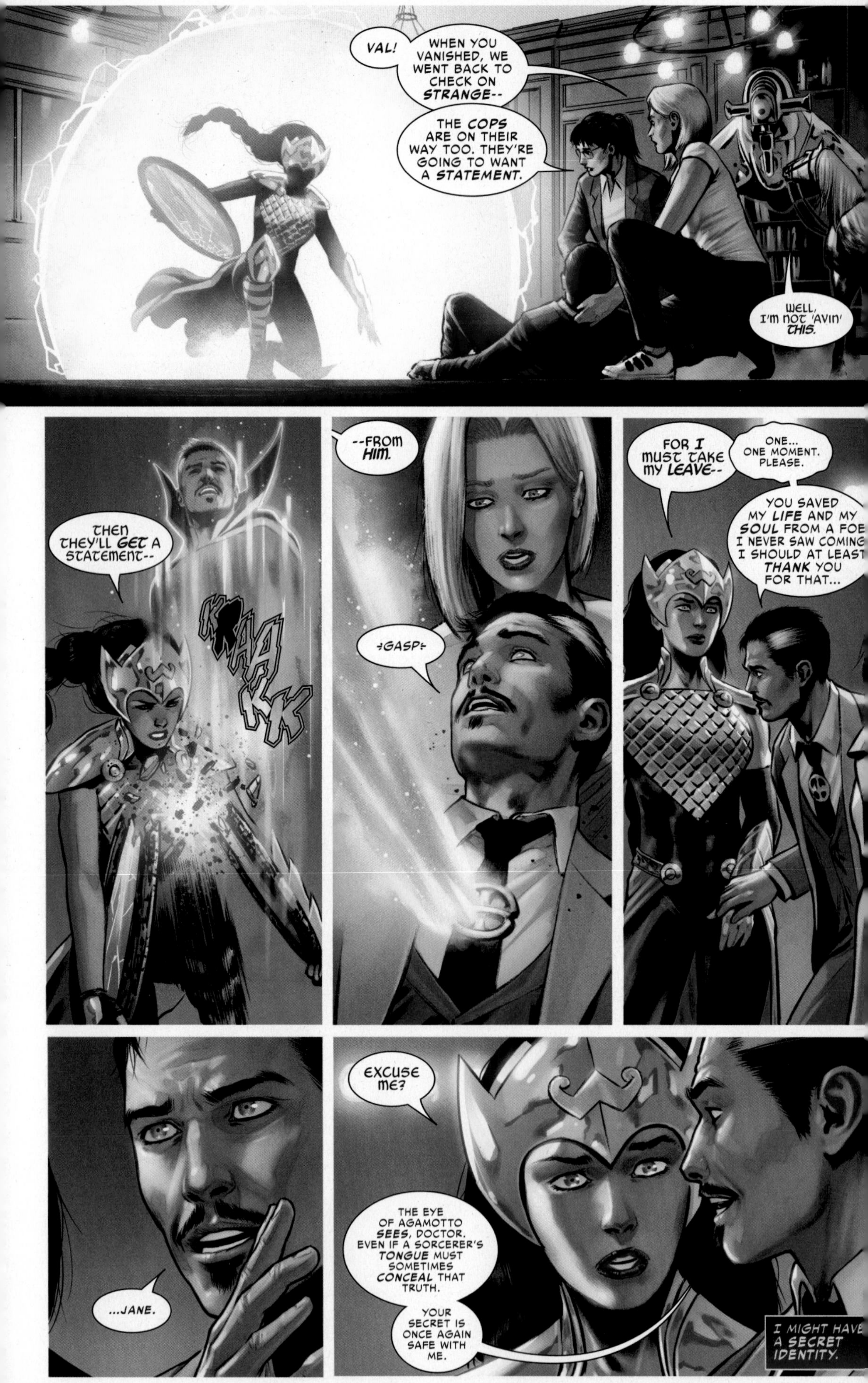

VAL!
WHEN YOU VANISHED, WE WENT BACK TO CHECK ON STRANGE--
THE COPS ARE ON THEIR WAY TOO. THEY'RE GOING TO WANT A STATEMENT.
WELL, I'M NOT 'AVIN' THIS.
THEN THEY'LL GET A STATEMENT--
KRAAKK
--FROM HIM.
-GASP-
FOR I MUST TAKE MY LEAVE--
ONE... ONE MOMENT. PLEASE.
YOU SAVED MY LIFE AND MY SOUL FROM A FOE I NEVER SAW COMING. I SHOULD AT LEAST THANK YOU FOR THAT...
...JANE.
EXCUSE ME?
THE EYE OF AGAMOTTO SEES, DOCTOR. EVEN IF A SORCERER'S TONGUE MUST SOMETIMES CONCEAL THAT TRUTH.
YOUR SECRET IS ONCE AGAIN SAFE WITH ME.
I MIGHT HAVE A SECRET IDENTITY.

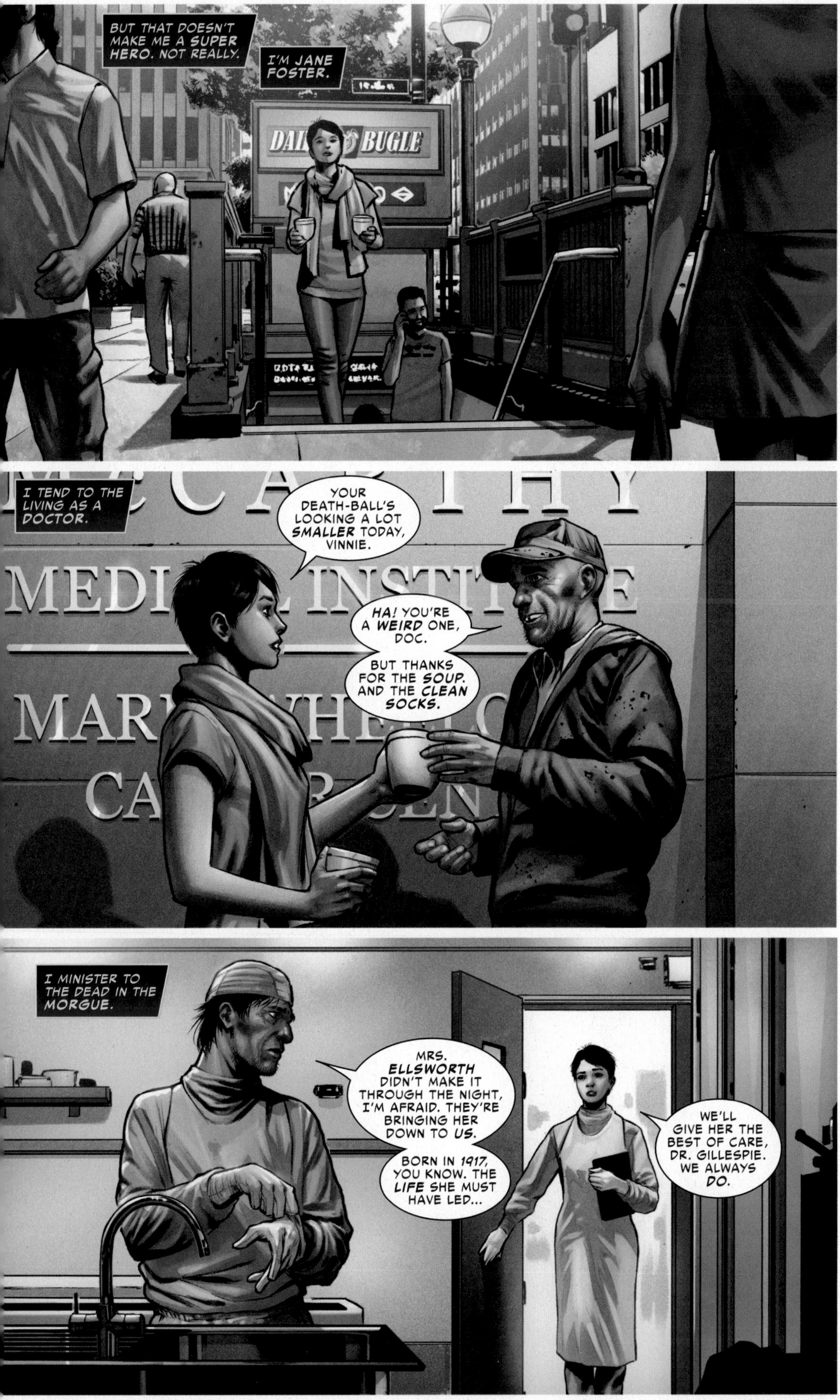
BUT THAT DOESN'T MAKE ME A SUPER HERO. NOT REALLY.
I'M JANE FOSTER.
DAILY BUGLE
I TEND TO THE LIVING AS A DOCTOR.
YOUR DEATH-BALL'S LOOKING A LOT SMALLER TODAY, VINNIE.
HA! YOU'RE A WEIRD ONE, DOC.
BUT THANKS FOR THE SOUP. AND THE CLEAN SOCKS.
I MINISTER TO THE DEAD IN THE MORGUE.
MRS. ELLSWORTH DIDN'T MAKE IT THROUGH THE NIGHT, I'M AFRAID. THEY'RE BRINGING HER DOWN TO US.
BORN IN 1917, YOU KNOW. THE LIFE SHE MUST HAVE LED...
WE'LL GIVE HER THE BEST OF CARE, DR. GILLESPIE. WE ALWAYS DO.

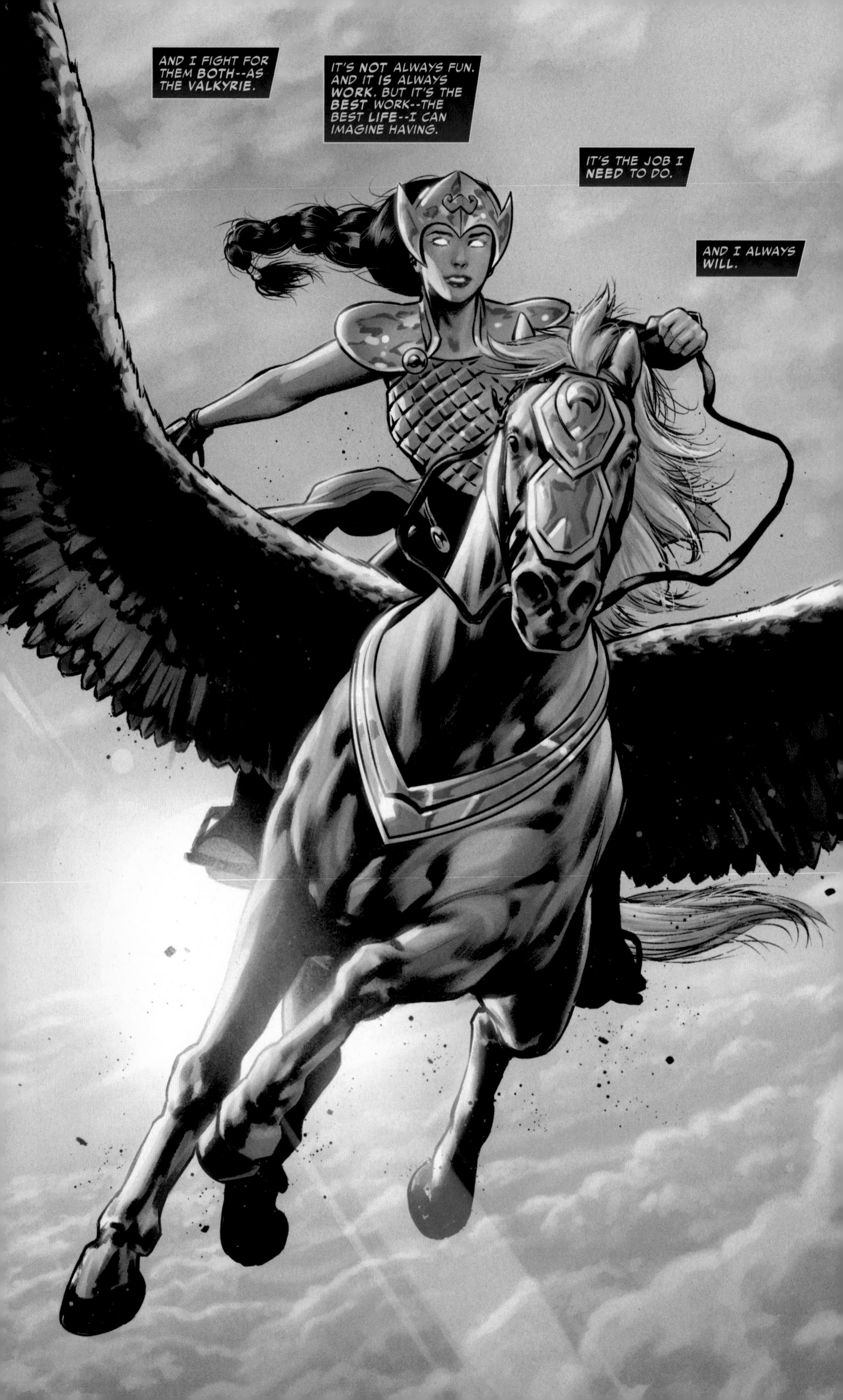
AND I FIGHT FOR THEM BOTH--AS THE VALKYRIE.
IT'S NOT ALWAYS FUN. AND IT IS ALWAYS WORK. BUT IT'S THE BEST WORK--THE BEST LIFE--I CAN IMAGINE HAVING.
IT'S THE JOB I NEED TO DO.
AND I ALWAYS WILL.

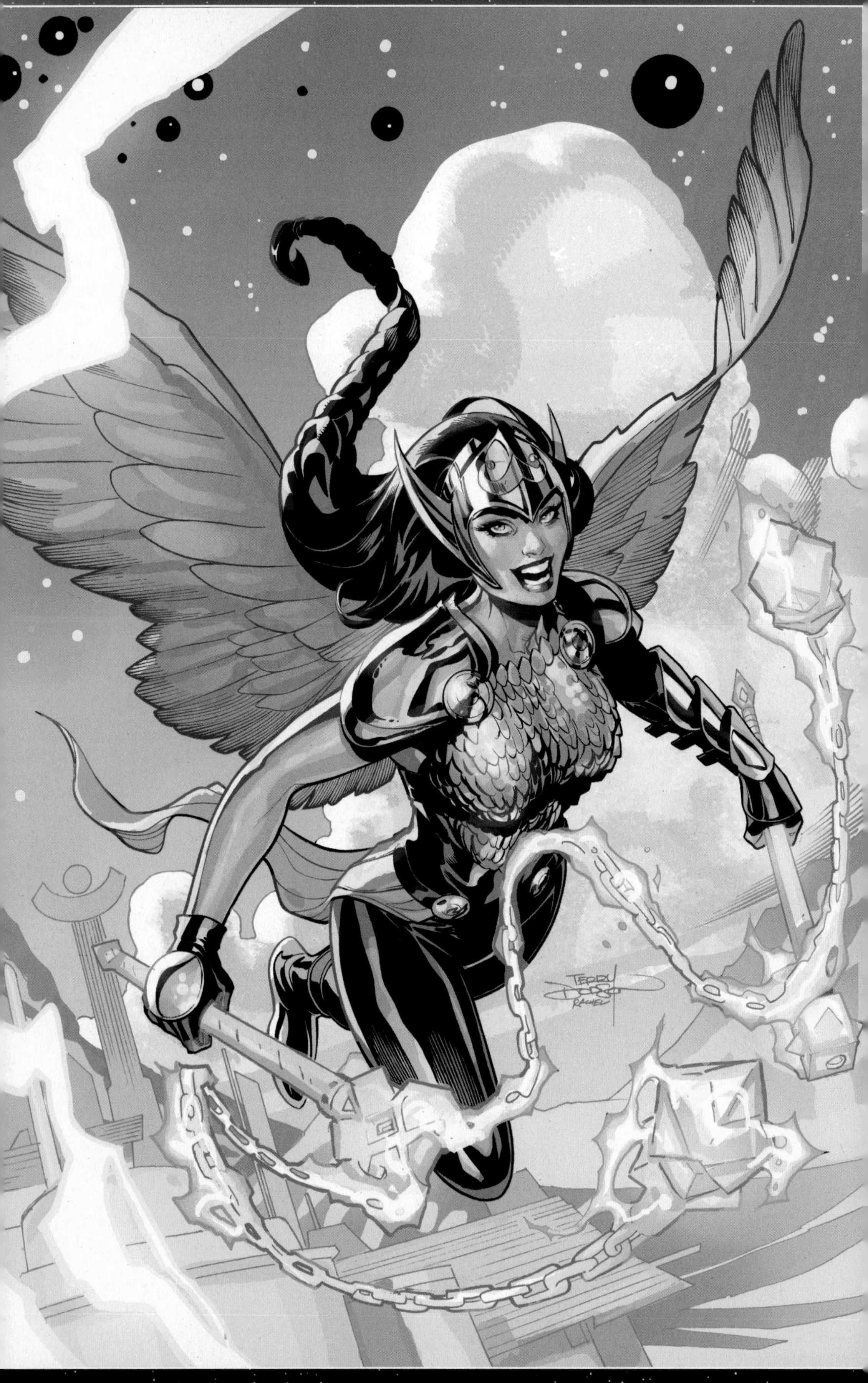

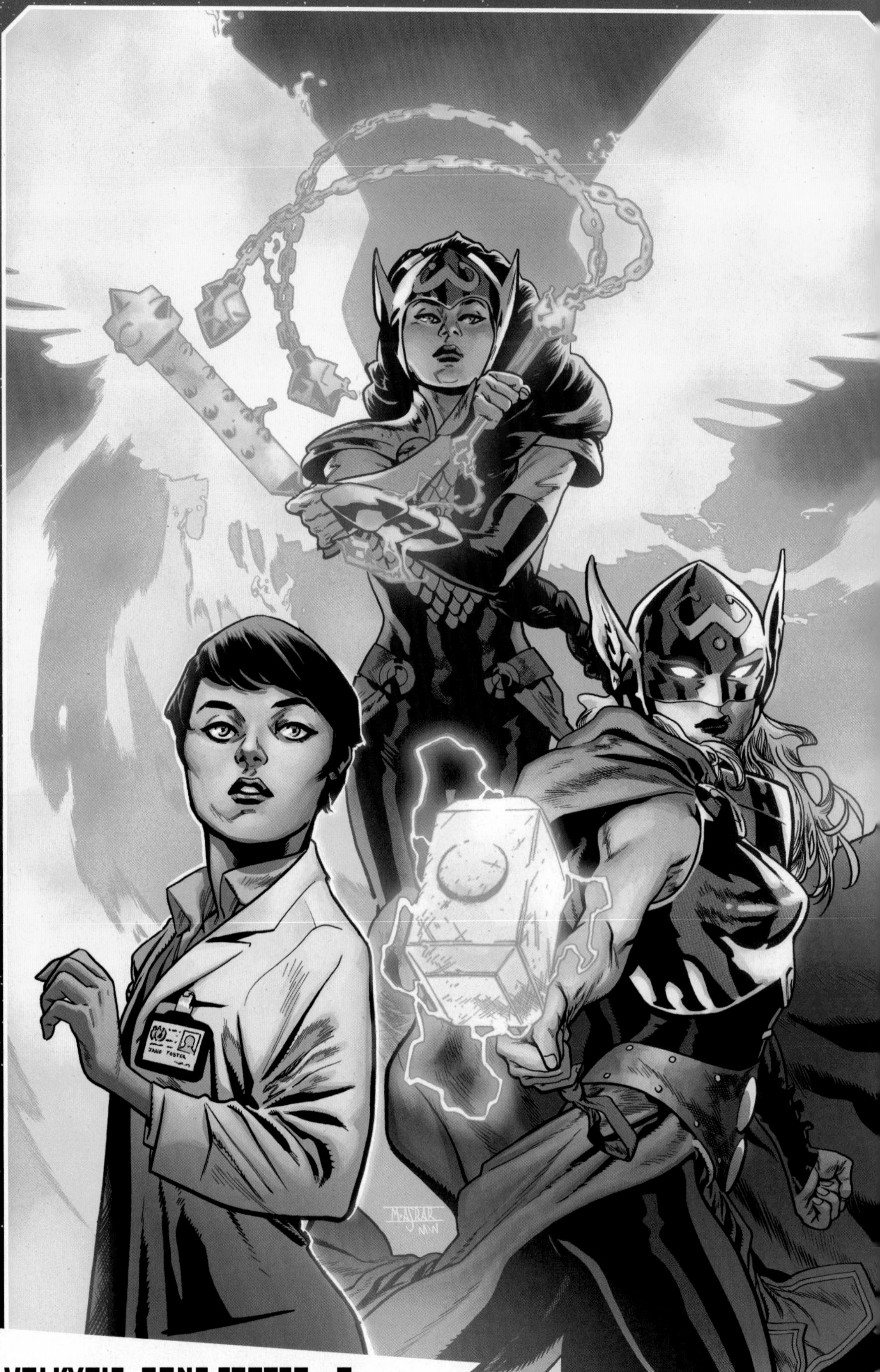
JANE FOSTER

VALKYRIE: JANE FOSTER #6

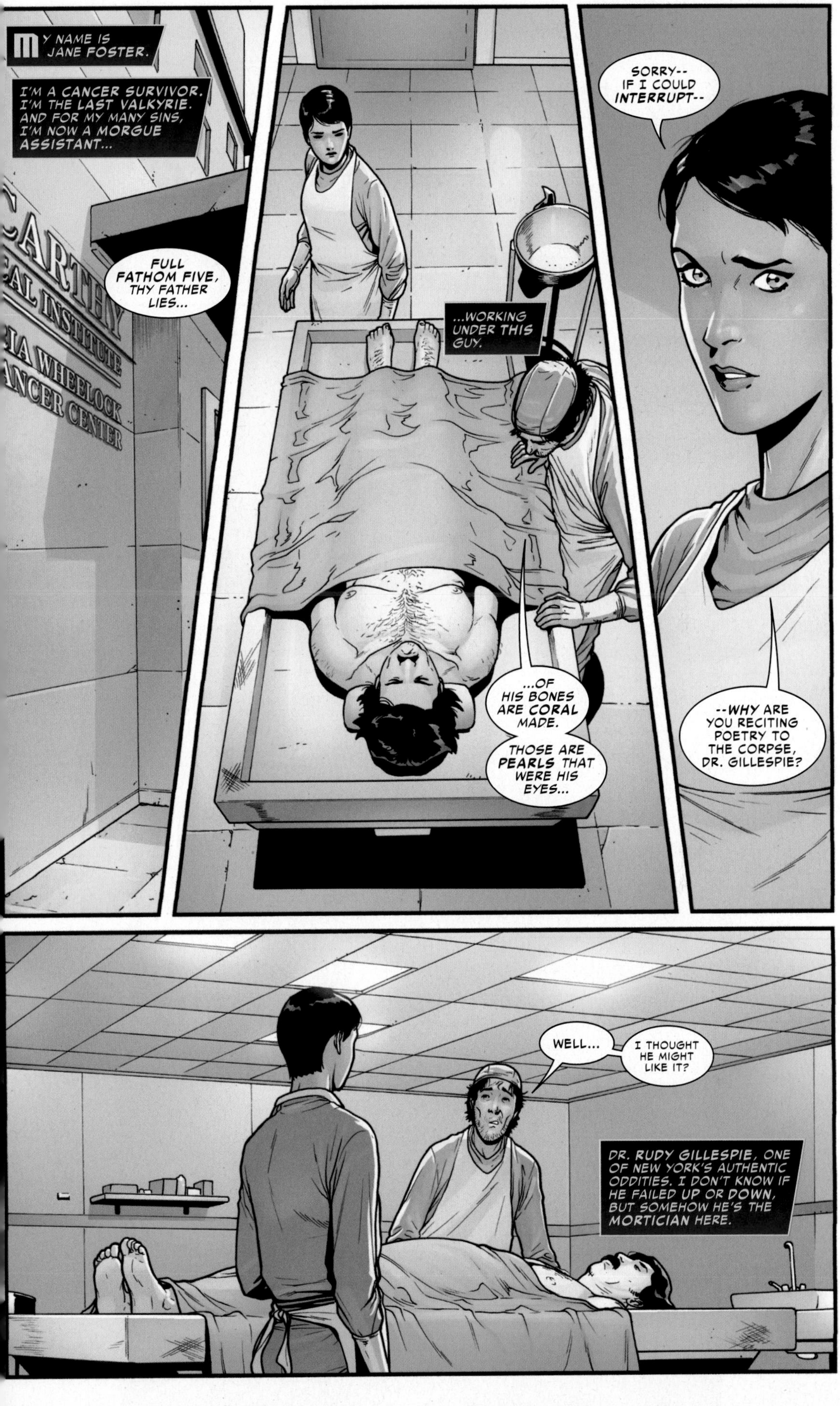
MY NAME IS JANE FOSTER.
I'M A CANCER SURVIVOR. I'M THE LAST VALKYRIE. AND FOR MY MANY SINS, I'M NOW A MORGUE ASSISTANT...
FULL FATHOM FIVE, THY FATHER LIES...
...WORKING UNDER THIS GUY.
...OF HIS BONES ARE CORAL MADE.
THOSE ARE PEARLS THAT WERE HIS EYES...
SORRY-- IF I COULD INTERRUPT--
--WHY ARE YOU RECITING POETRY TO THE CORPSE, DR. GILLESPIE?
WELL...
I THOUGHT HE MIGHT LIKE IT?
DR. RUDY GILLESPIE, ONE OF NEW YORK'S AUTHENTIC ODDITIES. I DON'T KNOW IF HE FAILED UP OR DOWN, BUT SOMEHOW HE'S THE MORTICIAN HERE.

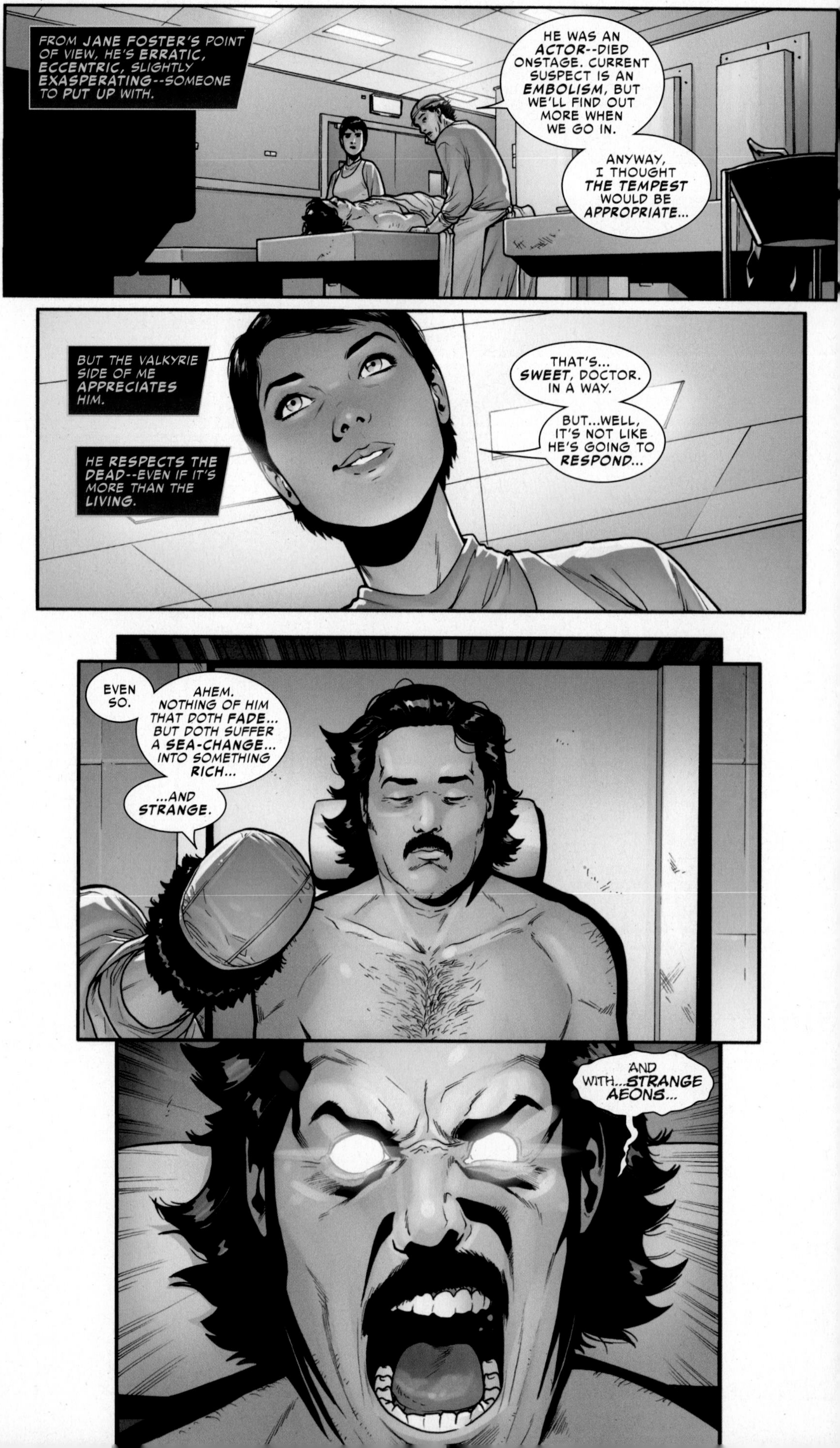
FROM JANE FOSTER'S POINT OF VIEW, HE'S ERRATIC, ECCENTRIC, SLIGHTLY EXASPERATING--SOMEONE TO PUT UP WITH.
HE WAS AN ACTOR--DIED ONSTAGE. CURRENT SUSPECT IS AN EMBOLISM, BUT WE'LL FIND OUT MORE WHEN WE GO IN.
ANYWAY, I THOUGHT THE TEMPEST WOULD BE APPROPRIATE...
BUT THE VALKYRIE SIDE OF ME APPRECIATES HIM.
HE RESPECTS THE DEAD--EVEN IF IT'S MORE THAN THE LIVING.
THAT'S... SWEET, DOCTOR. IN A WAY.
BUT...WELL, IT'S NOT LIKE HE'S GOING TO RESPOND...
EVEN SO.
AHEM. NOTHING OF HIM THAT DOTH FADE... BUT DOTH SUFFER A SEA-CHANGE... INTO SOMETHING RICH...
...AND STRANGE.
AND WITH... STRANGE AEONS...

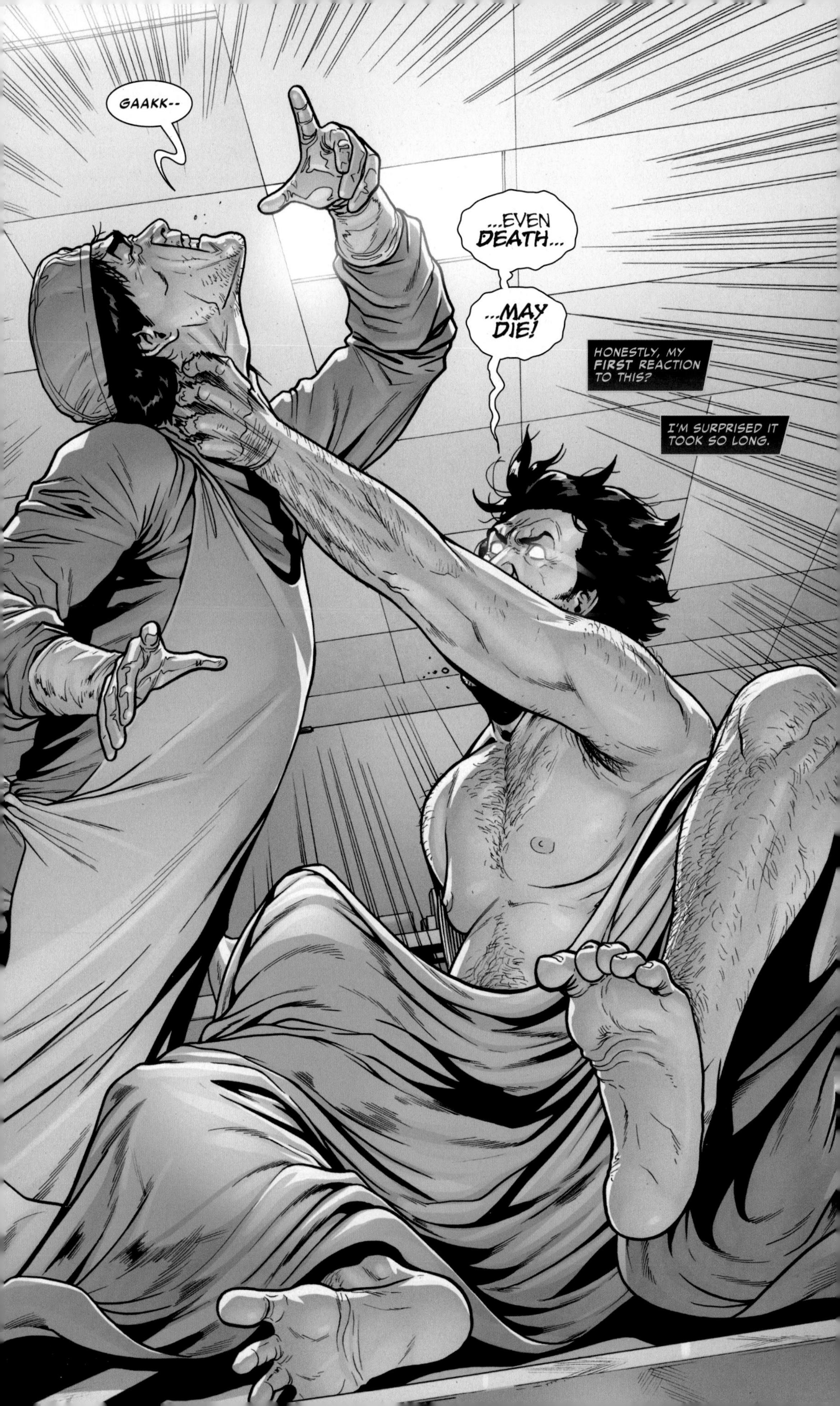
GAAKK--
...EVEN DEATH...
...MAY DIE!
HONESTLY, MY FIRST REACTION TO THIS?
I'M SURPRISED IT TOOK SO LONG.

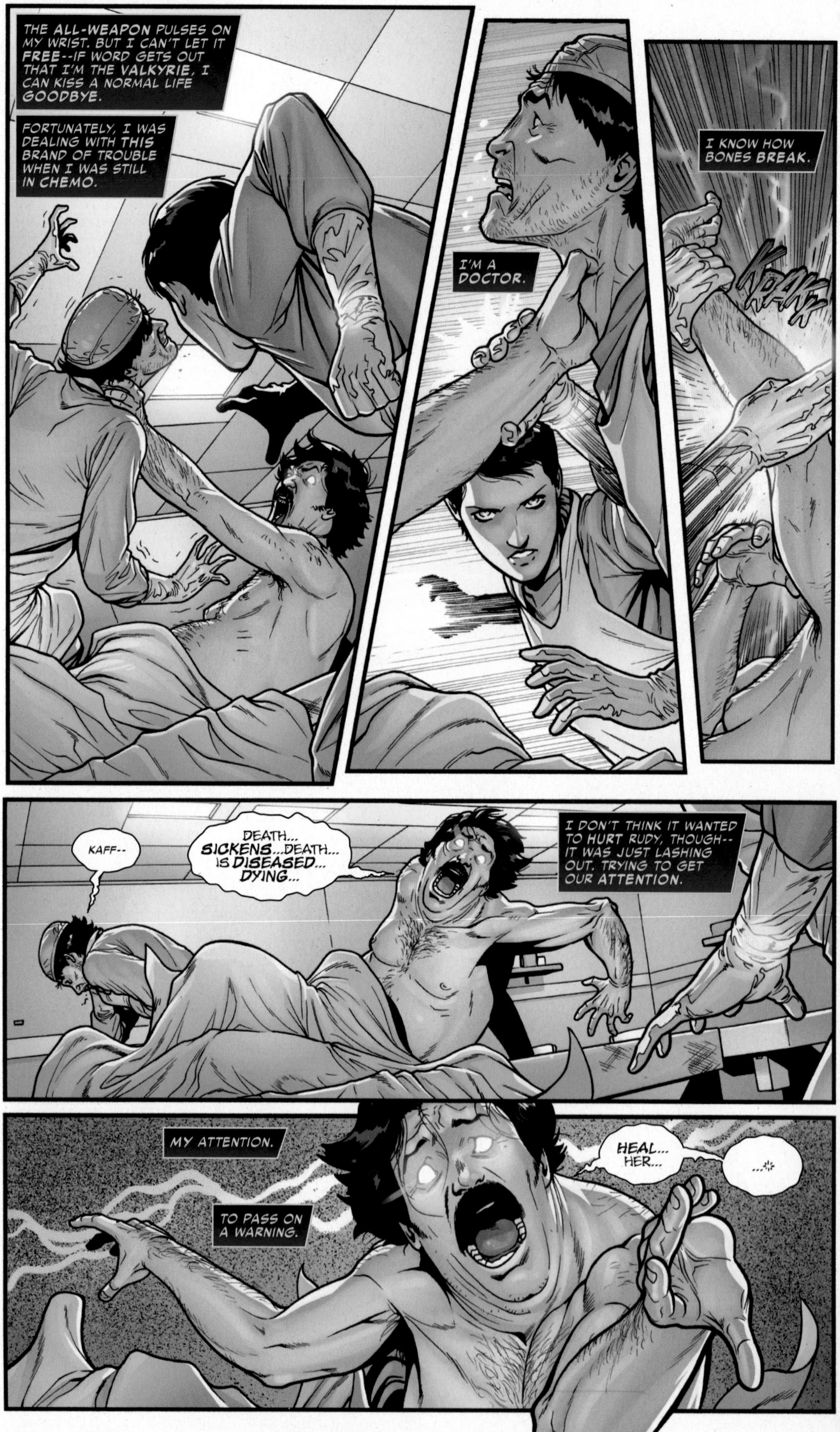

THE ALL-WEAPON PULSES ON MY WRIST. BUT I CAN'T LET IT FREE--IF WORD GETS OUT THAT I'M THE VALKYRIE, I CAN KISS A NORMAL LIFE GOODBYE.
FORTUNATELY, I WAS DEALING WITH THIS BRAND OF TROUBLE WHEN I WAS STILL IN CHEMO.
I'M A DOCTOR.
I KNOW HOW BONES BREAK.
KRAK
KAFF--
DEATH... SICKENS...DEATH... IS DISEASED... DYING...
I DON'T THINK IT WANTED TO HURT RUDY, THOUGH--IT WAS JUST LASHING OUT. TRYING TO GET OUR ATTENTION.
MY ATTENTION.
TO PASS ON A WARNING.
HEAL... HER...

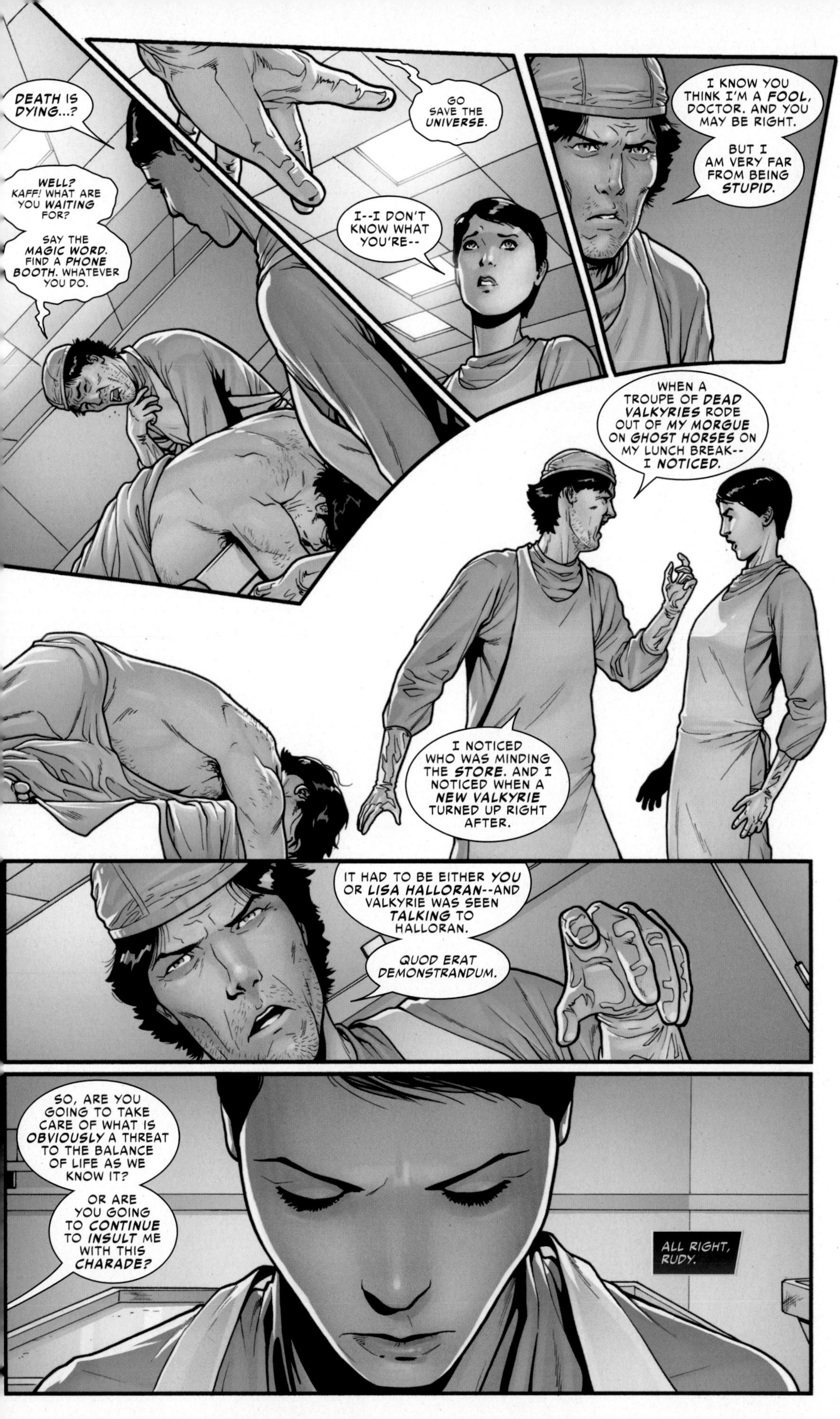

DEATH IS DYING...?
WELL? KAFF! WHAT ARE YOU WAITING FOR?
SAY THE MAGIC WORD. FIND A PHONE BOOTH. WHATEVER YOU DO.
GO SAVE THE UNIVERSE.
I--I DON'T KNOW WHAT YOU'RE--
I KNOW YOU THINK I'M A FOOL, DOCTOR. AND YOU MAY BE RIGHT.
BUT I AM VERY FAR FROM BEING STUPID.
WHEN A TROUPE OF DEAD VALKYRIES RODE OUT OF MY MORGUE ON GHOST HORSES ON MY LUNCH BREAK-- I NOTICED.
I NOTICED WHO WAS MINDING THE STORE. AND I NOTICED WHEN A NEW VALKYRIE TURNED UP RIGHT AFTER.
IT HAD TO BE EITHER YOU OR LISA HALLORAN--AND VALKYRIE WAS SEEN TALKING TO HALLORAN.
QUOD ERAT DEMONSTRANDUM.
SO, ARE YOU GOING TO TAKE CARE OF WHAT IS OBVIOUSLY A THREAT TO THE BALANCE OF LIFE AS WE KNOW IT?
OR ARE YOU GOING TO CONTINUE TO INSULT ME WITH THIS CHARADE?
ALL RIGHT, RUDY.

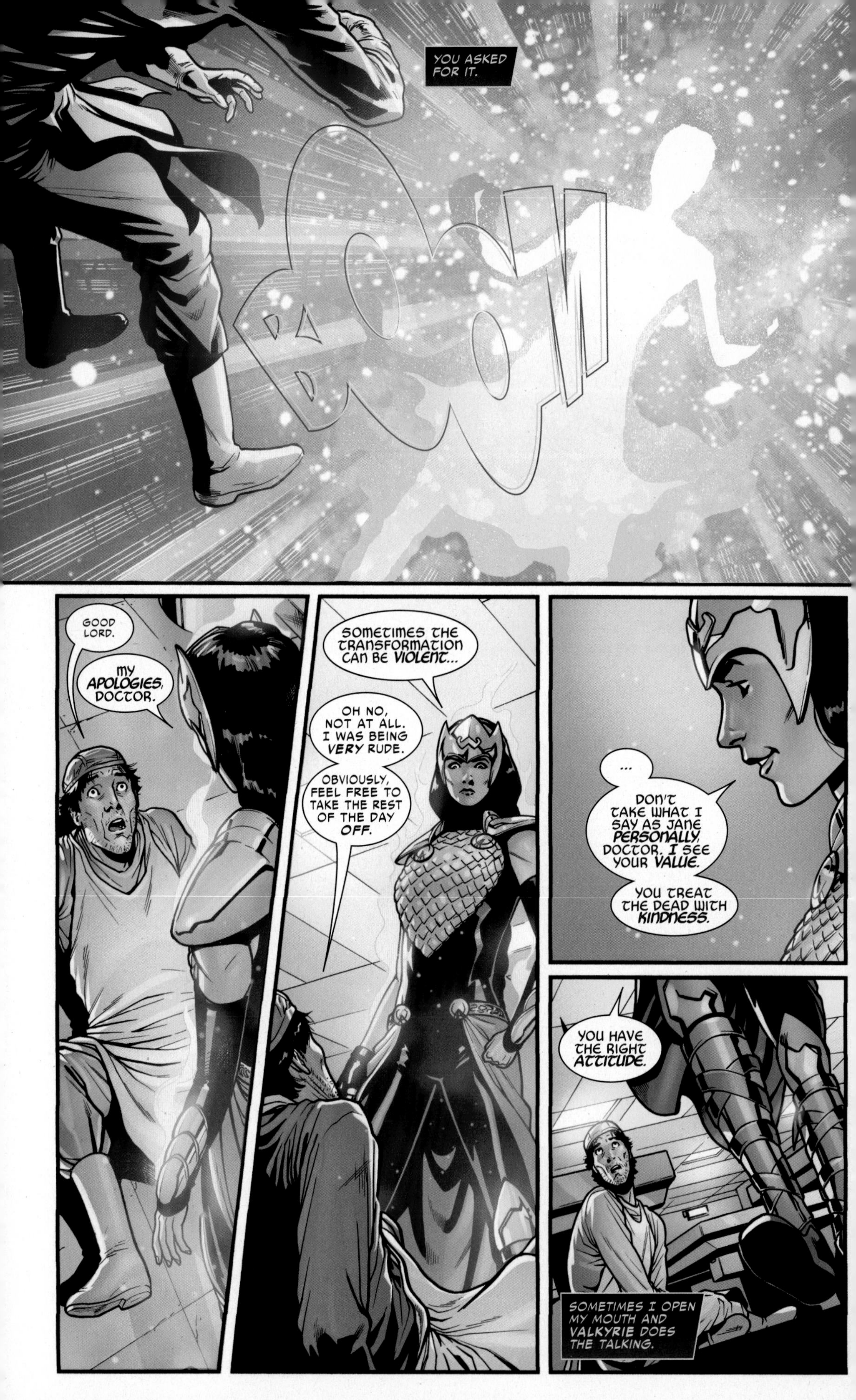
YOU ASKED FOR IT.
BOOOM
GOOD LORD.
MY APOLOGIES, DOCTOR.
SOMETIMES THE TRANSFORMATION CAN BE VIOLENT...
OH NO, NOT AT ALL. I WAS BEING VERY RUDE.
OBVIOUSLY, FEEL FREE TO TAKE THE REST OF THE DAY OFF.
...
DON'T TAKE WHAT I SAY AS JANE PERSONALLY, DOCTOR. I SEE YOUR VALUE.
YOU TREAT THE DEAD WITH KINDNESS.
YOU HAVE THE RIGHT ATTITUDE.
SOMETIMES I OPEN MY MOUTH AND VALKYRIE DOES THE TALKING.

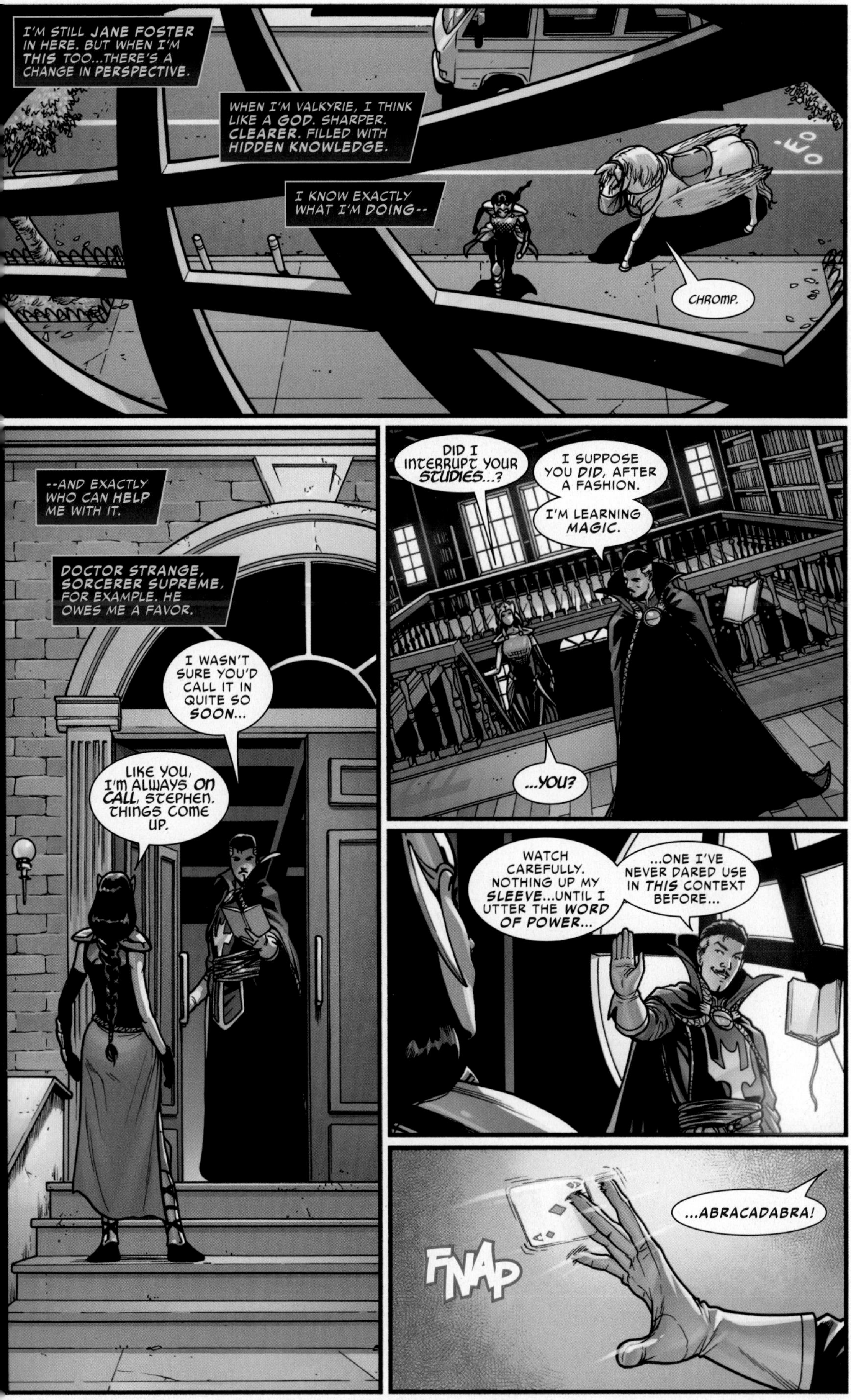

I'M STILL JANE FOSTER IN HERE. BUT WHEN I'M THIS TOO...THERE'S A CHANGE IN PERSPECTIVE.
WHEN I'M VALKYRIE, I THINK LIKE A GOD. SHARPER. CLEARER. FILLED WITH HIDDEN KNOWLEDGE.
I KNOW EXACTLY WHAT I'M DOING--
CHROMP.
--AND EXACTLY WHO CAN HELP ME WITH IT.
DOCTOR STRANGE, SORCERER SUPREME, FOR EXAMPLE. HE OWES ME A FAVOR.
I WASN'T SURE YOU'D CALL IT IN QUITE SO SOON...
LIKE YOU, I'M ALWAYS ON CALL, STEPHEN. THINGS COME UP.
DID I INTERRUPT YOUR STUDIES...?
I SUPPOSE YOU DID, AFTER A FASHION.
I'M LEARNING MAGIC.
...YOU?
WATCH CAREFULLY. NOTHING UP MY SLEEVE...UNTIL I UTTER THE WORD OF POWER...
...ONE I'VE NEVER DARED USE IN THIS CONTEXT BEFORE...
...ABRACADABRA!
FNAP

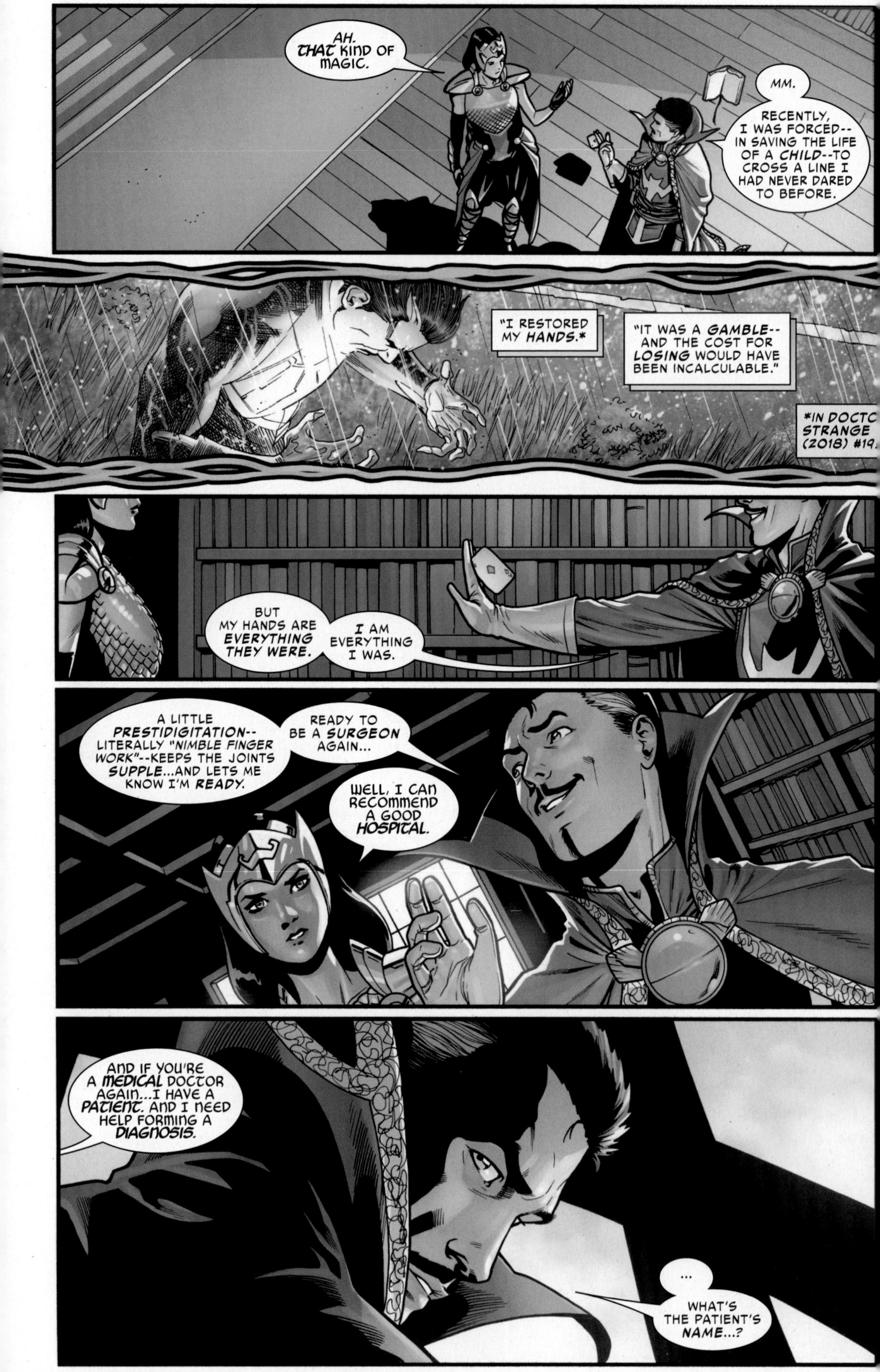
AH. THAT KIND OF MAGIC.
MM.
RECENTLY, I WAS FORCED-- IN SAVING THE LIFE OF A CHILD--TO CROSS A LINE I HAD NEVER DARED TO BEFORE.
"I RESTORED MY HANDS.*
"IT WAS A GAMBLE-- AND THE COST FOR LOSING WOULD HAVE BEEN INCALCULABLE."
*IN DOCTOR STRANGE (2018) #19.
BUT MY HANDS ARE EVERYTHING THEY WERE.
I AM EVERYTHING I WAS.
A LITTLE PRESTIDIGITATION-- LITERALLY "NIMBLE FINGER WORK"--KEEPS THE JOINTS SUPPLE...AND LETS ME KNOW I'M READY.
READY TO BE A SURGEON AGAIN...
WELL, I CAN RECOMMEND A GOOD HOSPITAL.
AND IF YOU'RE A MEDICAL DOCTOR AGAIN...I HAVE A PATIENT. AND I NEED HELP FORMING A DIAGNOSIS.
...
WHAT'S THE PATIENT'S NAME...?

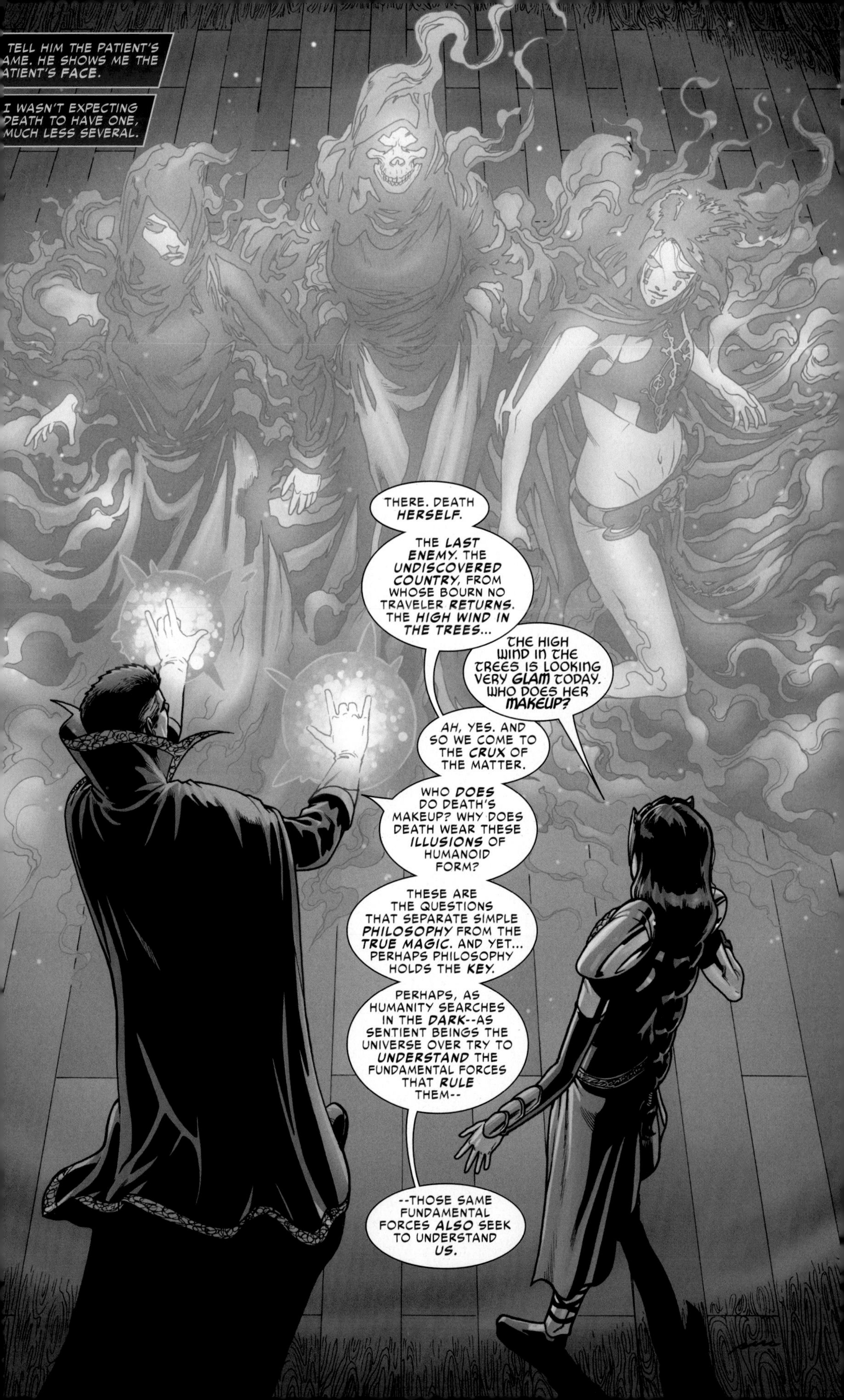
TELL HIM THE PATIENT'S
AME. HE SHOWS ME THE
ATIENT'S FACE.
I WASN'T EXPECTING DEATH TO HAVE ONE, MUCH LESS SEVERAL.
THERE. DEATH HERSELF.
THE LAST ENEMY. THE UNDISCOVERED COUNTRY, FROM WHOSE BOURN NO TRAVELER RETURNS. THE HIGH WIND IN THE TREES...
THE HIGH WIND IN THE TREES IS LOOKING VERY GLAM TODAY. WHO DOES HER MAKEUP?
AH, YES. AND SO WE COME TO THE CRUX OF THE MATTER.
WHO DOES DO DEATH'S MAKEUP? WHY DOES DEATH WEAR THESE ILLUSIONS OF HUMANOID FORM?
THESE ARE THE QUESTIONS THAT SEPARATE SIMPLE PHILOSOPHY FROM THE TRUE MAGIC. AND YET... PERHAPS PHILOSOPHY HOLDS THE KEY.
PERHAPS, AS HUMANITY SEARCHES IN THE DARK--AS SENTIENT BEINGS THE UNIVERSE OVER TRY TO UNDERSTAND THE FUNDAMENTAL FORCES THAT RULE THEM--
--THOSE SAME FUNDAMENTAL FORCES ALSO SEEK TO UNDERSTAND US.

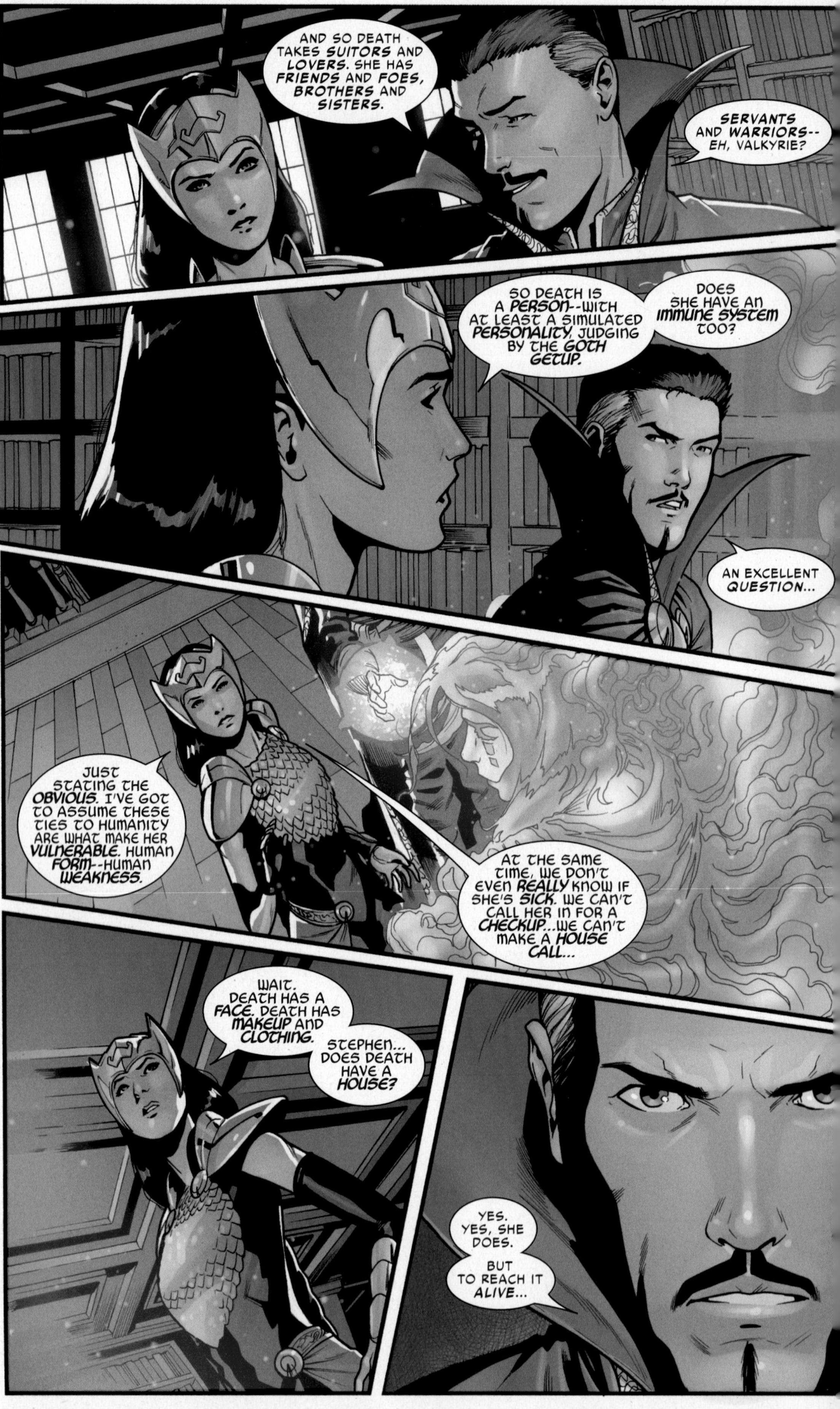
AND SO DEATH TAKES SUITORS AND LOVERS. SHE HAS FRIENDS AND FOES, BROTHERS AND SISTERS.
SERVANTS AND WARRIORS-- EH, VALKYRIE?
SO DEATH IS A PERSON--WITH AT LEAST A SIMULATED PERSONALITY, JUDGING BY THE GOTH GETUP.
DOES SHE HAVE AN IMMUNE SYSTEM TOO?
AN EXCELLENT QUESTION...
JUST STATING THE OBVIOUS. I'VE GOT TO ASSUME THESE TIES TO HUMANITY ARE WHAT MAKE HER VULNERABLE. HUMAN FORM--HUMAN WEAKNESS.
AT THE SAME TIME, WE DON'T EVEN REALLY KNOW IF SHE'S SICK. WE CAN'T CALL HER IN FOR A CHECKUP...WE CAN'T MAKE A HOUSE CALL...
WAIT. DEATH HAS A FACE. DEATH HAS MAKEUP AND CLOTHING.
STEPHEN... DOES DEATH HAVE A HOUSE?
YES. YES, SHE DOES.
BUT TO REACH IT ALIVE...

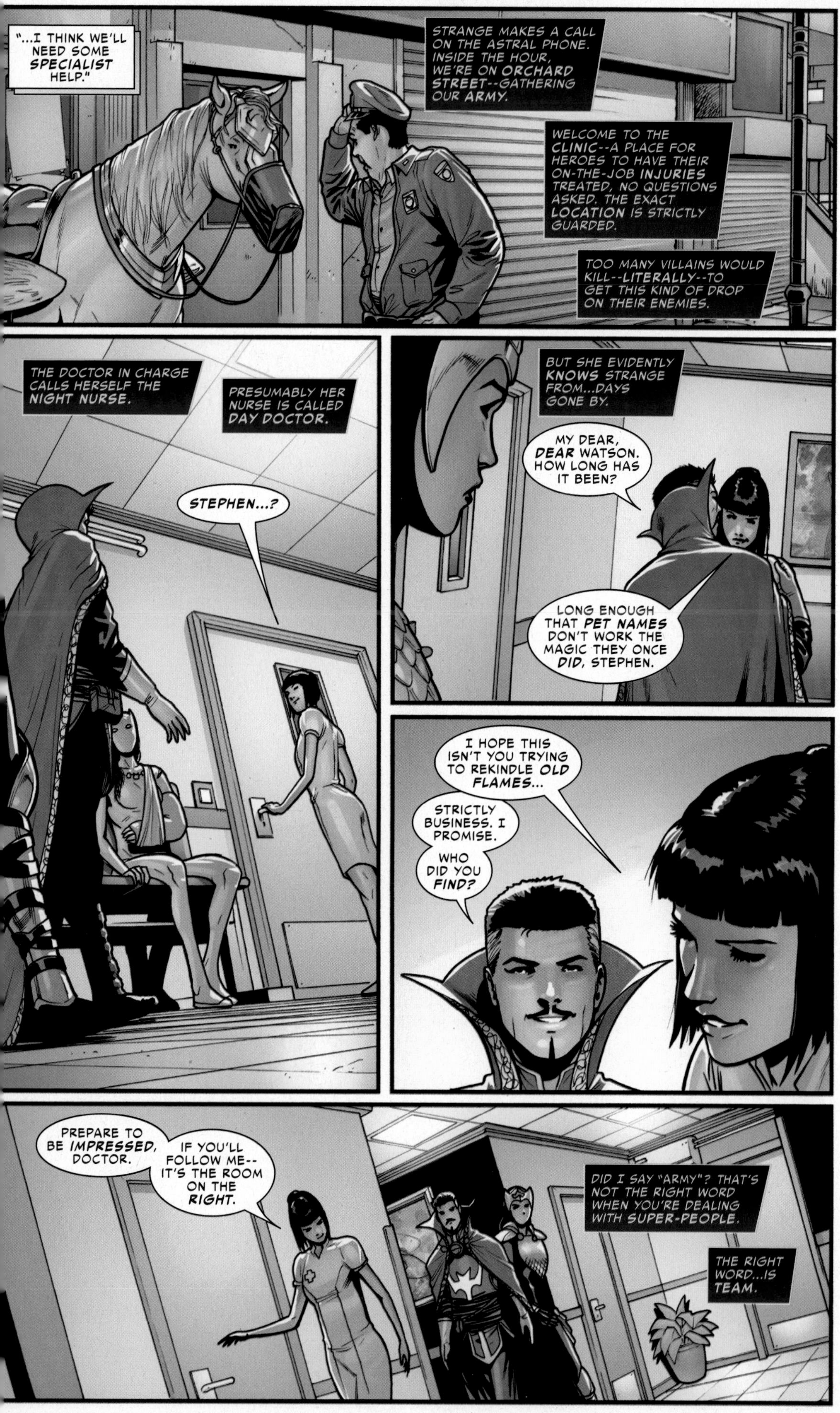
"...I THINK WE'LL NEED SOME SPECIALIST HELP."
STRANGE MAKES A CALL ON THE ASTRAL PHONE. INSIDE THE HOUR, WE'RE ON ORCHARD STREET--GATHERING OUR ARMY.
WELCOME TO THE CLINIC--A PLACE FOR HEROES TO HAVE THEIR ON-THE-JOB INJURIES TREATED, NO QUESTIONS ASKED. THE EXACT LOCATION IS STRICTLY GUARDED.
TOO MANY VILLAINS WOULD KILL--LITERALLY--TO GET THIS KIND OF DROP ON THEIR ENEMIES.
THE DOCTOR IN CHARGE CALLS HERSELF THE NIGHT NURSE.
PRESUMABLY HER NURSE IS CALLED DAY DOCTOR.
STEPHEN...?
BUT SHE EVIDENTLY KNOWS STRANGE FROM...DAYS GONE BY.
MY DEAR, DEAR WATSON. HOW LONG HAS IT BEEN?
LONG ENOUGH THAT PET NAMES DON'T WORK THE MAGIC THEY ONCE DID, STEPHEN.
I HOPE THIS ISN'T YOU TRYING TO REKINDLE OLD FLAMES...
STRICTLY BUSINESS. I PROMISE.
WHO DID YOU FIND?
PREPARE TO BE IMPRESSED, DOCTOR.
IF YOU'LL FOLLOW ME--IT'S THE ROOM ON THE RIGHT.
DID I SAY "ARMY"? THAT'S NOT THE RIGHT WORD WHEN YOU'RE DEALING WITH SUPER-PEOPLE.
THE RIGHT WORD...IS TEAM.

A MEDICAL TEAM.

SOUND OFF, EVERYBODY...

PERSEVERANCE
THE JOURNEY OF A MILLION MILES BEGINS WITH A SINGLE STEP

CARDIAC.

I STRIKE AT EVIL'S HEART.

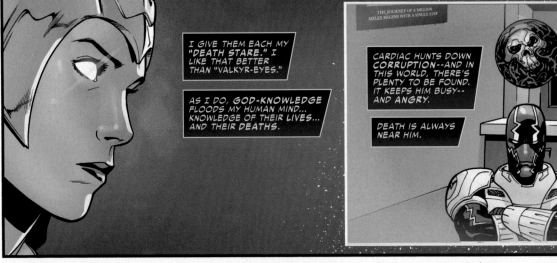

I GIVE THEM EACH MY "DEATH STARE." I LIKE THAT BETTER THAN "VALKYR-EYES."

AS I DO, GOD-KNOWLEDGE FLOODS MY HUMAN MIND... KNOWLEDGE OF THEIR LIVES... AND THEIR DEATHS.

THE JOURNEY OF A MILLION MILES BEGINS WITH A SINGLE STEP

CARDIAC HUNTS DOWN CORRUPTION--AND IN THIS WORLD, THERE'S PLENTY TO BE FOUND. IT KEEPS HIM BUSY-- AND ANGRY.

DEATH IS ALWAYS NEAR HIM.

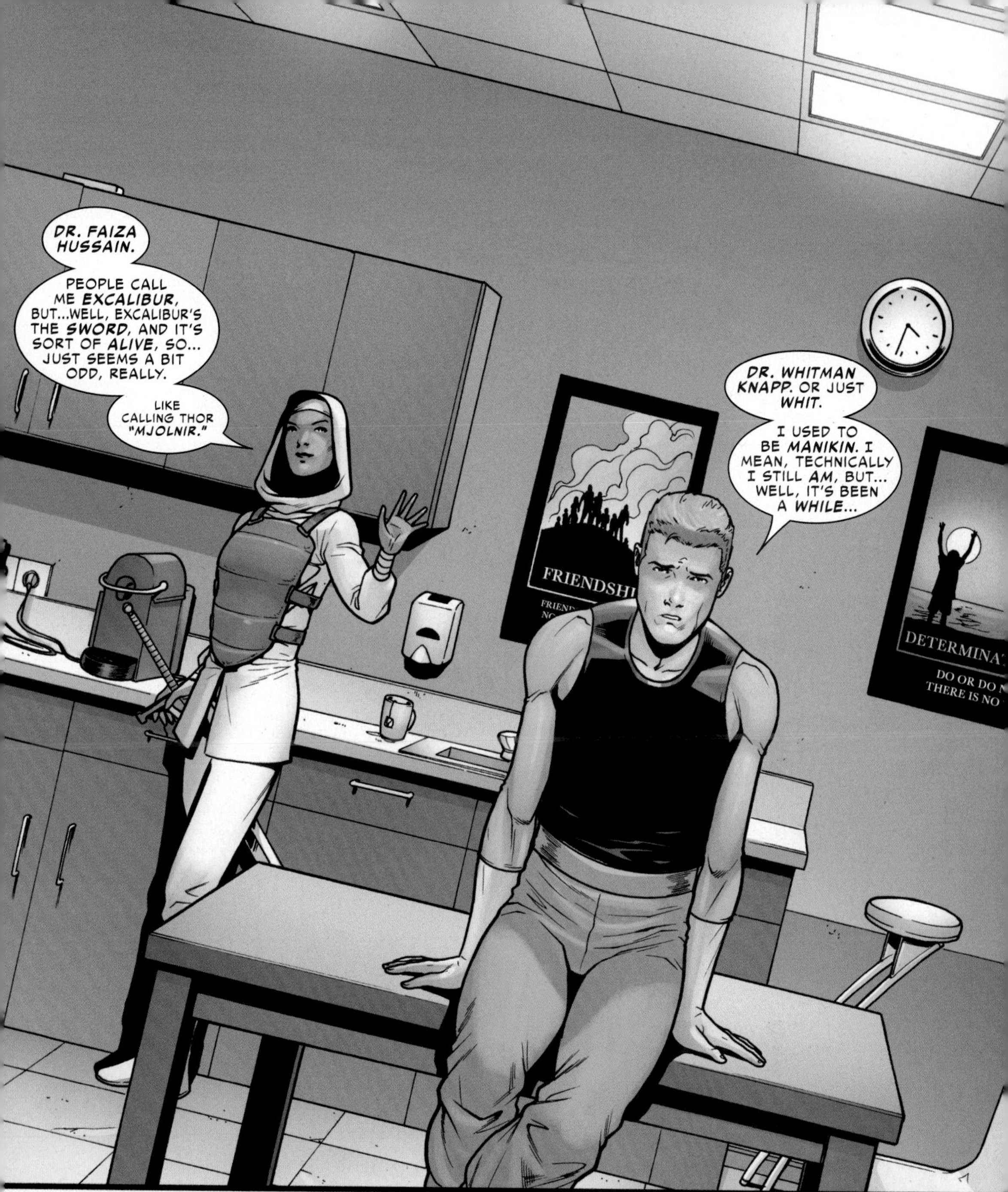
DR. FAIZA HUSSAIN.
PEOPLE CALL ME EXCALIBUR, BUT...WELL, EXCALIBUR'S THE SWORD, AND IT'S SORT OF ALIVE, SO... JUST SEEMS A BIT ODD, REALLY.
LIKE CALLING THOR "MJOLNIR."
DR. WHITMAN KNAPP. OR JUST WHIT.
I USED TO BE MANIKIN. I MEAN, TECHNICALLY I STILL AM, BUT... WELL, IT'S BEEN A WHILE...
FRIENDSHI
DETERMINA
DO OR DO N
THERE IS NO

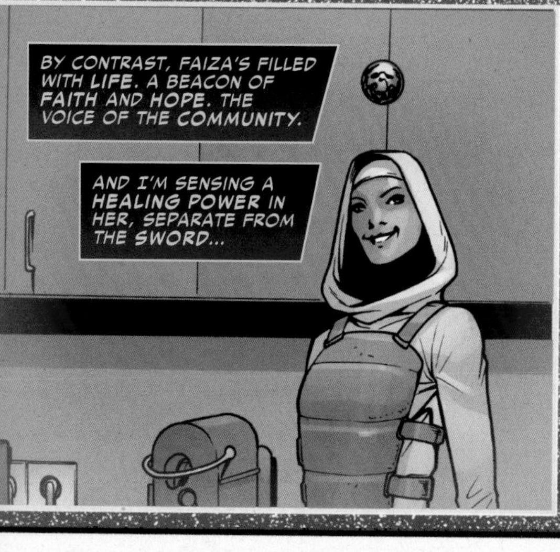
BY CONTRAST, FAIZA'S FILLED WITH LIFE. A BEACON OF FAITH AND HOPE. THE VOICE OF THE COMMUNITY.
AND I'M SENSING A HEALING POWER IN HER, SEPARATE FROM THE SWORD...

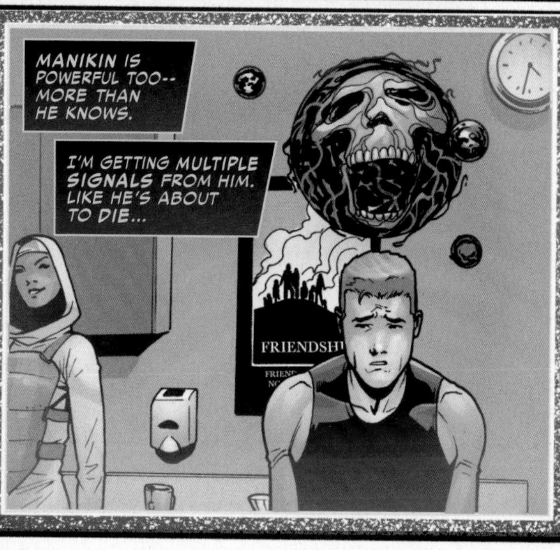
MANIKIN IS POWERFUL TOO-- MORE THAN HE KNOWS.
I'M GETTING MULTIPLE SIGNALS FROM HIM. LIKE HE'S ABOUT TO DIE...
FRIENDSHI

...AND ABOUT TO LIVE.

THE *TRUE EXCALIBUR*. IT'S BEEN MANY YEARS SINCE I LAST BEHELD THIS TREASURE.

THE SWORD THAT HEALS...

DON'T BE RIDICULOUS. HOW CAN A SWORD *HEAL?*

I SHOULD FIND OUT MORE...

HOW MUCH WERE YOU *TOLD* ABOUT THIS MISSION, WHIT?

YOU AND *STRANGE* NEED A TEAM OF DOCTORS TO DIAGNOSE *DEATH* AND STOP THE UNIVERSE FROM *BREAKING.*

DON'T WORRY ABOUT *ME.* I HANDLED *WEIRDER* STUFF WHEN I WAS IN *ALPHA FLIGHT.*

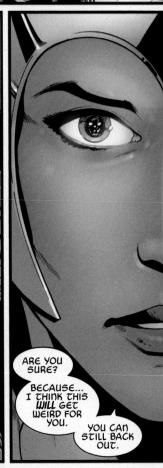

ARE YOU SURE?

BECAUSE... I THINK THIS *WILL* GET WEIRD FOR YOU.

YOU CAN STILL BACK OUT.

...

NO, I DON'T THINK I CAN. NIGHT NURSE SAID YOU NEEDED A *DOCTOR*--THAT'S WHAT I AM.

AND I'VE NEVER TURNED A PATIENT AWAY YET.

IF NONE OF US ARE SITTING THIS ONE OUT--LET'S GET MOVING.

I ASSUME YOU'RE OUR *TRANSPORT,* STRANGE--

I AM INDEED. *BRACE* YOURSELVES...

...FOR THE WAY IS *DARK.*

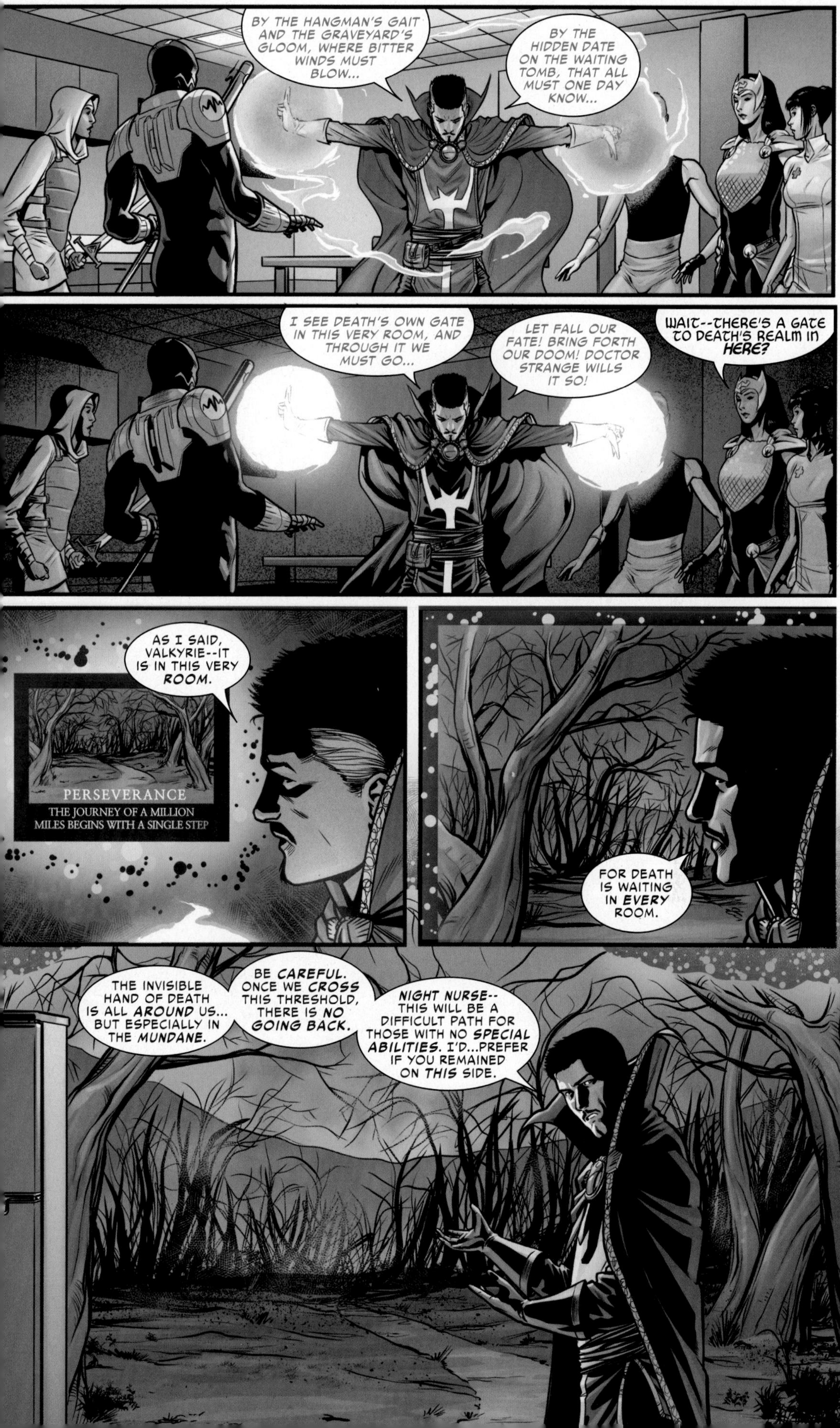

BY THE HANGMAN'S GAIT AND THE GRAVEYARD'S GLOOM, WHERE BITTER WINDS MUST BLOW...
BY THE HIDDEN DATE ON THE WAITING TOMB, THAT ALL MUST ONE DAY KNOW...
I SEE DEATH'S OWN GATE IN THIS VERY ROOM, AND THROUGH IT WE MUST GO...
LET FALL OUR FATE! BRING FORTH OUR DOOM! DOCTOR STRANGE WILLS IT SO!
WAIT--THERE'S A GATE TO DEATH'S REALM IN HERE?
AS I SAID, VALKYRIE--IT IS IN THIS VERY ROOM.
PERSEVERANCE
THE JOURNEY OF A MILLION MILES BEGINS WITH A SINGLE STEP
FOR DEATH IS WAITING IN EVERY ROOM.
THE INVISIBLE HAND OF DEATH IS ALL AROUND US... BUT ESPECIALLY IN THE MUNDANE.
BE CAREFUL. ONCE WE CROSS THIS THRESHOLD, THERE IS NO GOING BACK.
NIGHT NURSE-- THIS WILL BE A DIFFICULT PATH FOR THOSE WITH NO SPECIAL ABILITIES. I'D...PREFER IF YOU REMAINED ON THIS SIDE.

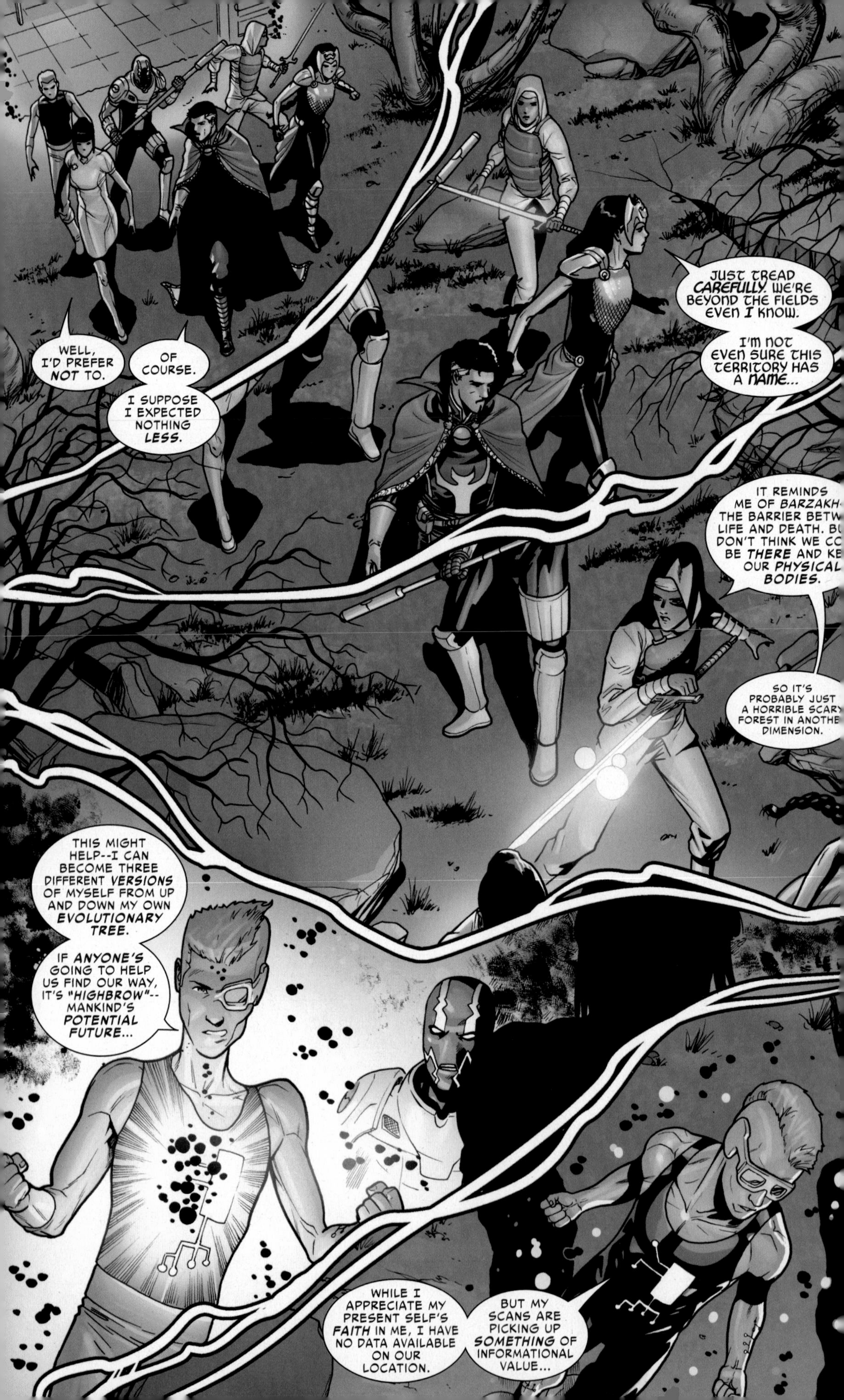
WELL, I'D PREFER NOT TO.
OF COURSE.
I SUPPOSE I EXPECTED NOTHING LESS.
JUST TREAD CAREFULLY. WE'RE BEYOND THE FIELDS EVEN I KNOW.
I'M NOT EVEN SURE THIS TERRITORY HAS A NAME...
IT REMINDS ME OF BARZAKH-- THE BARRIER BETW LIFE AND DEATH. BU DON'T THINK WE CO BE THERE AND KE OUR PHYSICAL BODIES.
SO IT'S PROBABLY JUST A HORRIBLE SCARY FOREST IN ANOTHE DIMENSION.
THIS MIGHT HELP--I CAN BECOME THREE DIFFERENT VERSIONS OF MYSELF FROM UP AND DOWN MY OWN EVOLUTIONARY TREE.
IF ANYONE'S GOING TO HELP US FIND OUR WAY, IT'S "HIGHBROW"-- MANKIND'S POTENTIAL FUTURE...
WHILE I APPRECIATE MY PRESENT SELF'S FAITH IN ME, I HAVE NO DATA AVAILABLE ON OUR LOCATION.
BUT MY SCANS ARE PICKING UP SOMETHING OF INFORMATIONAL VALUE...

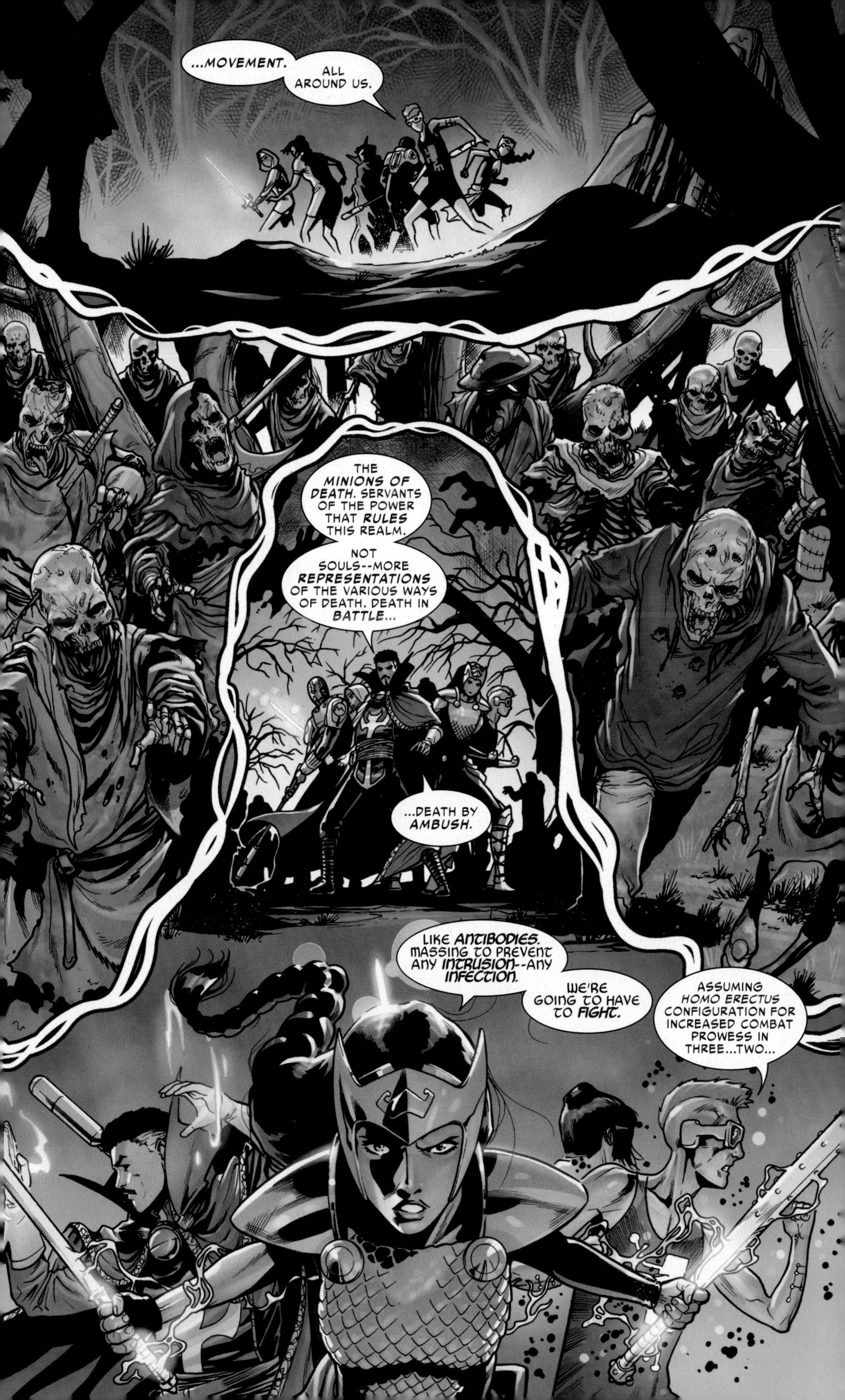
...MOVEMENT.
ALL AROUND US.
THE MINIONS OF DEATH. SERVANTS OF THE POWER THAT RULES THIS REALM.
NOT SOULS--MORE REPRESENTATIONS OF THE VARIOUS WAYS OF DEATH. DEATH IN BATTLE...
...DEATH BY AMBUSH.
LIKE ANTIBODIES. MASSING TO PREVENT ANY INTRUSION--ANY INFECTION.
WE'RE GOING TO HAVE TO FIGHT.
ASSUMING HOMO ERECTUS CONFIGURATION FOR INCREASED COMBAT PROWESS IN THREE...TWO...

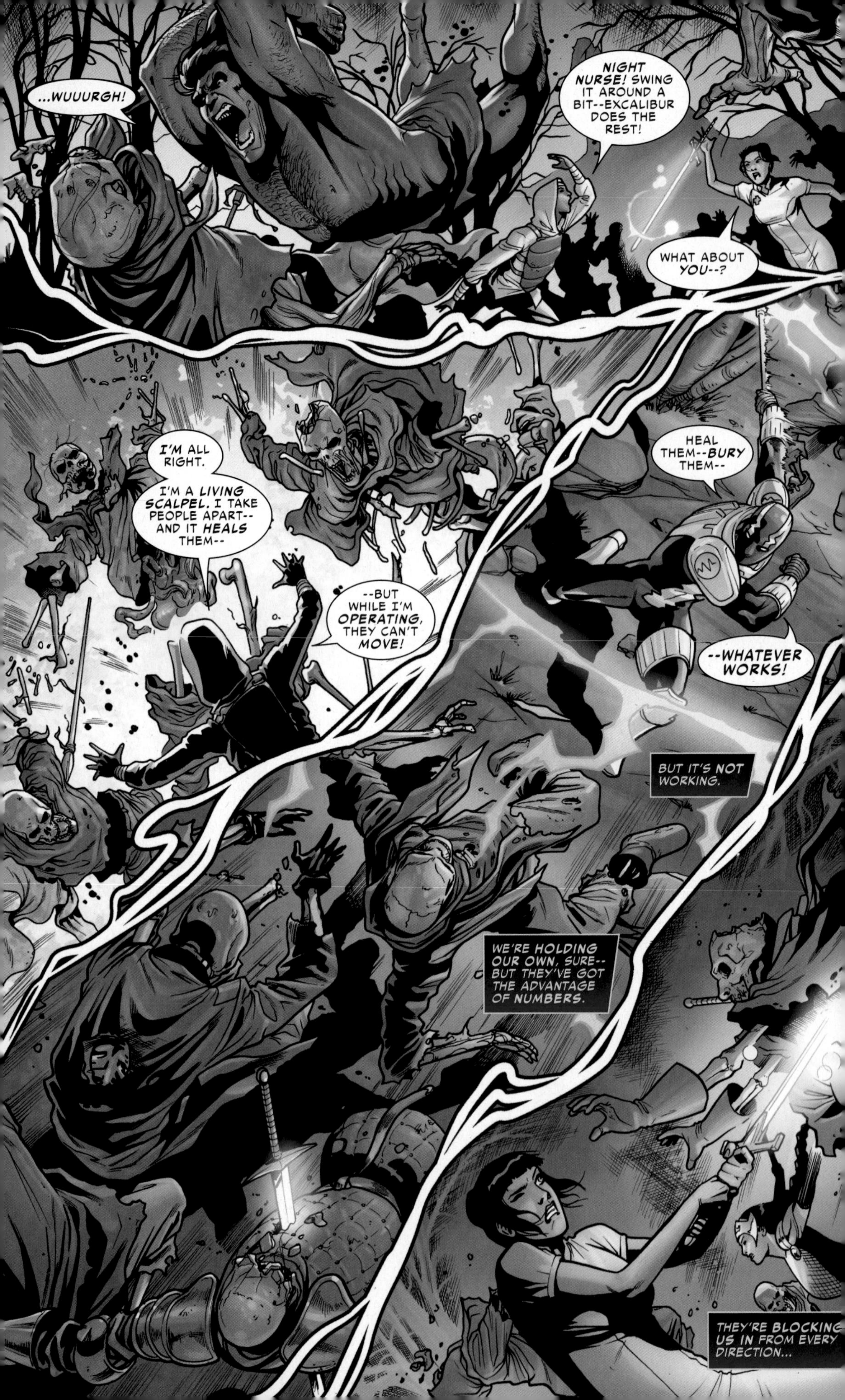
...WUUURGH!
NIGHT NURSE! SWING IT AROUND A BIT--EXCALIBUR DOES THE REST!
WHAT ABOUT YOU--?
I'M ALL RIGHT.
I'M A LIVING SCALPEL. I TAKE PEOPLE APART-- AND IT HEALS THEM--
--BUT WHILE I'M OPERATING, THEY CAN'T MOVE!
HEAL THEM--BURY THEM--
--WHATEVER WORKS!
BUT IT'S NOT WORKING.
WE'RE HOLDING OUR OWN, SURE-- BUT THEY'VE GOT THE ADVANTAGE OF NUMBERS.
THEY'RE BLOCKING US IN FROM EVERY DIRECTION...

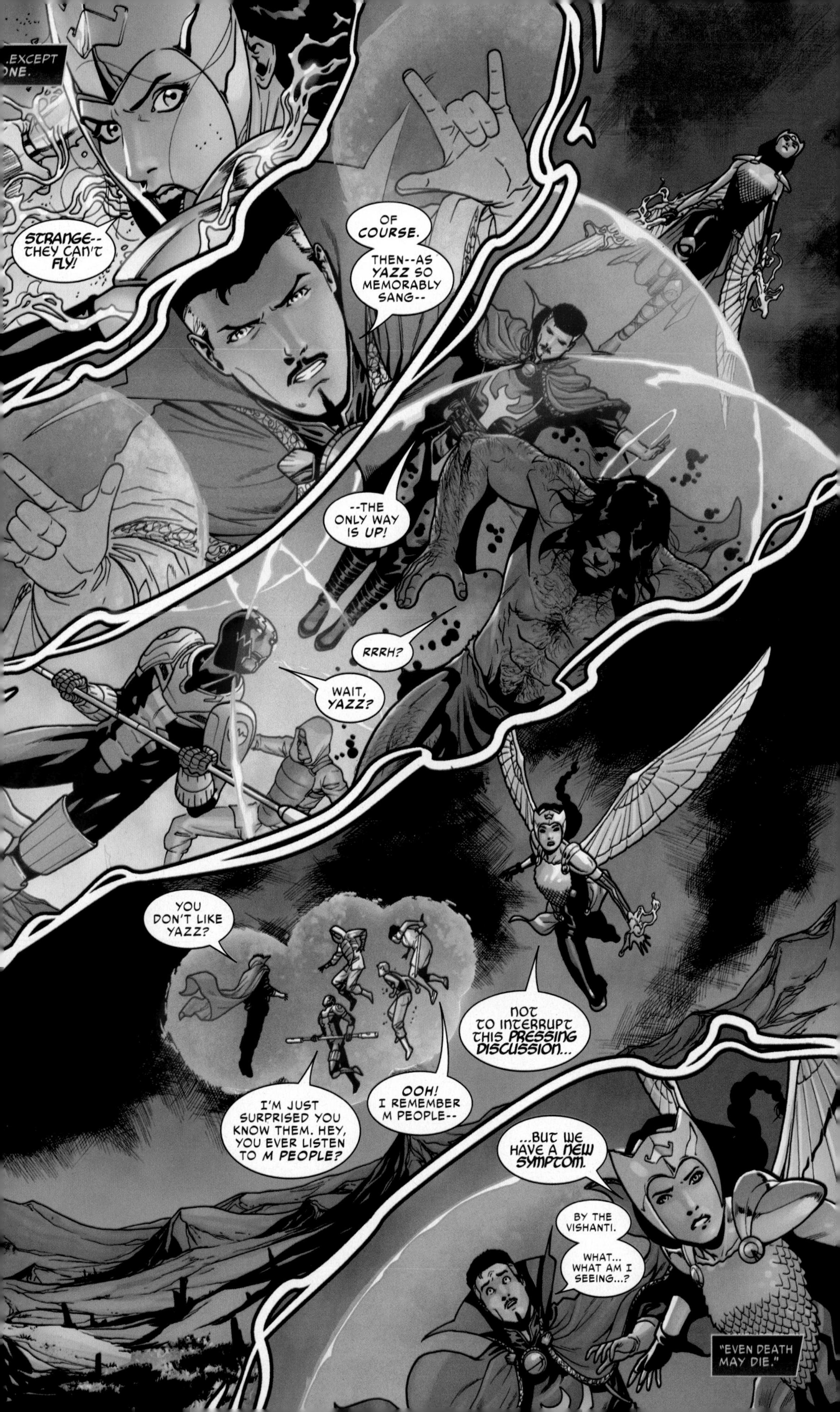

...EXCEPT ONE.
STRANGE--THEY CAN'T FLY!
OF COURSE.
THEN--AS YAZZ SO MEMORABLY SANG--
--THE ONLY WAY IS UP!
RRRH?
WAIT, YAZZ?
YOU DON'T LIKE YAZZ?
I'M JUST SURPRISED YOU KNOW THEM. HEY, YOU EVER LISTEN TO M PEOPLE?
OOH! I REMEMBER M PEOPLE--
NOT TO INTERRUPT THIS PRESSING DISCUSSION...
...BUT WE HAVE A NEW SYMPTOM.
BY THE VISHANTI.
WHAT... WHAT AM I SEEING...?
"EVEN DEATH MAY DIE."

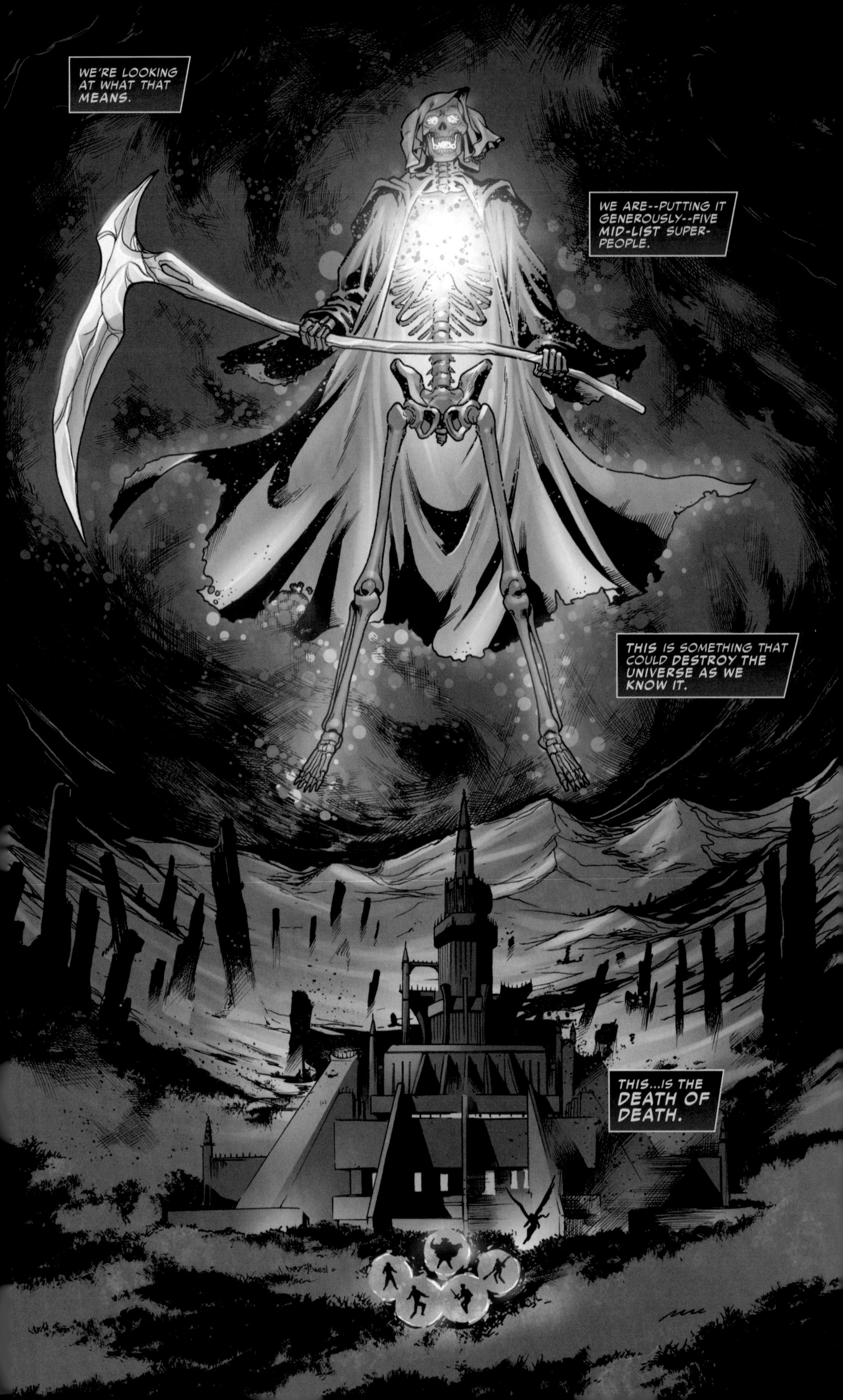
WE'RE LOOKING AT WHAT THAT MEANS.
WE ARE--PUTTING IT GENEROUSLY--FIVE MID-LIST SUPER-PEOPLE.
THIS IS SOMETHING THAT COULD DESTROY THE UNIVERSE AS WE KNOW IT.
THIS...IS THE DEATH OF DEATH.

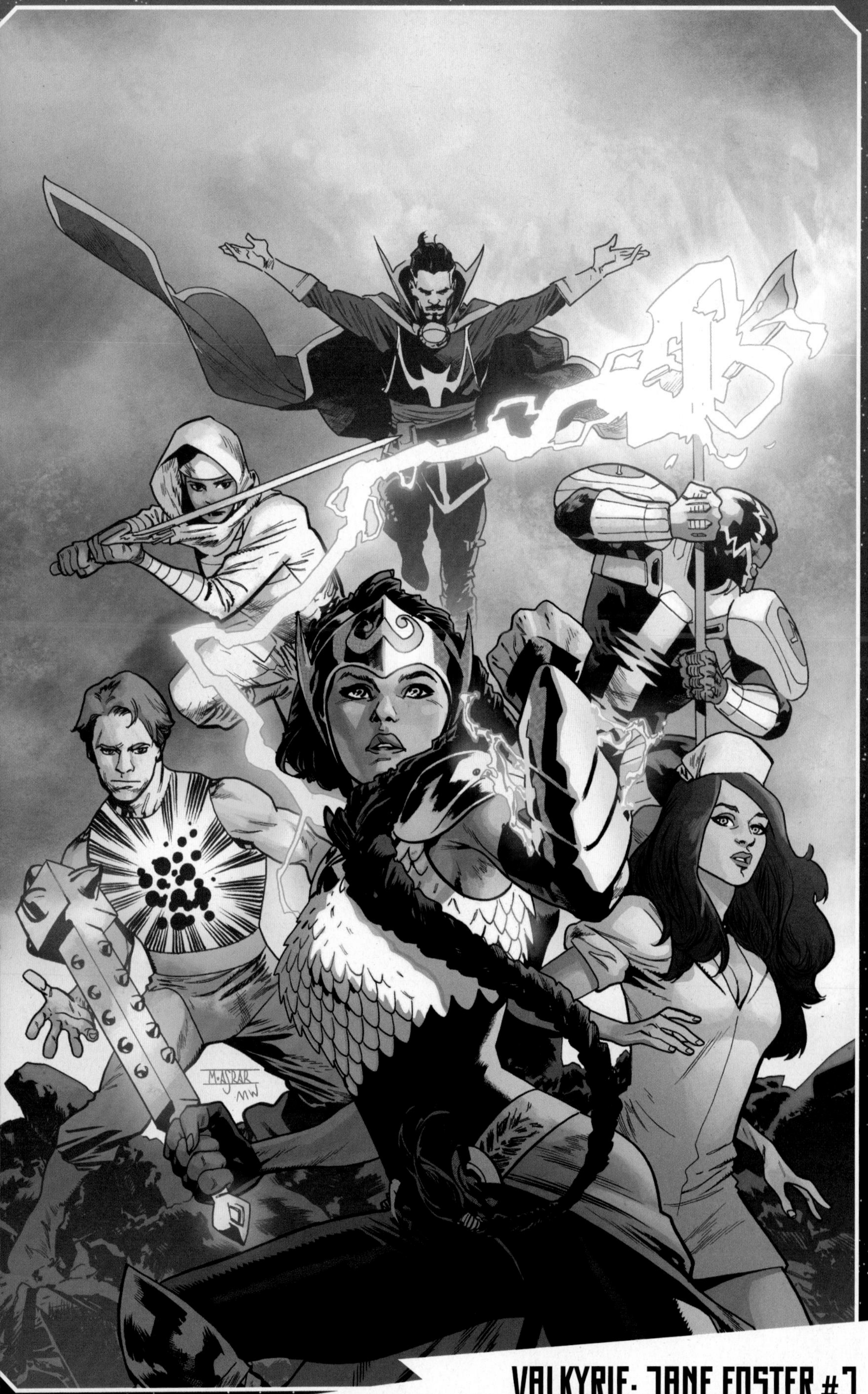
M.ASRAR
MW

VALKYRIE: JANE FOSTER #7

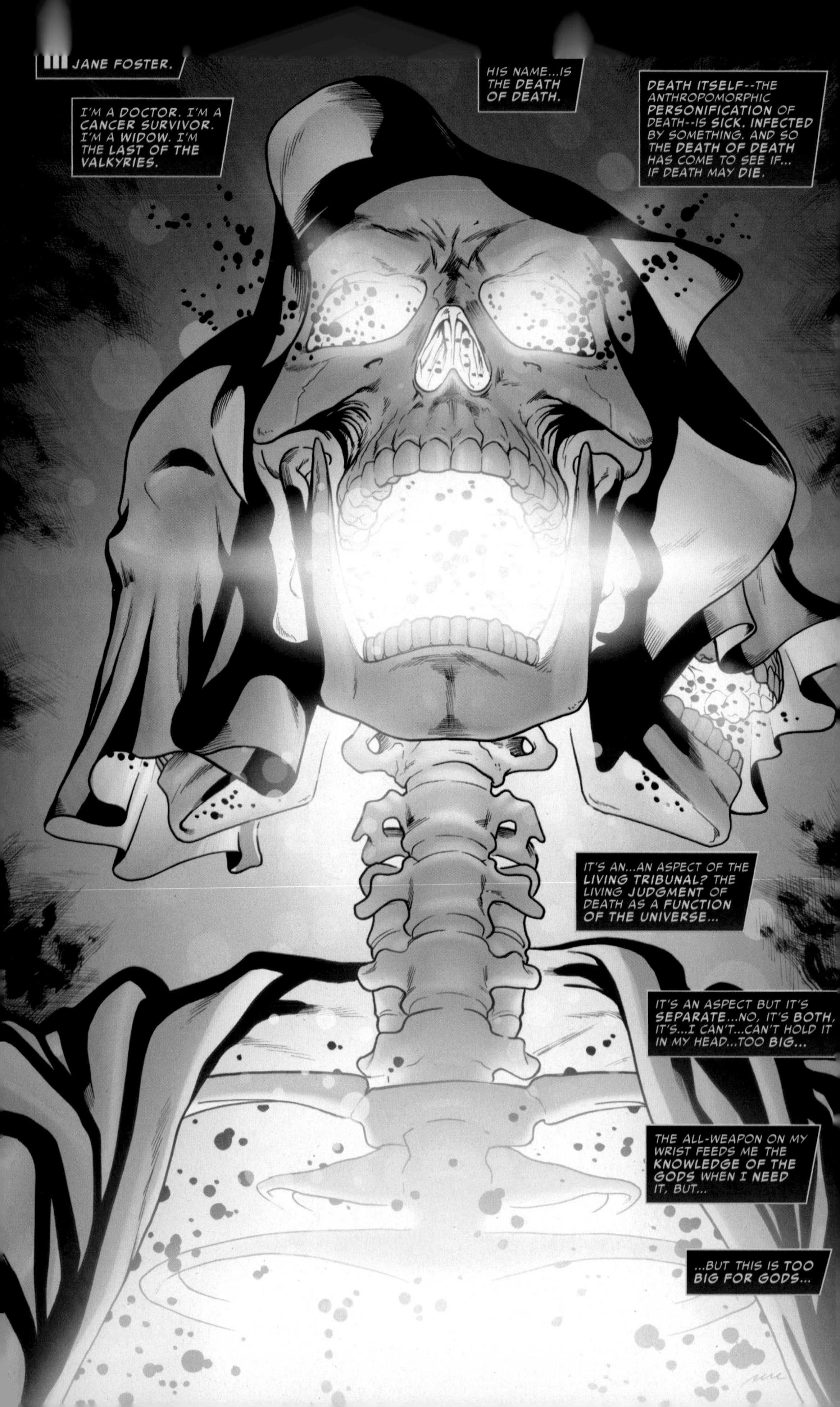
JANE FOSTER.
I'M A DOCTOR. I'M A CANCER SURVIVOR. I'M A WIDOW. I'M THE LAST OF THE VALKYRIES.
HIS NAME...IS THE DEATH OF DEATH.
DEATH ITSELF--THE ANTHROPOMORPHIC PERSONIFICATION OF DEATH--IS SICK. INFECTED BY SOMETHING. AND SO THE DEATH OF DEATH HAS COME TO SEE IF... IF DEATH MAY DIE.
IT'S AN...AN ASPECT OF THE LIVING TRIBUNAL? THE LIVING JUDGMENT OF DEATH AS A FUNCTION OF THE UNIVERSE...
IT'S AN ASPECT BUT IT'S SEPARATE...NO, IT'S BOTH, IT'S...I CAN'T...CAN'T HOLD IT IN MY HEAD...TOO BIG...
THE ALL-WEAPON ON MY WRIST FEEDS ME THE KNOWLEDGE OF THE GODS WHEN I NEED IT, BUT...
...BUT THIS IS TOO BIG FOR GODS...

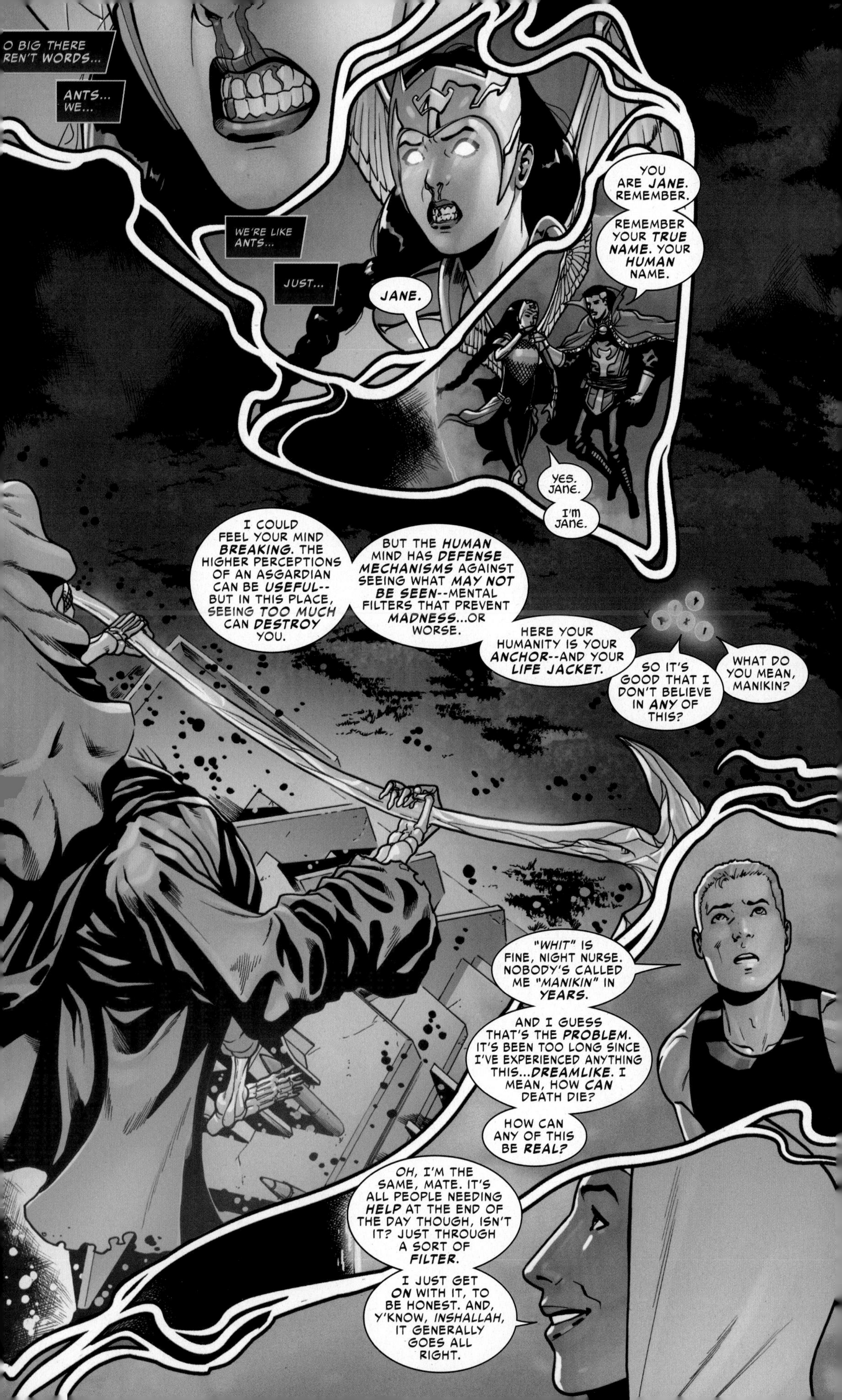

O BIG THERE
REN'T WORDS...
ANTS...
WE...
WE'RE LIKE ANTS...
JUST...
JANE.
YOU ARE JANE. REMEMBER.
REMEMBER YOUR TRUE NAME. YOUR HUMAN NAME.
YES. JANE.
I'M JANE.
I COULD FEEL YOUR MIND BREAKING. THE HIGHER PERCEPTIONS OF AN ASGARDIAN CAN BE USEFUL--BUT IN THIS PLACE, SEEING TOO MUCH CAN DESTROY YOU.
BUT THE HUMAN MIND HAS DEFENSE MECHANISMS AGAINST SEEING WHAT MAY NOT BE SEEN--MENTAL FILTERS THAT PREVENT MADNESS...OR WORSE.
HERE YOUR HUMANITY IS YOUR ANCHOR--AND YOUR LIFE JACKET.
SO IT'S GOOD THAT I DON'T BELIEVE IN ANY OF THIS?
WHAT DO YOU MEAN, MANIKIN?
"WHIT" IS FINE, NIGHT NURSE. NOBODY'S CALLED ME "MANIKIN" IN YEARS.
AND I GUESS THAT'S THE PROBLEM. IT'S BEEN TOO LONG SINCE I'VE EXPERIENCED ANYTHING THIS...DREAMLIKE. I MEAN, HOW CAN DEATH DIE?
HOW CAN ANY OF THIS BE REAL?
OH, I'M THE SAME, MATE. IT'S ALL PEOPLE NEEDING HELP AT THE END OF THE DAY THOUGH, ISN'T IT? JUST THROUGH A SORT OF FILTER.
I JUST GET ON WITH IT, TO BE HONEST. AND, Y'KNOW, INSHALLAH, IT GENERALLY GOES ALL RIGHT.

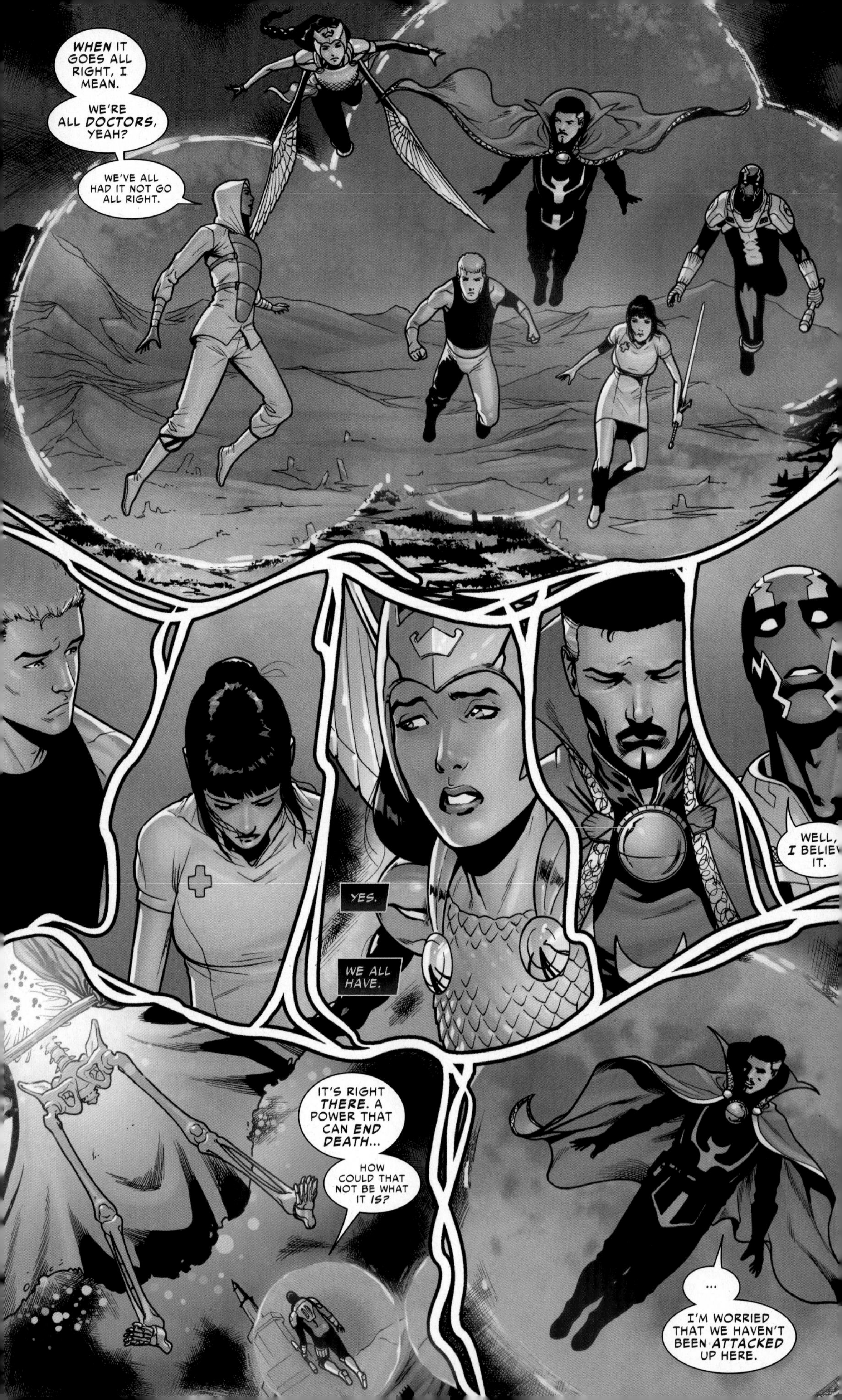
WHEN IT GOES ALL RIGHT, I MEAN.
WE'RE ALL DOCTORS, YEAH?
WE'VE ALL HAD IT NOT GO ALL RIGHT.
YES.
WE ALL HAVE.
WELL, I BELIE IT.
IT'S RIGHT THERE. A POWER THAT CAN END DEATH...
HOW COULD THAT NOT BE WHAT IT IS?
...
I'M WORRIED THAT WE HAVEN'T BEEN ATTACKED UP HERE.

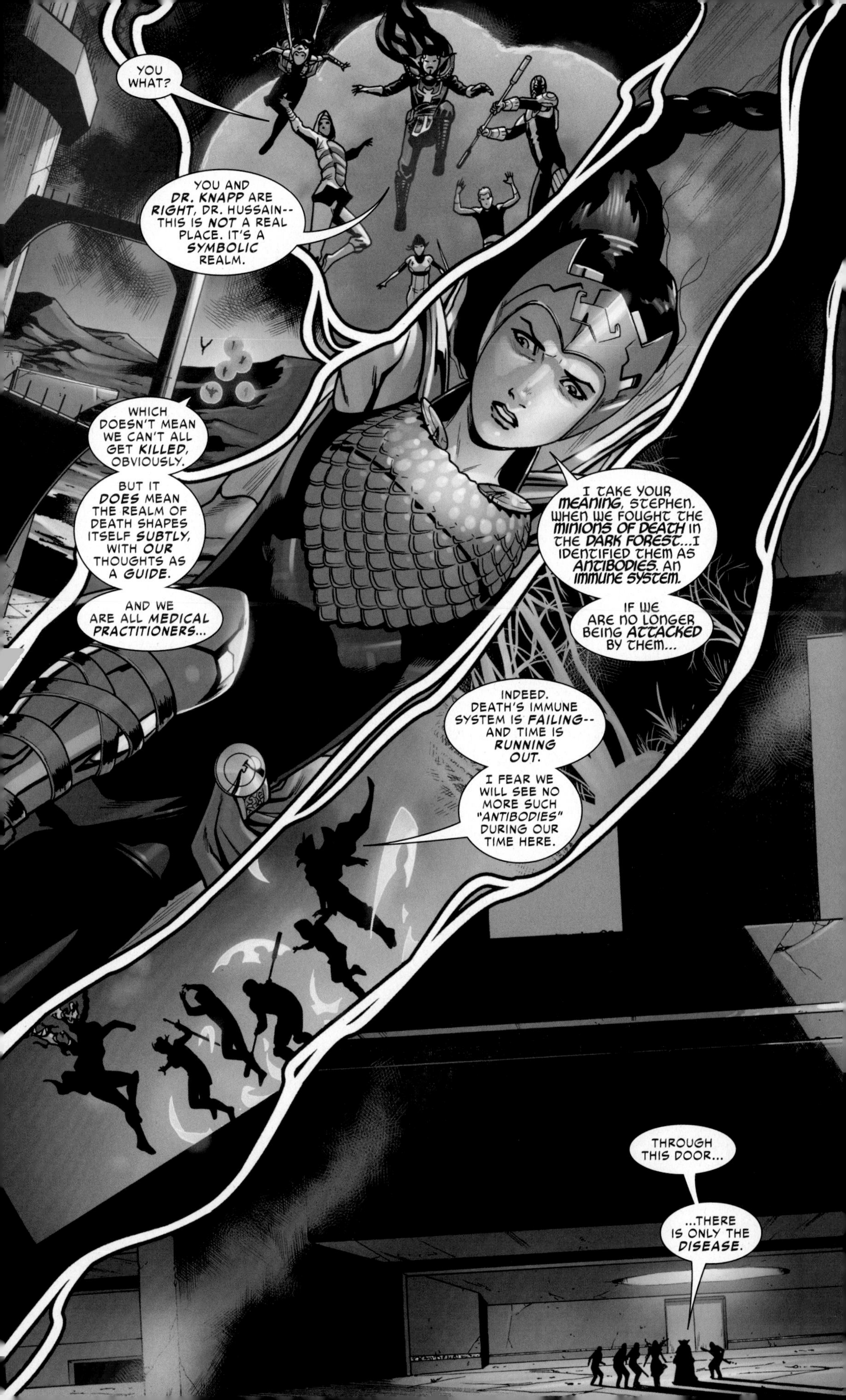
YOU WHAT?
YOU AND DR. KNAPP ARE RIGHT, DR. HUSSAIN-- THIS IS NOT A REAL PLACE. IT'S A SYMBOLIC REALM.
WHICH DOESN'T MEAN WE CAN'T ALL GET KILLED, OBVIOUSLY.
BUT IT DOES MEAN THE REALM OF DEATH SHAPES ITSELF SUBTLY, WITH OUR THOUGHTS AS A GUIDE.
AND WE ARE ALL MEDICAL PRACTITIONERS...
I TAKE YOUR MEANING, STEPHEN. WHEN WE FOUGHT THE MINIONS OF DEATH IN THE DARK FOREST...I IDENTIFIED THEM AS ANTIBODIES. AN IMMUNE SYSTEM.
IF WE ARE NO LONGER BEING ATTACKED BY THEM...
INDEED. DEATH'S IMMUNE SYSTEM IS FAILING-- AND TIME IS RUNNING OUT.
I FEAR WE WILL SEE NO MORE SUCH "ANTIBODIES" DURING OUR TIME HERE.
THROUGH THIS DOOR...
...THERE IS ONLY THE DISEASE.

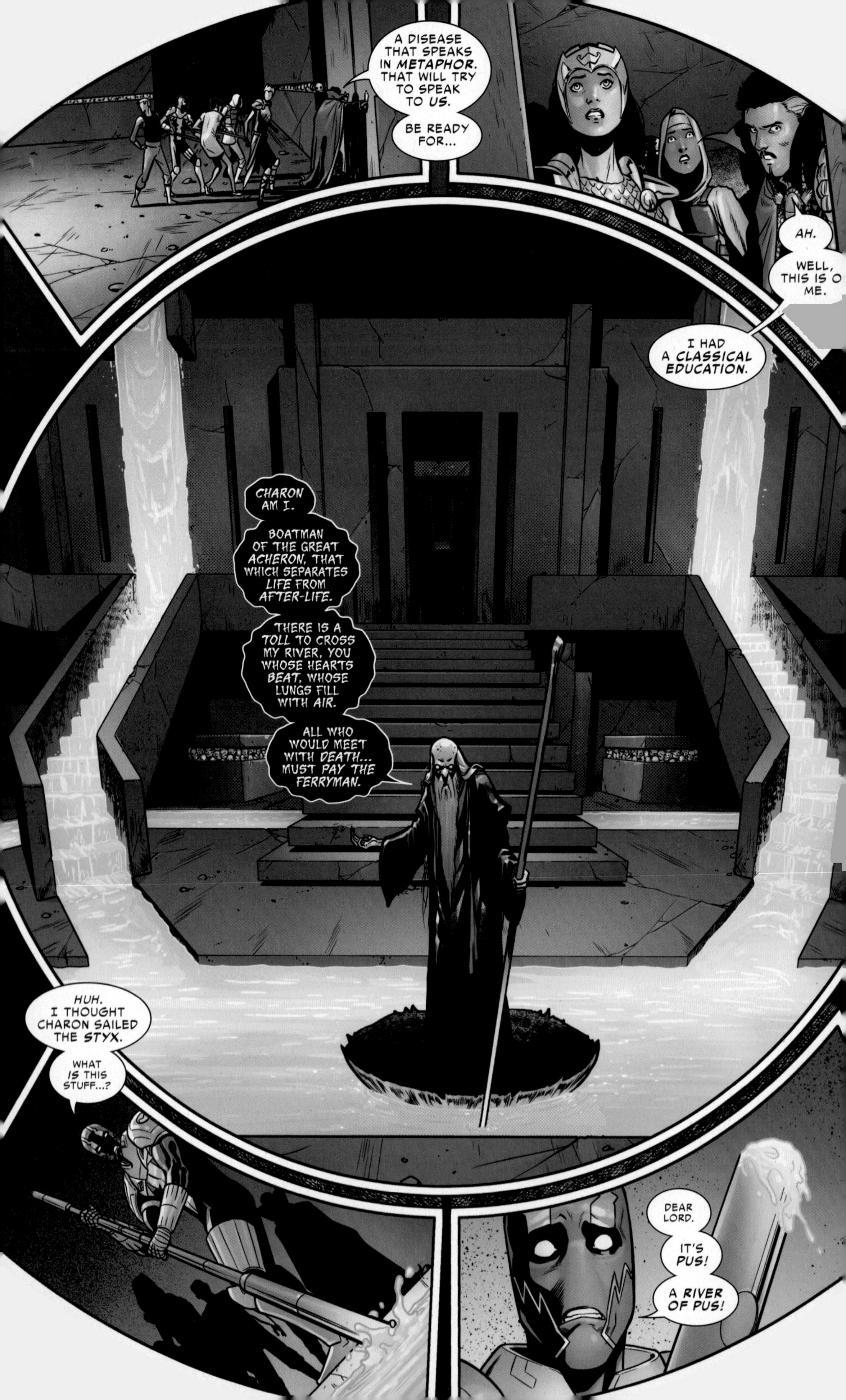
A DISEASE THAT SPEAKS IN *METAPHOR*. THAT WILL TRY TO SPEAK TO *US*.
BE READY FOR...
AH.
WELL, THIS IS O ME.
I HAD A *CLASSICAL* EDUCATION.
CHARON AM I.
BOATMAN OF THE GREAT *ACHERON*, THAT WHICH SEPARATES *LIFE* FROM *AFTER-LIFE*.
THERE IS A TOLL TO CROSS MY RIVER, YOU WHOSE HEARTS *BEAT*, WHOSE LUNGS FILL WITH *AIR*.
ALL WHO WOULD MEET WITH *DEATH*... MUST PAY THE FERRYMAN.
HUH. I THOUGHT CHARON SAILED THE *STYX*.
WHAT *IS* THIS STUFF...?
DEAR LORD.
IT'S *PUS*!
A *RIVER* OF *PUS*!

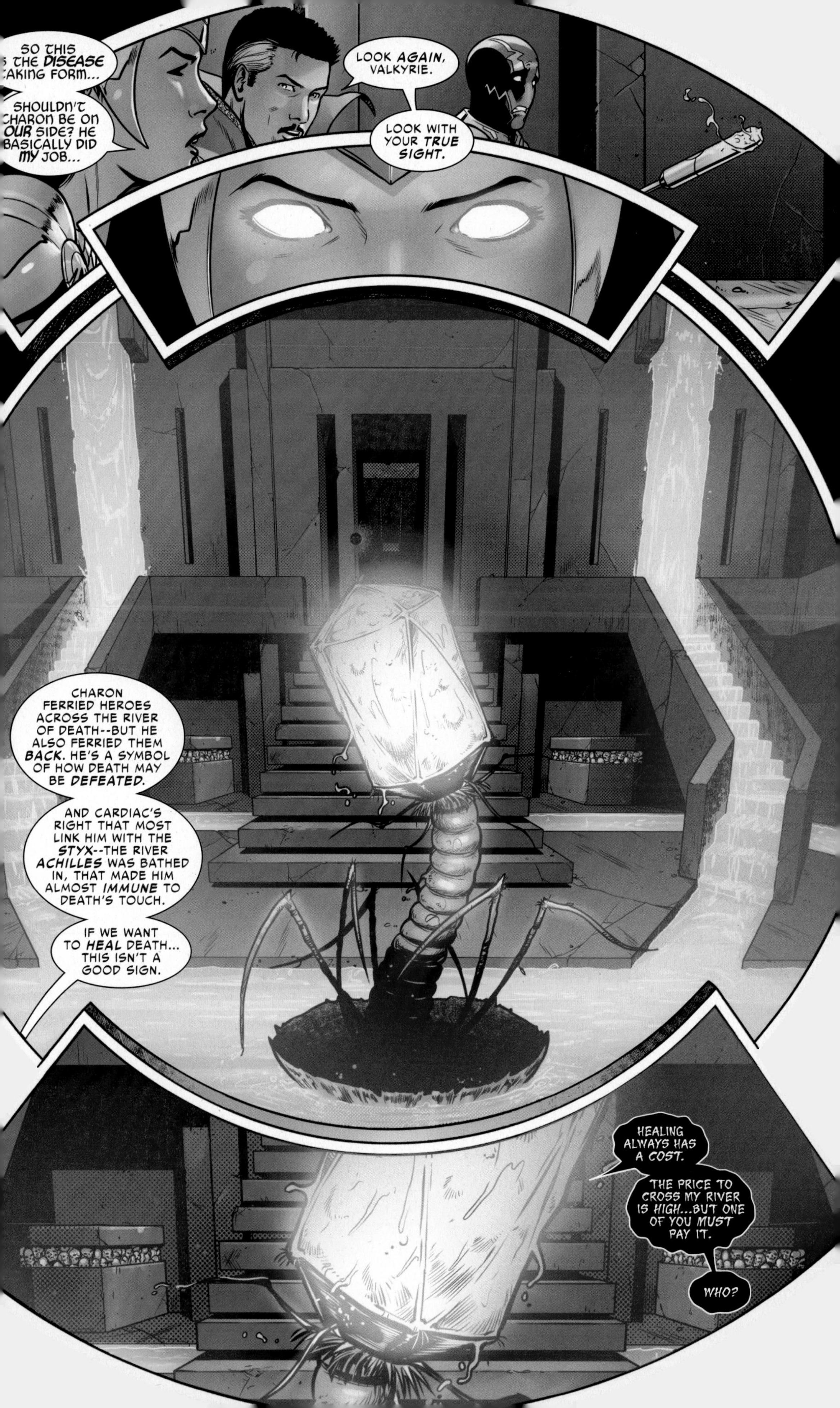

SO THIS IS THE DISEASE TAKING FORM...
SHOULDN'T CHARON BE ON OUR SIDE? HE BASICALLY DID MY JOB...
LOOK AGAIN, VALKYRIE.
LOOK WITH YOUR TRUE SIGHT.
CHARON FERRIED HEROES ACROSS THE RIVER OF DEATH--BUT HE ALSO FERRIED THEM BACK. HE'S A SYMBOL OF HOW DEATH MAY BE DEFEATED.
AND CARDIAC'S RIGHT THAT MOST LINK HIM WITH THE STYX--THE RIVER ACHILLES WAS BATHED IN, THAT MADE HIM ALMOST IMMUNE TO DEATH'S TOUCH.
IF WE WANT TO HEAL DEATH... THIS ISN'T A GOOD SIGN.
HEALING ALWAYS HAS A COST.
THE PRICE TO CROSS MY RIVER IS HIGH...BUT ONE OF YOU MUST PAY IT.
WHO?

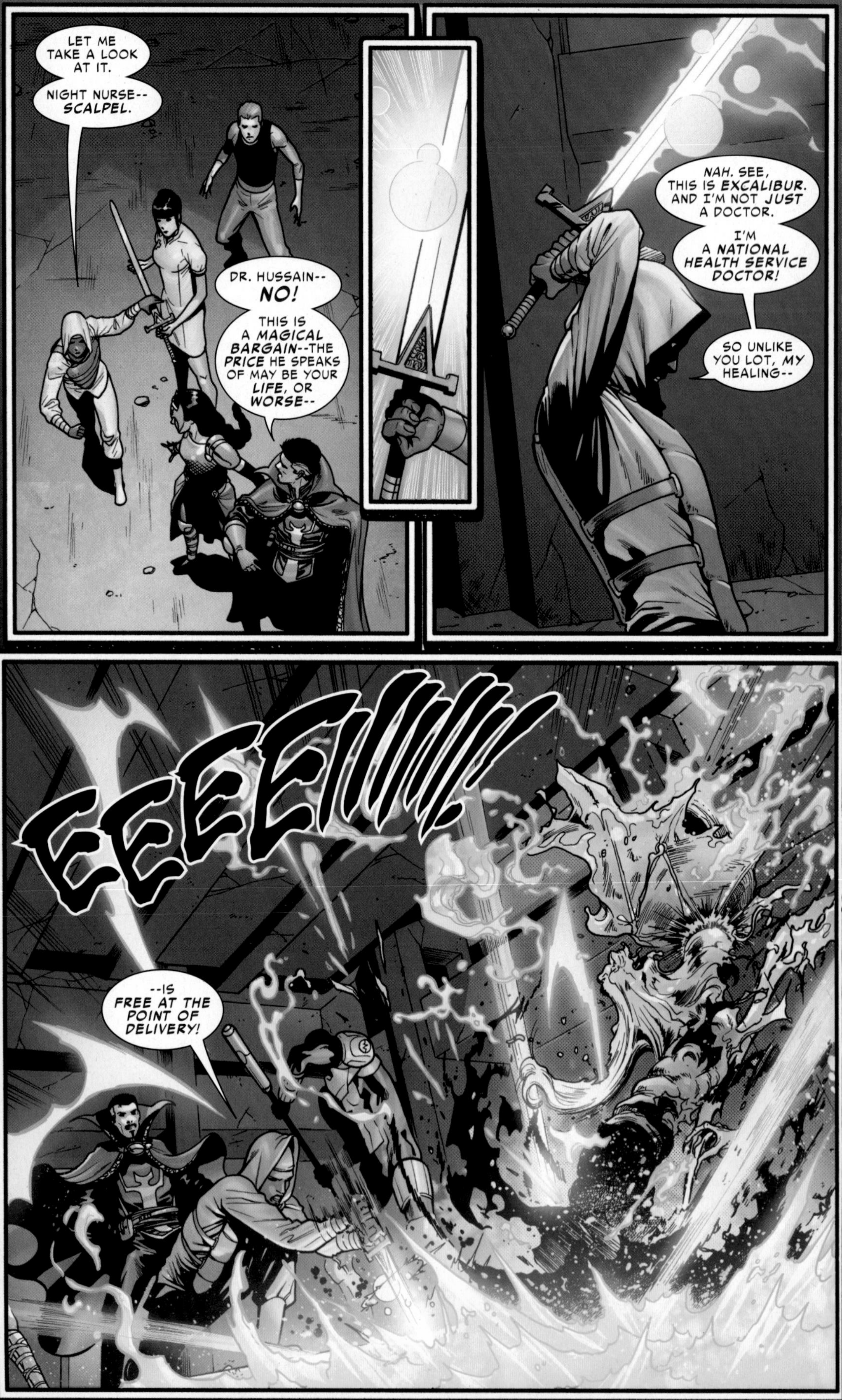

LET ME TAKE A LOOK AT IT.
NIGHT NURSE-- SCALPEL.
DR. HUSSAIN-- NO!
THIS IS A MAGICAL BARGAIN--THE PRICE HE SPEAKS OF MAY BE YOUR LIFE, OR WORSE--
NAH. SEE, THIS IS EXCALIBUR. AND I'M NOT JUST A DOCTOR.
I'M A NATIONAL HEALTH SERVICE DOCTOR!
SO UNLIKE YOU LOT, MY HEALING--
EEEEIIIIIII!
--IS FREE AT THE POINT OF DELIVERY!

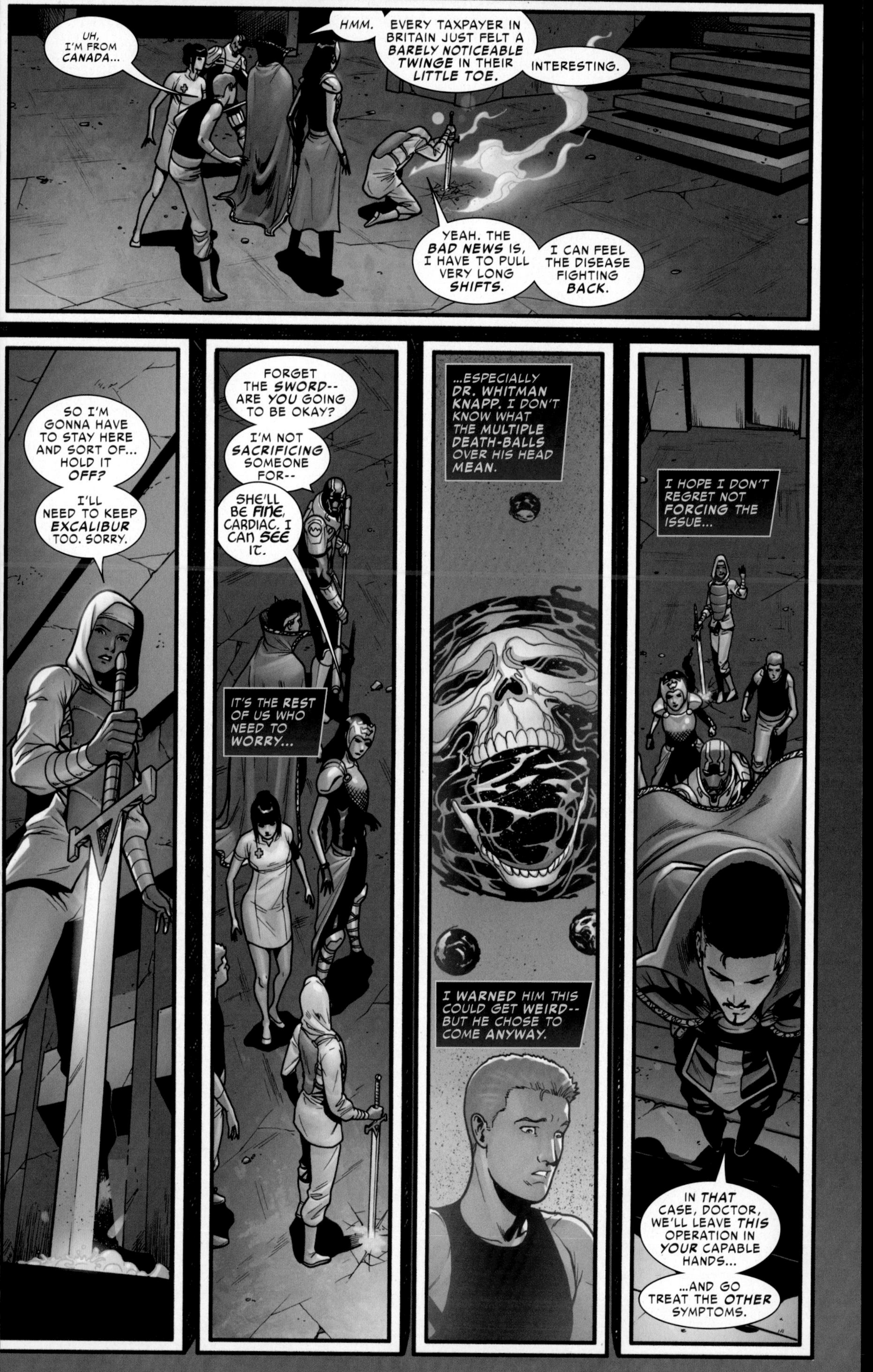
UH, I'M FROM CANADA...
HMM.
EVERY TAXPAYER IN BRITAIN JUST FELT A BARELY NOTICEABLE TWINGE IN THEIR LITTLE TOE.
INTERESTING.
YEAH. THE BAD NEWS IS, I HAVE TO PULL VERY LONG SHIFTS.
I CAN FEEL THE DISEASE FIGHTING BACK.
SO I'M GONNA HAVE TO STAY HERE AND SORT OF... HOLD IT OFF?
I'LL NEED TO KEEP EXCALIBUR TOO. SORRY.
FORGET THE SWORD-- ARE YOU GOING TO BE OKAY?
I'M NOT SACRIFICING SOMEONE FOR--
SHE'LL BE FINE, CARDIAC. I CAN SEE IT.
IT'S THE REST OF US WHO NEED TO WORRY...
...ESPECIALLY DR. WHITMAN KNAPP. I DON'T KNOW WHAT THE MULTIPLE DEATH-BALLS OVER HIS HEAD MEAN.
I WARNED HIM THIS COULD GET WEIRD-- BUT HE CHOSE TO COME ANYWAY.
I HOPE I DON'T REGRET NOT FORCING THE ISSUE...
IN THAT CASE, DOCTOR, WE'LL LEAVE THIS OPERATION IN YOUR CAPABLE HANDS...
...AND GO TREAT THE OTHER SYMPTOMS.

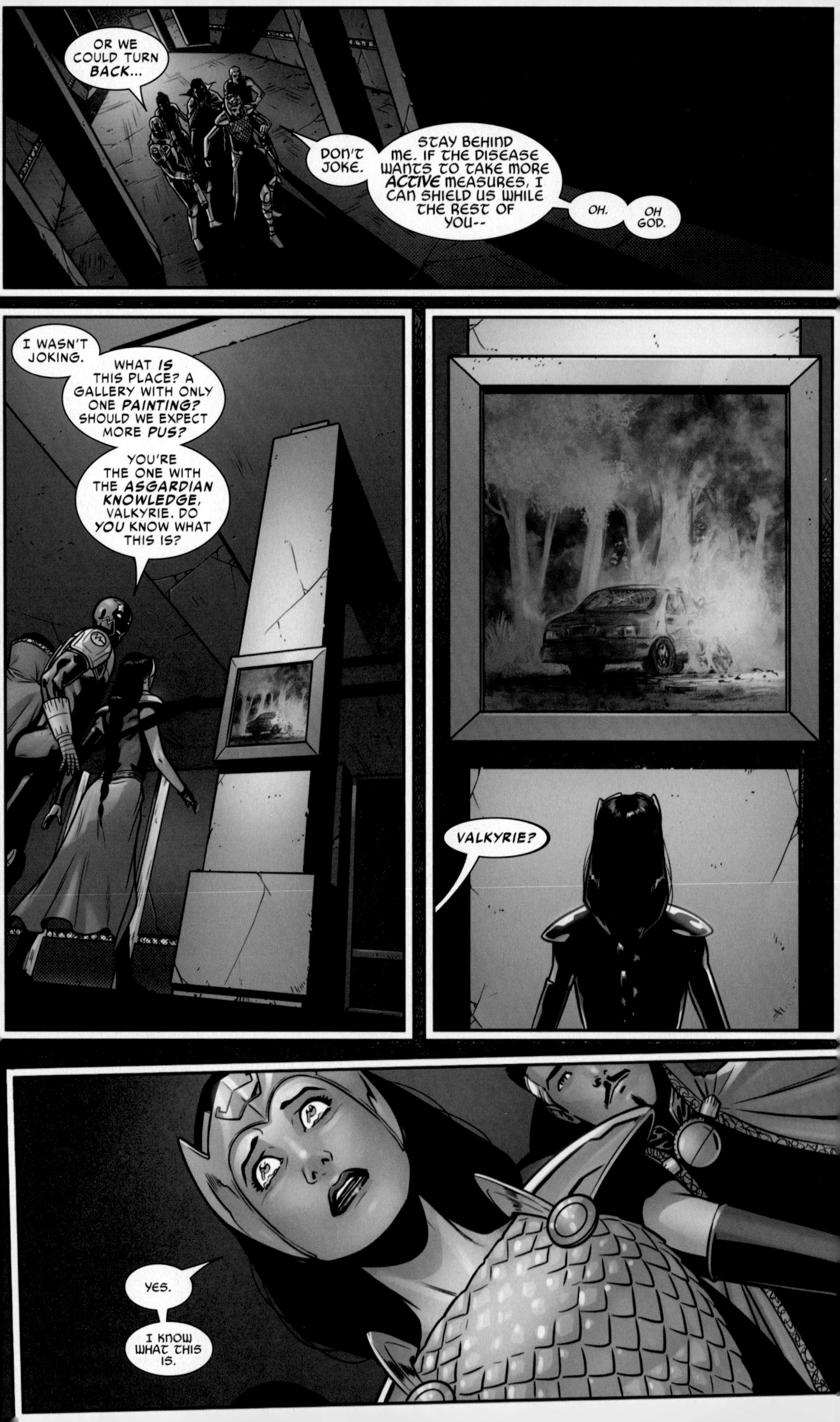

OR WE COULD TURN BACK...
DON'T JOKE.
STAY BEHIND ME. IF THE DISEASE WANTS TO TAKE MORE ACTIVE MEASURES, I CAN SHIELD US WHILE THE REST OF YOU--
OH.
OH GOD.
I WASN'T JOKING.
WHAT IS THIS PLACE? A GALLERY WITH ONLY ONE PAINTING? SHOULD WE EXPECT MORE PUS?
YOU'RE THE ONE WITH THE ASGARDIAN KNOWLEDGE, VALKYRIE. DO YOU KNOW WHAT THIS IS?
VALKYRIE?
YES.
I KNOW WHAT THIS IS.

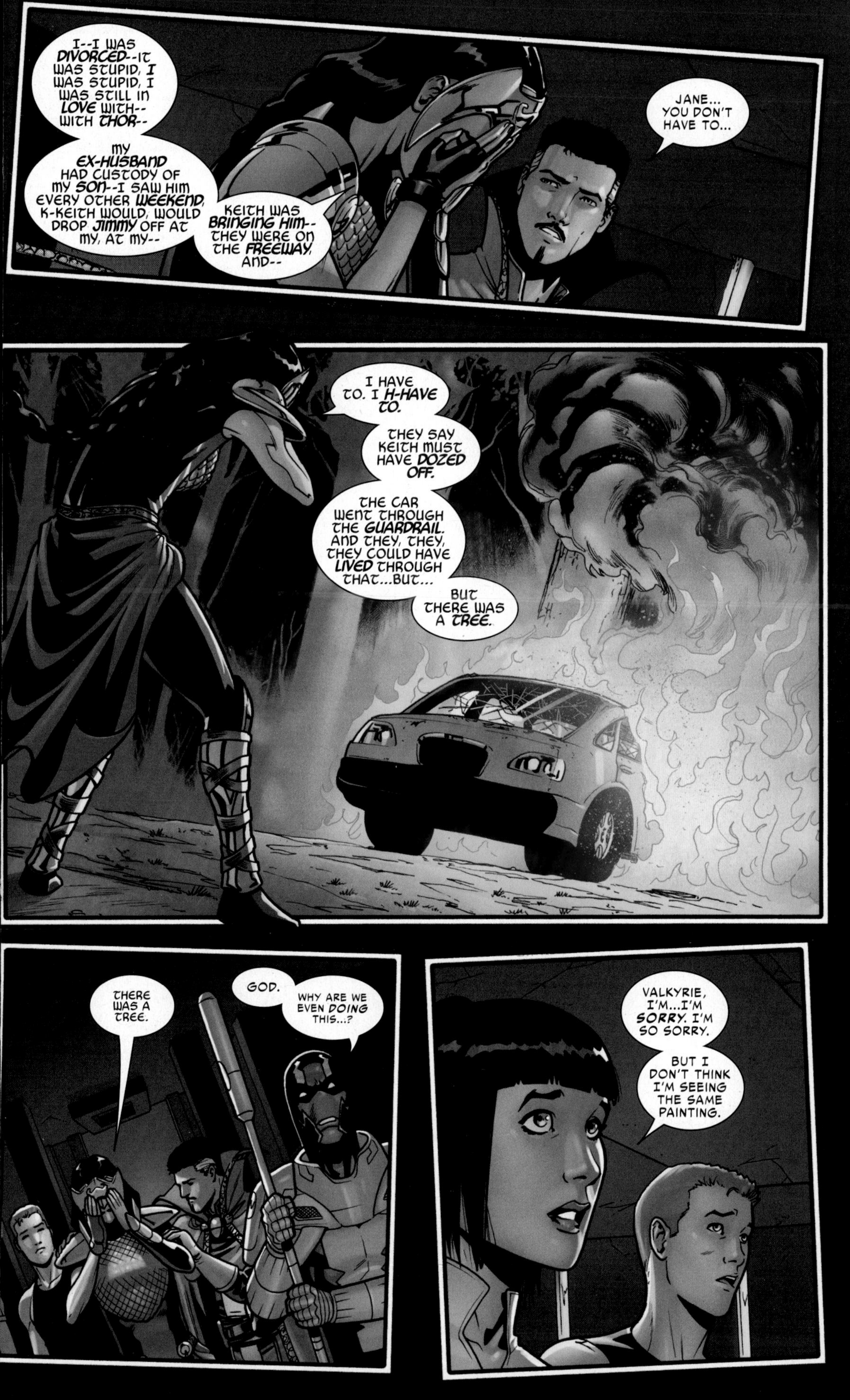

I--I WAS DIVORCED--IT WAS STUPID, I WAS STUPID, I WAS STILL IN LOVE WITH--WITH THOR--
MY EX-HUSBAND HAD CUSTODY OF MY SON--I SAW HIM EVERY OTHER WEEKEND, K-KEITH WOULD, WOULD DROP JIMMY OFF AT MY, AT MY--
KEITH WAS BRINGING HIM--THEY WERE ON THE FREEWAY, AND--
JANE... YOU DON'T HAVE TO...
I HAVE TO. I H-HAVE TO.
THEY SAY KEITH MUST HAVE DOZED OFF.
THE CAR WENT THROUGH THE GUARDRAIL. AND THEY, THEY, THEY COULD HAVE LIVED THROUGH THAT...BUT...
BUT THERE WAS A TREE.
THERE WAS A TREE.
GOD.
WHY ARE WE EVEN DOING THIS...?
VALKYRIE, I'M...I'M SORRY. I'M SO SORRY.
BUT I DON'T THINK I'M SEEING THE SAME PAINTING.

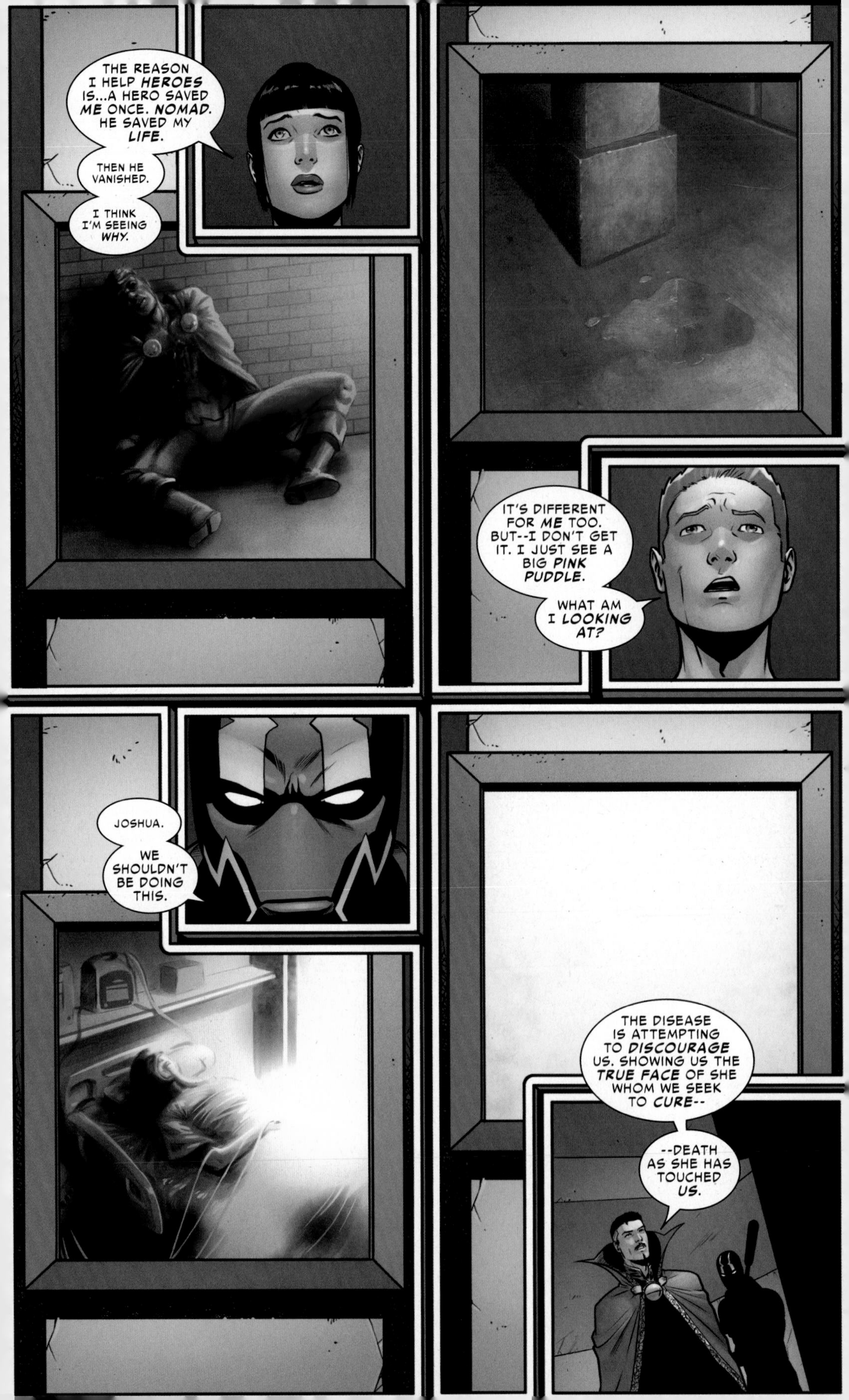
THE REASON I HELP HEROES IS...A HERO SAVED ME ONCE. NOMAD. HE SAVED MY LIFE.
THEN HE VANISHED.
I THINK I'M SEEING WHY.
IT'S DIFFERENT FOR ME TOO. BUT--I DON'T GET IT. I JUST SEE A BIG PINK PUDDLE.
WHAT AM I LOOKING AT?
JOSHUA.
WE SHOULDN'T BE DOING THIS.
THE DISEASE IS ATTEMPTING TO DISCOURAGE US. SHOWING US THE TRUE FACE OF SHE WHOM WE SEEK TO CURE--
--DEATH AS SHE HAS TOUCHED US.

FOR ME, THE CANVAS IS *BLANK.* PURE *NOTHINGNESS*-- THE DEATH OF AN *ENTIRE* REALITY.

A SIGHT I HAVE SEEN *TOO OFTEN* AS THE SORCERER--

--SUPRE*EAAGGGHH!*

SORRY, DOCTOR.

SH*RRZAKK*

BUT I HAD TO TAKE YOU *OUT,* AND A *SURPRISE SHOCK* TO THE *BRAIN* WAS THE ONLY WAY TO DO IT.

HOPE YOU'RE *OKAY...*

ARE YOU INSANE? STRANGE WAS OUR *GUIDE* TO THIS REALM! IF WE'RE GOING TO *SAVE DEATH'S LIFE,* WE *NEED* HIM--

LORD, LISTEN TO YOURSELF! *SAVE DEATH'S LIFE!* IT'S LIKE A *SICK JOKE!*

WE CAN SAVE AN *INFINITY* OF LIVES--LIKE YOUR *SON,* LIKE MY *BROTHER*--JUST BY *WITHHOLDING TREATMENT!* LETTING THIS HAPPEN!

WHY? WHY DO WE NEED *DEATH?!*

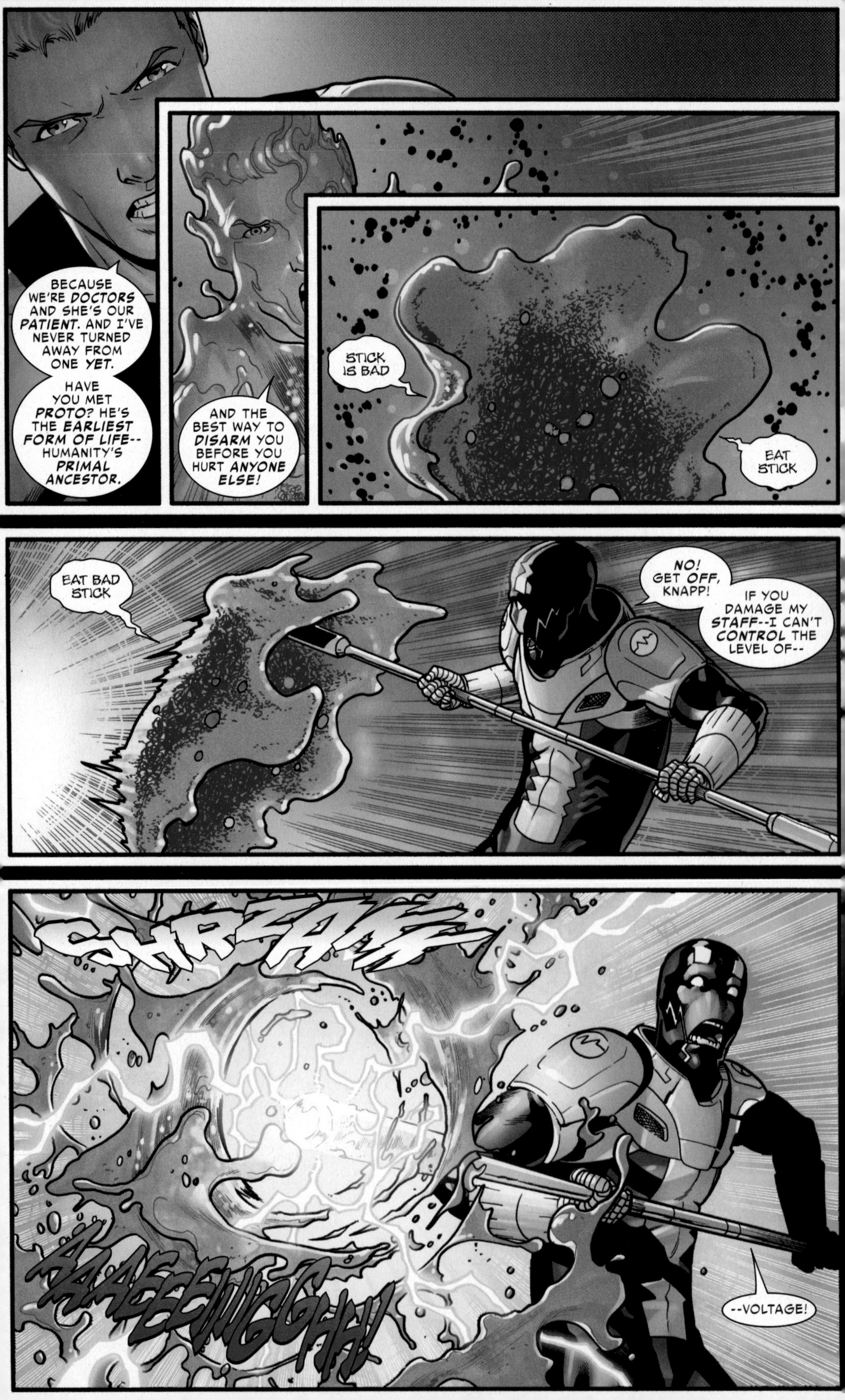
BECAUSE WE'RE DOCTORS AND SHE'S OUR PATIENT. AND I'VE NEVER TURNED AWAY FROM ONE YET.
HAVE YOU MET PROTO? HE'S THE EARLIEST FORM OF LIFE-- HUMANITY'S PRIMAL ANCESTOR.
AND THE BEST WAY TO DISARM YOU BEFORE YOU HURT ANYONE ELSE!
STICK IS BAD
EAT STICK
EAT BAD STICK
NO! GET OFF, KNAPP!
IF YOU DAMAGE MY STAFF--I CAN'T CONTROL THE LEVEL OF--
SHRZAAM
AAAEEEIIIGGHH!
--VOLTAGE!

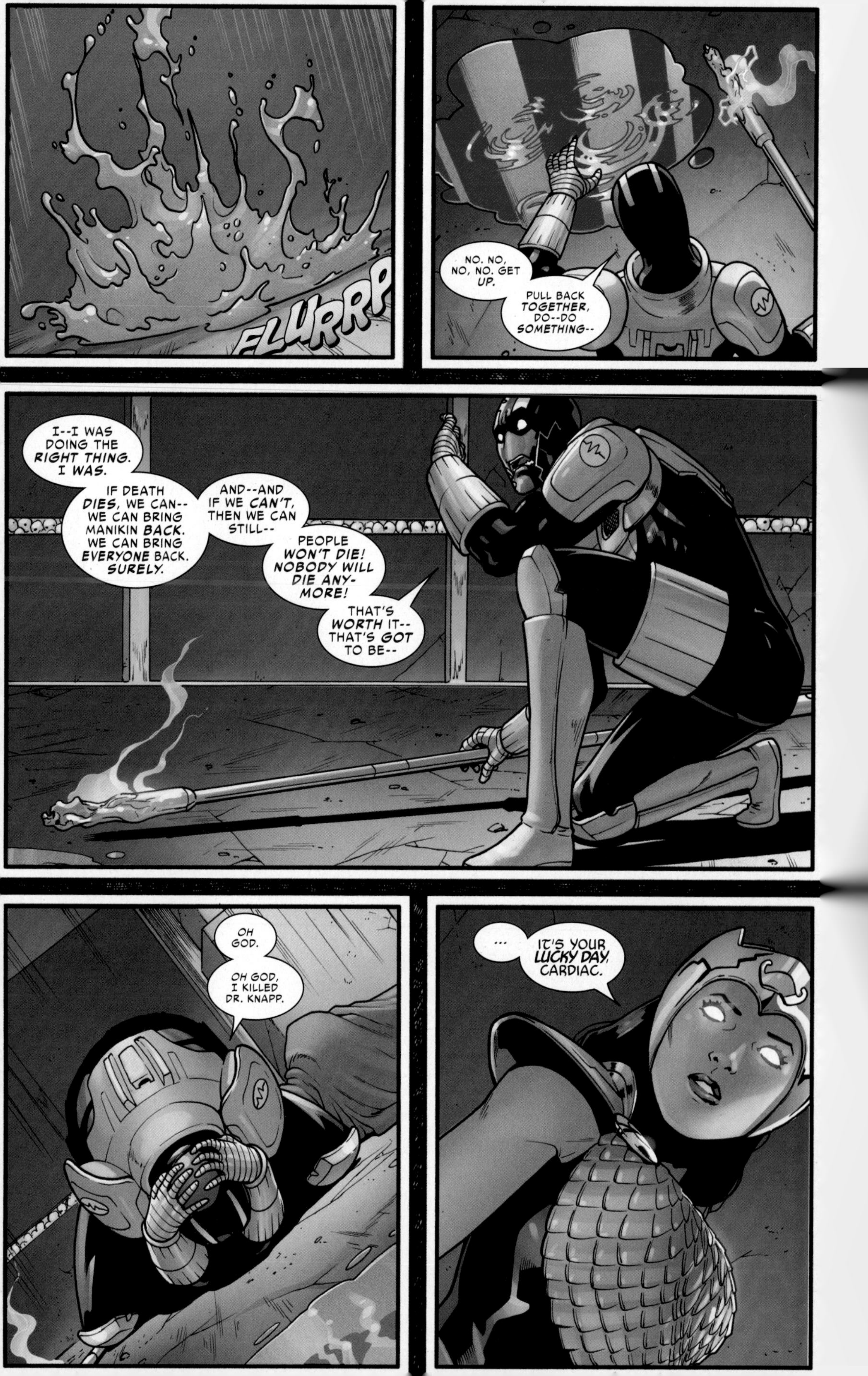

FLURRP
NO. NO, NO, NO. GET UP.
PULL BACK TOGETHER, DO--DO SOMETHING--
I--I WAS DOING THE RIGHT THING. I WAS.
IF DEATH DIES, WE CAN--WE CAN BRING MANIKIN BACK. WE CAN BRING EVERYONE BACK. SURELY.
AND--AND IF WE CAN'T, THEN WE CAN STILL--
PEOPLE WON'T DIE! NOBODY WILL DIE ANY-MORE!
THAT'S WORTH IT--THAT'S GOT TO BE--
OH GOD.
OH GOD, I KILLED DR. KNAPP.
...
IT'S YOUR LUCKY DAY, CARDIAC.

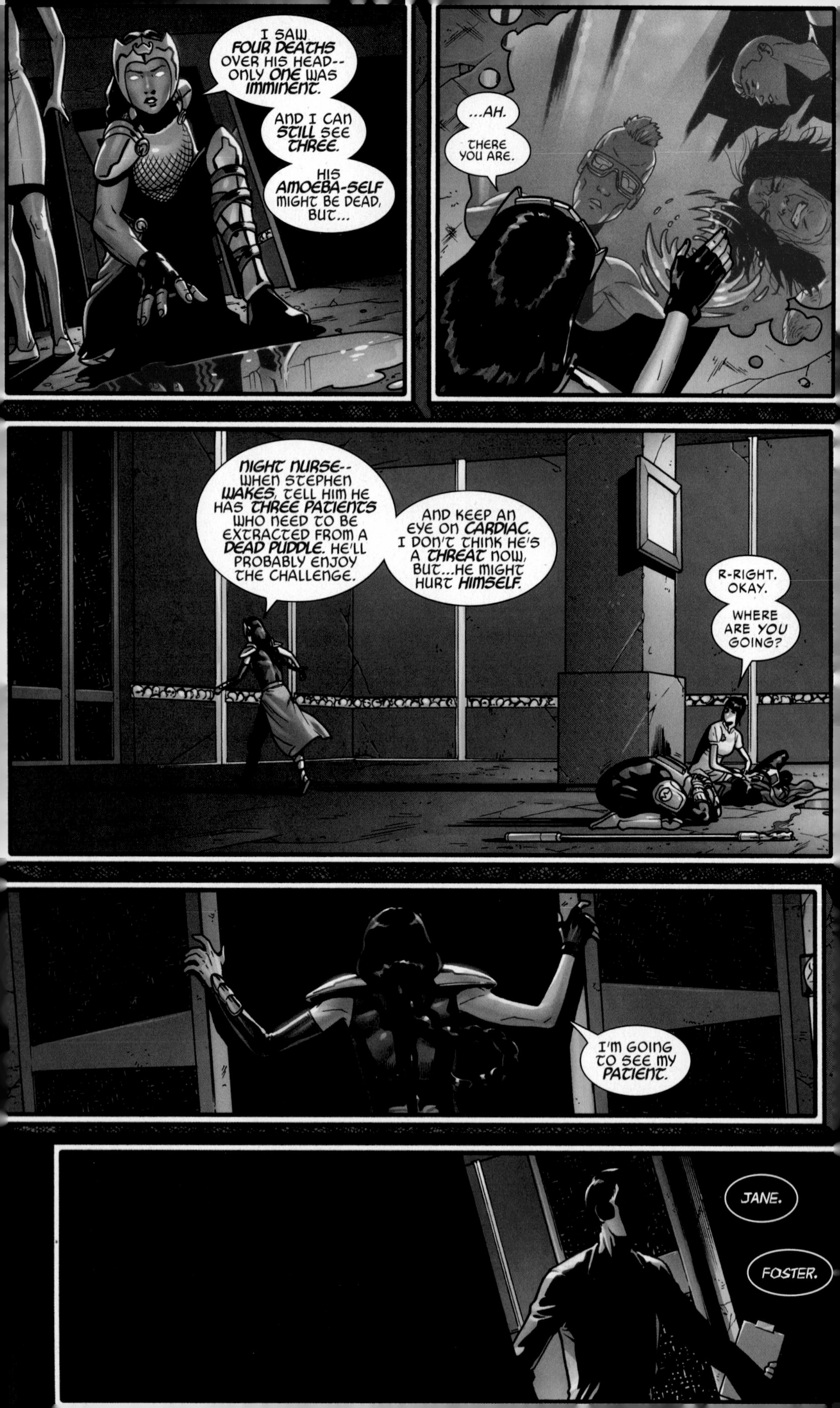
I SAW FOUR DEATHS OVER HIS HEAD-- ONLY ONE WAS IMMINENT.
AND I CAN STILL SEE THREE.
HIS AMOEBA-SELF MIGHT BE DEAD, BUT...
...AH.
THERE YOU ARE.
NIGHT NURSE-- WHEN STEPHEN WAKES, TELL HIM HE HAS THREE PATIENTS WHO NEED TO BE EXTRACTED FROM A DEAD PUDDLE. HE'LL PROBABLY ENJOY THE CHALLENGE.
AND KEEP AN EYE ON CARDIAC. I DON'T THINK HE'S A THREAT NOW, BUT...HE MIGHT HURT HIMSELF.
R-RIGHT. OKAY.
WHERE ARE YOU GOING?
I'M GOING TO SEE MY PATIENT.
JANE.
FOSTER.

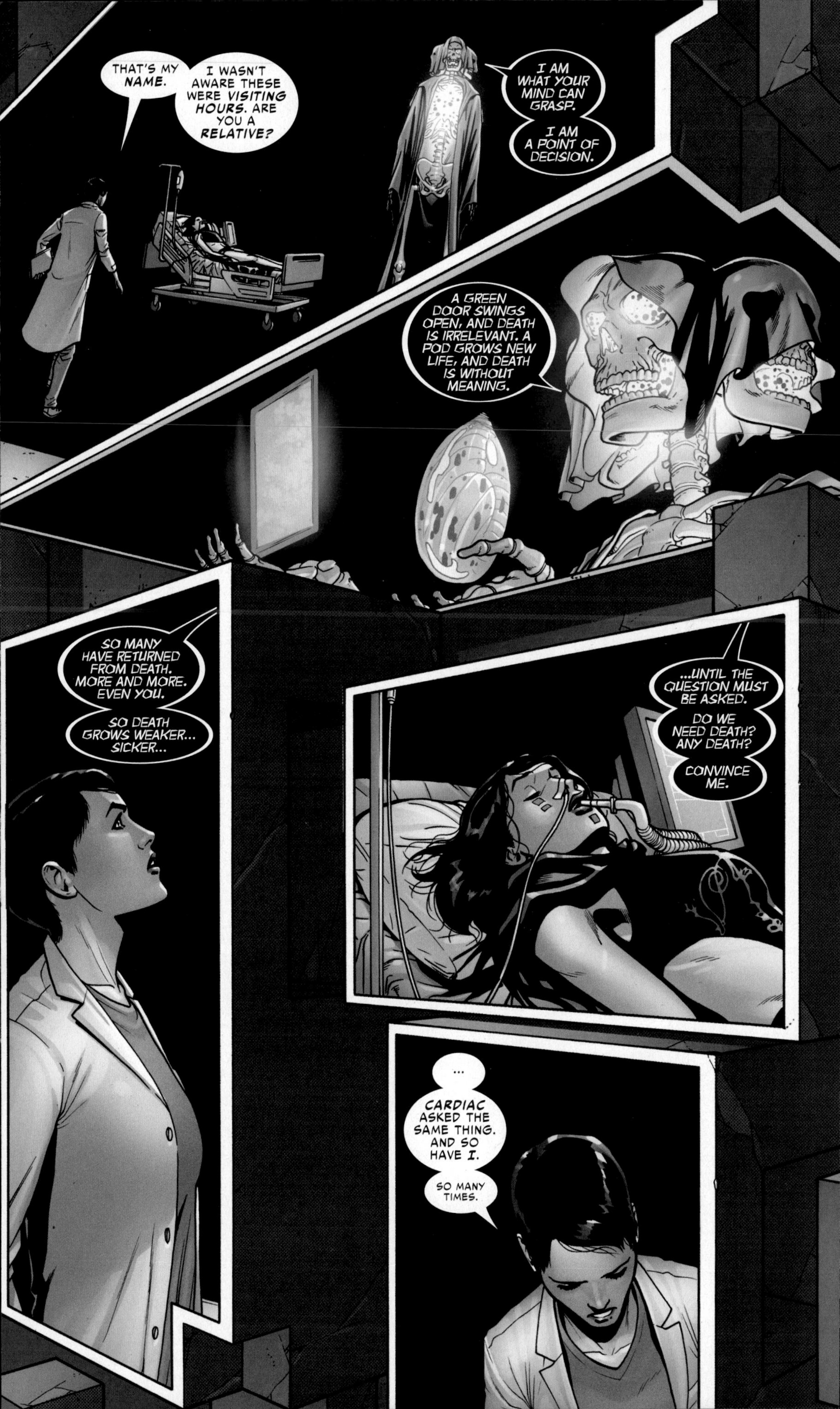
THAT'S MY NAME.
I WASN'T AWARE THESE WERE VISITING HOURS. ARE YOU A RELATIVE?
I AM WHAT YOUR MIND CAN GRASP.
I AM A POINT OF DECISION.
A GREEN DOOR SWINGS OPEN, AND DEATH IS IRRELEVANT. A POD GROWS NEW LIFE, AND DEATH IS WITHOUT MEANING.
SO MANY HAVE RETURNED FROM DEATH. MORE AND MORE. EVEN YOU.
SO DEATH GROWS WEAKER... SICKER...
...UNTIL THE QUESTION MUST BE ASKED.
DO WE NEED DEATH? ANY DEATH?
CONVINCE ME.
...
CARDIAC ASKED THE SAME THING. AND SO HAVE I.
SO MANY TIMES.

IMAGING A WORLD WHERE KEITH AND JIMMY *DIDN'T DIE.*

WHERE NOBODY EVER HAS TO...TO GO *THROUGH* THAT...

...BUT THAT'S NOT A WORLD WITHOUT *ANY DEATH,* IS IT? THAT'S A WORLD WITHOUT *PEOPLE DYING.*

THAT'S NOT WHAT YOU *ASKED.*

I'M NOT THINKING LIKE *VALKYRIE* HERE. SHE SEES DEATH AS A *JOURNEY.*

YOU'D THINK I'D TAKE SOME COMFORT IN THAT.

NO.

I'M THINKING LIKE A *DOCTOR.*

AND NOBODY RESPECTS DEATH LIKE A DOCTOR.

IF THERE WAS NO DEATH AT *ALL.* IF *NOTHING* DIED.

NOT *PEOPLE,* NOT *ANIMALS* OR *PLANTS*...NOT *GERMS*...

NOT *CELLS.*

A UNIVERSE OF LIVING CELLS THAT DIDN'T *DIE* BUT STILL *REPRODUCED.*

I'D CALL THAT A *CANCERVERSE.* AND I DON'T THINK I'D WANT TO *LIVE* THERE.

THE END OF *PAIN*...AND *FEAR*...AND *SORROW*...THESE ARE THINGS TO *STRIVE* FOR. FOR ALL OUR DAYS.

THE END OF *DEATH*...

...

I DON'T THINK THAT MEANS *LIFE.*

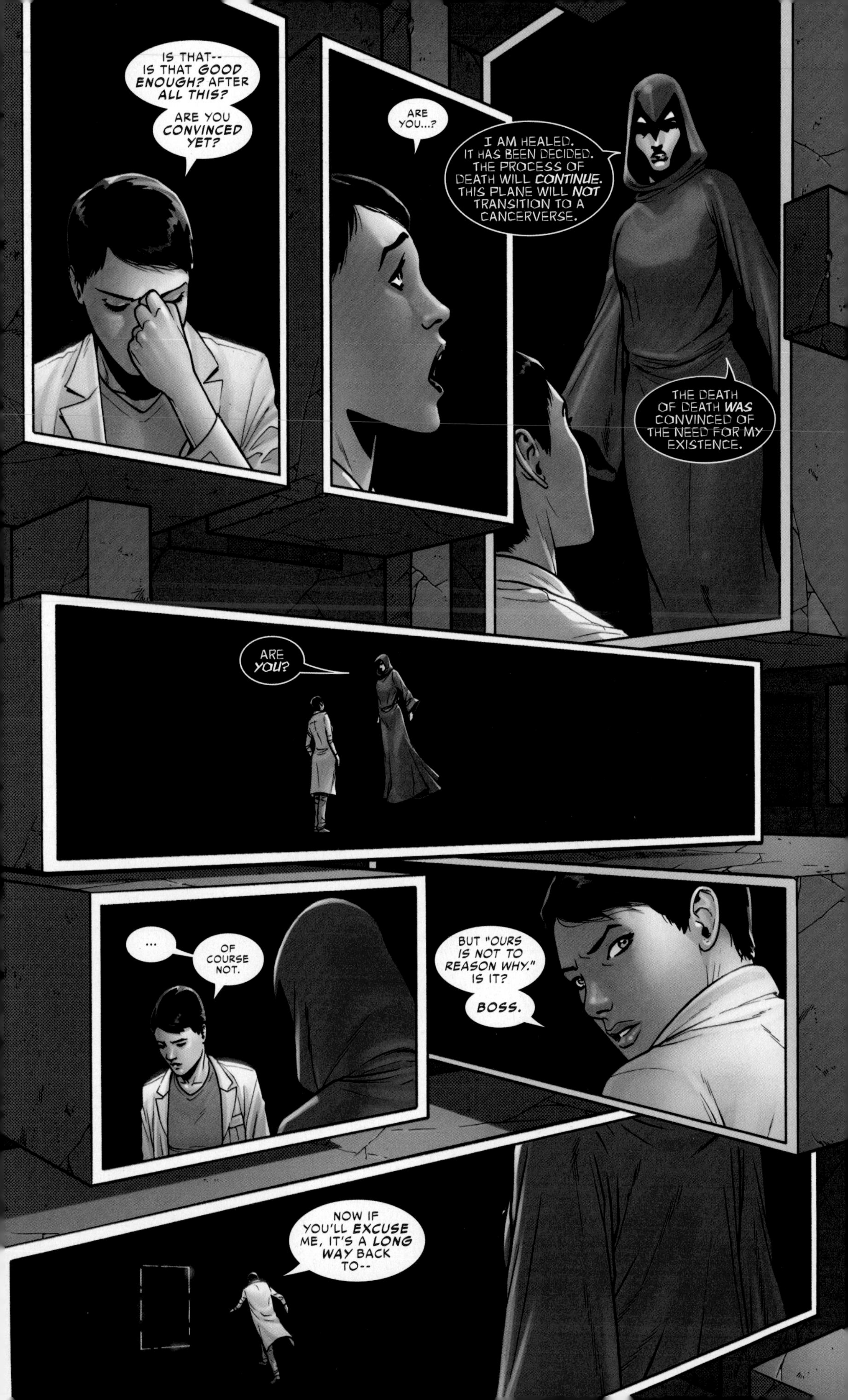
IS THAT-- IS THAT GOOD ENOUGH? AFTER ALL THIS?
ARE YOU CONVINCED YET?
ARE YOU...?
I AM HEALED. IT HAS BEEN DECIDED. THE PROCESS OF DEATH WILL CONTINUE. THIS PLANE WILL NOT TRANSITION TO A CANCERVERSE.
THE DEATH OF DEATH WAS CONVINCED OF THE NEED FOR MY EXISTENCE.
ARE YOU?
...
OF COURSE NOT.
BUT "OURS IS NOT TO REASON WHY." IS IT?
BOSS.
NOW IF YOU'LL EXCUSE ME, IT'S A LONG WAY BACK TO--

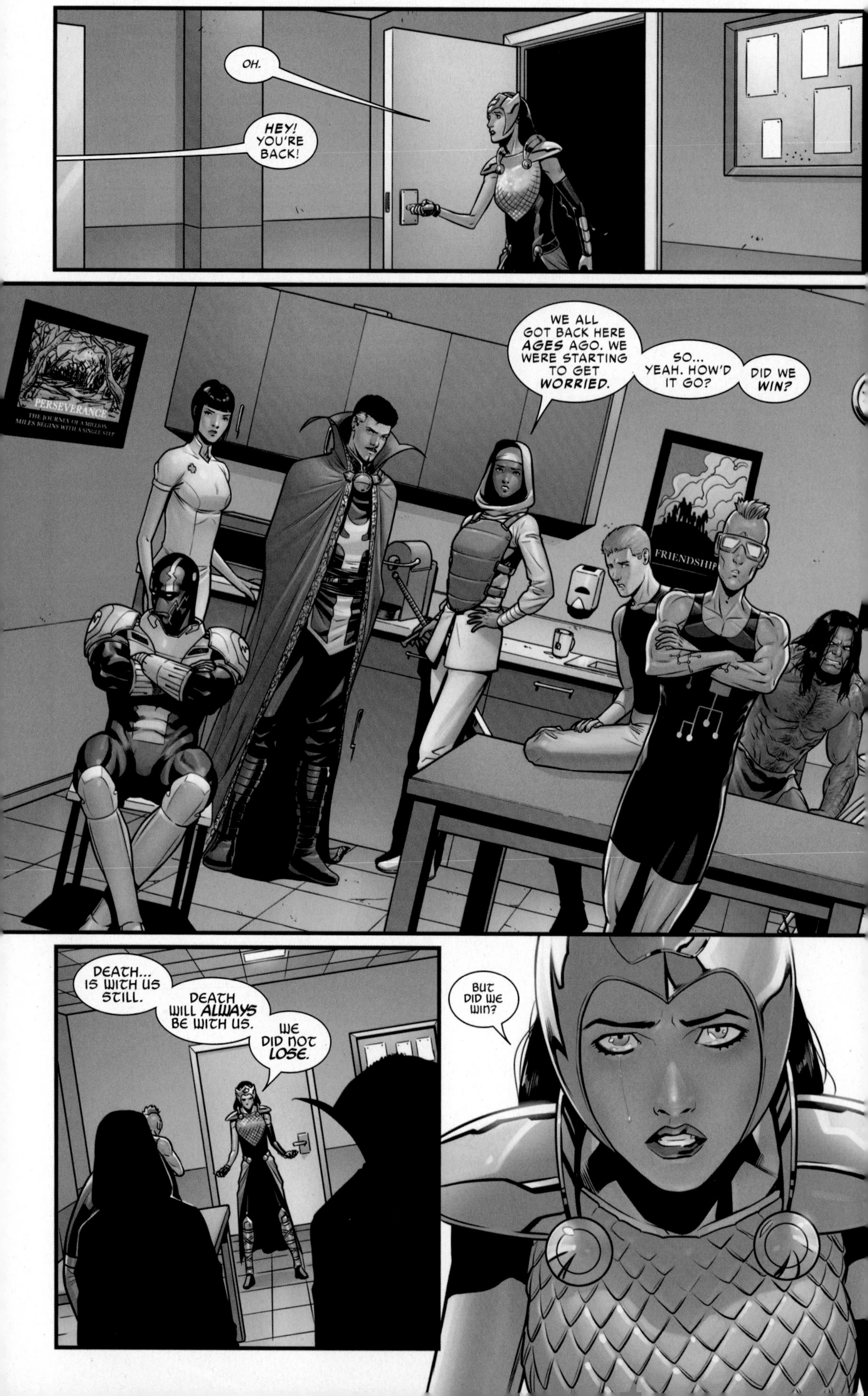

OH.
HEY! YOU'RE BACK!
WE ALL GOT BACK HERE AGES AGO. WE WERE STARTING TO GET WORRIED.
SO... YEAH. HOW'D IT GO?
DID WE WIN?
PERSEVERANCE
THE JOURNEY OF A MILLION MILES BEGINS WITH A SINGLE STEP
FRIENDSHIP
DEATH... IS WITH US STILL.
DEATH WILL ALWAYS BE WITH US.
WE DID NOT LOSE.
BUT DID WE WIN?

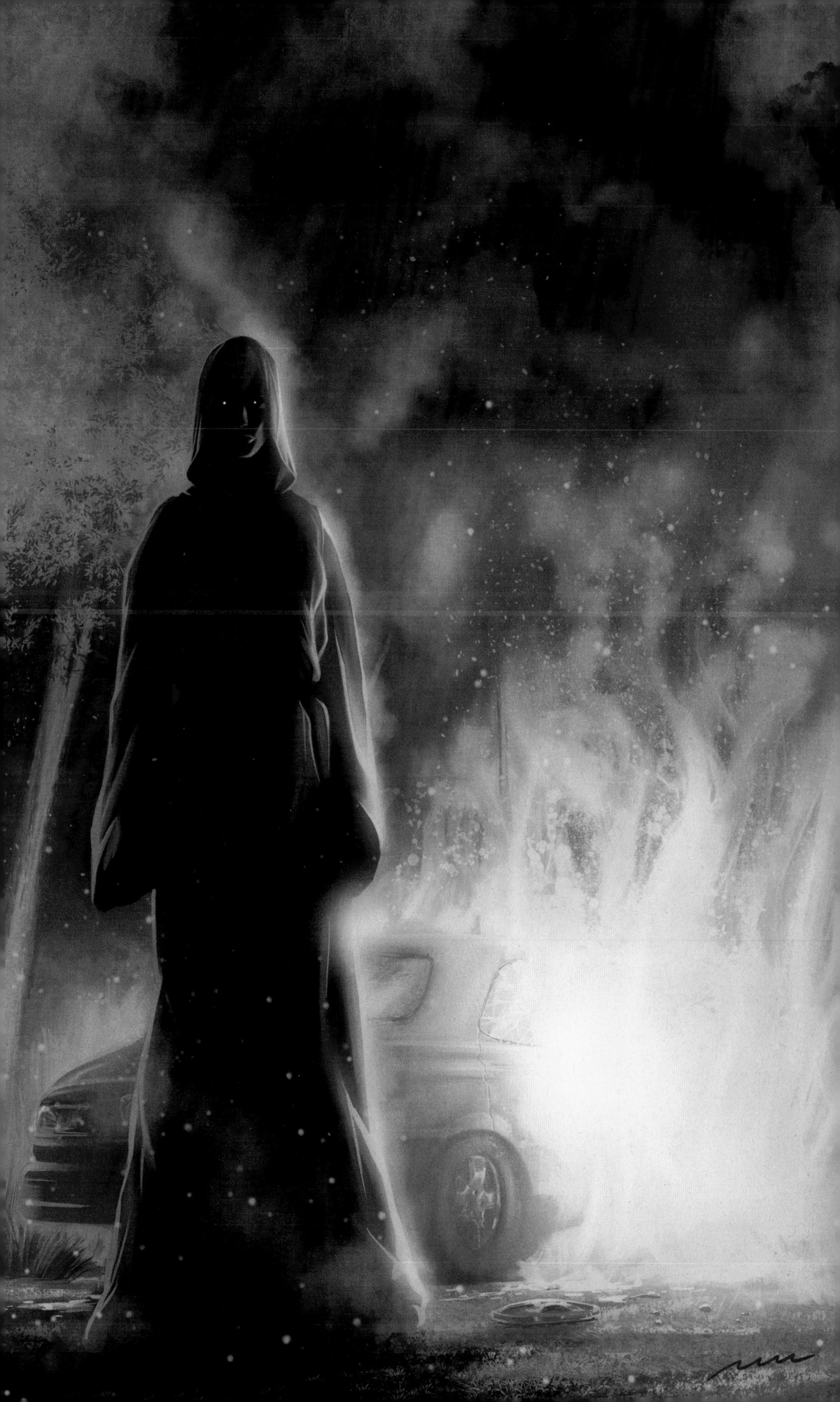

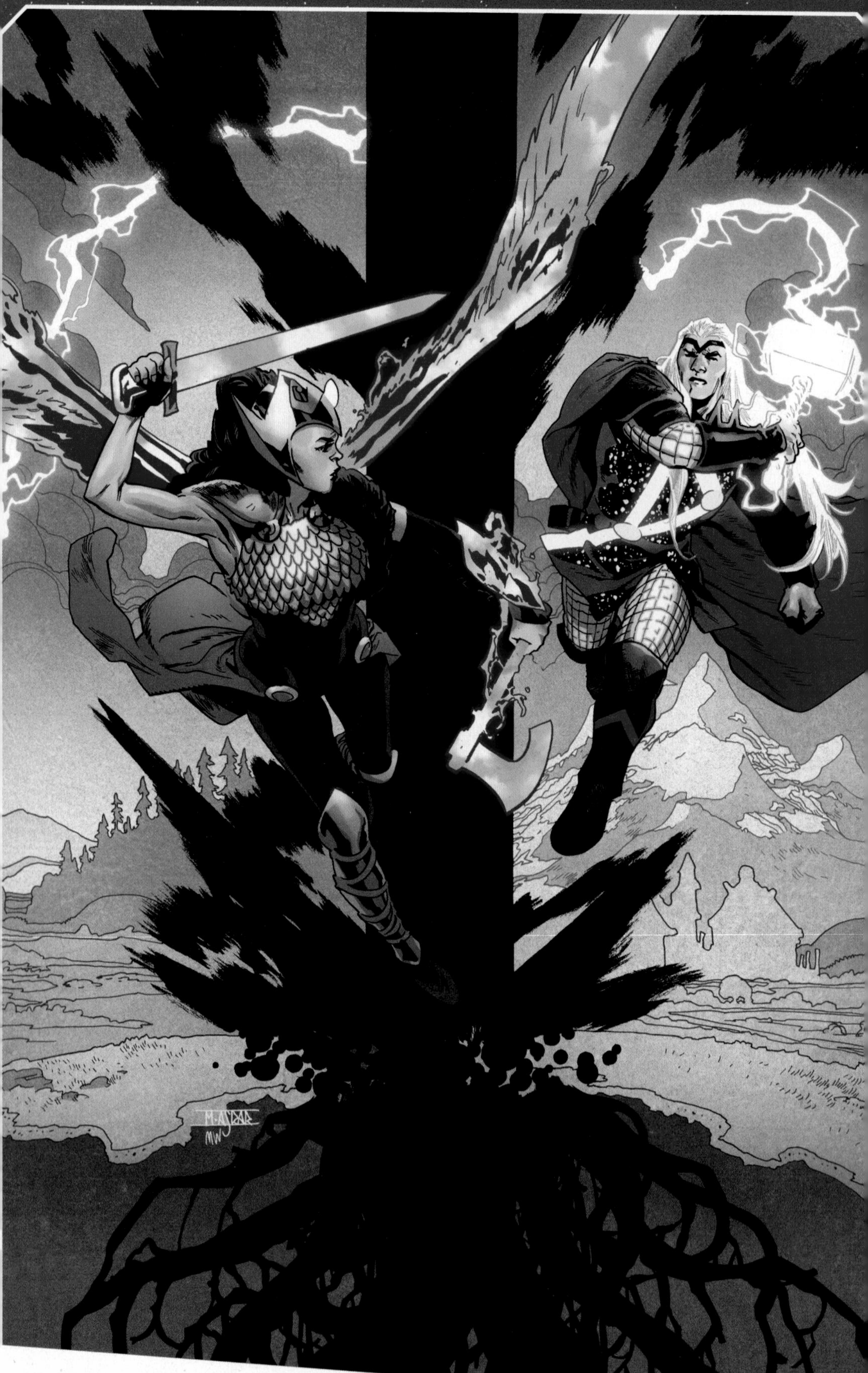
M.AYDAR
MW

VALKYRIE: JANE FOSTER #8

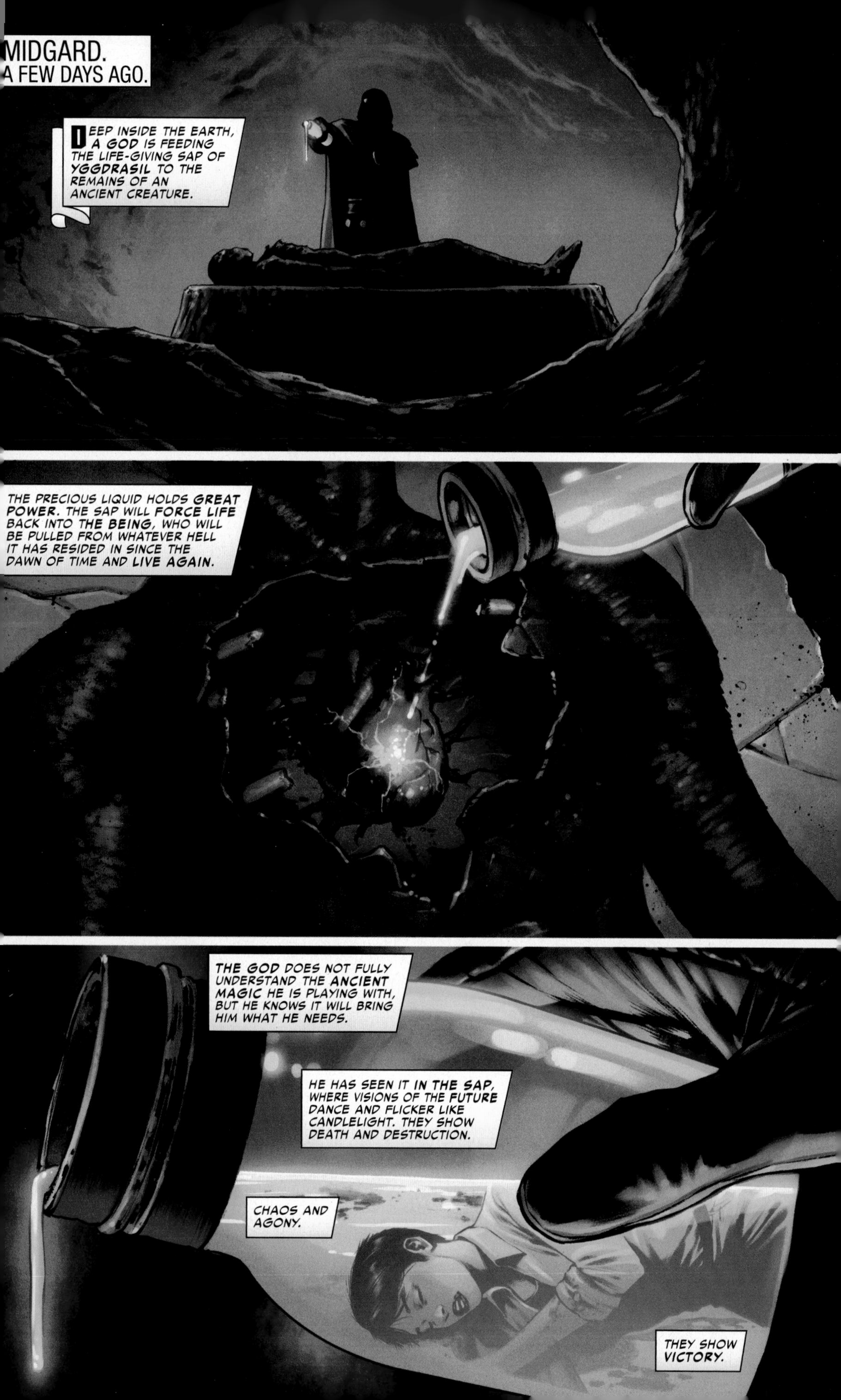
MIDGARD. A FEW DAYS AGO.
DEEP INSIDE THE EARTH, A GOD IS FEEDING THE LIFE-GIVING SAP OF YGGDRASIL TO THE REMAINS OF AN ANCIENT CREATURE.
THE PRECIOUS LIQUID HOLDS GREAT POWER. THE SAP WILL FORCE LIFE BACK INTO THE BEING, WHO WILL BE PULLED FROM WHATEVER HELL IT HAS RESIDED IN SINCE THE DAWN OF TIME AND LIVE AGAIN.
THE GOD DOES NOT FULLY UNDERSTAND THE ANCIENT MAGIC HE IS PLAYING WITH, BUT HE KNOWS IT WILL BRING HIM WHAT HE NEEDS.
HE HAS SEEN IT IN THE SAP, WHERE VISIONS OF THE FUTURE DANCE AND FLICKER LIKE CANDLELIGHT. THEY SHOW DEATH AND DESTRUCTION.
CHAOS AND AGONY.
THEY SHOW VICTORY.

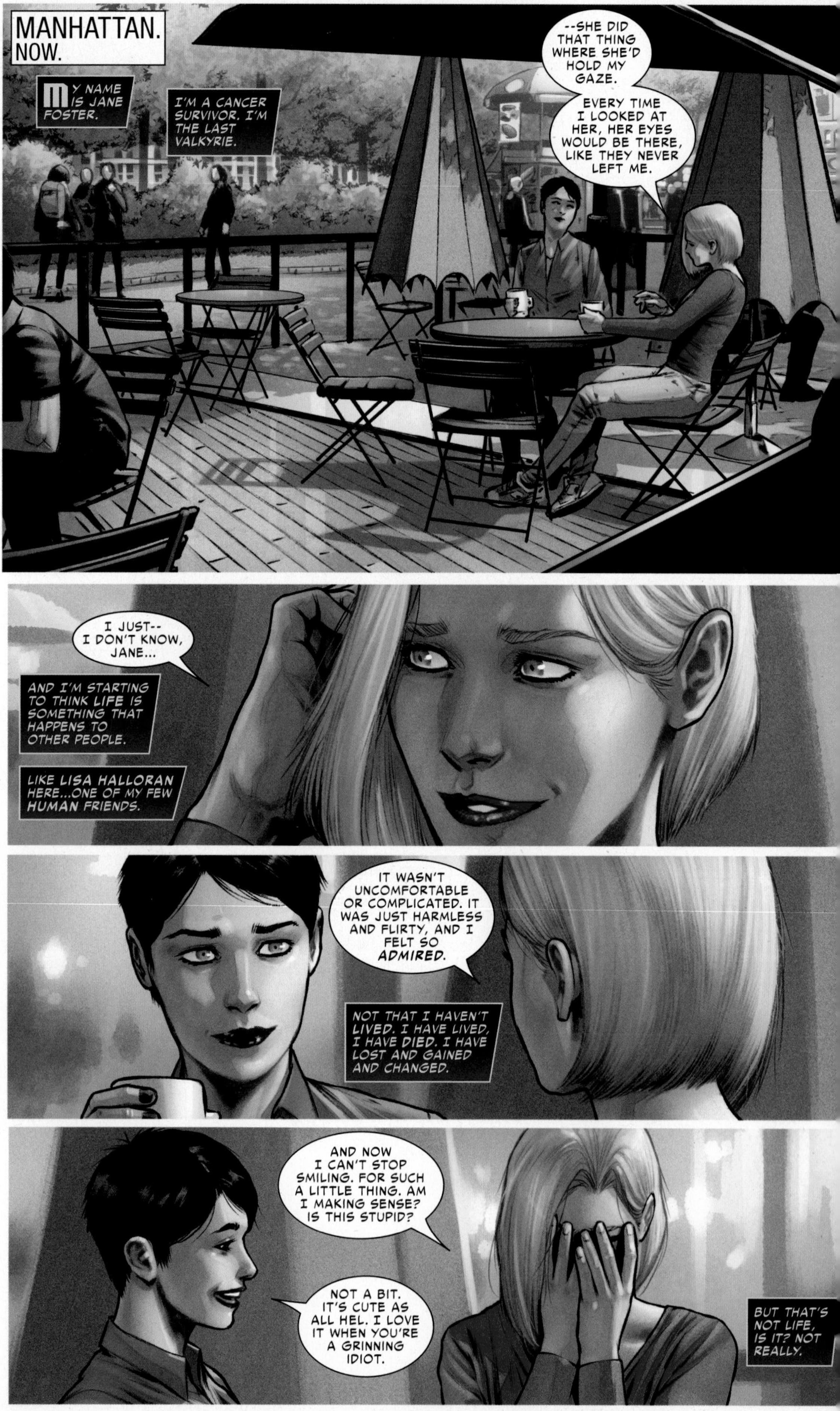
MANHATTAN. NOW.
MY NAME IS JANE FOSTER.
I'M A CANCER SURVIVOR. I'M THE LAST VALKYRIE.
--SHE DID THAT THING WHERE SHE'D HOLD MY GAZE.
EVERY TIME I LOOKED AT HER, HER EYES WOULD BE THERE, LIKE THEY NEVER LEFT ME.
I JUST-- I DON'T KNOW, JANE...
AND I'M STARTING TO THINK LIFE IS SOMETHING THAT HAPPENS TO OTHER PEOPLE.
LIKE LISA HALLORAN HERE...ONE OF MY FEW HUMAN FRIENDS.
IT WASN'T UNCOMFORTABLE OR COMPLICATED. IT WAS JUST HARMLESS AND FLIRTY, AND I FELT SO ADMIRED.
NOT THAT I HAVEN'T LIVED. I HAVE LIVED, I HAVE DIED. I HAVE LOST AND GAINED AND CHANGED.
AND NOW I CAN'T STOP SMILING. FOR SUCH A LITTLE THING. AM I MAKING SENSE? IS THIS STUPID?
NOT A BIT. IT'S CUTE AS ALL HEL. I LOVE IT WHEN YOU'RE A GRINNING IDIOT.
BUT THAT'S NOT LIFE, IS IT? NOT REALLY.

HEY, SPEAKING OF GRINNING IDIOTS, DIDN'T *YOU* HAVE A DATE LAST WEEK? WITH THE CUTE-BUT-BORING BANKER?

WELL...I TRIED TO MAKE IT. I *REALLY* DID.

IT MIGHT BE PART OF THE PROBLEM.

OH, JANE...

..I DID CALL HIM THAT, DIDN'T I?

"BORING" MIGHT BE UNFAIR. MY SCALE IS A BIT OFF.

BUT I WAS A BIT *BUSY* THAT NIGHT--SMALL KREE INCURSION, PROTECTING THE EARTH, YOU KNOW...AND BY THE TIME I WAS DONE, I WAS *TOO* TOO LATE...

SO, WHAT ABOUT CUTE-BUT-*COMPLICATED?* YOU KNOW, THE ONE WITH THE *WINGS?*

*SAM?** WELL, IT'S ALL VERY *FRIENDLY.* AND I HAVEN'T TOLD H--

*SHE MEANS SAM WILSON, A.K.A. THE FALCON! REMEMBER THEIR KISS BACK IN ALL-NEW, ALL-DIFFERENT AVENGERS #4? --WIL

CAN YOU FEEL THAT?

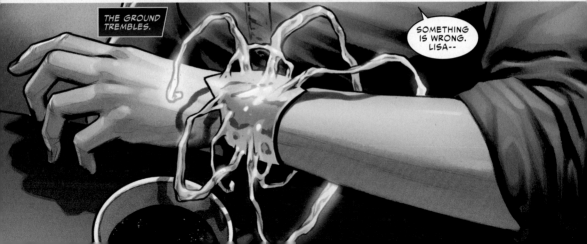

THE GROUND TREMBLES.

SOMETHING IS WRONG. LISA--

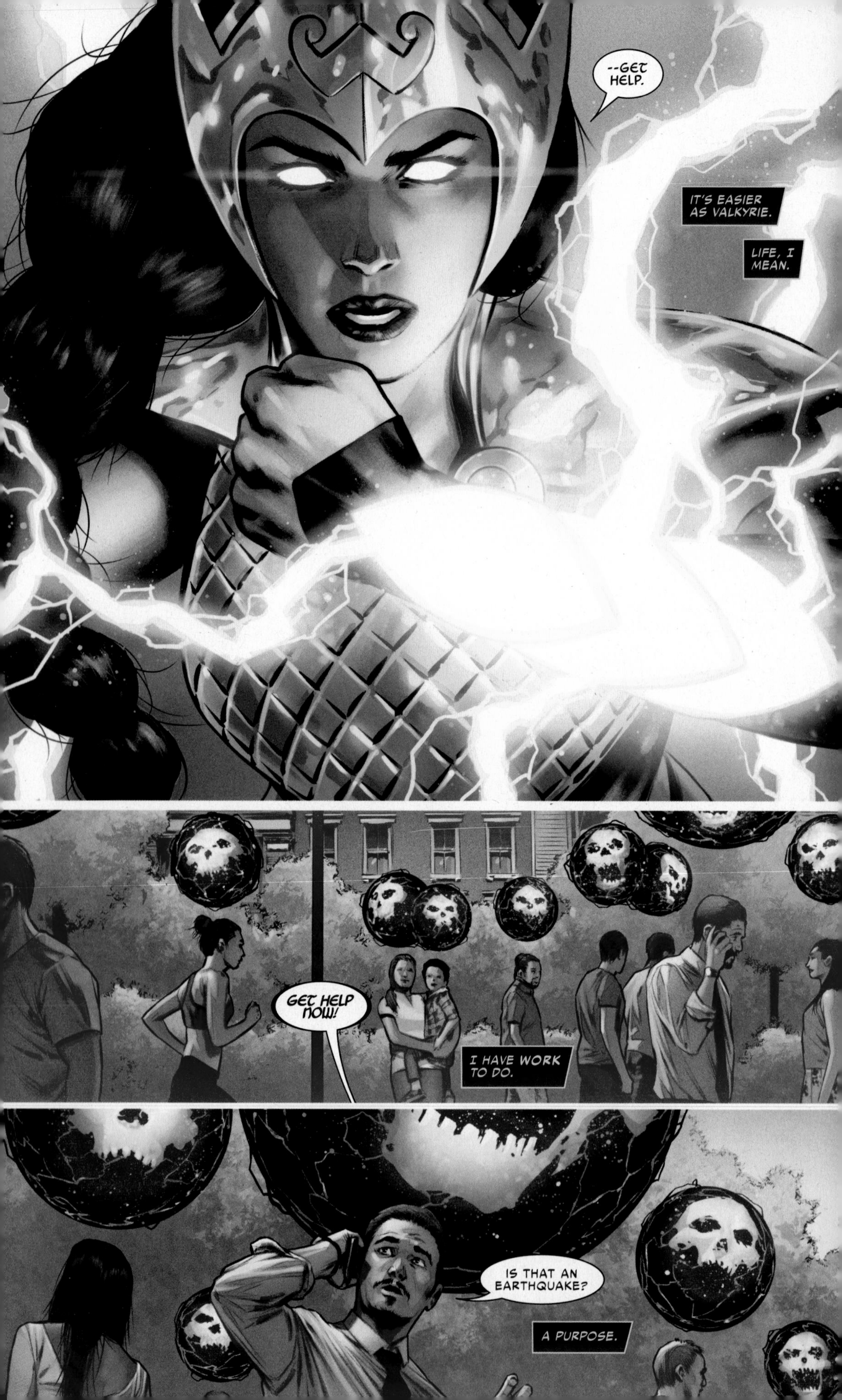
--GET HELP.
IT'S EASIER AS VALKYRIE.
LIFE, I MEAN.
GET HELP NOW!
I HAVE WORK TO DO.
IS THAT AN EARTHQUAKE?
A PURPOSE.

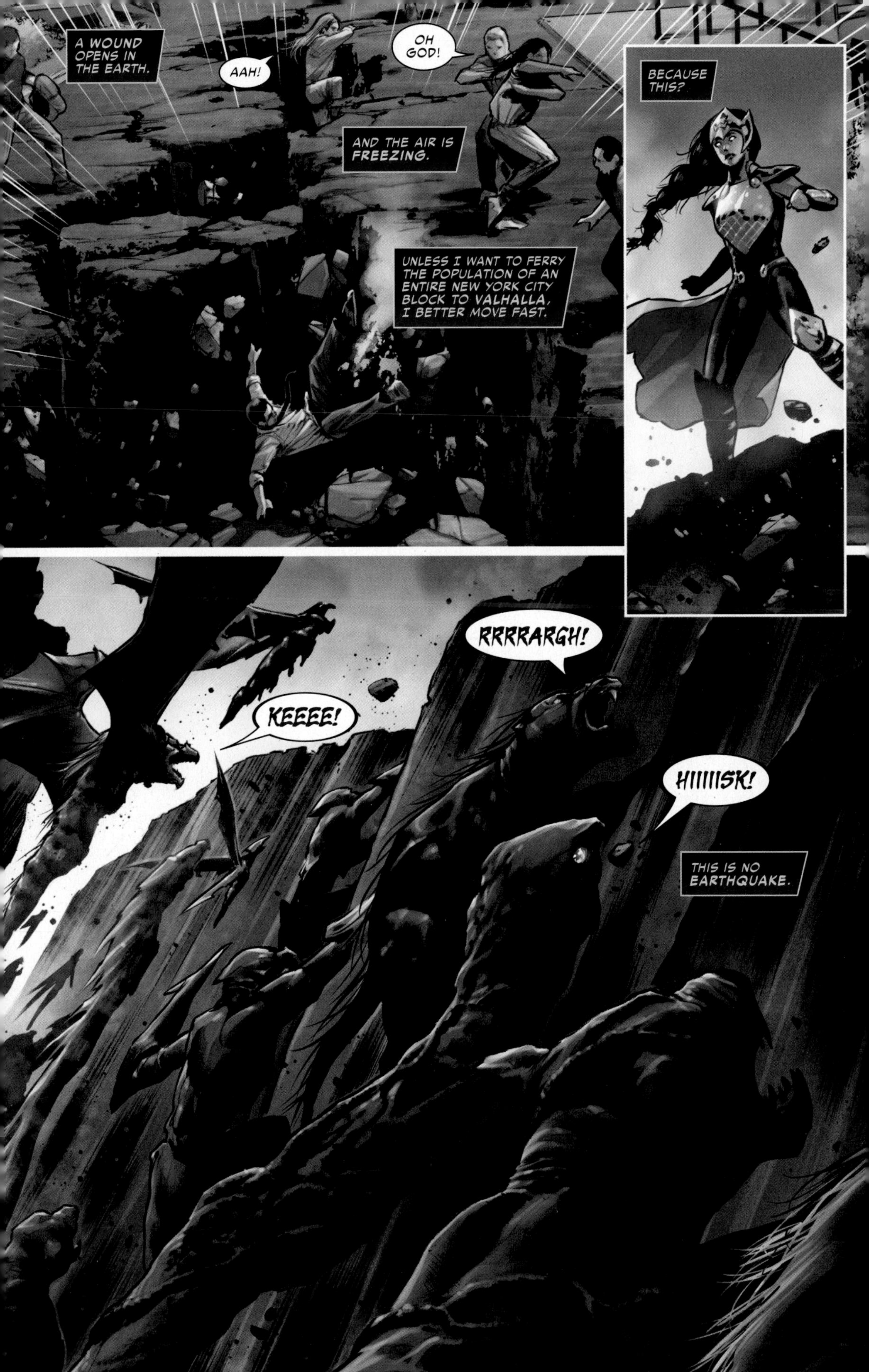
A WOUND OPENS IN THE EARTH.
AAH!
OH GOD!
AND THE AIR IS FREEZING.
UNLESS I WANT TO FERRY THE POPULATION OF AN ENTIRE NEW YORK CITY BLOCK TO VALHALLA, I BETTER MOVE FAST.
BECAUSE THIS?
RRRRARGH!
KEEEE!
HIIIIISK!
THIS IS NO EARTHQUAKE.

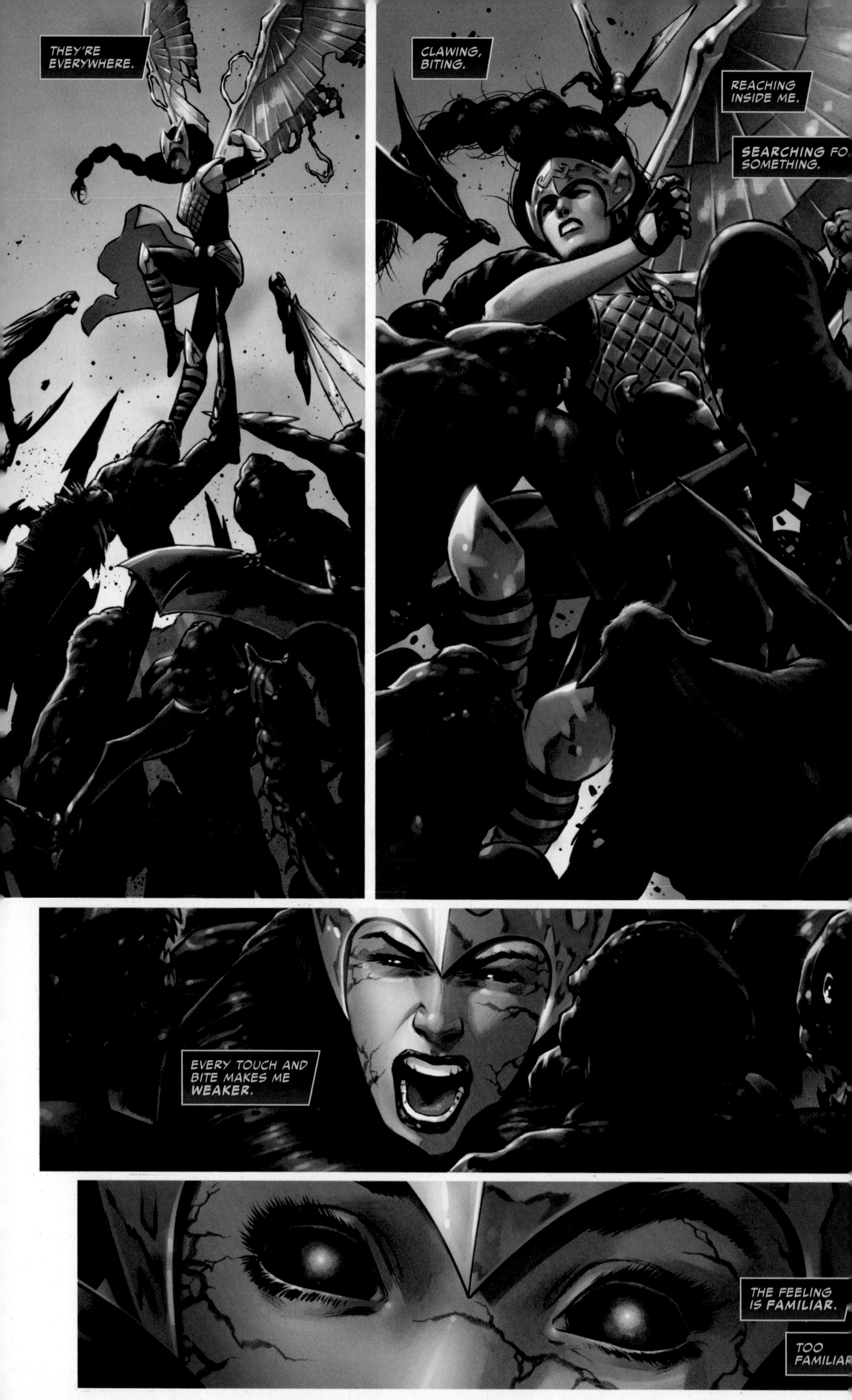
THEY'RE EVERYWHERE.
CLAWING, BITING.
REACHING INSIDE ME.
SEARCHING FO
SOMETHING.
EVERY TOUCH AND BITE MAKES ME WEAKER.
THE FEELING IS FAMILIAR.
TOO FAMILIAR

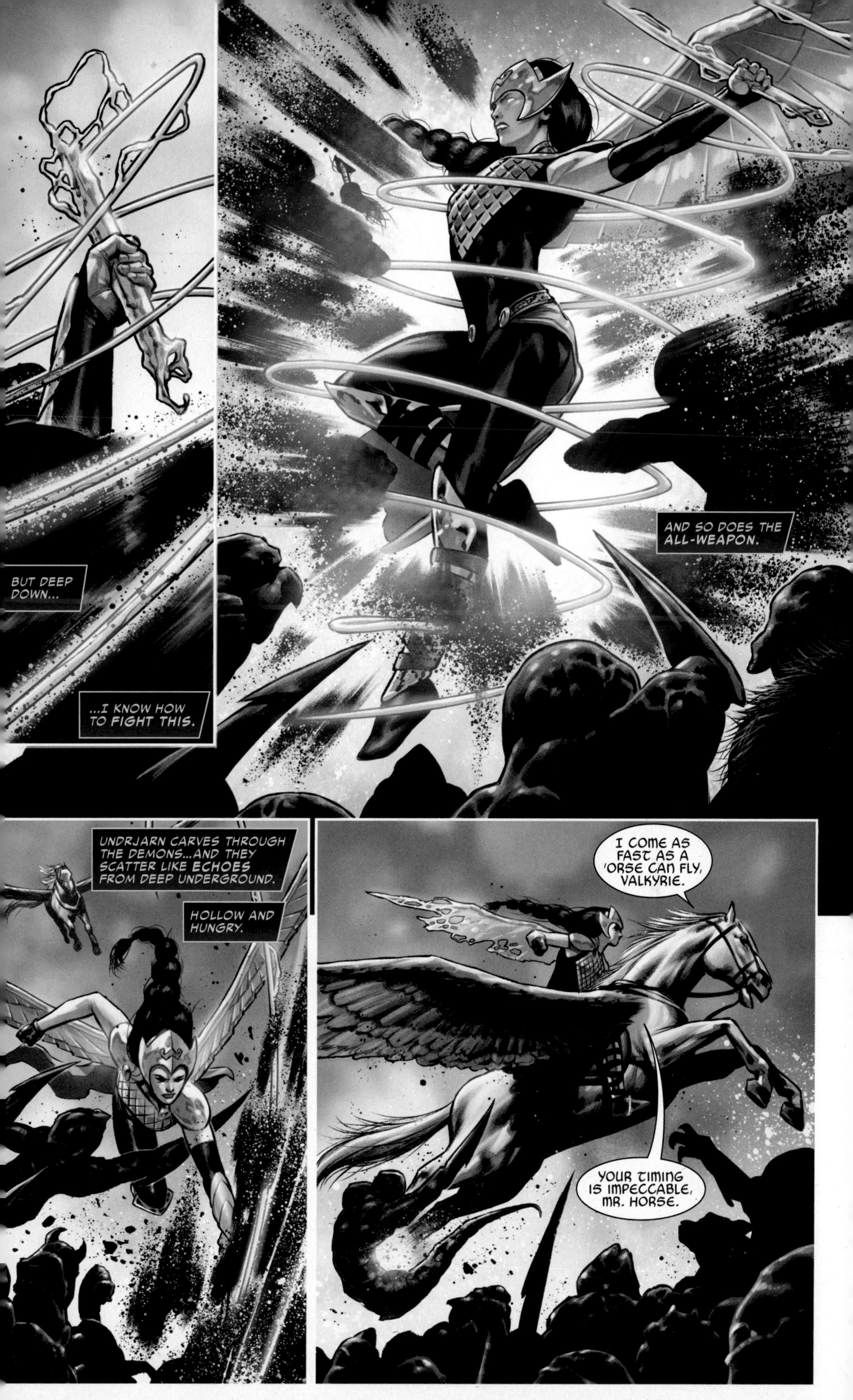
BUT DEEP DOWN...
...I KNOW HOW TO FIGHT THIS.
AND SO DOES THE ALL-WEAPON.
UNDRJARN CARVES THROUGH THE DEMONS...AND THEY SCATTER LIKE ECHOES FROM DEEP UNDERGROUND.
HOLLOW AND HUNGRY.
I COME AS FAST AS A 'ORSE CAN FLY, VALKYRIE.
YOUR TIMING IS IMPECCABLE, MR. HORSE.

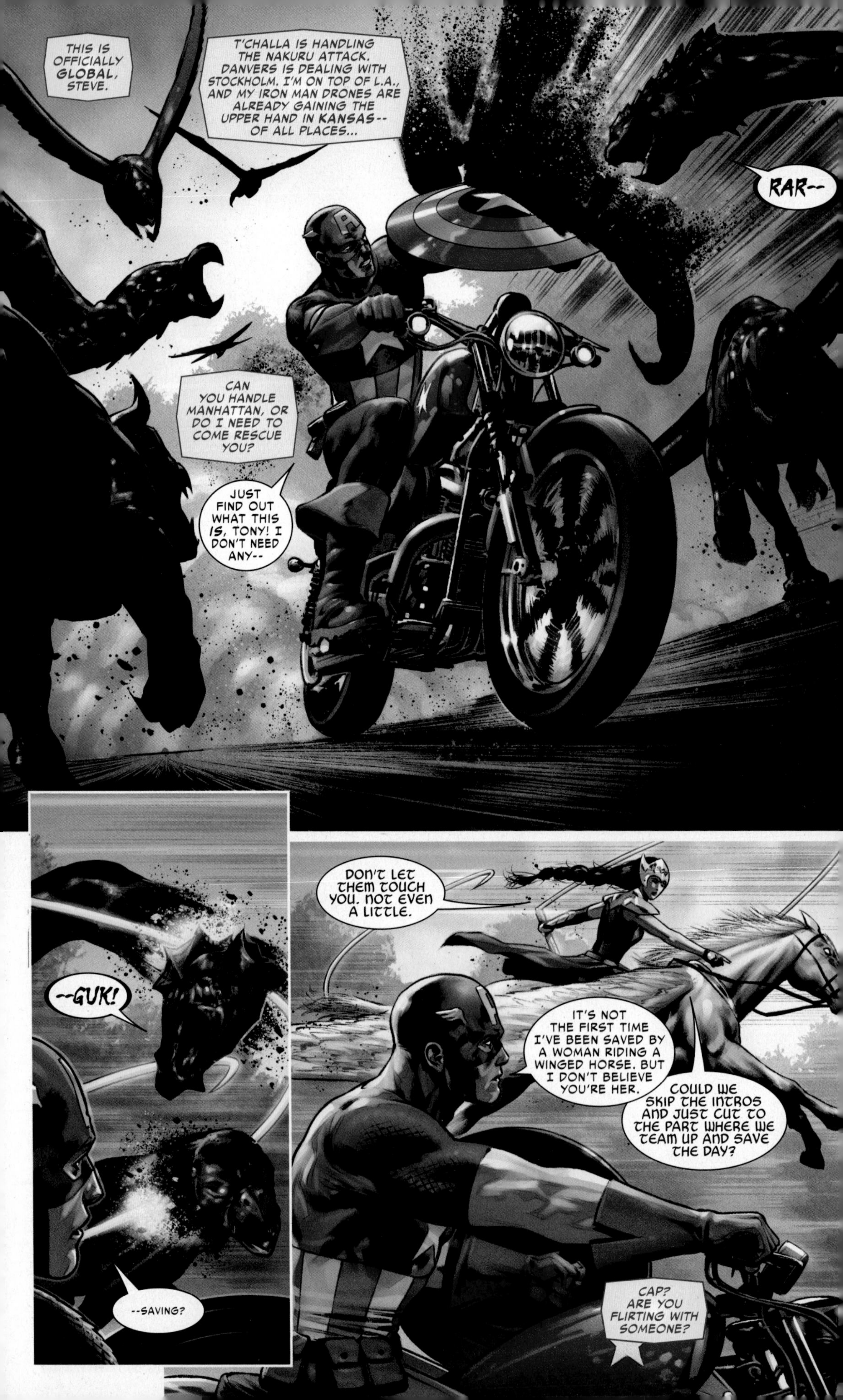
THIS IS OFFICIALLY GLOBAL, STEVE.
T'CHALLA IS HANDLING THE NAKURU ATTACK. DANVERS IS DEALING WITH STOCKHOLM. I'M ON TOP OF L.A., AND MY IRON MAN DRONES ARE ALREADY GAINING THE UPPER HAND IN KANSAS-- OF ALL PLACES...
RAR--
CAN YOU HANDLE MANHATTAN, OR DO I NEED TO COME RESCUE YOU?
JUST FIND OUT WHAT THIS IS, TONY! I DON'T NEED ANY--
--GUK!
--SAVING?
DON'T LET THEM TOUCH YOU. NOT EVEN A LITTLE.
IT'S NOT THE FIRST TIME I'VE BEEN SAVED BY A WOMAN RIDING A WINGED HORSE. BUT I DON'T BELIEVE YOU'RE HER.
COULD WE SKIP THE INTROS AND JUST CUT TO THE PART WHERE WE TEAM UP AND SAVE THE DAY?
CAP? ARE YOU FLIRTING WITH SOMEONE?

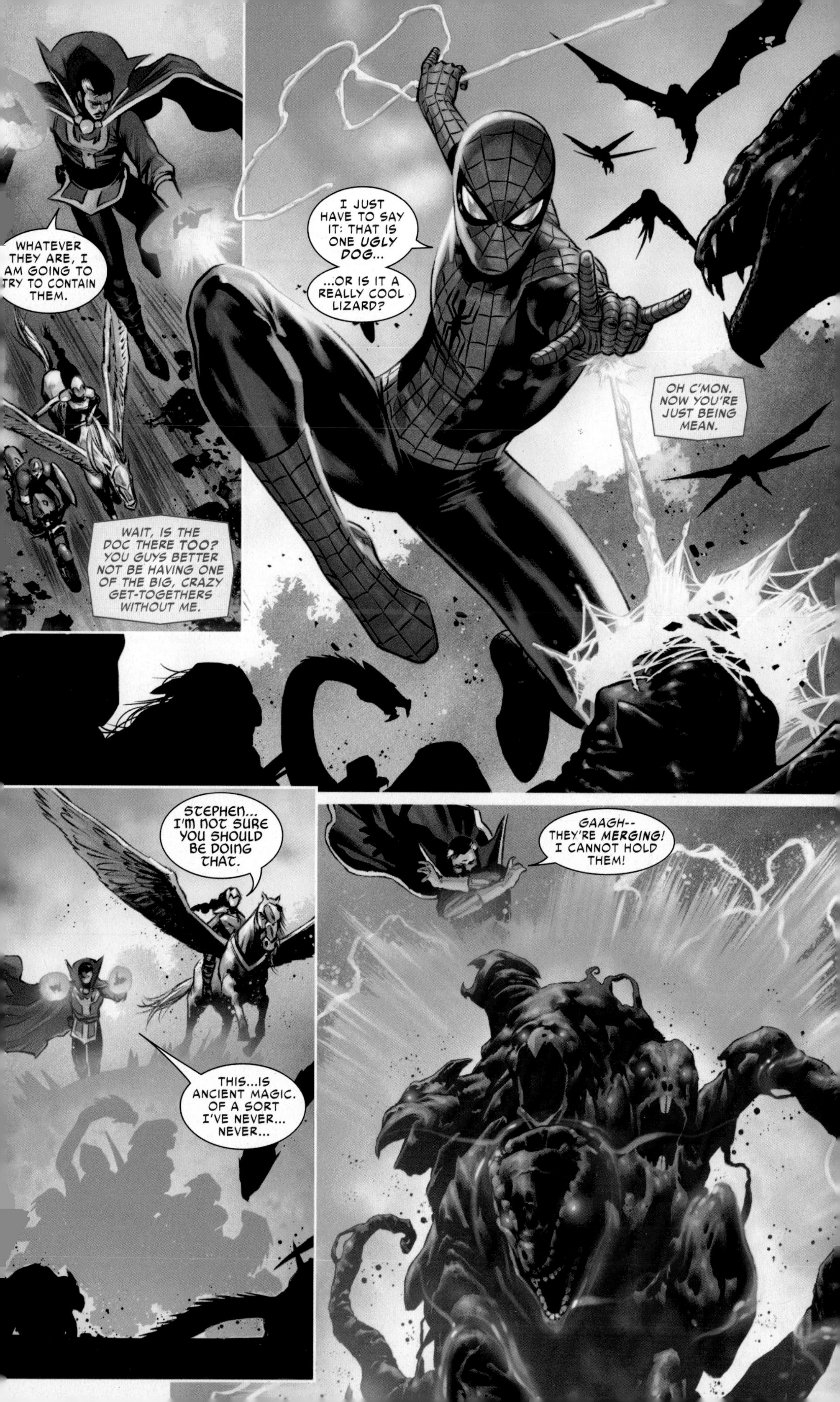

WHATEVER THEY ARE, I AM GOING TO TRY TO CONTAIN THEM.
WAIT, IS THE DOC THERE TOO? YOU GUYS BETTER NOT BE HAVING ONE OF THE BIG, CRAZY GET-TOGETHERS WITHOUT ME.
I JUST HAVE TO SAY IT: THAT IS ONE UGLY DOG...
...OR IS IT A REALLY COOL LIZARD?
OH C'MON. NOW YOU'RE JUST BEING MEAN.
STEPHEN... I'M NOT SURE YOU SHOULD BE DOING THAT.
THIS...IS ANCIENT MAGIC. OF A SORT I'VE NEVER... NEVER...
GAAGH-- THEY'RE MERGING! I CANNOT HOLD THEM!

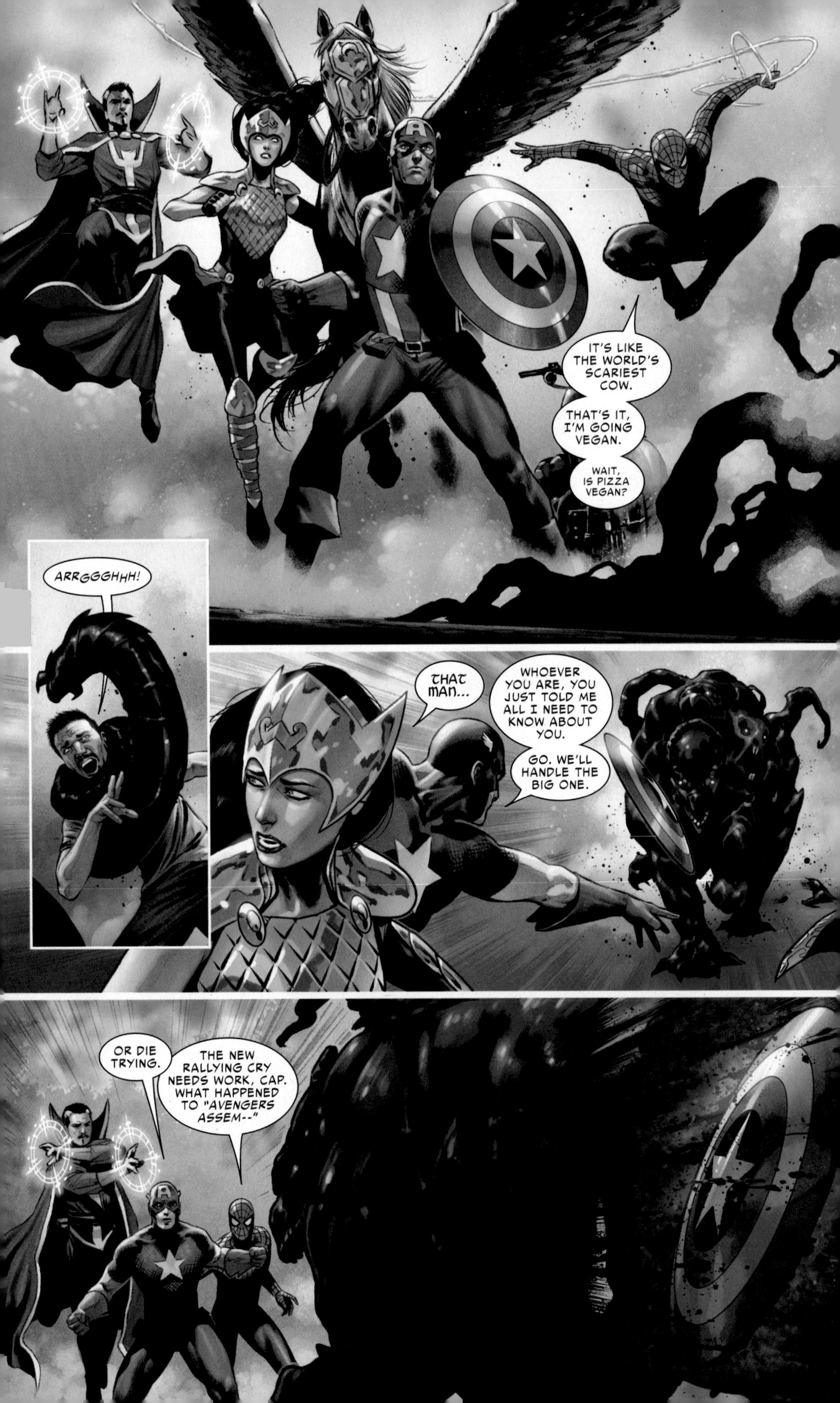
IT'S LIKE THE WORLD'S SCARIEST COW.
THAT'S IT, I'M GOING VEGAN.
WAIT, IS PIZZA VEGAN?
ARRGGGHHH!
THAT MAN...
WHOEVER YOU ARE, YOU JUST TOLD ME ALL I NEED TO KNOW ABOUT YOU.
GO. WE'LL HANDLE THE BIG ONE.
OR DIE TRYING.
THE NEW RALLYING CRY NEEDS WORK, CAP. WHAT HAPPENED TO "AVENGERS ASSEM--"

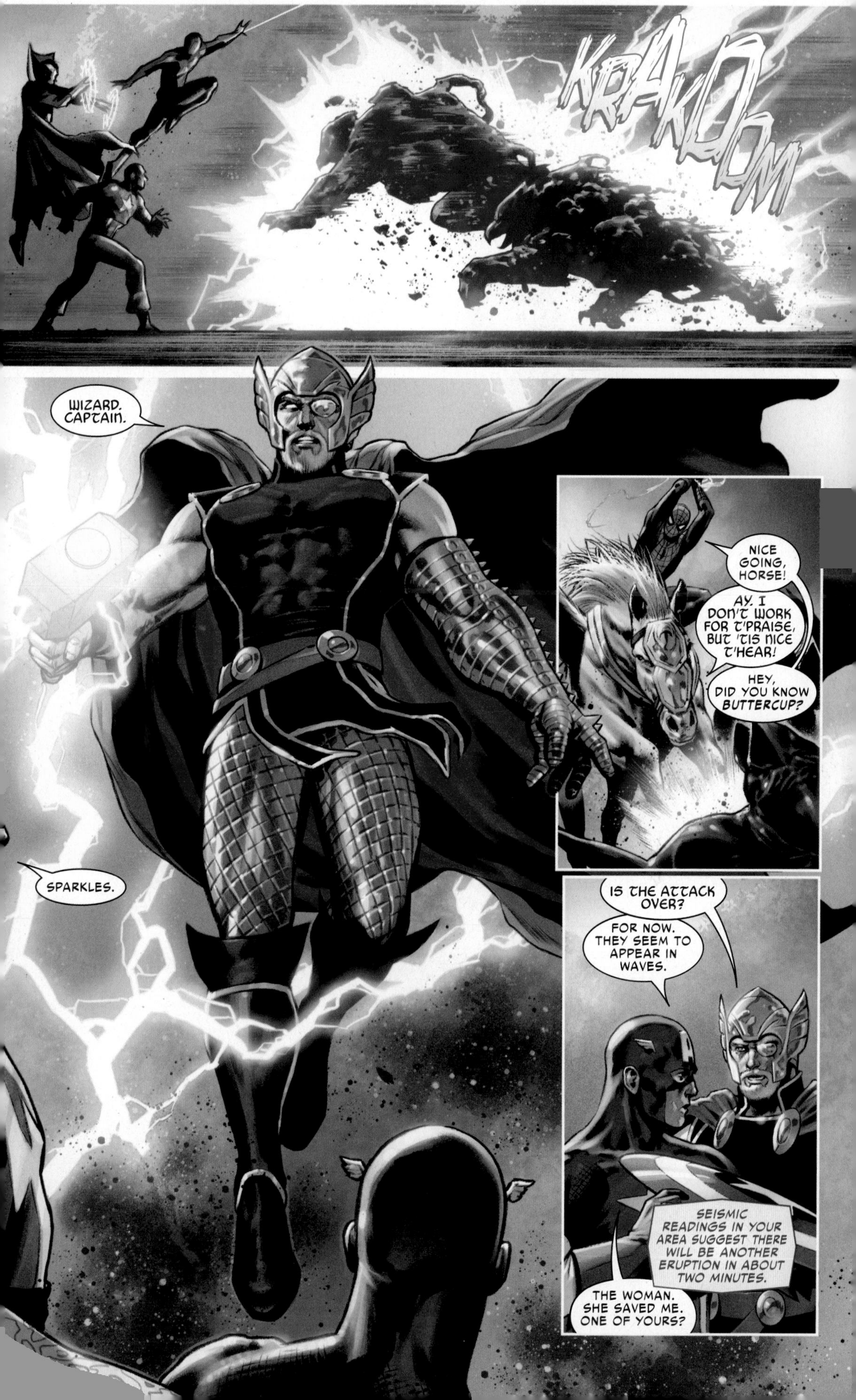
KRAKOOM
WIZARD. CAPTAIN.
SPARKLES.
NICE GOING, HORSE!
AY. I DON'T WORK FOR T'PRAISE, BUT 'TIS NICE T'HEAR!
HEY, DID YOU KNOW BUTTERCUP?
IS THE ATTACK OVER?
FOR NOW. THEY SEEM TO APPEAR IN WAVES.
SEISMIC READINGS IN YOUR AREA SUGGEST THERE WILL BE ANOTHER ERUPTION IN ABOUT TWO MINUTES.
THE WOMAN. SHE SAVED ME. ONE OF YOURS?

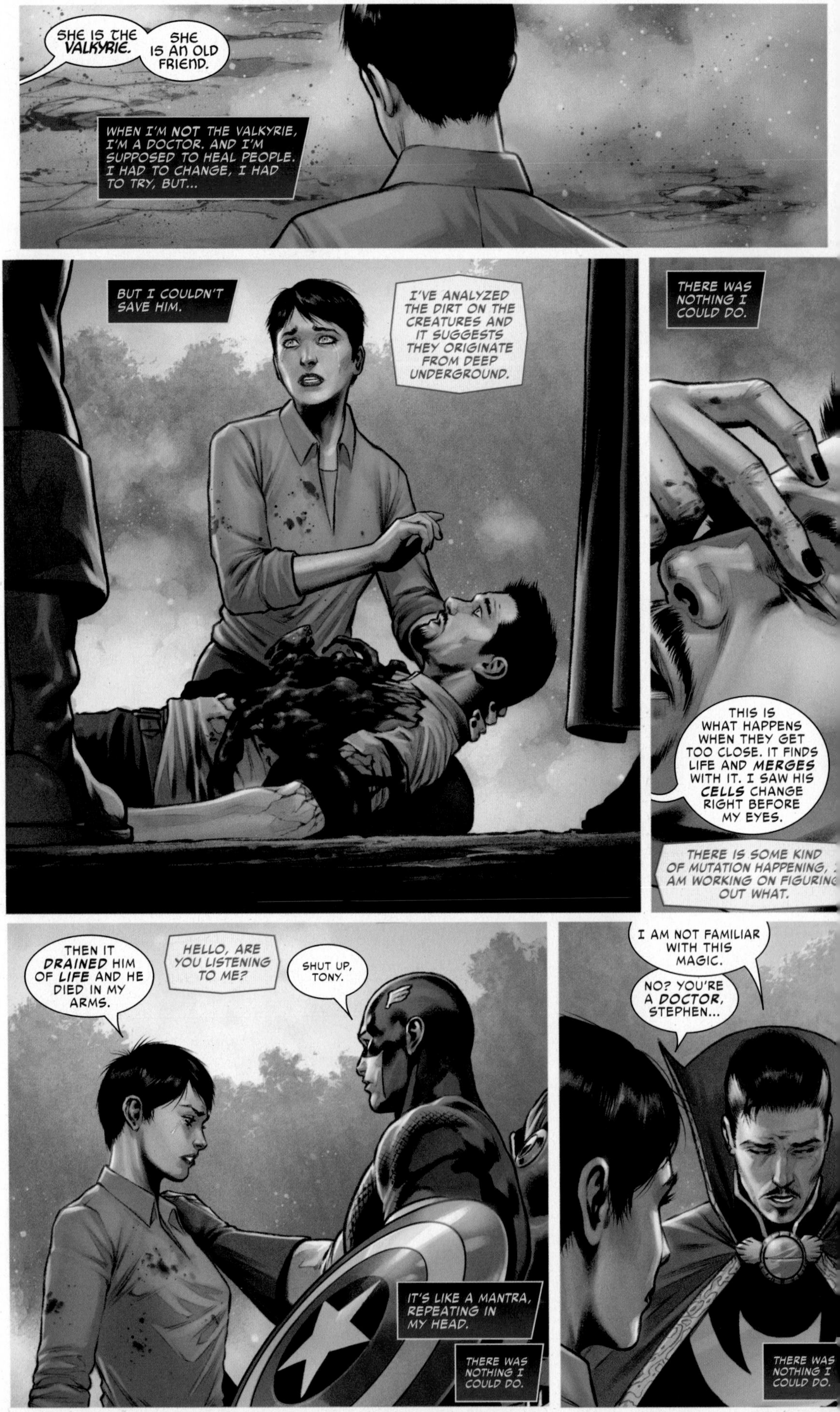
SHE IS THE VALKYRIE.
SHE IS AN OLD FRIEND.
WHEN I'M NOT THE VALKYRIE, I'M A DOCTOR. AND I'M SUPPOSED TO HEAL PEOPLE. I HAD TO CHANGE, I HAD TO TRY, BUT...
BUT I COULDN'T SAVE HIM.
I'VE ANALYZED THE DIRT ON THE CREATURES AND IT SUGGESTS THEY ORIGINATE FROM DEEP UNDERGROUND.
THERE WAS NOTHING I COULD DO.
THIS IS WHAT HAPPENS WHEN THEY GET TOO CLOSE. IT FINDS LIFE AND MERGES WITH IT. I SAW HIS CELLS CHANGE RIGHT BEFORE MY EYES.
THERE IS SOME KIND OF MUTATION HAPPENING. I AM WORKING ON FIGURING OUT WHAT.
THEN IT DRAINED HIM OF LIFE AND HE DIED IN MY ARMS.
HELLO, ARE YOU LISTENING TO ME?
SHUT UP, TONY.
IT'S LIKE A MANTRA, REPEATING IN MY HEAD.
THERE WAS NOTHING I COULD DO.
I AM NOT FAMILIAR WITH THIS MAGIC.
NO? YOU'RE A DOCTOR, STEPHEN...
THERE WAS NOTHING I COULD DO.

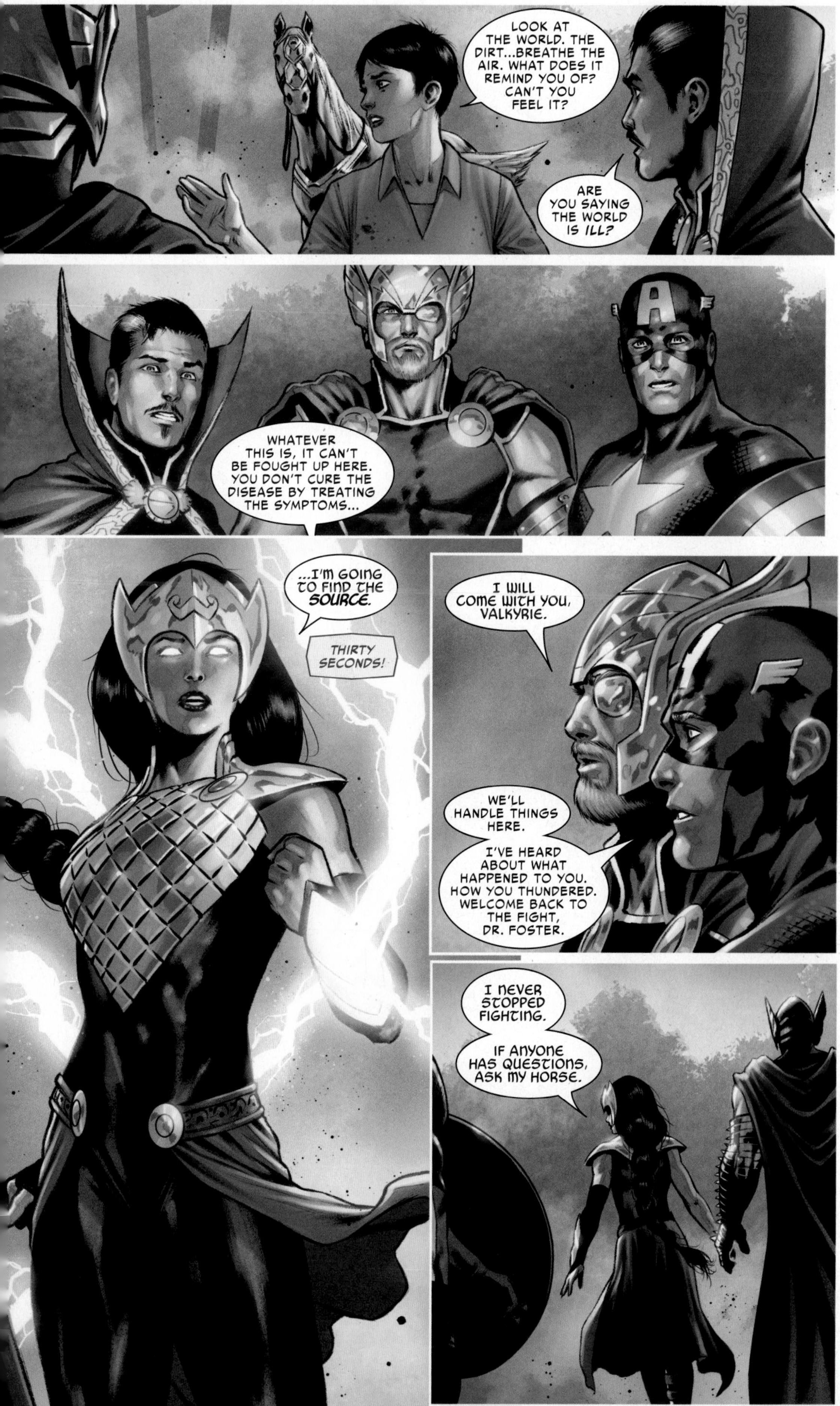

LOOK AT THE WORLD. THE DIRT...BREATHE THE AIR. WHAT DOES IT REMIND YOU OF? CAN'T YOU FEEL IT?
ARE YOU SAYING THE WORLD IS ILL?
WHATEVER THIS IS, IT CAN'T BE FOUGHT UP HERE. YOU DON'T CURE THE DISEASE BY TREATING THE SYMPTOMS...
...I'M GOING TO FIND THE SOURCE.
THIRTY SECONDS!
I WILL COME WITH YOU, VALKYRIE.
WE'LL HANDLE THINGS HERE.
I'VE HEARD ABOUT WHAT HAPPENED TO YOU. HOW YOU THUNDERED. WELCOME BACK TO THE FIGHT, DR. FOSTER.
I NEVER STOPPED FIGHTING.
IF ANYONE HAS QUESTIONS, ASK MY HORSE.

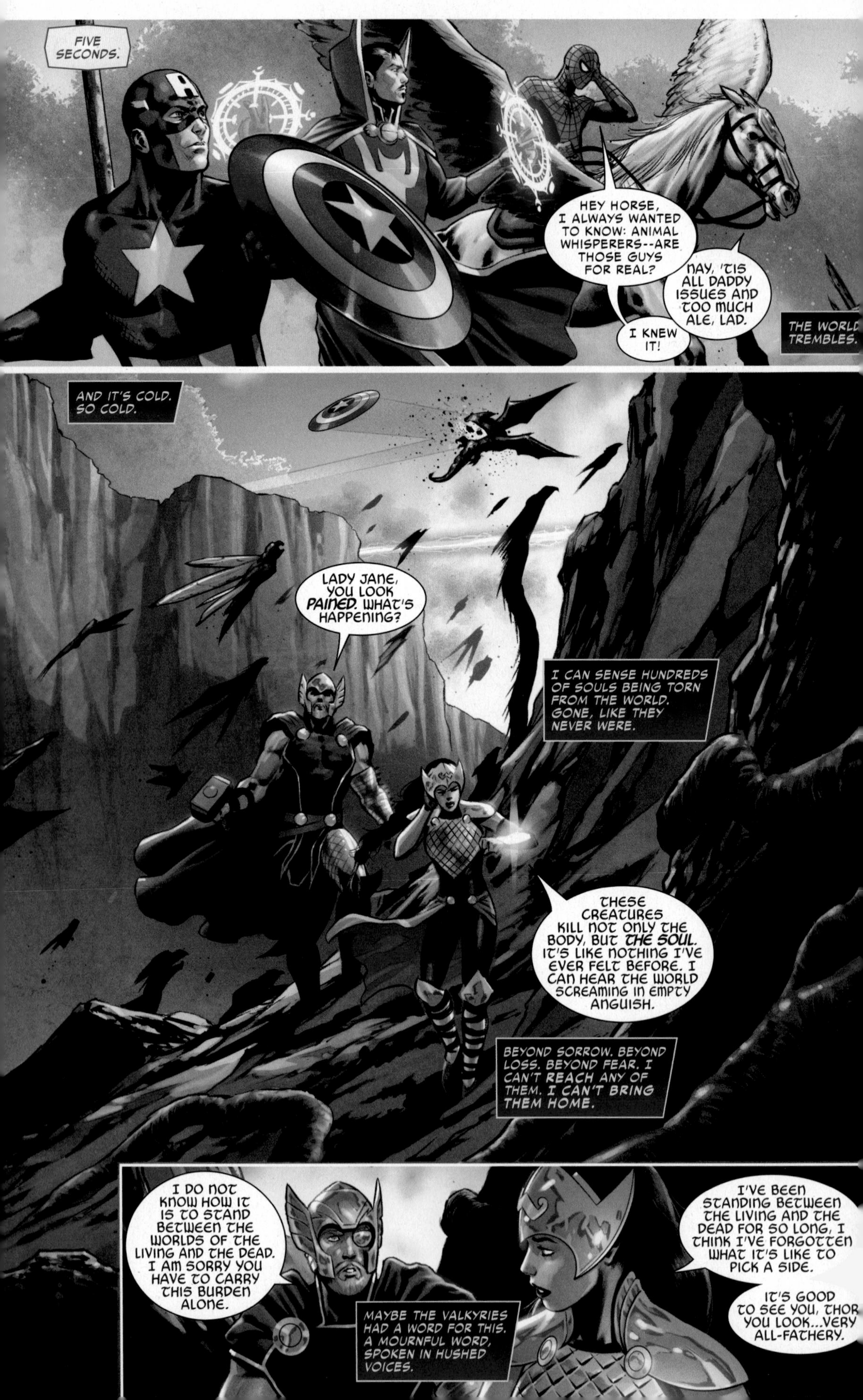
FIVE SECONDS.
HEY HORSE, I ALWAYS WANTED TO KNOW: ANIMAL WHISPERERS--ARE THOSE GUYS FOR REAL?
NAY, 'TIS ALL DADDY ISSUES AND TOO MUCH ALE, LAD.
I KNEW IT!
THE WORLD TREMBLES.
AND IT'S COLD. SO COLD.
LADY JANE, YOU LOOK PAINED. WHAT'S HAPPENING?
I CAN SENSE HUNDREDS OF SOULS BEING TORN FROM THE WORLD. GONE, LIKE THEY NEVER WERE.
THESE CREATURES KILL NOT ONLY THE BODY, BUT THE SOUL. IT'S LIKE NOTHING I'VE EVER FELT BEFORE. I CAN HEAR THE WORLD SCREAMING IN EMPTY ANGUISH.
BEYOND SORROW. BEYOND LOSS. BEYOND FEAR. I CAN'T REACH ANY OF THEM. I CAN'T BRING THEM HOME.
I DO NOT KNOW HOW IT IS TO STAND BETWEEN THE WORLDS OF THE LIVING AND THE DEAD. I AM SORRY YOU HAVE TO CARRY THIS BURDEN ALONE.
MAYBE THE VALKYRIES HAD A WORD FOR THIS. A MOURNFUL WORD, SPOKEN IN HUSHED VOICES.
I'VE BEEN STANDING BETWEEN THE LIVING AND THE DEAD FOR SO LONG, I THINK I'VE FORGOTTEN WHAT IT'S LIKE TO PICK A SIDE.
IT'S GOOD TO SEE YOU, THOR. YOU LOOK...VERY ALL-FATHERY.

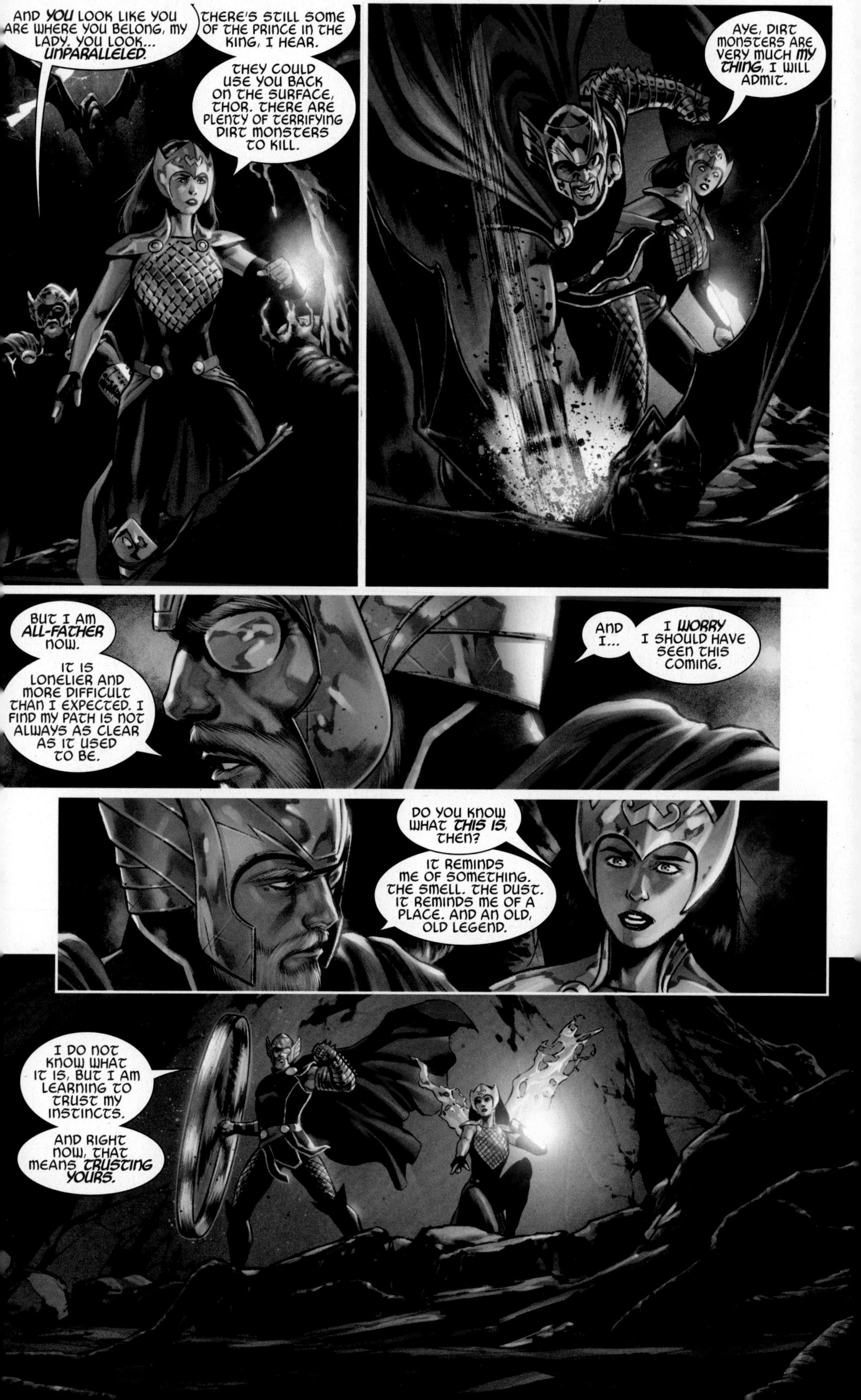

AND YOU LOOK LIKE YOU ARE WHERE YOU BELONG, MY LADY. YOU LOOK... UNPARALLELED.
THERE'S STILL SOME OF THE PRINCE IN THE KING, I HEAR.
THEY COULD USE YOU BACK ON THE SURFACE, THOR. THERE ARE PLENTY OF TERRIFYING DIRT MONSTERS TO KILL.
AYE, DIRT MONSTERS ARE VERY MUCH MY THING, I WILL ADMIT.
BUT I AM ALL-FATHER NOW.
IT IS LONELIER AND MORE DIFFICULT THAN I EXPECTED. I FIND MY PATH IS NOT ALWAYS AS CLEAR AS IT USED TO BE.
AND I...
I WORRY I SHOULD HAVE SEEN THIS COMING.
DO YOU KNOW WHAT THIS IS, THEN?
IT REMINDS ME OF SOMETHING. THE SMELL. THE DUST. IT REMINDS ME OF A PLACE. AND AN OLD, OLD LEGEND.
I DO NOT KNOW WHAT IT IS, BUT I AM LEARNING TO TRUST MY INSTINCTS.
AND RIGHT NOW, THAT MEANS TRUSTING YOURS.

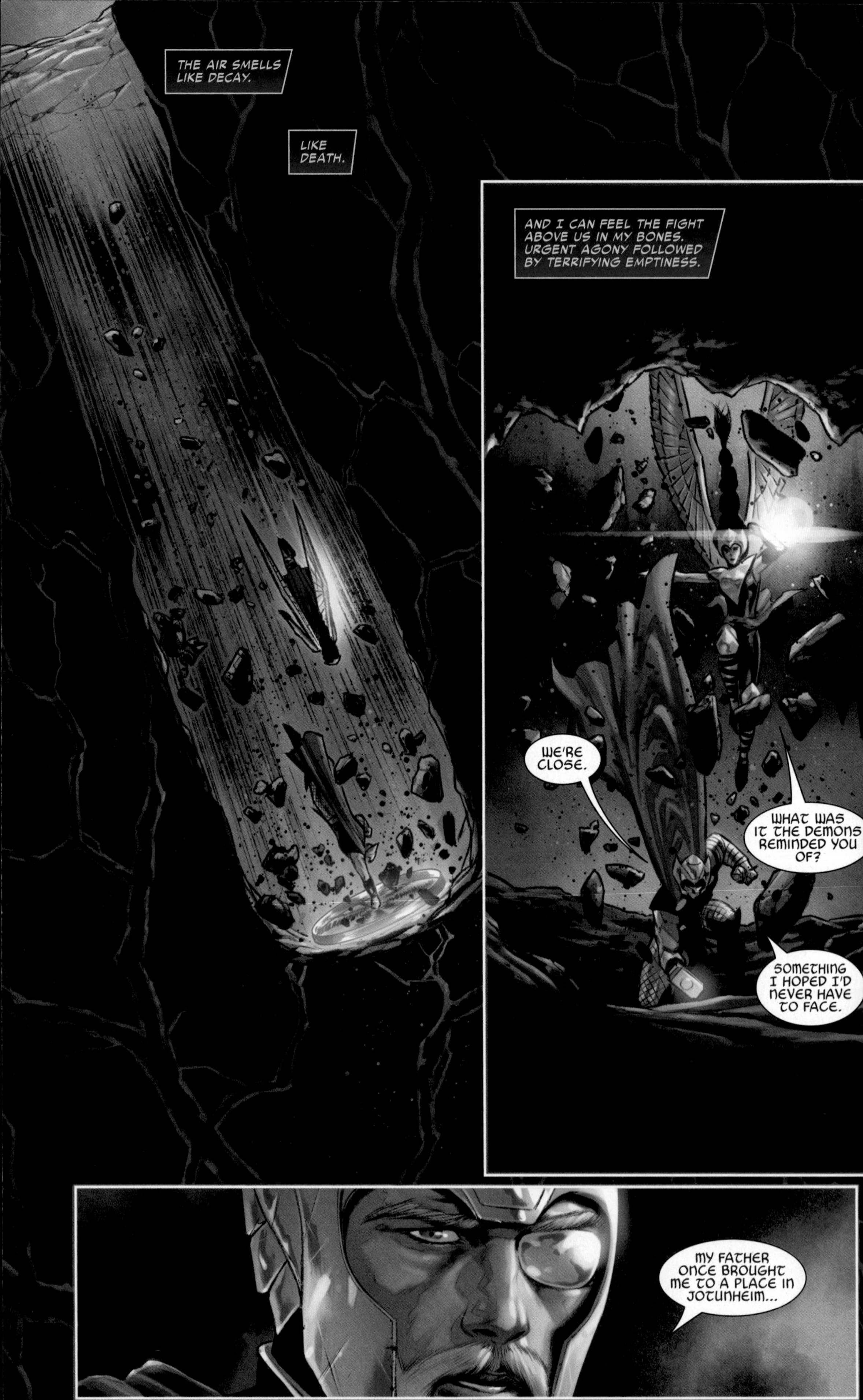
THE AIR SMELLS LIKE DECAY.
LIKE DEATH.
AND I CAN FEEL THE FIGHT ABOVE US IN MY BONES. URGENT AGONY FOLLOWED BY TERRIFYING EMPTINESS.
WE'RE CLOSE.
WHAT WAS IT THE DEMONS REMINDED YOU OF?
SOMETHING I HOPED I'D NEVER HAVE TO FACE.
MY FATHER ONCE BROUGHT ME TO A PLACE IN JOTUNHEIM...

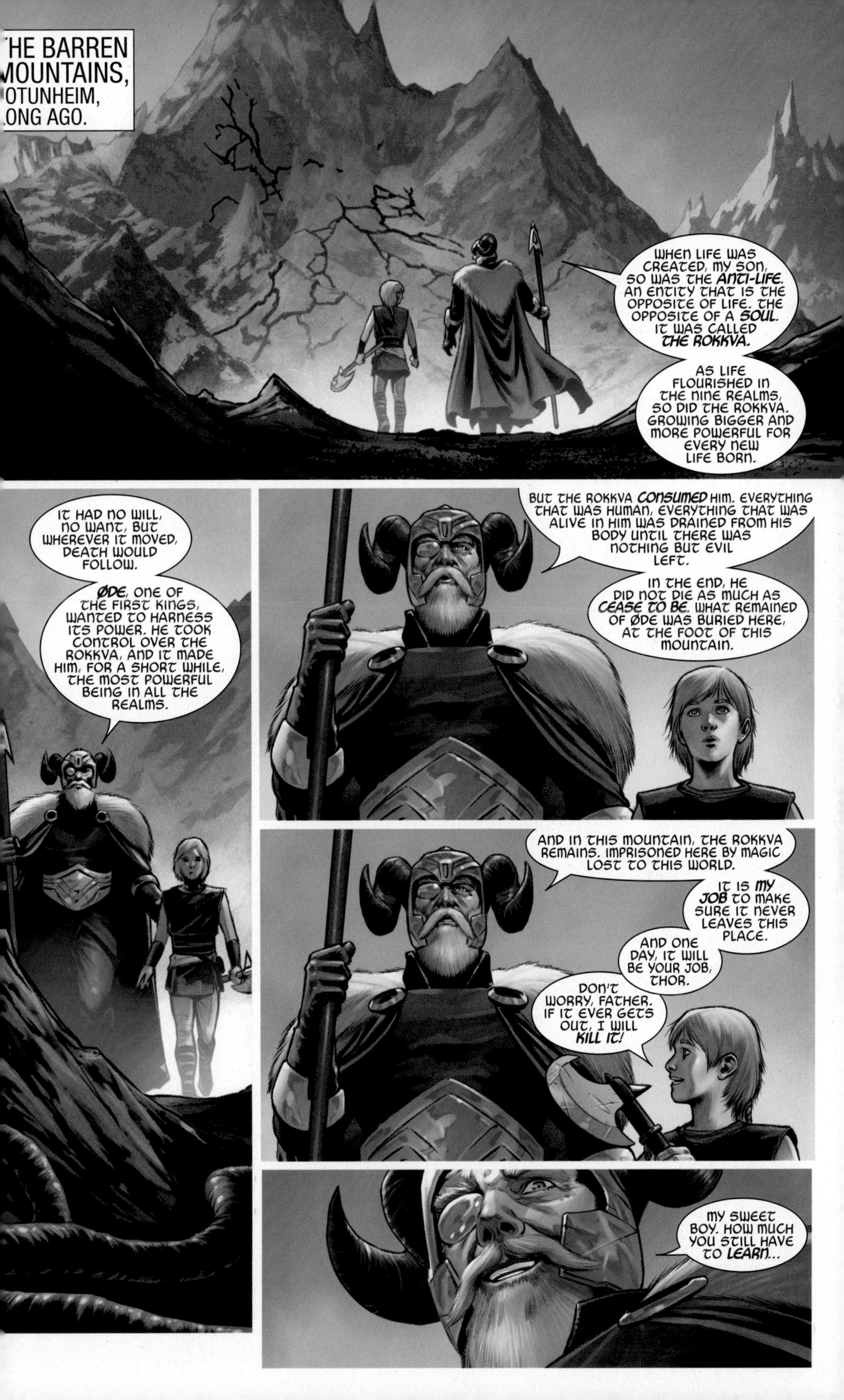
THE BARREN MOUNTAINS, JOTUNHEIM, LONG AGO.
WHEN LIFE WAS CREATED, MY SON, SO WAS THE ANTI-LIFE. AN ENTITY THAT IS THE OPPOSITE OF LIFE. THE OPPOSITE OF A SOUL. IT WAS CALLED THE ROKKVA.
AS LIFE FLOURISHED IN THE NINE REALMS, SO DID THE ROKKVA. GROWING BIGGER AND MORE POWERFUL FOR EVERY NEW LIFE BORN.
IT HAD NO WILL, NO WANT, BUT WHEREVER IT MOVED, DEATH WOULD FOLLOW.
ØDE, ONE OF THE FIRST KINGS, WANTED TO HARNESS ITS POWER. HE TOOK CONTROL OVER THE ROKKVA, AND IT MADE HIM, FOR A SHORT WHILE, THE MOST POWERFUL BEING IN ALL THE REALMS.
BUT THE ROKKVA CONSUMED HIM. EVERYTHING THAT WAS HUMAN, EVERYTHING THAT WAS ALIVE IN HIM WAS DRAINED FROM HIS BODY UNTIL THERE WAS NOTHING BUT EVIL LEFT.
IN THE END, HE DID NOT DIE AS MUCH AS CEASE TO BE. WHAT REMAINED OF ØDE WAS BURIED HERE, AT THE FOOT OF THIS MOUNTAIN.
AND IN THIS MOUNTAIN, THE ROKKVA REMAINS. IMPRISONED HERE BY MAGIC LOST TO THIS WORLD.
IT IS MY JOB TO MAKE SURE IT NEVER LEAVES THIS PLACE.
AND ONE DAY, IT WILL BE YOUR JOB, THOR.
DON'T WORRY, FATHER. IF IT EVER GETS OUT, I WILL KILL IT!
MY SWEET BOY. HOW MUCH YOU STILL HAVE TO LEARN...

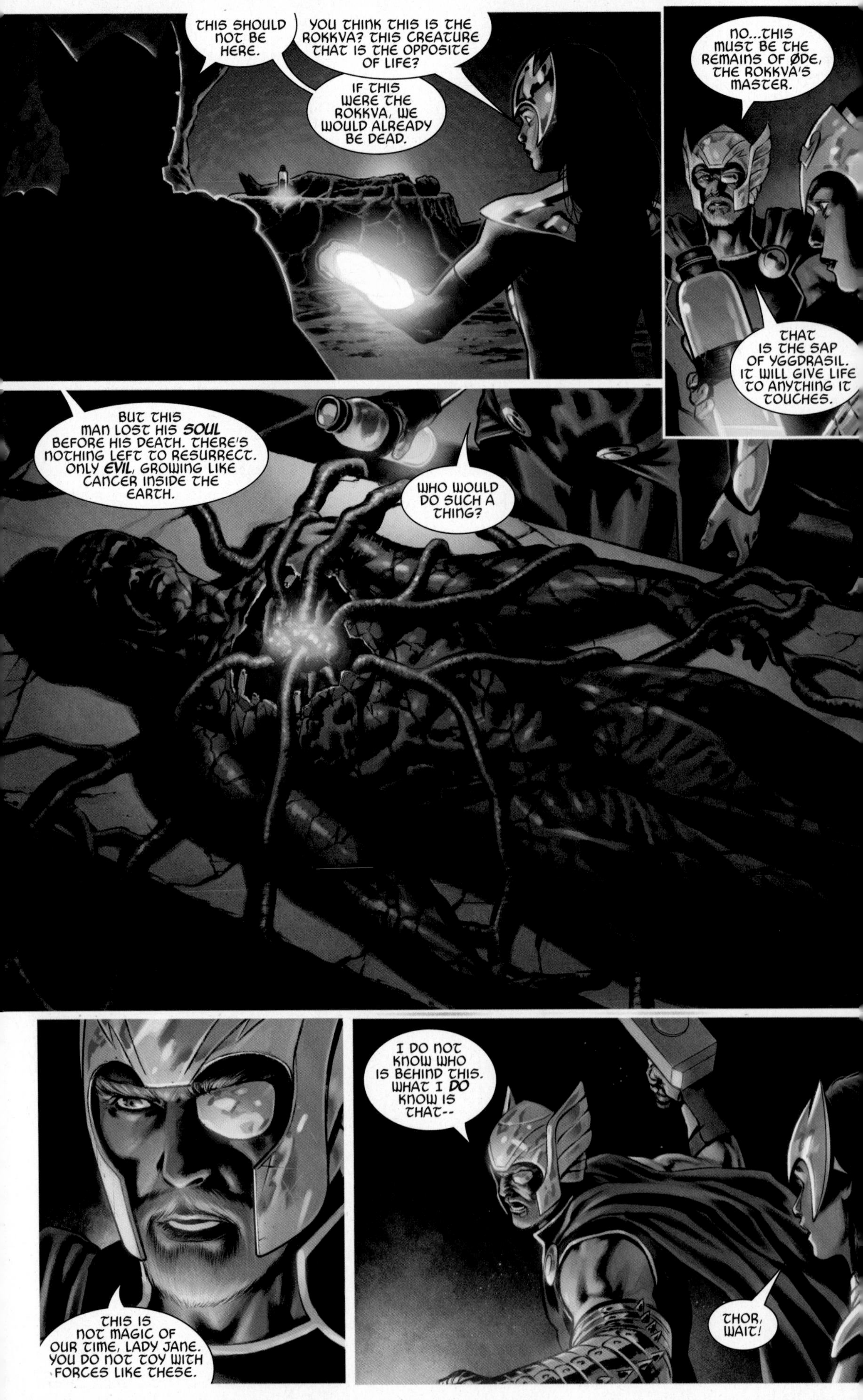

THIS SHOULD NOT BE HERE.
YOU THINK THIS IS THE ROKKVA? THIS CREATURE THAT IS THE OPPOSITE OF LIFE?
IF THIS WERE THE ROKKVA, WE WOULD ALREADY BE DEAD.
NO...THIS MUST BE THE REMAINS OF ØDE, THE ROKKVA'S MASTER.
THAT IS THE SAP OF YGGDRASIL. IT WILL GIVE LIFE TO ANYTHING IT TOUCHES.
BUT THIS MAN LOST HIS SOUL BEFORE HIS DEATH. THERE'S NOTHING LEFT TO RESURRECT. ONLY EVIL, GROWING LIKE CANCER INSIDE THE EARTH.
WHO WOULD DO SUCH A THING?
THIS IS NOT MAGIC OF OUR TIME, LADY JANE. YOU DO NOT TOY WITH FORCES LIKE THESE.
I DO NOT KNOW WHO IS BEHIND THIS. WHAT I DO KNOW IS THAT--
THOR, WAIT!

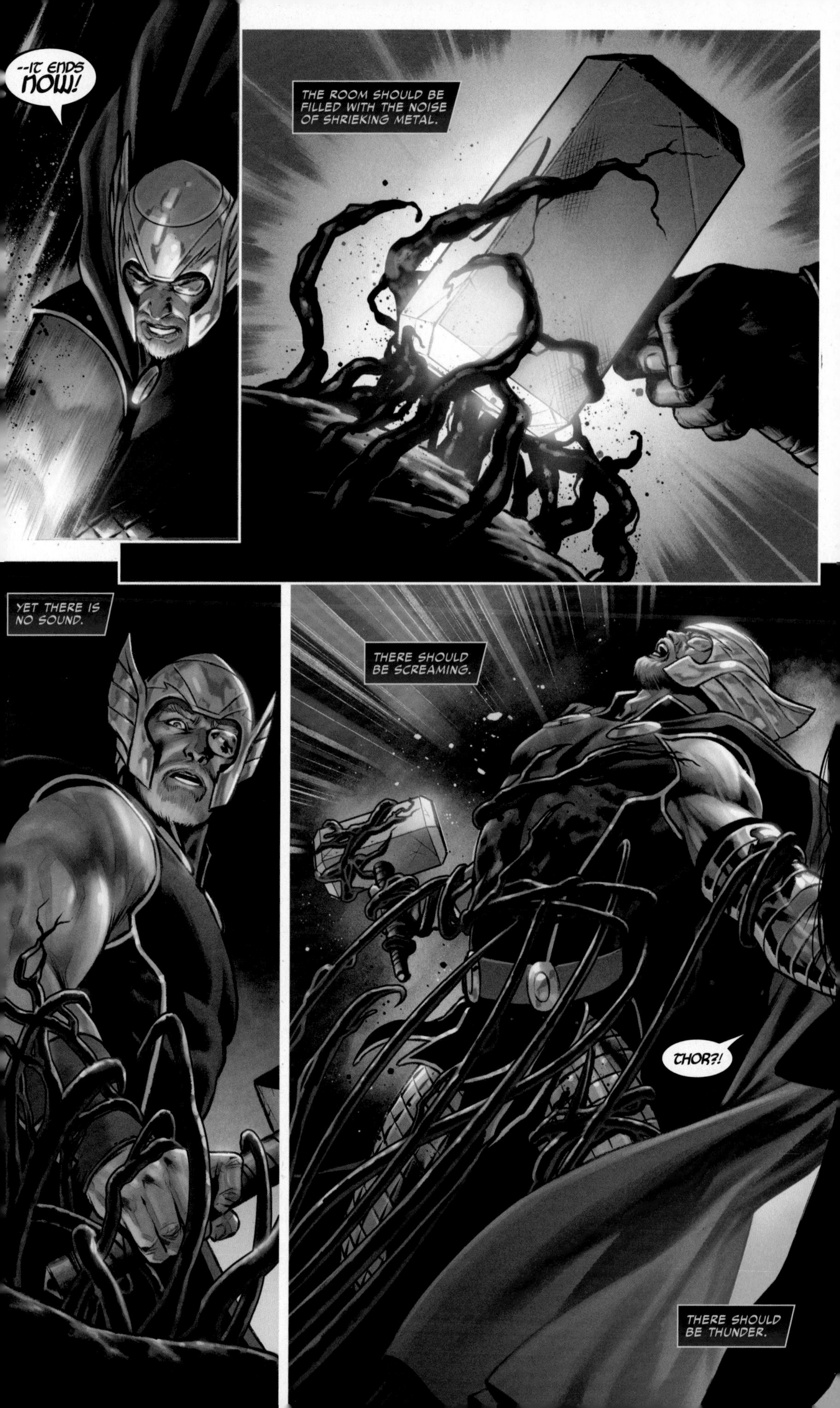
--IT ENDS NOW!
THE ROOM SHOULD BE FILLED WITH THE NOISE OF SHRIEKING METAL.
YET THERE IS NO SOUND.
THERE SHOULD BE SCREAMING.
THOR?!
THERE SHOULD BE THUNDER.

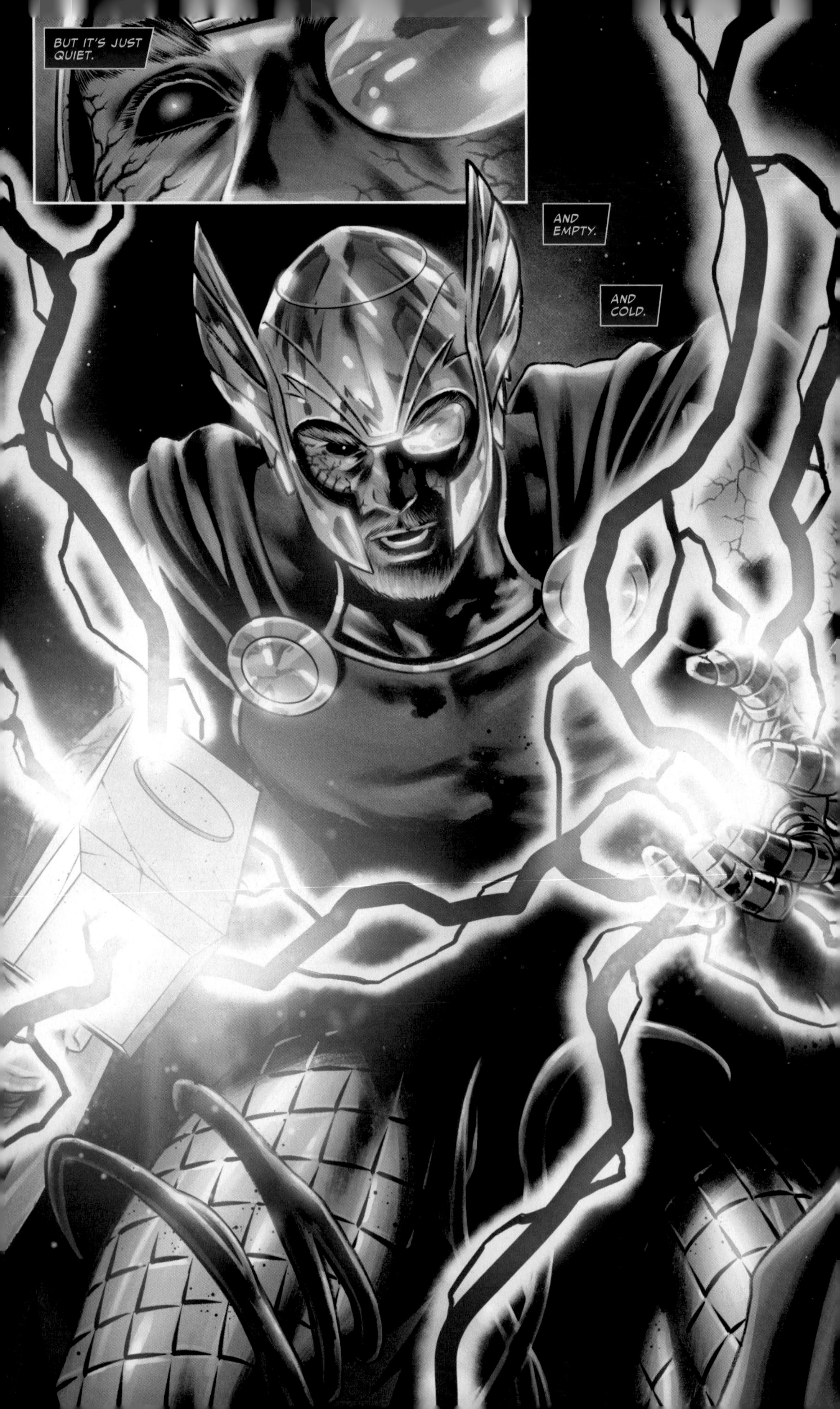
BUT IT'S JUST QUIET.
AND EMPTY.
AND COLD.

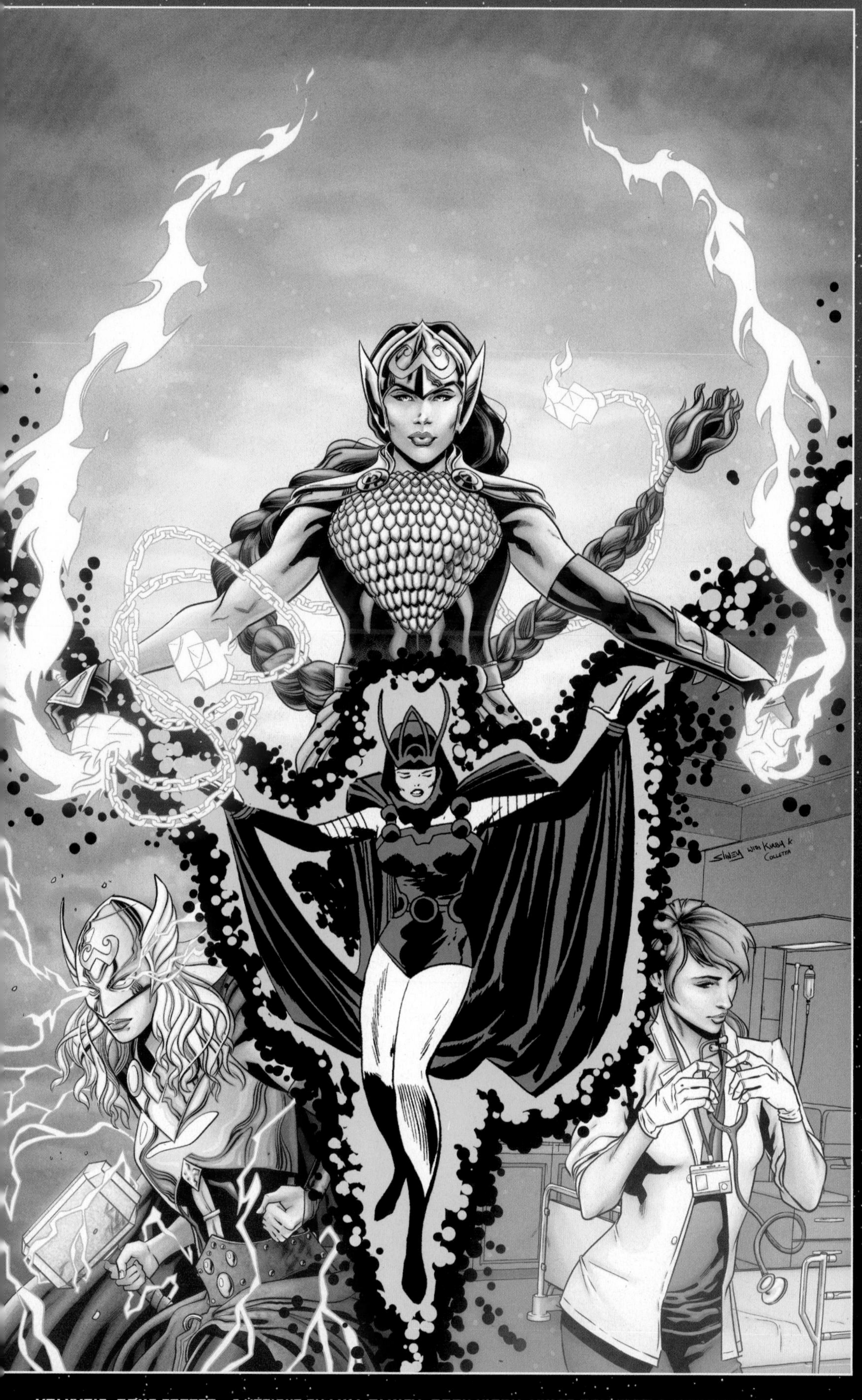
SLINEY WITH KIRBY & COLLETTA

VALKYRIE: JANE FOSTER #1 VARIANT BY WILL SLINEY, JACK KIRBY, VINCE COLLETTA & MORRY HOLLOWELL

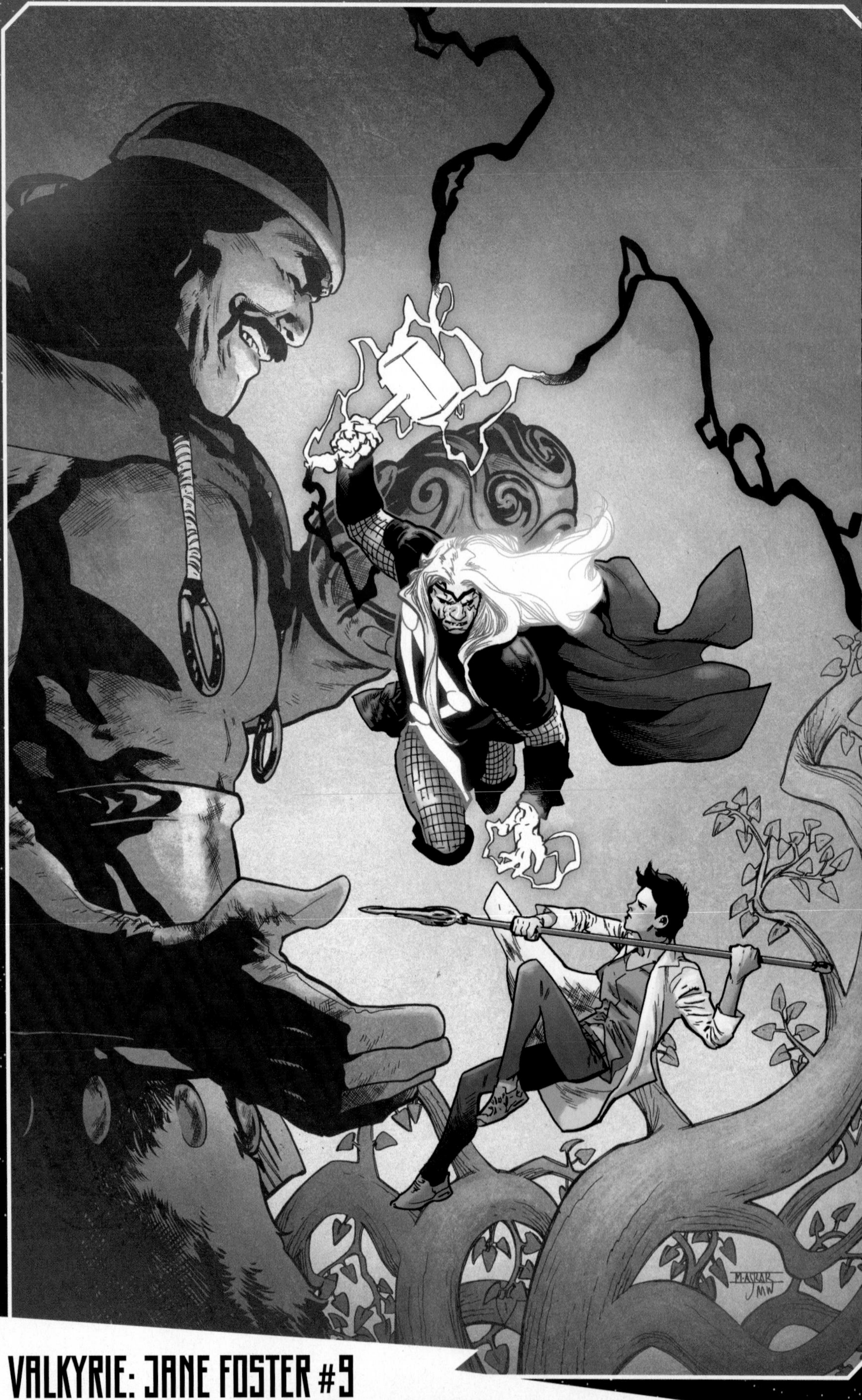
MEDKAR MW

VALKYRIE: JANE FOSTER #9

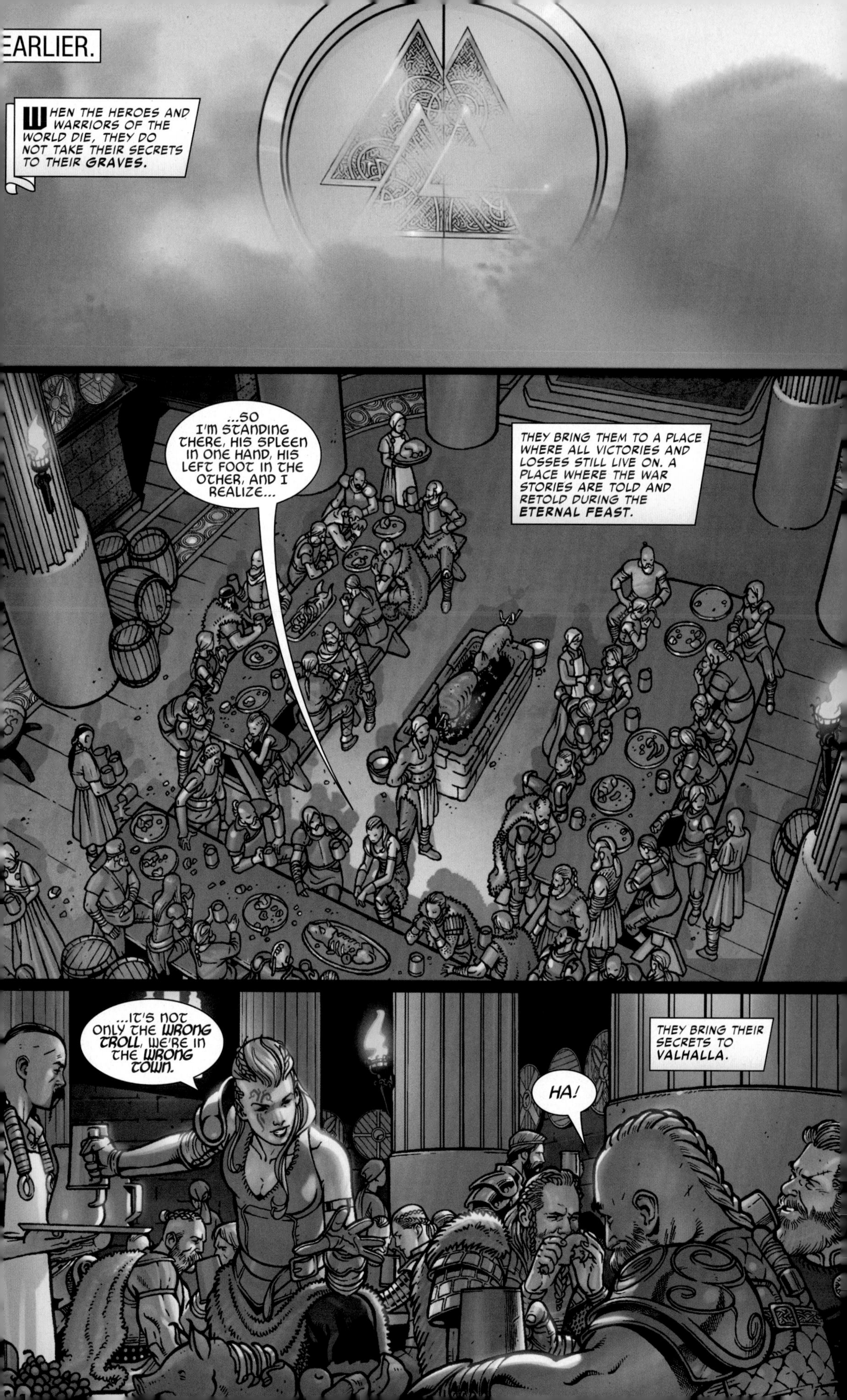
EARLIER.
WHEN THE HEROES AND WARRIORS OF THE WORLD DIE, THEY DO NOT TAKE THEIR SECRETS TO THEIR GRAVES.
...SO I'M STANDING THERE, HIS SPLEEN IN ONE HAND, HIS LEFT FOOT IN THE OTHER, AND I REALIZE...
THEY BRING THEM TO A PLACE WHERE ALL VICTORIES AND LOSSES STILL LIVE ON. A PLACE WHERE THE WAR STORIES ARE TOLD AND RETOLD DURING THE ETERNAL FEAST.
...IT'S NOT ONLY THE WRONG TROLL, WE'RE IN THE WRONG TOWN.
THEY BRING THEIR SECRETS TO VALHALLA.
HA!

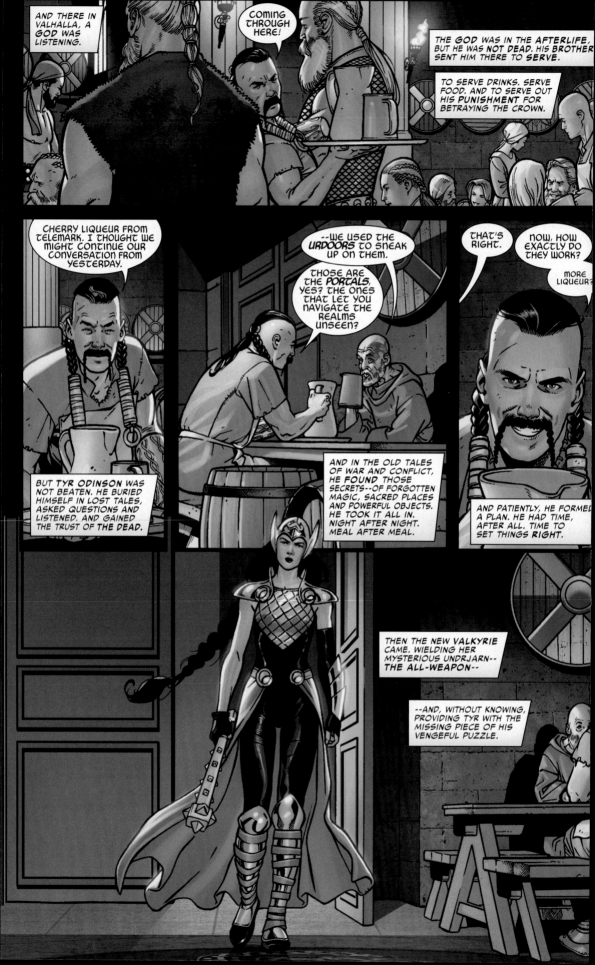

AND THERE IN VALHALLA, A GOD WAS LISTENING.

COMING THROUGH HERE!

THE GOD WAS IN THE AFTERLIFE, BUT HE WAS NOT DEAD. HIS BROTHER SENT HIM THERE TO SERVE.

TO SERVE DRINKS. SERVE FOOD. AND TO SERVE OUT HIS PUNISHMENT FOR BETRAYING THE CROWN.

CHERRY LIQUEUR FROM TELEMARK. I THOUGHT WE MIGHT CONTINUE OUR CONVERSATION FROM YESTERDAY.

--WE USED THE *URDOORS* TO SNEAK UP ON THEM.

THOSE ARE THE *PORTALS*, YES? THE ONES THAT LET YOU NAVIGATE THE REALMS UNSEEN?

THAT'S RIGHT.

NOW, HOW EXACTLY DO THEY WORK?

MORE LIQUEUR?

BUT TYR ODINSON WAS NOT BEATEN. HE BURIED HIMSELF IN LOST TALES, ASKED QUESTIONS AND LISTENED. AND GAINED THE TRUST OF THE DEAD.

AND IN THE OLD TALES OF WAR AND CONFLICT, HE FOUND THOSE SECRETS--OF FORGOTTEN MAGIC, SACRED PLACES AND POWERFUL OBJECTS. HE TOOK IT ALL IN. NIGHT AFTER NIGHT. MEAL AFTER MEAL.

AND PATIENTLY, HE FORMED A PLAN. HE HAD TIME, AFTER ALL. TIME TO SET THINGS RIGHT.

THEN THE NEW VALKYRIE CAME. WIELDING HER MYSTERIOUS UNDRJARN-- THE ALL-WEAPON--

--AND, WITHOUT KNOWING, PROVIDING TYR WITH THE MISSING PIECE OF HIS VENGEFUL PUZZLE.

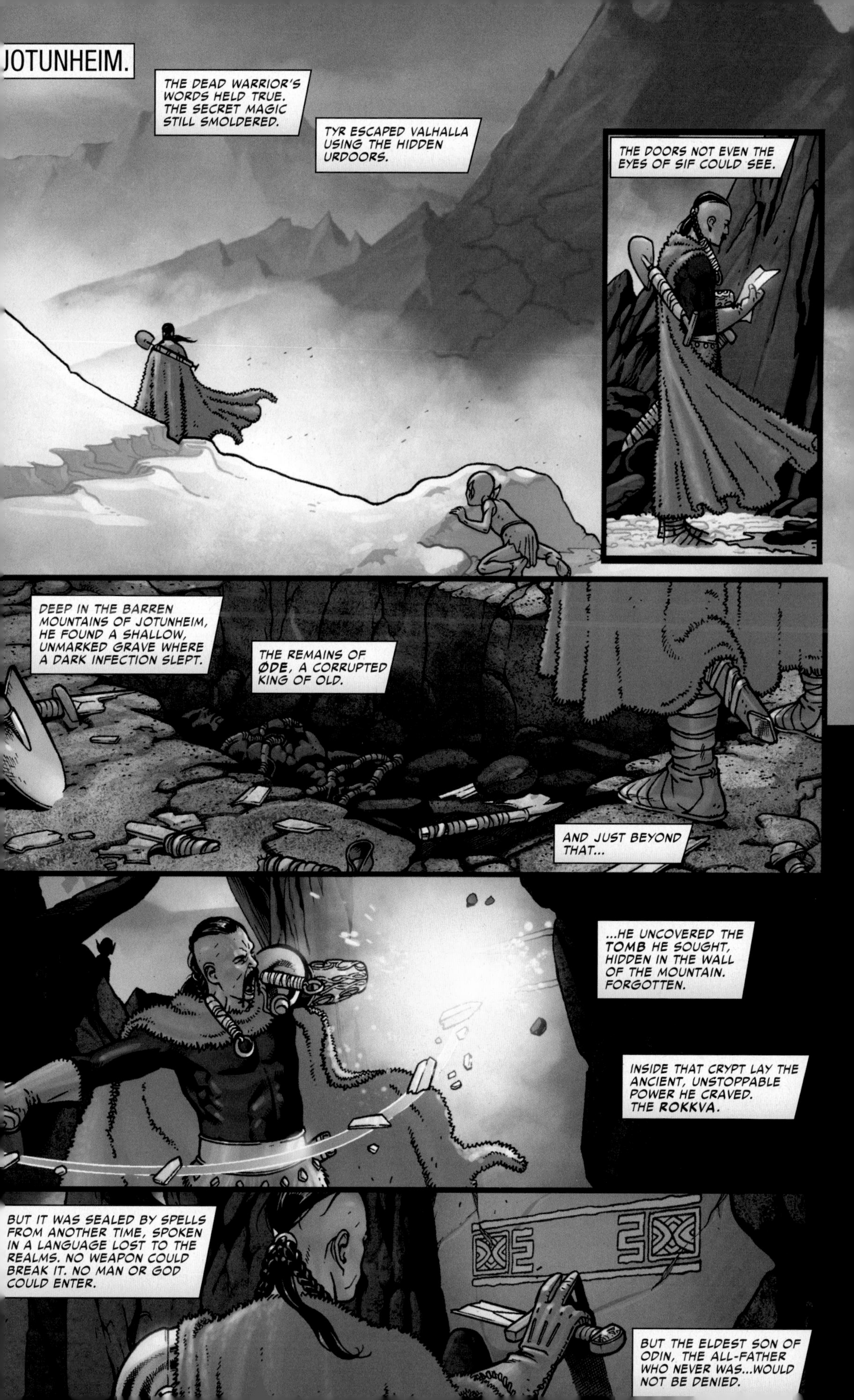
JOTUNHEIM.
THE DEAD WARRIOR'S WORDS HELD TRUE. THE SECRET MAGIC STILL SMOLDERED.
TYR ESCAPED VALHALLA USING THE HIDDEN URDOORS.
THE DOORS NOT EVEN THE EYES OF SIF COULD SEE.
DEEP IN THE BARREN MOUNTAINS OF JOTUNHEIM, HE FOUND A SHALLOW, UNMARKED GRAVE WHERE A DARK INFECTION SLEPT.
THE REMAINS OF ØDE, A CORRUPTED KING OF OLD.
AND JUST BEYOND THAT...
...HE UNCOVERED THE TOMB HE SOUGHT, HIDDEN IN THE WALL OF THE MOUNTAIN. FORGOTTEN.
INSIDE THAT CRYPT LAY THE ANCIENT, UNSTOPPABLE POWER HE CRAVED. THE ROKKVA.
BUT IT WAS SEALED BY SPELLS FROM ANOTHER TIME, SPOKEN IN A LANGUAGE LOST TO THE REALMS. NO WEAPON COULD BREAK IT. NO MAN OR GOD COULD ENTER.
BUT THE ELDEST SON OF ODIN, THE ALL-FATHER WHO NEVER WAS...WOULD NOT BE DENIED.

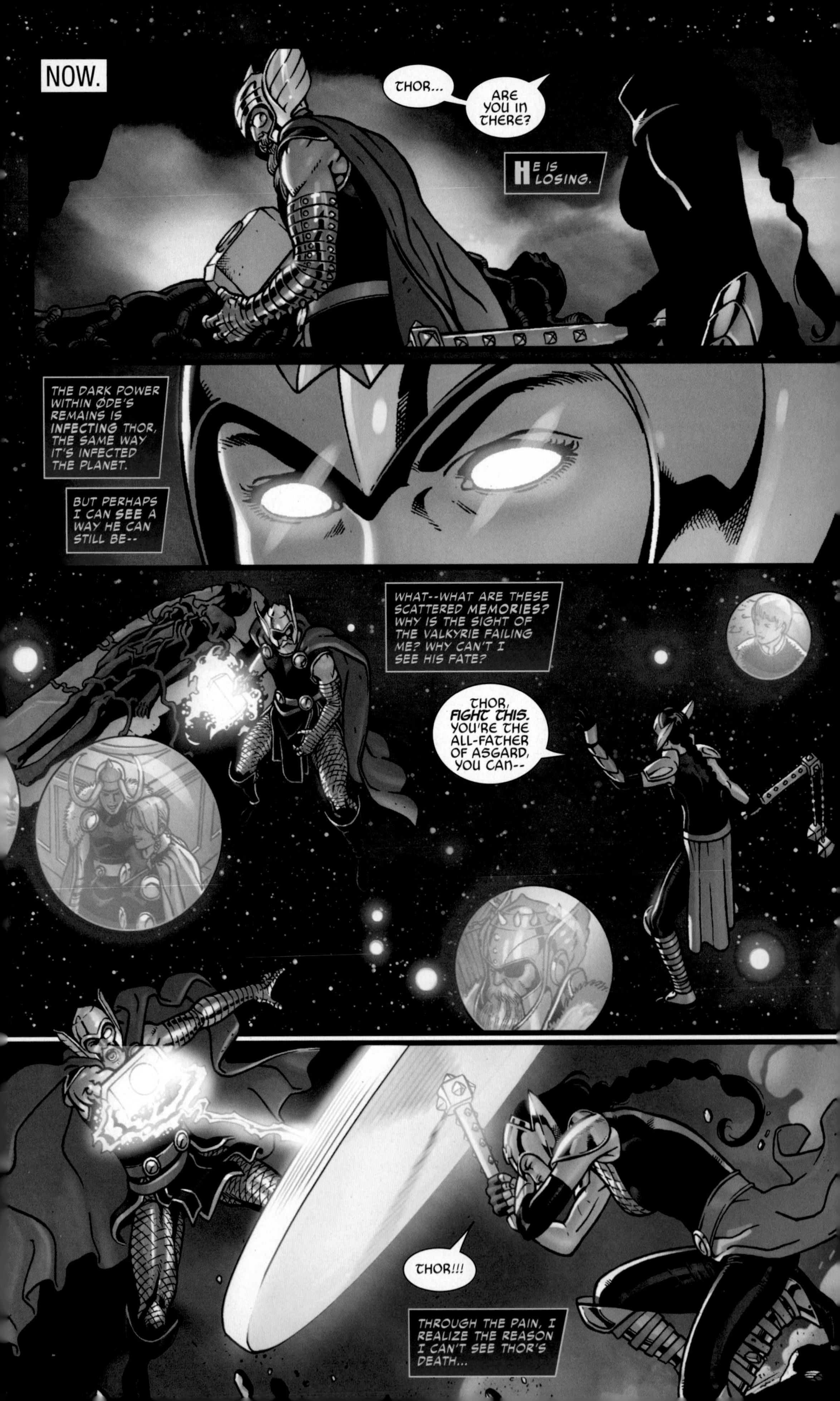
NOW.
THOR...
ARE YOU IN THERE?
HE IS LOSING.
THE DARK POWER WITHIN ØDE'S REMAINS IS INFECTING THOR, THE SAME WAY IT'S INFECTED THE PLANET.
BUT PERHAPS I CAN SEE A WAY HE CAN STILL BE--
WHAT--WHAT ARE THESE SCATTERED MEMORIES? WHY IS THE SIGHT OF THE VALKYRIE FAILING ME? WHY CAN'T I SEE HIS FATE?
THOR, FIGHT THIS. YOU'RE THE ALL-FATHER OF ASGARD, YOU CAN--
THOR!!!
THROUGH THE PAIN, I REALIZE THE REASON I CAN'T SEE THOR'S DEATH...

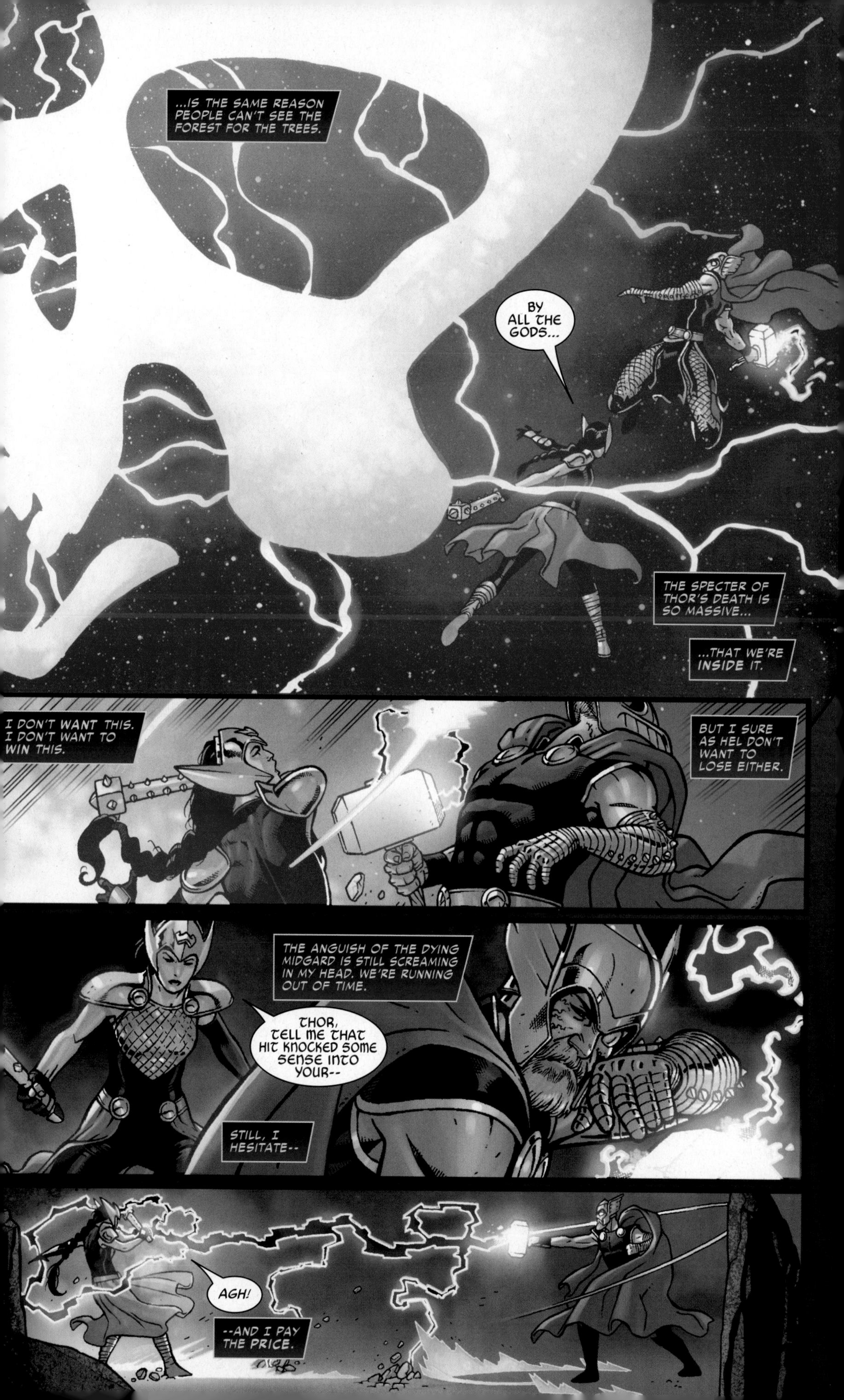
...IS THE SAME REASON PEOPLE CAN'T SEE THE FOREST FOR THE TREES.
BY ALL THE GODS...
THE SPECTER OF THOR'S DEATH IS SO MASSIVE...
...THAT WE'RE INSIDE IT.
I DON'T WANT THIS. I DON'T WANT TO WIN THIS.
BUT I SURE AS HEL DON'T WANT TO LOSE EITHER.
THE ANGUISH OF THE DYING MIDGARD IS STILL SCREAMING IN MY HEAD. WE'RE RUNNING OUT OF TIME.
THOR, TELL ME THAT HIT KNOCKED SOME SENSE INTO YOUR--
STILL, I HESITATE--
AGH!
--AND I PAY THE PRICE.

THIS IS NOT PAIN.

THIS IS SOMETHING

ELSE

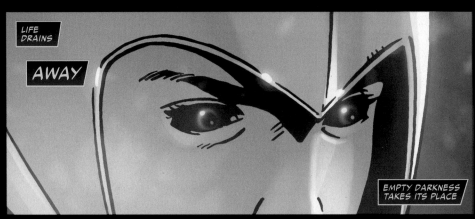

LIFE DRAINS

AWAY

EMPTY DARKNESS TAKES ITS PLACE

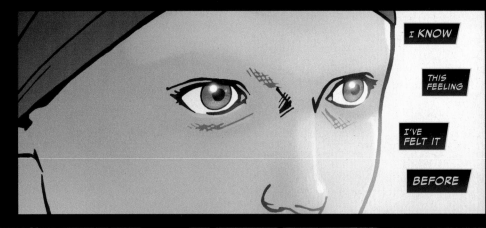

I KNOW

THIS FEELING

I'VE FELT IT

BEFORE

AND I KNOW HOW TO FIGHT THE DARKEST OF INFECTIONS.

AS A DOCTOR.

A PATIENT.

A THOR

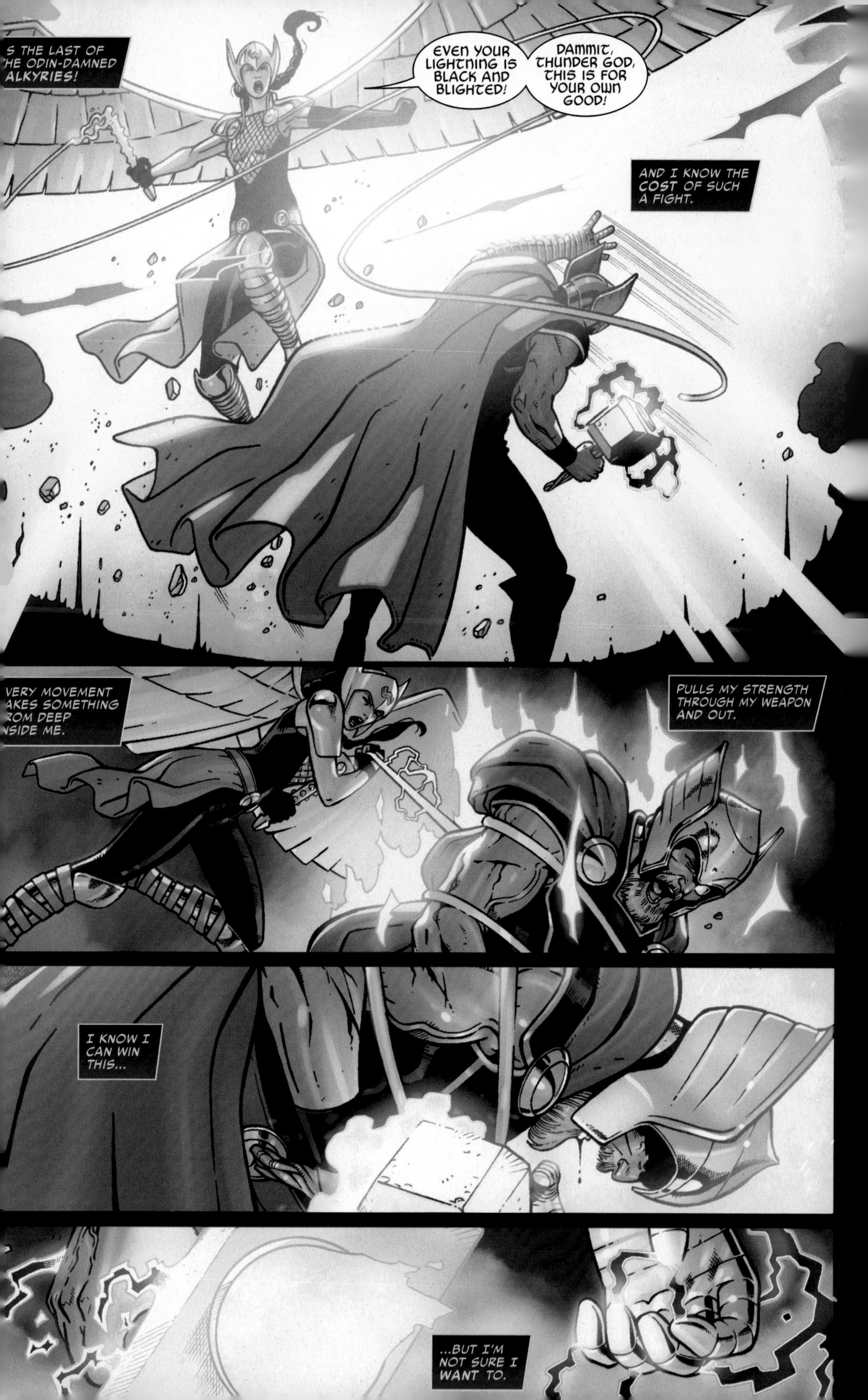
S THE LAST OF HE ODIN-DAMNED ALKYRIES!
EVEN YOUR LIGHTNING IS BLACK AND BLIGHTED!
DAMMIT, THUNDER GOD, THIS IS FOR YOUR OWN GOOD!
AND I KNOW THE COST OF SUCH A FIGHT.
VERY MOVEMENT AKES SOMETHING ROM DEEP NSIDE ME.
PULLS MY STRENGTH THROUGH MY WEAPON AND OUT.
I KNOW I CAN WIN THIS...
...BUT I'M NOT SURE I WANT TO.

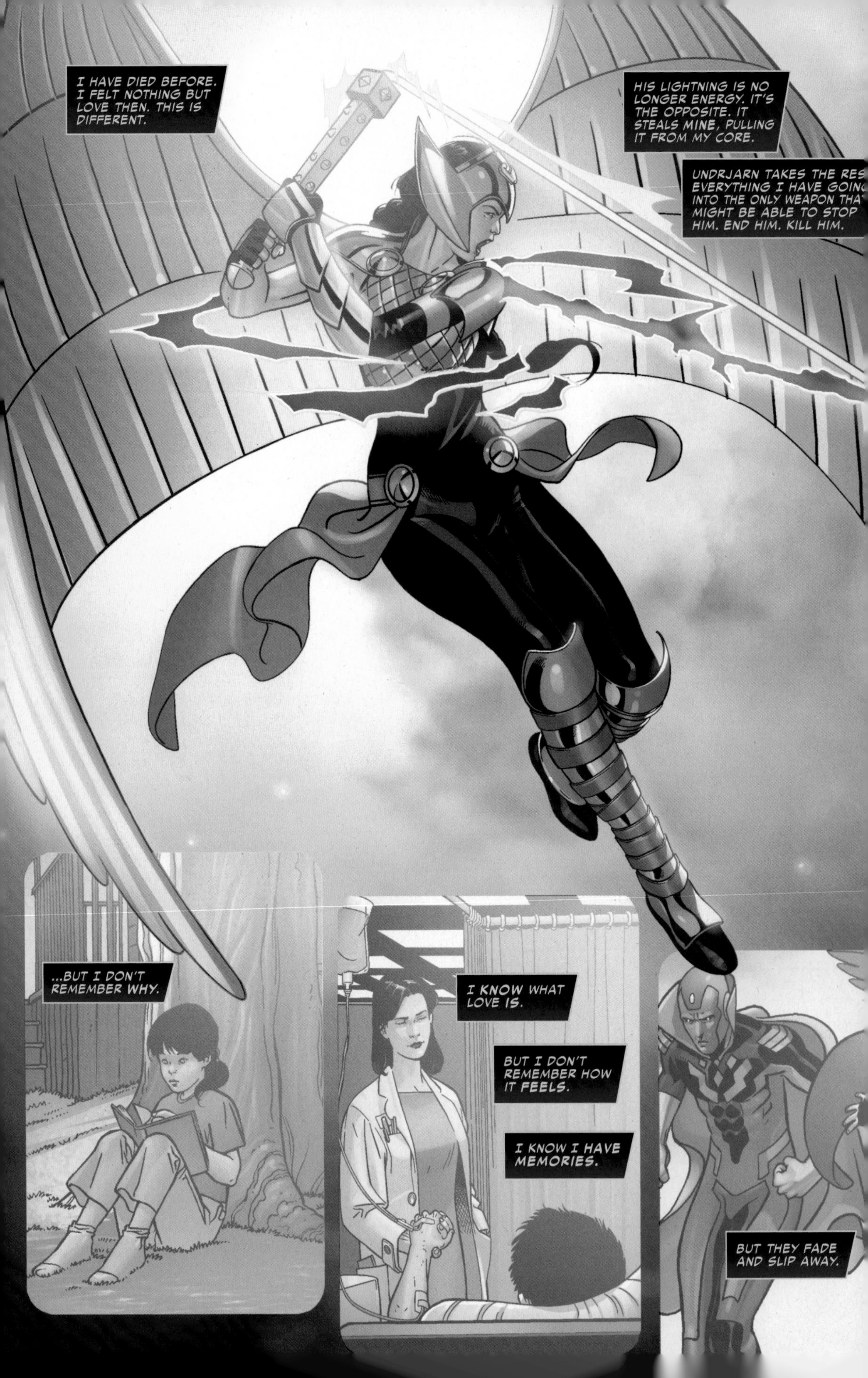
I HAVE DIED BEFORE. I FELT NOTHING BUT LOVE THEN. THIS IS DIFFERENT.
HIS LIGHTNING IS NO LONGER ENERGY. IT'S THE OPPOSITE. IT STEALS MINE, PULLING IT FROM MY CORE.
UNDRJARN TAKES THE RES EVERYTHING I HAVE GOIN INTO THE ONLY WEAPON THA MIGHT BE ABLE TO STOP HIM. END HIM. KILL HIM.
...BUT I DON'T REMEMBER WHY.
I KNOW WHAT LOVE IS.
BUT I DON'T REMEMBER HOW IT FEELS.
I KNOW I HAVE MEMORIES.
BUT THEY FADE AND SLIP AWAY.

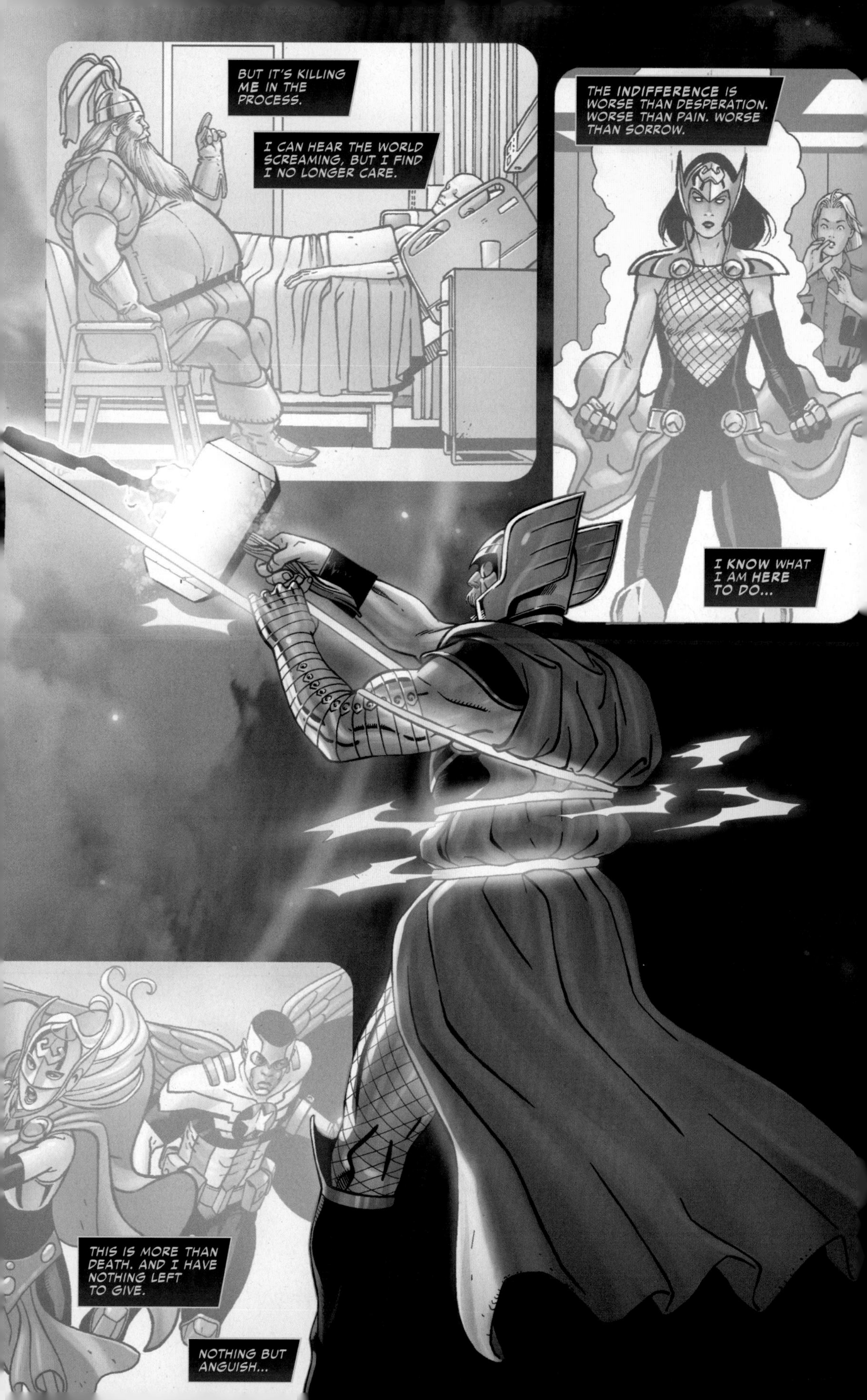
BUT IT'S KILLING ME IN THE PROCESS.
I CAN HEAR THE WORLD SCREAMING, BUT I FIND I NO LONGER CARE.
THE INDIFFERENCE IS WORSE THAN DESPERATION. WORSE THAN PAIN. WORSE THAN SORROW.
I KNOW WHAT I AM HERE TO DO...
THIS IS MORE THAN DEATH. AND I HAVE NOTHING LEFT TO GIVE.
NOTHING BUT ANGUISH...

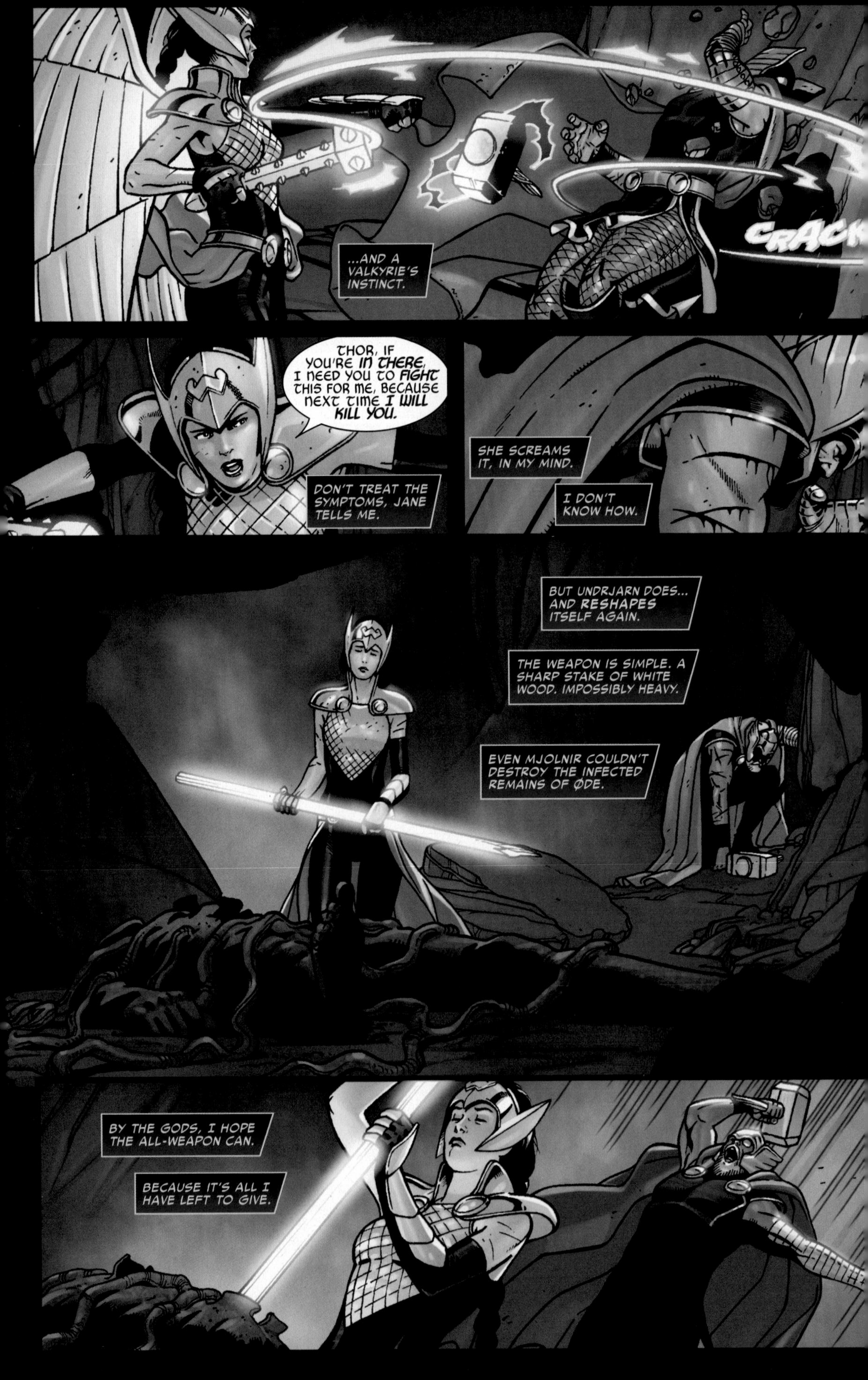
CRACK
...AND A VALKYRIE'S INSTINCT.
THOR, IF YOU'RE IN THERE, I NEED YOU TO FIGHT THIS FOR ME, BECAUSE NEXT TIME I WILL KILL YOU.
DON'T TREAT THE SYMPTOMS, JANE TELLS ME.
SHE SCREAMS IT, IN MY MIND.
I DON'T KNOW HOW.
BUT UNDRJARN DOES... AND RESHAPES ITSELF AGAIN.
THE WEAPON IS SIMPLE. A SHARP STAKE OF WHITE WOOD. IMPOSSIBLY HEAVY.
EVEN MJOLNIR COULDN'T DESTROY THE INFECTED REMAINS OF ØDE.
BY THE GODS, I HOPE THE ALL-WEAPON CAN.
BECAUSE IT'S ALL I HAVE LEFT TO GIVE.

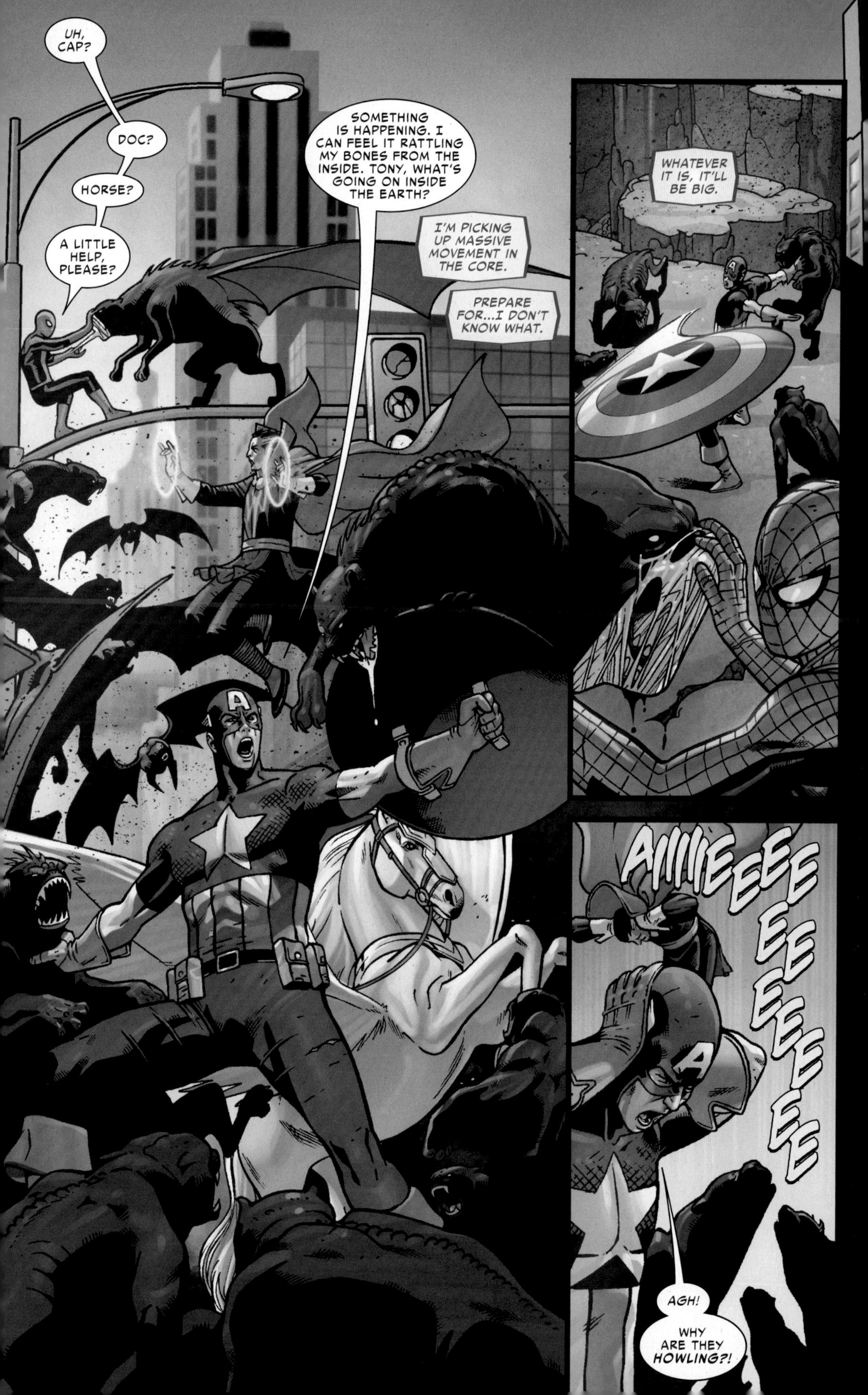
UH, CAP?
DOC?
HORSE?
A LITTLE HELP, PLEASE?
SOMETHING IS HAPPENING. I CAN FEEL IT RATTLING MY BONES FROM THE INSIDE. TONY, WHAT'S GOING ON INSIDE THE EARTH?
I'M PICKING UP MASSIVE MOVEMENT IN THE CORE.
PREPARE FOR...I DON'T KNOW WHAT.
WHATEVER IT IS, IT'LL BE BIG.
AIIIIEEEEEEEEEEEEE
AGH!
WHY ARE THEY HOWLING?!

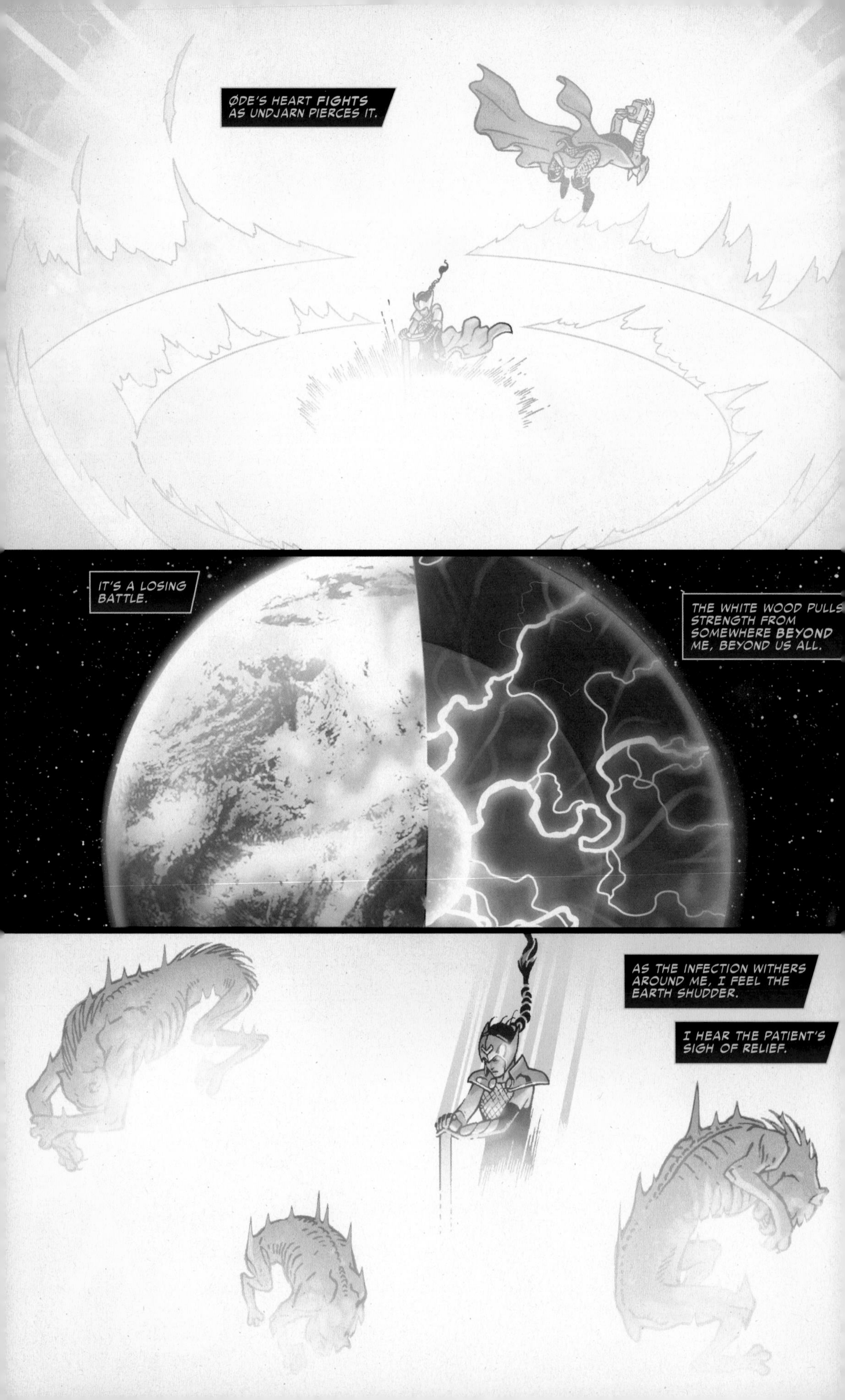
ØDE'S HEART FIGHTS AS UNDJARN PIERCES IT.
IT'S A LOSING BATTLE.
THE WHITE WOOD PULLS STRENGTH FROM SOMEWHERE BEYOND ME, BEYOND US ALL.
AS THE INFECTION WITHERS AROUND ME, I FEEL THE EARTH SHUDDER.
I HEAR THE PATIENT'S SIGH OF RELIEF.

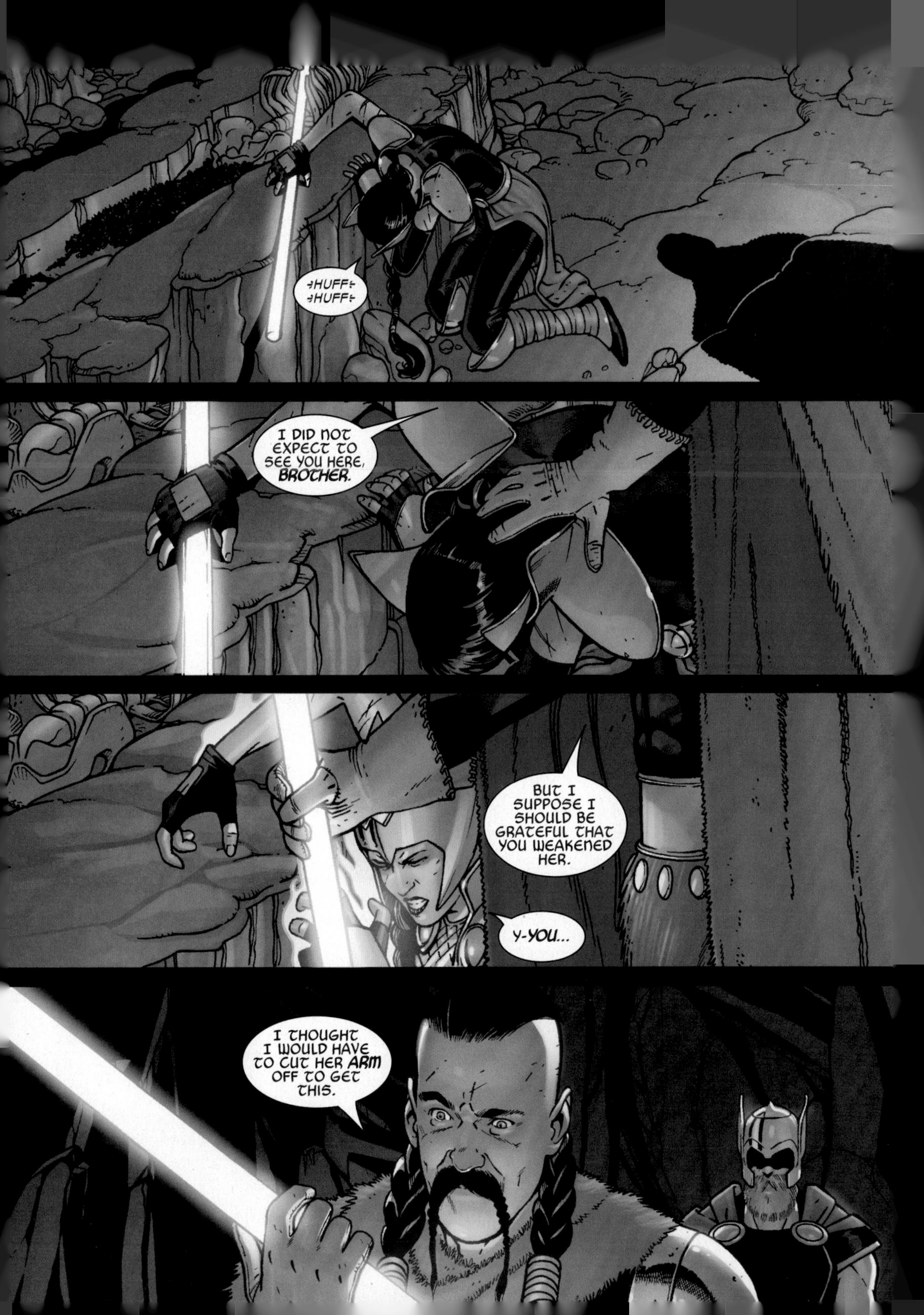

HUFF HUFF
I DID NOT EXPECT TO SEE YOU HERE, BROTHER.
BUT I SUPPOSE I SHOULD BE GRATEFUL THAT YOU WEAKENED HER.
Y-YOU...
I THOUGHT I WOULD HAVE TO CUT HER ARM OFF TO GET THIS.

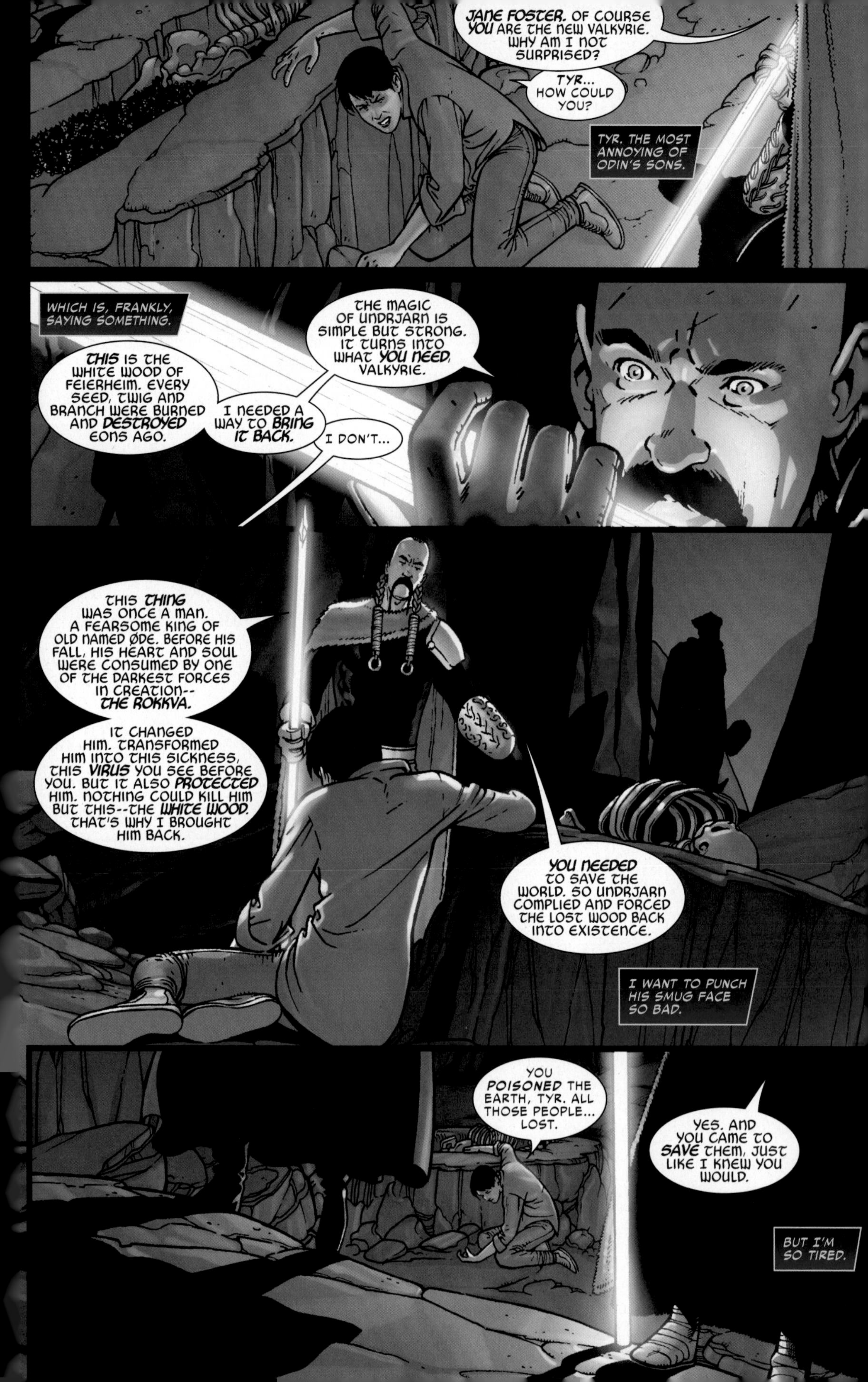
JANE FOSTER. OF COURSE YOU ARE THE NEW VALKYRIE. WHY AM I NOT SURPRISED?
TYR... HOW COULD YOU?
TYR. THE MOST ANNOYING OF ODIN'S SONS.
WHICH IS, FRANKLY, SAYING SOMETHING.
THIS IS THE WHITE WOOD OF FEIERHEIM. EVERY SEED, TWIG AND BRANCH WERE BURNED AND DESTROYED EONS AGO.
I NEEDED A WAY TO BRING IT BACK.
THE MAGIC OF UNDRJARN IS SIMPLE BUT STRONG. IT TURNS INTO WHAT YOU NEED, VALKYRIE.
I DON'T...
THIS THING WAS ONCE A MAN. A FEARSOME KING OF OLD NAMED ØDE. BEFORE HIS FALL, HIS HEART AND SOUL WERE CONSUMED BY ONE OF THE DARKEST FORCES IN CREATION-- THE ROKKVA.
IT CHANGED HIM. TRANSFORMED HIM INTO THIS SICKNESS, THIS VIRUS YOU SEE BEFORE YOU. BUT IT ALSO PROTECTED HIM. NOTHING COULD KILL HIM BUT THIS--THE WHITE WOOD. THAT'S WHY I BROUGHT HIM BACK.
YOU NEEDED TO SAVE THE WORLD. SO UNDRJARN COMPLIED AND FORCED THE LOST WOOD BACK INTO EXISTENCE.
I WANT TO PUNCH HIS SMUG FACE SO BAD.
YOU POISONED THE EARTH, TYR. ALL THOSE PEOPLE... LOST.
YES. AND YOU CAME TO SAVE THEM, JUST LIKE I KNEW YOU WOULD.
BUT I'M SO TIRED.

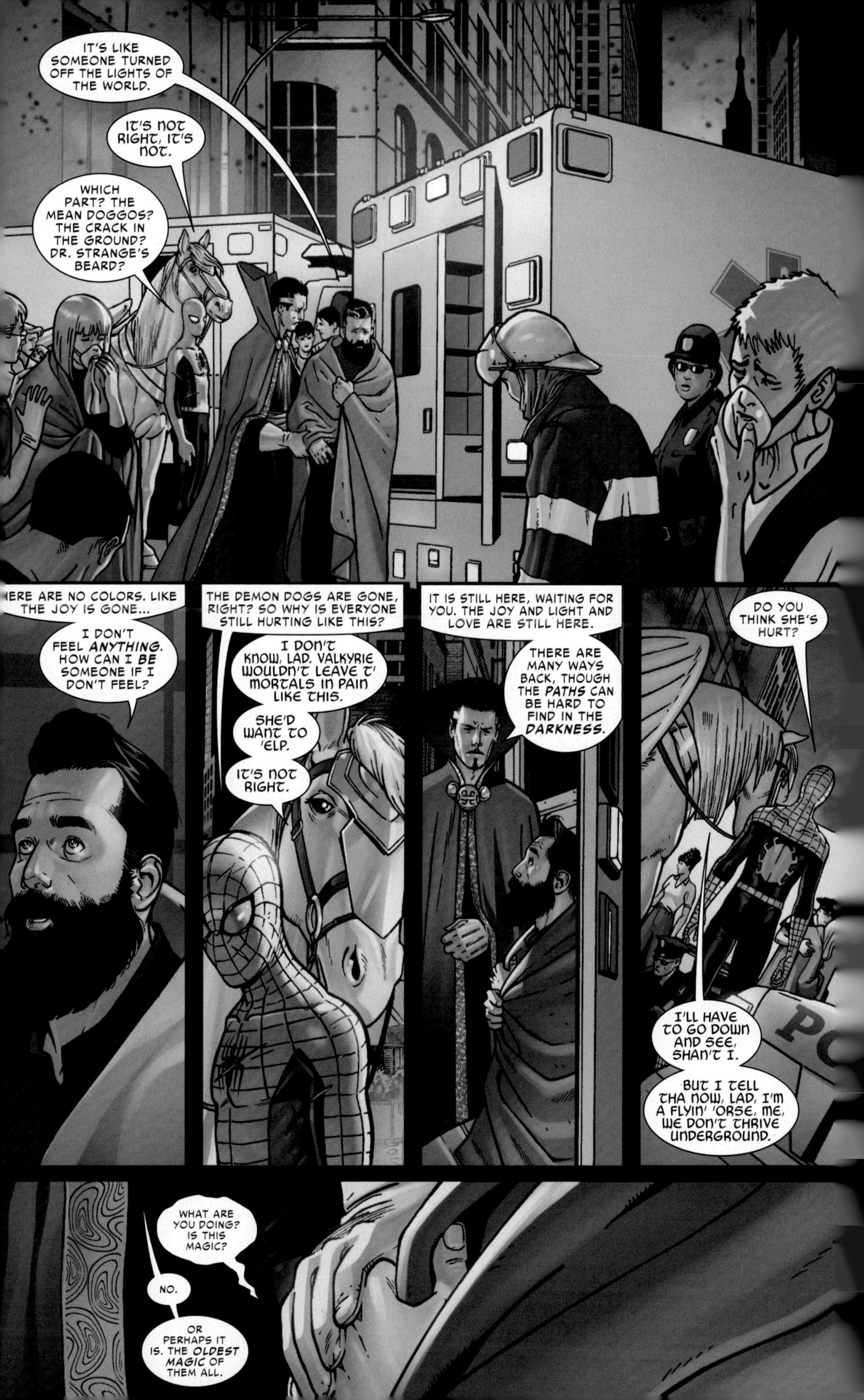
IT'S LIKE SOMEONE TURNED OFF THE LIGHTS OF THE WORLD.
IT'S NOT RIGHT, IT'S NOT.
WHICH PART? THE MEAN DOGGOS? THE CRACK IN THE GROUND? DR. STRANGE'S BEARD?
HERE ARE NO COLORS. LIKE THE JOY IS GONE...
I DON'T FEEL *ANYTHING*. HOW CAN I *BE* SOMEONE IF I DON'T FEEL?
THE DEMON DOGS ARE GONE, RIGHT? SO WHY IS EVERYONE STILL HURTING LIKE THIS?
I DON'T KNOW, LAD. VALKYRIE WOULDN'T LEAVE T' MORTALS IN PAIN LIKE THIS.
SHE'D WANT TO 'ELP.
IT'S NOT RIGHT.
IT IS STILL HERE, WAITING FOR YOU. THE JOY AND LIGHT AND LOVE ARE STILL HERE.
THERE ARE MANY WAYS BACK, THOUGH THE *PATHS* CAN BE HARD TO FIND IN THE *DARKNESS*.
DO YOU THINK SHE'S HURT?
I'LL HAVE TO GO DOWN AND SEE, SHAN'T I.
BUT I TELL THA NOW, LAD, I'M A FLYIN' 'ORSE, ME, WE DON'T THRIVE UNDERGROUND.
PO
WHAT ARE YOU DOING? IS THIS MAGIC?
NO.
OR PERHAPS IT IS. THE *OLDEST MAGIC* OF THEM ALL.

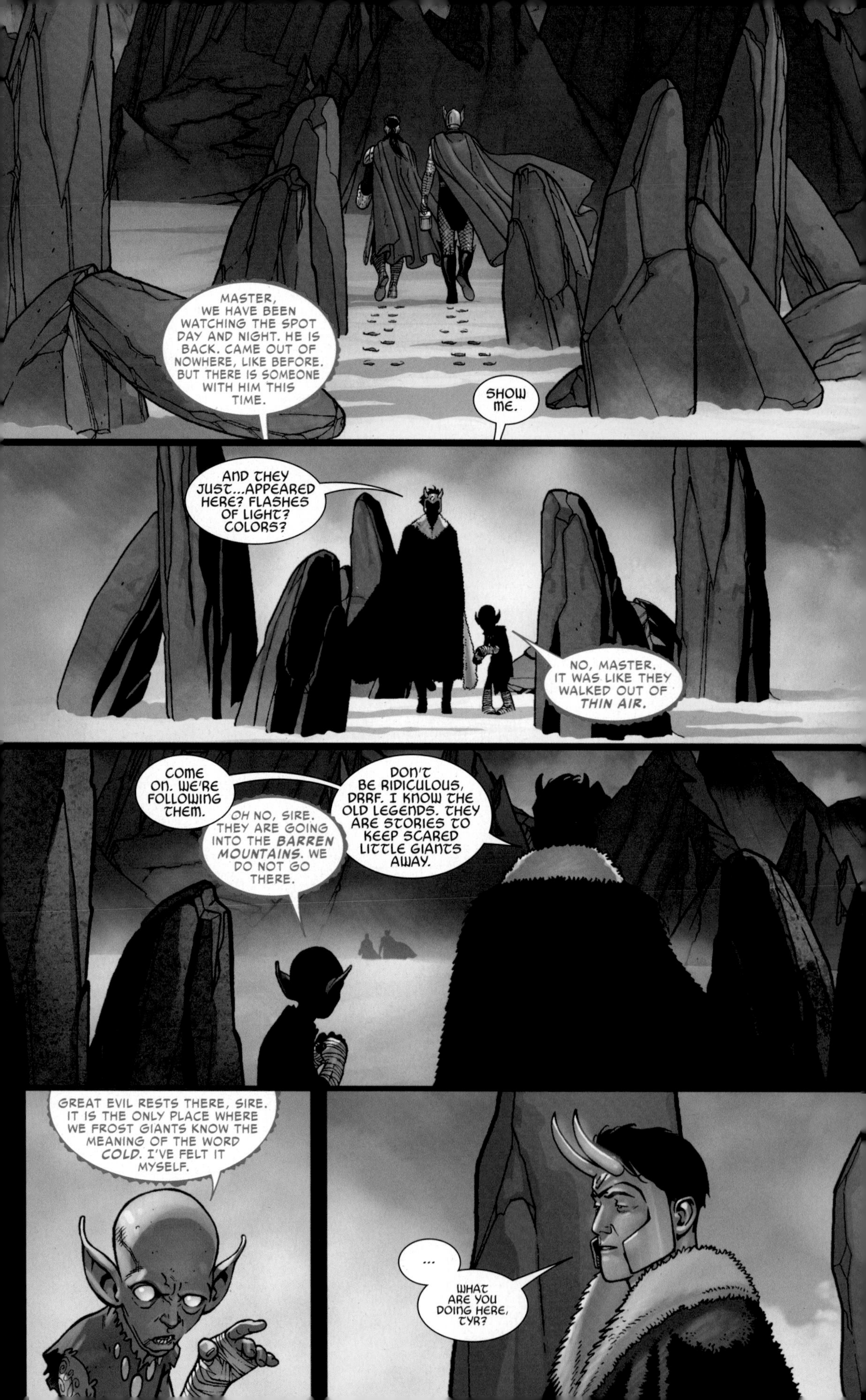
MASTER, WE HAVE BEEN WATCHING THE SPOT DAY AND NIGHT. HE IS BACK. CAME OUT OF NOWHERE, LIKE BEFORE. BUT THERE IS SOMEONE WITH HIM THIS TIME.
SHOW ME.
AND THEY JUST...APPEARED HERE? FLASHES OF LIGHT? COLORS?
NO, MASTER. IT WAS LIKE THEY WALKED OUT OF *THIN AIR.*
COME ON. WE'RE FOLLOWING THEM.
OH NO, SIRE. THEY ARE GOING INTO THE *BARREN MOUNTAINS.* WE DO NOT GO THERE.
DON'T BE RIDICULOUS, DRRF. I KNOW THE OLD LEGENDS. THEY ARE STORIES TO KEEP SCARED LITTLE GIANTS AWAY.
GREAT EVIL RESTS THERE, SIRE. IT IS THE ONLY PLACE WHERE WE FROST GIANTS KNOW THE MEANING OF THE WORD *COLD.* I'VE FELT IT MYSELF.
...
WHAT ARE YOU DOING HERE, TYR?

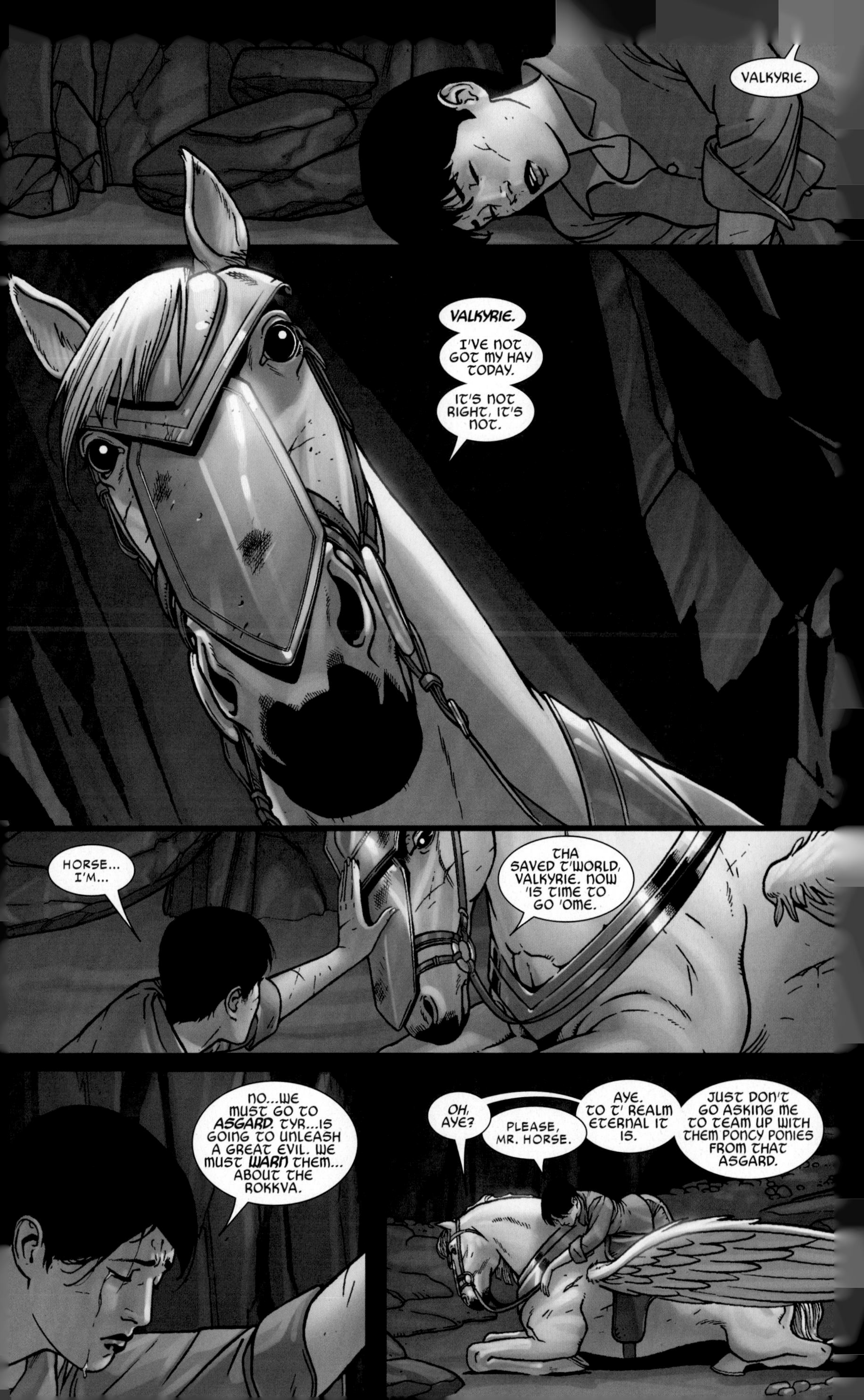
VALKYRIE.
VALKYRIE.
I'VE NOT GOT MY HAY TODAY.
IT'S NOT RIGHT, IT'S NOT.
HORSE... I'M...
THA SAVED T'WORLD, VALKYRIE. NOW 'IS TIME TO GO 'OME.
NO...WE MUST GO TO ASGARD. TYR...IS GOING TO UNLEASH A GREAT EVIL. WE MUST WARN THEM... ABOUT THE ROKKVA.
OH, AYE?
PLEASE, MR. HORSE.
AYE. TO T' REALM ETERNAL IT IS.
JUST DON'T GO ASKING ME TO TEAM UP WITH THEM PONCY PONIES FROM THAT ASGARD.

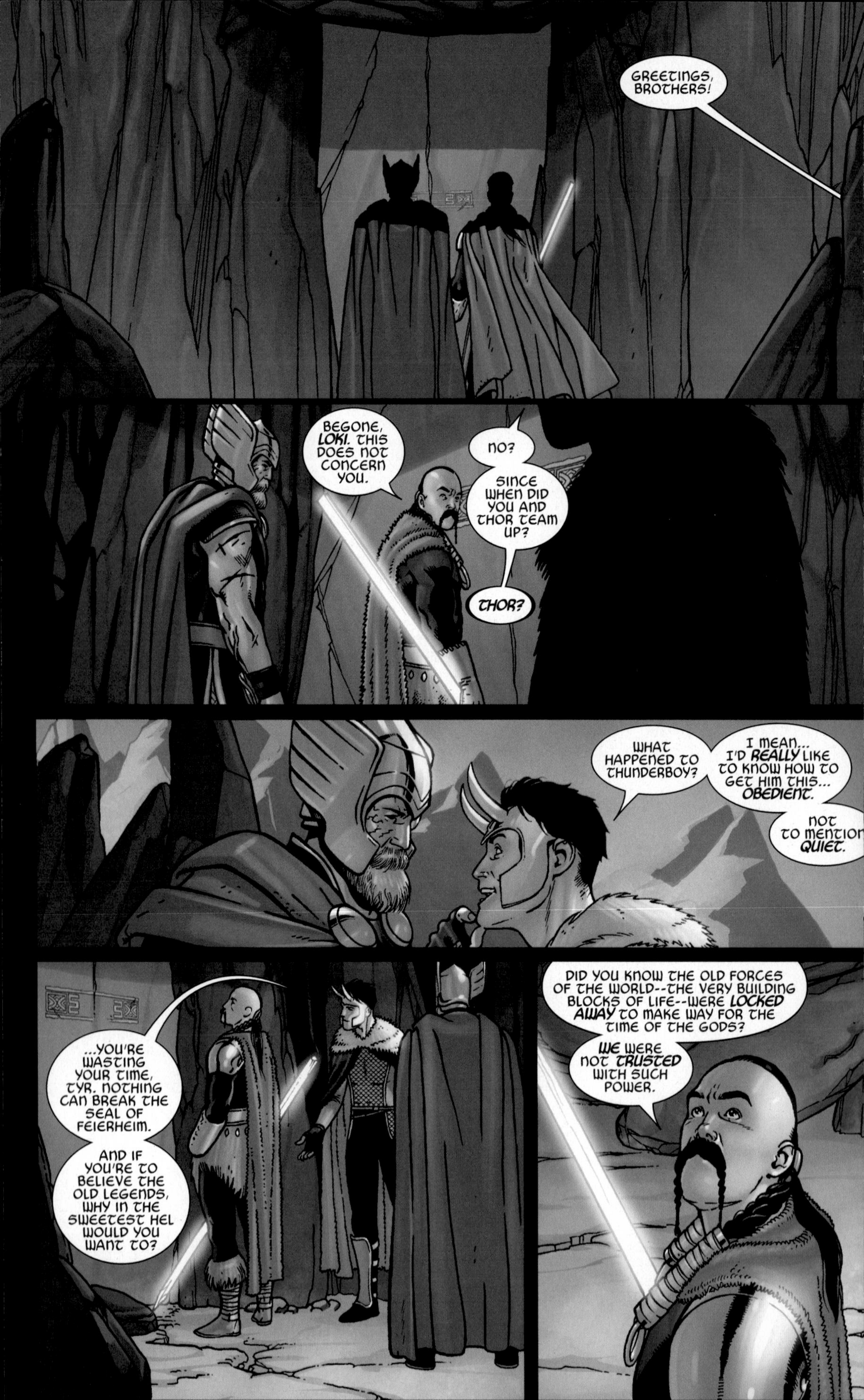
GREETINGS, BROTHERS!
BEGONE, LOKI. THIS DOES NOT CONCERN YOU.
NO?
SINCE WHEN DID YOU AND THOR TEAM UP?
THOR?
WHAT HAPPENED TO THUNDERBOY?
I MEAN... I'D REALLY LIKE TO KNOW HOW TO GET HIM THIS... OBEDIENT.
NOT TO MENTION QUIET.
...YOU'RE WASTING YOUR TIME, TYR. NOTHING CAN BREAK THE SEAL OF FEIERHEIM.
AND IF YOU'RE TO BELIEVE THE OLD LEGENDS, WHY IN THE SWEETEST HEL WOULD YOU WANT TO?
DID YOU KNOW THE OLD FORCES OF THE WORLD--THE VERY BUILDING BLOCKS OF LIFE--WERE LOCKED AWAY TO MAKE WAY FOR THE TIME OF THE GODS?
WE WERE NOT TRUSTED WITH SUCH POWER.

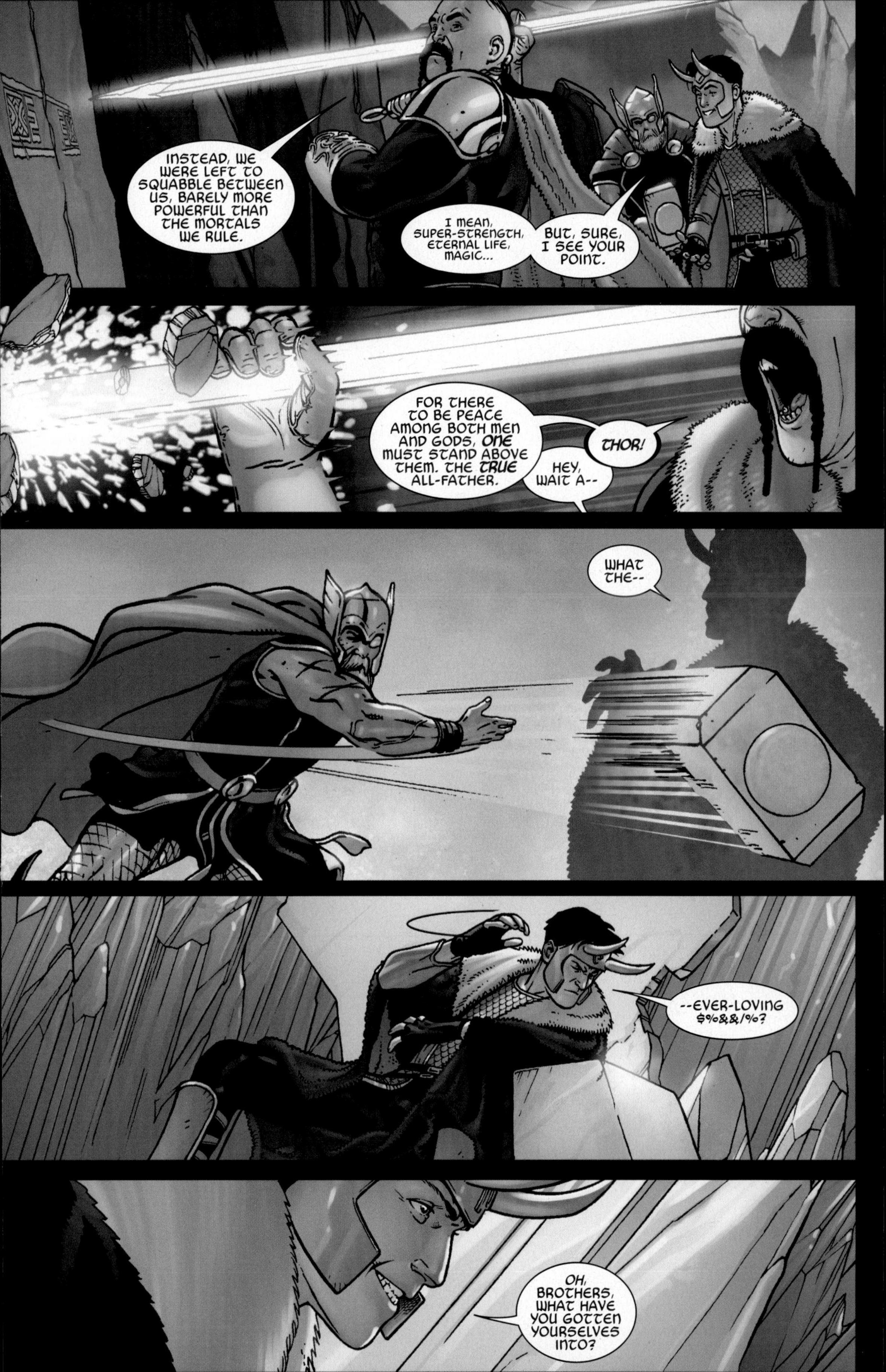
INSTEAD, WE WERE LEFT TO SQUABBLE BETWEEN US, BARELY MORE POWERFUL THAN THE MORTALS WE RULE.
I MEAN, SUPER-STRENGTH, ETERNAL LIFE, MAGIC...
BUT, SURE, I SEE YOUR POINT.
FOR THERE TO BE PEACE AMONG BOTH MEN AND GODS, ONE MUST STAND ABOVE THEM. THE TRUE ALL-FATHER.
THOR!
HEY, WAIT A--
WHAT THE--
--EVER-LOVING $%&&/%?
OH, BROTHERS, WHAT HAVE YOU GOTTEN YOURSELVES INTO?

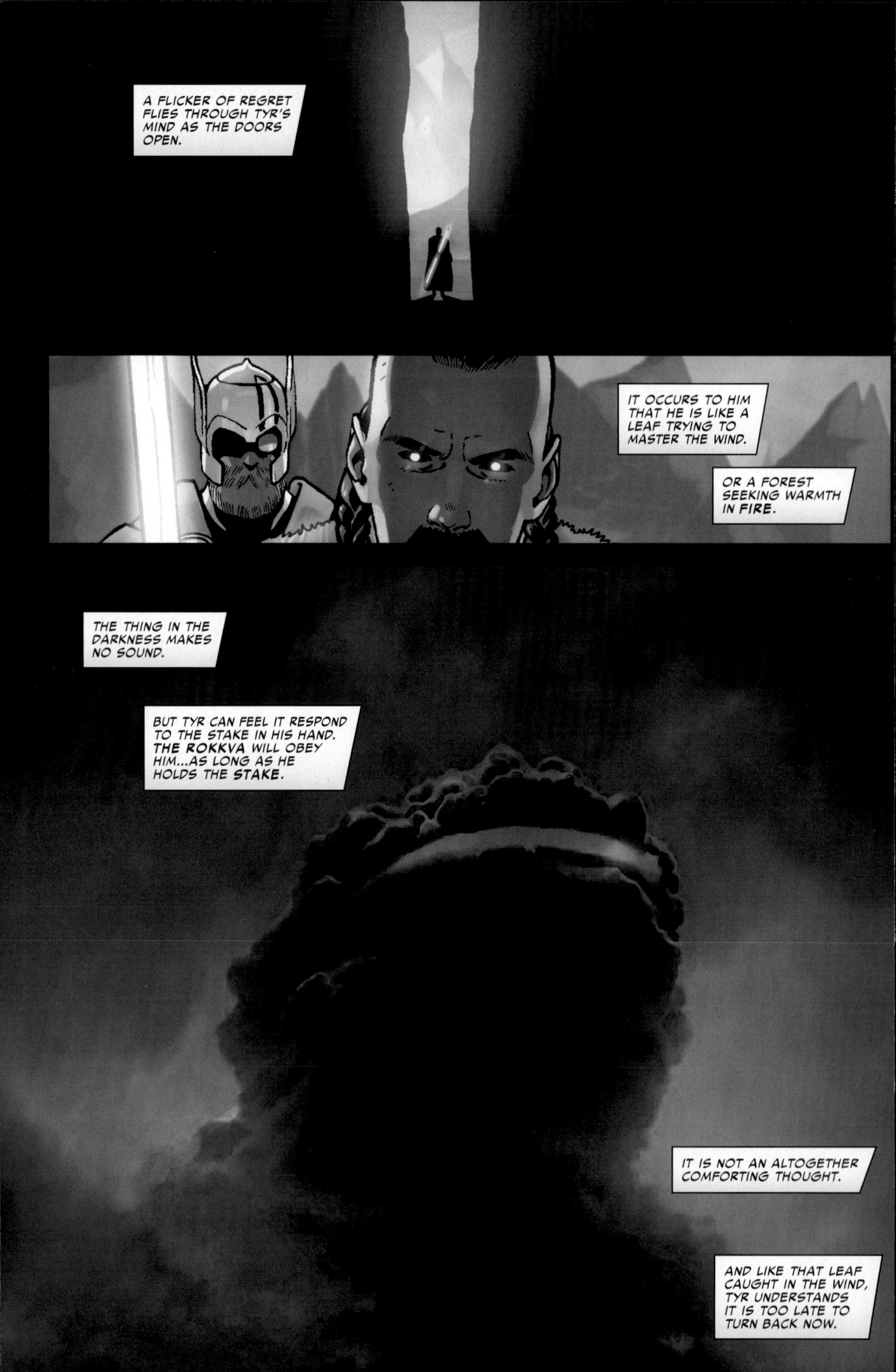
A FLICKER OF REGRET FLIES THROUGH TYR'S MIND AS THE DOORS OPEN.
IT OCCURS TO HIM THAT HE IS LIKE A LEAF TRYING TO MASTER THE WIND.
OR A FOREST SEEKING WARMTH IN FIRE.
THE THING IN THE DARKNESS MAKES NO SOUND.
BUT TYR CAN FEEL IT RESPOND TO THE STAKE IN HIS HAND. THE ROKKVA WILL OBEY HIM...AS LONG AS HE HOLDS THE STAKE.
IT IS NOT AN ALTOGETHER COMFORTING THOUGHT.
AND LIKE THAT LEAF CAUGHT IN THE WIND, TYR UNDERSTANDS IT IS TOO LATE TO TURN BACK NOW.

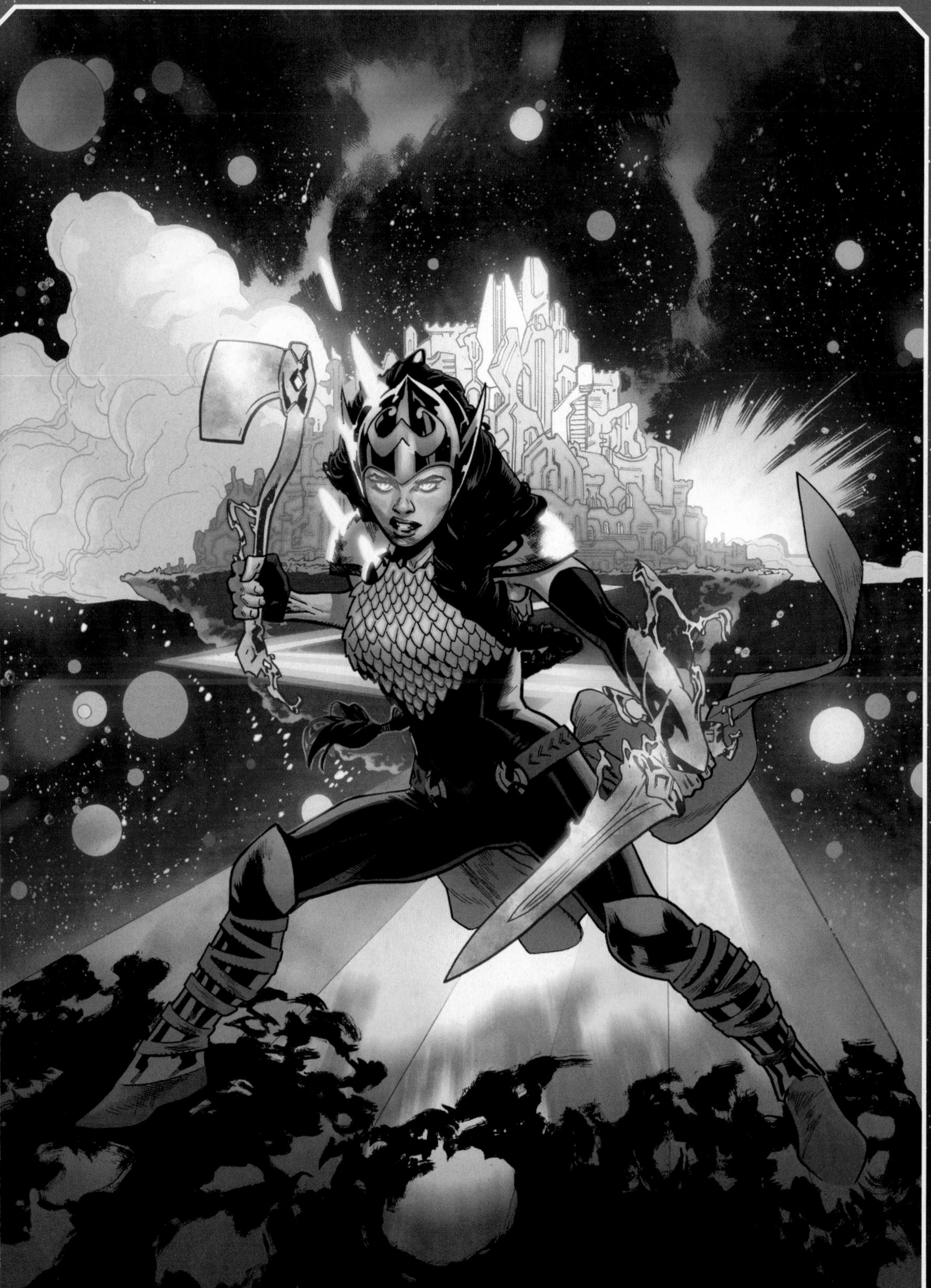

M. ASRAR
MW

VALKYRIE: JANE FOSTER #10

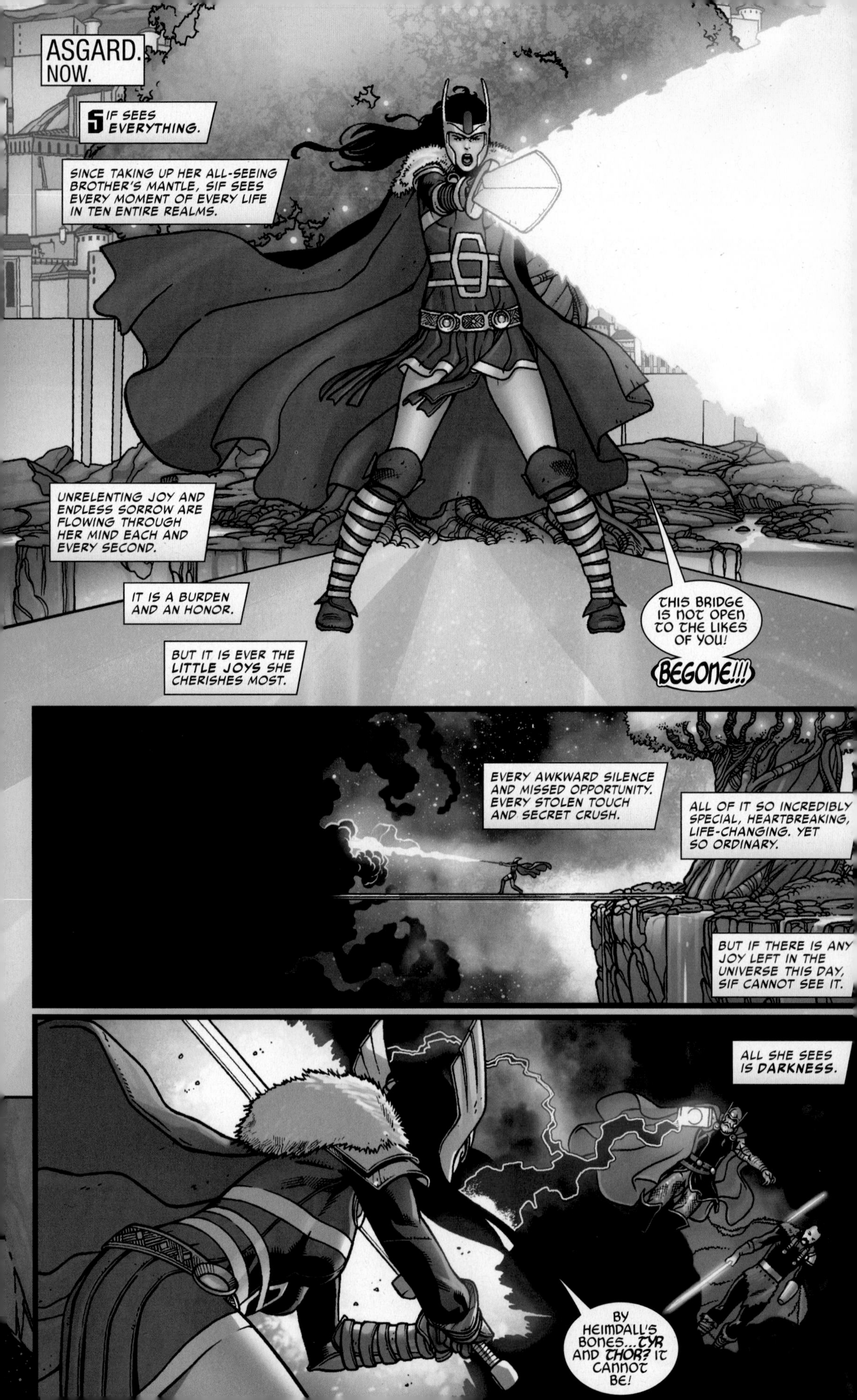
ASGARD. NOW.
SIF SEES EVERYTHING.
SINCE TAKING UP HER ALL-SEEING BROTHER'S MANTLE, SIF SEES EVERY MOMENT OF EVERY LIFE IN TEN ENTIRE REALMS.
UNRELENTING JOY AND ENDLESS SORROW ARE FLOWING THROUGH HER MIND EACH AND EVERY SECOND.
IT IS A BURDEN AND AN HONOR.
BUT IT IS EVER THE LITTLE JOYS SHE CHERISHES MOST.
THIS BRIDGE IS NOT OPEN TO THE LIKES OF YOU!
BEGONE!!!
EVERY AWKWARD SILENCE AND MISSED OPPORTUNITY. EVERY STOLEN TOUCH AND SECRET CRUSH.
ALL OF IT SO INCREDIBLY SPECIAL, HEARTBREAKING, LIFE-CHANGING. YET SO ORDINARY.
BUT IF THERE IS ANY JOY LEFT IN THE UNIVERSE THIS DAY, SIF CANNOT SEE IT.
ALL SHE SEES IS DARKNESS.
BY HEIMDALL'S BONES... TYR AND THOR? IT CANNOT BE!

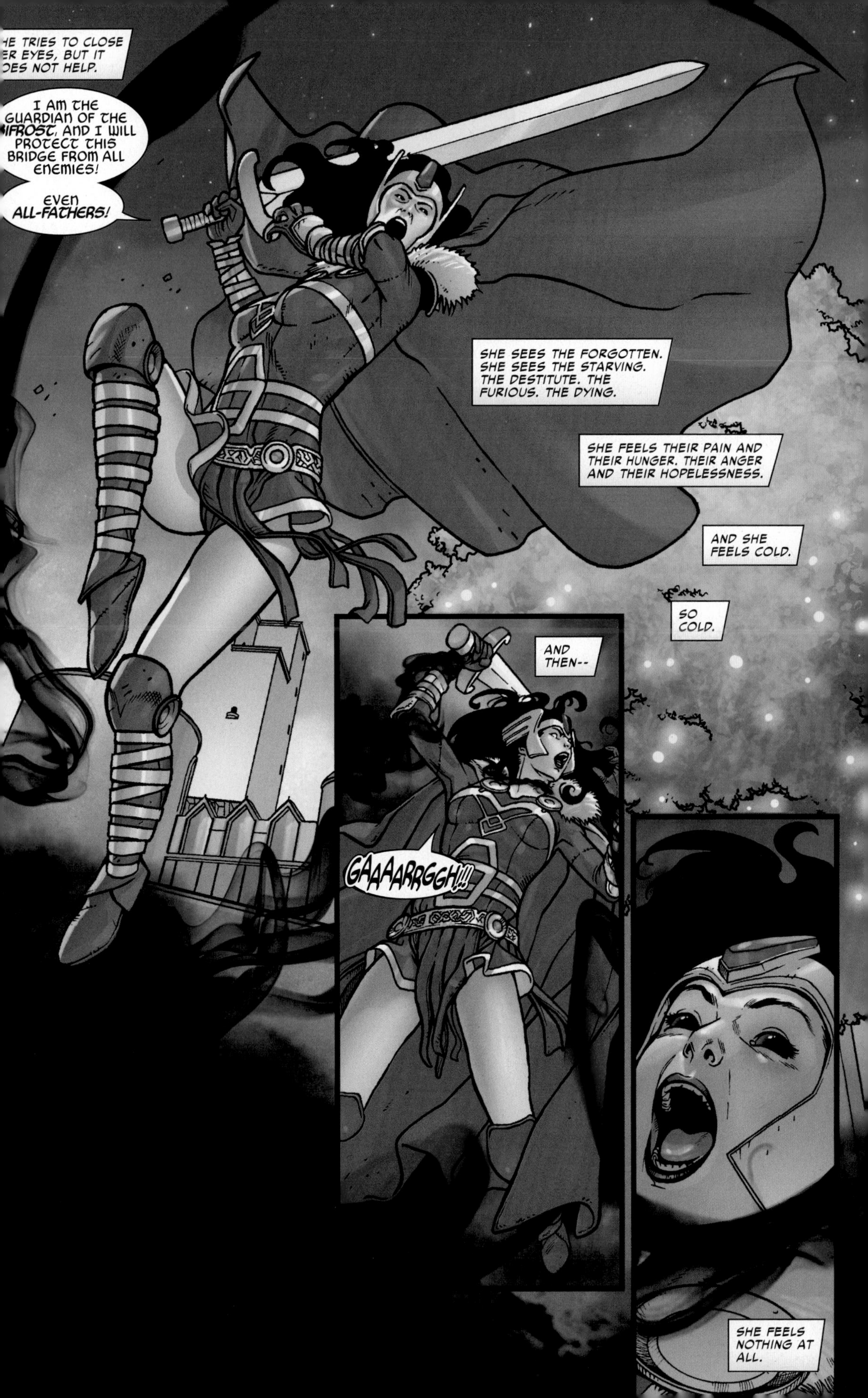
HE TRIES TO CLOSE ER EYES, BUT IT OES NOT HELP.
I AM THE GUARDIAN OF THE IFROST, AND I WILL PROTECT THIS BRIDGE FROM ALL ENEMIES!
EVEN ALL-FATHERS!
SHE SEES THE FORGOTTEN. SHE SEES THE STARVING. THE DESTITUTE. THE FURIOUS. THE DYING.
SHE FEELS THEIR PAIN AND THEIR HUNGER. THEIR ANGER AND THEIR HOPELESSNESS.
AND SHE FEELS COLD.
SO COLD.
AND THEN--
GAAAARRGGH!!!
SHE FEELS NOTHING AT ALL.

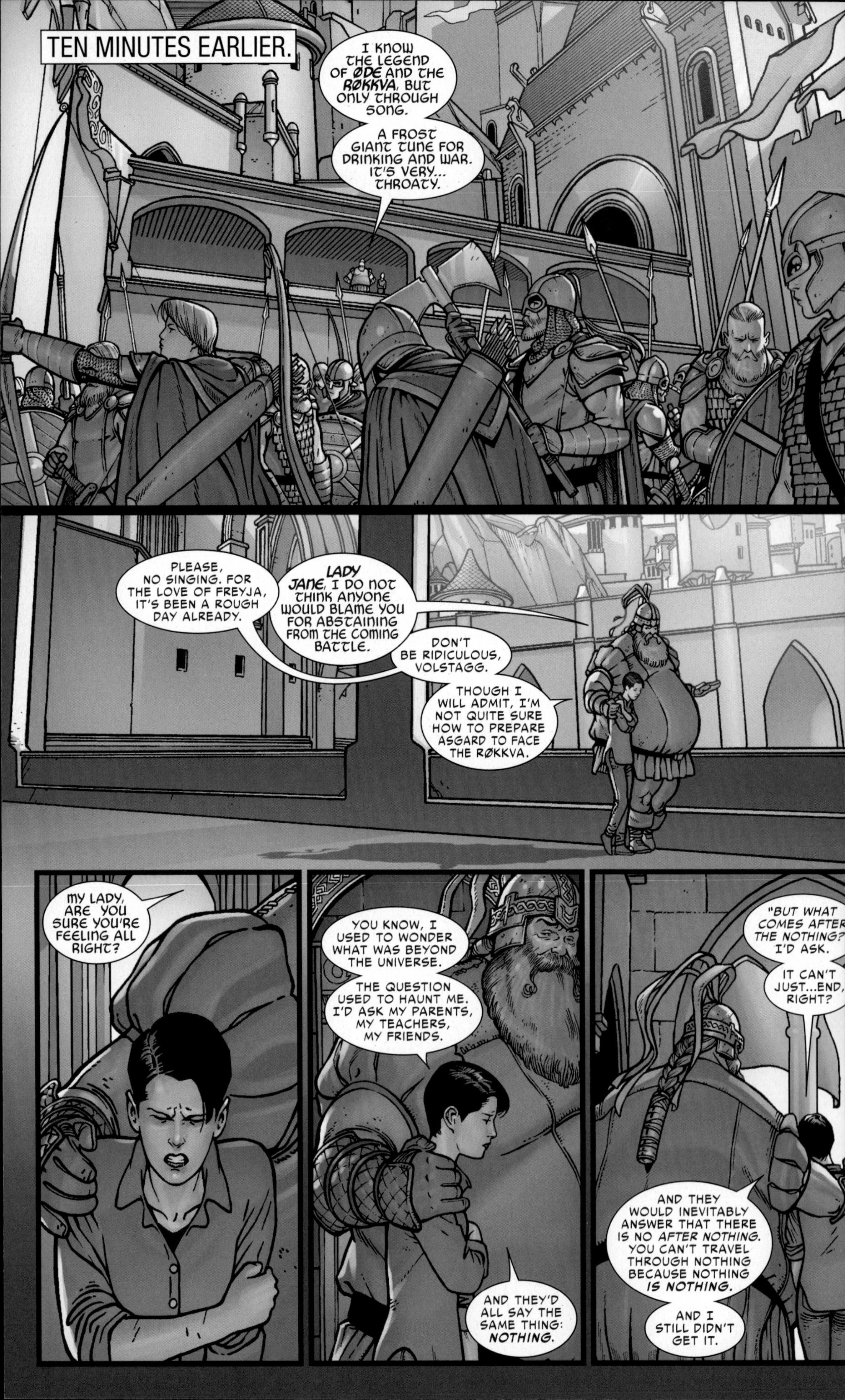
TEN MINUTES EARLIER.
I KNOW THE LEGEND OF ØDE AND THE RØKKVA, BUT ONLY THROUGH SONG.
A FROST GIANT TUNE FOR DRINKING AND WAR. IT'S VERY... THROATY.
PLEASE, NO SINGING. FOR THE LOVE OF FREYJA, IT'S BEEN A ROUGH DAY ALREADY.
LADY JANE, I DO NOT THINK ANYONE WOULD BLAME YOU FOR ABSTAINING FROM THE COMING BATTLE.
DON'T BE RIDICULOUS, VOLSTAGG.
THOUGH I WILL ADMIT, I'M NOT QUITE SURE HOW TO PREPARE ASGARD TO FACE THE RØKKVA.
MY LADY, ARE YOU SURE YOU'RE FEELING ALL RIGHT?
YOU KNOW, I USED TO WONDER WHAT WAS BEYOND THE UNIVERSE.
THE QUESTION USED TO HAUNT ME. I'D ASK MY PARENTS, MY TEACHERS, MY FRIENDS.
AND THEY'D ALL SAY THE SAME THING: NOTHING.
"BUT WHAT COMES AFTER THE NOTHING?" I'D ASK.
IT CAN'T JUST...END, RIGHT?
AND THEY WOULD INEVITABLY ANSWER THAT THERE IS NO AFTER NOTHING. YOU CAN'T TRAVEL THROUGH NOTHING BECAUSE NOTHING IS NOTHING.
AND I STILL DIDN'T GET IT.

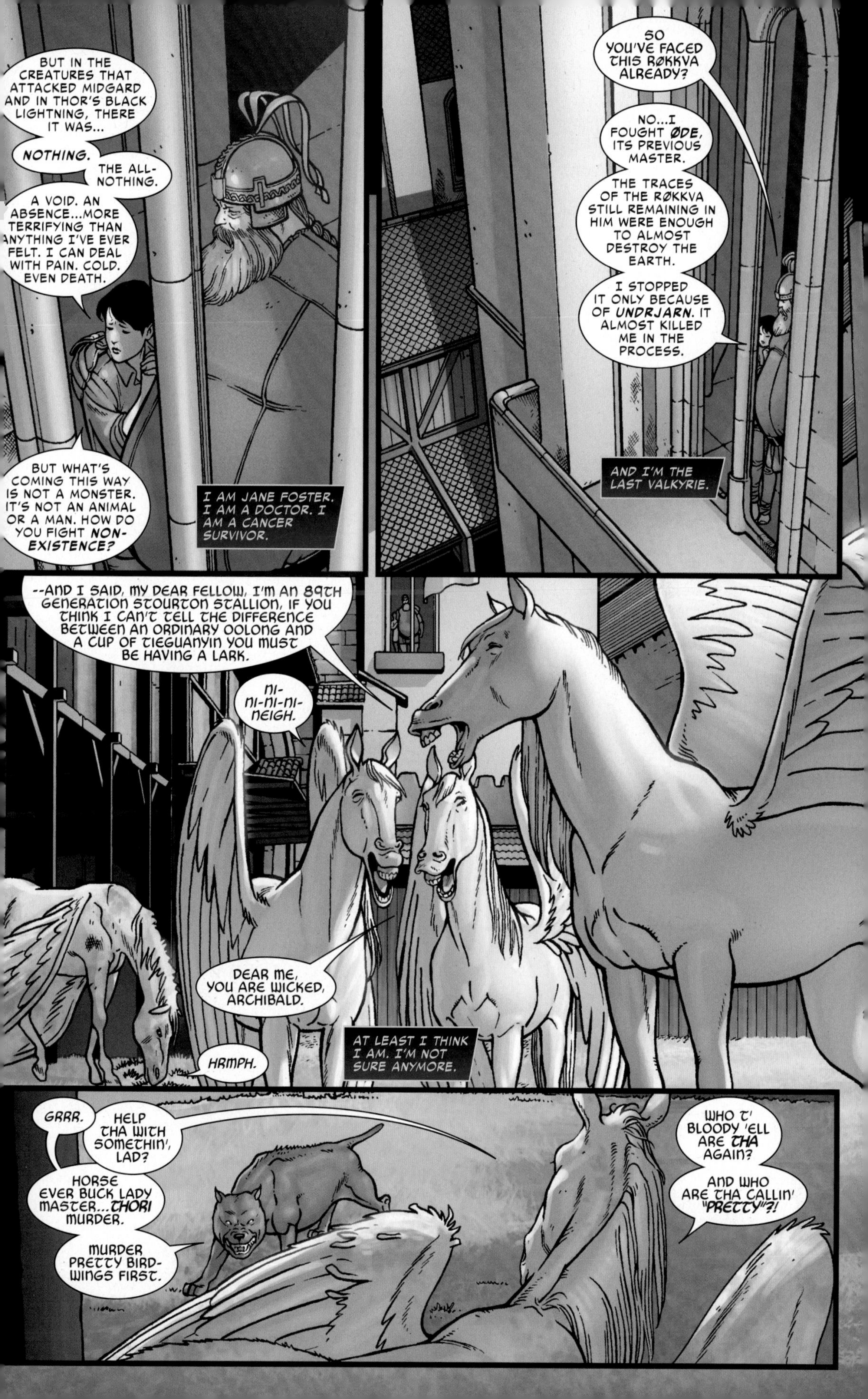

BUT IN THE CREATURES THAT ATTACKED MIDGARD AND IN THOR'S BLACK LIGHTNING, THERE IT WAS...
NOTHING.
THE ALL-NOTHING.
A VOID. AN ABSENCE...MORE TERRIFYING THAN ANYTHING I'VE EVER FELT. I CAN DEAL WITH PAIN. COLD. EVEN DEATH.
BUT WHAT'S COMING THIS WAY IS NOT A MONSTER. IT'S NOT AN ANIMAL OR A MAN. HOW DO YOU FIGHT NON-EXISTENCE?
I AM JANE FOSTER. I AM A DOCTOR. I AM A CANCER SURVIVOR.
SO YOU'VE FACED THIS RØKKVA ALREADY?
NO...I FOUGHT ØDE, ITS PREVIOUS MASTER.
THE TRACES OF THE RØKKVA STILL REMAINING IN HIM WERE ENOUGH TO ALMOST DESTROY THE EARTH.
I STOPPED IT ONLY BECAUSE OF UNDRJARN. IT ALMOST KILLED ME IN THE PROCESS.
AND I'M THE LAST VALKYRIE.
--AND I SAID, MY DEAR FELLOW, I'M AN 89TH GENERATION STOURTON STALLION, IF YOU THINK I CAN'T TELL THE DIFFERENCE BETWEEN AN ORDINARY OOLONG AND A CUP OF TIEGUANYIN YOU MUST BE HAVING A LARK.
NI-NI-NI-NI-NEIGH.
DEAR ME, YOU ARE WICKED, ARCHIBALD.
HRMPH.
AT LEAST I THINK I AM. I'M NOT SURE ANYMORE.
GRRR.
HELP THA WITH SOMETHIN', LAD?
HORSE EVER BUCK LADY MASTER...THORI MURDER.
MURDER PRETTY BIRD-WINGS FIRST.
WHO T' BLOODY 'ELL ARE THA AGAIN?
AND WHO ARE THA CALLIN' "PRETTY"?!

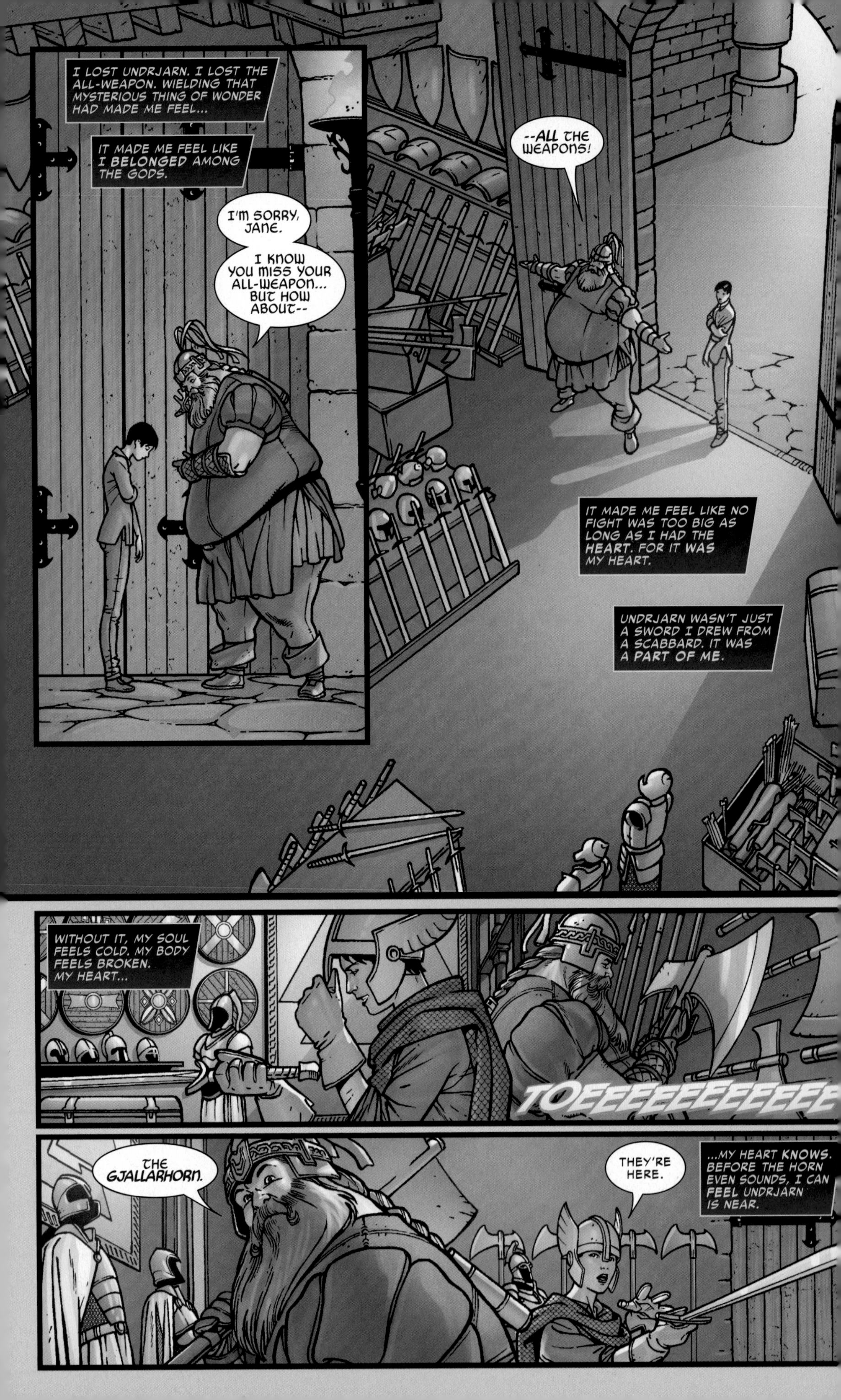

I LOST UNDRJARN. I LOST THE ALL-WEAPON. WIELDING THAT MYSTERIOUS THING OF WONDER HAD MADE ME FEEL...
IT MADE ME FEEL LIKE I BELONGED AMONG THE GODS.
I'M SORRY, JANE.
I KNOW YOU MISS YOUR ALL-WEAPON... BUT HOW ABOUT--
--ALL THE WEAPONS!
IT MADE ME FEEL LIKE NO FIGHT WAS TOO BIG AS LONG AS I HAD THE HEART. FOR IT WAS MY HEART.
UNDRJARN WASN'T JUST A SWORD I DREW FROM A SCABBARD. IT WAS A PART OF ME.
WITHOUT IT, MY SOUL FEELS COLD. MY BODY FEELS BROKEN. MY HEART...
TOEEEEEEEEEEEE
THE GJALLARHORN.
THEY'RE HERE.
...MY HEART KNOWS. BEFORE THE HORN EVEN SOUNDS, I CAN FEEL UNDRJARN IS NEAR.

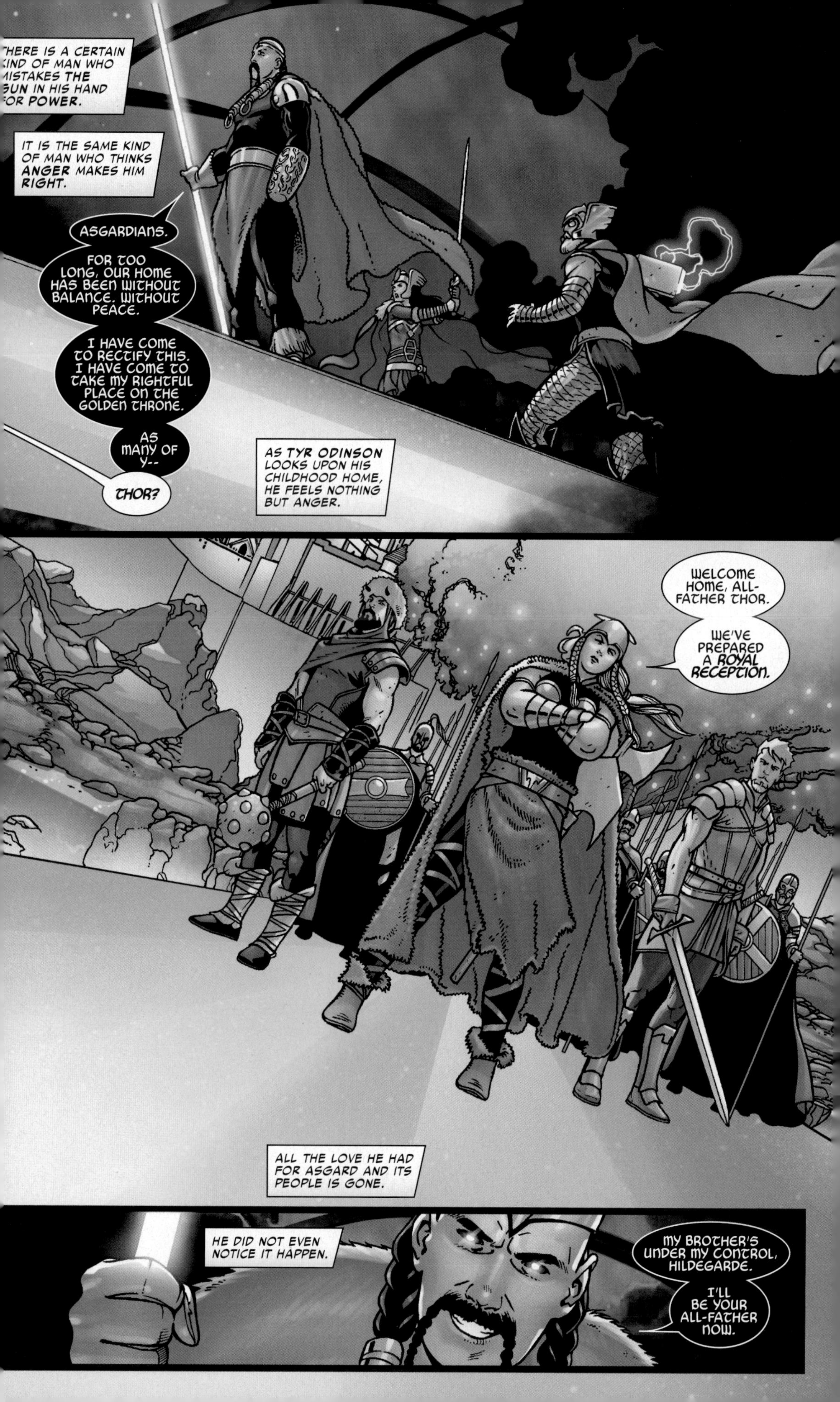

THERE IS A CERTAIN KIND OF MAN WHO MISTAKES THE GUN IN HIS HAND FOR POWER.
IT IS THE SAME KIND OF MAN WHO THINKS ANGER MAKES HIM RIGHT.
ASGARDIANS.
FOR TOO LONG, OUR HOME HAS BEEN WITHOUT BALANCE. WITHOUT PEACE.
I HAVE COME TO RECTIFY THIS. I HAVE COME TO TAKE MY RIGHTFUL PLACE ON THE GOLDEN THRONE.
AS MANY OF Y--
THOR?
AS TYR ODINSON LOOKS UPON HIS CHILDHOOD HOME, HE FEELS NOTHING BUT ANGER.
WELCOME HOME, ALL-FATHER THOR.
WE'VE PREPARED A ROYAL RECEPTION.
ALL THE LOVE HE HAD FOR ASGARD AND ITS PEOPLE IS GONE.
HE DID NOT EVEN NOTICE IT HAPPEN.
MY BROTHER'S UNDER MY CONTROL, HILDEGARDE.
I'LL BE YOUR ALL-FATHER NOW.

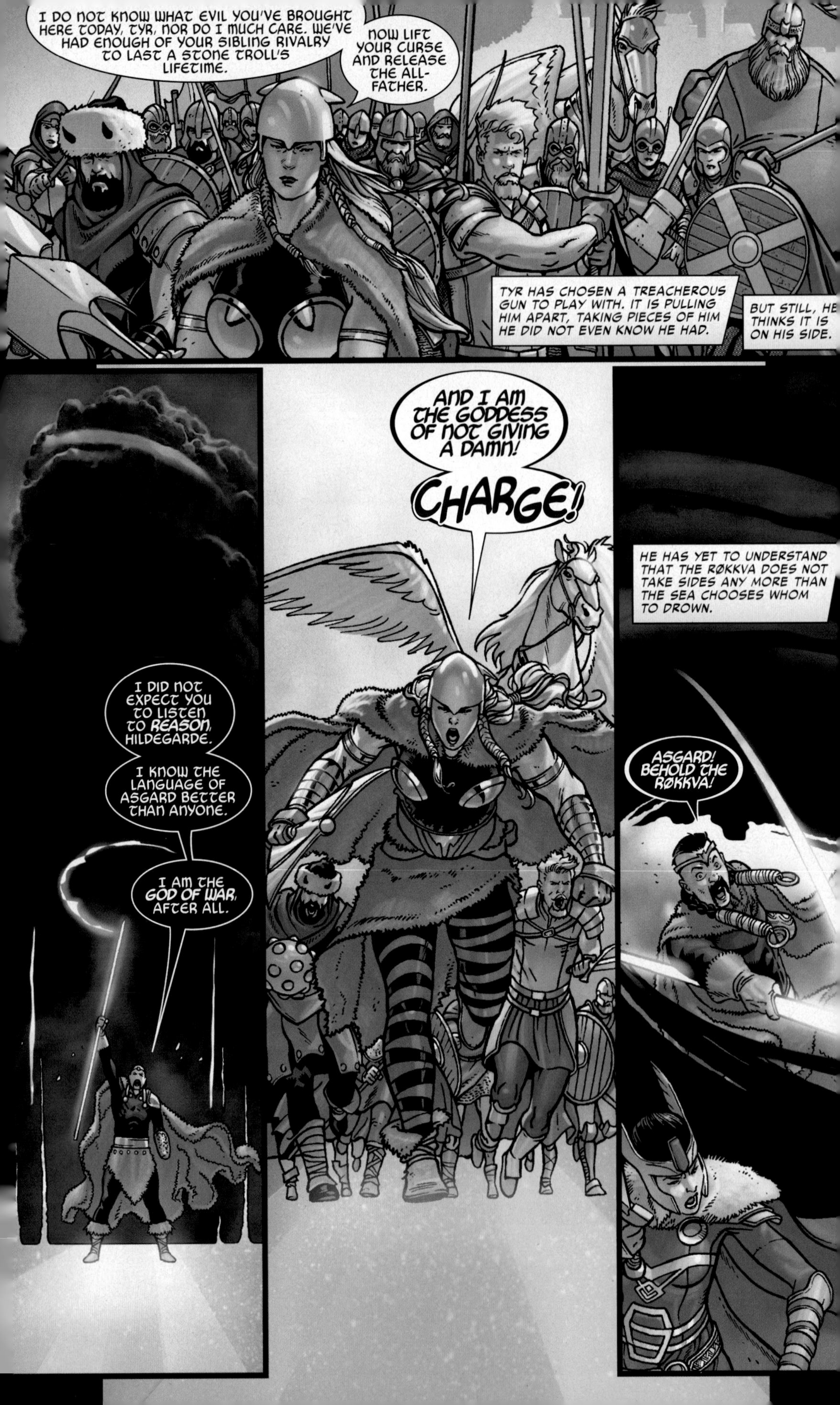

I DO NOT KNOW WHAT EVIL YOU'VE BROUGHT HERE TODAY, TYR, NOR DO I MUCH CARE. WE'VE HAD ENOUGH OF YOUR SIBLING RIVALRY TO LAST A STONE TROLL'S LIFETIME.
NOW LIFT YOUR CURSE AND RELEASE THE ALL-FATHER.
TYR HAS CHOSEN A TREACHEROUS GUN TO PLAY WITH. IT IS PULLING HIM APART, TAKING PIECES OF HIM HE DID NOT EVEN KNOW HE HAD.
BUT STILL, HE THINKS IT IS ON HIS SIDE.
I DID NOT EXPECT YOU TO LISTEN TO REASON, HILDEGARDE.
I KNOW THE LANGUAGE OF ASGARD BETTER THAN ANYONE.
I AM THE GOD OF WAR, AFTER ALL.
AND I AM THE GODDESS OF NOT GIVING A DAMN!
CHARGE!
HE HAS YET TO UNDERSTAND THAT THE RØKKVA DOES NOT TAKE SIDES ANY MORE THAN THE SEA CHOOSES WHOM TO DROWN.
ASGARD! BEHOLD THE RØKKVA!

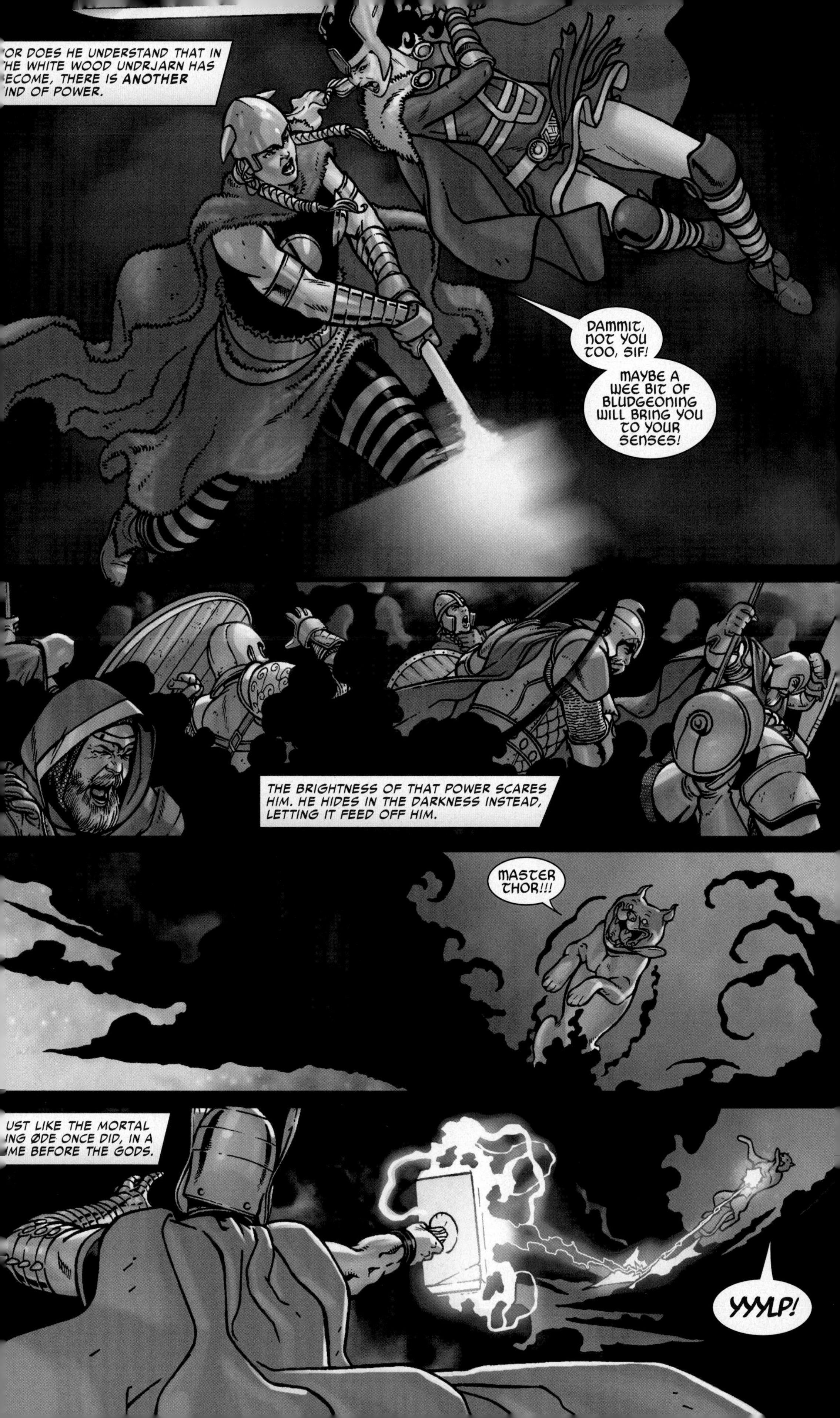

'OR DOES HE UNDERSTAND THAT IN
'HE WHITE WOOD UNDRJARN HAS
ECOME, THERE IS ANOTHER
IND OF POWER.
DAMMIT, NOT YOU TOO, SIF!
MAYBE A WEE BIT OF BLUDGEONING WILL BRING YOU TO YOUR SENSES!
THE BRIGHTNESS OF THAT POWER SCARES HIM. HE HIDES IN THE DARKNESS INSTEAD, LETTING IT FEED OFF HIM.
MASTER THOR!!!
UST LIKE THE MORTAL
ING ØDE ONCE DID, IN A
ME BEFORE THE GODS.
YYYLP!

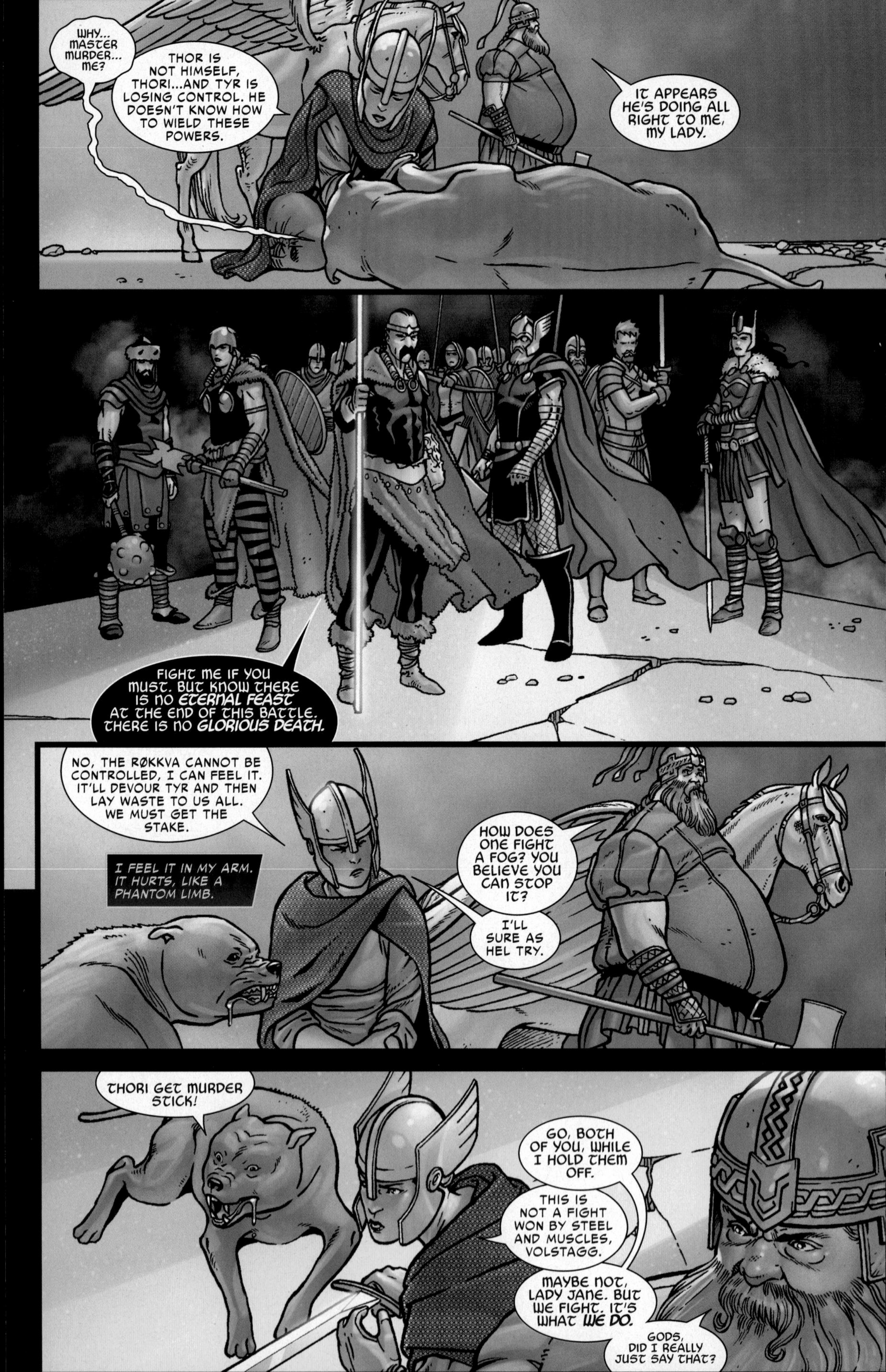
WHY... MASTER MURDER... ME?
THOR IS NOT HIMSELF, THORI...AND TYR IS LOSING CONTROL. HE DOESN'T KNOW HOW TO WIELD THESE POWERS.
IT APPEARS HE'S DOING ALL RIGHT TO ME, MY LADY.
FIGHT ME IF YOU MUST. BUT KNOW THERE IS NO ETERNAL FEAST AT THE END OF THIS BATTLE. THERE IS NO GLORIOUS DEATH.
NO, THE RØKKVA CANNOT BE CONTROLLED, I CAN FEEL IT. IT'LL DEVOUR TYR AND THEN LAY WASTE TO US ALL. WE MUST GET THE STAKE.
I FEEL IT IN MY ARM. IT HURTS, LIKE A PHANTOM LIMB.
HOW DOES ONE FIGHT A FOG? YOU BELIEVE YOU CAN STOP IT?
I'LL SURE AS HEL TRY.
THORI GET MURDER STICK!
GO, BOTH OF YOU, WHILE I HOLD THEM OFF.
THIS IS NOT A FIGHT WON BY STEEL AND MUSCLES, VOLSTAGG.
MAYBE NOT, LADY JANE. BUT WE FIGHT. IT'S WHAT WE DO.
GODS, DID I REALLY JUST SAY THAT?

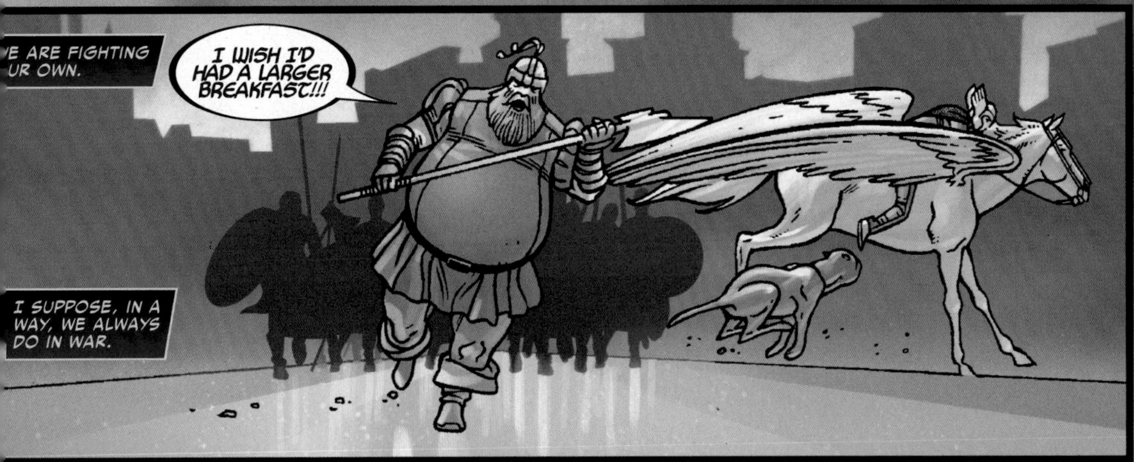

E ARE FIGHTING
UR OWN.
I WISH I'D HAD A LARGER BREAKFAST!!!
I SUPPOSE, IN A WAY, WE ALWAYS DO IN WAR.

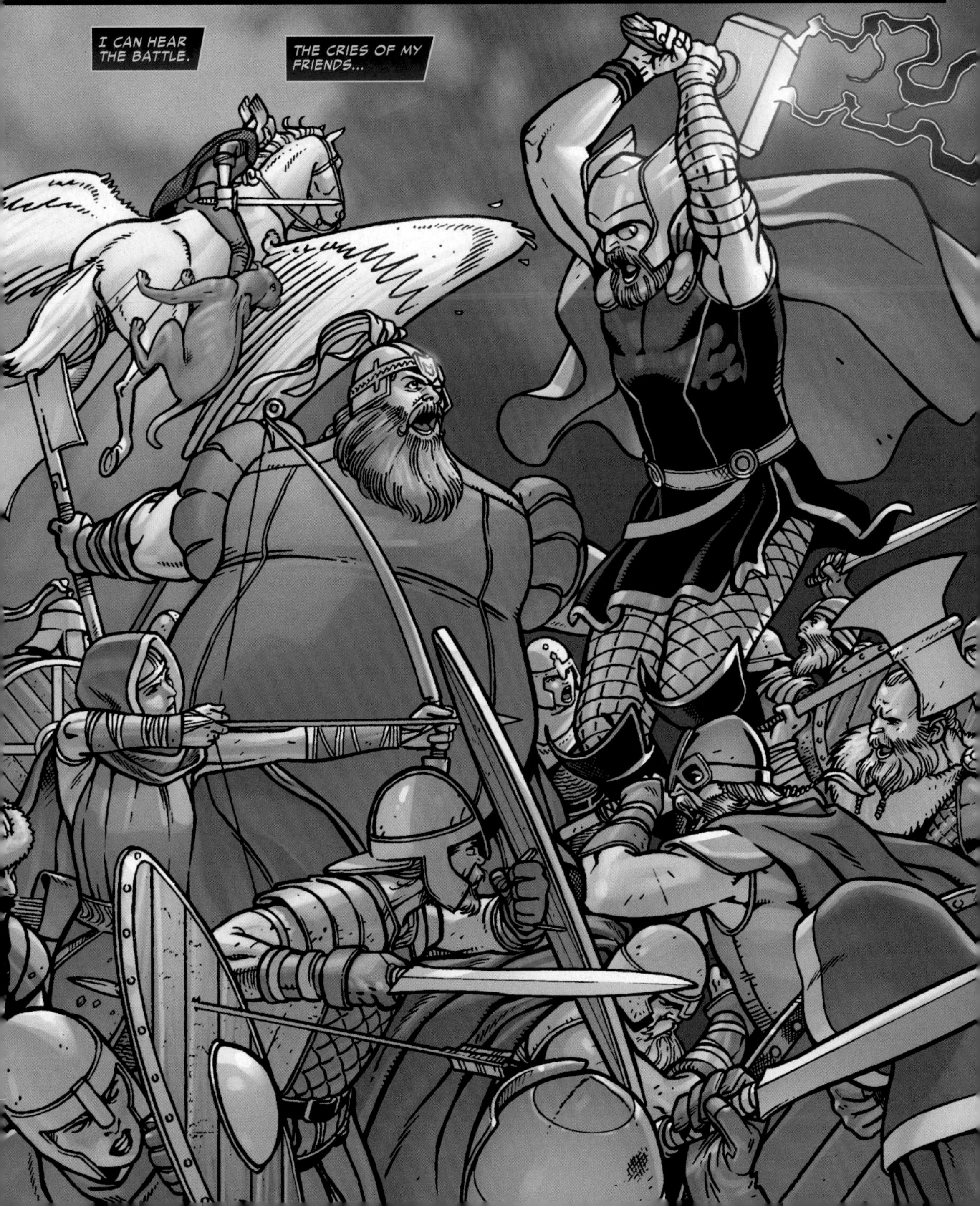

I CAN HEAR THE BATTLE.
THE CRIES OF MY FRIENDS...

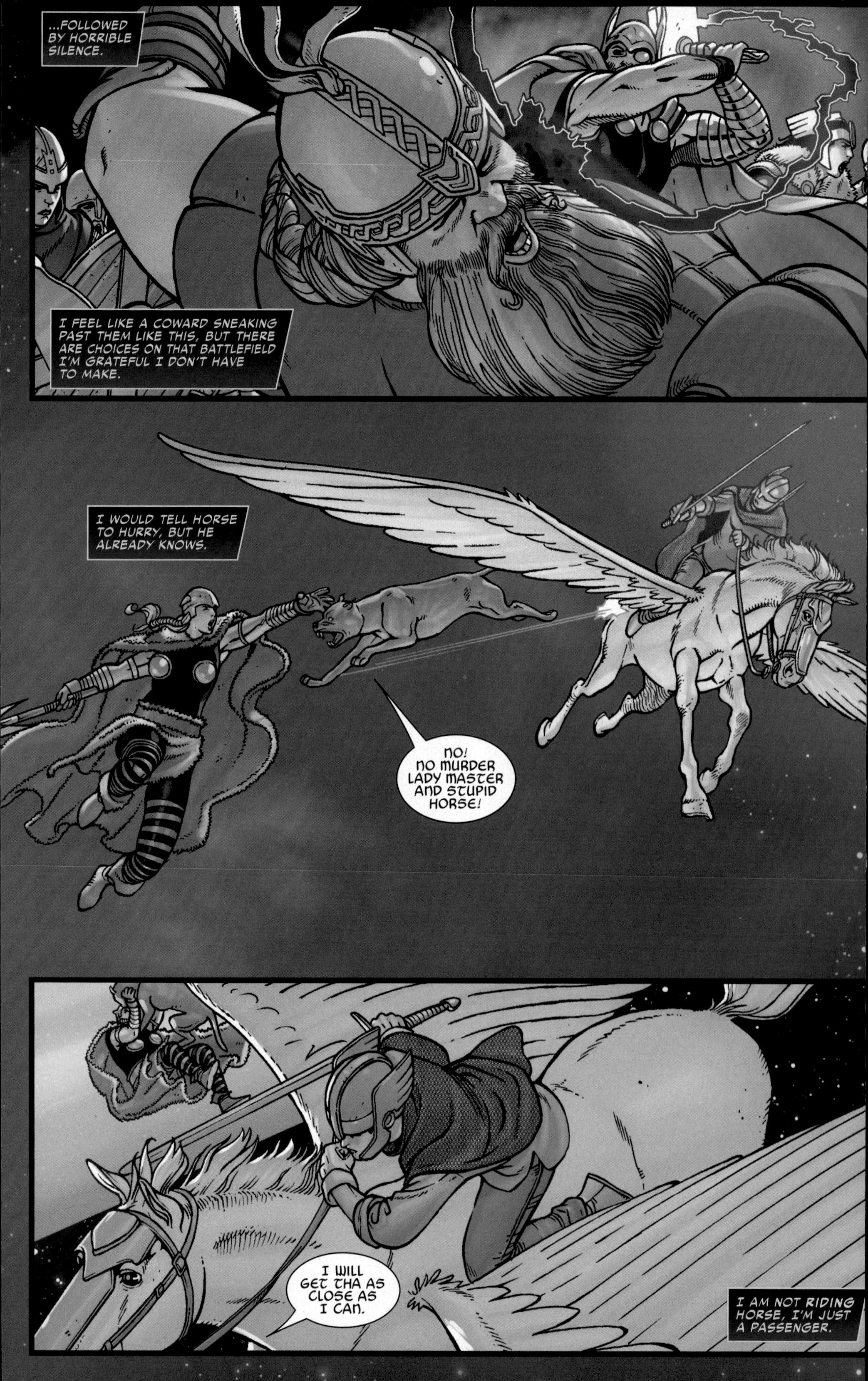
...FOLLOWED BY HORRIBLE SILENCE.
I FEEL LIKE A COWARD SNEAKING PAST THEM LIKE THIS, BUT THERE ARE CHOICES ON THAT BATTLEFIELD I'M GRATEFUL I DON'T HAVE TO MAKE.
I WOULD TELL HORSE TO HURRY, BUT HE ALREADY KNOWS.
NO! NO MURDER LADY MASTER AND STUPID HORSE!
I WILL GET THA AS CLOSE AS I CAN.
I AM NOT RIDING HORSE, I'M JUST A PASSENGER.

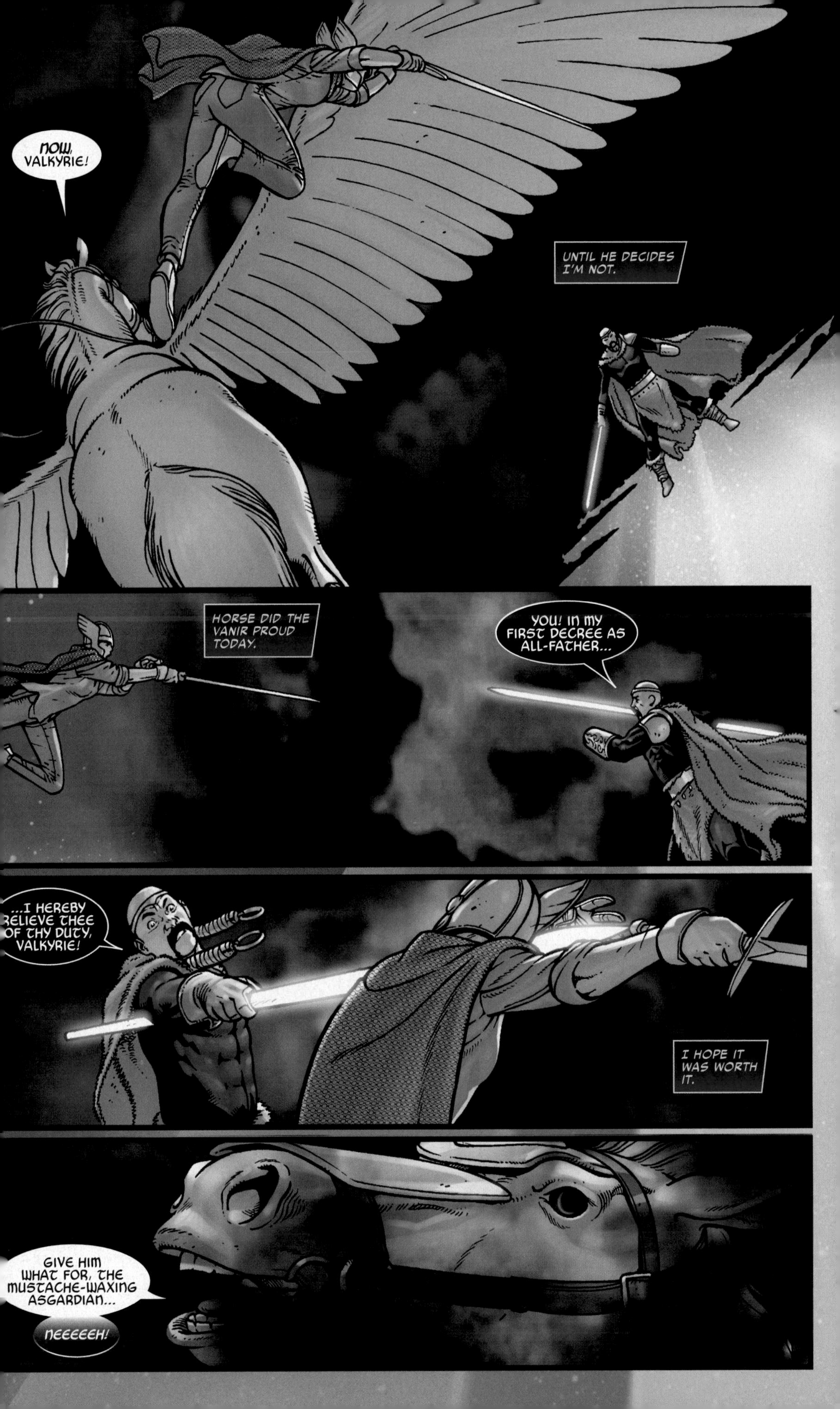
NOW, VALKYRIE!
UNTIL HE DECIDES I'M NOT.
HORSE DID THE VANIR PROUD TODAY.
YOU! IN MY FIRST DECREE AS ALL-FATHER...
...I HEREBY RELIEVE THEE OF THY DUTY, VALKYRIE!
I HOPE IT WAS WORTH IT.
GIVE HIM WHAT FOR, THE MUSTACHE-WAXING ASGARDIAN...
NEEEEEH!

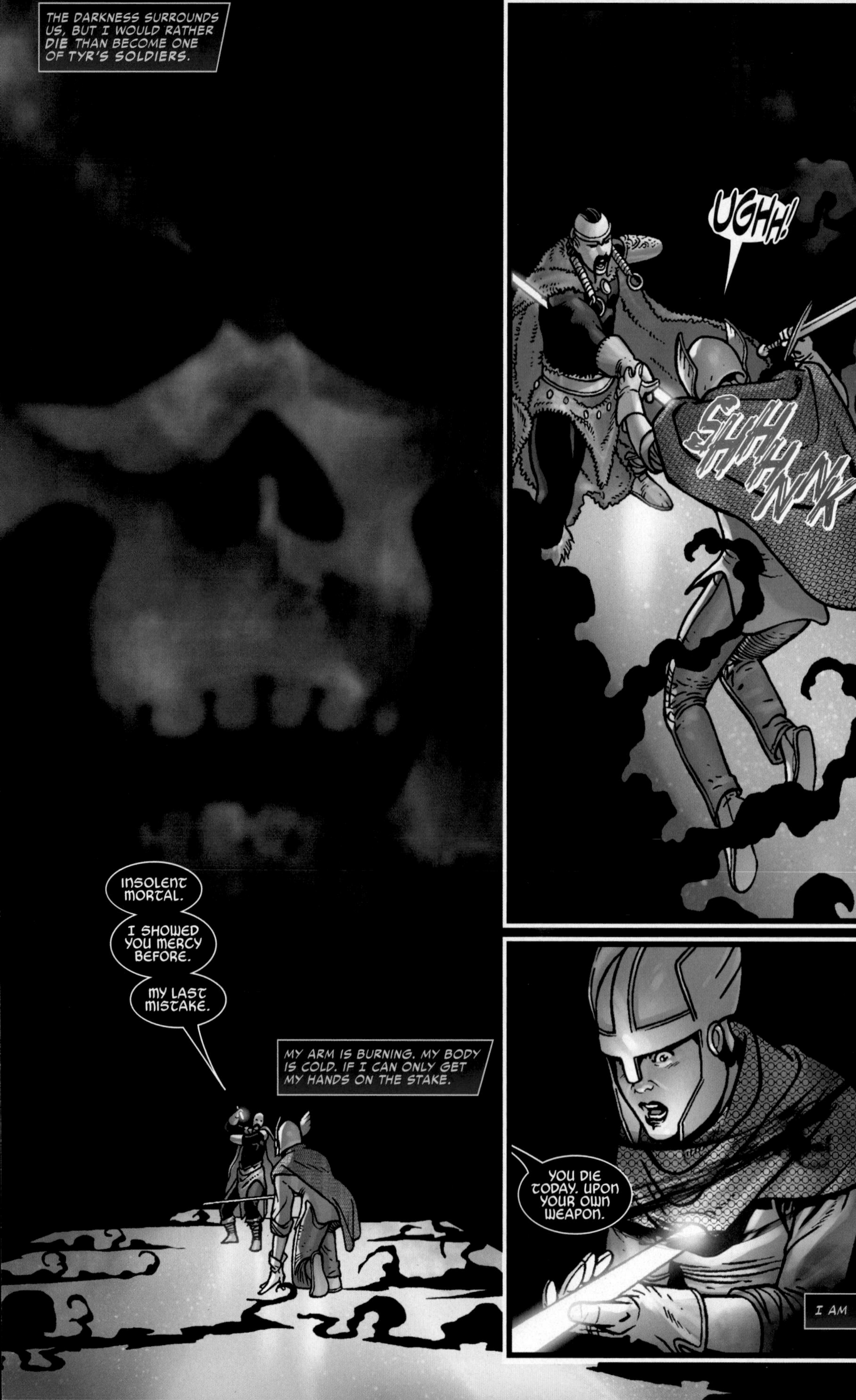
THE DARKNESS SURROUNDS US, BUT I WOULD RATHER DIE THAN BECOME ONE OF TYR'S SOLDIERS.
INSOLENT MORTAL.
I SHOWED YOU MERCY BEFORE.
MY LAST MISTAKE.
MY ARM IS BURNING. MY BODY IS COLD. IF I CAN ONLY GET MY HANDS ON THE STAKE.
UGHH!
SHHHNK
YOU DIE TODAY. UPON YOUR OWN WEAPON.
I AM

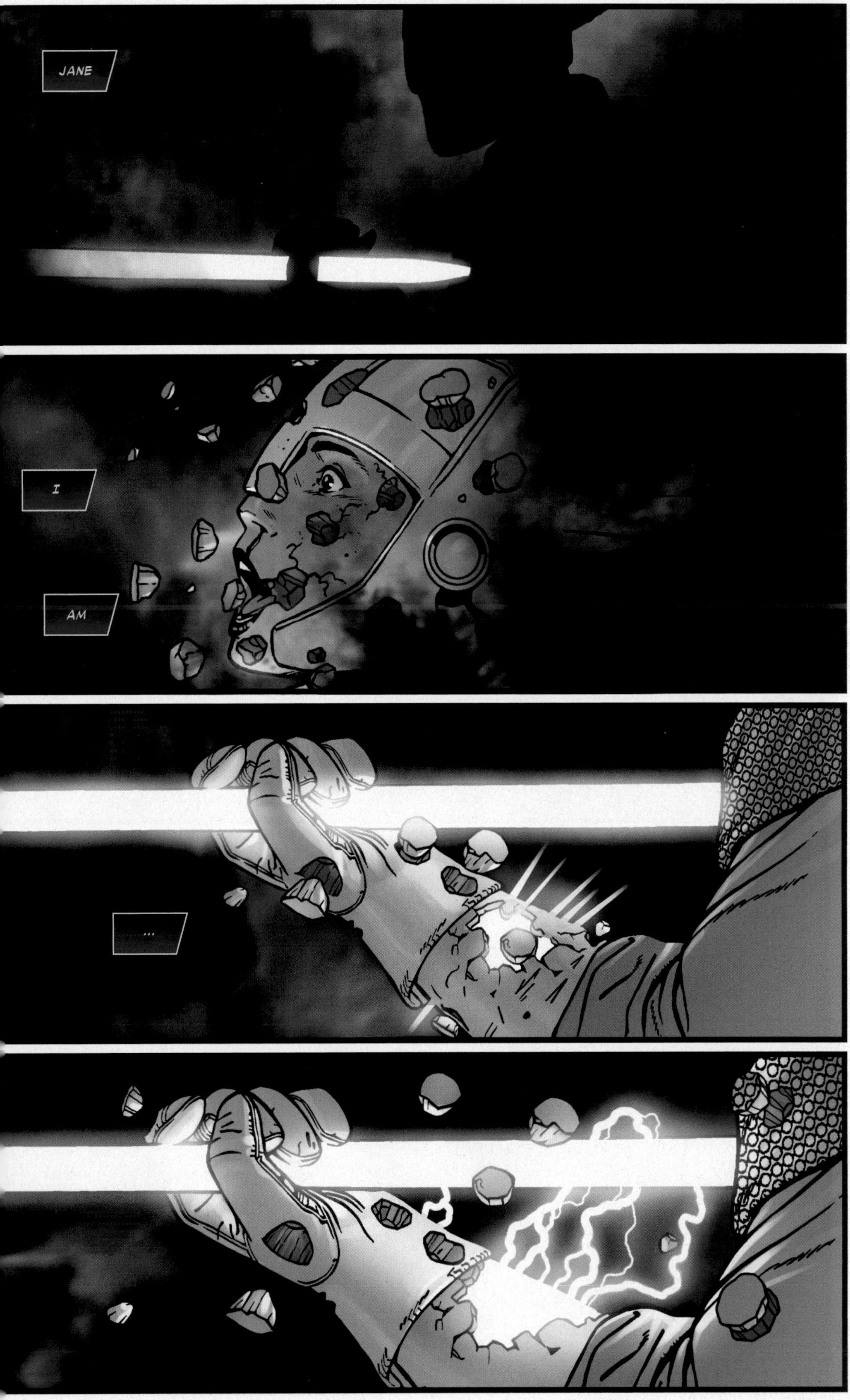

JANE
I
AM
...

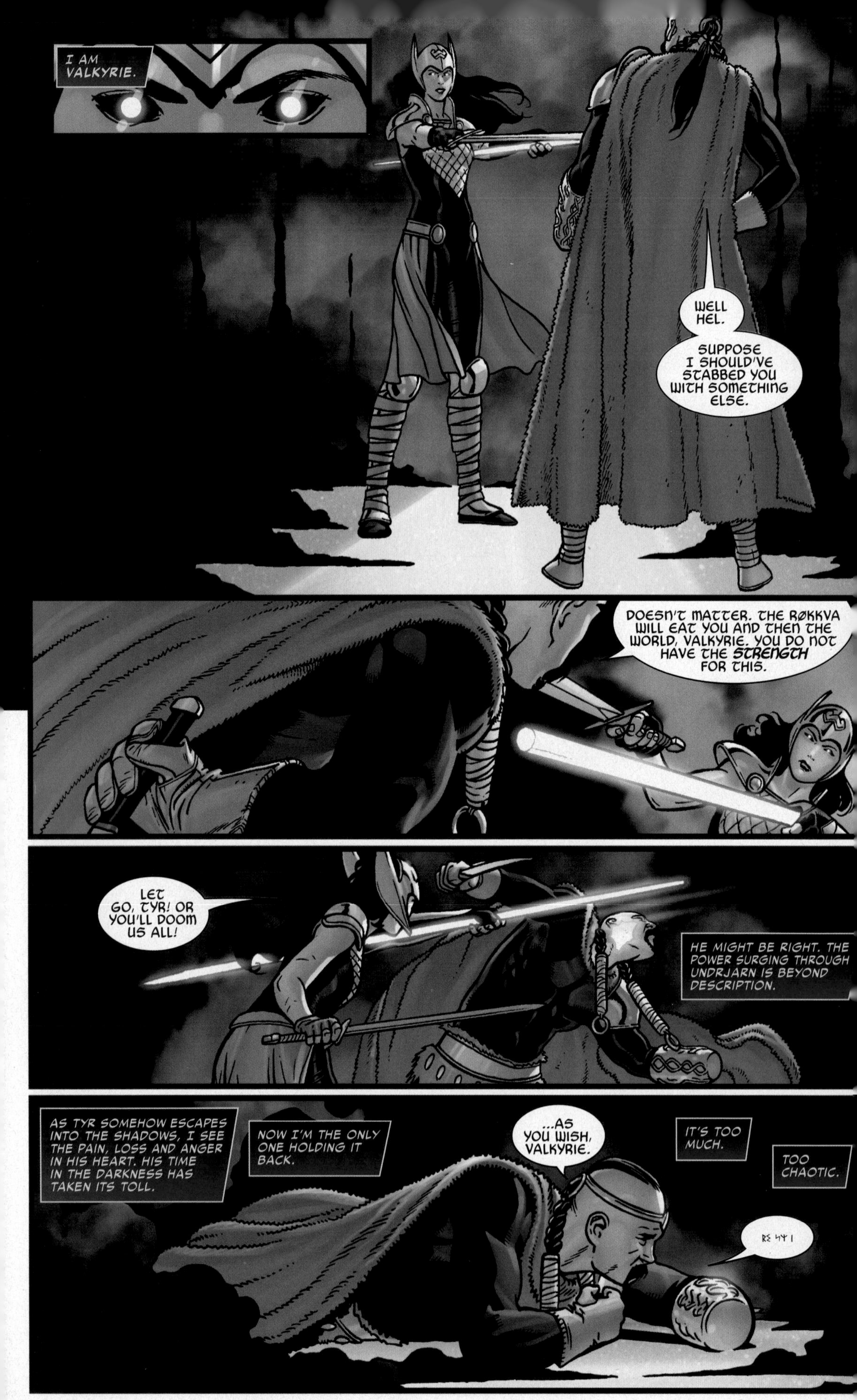
I AM VALKYRIE.
WELL HEL.
SUPPOSE I SHOULD'VE STABBED YOU WITH SOMETHING ELSE.
DOESN'T MATTER. THE RØKKVA WILL EAT YOU AND THEN THE WORLD, VALKYRIE. YOU DO NOT HAVE THE STRENGTH FOR THIS.
LET GO, TYR! OR YOU'LL DOOM US ALL!
HE MIGHT BE RIGHT. THE POWER SURGING THROUGH UNDRJARN IS BEYOND DESCRIPTION.
AS TYR SOMEHOW ESCAPES INTO THE SHADOWS, I SEE THE PAIN, LOSS AND ANGER IN HIS HEART. HIS TIME IN THE DARKNESS HAS TAKEN ITS TOLL.
NOW I'M THE ONLY ONE HOLDING IT BACK.
...AS YOU WISH, VALKYRIE.
IT'S TOO MUCH.
TOO CHAOTIC.

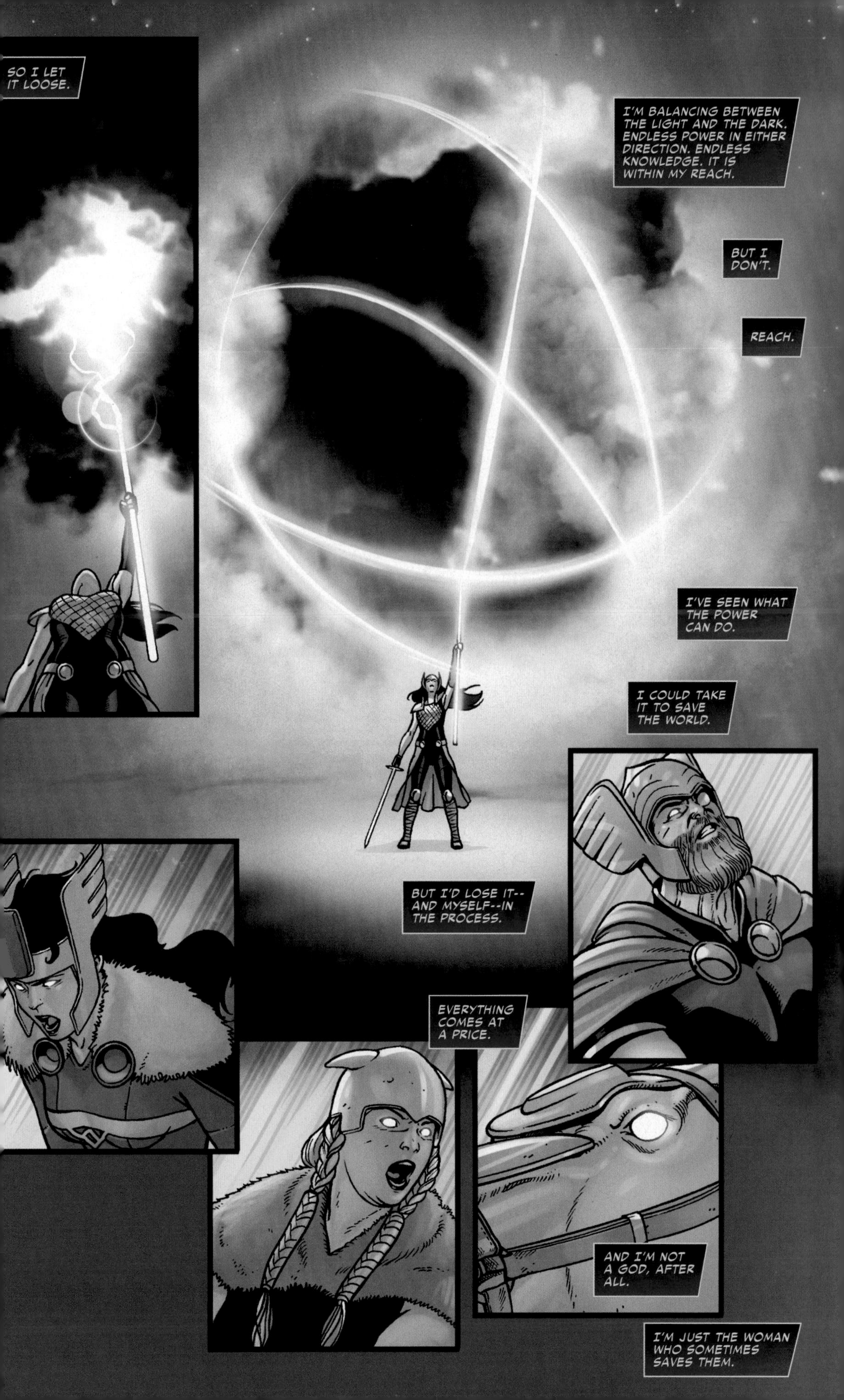
SO I LET IT LOOSE.
I'M BALANCING BETWEEN THE LIGHT AND THE DARK. ENDLESS POWER IN EITHER DIRECTION. ENDLESS KNOWLEDGE. IT IS WITHIN MY REACH.
BUT I DON'T.
REACH.
I'VE SEEN WHAT THE POWER CAN DO.
I COULD TAKE IT TO SAVE THE WORLD.
BUT I'D LOSE IT--AND MYSELF--IN THE PROCESS.
EVERYTHING COMES AT A PRICE.
AND I'M NOT A GOD, AFTER ALL.
I'M JUST THE WOMAN WHO SOMETIMES SAVES THEM.

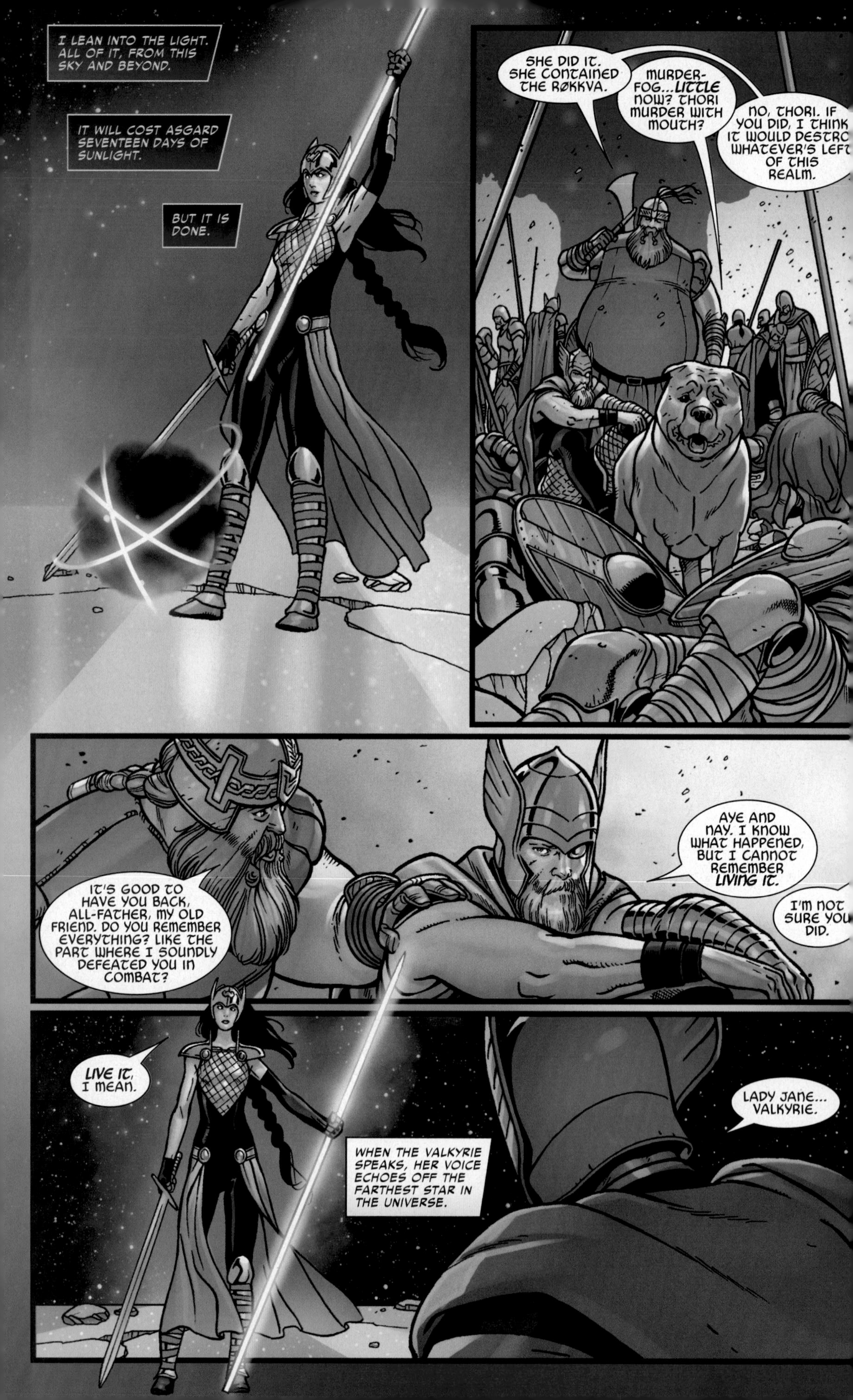
I LEAN INTO THE LIGHT. ALL OF IT, FROM THIS SKY AND BEYOND.
IT WILL COST ASGARD SEVENTEEN DAYS OF SUNLIGHT.
BUT IT IS DONE.
SHE DID IT. SHE CONTAINED THE RØKKVA.
MURDER-FOG...LITTLE NOW? THORI MURDER WITH MOUTH?
NO, THORI. IF YOU DID, I THINK IT WOULD DESTRO WHATEVER'S LEFT OF THIS REALM.
IT'S GOOD TO HAVE YOU BACK, ALL-FATHER, MY OLD FRIEND. DO YOU REMEMBER EVERYTHING? LIKE THE PART WHERE I SOUNDLY DEFEATED YOU IN COMBAT?
AYE AND NAY. I KNOW WHAT HAPPENED, BUT I CANNOT REMEMBER LIVING IT.
I'M NOT SURE YOU DID.
LIVE IT, I MEAN.
WHEN THE VALKYRIE SPEAKS, HER VOICE ECHOES OFF THE FARTHEST STAR IN THE UNIVERSE.
LADY JANE... VALKYRIE.

THE WEEKS THAT FOLLOW, THE VALKYRIE WILL WONDER WHAT SECRETS SHE COULD HAVE UNLOCKED IN THE LIGHT.

TYR ESCAPED. BUT HE IS NOT A THREAT TO ANYONE IN HIS CURRENT STATE.

EVEN SO, MY BROTHER MUST ANSWER FOR HIS CRIMES. ASGARD WILL SEE TO IT.

I MUST GO. PLEASE, TAKE CARE OF MY HORSE UNTIL I'M BACK.

SHE WILL WONDER IF SHE MADE THE RIGHT CALL, GIVING IT UP.

JANE... WOULD YOU HAVE *KILLED* ME? BACK THERE, IN THE CENTER OF MIDGARD?

TO SAVE THE EARTH? YES, I WOULD.

BUT I HOPE YOU KNOW IT WOULD HAVE KILLED ME TOO.

COME, DEAR HORSE... THE STABLES OF ASGARD WILL WELCOME YOU.

I'M NOT ONE O' THEM POSH PONIES THA GOT 'ERE IN ASGARD. A ROOM IN T' CASTLE WILL DO JUST FINE, LAD.

I'LL NEED SOME HAY, MIND.

AS TIME PASSES, SHE WILL WONDER IF WHAT SHE SAW IN THE LIGHT WAS REAL AT ALL.

AND IN THE END, SHE WILL COME TO REALIZE IT DOES NOT MATTER.

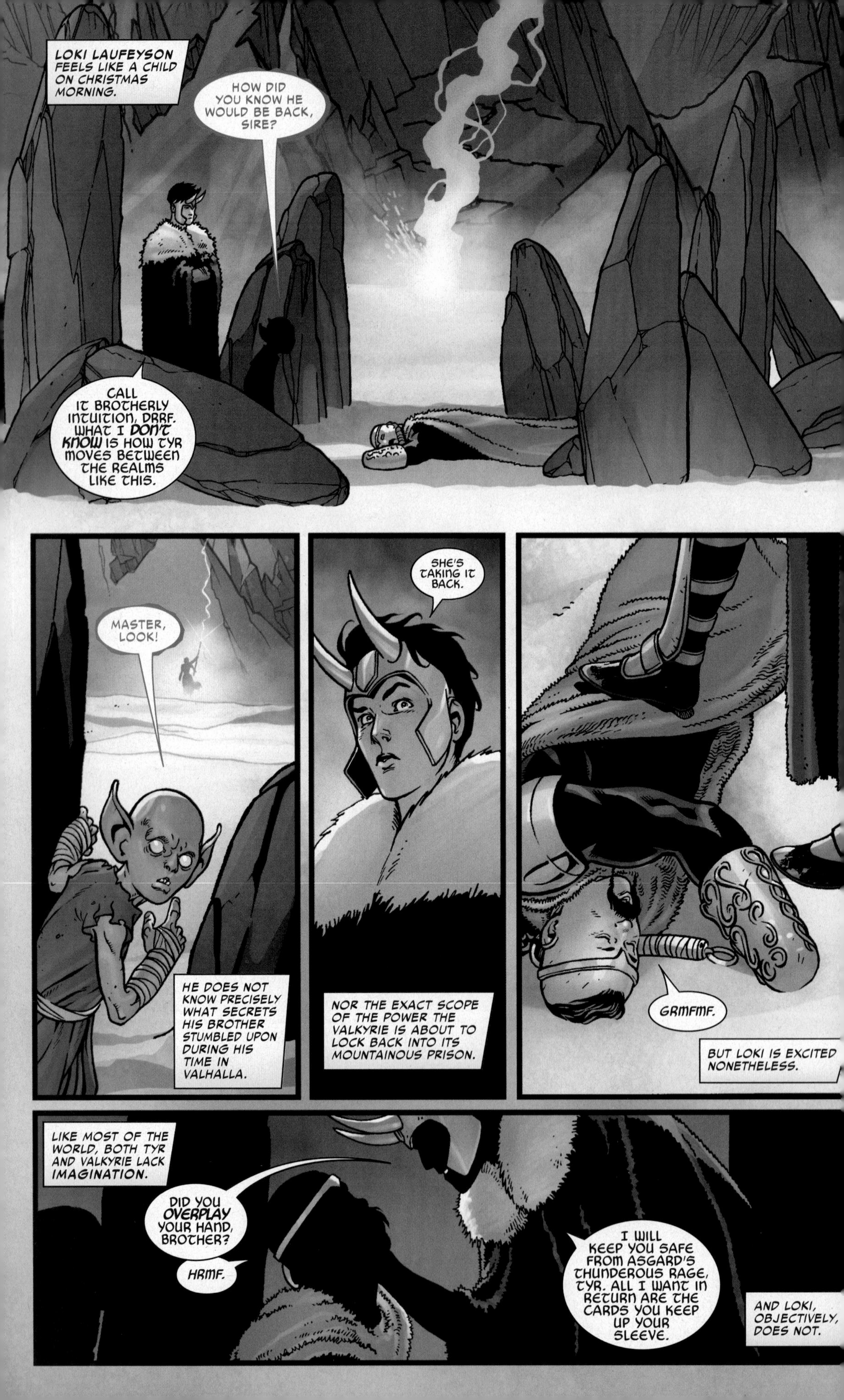

LOKI LAUFEYSON FEELS LIKE A CHILD ON CHRISTMAS MORNING.
HOW DID YOU KNOW HE WOULD BE BACK, SIRE?
CALL IT BROTHERLY INTUITION, DRRF. WHAT I DON'T KNOW IS HOW TYR MOVES BETWEEN THE REALMS LIKE THIS.
MASTER, LOOK!
HE DOES NOT KNOW PRECISELY WHAT SECRETS HIS BROTHER STUMBLED UPON DURING HIS TIME IN VALHALLA.
SHE'S TAKING IT BACK.
NOR THE EXACT SCOPE OF THE POWER THE VALKYRIE IS ABOUT TO LOCK BACK INTO ITS MOUNTAINOUS PRISON.
GRMFMF.
BUT LOKI IS EXCITED NONETHELESS.
LIKE MOST OF THE WORLD, BOTH TYR AND VALKYRIE LACK IMAGINATION.
DID YOU OVERPLAY YOUR HAND, BROTHER?
HRMF.
I WILL KEEP YOU SAFE FROM ASGARD'S THUNDEROUS RAGE, TYR. ALL I WANT IN RETURN ARE THE CARDS YOU KEEP UP YOUR SLEEVE.
AND LOKI, OBJECTIVELY, DOES NOT.

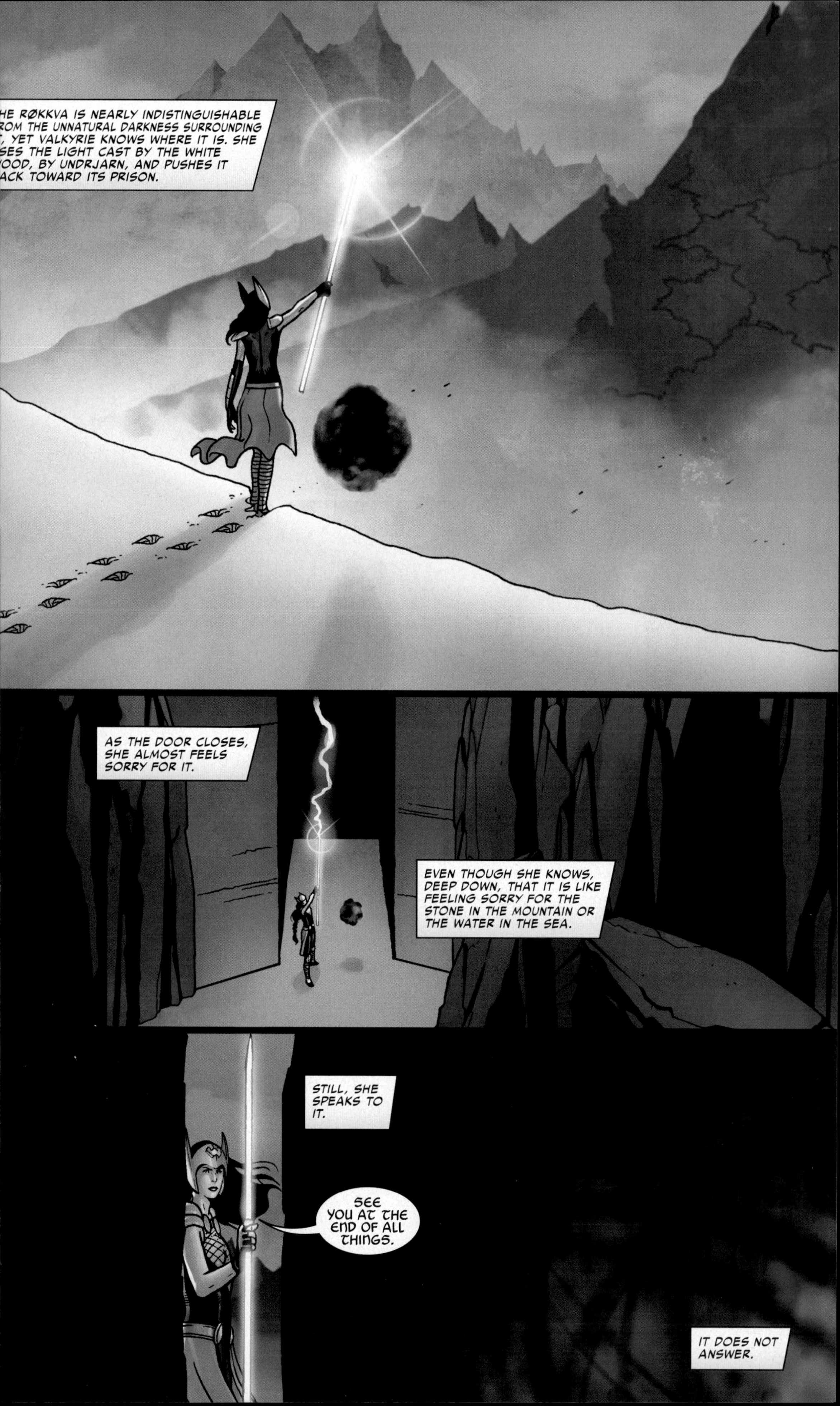
HE RØKKVA IS NEARLY INDISTINGUISHABLE ROM THE UNNATURAL DARKNESS SURROUNDING , YET VALKYRIE KNOWS WHERE IT IS. SHE SES THE LIGHT CAST BY THE WHITE OOD, BY UNDRJARN, AND PUSHES IT ACK TOWARD ITS PRISON.
AS THE DOOR CLOSES, SHE ALMOST FEELS SORRY FOR IT.
EVEN THOUGH SHE KNOWS, DEEP DOWN, THAT IT IS LIKE FEELING SORRY FOR THE STONE IN THE MOUNTAIN OR THE WATER IN THE SEA.
STILL, SHE SPEAKS TO IT.
SEE YOU AT THE END OF ALL THINGS.
IT DOES NOT ANSWER.

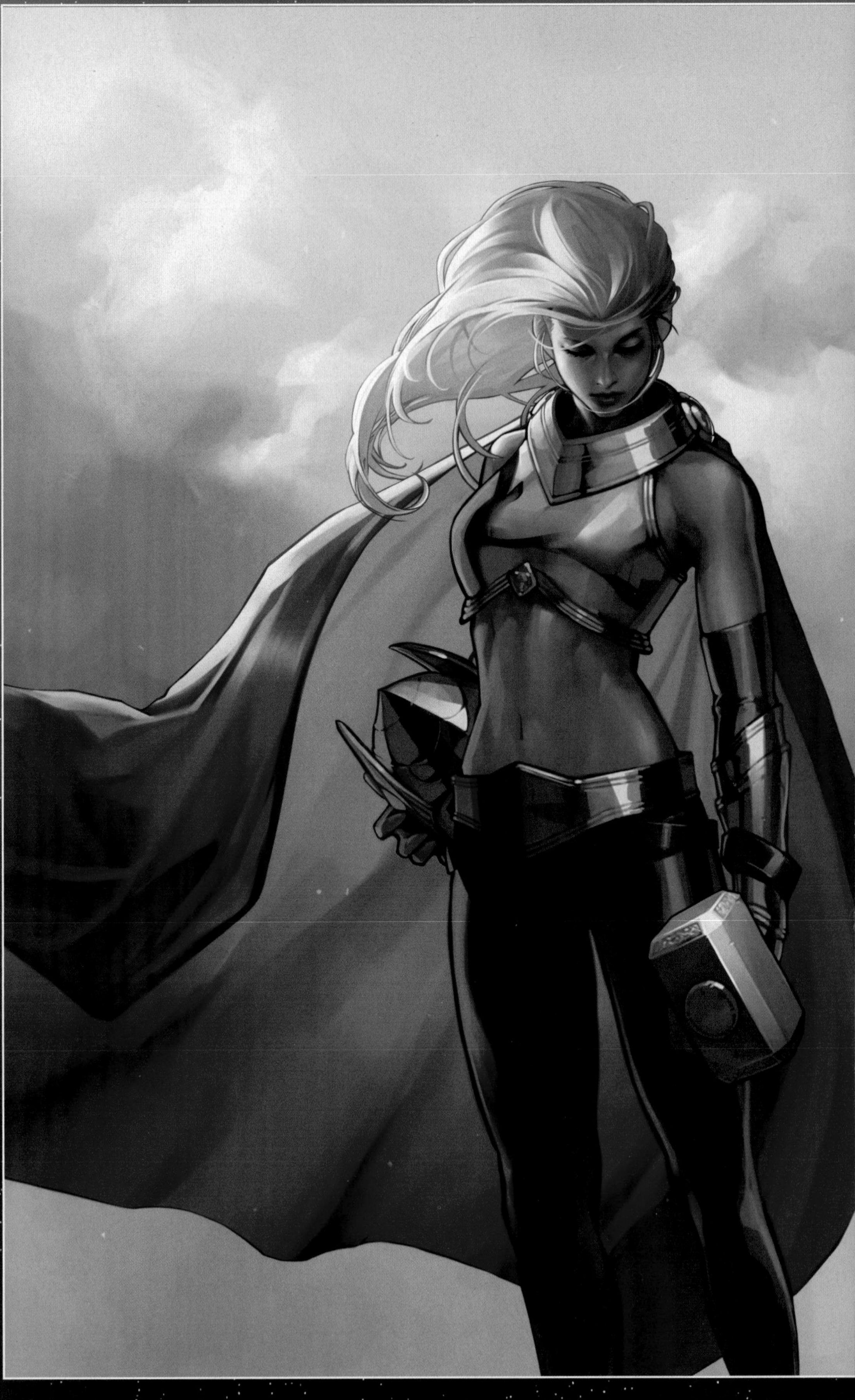

MIGHTY THOR #705 VARIANT BY JEEHYUNG LEE

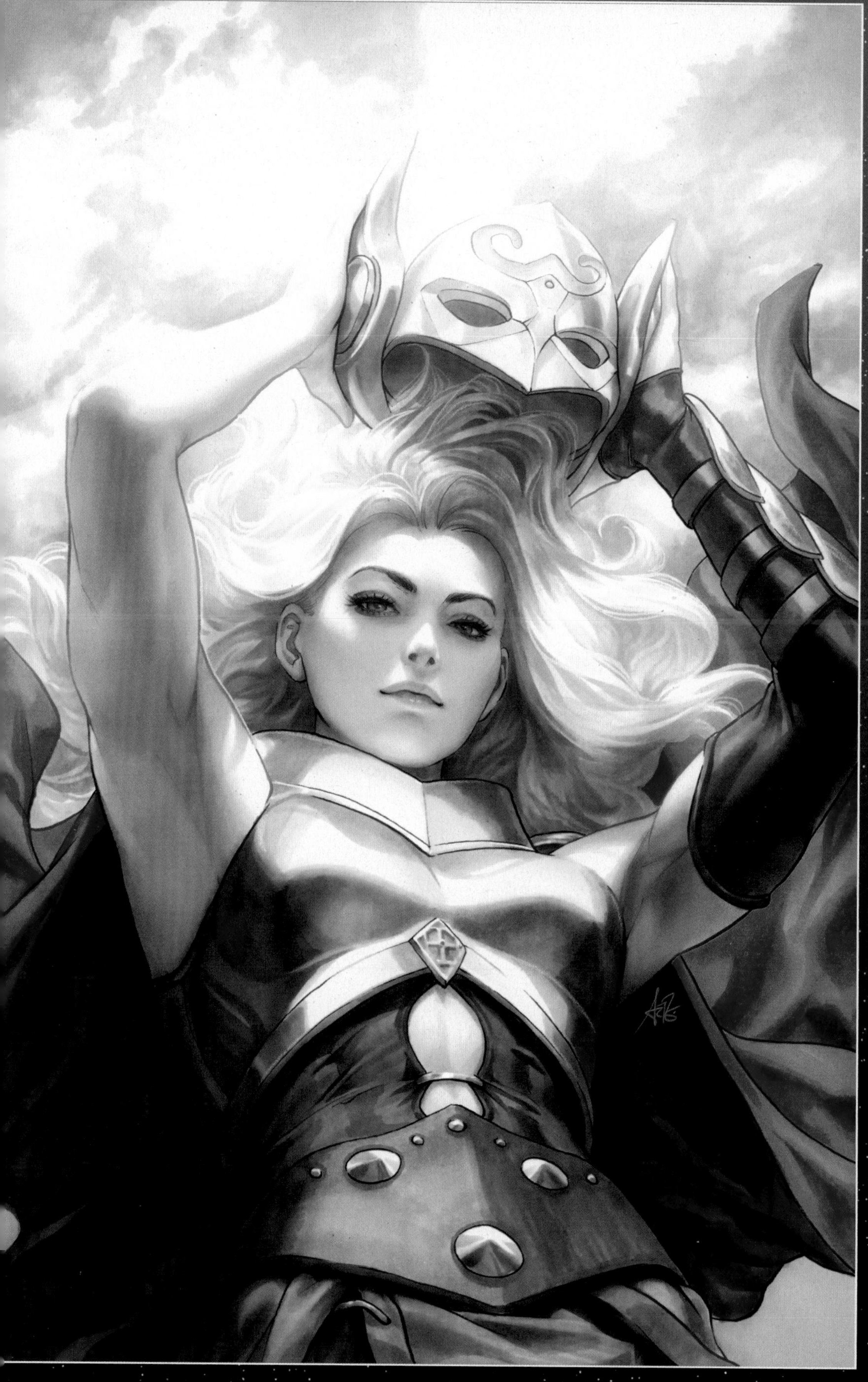

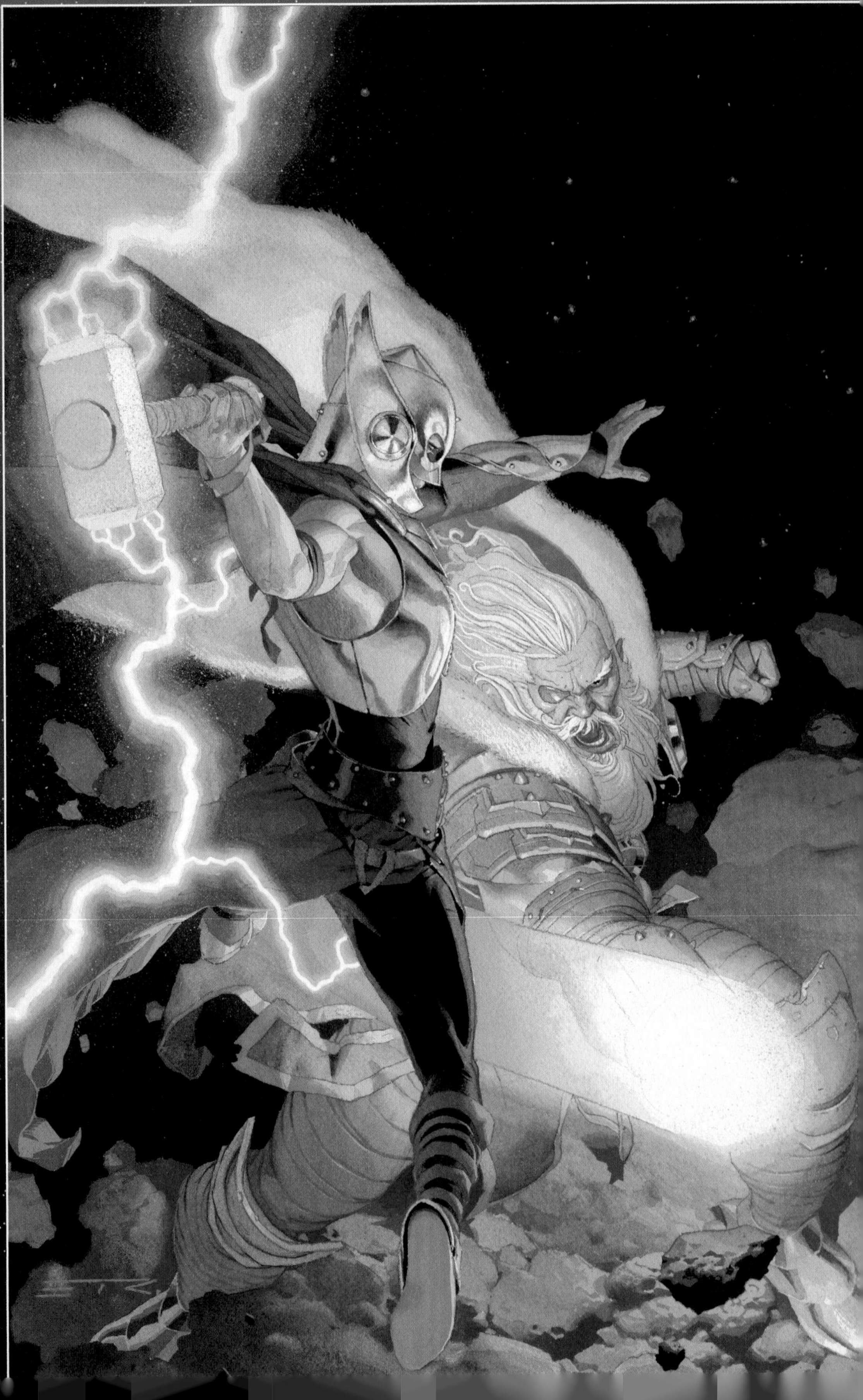

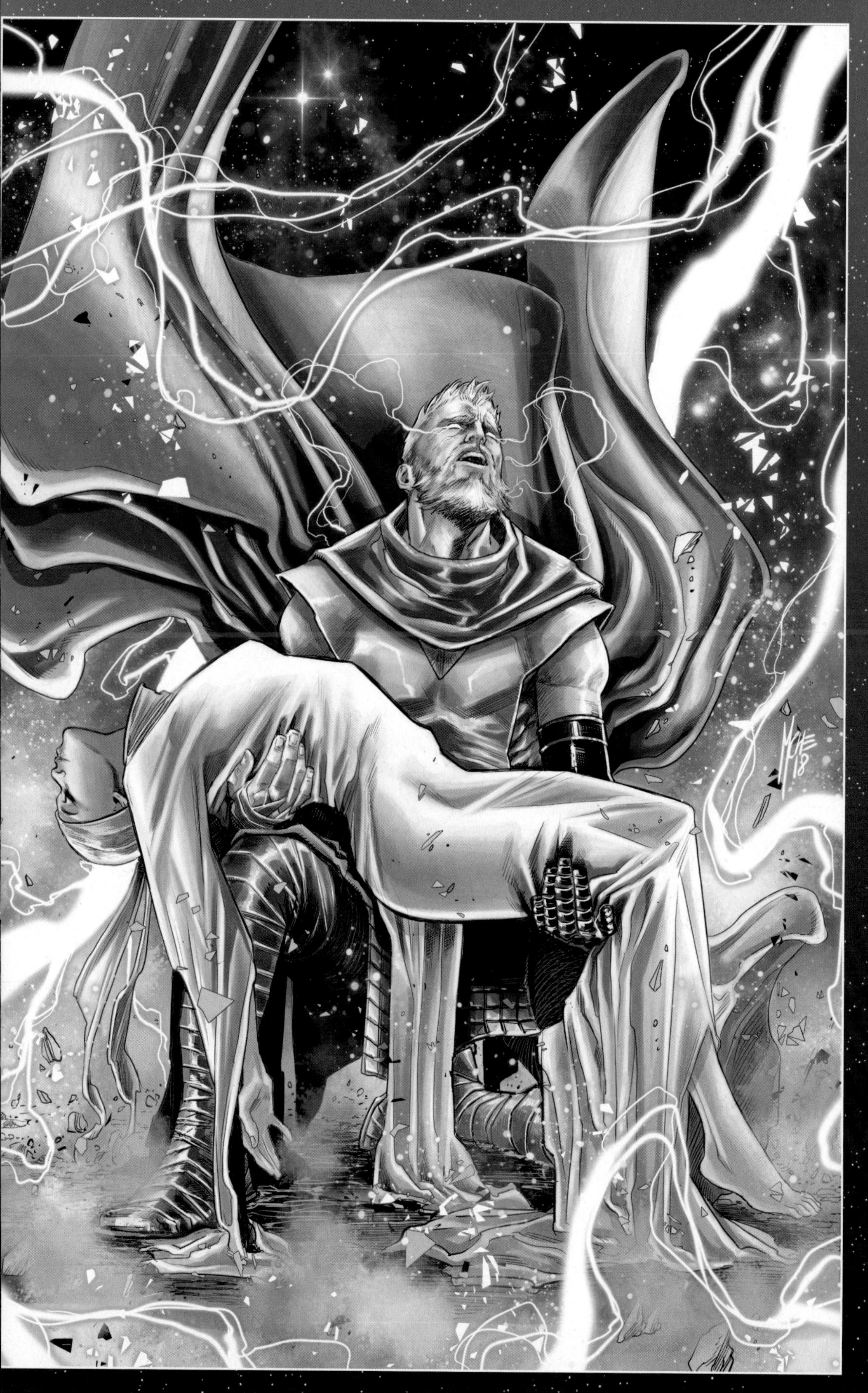

MIGHTY THOR #706 VARIANT BY MARCO CHECCHETTO

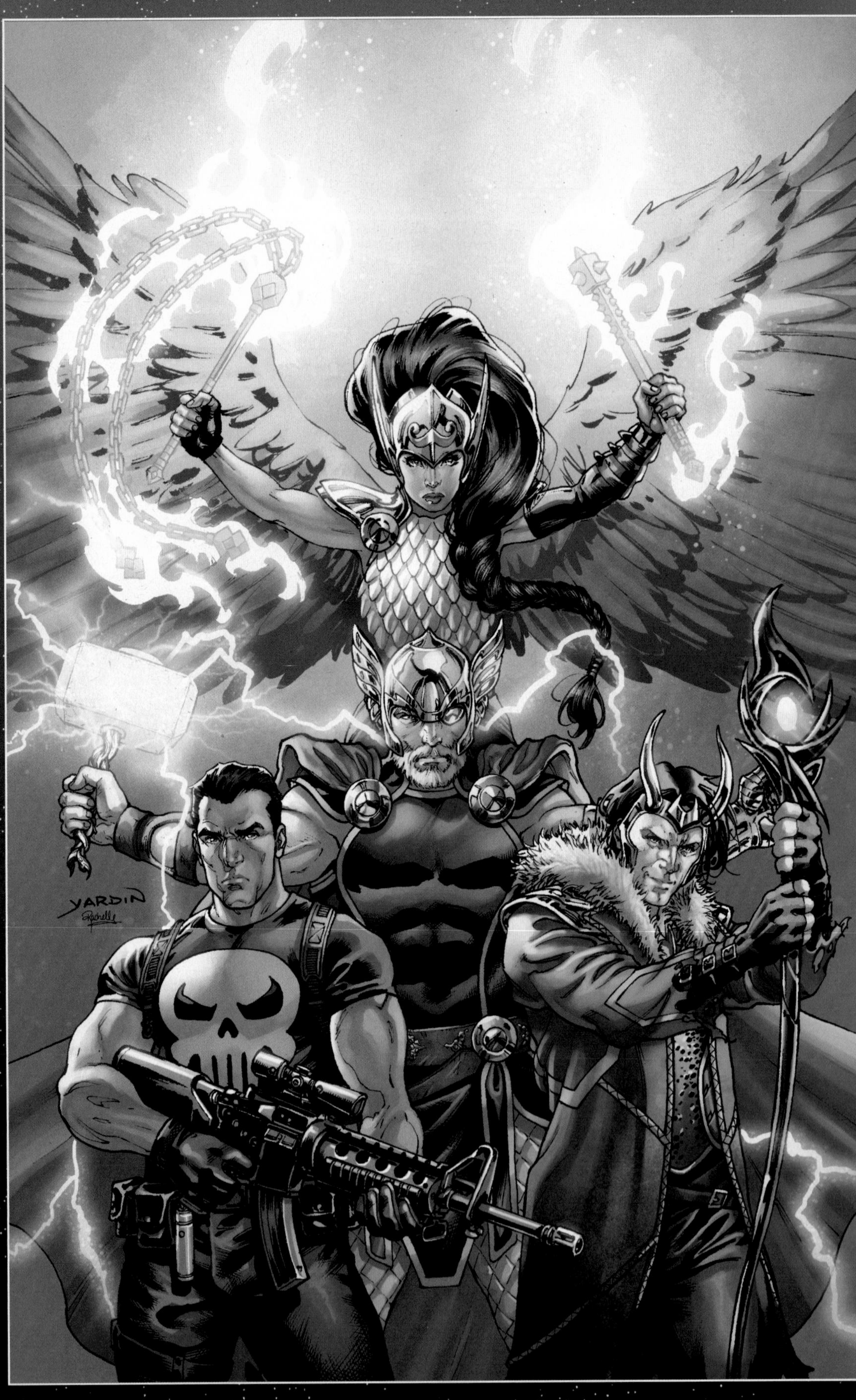
YARDIN

WAR OF THE REALMS OMEGA #1 VARIANT BY DAVID YARDIN & RACHELLE ROSENBERG

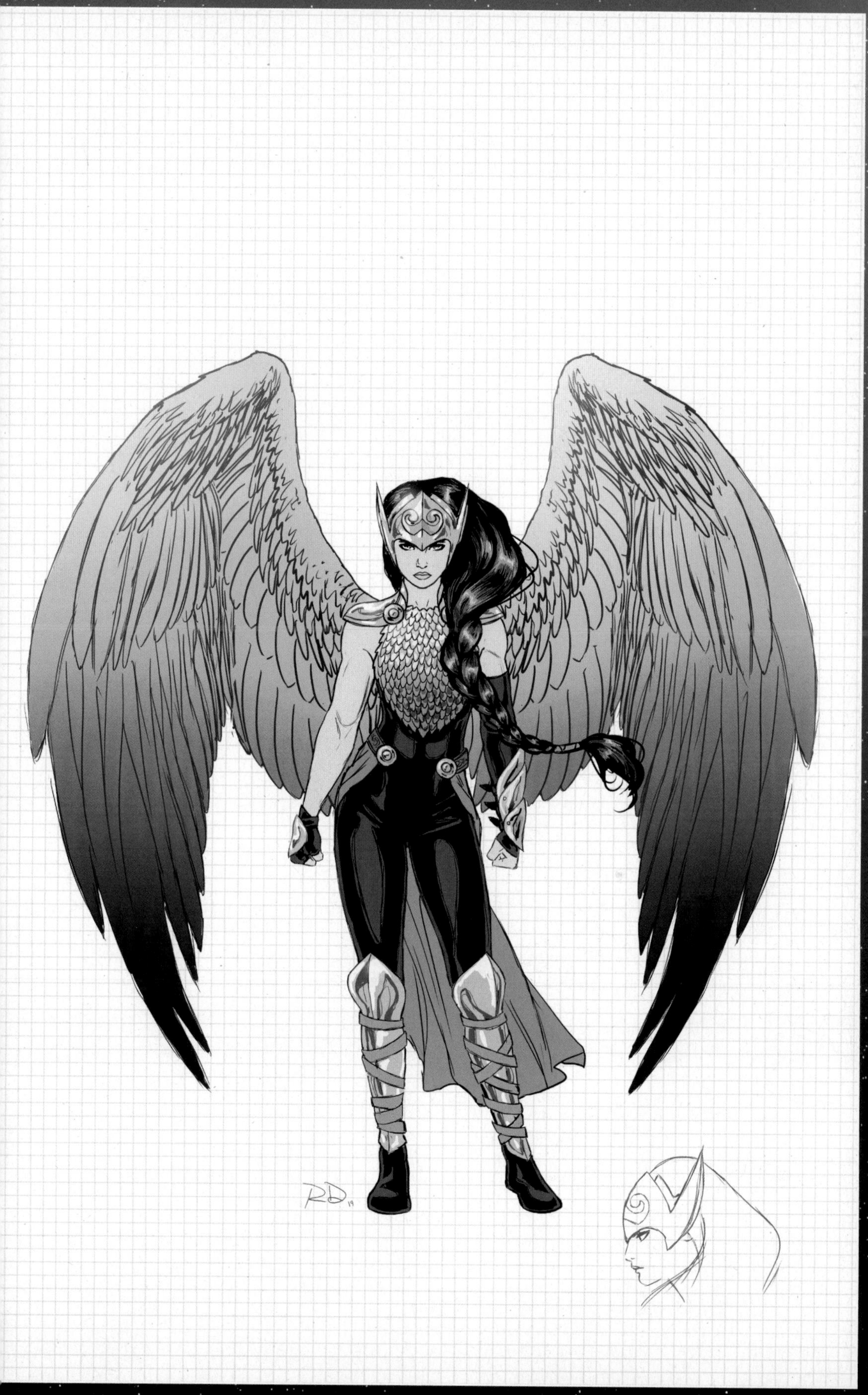
RD

VALKYRIE: JANE FOSTER #1 2ND PRINTING DESIGN VARIANT BY RUSSELL DAUTERMAN

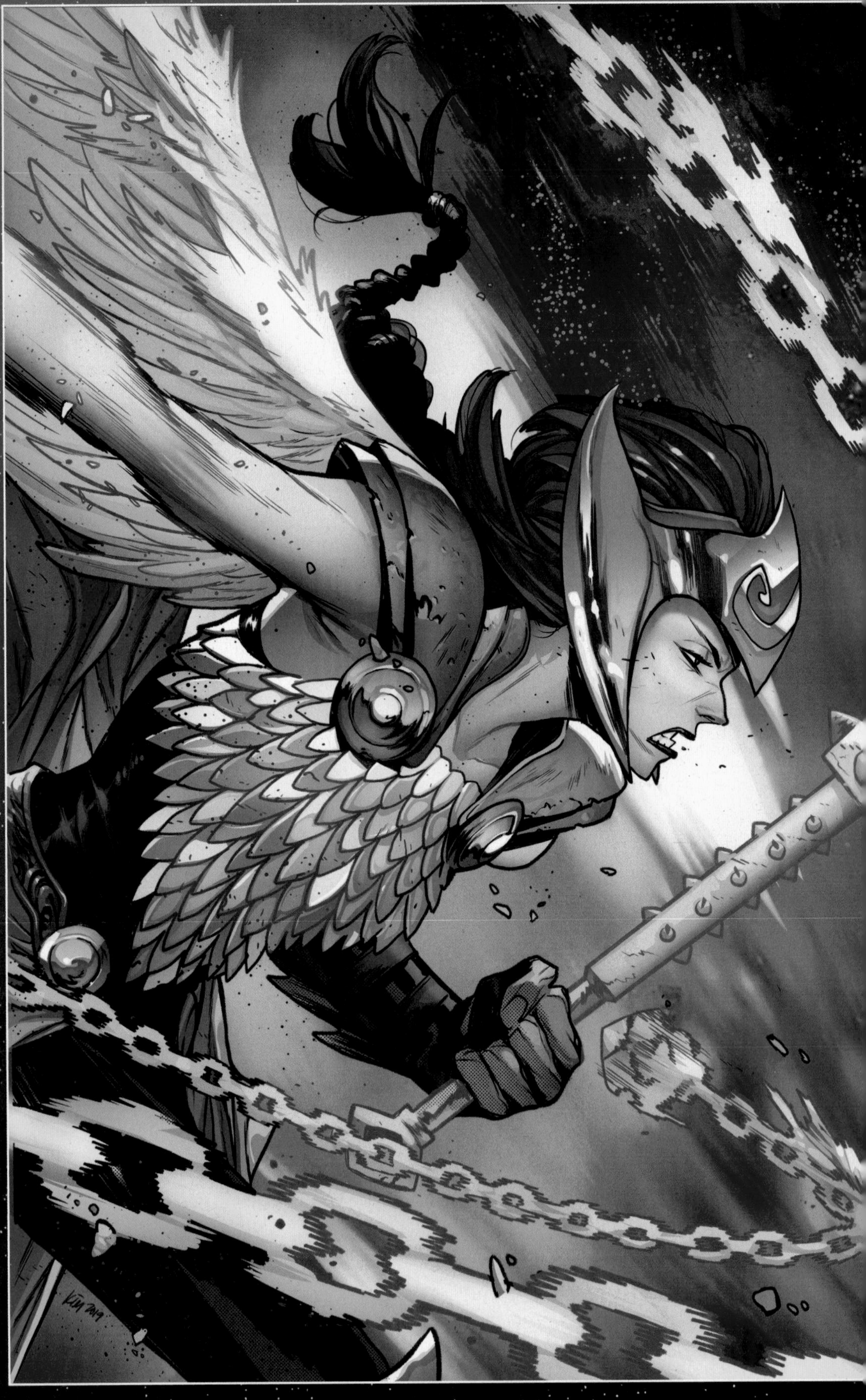

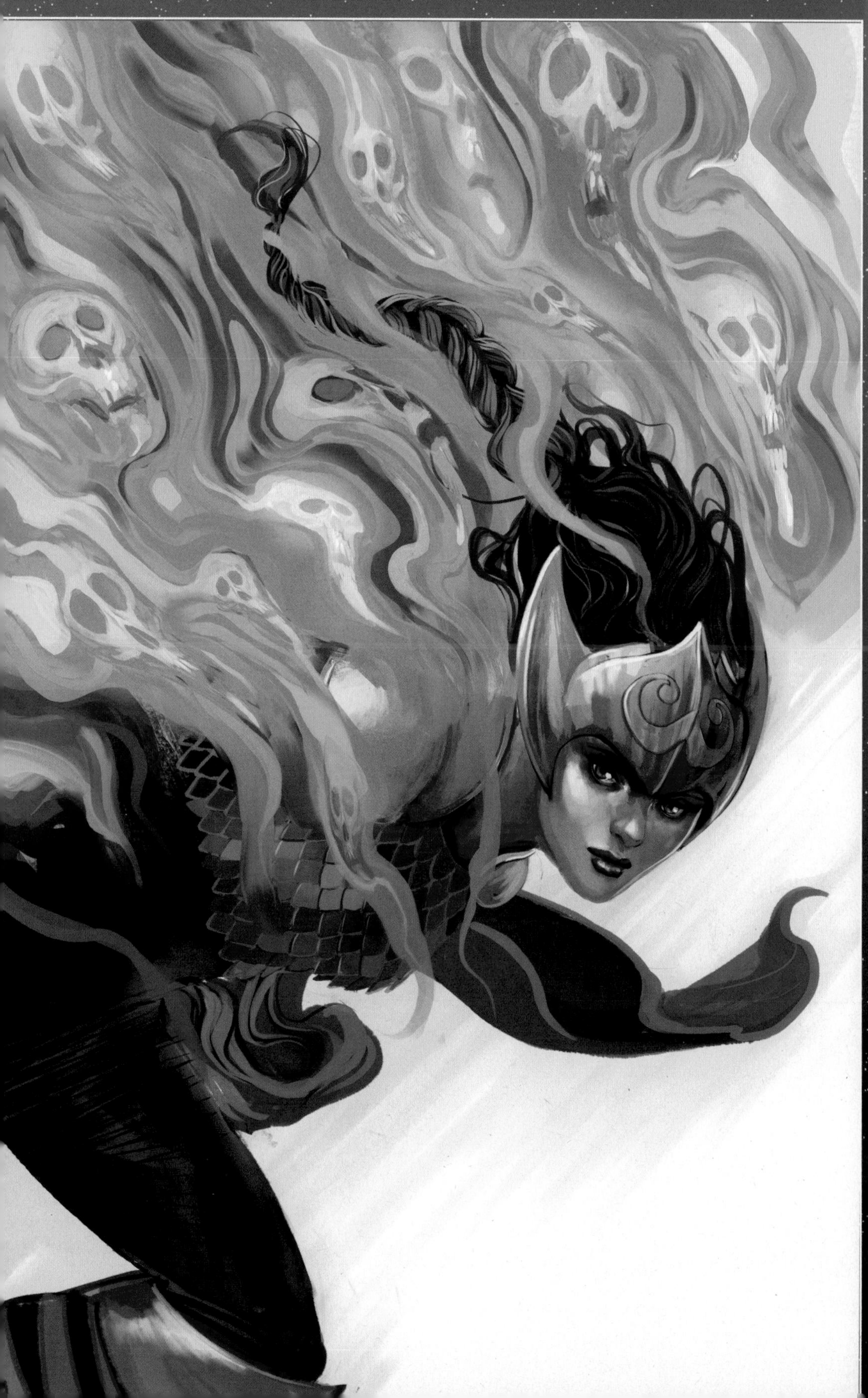

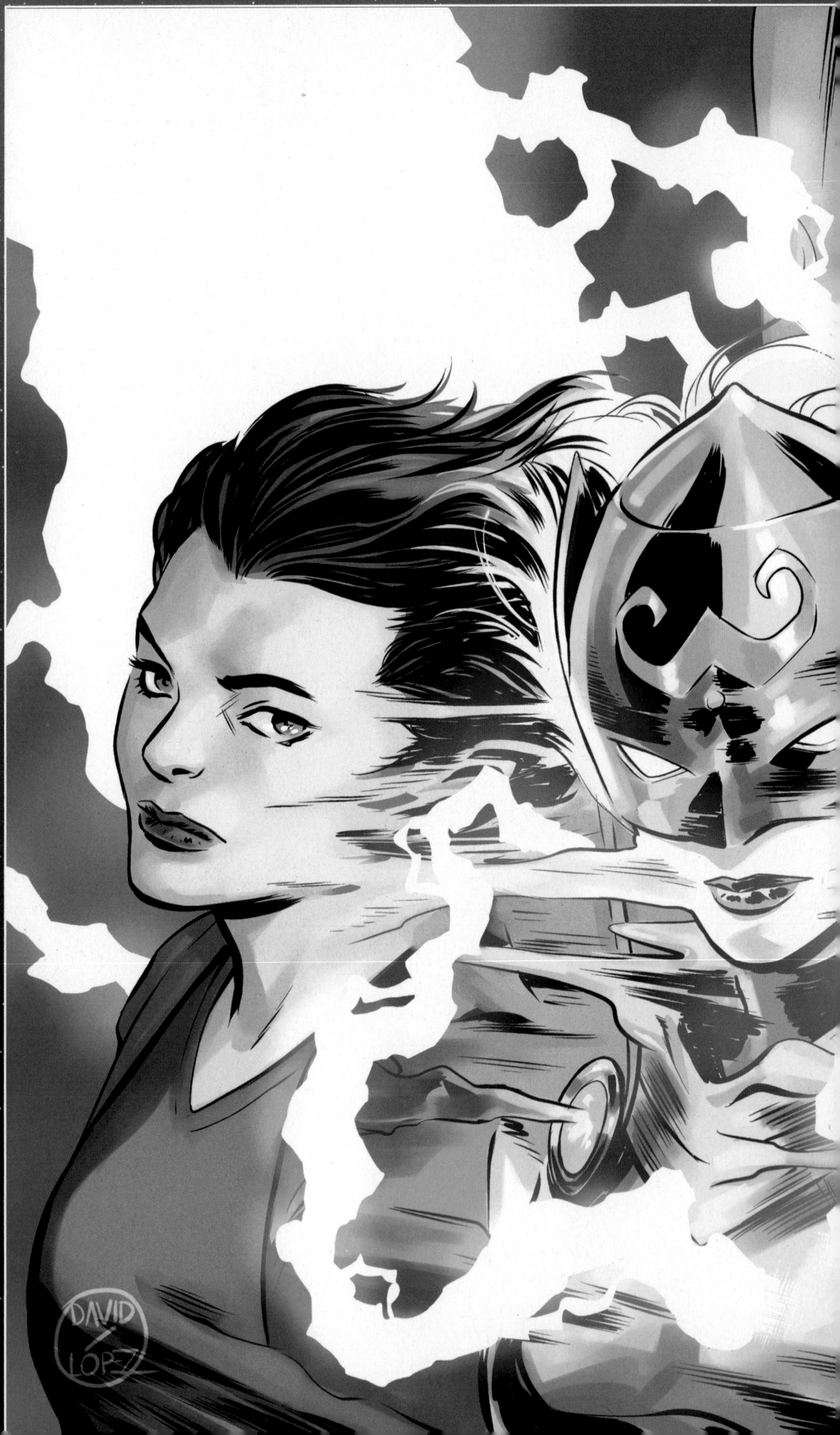
DAVID LOPEZ

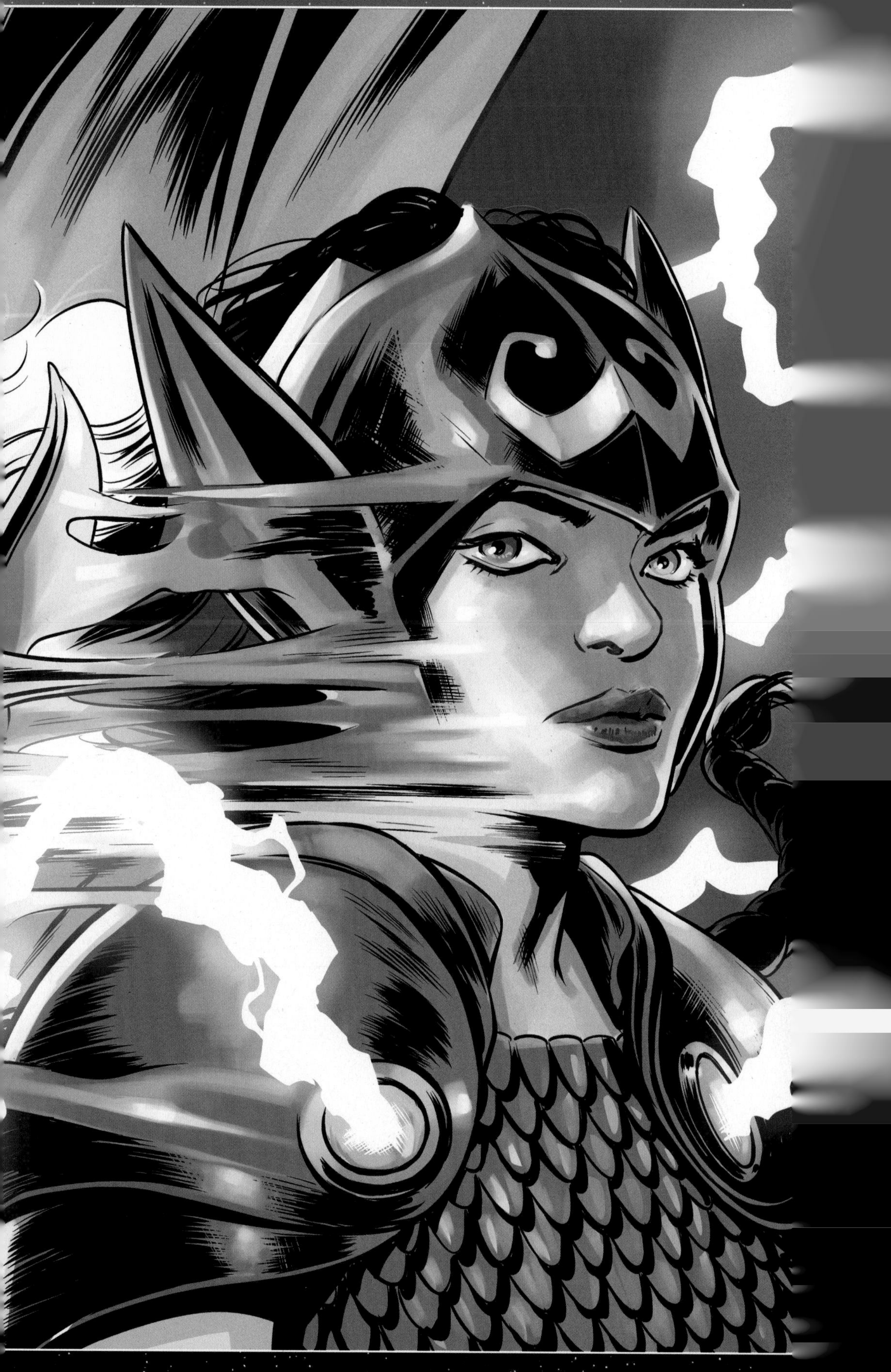

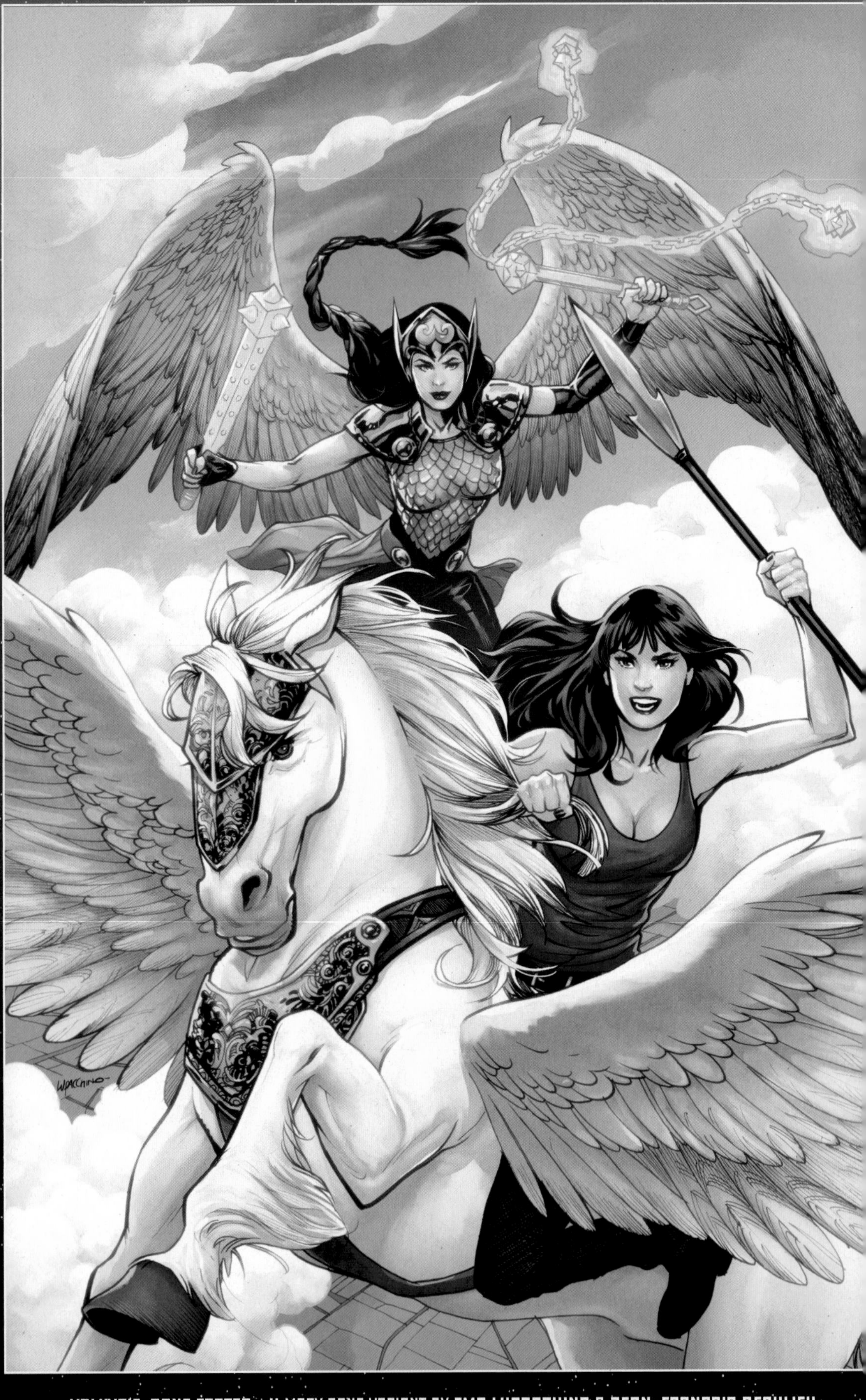

VALKYRIE: JANE FOSTER #4 MARY JANE VARIANT BY EMA LUPACCHINO & JEAN-FRANCOIS BEAULIEU

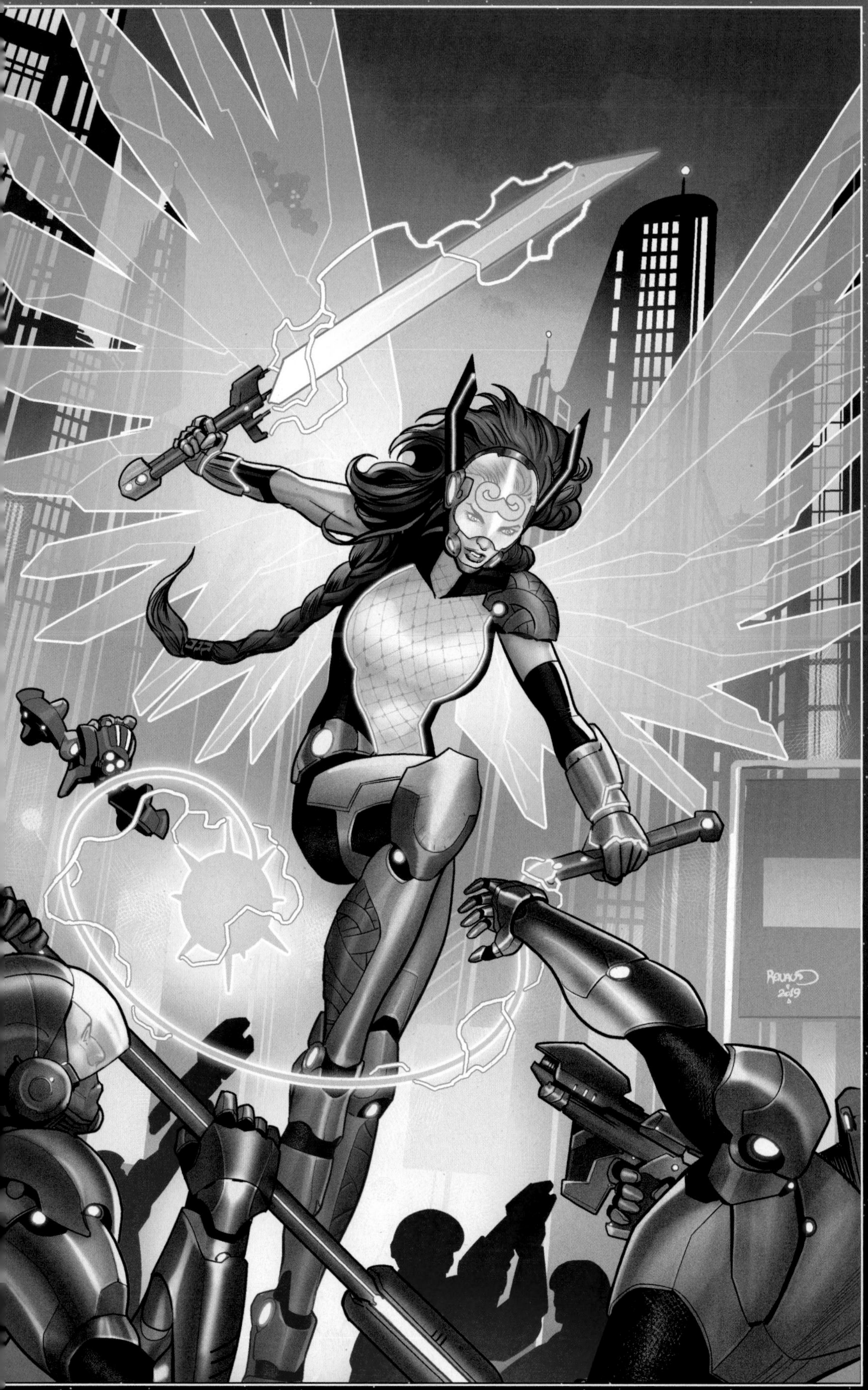

VALKYRIE: JANE FOSTER #5 2099 VARIANT BY PAUL RENAUD

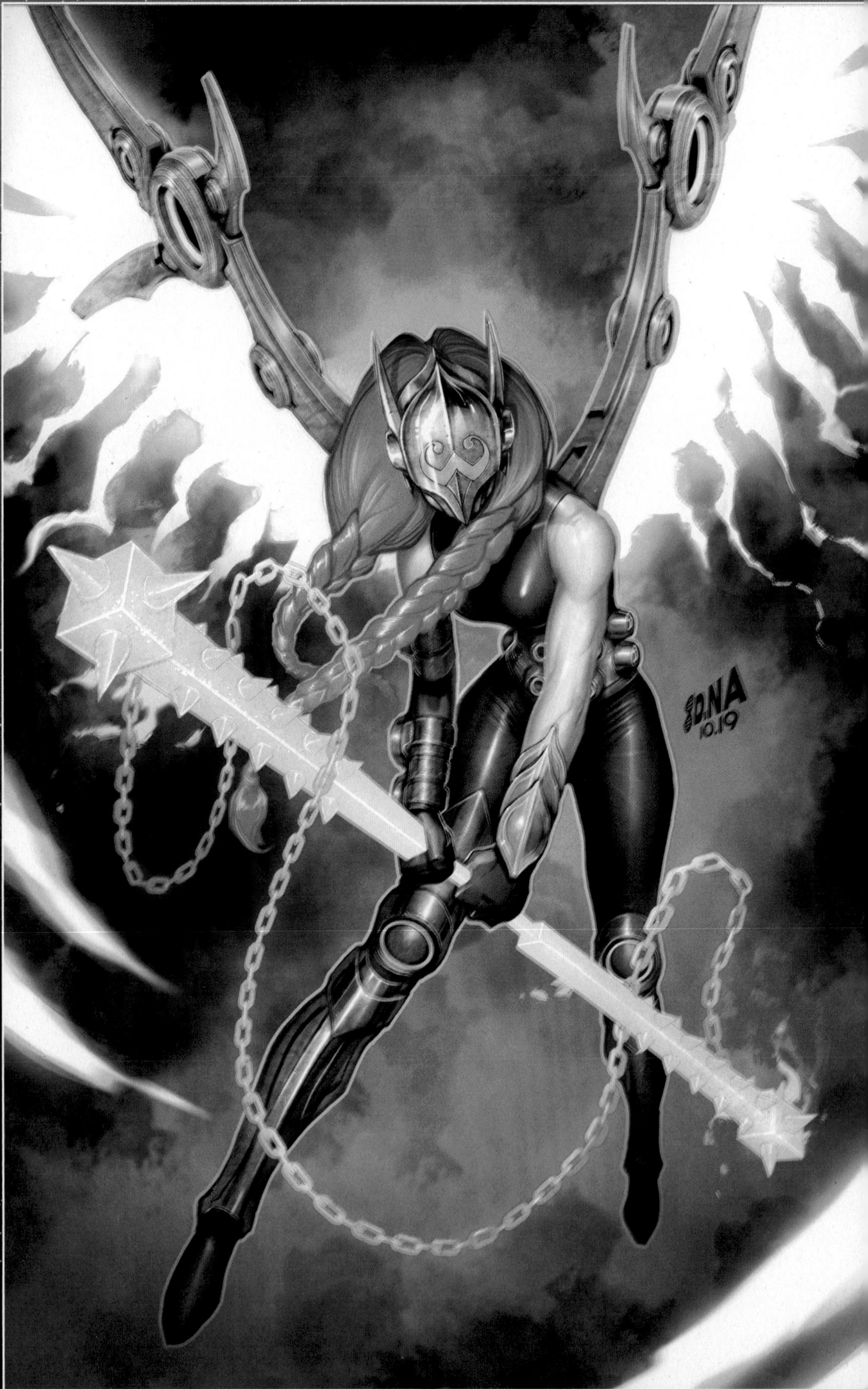
D.NA
10.19

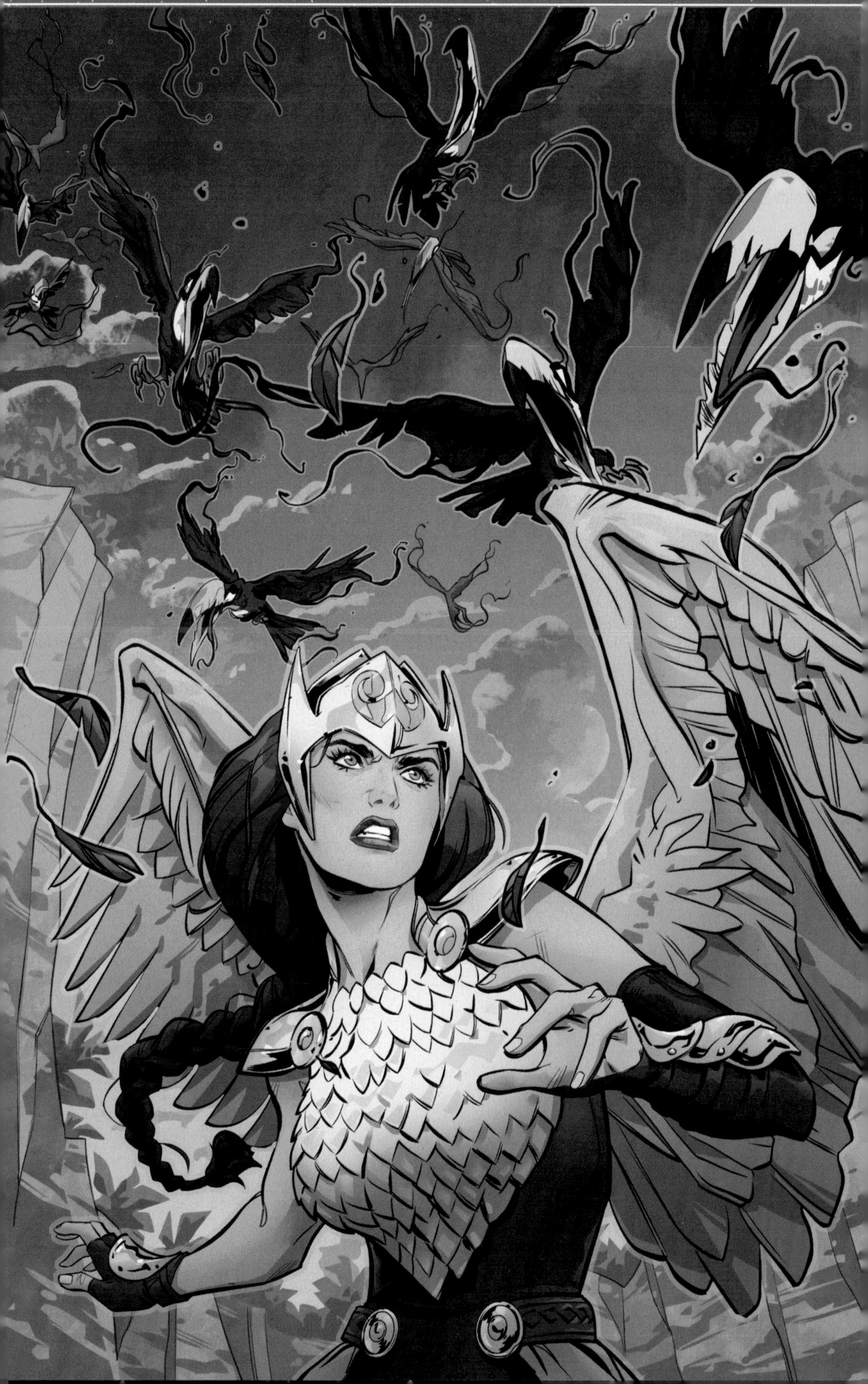

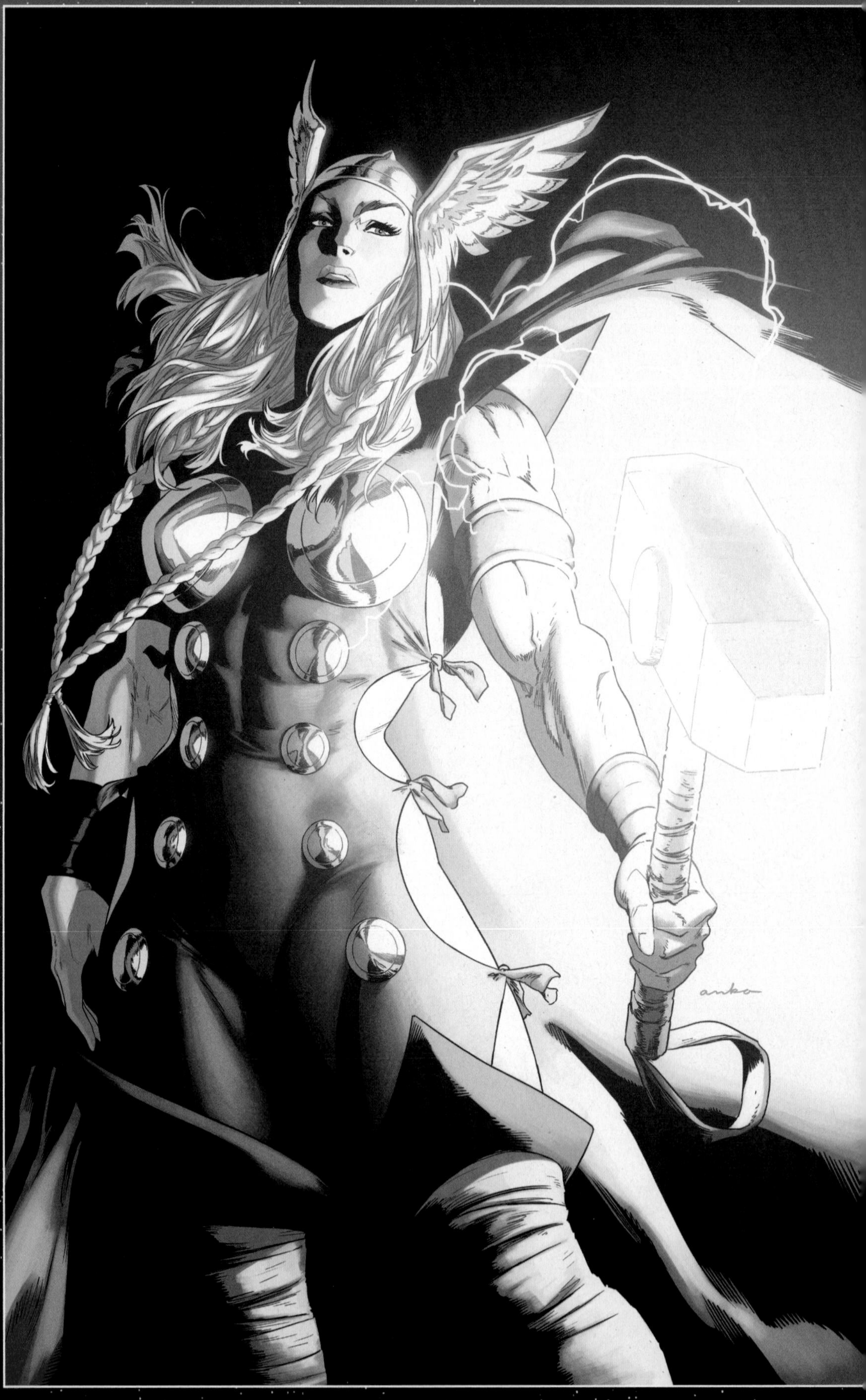

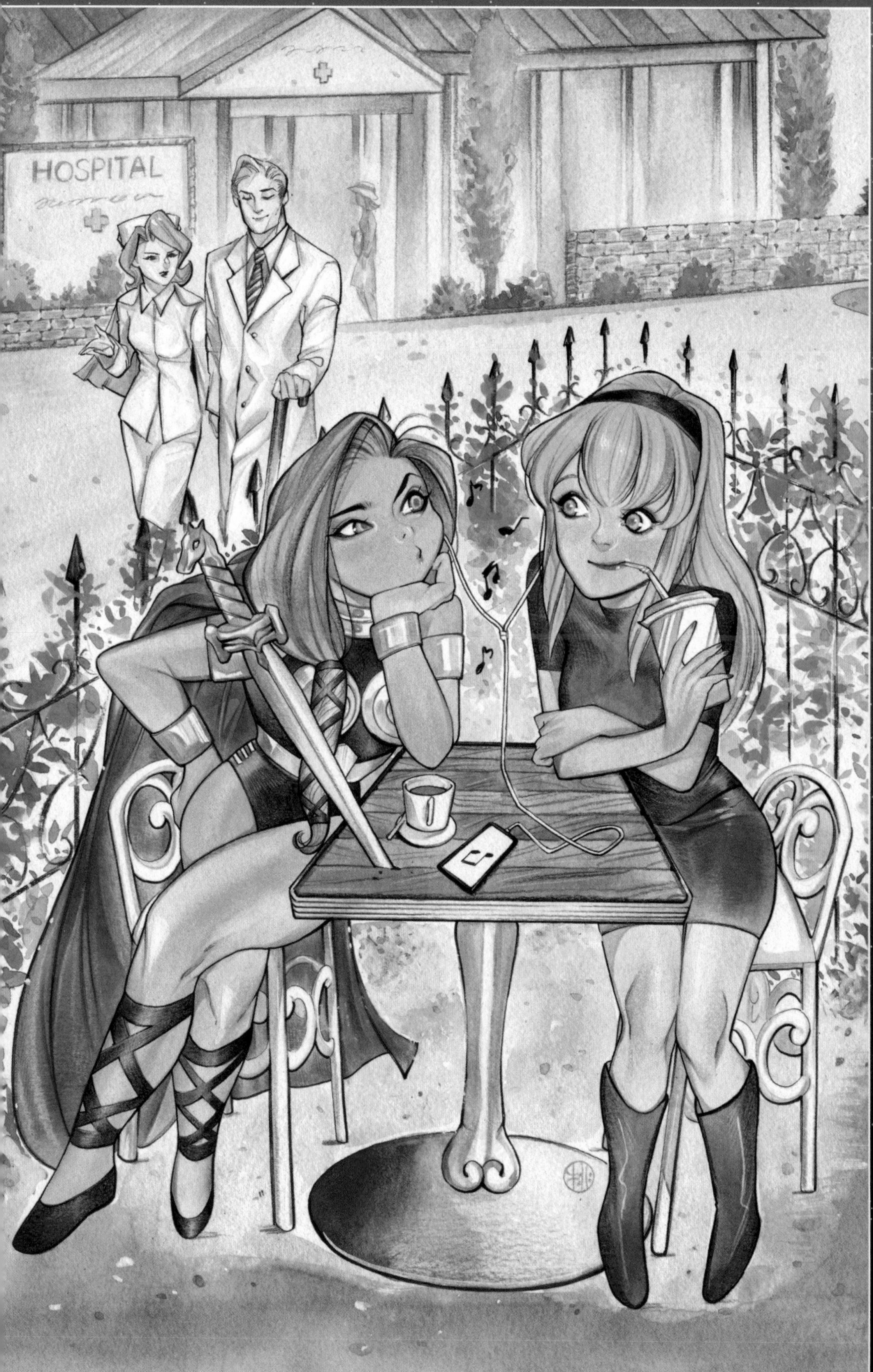
HOSPITAL

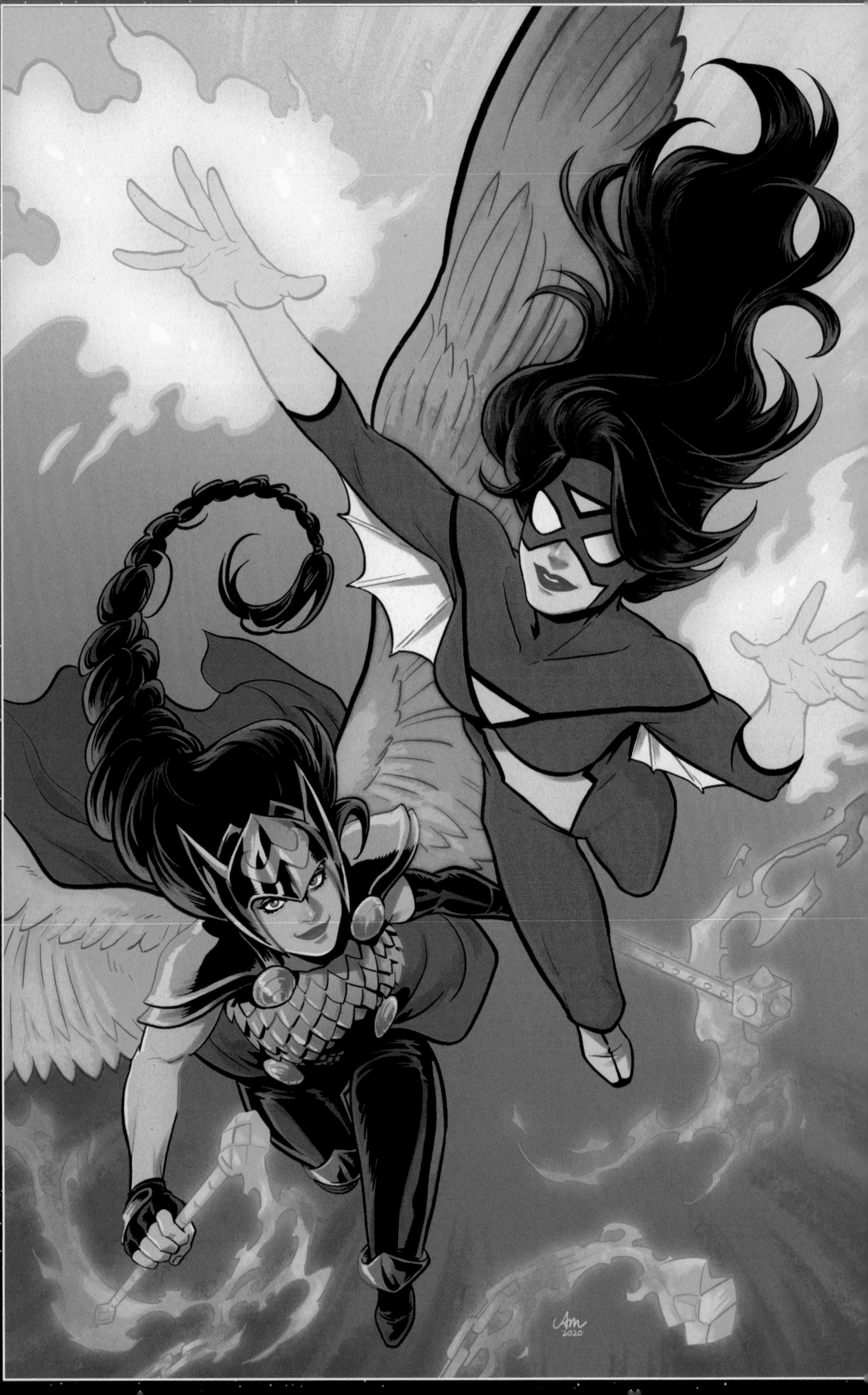

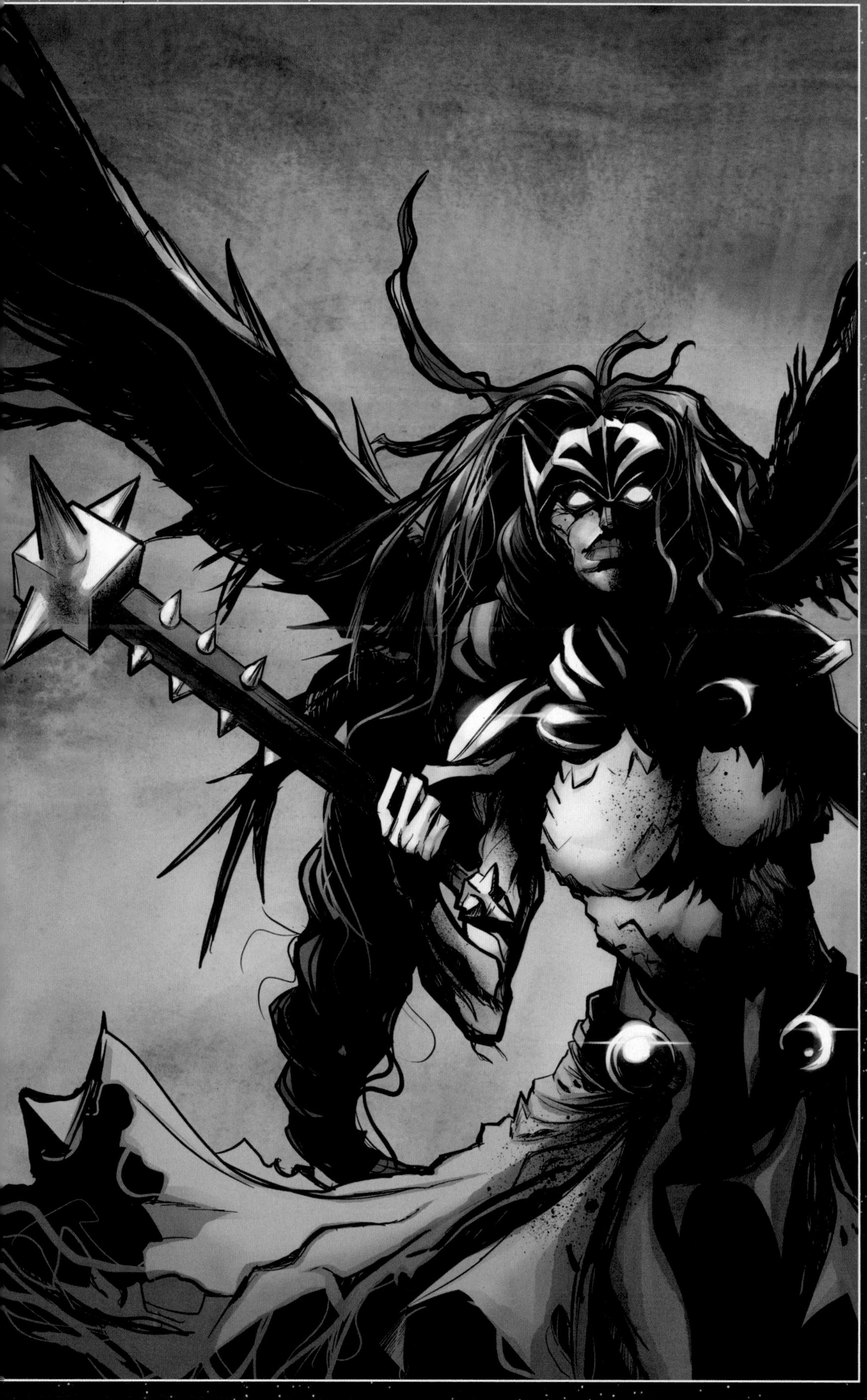

VALKYRIE: JANE FOSTER #10 MARVEL ZOMBIES VARIANT BY ROBBI RODRIGUEZ & JASON KEITH

HOW TO HORSE – A GUIDE TO PHONETIC YORKSHIRE
BY AL EWING

Mr. Horse speaks with a Yorkshire accent. Sean Bean is my go-to — his native accent is a little mild, but he's a good voice to keep in the head.

There's a method to this madness — Yorkshire has strong roots with the Vikings. Take a look at the BBC video on the Yorkshire dialect from their *Story of English* series.

So here's a glossary, running from the basics to more advanced bits and pieces. There are exceptions to all of this — for instance, "where the action is" sounds better than "where t'action is" — but this is, at least, a guide.

- [ ] The: T'. "There's trouble at t'mill."
- [ ] You: Thee or Tha, usually Tha. "Aye, tha knows."
- [ ] You've: Tha's. "Tha's been Valkyrie long enough to know that."
- [ ] You're: Tha's. "Tha's Valkyrie now, and there's an end on't."
- [ ] Your: Thy. "I got thy All-Weapon signal, Valkyrie."
- [ ] Yourself: Thissen. ("Thyself" will do on the page, since this one's advanced.)
- [ ] Those: Them. "I'm not like them posh ponies from that Asgard."
- [ ] Was: Were. "I were feelin' a bit awkward." "She were here a minute ago, like."
- [ ] Yes: Aye.
- [ ] Is that so?: Oh, aye?
- [ ] Oh, yes.: Oh, aye.
- [ ] Oh, I see how it is.: Oh, aye.
- [ ] I don't believe you.: Oh, aye.
- [ ] Hello: Ey up. "Ey up, lad."
- [ ] MALE CHARACTERS are addressed by name or as "lad." FEMALE CHARACTERS are addressed by name or as "lass," barring Valkyrie, who's always addressed as "Valkyrie," being the boss. Everyone Mr. Horse meets is younger than him, so "lad" or "lass" works, though non-binary characters should probably just be addressed by name.
- [ ] Anything: Owt.
- [ ] Nothing: Nowt.

- [ ] Nothing but, just: Nobbut. "I'm nobbut middlin'."
- [ ] Average, neither good nor bad: Middlin'.
- [ ] Just average: Nobbut middlin'. "Aye, I'm nobbut middlin'."
- [ ] Perhaps, maybe, possibly: 'Appen. "'Appen I've an idea."
- [ ] Great: Champion, grand. "Aye, that's champion, that is." "Aye, that's grand."
- [ ] Making a fuss: Mithering. Actually pronounced my-the-ring, so "Mitherin' and ditherin'" only rhymes on paper.
- [ ] Asgard: That Asgard. As in "that London." "Oh, aye, from that Asgard, I shouldn't wonder."

GENERAL NOTES

- [ ] Drop g's and h's as a rule. "Hay" keeps its h so it's easier to read — there'll be others like that.
- [ ] "Like" can be sprinkled at the end of sentences where it feels right. This is advanced stuff, though, so use sparingly.
- [ ] At the end of sentences about himself — "I'm good Vanir stock," for example — "I am" or "me" can be added. "I'm good Vanir stock, I am." "I'm a workin' 'orse, me."

NOTES ON PERSONALITY

- [ ] Mr. Horse is "good Vanir stock, not like them posh ponies from that Asgard" and isn't shy about mentioning it. He has a solid disrespect for Asgard in general — he sees them as a bunch of upper-class toffee-nosed ponces who've not done a day's proper work in their lives. No Asgardian has ever impressed him or ever will, including Thor, Odin, Balder and the rest. Jane gets a pass for not being from Asgard.
- [ ] Mr. Horse is a paid-up member of the union and expects fair recompense for his labor. In practice, this means eating a lot of food. I don't know if he'd ever go on strike, but he'd definitely threaten to.
- [ ] He lives in Jane's apartment. He can't or won't flush the toilet — more than that we've glossed over. Presumably there's some means for him to get out and into the air — an open balcony window, maybe?
- [ ] He doesn't have a name because he doesn't need one. "Mr. Horse" is just to make things easier on humans — he's

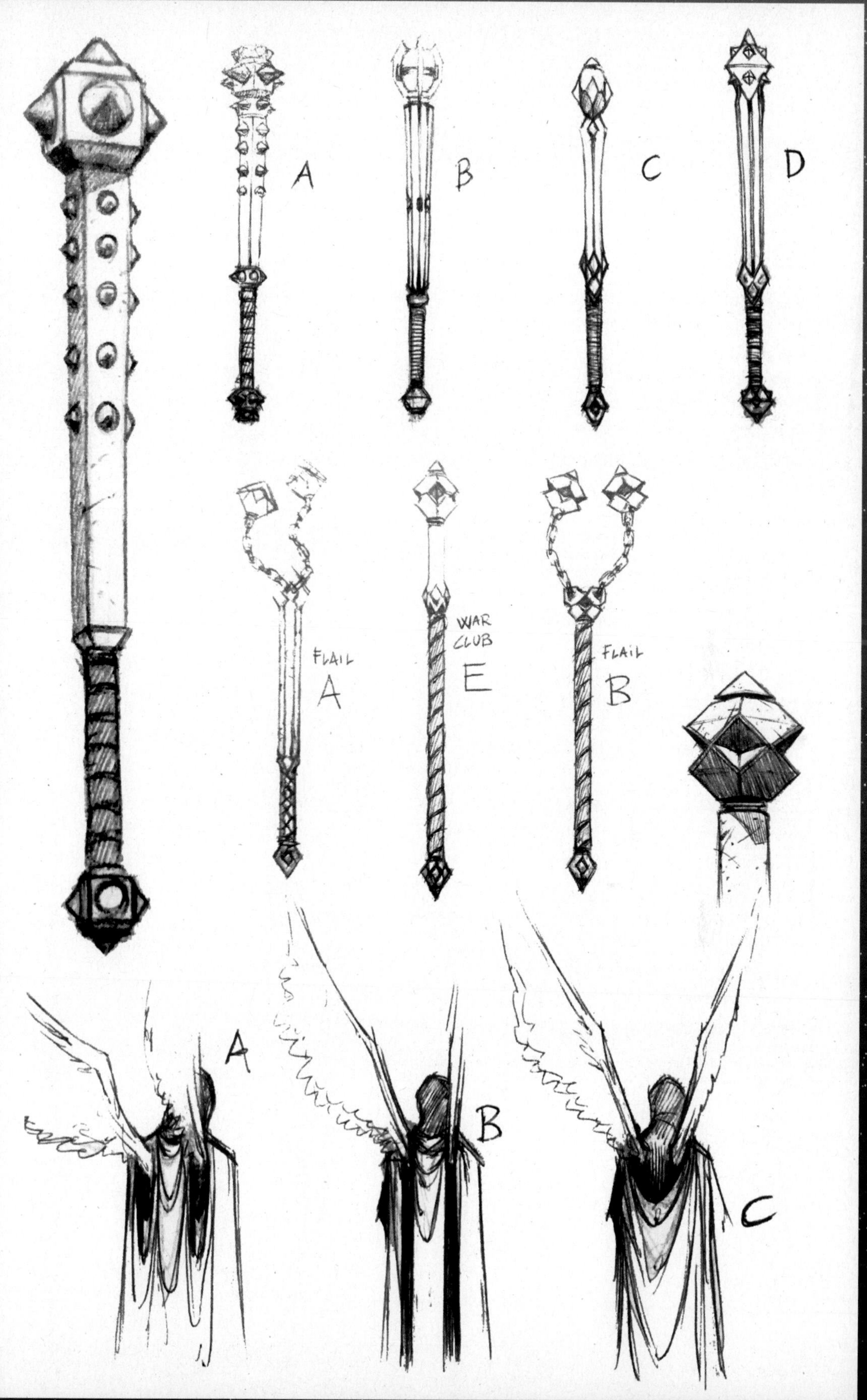
A
B
C
D
FLAIL
A
WAR
CLUB
E
FLAIL
B
A
B
C

WEAPON AND COSTUME DESIGNS BY CAFU

Jane Foster refused to die.

I mean, I did straight up kill her back in THE MIGHTY THOR #705, which is definitely one of the issues I'm most proud of from my entire career. I cried writing that issue. Cried when Russell Dauterman's pages came in. Cried with fans after they read it. It was the culmination of a story I'd been working on for years. The story of Jane as cancer fighter/super hero.

That story ended, but Jane just wouldn't stay dead. I couldn't leave her dead. Even as she stood at the gates of Valhalla, poised to go on to the other side, to her well-earned eternal reward...she held back. Because she knew what I knew.

Jane Foster's story wasn't finished.

Her evolution into Valkyrie has been in the works ever since then. Since before then, really. Because I wanted Jane to fly again. To find a new place in the Marvel Universe. A new mission. New challenges.

And boy, does she have challenges coming her way. You ever tried to find a New York City apartment big enough for a winged horse?

Just like Jane's time as Thor, this will be a story set firmly in both the gritty mortal world and the ethereal, fantastical realms beyond this one. This is a story about life in New York City and death in Valhalla. About the cold slab of a hospital morgue and the golden throne of Asgard.

The Valkyries are dead, casualties of the greatest war the realms have ever known.

Who better to take up the mantle of the Choosers of the Slain...than the woman who refused to die?

Welcome back, Jane.

And as ever...stay worthy.

Jason Aaron
KC, June 2019

I've been thinking about death.

Partly for work. I write the IMMORTAL HULK book—death comes up. Partly...well, I'm not getting any younger, and the world isn't getting any safer. And even in the best possible circumstances, given a long enough time frame, the human body has a 100% failure rate.

The thing about death is what comes after. See, I'm more an agnostic than an atheist, but even so—I never quite got my head around that part.

Is it scary? Is it nirvanic? Am I missing the point?

Opinions differ.

It'd be nice if there were someone there for you, when the time came. Someone who could take your hand and show you what's next—maybe take you into it. Someone who was a little like a doctor. Someone who was a little like a super hero. Someone who would stand up for you and fight in your corner whether you were alive or dead or somewhere in between.

I mean, maybe this someone's learning the ropes a little. Maybe she's got a day job she has to keep and friends she has to look after, and maybe one of those friends is a horse. Maybe she's being targeted by the deadliest killer on the planet on the orders of a mysterious figure with an agenda of their own.

But still. It'd be nice.

Welcome to VALKYRIE, Jane Foster. Hope you survive the...

...hmmm.

Al Ewing